GREGOR DALLAS

AT THE HEART OF A TIGER

CLEMENCEAU AND HIS WORLD
1841–1929

Carroll & Graf Publishers, Inc.
New York

Copyright © 1993 by Gregor Dallas

Published by arrangement with Macmillan London Limited, a division of Pan Macmillan Limited.

First Carroll & Graf edition 1993

Carroll & Graf Publishers, Inc.
260 Fifth Avenue
New York, NY 10001

Library of Congress Cataloging-in-Publication Data

Dallas, Gregor.
    At the heart of a tiger : Clemenceau and his world, 1841–1929 / Gregor Dallas.
        p.   cm.
    Includes bibliographical references and index.
    ISBN 0-7867-0000-9
    1. Clemenceau, Georges, 1841–1929.   2. Heads of state—France—Biography.   3. France—Politics and government—1870–1940.   4. World War, 1914–1918—Participation, French.
    I. Title.
    DC342.8.C6D28   1993
    944.081′4′092—dc20
    [B]   93-27038
                                                                        CIP

Manufactured in the United States of America

To my father,
William Thomas Dallas

CONTENTS

LIST OF ILLUSTRATIONS

The father, Benjamin Clemenceau
The mother, Emma Gautreau Clemenceau
The Château de l'Aubraie
Georges at 16
Paris in the Second Empire
Professor Charles Robin
Georges Clemenceau in 1862
Clemenceau in 1865
William Tweed
New York in the 1860s
H. Dupray's *Dragoons at Gravelotte*, 18 August 1870
Bazeilles, near Sedan, September 1870
Crowds invade the Corps Législatif, 4 September 1870
Clemenceau as Mayor of Montmartre
Place de la Concorde, 1871
E. Betsellère's *L'Oublié*
Louis Michel, 1871
Dolivet, National Guard
One of the Red Clubs holds a meeting during the Siege
The Hôtel de Ville under the Commune

J.E. Raffaëlli, *Georges Clemenceau at a public meeting, Cirque Fernando (1885)*
Marshal MacMahon
Gambetta
Jules Ferry
Opening of the new Chamber of Deputies, 5 March 1876
Boulevard des Italiens on election night, 14 October 1877
Gambetta speaking in the Chamber
E. Detaille's *Distribution of the flags at Longchamp*, 14 July 1880
General Boulanger leading the troops, 1887
Edouard Drumont
Cartoon of Clemenceau
The Marquis de Morès
Emile Zola in court, February 1898
Albert Clemenceau pleads
Sketch of Alfred Dreyfus
Dreyfus at Rennes
Office of the minister of the interior, 5 May 1906

Coffins at Courrières, March 1906
Jean Jaurès, June 1906

The Senate Army Committee, May 1916
Clemenceau visits the battlefield of Maurepas in the Somme, October 1916
Fatigue duty behind the Chemin des Dames, 1917
A stretch of the Chemin des Dames
Aristide Briand
Joseph Caillaux
Louis Malvy
Bolo Pasha
French infantry in rifle pits, April 1918
Clemenceau announces the proclamation of armistice, 11 November 1918
Aerial view of Versailles, 28 June 1919
Last page of the Peace Treaty
Clemenceau and Monet at Giverny
Clemenceau at Monet's funeral
Clemenceau's last home in the Vendée
Clemenceau at Belébat
Clemenceau catches a rose

PICTURE ACKNOWLEDGEMENTS

The author and publishers are grateful to the following for permission to reproduce pictures:

Bibliothèque Nationale: numbers 13, 15, 16, 17, 19, 21, 23, 24, 25, 26, 27, 29, 31, 32, 33, 34, 35, 36, 37, 38, 39, 40, 43, 44, 45, 46, 47, 48, 50, 51, 56

Hulton-Deutsch Collection Ltd: number 9

Illustration magazine, no. 4526, 30 November 1929: numbers 1, 2, 3, 4, 7, 8, 49, 54

Musée de l'Armée, Paris: numbers 11, 12, 14, 18, 20, 22, 28

Musée d'Histoire Contemporaine – BDIC: numbers 41 and 42

New York Historical Society: number 10

© Collection Roger Viollet: numbers 6, 30, 52, 53

Collection Sirot-Angel: numbers 5 and 55

PREFACE

OF ALL the major war leaders in recent times certainly the least known to English-speaking readers today is Georges Benjamin Clemenceau. That is partly his own fault. He left no memoirs, he destroyed much of his correspondence and spent the last years of his life preoccupied with flowers, paintings and ancient Greeks. Though a statesman of the first rank, Clemenceau hated politicians and refused to attach himself to a political party. He was the bane of the Socialists and for more than a generation he has also been the bane of professional historians. Journalists started referring to Clemenceau as 'the Tiger' after 1906 because of his independence, which was combined with a certain ruthlessness.

But the fundamental reason why we have forgotten Clemenceau is because after the First World War came a Second World War; much of the drama and the sorrow of the First has consequently been thrown to the winds. Recent histories may have rekindled some of our memories of the ordinary soldiers of the First War but, paradoxically, they tell us little of the man who led them and their Allies to victory in 1918. And a victory it certainly was.

Clemenceau was a great friend of Britain – he was probably more popular among British troops in 1918 than their own political leaders. For Winston Churchill, who was frequently with him during that last critical year of the war, Clemenceau would become a model of defiance. Re-read Churchill's wartime speeches: you will find there the phrases of Clemenceau. 'It is already certain that Clemenceau was one of the world's great men,' wrote Churchill in *The Strand* in 1930. 'As much as any single human being, miraculously magnified, can ever be a nation, he was France.' When de Gaulle came to Britain in 1940 he too would evoke the memory of Clemenceau: 'From the depth of your Vendéen tomb, Clemenceau, you do not sleep.'

Why were both Churchill and de Gaulle so attracted to Clemenceau? There was more involved here than the war leader. Few people in politics have been able to transform their careers into a work of art. Clemenceau was one of the exceptions: for him art, science and politics were simply different perspectives on the same phenomenon, the human being, and he moulded his own life accordingly. His understanding of human nature was an eighteenth-century understanding, his models were Condorcet, Helvetius and d'Holbach, his philosophy – if philosophy it was – was based on an old view of life that existed before the lines of discipline were drawn, the arguments polarised, the departments set up and the

specialists called in. *Uomo universale?* He came as close to it as any
politician can.

Yet one of the greatest ambiguities about Clemenceau is that, despite his
active presence in virtually every important political event that occurred
in France between the Franco–Prussian War and the First World War, he
was a very private man. That is why he destroyed so many documents,
so many of his letters. The biographers curse. But is it really important
to know every minute of a great statesman's life? Do we have to be fed
every tedious detail? The most essential thing is surely to be able to step
into his world – the world that created him – and attempt to assess what
he, in his turn, did for it.

So let Clemenceau (as he would have wished) disappear now and
again. I never wanted this to be a definitive biography; others have
made attempts at that. Instead, woven into the biographical account you
will find here the story of the various human worlds Clemenceau and his
generation embodied: the rural world of western France where he passed
the best years of his childhood; the political world of nineteenth-century
Jacobins, the insurgents of the Second Empire, a world immersed in the
writings of Michelet, Hugo, Lamartine and Vigny; a world of science –
not our science, but the eclectic science of the arts, the science of Comte
and the 'spontaneous generationists'; the world of Paris and New York,
of the American Radical and the French Radical; the world that gave us
Impressionism, photography, railways . . . and the machine gun.

Six full years went into this book, years which have brought many
lessons home to me. I have studied in libraries, sifted through thick
cartons of papers in several archives; I have visited numerous museums.
But places – bricks, stones, fields and hedges – have become historical
documents for me too; Clemenceau would have understood why. I now
know how most of those battlefields look today, I have been to the mairies,
I have sat through debates at the Palais-Bourbon. I even tried to descend
a coalmine in the northern fields; but the pits have now all been closed;
yet I saw the old miners' villages, the pithead towers, the slagheaps. So
this is the road where a famous riot took place, that's where the police
stood and that's where the shot was fired; but, just a moment, look once
more, what was going on up that neighbouring alley?

Some of these places exert a quite magical effect on the person who
wants to remember: a street in Paris as the red sun sets in the third week
of May, the coast at Arcachon in the New Year as a flight of gulls wings
by, the rolling autumnal hills overlooking Sedan, a forest near Verdun.
If those trees could whisper, if those walls could talk, if the sea had
words . . .

These places furnish the main themes of this book. The idea – it is
Clemenceau's – that 'History' is not an abstract rational process but a
very haphazard living phenomenon is expressed in the muddled terrain

and hybrid architectures our forebears left behind. Place, moreover, tells of the style of past political debate. If you sit in the Palais-Bourbon you can see how the politicians of the Third Republic could view politics as theatre, an extension of the Odéon and the Comédie Française. And there is another theme: the nature of power. Power is not something you can touch, it is not a commodity you can buy, auction, like a field or a house; it has no centre and its oppositions are multiple. Walk from Belleville to Montmartre and you'll understand what I mean. Related to this is the problem of 'class' (reflect on it for a moment as you peruse the hidden courtyards off rue de la Goutte d'Or). Clemenceau could talk with authority about the 'working class' because he knew Montmartre.

Theatre and politics? Let me suggest to you one more theme: the rhetoric of war and its ally, old-fashioned political oratory. I have only heard one recording of the voice of Clemenceau; it is theatrical. No politician could speak like that today. But have you recently heard the recordings of Churchill? of de Gaulle? of André Malraux' oration (how else would you describe it?) as the casket of the Resistance hero Jean Moulin was transferred to the Panthéon? It is the voice of Hugo, the voice of the printed media and of the theatre, the voice of another time.

Those sacred places I visited also spoke of a silence, of the history that has not been recorded, of words that have never been said, of unbearable fears, of intolerable passions, of untold sentiments. How many have dared write this history of silence? You have to go back to Michelet. Clemenceau always went back to the historian Michelet.

Six years of work have brought me many friends and put me in contact with several generous institutions. I have first to thank the Authors' Foundation in London which provided critical financial support. I am also most heavily indebted to archivists and librarians in France, and I would like most especially to thank the staff of the Bibliothèque de Documentation Internationale Contemporaine at Nanterre, the staff of the Sorbonne library, of the Bibliothèque Historique de la Ville de Paris and of the Bibliothèque Nationale for their help. In the course of my research, Emmanuel Reveneau helped me track down documents which enabled me to add to this book much colour. I have also benefited from the help of the curator of the BDIC's 'Photothèque', housed in a top floor of the Invalides; Thérèse Blondet-Bisch is a professional artist and her eagle eye helped me examine the extraordinary photographic collection which is preserved there. Downstairs, in the library of the Musée de l'Armée, Anne Pavard provided similar aid. I am most grateful to the small staff of the Archives du Sénat in the Palais de Luxembourg for giving me access to the rich documentation they possess on the First World War. Most helpful too were the administrators of the Goncourt archives (containing several cartons of Clemenceau's correspondence) which are now kept at the Archives municipales in Lorraine's magnificent provincial capital, Nancy.

My experience with my publishers, Macmillan London, has been a most productive and happy one. I give special thanks to Adam Sisman who so encouraged me at an early stage of my work and I wish him every success in his new profession as author. Roland Philipps has provided enthusiastic guidance through the complex world of modern publishing. I also thank Katie Owen for showing such patience and good sense in our detailed discussions of the manuscript. And I am grateful to Caroline Dawnay whose professional advice and understanding of books have demonstrated to me the high value of a literary agent today.

Finally I thank those essential friends who made the whole project possible. Micheline Herz, though so ill, worked with me over the first tentative drafts and I am deeply saddened that she did not live long enough to witness the results of her encouragement. Jean Collignon was also an early source of strength. A thousand inner *thank-you*'s are owed to Christine Reveneau-Heiberger, who has supported my moods, my obsessions, my madness, my delights.

I dedicate this book to my father. Those who knew him well and turn to the following pages will understand why.

My gratitude, however, extends to all these kind people, and many others besides, who have helped me bring you a book about a world just beyond living memory, a world just the other side of our horizon.

G.D.
Chambourcy
January 1992

CHAPTER ONE

Bocages and Plain

IF YOU are ever in the west of France, take a trip south of Nantes down
what is today the *N 137* towards an old Atlantic citadel, La Rochelle:
this is a land of frontiers and crossroads. You will pass through three
administrative departments, four separate natural regions and a border
zone – the 'marches' – of two former provinces. But the locals will tell
you that this is all one region. La Rochelle, they'll say, is as much a part
of their *pays* as Nantes. Mention Rochefort and you will probably get a
quizzical look; anything south of La Rochelle is 'elsewhere'. Speak of La
Baule or Châteaubriant and they will shrug their shoulders; everything
north of Nantes is 'foreign'.

History gave this region its identity, not the administrators in Paris.
They only lent it a name. When, at the outbreak of the Revolution, they
carved up the ancient provinces into departments they called the unit south
of Nantes the 'Deux Lays', for the Grand Lay and the Petit Lay flow right
across its centre. But the two new locally elected deputies turned out to be
so ugly that the administrators, scared of the obvious joke – *les deux laids*
–, decided to change the name of their department to that of a still tinier
stream, the Vendée. It would have been of small consequence had not a
bloody civil war broken out in the area three years later. The 'Vendée'
suddenly became something of epic proportions, stretching well beyond
its formal administrative limits. As a geographer once put it, 'While all
the provinces became departments, the Vendée was the only department
to become a province.' Between Nantes and La Rochelle lies the 'province'
of the Vendée.

Over the high bridge that crosses the Loire, through Nantes' southern
suburb of Rezé, the road will lead you first into an area of vineyards. The
rows of well-pruned creepers, which retain the heat and release the frosts,
appear from the car as fields of unbroken foliage hugging the hollows and
nubs of the ground. Periodically you will spy a village – Châteauthébaud,
Aigrefeuille, Remouillet; little parthenons set up on hills, whose red tiled
roofs and stuccoed walls will make you think you are in some backcountry
area near the Mediterranean, not Biscay Bay.

But it may be raining. 'Rain is a companion in Loire-Inférieure, the faithful half of a life,' writes the novelist Jean Rouaud. Every peasant from Nantes to La Rochelle has blessed those clouds charged with the Ocean's vapours; every farmer today grouses about recent summers when the 'faithful half' failed to come home. Even when the sun is shining you are aware of the Ocean. Sea gulls soar in an air which is visible, alive and scented with salt and moisture; you can see it settle in the valleys, slightly blue and nuzzling up against the streams.

The vineyards fade into trees and hedges after Montaigu, in the Vendée proper, although you may find, between the advertisement for one of E. Leclerc's supermarkets and Gilbert Borrod's '*auto-école*', a sign chalked on cardboard, '*Dégustation de Muscadet – Frites*', which tells you what the natives here like best: drink.

Vendéens drank because they were poor.

You see those ugly modern homes out in the country? They belong to the peasants. They like modern architecture, not the old creviced stone walls, the sagging roofs, the tilted chimney-pots; the scenes of their past. Michel Ragon remembers how, shortly before his Vendéen mother died in the 1960's, she turned her back on the window overlooking the rural fields; '*Ne me montre pas* ça!' the poor woman cried in contempt of the ancient landscape.

But really, it is worth your examination. Let the wheels of time stop and reverse themselves. As you travel forward, take your mind backward. The walls of those old houses appear to have no windows, no door, because Vendéens refused to face the road and foreigners; you must enter by the other side. There is a cross whitewashed on the outside wall? It is not God's cross. It represents a yoke for oxen; a ploughman lived here. You would never find it on a shopkeeper's home, or an artisan's. They say it is a pagan sign, put there to keep away evil spirits.

More crosses, in stone or in iron, towering over each major intersection, called a *queru* by Vendéens. Yes, these crosses are to Christ. Sometimes you will find a statue to Mary by a *queru*, sometimes you will find both. Most were built in the nineteenth century. The Vendée had not always been Catholic.

There is one statue, at the crossroads of Sainte-Hermine, which is neither to Jesus nor His mother; it is a group of *poilus* – soldiers of the Fourteen–Eighteen War – looking upward at the representation of an old man in a hat. In the last war, the Nazis knocked its head off; they had their reasons. The statue was reconstructed in 1944.

The hedgerows came first. From a hill you will see how far they go. And if you think it is all just greenery, step up closer and you will find dog rose, honeysuckle, willow, hawthorn, elderberry and vetch. The blue flower of borage was used to combat colds and indigestion; the violet of mallow cured sore throats and bronchitis. You can tell the age of these hedges from what grows in them. Most of them have been there for more than a millennium, marking out lines, following the borders of the old hollow lanes that fifty generations of oxen and carts have sunk in the land.

Formalised lines came late to the Vendée. Napoleon ordered a national land survey, but it was only in Louis-Philippe's reign that the *arpenteur* – the surveyor, in his high hat, white collar and his instruments in a brief case – arrived here. From then on it was all marked down on paper, kept in large volumes you can still consult at the mairie. The *arpenteur* used his instruments and the hedges. At this point of gorse, blackthorn and hazel begins lot number *quinze-dix-sept* of the Vendée's cadastre. There it is *quinze-dix-huit*. Baptiste Meriau *et héritiers* lay claim to this one. They call those plots of land *borderies* and *métairies* which, if elsewhere designate the kind of lease employed, here only refer to the size of the farm, rather like one speaks in the Vendée of a *journeau* of vines.

And so the hedges go on to divide and define. Here the cattle shall graze for a year; there, there will be wheat. On this side barley; on that, a red-stalked patch of buckwheat. The hedges also give the terrain its name. In England we would call it 'bosky country'. In France it is the 'bocages'.

There did exist in the past a few Vendéen aristocrats. But they were either absent or poor. Ask the locals again: the bocages have always belonged to the peasants, small peasant property-holders. When in the Fourteen–Eighteen War the prime minister of France called on them to defend their *patrie*, they knew what he was talking about . . . for the prime minister, like them, was a Vendéen.

Terrain, culture, religion and politics are overlapping worlds in the Vendée. After the crossroads and the statue at Sainte-Hermine you leave the bocages and enter the 'plain' – flatlands stretching from the coast to the interior of Poitou, where the quail fly, where maize and sunflowers are grown. The plain boasts of several large towns, it is one of Rabelais' homelands and the heart of a Protestant and republican tradition. This is where the sea drew back a few million years ago. But the boundary between land and sea is still not very clear; after Luçon you will cross marshlands that extend all the way to La Rochelle.

The people of the plain might vote differently, but they still consider themselves Vendéen for they share the same history, they are children of the same mythologies.

Phantoms, fairies, ogres and giants – the lands of the Vendée are roamed by them. Stop at the crossroads and frontiers and listen. The Fairy Melusina, half-woman, half-sea-serpent, was a Vendéenne. Bluebeard was a Vendéen. He haunts the ruins of his castle at Tiffauges which, as you might expect, is in a border region, on the frontiers of ancient Poitou, Brittany and Anjou.

When war came to the region the peasants themselves became ogres and giants. In 1793 an army of eighty thousand of them, armed with arquebuses, hunting guns, scythes and pitch-forks marched on Nantes. They were destroyed at Savenay; the Parisian Republic then ordered the 'transformation of this country into a desert'.

Until the Revolution, there were still many Protestants living in the bocages, in villages like Pouzauges, Le Baupère, Mouchamps, Sainte-Hermine and Mouillerons-en-Pareds. But in August 1793 a great exodus began; they fled to the republican plain. Another line had been drawn across the Vendée.

These are the events, then, which have created the hedges, the roads, the crosses to Christ and to the ploughman, the modern homes, the old statues and the sign *Dégustation de Muscadet – Frites*.

I think you have it; you begin to see and hear it all now. Yes.

So close your ears to the roar of the motorbicycle and the purr of the car. Don't think of tomorrow: I have a true story of ogres and giants to tell.

Imagine the tarmac gone and in its place a road with a dusted white surface – potholed and rutted – engrafted like the vine to the land and twisting in strange detours. Atop every hill stands a windmill with its slatted sails circling lazily to the breeze. At the crossing of the river is a humpback bridge built in black stone; you have time to contemplate the water rippling over white pebbles and glimpse, through the foliage of alder, the water-lilies which open their petals to the sun. A gaggle of geese hold parliament on the river's edge; they are all orating simultaneously. The lowing of cattle, the regular step of mules charged with sacks of grain, the crack of the whip, the slow and monotonous creak of the watermill's wheel; these are the sounds of the Vendée when Louis-Philippe ruled France.

In the distance you see the dust kicked up as a light carriage approaches, now at a trot, now at a canter; the driver has to watch his road. A thud of hoofs, the bounce of wheels. Past the hedges and haystacks the carriage emerges, disappears, then re-emerges. Soon it is upon you, drawn by a horse with shining, its nostrils flaring; the driver looks earnest. In a flash you see the passenger, a young woman wrapped in furs. She is on her way to Mouilleron-en-Pareds to bear a first son.

II

EMMA GAUTREAU'S parents' home was in the heart of the bocages. Her husband's home, the château de l'Aubraie, was on the border of the plain, not far from Sainte-Hermine.

The Gautreaus' sixteenth-century house, set on one of the main streets of Mouilleron-en-Pareds, was not a very impressive place. A few rough cobbles adjoined its stone façade to provide a narrow way for pedestrians fussy enough to want to avoid the mud of the road. It had five narrow windows overlooking the street and a tiny door, painted red, which opened into a hallway and a large living room furnished in greens and browns. Georges Clemenceau was born upstairs on 28 September 1841.

Benjamin Clemenceau, the father, did not attend though he was a trained doctor. This would hardly have been in the tradition of his middle-class household. Instead he remained at L'Aubraie where he enjoyed his horses, his library, some painting and a brisk walk along the country paths of his parents' properties. He was a cultivated man and well known among local republican politicians. He had married Emma Gautreau two years earlier before a Protestant pastor – perhaps the first and certainly the last religious act of his life. The couple already had one child – a daughter, another Emma.

Emma Gautreau had been uncomfortable at L'Aubraie. Her father-in-law, Paul-Jean Clemenceau, was principally interested in his cattle, which he would inspect in a white tie and a top hat. Her brother-in-law, a practising Catholic, plumped for dogs. Paul-Jean's wife was well read, her conversation lively. But this could not repair the low opinion Benjamin had developed for the other two men, a tension that Emma, as his wife, had to absorb in silence.

The château itself was a silent, secret place. When Georges Clemenceau's private secretary visited the château in the 1920's he described it as 'a thing fierce and proud'. Its outer walls had been built at the same time as Bluebeard's castle. They rose two storeys high from the surrounding moat; a drawbridge, which had been converted to stone, dominated the approach. Inside the former guardroom had rafters which still bore the burn marks of an attack by soldiers of the Catholic League; its walls had been gilded in the distant past, its stone floors were worn smooth by peasants' wooden clogs. The Clemenceaus had acquired the property in 1809 when Paul-Jean's father, who had once been a member of the Council of Five Hundred under the Directory and by then had become a local notable of the Empire, married Gabrielle Joubert. The château was never a *bien national*, property confiscated from the aristocracy during the Revolution; the Jouberts had acquired it and its dependent farms sometime in the late eighteenth century – perhaps in 1790 – after its aristocratic

owner had gone bankrupt. None the less, families like the Jouberts and
the Clemenceaus had clearly benefited from the change in regimes, and this
was probably why L'Aubraie was decorated in every corner with busts and
portraits of Robespierre, Saint-Just and other heroes of the Revolution.

It was hardly a homely atmosphere. So whenever the opportunity
presented itself Emma would leave for Mouilleron, sometimes in the
company of her husband, but often without. Emma in flight. Such
triumph would rush over her when the carriage pulled up in rue de
la Chapelle. There was music in this house, dance, a gala. Her parents
might have been Protestants, but not of the dull, bookwormish kind: they
read the Bible, yes, but read it with passion.

Small wonder that she wanted her confinement to be in Mouilleron.

Thus Georges Clemenceau was a child of the Vendée's frontiers. His first
fleeting images of life lay on either side of them: there, on his father's
side, stood a small chilly château, of medieval origin, near the plain of
Sainte-Hermine; on his mother's side he would remember with great
affection a Protestant home in the thick of the bocages.

Clemenceau never spoke with much fondness of the château de
l'Aubraie. The only time he wrote about it was in a novel composed after
he had lost his seat in parliament and which emphasised its alienating
atmosphere. He damned his daughter when she wrote a short novel about
the place; 'it disgusted me to read the text.' He seems to have shared
something of the spirit of Emma's flight, for his best memories were of
his moments of escape. 'When I was able to mount my horse and gallop
in the fields, life was beautiful. Until then, it was deadly.' Clemenceau
certainly loved the plain, the hunts for quail and partridge, the open sky,
the view of a steeple in the distance: 'My joy was to run, to see the sky,
the wind, the rain, the sun, to get drunk on the perfumes of the grass, to
marvel at the spectacles of the land.'

In 1843, when Georges was only two, Benjamin Clemenceau, Emma
and the two children moved into a house on rue Calvaire which was in
the fashionable new western district of Nantes. Not far away were the
two establishments which for the next decade dominated Benjamin's life,
the reading club and the Théâtre Graslin, dominant not because of their
literary influence, but their politics. It was only with Paul-Jean's death
in 1860 that L'Aubraie came into Benjamin's hands. Yet ties with the
Vendée were never broken. Long stays at the château were part of the
annual regimen. It was considered rather chic by Nantes' elite (and in
the 1840's there were some good health reasons) to disappear into the
countryside for several months of the year. Doctor Benjamin Clemenceau,
for all his democratic talk, was no exception.

Four other children followed. Letters written much later suggest that the ties between them were strong and affectionate – crucial, indeed, in the development of Georges' subsequent political career; this would not be a solo effort. Emma, his elder sister, continued to occupy Georges' thoughts throughout his life; she was born one year before him, she also died one year before him. She was protective and, possibly because of this, Georges turned his own parental sentiments – which were considerable – in the direction of his younger brother, Albert, twenty years his junior and destined to become a lawyer. There were two other sisters, Adrienne (about whom little is known beyond the fact that she was physically disabled and thus condemned by the social norms of every era to a spinster's life), who was born in 1850, and Sophie, born in 1854. Sophie was quite a character. According to one of her nephews she was a tall and bony-framed lady, and correspondence suggests that she played an important and mostly successful role in maintaining the family ties, especially when tensions were great. She was less effective when it came to estranged spouses: 'Clemenceaus,' she once concluded in exasperation, 'only get on with Clemenceaus.'

Clemenceau's brother Paul, who would become a wealthy engineer, was born in 1857. He seems to have played an important part in the background of Georges' early political career, particularly where financial matters were concerned. But after the 1890's relations deteriorated for several reasons (none directly connected to Paul's inheritance of L'Aubraie on Benjamin's death in 1897). By the end of the Great War the two were no longer on speaking terms. Sophie's magic did not work here.

Clemenceau's relationship with his parents corresponded to what one might expect of a well-to-do family of the time; his father was rational and dominant, his mother spiritual and affectionate. But this psychological division of labour was much greater than what most sons of the nineteenth century experienced. That strong sentimental element, that religious ardour you will find in his speech, came from his mother. A small but significant fact: when he was still an infant his mother gave him a casket into which every year, on his birthday, she put a gift, sometimes a book sometimes money. The image of birth, death and a repeated resurrection crops up again and again in Clemenceau's writing and speeches: that casket, a celebration of birth, accompanied him to his grave.

There was something else in Clemenceau's speech which is frequently (for good reason) overlooked, and that is his knowledge of the Bible. He would often accompany his mother to Mouilleron, which was as much a relief for him as it was for her, although it is quite ironic that this man, who would be remembered by historians as an opponent of all organised religions, should pass the happiest moments of his childhood in a household of believers. When Clemenceau spoke of '*mon village*', he was referring not to the distinctly unattractive settlement of Féaule that straddles the main road just beyond the château de l'Aubraie; he was talking about Mouilleron.

At Mouilleron Clemenceau learned his Bible and adopted for life its intensity of language. The grandfather, who had a somewhat rustic manner, must have spotted some talent in Georges' reading: 'When I get to heaven,' he declared, bouncing the grandson on his knees, 'it would give me great pleasure to learn that you've made a fine speech like Jules Favre.' Nobody knows whether Grandfather Gautreau fulfilled his side of the pledge, but little Georges did his.

Talk of heaven could draw out every fury from his father. He had forced a vow out of Emma that should he die she would never permit her children baptism or a religious education – 'and if you should fail to do so, I would feel constrained to hate you.' The only gods Benjamin Clemenceau knew, and of these alone could his family speak, were the heroes of the Revolution.

III

ON THE surface, Benjamin Clemenceau's anticlericalism is easy enough to explain. In France, identification with the Revolution has always been accompanied by hostility towards the Church. It might be latent, as was arguably the case of such a secularly minded bishop as Talleyrand; it might be open, as was certainly the case of Robespierre and the Committee of Twelve; it was never, it could never, be compromising. 'I define the Revolution, the accession of Law, the resurrection of Right, the reaction of Justice,' wrote the historian Benjamin Clemenceau liked to quote most, Jules Michelet. 'The Law, such as it appeared in the Revolution, is it in conformity or is it against the religious law which preceded it? Otherwise said: the Revolution, is it Christian, or anti-Christian?' Even Napoleon, who would have borne more than one cross to keep an army of citizens behind him, never managed to pull off more than a truce, the Concordat, which eventually brought the pope a sentence of exile, two emperors distrust from all quarters, the nation the debate of the century. At a national level, defenders of the Church and defenders of the Revolution were in opposite camps.

But the ideology was only part of a whole culture that Benjamin Clemenceau had absorbed from his family and his profession.

Benjamin Clemenceau was a doctor. His father was a doctor. His grandfather was a doctor ... The medical profession, if it was known in France as 'liberal', was throughout the nineteenth century to a large extent hereditary. In Rouen, there was a family called Flaubert. At Reims, there was Henrot. At Bordeaux, it was Gintrac. At Tours, Herpin. Not that the recruitment of the medical corps lacked rigour. Even the humble *officiers de santé* (immortalised in the character of Charles Bovary) had to pass three examinations before the local department's medical jury, made up of two doctors and a professor of medicine. To earn the title of 'doctor', a candidate would have to study for four years at a faculty of medicine (as a formal requirement – the average student would, in fact, take more than double that time), sit for five exams and then produce a thesis. So Benjamin, who had left for Paris at the propitious time of spring 1830 and got his doctorate five years later, was moving rather more rapidly than most.

But in those days it was the family, with its money and connections, which provided the vital element for survival (let alone success) in medicine. The Clemenceaus were not rich, but comfortable. Again following a common pattern among the well-to-do of the period, their principal income was not earned but came instead from their landed properties (Le Colombier, Féaule and L'Aubraie), most of which had been acquired in the seventeenth and eighteenth centuries. Money made the study of medicine a less harrowing experience for Clemenceaus than was normally the case.

It is not surprising that students, especially medical students, in the nineteenth century identified with the 'working classes'. Their conditions were frightful. Students at the faculty of medicine in Paris rented small, inadequately heated rooms in the Latin Quarter; if they hadn't acquired a *pension bourgeoise*, where cheap meals were provided, food could also become a major problem. Disease already was: one student out of fifty literally died before achieving his doctorate (your chances of avoiding a serious disease were somewhat better if you had chosen to study at the faculty of law where only one in eighty died). When doctors started to express interest in the famous '*question sociale*', they did so not only out of philanthropy or as the result of treating the poor, they did it because so many of them had experienced misery first hand – and misery even with families forking out sums ranging between 15 and 25,000 francs (depending on the period) for the total costs of study.

Family connections played an even greater role in the placement once one had got the doctorate, and the Clemenceaus were well connected with the local doctors of Nantes and the Vendée. Benjamin Clemenceau was close to Ange Guépin, the ophthalmologist at Nantes and author of numerous works (on politics, geography and history!), as well as his colleagues like Eugène Bonamy, Bertin and Gabriel Simon. He knew Doctor Armand Trastour who, as mayor of nearby Montaigu between 1837 and 1870, directed an ambitious local programme of building and sanitary improvement – one of those water-and-sewer men who bettered the lives of his contemporaries and delighted scholars of urban history ever since. These men were celebrities and good republicans. When Ange Guépin died in May 1873, the people of Nantes spent two days filing past his open coffin, touching his hands, whispering to him and bringing him flowers before attending a mass civic funeral.

Lay republicanism was what mattered. The last thing that concerned a doctor like Benjamin Clemenceau was the practice of medicine. Georges Clemenceau claimed that his father had had, in all his life, only one patient and he had managed to kill him.

When one spoke of the medical profession being 'liberal' it was really because of the politics and above all the leisure, not the method of recruitment. The Clemenceaus might have been exceptional in the small number of patients that they treated, but this was only a matter of degree. Most doctors in the nineteenth century had very few clients and they would spend days in their homes waiting for business. What they did with their leisure obviously varied according to taste, personality and education – a medical degree didn't guarantee brilliant conversation in the salons and the reading clubs of cities like Nantes. But for the most educated, an appreciation of art, sociology – doctors were among the first to provide empirical evidence in this new field – and an unbreachable faith in science were the principal guides in their intellectual pursuits outside medicine.

In fact, the French doctor played a major role in perpetuating the link between art and science, a link which Georges Clemenceau would never abandon.

Benjamin Clemenceau enjoyed sketching and was fairly accomplished as a landscape and portrait artist. He spent much of his time copying the paintings of Jean-Baptiste Greuze whose romantic and rather splendid scenes of noble peasants, adoring children and happy hens on the kitchen floor would, at a later time, have been considered totally inappropriate for a man of science. But this was not the sort of contradiction his own age confronted. A fury of pity, as Michelet called it, clung to the progressive man's hopes in the future of mankind. The sight and experience of human suffering was not enough; you would have to ennoble it if you held out any prospect for its relief. It was, as Hugo put it, the fault of Voltaire, the fault of Rousseau: for more than a generation after the Revolution the eighteenth-century Greuze projected the spirit of Rousseau on canvas – a form of socialist realism *avant la lettre* (though more amusing) that gave pictorial substance to the People, so much the object of pity in Benjamin's day.

The pastel that Benjamin Clemenceau drew of Georges at the age of ten shows the influence of Greuze but tells us little of his son. He is well dressed, his hair is tidy, and he is not looking at the portraitist.

More important than painting was Benjamin Clemenceau's readings. He would disappear for hours into his library and was not very polite if anyone disturbed him: 'Georges, get out of here: you are not in your place.' He concentrated on books about revolution, republicanism and science. Dinners at L'Aubraie or at Nantes were spent listening to Benjamin's thoughts on these various subjects. Robespierre he considered a deity and Danton a traitor. Napoleon had betrayed the popular cause and reverted to tyranny and a futile flirtation with the Church. The Church, of course, embodied tyranny, it obstructed all science and progress, and any association with it would lead one ineluctably down the same path; kings and emperors were not popular in Benjamin Clemenceau's house.

IV

THAT HOUSE in Nantes could be as silent as the château de l'Aubraie. There were moments when one could believe one was in the country. From an upstairs window the infant Georges would look out on the plane trees bared of all foliage, a few old men on the benches, the empty streets. On Sundays there was a regular clanging of cathedral bells, on busy days the rumble of wagons. Most of the people were dressed as if it were Sunday, though a few peasants with long hair and wide hats might be pushing their carts to the markets on the Erdre; a black man in rags sat on one corner, with his five children, begging for pennies. The whinny of horses. The cry of a jay in one of the trees. Heaven knows where father was!

One morning in February, when Georges was six, he saw his father crossing the street in a very agitated state. 'The King is probably dead,' joked his elder sister.

But it was better than that. There had been a revolution in Paris. A Second Republic had just been proclaimed.

In 1843 Benjamin had joined a 'Republican Commission of Nantes' and spent most of the next five years consorting with businessmen and professionals who sought to get rid of the King. The news that republicans had established a new Provisional Government (which included his friend, Etienne Arago) in Paris was like a fantasy come true. He signed the congratulatory message his reading club sent to Paris and then he left with his whole family for the annual sojourn in the Vendée.

At Le Colombier, the Clemenceaus' ancestral home north of Mouilleron, he planted a liberty tree. At L'Aubraie he found his brother Paul manufacturing bullets on the kitchen table with the obvious intent of joining

General Cavaignac's 'forces of order'. Benjamin threatened to go to Paris
and join the other side. Neither brother actually made the trip.

It was too late. June 1848 was a shock for Benjamin Clemenceau; and
every following winter the news got worse.

Living history was not like reading it. History, once written, has the
illusion of inevitability, and nowhere is this probably more true than in
the histories we have of the short-lived Second Republic. As politicians
prepared Europe for its first democracy, philosophers, journalists, political
arithmeticians and men of letters were producing what can be fairly
regarded as the first social sciences. They were the ones who created
the illusion of inevitability. One dramatic event followed on the other;
the scientists of humanity took notes, they lectured, they wrote about
society on the grander plan, of class and collectivity, and kept a respectful
distance from the fussiness of little lives and fortunes. When it was all over,
the fall of the Second Republic seemed to fit the historical order of things;
bourgeois fear and the immaturity of the working classes were the main
explanations.

But the harshness and peculiar character of repression was unforeseen,
unforeseeable. In the beginning, *all* had stood for progress, save a minority
of ultra-royalists. Future figures of conservativism, like General Cavaignac
and even Prince Louis-Napoleon, thought of themselves as liberal. In
early 1848 Benjamin Clemenceau and his political friends could not have
found it easy to distinguish 'progressives' from 'reactionaries'. But by 1849
they did.

The developments in France over the four years of the Republic set the
tone for Georges Clemenceau's own early training in politics. Benjamin,
turning forty, was now further isolated from brother and father, his
anticlericalism pushed yet deeper into the steely runnels of doctrine, his
republican energy made more combative. He began to turn his attention
to the education of his son.

Georges entered Nantes' lycée the year Louis-Napoleon assumed the
title of Emperor. The main emphasis of the curriculum at Nantes was
on rhetoric, elocution and the classics, all of which Georges Clemenceau
would one day put to great profit. But at the time he found himself 'caught
between two fires': the effort, by day, of his school to instil a religious
sense of morality and self-discipline, and the intensive interrogation he
then got from his father every night at supper. Not surprisingly, he
identified with his father, challenged his teachers and was dismissed
from class on at least one occasion. One of his worst memories was
being forced to read Demosthenes' *On the Crown* in its original Greek. His
unsmiling master placed 'this masterpiece into our hands in order to give
us lessons of grammar, with an absolute prohibition to read a translation

that would have given us a general view of the drama which played out the future of our civilisation'. Yet, despite it all, Georges managed to earn distinguished marks, *accessits*, in classics, recitation, English and chemistry: he received first prizes in French speech and Latin in his last year.

In the meantime his father was getting further embroiled in politics. He had been considered sufficiently important by Napoleon's police to receive the honour of a prison sentence in the aftermath of the *coup d'état* of December 1851. He was released within a few months. During the government's crackdown that followed Orsini's attempt on the Emperor's life he faced further imprisonment and, worse, transportation.

It was one of the most dramatic events of his life. He was arrested at his reading club in the presence of his seventeen-year-old son late on a Sunday afternoon in March, 1858. For a month he was guarded at Nantes while the prefect prepared a case for the prosecution, and was then sentenced to be deported to Algeria. His daughter Emma had a nervous collapse. Georges began to assume the mantle of authority.

He relates that he was witness to his father's departure from Nantes for Marseille. Georges cried out to his father, abandoned by all of his friends but two, Hannibal's oath, 'I will avenge you!' to which Benjamin replied, 'If you want to avenge me, work.'

A crowd had gathered round the departing wagonette and posed enough of a threat for the prefect to call out the troops. Street demonstrations continued for several days. They must have had an effect because when Benjamin arrived in Marseille he received the glad tidings that he was not going to North Africa after all, the Minister of the Interior had just granted a pardon; he took a carriage back to the Vendée and L'Aubraie. It was an appreciable achievement in a period of the Second Empire that is usually regarded as authoritarian. By now, Benjamin Clemenceau was a local hero.

V

THIS WAS the image he wanted: back to the wall, daggers drawn, the romantic hero ready to challenge God Himself if He stood in the way of man's liberty and justice. This was the way he saw himself: a man of action, passionate and alone in the universe. The hero: the kind of man psychologists say engages his enemies outside to overcome the great holy war within. For Benjamin, it was an internal war alright. Part of this arose from tensions with his own father, who had never really approved of his marriage into a modest Protestant family from the bocages.

But the age bred great romantic battles. Benjamin Clemenceau had gone to Paris as a medical student the very month Hugo's *Hernani* opened at the Comédie Française. He had attended and must have witnessed Hugo's supporters arriving in their capes and fancy hats, with their flowing hair – Théophile Gautier wearing his legendary red waistcoat (which was actually a brilliant pink). Theatre was more than the performance; it was a social occasion, a political event and, in this instance, war: 'two systems, two parties, two armies, two civilisations – it is not saying too much – were present, cordially hating each other, as one hates one another in literary hatreds,' said Gautier of the opening night. 'The general attitude was hostile, arms folded, the quarrel waiting to fly out at the slightest contact.'

The romantic hero – angry defender of genius, youth, and humanity – caught the ambivalent tone of this serious, serious era. No jokes. No ridicule. None of the biting satire of a Voltaire or a Diderot. Nobody jousted with windmills here, no Candide after ugly ladies washing dishes by the sea of Marmora. You had to be serious when addressing the people. The early nineteenth century speaks to us, in the first person, about the gravest matters of life and love. Look at the photographs of Benjamin Clemenceau. 'My father,' said Georges, 'was at bottom a romantic who carried into politics, into sociology, the literary ideas of Victor Hugo and those fellows.'

Romantic sociology? What Benjamin had picked up in Paris and passed on to his son were the two voices of romanticism, the solitary genius groaning in an environment of mediocrities, and the cry of the crowd, the people, to be freed of brutish poverty and oppression. An earnest, self-fashioned ego had managed to combine itself with the curious idea that the mass had a consciousness, though nobody ever thought of inviting one in to tea and asking it. 'The people,' wrote Hugo in his preface to *Ruy Blas*, 'who have the future but have not the present; the people, orphaned, poor, intelligent and strong ... The people, it would be Ruy Blas.' Whatever he meant – and one cannot be sure what he meant – it was most appealing to think that somehow ego and the consciousness of the people could be embodied in a single individual. 'The people, it would be . . .' Who next? No telling on whose shoulders the hand of creation and destiny tomorrow might fall.

Vanity was not the sole ingredient of Benjamin's philosophy. He had received a medal for his part in the July Days in Nantes in 1830. We do not know of his whereabouts when the barricades went up again in Paris in June 1832. But his solid embrace of republic and revolution captures the enthusiasm and subsequent disappointment these two years had kindled in his generation – the period of revelation so central to Hugo's *Les Misérables*: 'The modern ideal,' Hugo comments as he describes the final assault on the barricade, rué de la Chanvrerie, 'the modern idea! finds its pattern in art, and its means in science. It is by science that one will realise that august vision of the poets: *le beau social*, the social aesthetic.' A thrilling idea at the time. That passing, rejoicing experience of beauty, best expressed in art (but known by anyone with the passion to love), has a social function and direction if applied by our romantic *with science*, an understanding of the group, the people, their ugliness, their misery. The romantic's social science was an altruistic science which lighted the way to human progress. Art and science, love and intelligence: this is what would save the people from injustice, pull them out of their *darkness* and *bestiality* (the words of the romantics). But do not try to move too fast; *Malheur à qui tente de lui forcer la main!*

The greatest single influence on Benjamin was the historian Jules Michelet if one is to believe his son; he used to speak of Michelet 'always with the greatest respect'. Here again was a passionate appeal for a social understanding combined with isolated genius: '*Me*, poor solitary dreamer, what could I give to this great silent people? What I had, my voice.' When Benjamin arrived in Paris, Michelet was in Italy with the 'new science' of Giovanni Vico buzzing in his head. Already, in his early thirties, he had achieved some renown as a professor at the Ecole préparatoire (not yet the Normale). Benjamin might have heard of him, though it would be stretching the imagination to think of Michelet as exerting much effect at this time; the influence must have come early in the 1840's when Michelet, at the Collège de France, abandoned the Middle Ages for the Revolution and contemporary history; his reasons were pressing, to counter what he saw as a return of the old tyrannies of monarchy and clerical prejudice. He was planting, and dressing, the seeds of 1848.

There is something alluringly naïve about this singular hero setting up the New Jerusalem in Paris on behalf of the speechless masses. It was an article of faith for so many of his admirers and contemporaries, especially the professionals, the journalists, what we usually call the intellectuals who had completed their apprenticeship during the reign of the last French monarch. '*Les prophètes! Les prophètes!*' students had cried when greeting Michelet and Edgar Quinet at the first session of the College following the proclamation of the Republic. After the coup of 1851, Hugo went into voluntary exile – photos of him show him playing his part well, head in hands, like a Rodin statue, brooding on the rocks of Guernsey, Socrates summoning his genius; Michelet lost both his chair at the Collège de France and his position at the Archives Nationales, and spent many of the next years travelling in the provinces and abroad – in Nantes he recorded a meeting with Benjamin Clemenceau. These were the models for a generation. Benjamin could shut himself up in his library and still believe himself to be the representative man, the hero of art, of science and the people, dreaming of a second Renaissance.

The paradox of Benjamin Clemenceau is that he could rage about the rights of man and the Revolution in an almost mystical frenzy and at the same time embrace science as the means, the tool, by which the people could realise their full potential as practical, reasonable beings. Every creature had its place. The romantic hero could stretch out and engage the whole natural universe in dialogue, in one vast elan of love.

In one of the most extraordinary passages he wrote – it is from *La Mer* – Michelet speaks of the humble task of molluscs in the liberating scheme of History. They say nothing, their lives are to themselves: 'Solitude! (says a heart of woman) Grand and sad solitude!' No, no, responds Michelet, 'all is friend here,' for 'these poor little workers' pass their speech on to their sublime father, the Ocean, who will speak in their place. This Ocean has a 'grand voice': 'Between the silent earth and the mute tribes of the sea, it creates here the dialogue, grand, strong and grave, sympathetic – the harmonious concord of the *great Me* with itself, this beautiful debate which is nothing other than Love.'

The unity of aesthetics and science, ego and altruism, was rather appealing to a country doctor who lived in the presence of the bocages, the plain and the sea: the doctor on frontiers who saw no patients. But applied to the world of politics and public policy it was a formula that invited conflict. Benjamin Clemenceau never put it to the test; his son did.

CHAPTER TWO

Paris

THE TWO men, father and son, travelled together to Paris in the autumn of 1861. The son by now had more than two years of medical training behind him, including internships at the Hôtel Dieu and the Hôpital Général in Nantes. But it was in Paris that his political ideals were first put to task. His father, having installed him in lodgings on rue de l'Estrapade – a comforting, unusually clean street for the neighbourhood, that had been saved from demolition by its proximity to the Panthéon and the fact that it ran close to the peak of the hill – introduced him to Etienne Arago's circle of republican friends. It seemed an ideal gentlemanly setting wherein he could pursue politics and a medical degree.

But the next four years were to be a period of severe personal crisis for Georges Clemenceau. More than that, the years in Paris were for him, as they were for so many who had lived through the two decades of Napoleon III, a time when the historical myths of the romantics were confronted with material realities the earlier generation had not counted on: universal manhood suffrage and abundant wealth without democracy. The Republic of 1848 had failed. Some could accept this as the new truth and make the appropriate compromises; they would consider republican ideas as the bubbling infatuations of youth, good ideas but quite impractical – they would actively cooperate with the men of the Second Empire. But for many retreat was more attractive. Already in Montmartre and Montparnasse could be found followers of Leconte de Lisle, of Gautier and of the Parnassiens; and there were the plain and simple bohemians who followed nothing beyond a vague negative attitude that everything that was material, conformist and useful was ugly. Disinterested in politics, they made poverty or, if they had the talent, art the hub of their existence and the 'bourgeois' a figure of fun.

Clemenceau, not a tall man but fastidiously dressed with the high-chinned collar, black silk cravat, waistcoat and watch-chain that were to remain his style for the rest of his life, kept a distance from this kind of life. He vigorously rejected the isolating ideal of the new 'art for art's sake' movement; he wanted, like all romantics, to stretch out, move on, be sociable, which was why he was so damning when he described Alphonse Daudet's play, *La dernière idole* – 'We still want to believe in friendship and especially in love,' he confirmed. But that was in February 1862. He was shortly to find himself on his own desert island. Neither compromiser nor bohemian, Clemenceau would have difficulty defining his place in this city of two million.

I

LOOK AT Paris of the Second Empire and you see a Paris of clichés: lights, mirrors, gilded cafés and high-ceilinged restaurants, Left Bank cafés filled with conspiring intellectuals, foreigners, tables set for two, and the irresistible fallen woman staring out into nothingness, a glass of green-shaded absinthe placed neatly in front of her. It was a display of advertisements. Cobblers, glovemakers, small operators and tradesmen stuck notices at eye level on the yellow-brown walls that flanked the asphalt pavements of the new quarters; they glued them at the entrance of cafés, the doors locked open, beside the corkscrew staircase, on the backs of the chairs. Over your shoulders loomed bold, capital lettered proclamations running up to the roofs, announcing the presence of some clothes merchant, or a furniture house, that had just set up shop in the rue de la Chaussée d'Antin. The building sites were free game, always ready for a placard or bill-board that could stretch the length of a small street. One of the novelties of the age was the advertising carriage, carrying its signs on its roof and along its sides; it was usually gilded and complete with servants in livery. These would be scattered about the regular traffic of carriages, hired coaches – the open *cabriolets* numbered with small red figures, the closed *voitures* with larger yellow ones – and the odd commercial wagon. On the boulevards they ran four, and sometimes six, rows deep. The omnibuses of Paris had recently been reorganised into a single monopoly company, the CGO, which was supposed to provide a cheap way of getting round the city – six sous inside, three on top of the *impériale* as it was called. But they were inevitably overloaded and the offices which sold the tickets were scenes of Darwinian struggle and impolite French prose; flagging a bus down was an alternative, but it would require patience and set one head on into another impending hazard – the horses.

Horses presented a problem everywhere, and not only for the stinking mementos they left for careless feet. They took fright. The most busy time of the day was evening – the rich were eating out, the poor, walking home. Horses, in the congestion, took a beating; it was not surprising that some of the first measures on cruelty to animals had been taken at the dawning of the Second Empire.

Night added one more component. There *was* a show of lights, in the privileged sections. Gas lamps which nestled on posts of cast iron had largely replaced the oil lanterns, strung across the streets, that used to light Paris – intermittently according to the season – in the 1830's and 1840's. Electric lighting was known but was put off for a long time because it had been deemed injurious to the eyes by the city fathers. But it was not only street lamps that gave Paris its famous nickname. Shops remained open, kiosks lining the two sides of the larger boulevards, their gas brightened interiors flickering through the coloured window panes: gas illuminated letters on the front of every theatre; it was the activity on these streets, commercial, entertaining, that lent them light. 'On the western boulevards, and other fashionable parts of town,' read Galignani's *New Paris Guide*, 'it is difficult to fancy anything more tastefully brilliant than the Parisian coffee-rooms. When lit up at night, the effect, seen either from the exterior or within, is perfectly dazzling.'

Whether in the boulevards at night, or on the top of a hill, or upon one of the many monuments of Paris, that dazzling gorgeousness was constantly being thrown at the eyes of the visitor – 'How unlike the view from the top of St. Paul's in London, with its canopy of fogs and clouds, and its sickly sunbeams!' – and at anyone up from the provinces for the first time, for that matter. Not that the will to impress was new. The architects of Henry IV (the Place Royale, the Place Dauphine) and of Louis XIV (Jules Hardouin-Mansart's Place des Victoires, Place Louis-le-Grand – or the Vendôme as it was by now known) had established themselves as past masters of the art. But the scale of the monumental vistas and of the human traffic, the movement, which accompanied it, had never been seen before. The long boulevards of this period, looking down into a column, an arch, or a dome of stone, were expressions of a secular power, both economic and political, that no earlier regime had been able to approach. Their uniformity at once offended and excited a measure of content. They were comforting in an uncomforting world. They provided living space in a place where living space could only be bought at a premium. They were imposing. They were predictable: six or seven storeys high, the flanking apartment buildings rose straight up from the wide parallel pavements, the browed arches of the ground floor windows topped by the iron trellised line of balconies on the second, a plain cornice at the fourth, more balconies, and onward up to the grey mansard roofs housing maids and writers, red chimney-pots planted in threes, sixes and tens on broad stacks of lighter grey, and the whole line punctuated, here and there, by a small cupola.

Sensual, yes: urban life was touchable and erotic. Satisfying, no. If life on the wide modern streets of Paris offset some of the loneliness and fright

that could be found in every sad tenement block in the city, the thrill had
strings attached: tension, frustration, aimlessness. This could be seen in
the baggy pantaloons and threadbare coat that a stonemason or carpenter
exposed to ridicule as he stooped to pick up several huge copper sous on his
way back from work in a development site of the western quarters; in the
dilated, apprehensive eyes of the provincial 'celebrity' sitting alone among
a collection of empty pavement tables and chairs with all the serenity of
Michelangelo's God in judgment: 'I have no friends of any kind, and I do
not want any.' The wish to break ties and withdraw from the show was on
more than one poet's mind.

> *Je ne te vendrai pas mon ivresse ou mon mal,*
> *Je ne livrerai pas ma vie à tes huées,*
> *Je ne danserai pas sur ton tréteau banal*
> *Avec tes histrions et tes prostituées.* *

It was a sentiment that was found among several sections of the population,
not just the intellectuals. And it celebrated less a desire of falling in with the
crowd than a separation, a feeling of contempt for a regime and society that
seemed to cater solely to the greedy and the merciless.

In general, working people became increasingly agitated. There was
the inevitable printers' strike. That was in 1862. It was put down
with elephantine gentility by Napoleon's police. Liberalisation of the
association laws two years later did not improve the situation and soon
strikes, frequently violent, were to become a part of life in the capital, as
elsewhere.

Paris was changing; and it was changing before the architects started
drawing neat little lines across the city's map. In the first forty years of
the century, the population of Paris doubled; in the following twenty-five it
doubled again. More people meant more buildings; more buildings meant
more people, more work, more to be transported, more roads, more to
be levelled, more to be constructed. It was the second city in the world
to pass the million mark. One Frenchman in thirteen lived within its
boundaries, while only one-third of these had been born there. It was
a city of immigrants. It had the densest urban population in Europe,
although nobody could say exactly how dense because there was no
accurate means of measuring it. Rents went blazing forth in a fireworks
display. They were calculated according to the square metre, one more
sign of the shortage of space. In the early 1860's there were parts of Paris
where rents were raised, within a matter of weeks, from one franc to five

---

* 'I will not sell to you my ecstasy or my pain,/I will not surrender my life to your
jeers, I will not dance on your trite stage/ With your players and your prostitutes.'
Leconte de Lisle, *Les Montreurs* (1862).

and even ten a month, a devastating development for low-income families. Poverty compelled mobility.

Poor Paris moved in two directions: inward, into the invisible secret spaces between the boulevards and festooned streets; and outward, into the slopes and plains of Belleville, La Villette and still further, down the two sides of the Seine or, to the west, where already old landed estates were being bought up for cheap housing and industry – bankers had purchased land in Issy and Les Moulineaux: Nicolas Levallois, a former *compagnon* of the carpentry trade, was developing the chess-board settlement in a southern corner of Clichy that was soon to bear his name. Forces of concentration, forces of dispersion. Government did not possess the means of controlling them, though it could heighten their effect. The urban planners liked the free flow of human traffic, but they did not like the artifacts of industry. So they hid them. It was an industry of workshops they hid, of cobblers and hosiers, of printers, stationers and bookbinders, of machinists and locksmiths. Many of these people were organised in trade associations. Most were not, which allowed them to turn their skills in pursuit of the small profits that crowds made possible. Within the ring of fortifications that the diplomatically isolated governments of Louis-Philippe had felt compelled to construct and which became, in 1860, the formal boundary of the city, one could find the densest concentration of artisanry in the country, an area showing one of the lowest number of workers per *établissement* (they could hardly be described as 'businesses' in the English sense). These were the working people who crammed into the hidden islands of courtyards, haphazard staircases, ladders with missing rungs, a cobbled *rigole* or drain down the centre of the passageway carrying a dribble of human and animal effluent, the communal iron tap decorated with a gargoyle, feminine sphinx or some quaintly inapt cherub, thick wooden doors, tiny chambers, and at the end a cutler's shop, a small-ware dealer, or a maker of hand-guns; these islands that somebody without a map, or simply tired of the monotonous row of apartment blocks, might stumble on north of Hôtel de Ville and east of the new boulevard Sebastopol, or just further down, on the river's bank opposite Saint-Louis, or across the river in the Latin Quarter overlooking the cathedral of Notre Dame, or the rue Mouffetard. The hovels on the Ile de la Cité had been levelled; those on the slopes of Belleville, Ménilmontant and Montmartre multiplied.

Nobody planned poor Paris. What urban reforms were introduced highlighted the ineffectuality of government as an agent for social improvement; what actions were taken by Napoleon III and his indefatigable prefect, the baron Haussmann, merely exacerbated trends that could be traced back more than a generation. Most of the new avenues stopped short at the inner boulevards, that line of pomp and glitter which followed the old ramparts Louis XIV had ordered demolished. More of old Paris remained than the anti-government pamphleteers would lead one to believe. But it was not easily accessible – you could not take a carriage there – and anyway, it was not very pretty.

Large contractors did not build for the poor. In their quarters the most traditional forms of construction survived along with an inventive penchant for materials no architect could dream of: the tarpapered roof and bits of old metal and wood shoring up a wall or providing a chimney duct, quite divorced from the function for which they were originally intended. Animals found their place here: dogs, chicken, rabbits. Some of the most enterprising near the fortifications raised pigs. And gardens, or at least a patch, devoted to a few potatoes, some beans, or an incongruous sunflower looming over the black and secret vault of a home-made dwelling. Poverty in Paris belonged to only one social category, poverty. It had the rest, the haves, the have-nots, and the Mr. in-betweens. Most were the last. Urban peasants.

It was curious that one should speak, in such a town, of 'class', though there was probably no other place on earth where the culture of 'class' was more talked about, more intensely kindled, than in Paris. In the twenty-four years between 1827 and 1851 the barricades had been raised nine times. The bloodiest battle was still to come. The June Days of 1848 – when nearly every street east of the barrière Rochechouart and the barrière Saint-Jacques was occupied by the insurgent poor, artisans, petty tradesmen and students, when walls of hefty sandstone cobbles were thrown up at close to two hundred separate spots, when over 1500 lives were lost and another 12,000 persons arrested – seemed to confirm the depth of the war between the classes. Paris had become the human laboratory of Europe from which every universal social theory, and every fear, seemed to emanate. Even genuine workers were apt to look upon their world as split in two.

If there was one fundamental cause for such an ardent sense of 'class' in Paris, it was the general increase in population. Poor and rich were pressed together. You did not have to be a master of political economy to recognise in the Paris of the boulevards compensation for the other shortcomings of the city, the thankless lives and squalid dwellings. Avenues, advertisements, the trains, the carriages, the buses – this was a city in continual communication in a way that was visually striking. All visitors remarked about it. Yet there were whole sections of Paris that were shut out from one another; some residents even appeared to be unaware that they were living in Paris. There was also the violence in the way those avenues and boulevards were constructed. Gautier in 1855 spoke of the demolition squads felling houses 'as the pioneer of America fells trees.' But it was the Austrian architect, Camille Sitte, who probably came closest to the point by describing Haussmann's broad avenues and monumental perspectives as the embodiment of 'the modern disease of disengagement'. You had to admire it. You could feel at once a boundless power to control your own fate, and a sense of nothingness, an overwhelming helplessness.

Clemenceau's early years in Paris typified this. One extraordinary man's personal crisis in the 1860's – a will to control abdicating in helplessness and withdrawal – was the ordinary experience of thousands, hundreds of thousands.

II

Is IT very surprising that, in the midst of cities swelling in number, the science of the time should have been biology? The word itself was not used; at least, few of the educated had heard of 'biology.' But the sciences of life and of creation were developing quickly. And for a very short time they could be taken as the humanist's science, the science that a progressive philosopher might grasp as the hope and the cure for a suffering people.

Clemenceau wrote his thesis, *De la génération des éléments anatomiques*, over a period of about four months, between January and April 1865, and defended it on 13 May. He himself called it a compilation, a summary. Whole chapters are simply recapitulations of one or another article published by his director, Charles Robin, replete with long quotations and supporting footnotes. It was the sort of scissors-and-paste job that gave the medical thesis a very bad reputation in France; one could scan its 200-odd pages in vain to find an original piece of research, though there were passages that showed the excitement of the polemicist he already was, and it had style. Clemenceau describes the initial changes within a fertilised human egg, all thirteen hundredths of a millimetre, with the enthusiasm of a Carlyle or a Michelet describing a great historical event: '*Such* is the ovule at the moment that the phenomena, which follow fertilisation, are produced. *Now* begins that series of phenomena of which I spoke at the beginning. . .' He approached it with the same passion with which he would later regard his flowers at Saint-Vincent-sur-Jard or Monet's series of paintings of the cathedral at Rouen. Life erupts from what was moments earlier brute, amorphous matter, deprived of all structure, that becomes at that seminal instant structure, organised matter. 'A new individual has surged forth,' he explains, noting how the appearance of an organised living element out of apparently formless substances differed from the regular processes of nutrition and growth.

The individuality of life was one of the central concerns of the study. It is explained in terms of not just one, but several such surges, or 'apparitions' as Robin called these moments of creation. Clemenceau re-evokes a notion of one of Napoleon I's botanists, Buisseau de Mirbel, that an individual being, since it is made up of recurring minute internal births, is in effect a collective being, a federation of anatomic elements. No foreign matter was thought to influence this growth; what was already there within the body was simply supposed to create the conditions out of which tiny new organised living substances sprung. This internally confined process was also used to explain disease – due to 'bad conditions of milieu' such as a 'tainted atmosphere'. In Clemenceau's thesis, growth, adulthood, disease and death are all part of the same process, the generation of structured elements from amorphous matter.

In short, this was the theory of spontaneous generation, still popular in scientific circles in the 1860's, though it was dealt a mortal blow by a committee report, published the same year as Clemenceau's thesis, from the Academy of Sciences on Pasteur's experiments on fermentation – or rather the lack of it – in purified or filtered atmospheres.

Science was developing new premises, though not everyone saw it, not even the specialists. In his introduction to the second edition of *De la génération*, published two years later, Dr Charles Robin managed to reject, within the space of three pages, the theory of evolution, germ theory and the particle theory of light. It was not a promising base for Clemenceau's scientific ideas.

The influence of Robin is worth more than a passing thought. Clemenceau was not a philosopher and was not the type of person who would sink into deep reflection, even in periods of personal crisis such as he was facing when he wrote his thesis. A good phrase was irrepressible, regardless of whether it was at somebody else's expense or not, and it usually was. There are sentences in *De la génération* where he even seems to be taking a poke at the lumbering Teutonic sentences of his master. Clemenceau could move from a layman's language to the vocabulary of a pedant and back to simplicity again. *De la génération* is as much an exercise in style as anything else – like a schoolboy concocting good précis out of a civil servant's memorandum on salary scales.

But Charles Robin was not at all the man his scientific prose would suggest. When Clemenceau met him he was well past forty, but he did not look it. He was of medium height, wore a moustache, blonde hair, was slender, was fun to talk to and, as another contemporary of the time noted, 'was sufficiently worldly to amuse the ladies.' He was the first man in Paris to be offered a chair in histology, and it was from that position, enjoying the reputation as one of France's finest researchers to work with a microscope, that he expounded his theory about the generation of anatomic elements.

The 1860's were an exciting decade for a scientist. A debate raged between those who believed, like Darwin, Virchow and Pasteur, that the relationship between the species and individual variations were evidence that life came from outside the organism and was passed on, over time, from generation to generation, and those like Robin and Pasteur's great rivals, Pouchet, Joly, Musset, who understood life to be an internal force, born within, the only external agent being an environment of favourable conditions.

History is unkind to its losers. They are made the aficionados of quaint thoughts, like the inventors of aeroplanes with flapping wings, leg-driven carriages and mechanical brooms. The theory of spontaneous generation had its element of flapping wings. In the early seventeenth century a Flemish doctor and chemist, Jan Baptist van Helmont, proved that mice sprang spontaneously from the dirty shawls of old women. Flies were born out of ripe cheeses, they swarmed from rotting meat and faeces. But these fantastic phenomena had no serious defenders in the nineteenth century; spontaneous generation was by now a theory of tissues, molecules, cells, elements. Charles Robin in particular did not dismiss the existence of cells. He simply did not accept the cell as the building block of life. What he called an 'anatomic element' was less a physical unit than a time-mass unit that was under a continual process of change, a *phenomenon*, not just something you could touch.

Yet, if Robin showed more finesse than some of his colleagues (in fact, Pasteur even recommended him to the Academy of Sciences), he was also a man of his time, a humanist, a political animal, a man who believed that philosophy really could serve as a guide to the pursuit of scientific inquiry. The terrible truth had not yet dawned. For Robin and Clemenceau, Auguste Comte, the positivist philosopher, was as important an authority in science as the physiologists – Robin even took the physiologists to task for not being sufficiently well read in Comte. 'The misunderstanding of these ideas,' he writes in his introduction, 'is the source of systematic errors and contradictory hypotheses', of which Rudolph Virchow is singled out as one of the most guilty.

It is difficult today to imagine how a trained scientist could turn to a contemporary philosopher – or near contemporary, Comte had died in 1856, but it was only in the 1850's and 1860's that a following of any appreciable size developed – as a *source* for scientific theory. But this was an age when the natural sciences and the humanities were still on an equal footing, perhaps for the last time. In the mid-nineteenth century, the study of society was a science. The study of matter was a science. The great thing, however, was that they held one another in common respect. Both clung fervently to the same end, the perfectibility of mankind.

Development for Comte was social, not biological. Biology laid the conditions for existence, society provided the motor for change, an ever-increasing contact and borrowing between peoples that led, ultimately, to the irreversible development of civilisation. Biology was the material starting-point. Biology was what made society possible. Biologically, man was an emotional rather than an intellectual being, and it was from his innate emotional drive to be with others, for a 'solidarity' with his own kind, for altruism, that society was born and intellect began to evolve.

These notions were translated into Clemenceau's thesis, courtesy of Dr Charles Robin, by emphasising what we have already seen as the main aspects of his argument, the conditions of the milieu, spontaneous generation within the egg, and the succeeding string of generations as the organism developed. Life bursts tameless from an unstructured environment to create, by contact and borrowing, the structured organism, a federation of beings. The 'organic economy' (the term was becoming very popular) is an order of correlations, of matter reacting to matter, of small instrumental parts finding their place in the whole, of creating the whole, a circularity of substances. There is no room for the 'soul':

> Here the vitellus [egg yolk], a material endowed only with molecular renovation, and there the fœtus, an animated being. How can the first be born from the second? You say to me: it is between the two that the soul intervenes. All right. But at what moment? According to you, there is no life in the embryo before the introduction of the soul; with the soul life appears. You mean without doubt that the soul manifests its presence by some new phenomenon, which up to then was missing. Well, what is this phenomenon? Where, when, how does one observe it? What is the effect of the soul on the embryo? How can one distinguish the embryo without soul from the embryo with soul? ... The truth is that the birth of the embryo is composed of a series of *epigeneses*, that is to say, of the successive apparition in a determined order of anatomic elements of diverse types ... There is really nothing else there, other than the properties of organised matter, producing themselves within an organ which itself arises from an organism.

In a supporting footnote, Clemenceau cites Emile Littré's 1864 preface to Comte's *Cours de philosophie positive*: 'One undeniable fact is that one knows of no thought without brains.'

Clemenceau, the uncompromising materialist, was pushing the sciences into the cause of humanity. Beyond man, there was no intelligence. 'Mon père était *idéologue*.' From his father, Clemenceau had learnt the anti-clerical messages of the *idéologues*, a party of philosophers led by Georges Cabanis and Destutt de Tracy who, at the beginning of the century, reduced all thinking and all sentiment to the material organs of a material body – Descartes without the benefit of an autonomous mind. Now he applied them to a mid-nineteenth-century medical science. Man was alone with man, with the animals and the plants, the conditions of his existence. It was not only germs that were refused entry. Ideas, like disease, were born within. Clemenceau's humanism was a humanism with a vengeance, applied to what was at that time known, through microscopic analysis, of the private parts of frogs, molluscs, fish, insects, dogs and rabbits; and then turned on to man.

Louis Pasteur disliked this kind of philosophising. 'In the writings of M. Comte,' he wrote in a letter of reference that finally resulted in Robin gaining a chair at the Academy of Sciences, 'I have read only a few ridiculous passages; and in those of M. Littré, only the fine few pages inspired by his outstanding scholarship and some of his domestic virtues. My own philosophy is entirely of the heart, not the mind.' As for M. Robin himself, Pasteur was 'favourably inclined' because his work with the microscope was not so far represented at the Academy. 'I am not worried about his philosophical beliefs except for the harm they may do to his work; in the case of a scientist, a man must always be at grips with the experimental method . . .'

Clemenceau would go to his grave believing the contrary. He was an eclectic, like Robin, who was incapable of accepting the confines of the 'pure sciences' that were developing at the very time his thesis went to the press. Science, philosophy, journalism and politics were intertwined. 'To ignore questions,' he wrote in his discussion of the soul, citing spiced phrases from Comte and Littré, 'is to suppress them.' That, unfortunately, was precisely what the new science was all about.

Literary men, orators, the scholars, the politicians, those who loved the power of words and who were still willing to free themselves to human pity never accepted this. Edmond About, who could couple like a juggler intense anticlericalism with loyalty to the Empire, was one of them. He was a very well known playwright, and a journalist, and by the late 1850's a writer of science fiction. The year Charles Robin was made Professor of Histology at the Sorbonne, 1862, About published *L'Homme à l'oreille cassée*, *The Man with the Broken Ear*. One of its leading protagonists was Dr. Karl Nibor. The anagram was obvious.

Dr. Nibor's advice is solicited by a young man in Fontainebleau who has acquired in a Berlin pawnshop the desiccated remains of a colonel in Napoleon's army, captured by the Prussians at Danzig in the winter of 1813. Close to death from the cold, the colonel's body is subjected to the care of a German physician, a sort of Frankenstein, and for several months gradually strained, by pneumatic pump, of all vital liquids. Unfortunately, the physician dies before he is able to revive his patient. He leaves a will, but no directions. Dr. Nibor arrives in Fontainebleau, accompanied by members of the *Société de biologie*, on 15 August 1859, Assumption Day and the Emperor's birthday. He explains to an astonished audience how he intends to restore life to the patient: 'With a bath-tub and cauldron of boiling water, we will have everything we need. The colonel needs nothing but humidity.' For two days the colonel is bathed in water at body temperature. 'Organised matter has inherent properties which manifest themselves without the assistance of any foreign principle, whenever they are surrounded by certain conditions . . . Life will manifest itself in a few minutes. It is possible that the muscles will act first, and that their action may be convulsive, on account of not being regulated by the influence of the nervous system . . . I am quite hopeful, however, that the first spontaneous contractions will take place in the fibres of the heart. Such is the case in the embryo, where the rhythmic movements of the heart, precede the nervous functions.' The colonel's cheeks grow red, his eyes flash, the heart beats, the chest rises, the limbs violently contract, the body straightens up, and out comes the cry: '*Vive l'empéreur!*' In the meantime, Fontainebleau is rocked by a war of words between resurrectionists and Christians, to be joined by several *savants* in Paris. The resurrectionists argued that to resuscitate this man was in the interests of science and the right to life. The Christians argued that whoever tried this was a revolutionary, dangerous, and an enemy of the fundamental ideas on which society was based; the colonel must be buried. He eventually was. His second life lasted less than thirty-one days. He died of a broken heart.

It is a silly story. Robin was not a resurrectionist, or, at least, is not known to have dabbled in such radical forms of regeneration. But About had caught the vocabulary and, more, a philosophy of *life* cherished by one of the leading proponents of spontaneous generation. Moments before the colonel's cheeks begin to blush, Nibor is challenged by the young man's father, a good Catholic, who says in effect that you might get the heart to pump, you might get the brain to react, but you will never get the one to motivate the other and thus operate together because you are lacking the essential external agent, the vital principle. This kind of external force is, of course, anathema to Nibor, who replies that life will reveal itself at the instant that any organ – heart, brain, or whatever – which has 'the property of acting spontaneously' has taken on enough water to fulfil the conditions of its existence.

Life is an autonomous entity which creates itself; that is the message of the spontaneous generationists and it is their answer to the old chicken-and-egg problem of what comes first, life or matter: both arrive together, spontaneously; both depart together; before and after life there is nothing but structureless brute matter. There is some resemblance to Christ ordering Lazarus back to life, 'Arise now, walk and speak' (a romantic image that is found in much of Michelet's work). Only here there is no Christ; the order comes from within.

What was lost with the successes of Pasteur, Virchow and Darwin? It would be difficult to conclude that the humanities had not lost some status: a scientist could no longer call on a philosopher to give force to his argument, though the philosopher would often, almost with a sense of guilt-ridden obligation, turn to the scientist. Life itself was no longer such an issue once the mechanics of the two principal biological problems of the era, the related anatomy of different species and individual variation, had been worked out. Henceforth the question of the moment was not so much 'What is life?' as 'What makes this or that specific thing function?' and 'How are they related?'. It was undoubtedly progress. But questions *were* being suppressed. In the mid-nineteenth century, humanists and scientists saw distances developing between them, lines being drawn.

Clemenceau would one day admit to the folly of spontaneous generation. But life for him was always surging forth, creating its own meaning, annihilating disorder.

III

HE HAD come to Paris with the purpose of absorbing this culture of science, one that was in fact fast disappearing: the integrating science of his father and intellectual forebears. It was a political act. A commitment to science was, for Clemenceau, a commitment to the Revolution and its war against established religion.

Within a month of his arrival, he had joined the staff of a small student newspaper, *Le Travail*, which, like most left-bank journals of the day, only managed to squeeze out nine issues before it was closed by government order in the first week of March, 1862.

The paper was probably started with father and friends. At any rate, it was not an individual venture. Clemenceau, surrounded by a group of admiring bearded bohemians, leading the battle against Napoléon le Petit, is perhaps a nice thought, but stretches the imagination a bit. He was not a man who had an easy time making friends and an exception at this point in his life would seem odd. He hated the bohemian life, was a tidy man – a kind of genteel tidy disorder is reported by later observers – and his three apartments, first at rue de l'Estrapade, then rue de Bac and finally rue Saint-Sulpice, were respectable addresses which kept him a good arm's length from Grub Street. Unlike his father, who had made his first trip from their Vendée château to Paris by foot, Clemenceau

came in style, by *diligence*, with a couple of trunkloads of clothes strung
on top.

It was largely out of his father's effort that Clemenceau found himself
moving between two political circles. The first of these consisted almost
exclusively of old associates of the Second Republic who had managed
to put together the semblance of a social life now that Napoleon had
granted amnesty to all political criminals, offenders and persons previously
condemned as a danger to national security. Etienne Arago, the youngest
of four famous brothers from the Pyrenees, was the host. As a student, he
had been a close friend of Benjamin Clemenceau, a friendship that was
sealed for life with the Revolution of 1830. Accounts have described him
as a man with long flowing hair, but by the time the younger Clemenceau
was introduced to him in Paris it was clear that ten years of exile had had
a wearing effect on the epicranium.

The heroes of Arago's circle remained Michelet, Quinet and Hugo,
though Emile Littré had added a touch more 'science' by getting them
all to read Comte. Clemenceau had met Hugo on a trip he had made,
again with his father, in the summer of 1859 to that capital of the French
exiles, Brussels. His first impression was of a poet a little too full of himself,
but impressive. The only sight he was to get of Michelet was of an elderly
gentleman sitting in a balcony at the Odéon Theatre with sharp little black
eyes and long white hair (unlike Arago, his exile had been largely voluntary
and limited to Nantes and other such places).

Most of the visitors to Arago's home belonged to this generation of
romantics, born either in the last decade of the Napoleonic Empire
or some time during the Restoration. Within the inner sanctum were
Henri Lefort, Arthur Ranc and Eugène Pelletan. Pelletan was the
liveliest member of the group. He was a staunch believer in science
and progress, putting his thoughts together in a book, *La profession de
foi du XIXe siècle*, published the same year Louis-Napoleon proclaimed
his Empire. He also, as Clemenceau was soon to discover, knew his way
around prisons.

Around this nucleus revolved other figures, like François Lacour or the
radical marquis de Rochefort-Luçay, who preferred for the sake of his
clientele to be called Henri Rochefort, and various professors and literary
men. Charles Robin made an occasional appearance. Jules Simon was at
least talked about; one of those many faceted individuals who combined
heavy academic grime – he had made his name through a multi-volume
critical history of the Alexandrian School – with politics and studies of the
working class.

It is not difficult to guess how a young initiate to the group could
be induced to start a newspaper. All these people were newspapermen
and they did not suffer the obstacles that hampered later professionals;
founding a newspaper was the equivalent of founding a political party,

a new school of literary criticism, a social philosophy. It was a circle that exalted the written political word. One imagines a serious note in their sessions. They were the advocates of an older generation, the romantics.

If Clemenceau had ever known anything approaching the popular view of mid-nineteenth-century student meetings, where the tippling of a *canon* of rotten wine combines with the smoking of pipes and speeches delivered standing on a chair, then it must have been at Delestre's studio on rue des Fossés Saint-Jacques, not very far from his own flat. Jean-Baptiste Delestre was a well-forgotten painter who, in his thirties, had turned his talents to writing about his theory of the passions, as well as an inventive interest in 'pathological iconography' and Antoine Gros (Napoleon I's official artist who drowned himself in the Seine). That brought him into politics, opposition and, with the *coup d'état*, silence – or, more specifically, songs, photographs and a treatise on the human body.

There was a lot of debate at Delestre's, mostly about the French Revolution. They all thought the Revolution had been a good idea. But science couldn't determine who were its best proponents. Gustave Jourdan made a case for the Girondins, supporters of provincial rights, defended in a new book by Edgar Quinet. A convincing argument was made for the Jacobins by Ribert. One of the law students, Gustave Tridon, thought they were both wrong; science was obviously on the side of the Hébertists, they were the ones who considered it their first goal to bring science to the people. 'Science is your conquest, science belongs to all. Come and get it!'

It is clear that Clemenceau, from a very early point, was making an exception to these divisions. The Revolution in his eyes was a single entity, a single event. There was only one real division: you either accepted it, or you rejected it.

These were views he expressed as dramatic and literary editor of *Le Travail*. The editor-in-chief was Germain Casse, a former seminarist in his mid-twenties who had come over from Guadeloupe to study law. His friends described him as 'l'Abbé'. 'Socialist Republican, revolutionary, and atheist,' he said of himself, with a strong creole accent. Other members of the staff included fellow medical students such as Ferdinand Taule, E. N. J. Onimus (one of Robin's prize pupils) and Aristide Rey. There were the lawyers, Eugène Carré, Louis Andrieux and André Rousselle. Pierre Denis, who had already done some journalism in Lyon, was the closest the group came to recruiting a worker; he had been both a cobbler and a mason, and he did in fact spend the rest of his life in dire poverty.

The poet on the staff was a very nervous and quiet character called Emile Zola. Clemenceau was exasperated by him. 'Do anything you like,' he bluntly said after Zola had published a poem on 'Doubt'. 'Do anything you like. Sell mustard or women's hats. But give up literature. You will never be a writer.'

It is significant that Clemenceau should have picked theatre as his debut in journalism. His father's first political experience in Paris had been the staging of *Hernani* at the Comédie Française. In republican politics, science might have been the substance of the message, the people might have been its goal, but to transmit the first to the second required a channel that was accessible to everybody. The exchange had to be global. This is what gave the theatre a political role; it could be seen as something of a prototype for democracy because it was a medium directly accessible to 'the people'. 'I write,' said the popular melodramatist, Pixérécourt, 'for people who cannot read.' Perhaps this had special meaning for a man from the Vendée, one of the most illiterate corners of France.

At the age of twenty, Clemenceau was as adamant about the purpose of theatre as he was later about the defence of justice in parliament. 'The theatre is a tribune,' he wrote, 'take a moral idea and develop from it the consequences, this is how you will moralise the crowd that will come to applaud you.' It didn't matter whether you wrote to a public, painted for a public, or spoke to a public. Whatever. The social responsibility of the artist – this harks back to the altruism of Comte, Michelet and not a small part of Benjamin either – was to moralise the masses. Lift those people out of their chairs and let them celebrate their freedom.

The physical layout of the theatre could also be seen as a little replica of society too. The Odéon, in the middle of the Latin Quarter and the closest to Clemenceau's apartment, was fairly typical of the kind of theatre you found in Paris at the time. Cheap seats downstairs and cheap seats on top, they called that upper balcony 'paradise'; the rich sandwiched between the poor, like life between the garret and the sewer. The rich ate ice cream (it was already popular), the poor chewed apples. The main body of the ground floor was filled with orchestra seats and, behind them, was the pit. Women were not allowed in either the orchestra or the pit. It was from here that democracy spoke – often in the voices of hired hands, the *claque*, that were brought in by the director and friends of the playwright. The *claque* was no guarantee because if play-goers in Paris had abandoned the privilege of clapping when they heard something good, they had not surrendered their right to hiss at something they thought dreadful.

There was one play the staff of *Le Travail* had determined would not last a week. It was called *Gaëtana* and was written by the same man who had just published the spoof on Charles Robin, Edmond About. This was not a sin. Shaking hands with the Emperor was. Worse, like Pasteur, he was known to attend the imperial balls at Compiègne.

Gaëtana was not a masterpiece, even About admitted as much. To render the play more innocuous than its original script, the imperial censors – politely known as the *commission d'examen* – had cut out offending phrases like 'the custom of interrogations', 'absurd laws' or '*mon cher amour*'. *Gendarmes* were given, in the performance, a quaint old Italian term, 'sbires'.

Nobody heard this anyway. There were catcalls in the pit before the curtain went up on the first night. Occasional lines came through, such as the baron's jealous remark to Gaëtana. 'The young people of our century never part with just a fraternal kiss.'

'Don't insult the young,' screamed somebody from the pit.

When the requisite street urchin proclaimed, '*Je suis du peuple, moi!*' there were cries that it was the 'people' who were being insulted. And the romantic effect of the count's, 'I promise to snatch you from the arms of that old man and carry you, this very night, to a country where you will belong only to me, your lover!' was dampened by three explosive animal sounds from behind the orchestra. In the final act there was so much noise that the players simply mimed their parts.

About was humiliated and furious. This was on a Friday night in January – a few sonic booms from cold noses had added to the uproar. All weekend it continued. The management closed the play on Monday night in the middle of the performance, following which a band of students – About said a thousand young heroes – crossed the Seine to demonstrate in front of his apartment.

In retaliation he penned two articles, one in the fairly popular imperialist paper, *Le Constitutionnel*, the other in an obscure provincial instrument published in Troyes, *Le Napoléonien*. The second was much more provocative, referring to the young heroes as *polissons* or 'scoundrels' (*polisson* was the sort of term you expected an angry husband to use when he caught an adulterer at his trade).

Clemenceau's reply was in the character of *Le Travail*:

> We hold it an honour to be placed among the number of *polissons* of which M. Edmond About speaks in his indescribable letter. We return to its author all the contempt that it inspires in us, contempt that all the youth of the Schools certainly share. M. About is a bumptious and violent-tempered scamp. We despise him in Paris and we tell him so. He insults us in Champagne without letting us know. The public will appreciate his behaviour and ours.

IV

WELL, NEWSPAPERS were not designed to be objective. The kind of separation that was to develop in the more sedate corners of the Anglo-Saxon press between 'news' and 'editorial', 'fact' and 'opinion' was quite out of place in Napoleon III's France. The emphasis in France was on opinion. An opposition press had from the very beginning of the Empire commanded the majority of readers. This was rather surprising, considering that the *coup* of 1851 had actually started with a takeover of the Imprimerie Nationale: an implicit recognition by those who craved power that its secret lay in the written word. Yet power was never monolithic, it had no name and address and, once more than two persons were involved, its perpetrators could move on and off the visible stage like people on a bus. Its centre was elusive, its opposites multiple. Everybody had it, nobody had it. Power could surge forth like the cells of anatomy the scientists described; emerging, fading.

You could create meaning and order by a shout in the theatre. You had your place there, a seat in the hierarchy. But it was only with the written word that you registered your commitment, nourished an idea. That is what created the fragments of power as reflected in the enormous number of newspapers that appeared in the 1850's and 1860's. 'How beautiful was the Republic under the Empire!' became the stock cliché of the Third Republic as one government replaced another against a background of scattering political forces. Obviously the division was not so evident under the dictatorship of Napoleon III, but it was already there, in writing, in the newspapers.

During its brief existence, *Le Travail* was involved in polemics against fellow republican papers, the angriest being with the liberal *Le Courrier du Dimanche* under J. J. Weiss and Prévost-Parodol. At the same time, it made a bid for the unity of all republicans under the flag of the French Revolution, a reflection perhaps of the kind of discussion that went on at Delestre's. In one of its last issues, Clemenceau wrote:

> There is no lack of people who believe themselves to be very advanced and who tell us seriously – 'We accept, with all their consequences, the principles of '92, but we reject with horror the violence of the Revolution.' Now, those who talk like that are simpletons or men in poor faith. They apparently do not realise that such violence can only be the fatal consequence of the *appearance* of these principles on the political stage [*l'apparition de ces principes sur la scène politique*].

Clemenceau's distaste for division among defenders of the republican

Revolution of 1792 was mixed with a language that clearly wasn't very conciliatory. Was he deluding himself? How could anyone expect a solidarity to develop with words like these being thrown around?

The contradiction is revealing. Solidarity in Comte's order of things was not intellectual but biological, an innate emotional drive for contact and borrowing, which Clemenceau soon expressed in his thesis in the form of the generation or, as his master said, of the 'apparition', of a federation of beings: acting self-intentioned beings. This was the side of science that microbiology was about to abandon. Crudely put, you would bring people together not with reason, but a scream. In Clemenceau's science it was the *'principes immédiats'* of the surrounding milieu that combined with the autonomous generation of elements to give life. In his journalism it was the principles of '92 combined with the political act which put the Revolution in the history books.

The young Clemenceau rather liked this parallel between individual existence and the course of humanity. 'Man instructs himself with each step he makes in life,' he wrote in a passage which bears some comparison with Saint Augustine's call for a union with God. 'Man profits from the faults of his youth, the generations of today from those of yesterday. Man and humanity! the small and the great! one and all!'

This put him squarely within the school of progress, which provided for him a way of sifting out the good from the evil. Thus he attacked Guizot and Thiers for fatalism in a review of one of Michelet's volumes of the *Histoire de France* – time, he said, does not lend legitimacy to despotism, while making the glorious defenders of progress anathema. Michelet could see this because, like a good painter, he could look at society from a distance; he could appreciate the whole and avoid the useless details. But, again like a painter, he could feel the movement, not just describe it. History is not a narrative, concluded Clemenceau, imitating the historian, it is a resurrection.

This must have made About chuckle.

Clemenceau's last contribution to *Le Travail* was entitled, appropriately, 'The Martyrs of History'. It was published on 22 February 1862. Once more he emphasised the moral lessons of history, not its details. History is a story of suffering genius, the 'holy martyrs of society', at the hands of despots and the mob: 'It is beautiful to suffer and die for a principle, for an idea, as did Socrates or Jesus Christ.' Spartacus and Brutus (whose reputation as the Emperor's assassin was not exactly glowing at this moment) numbered among Clemenceau's martyrs, as were of course the men of 1793: 'No price was too high to pay for the triumph of the principles. Without them, I ask you, where would we be today?'

Perhaps it was meant to be a rhetorical question. But four days later, Georges Clemenceau was in gaol.

V

MONDAY, 24 FEBRUARY, was the fourteenth anniversary of the declaration of the Second Republic, a good occasion, Clemenceau and his colleagues thought, for workers and students to show their solidarity by demonstrating at the Bastille. The workers failed to turn up, but a few policemen did. Taule and Carré were arrested and taken to Sainte-Pélagie. Clemenceau apparently considered working-class struggle, like history and painting, as something best viewed from a distance. 'Luckily for him he was arrested at his home and not at the Bastille,' his father reported to his wife three and a half weeks later, 'for the ones who were taken there were beaten with cudgels and carried off like dead bodies.' He had been arrested on the 26th and carted off to Mazas.

Mazas was officially known as 'La Nouvelle Force'. It replaced an old aristocratic residence in the Marais that had been converted into a prison at the end of the eighteenth century and had been the site of some of the worst massacres of the Revolution. Mazas was no temporary structure. It had been built with meticulous care along the lines of a new humanitarian science of punishment which emphasised silence, separation and routine under the scrutinising eye of unseen authority.

There were questions to answer when you were brought in. Name. Age. Height. Religion. Scars. The colour of your eyes. The length of your right foot. A photograph was taken, among the first photographs of prisoner identity ever taken, and a number was given – you lost your name. And at some point you had to be cleaned. The common bath at Mazas was, Clemenceau said later, the colour of a *café au lait*. He told the guard that he simply would not get in it, was forced to do so, and had a wash up to his knees. After three days at Mazas Clemenceau was prepared to confess anything.

He was allowed to write but not to see relatives. The first to try unsuccessfully to secure his release was an unnamed cousin in Paris. He had also been in contact with two of his sisters, Adrienne, who was only twelve, and Emma, the eldest of the family, who seems to have played some part in keeping his position as a medical *externe* open. He wrote to his father in the Vendée on 15 March to tell him that he had been taken in front of a *juge d'instruction* twice and could not expect an early release. His medical post, he added, was not in jeopardy, at least for the time being. The father received the letter on the 18th (quicker than many twentieth-century postal deliveries). The formal tone that marks this letter is not unusual, but it is odd, given what one can only assume to have been a mutually close relationship, that almost a month had passed from the arrest before

Benjamin was in Paris. Is there an element of parental rejection here? It must have been a very grim time for the son.

At any rate, two days after receiving the letter, Benjamin is in Paris knocking at 'this awful door of Mazas'. To his astonishment he was granted a meeting with his son the very next day, between eleven in the morning and three in the afternoon. There is no record of what passed between them.

For the rest of his life Clemenceau was to harbour bitter feelings about prison reformers. It was only on 11 April, or more than six weeks from the day of his arrest, that he was carried in a *panier à salade*, or black maria, with what he took as a butcher accused of murder on his knee, to face a full court, the *sixième Chambre correctionnelle*. He appeared with Ferdinand Taule, still detained at Sainte-Pélagie. Two weeks earlier, Eugène Carré had been given a two month sentence and a 500 franc fine. Taule, on that day in April, also got two months. But sieur Clemenceau, perhaps because he had not been arrested at the scene, only got a month. He was also sentenced to pay half his prison expenses. The court found him guilty of a misdemeanour, a *délit*, of 'direct provocation, not followed with effect, of armed assembly'. In the formal notice of conviction it was specified that he had 'written, distributed to be posted, and had posted himself a certain number of placards in which he convoked a category of individuals to meet in a determined place, with the end of forming an assembly that might trouble public order'.

He was released in the first weeks of May and, like his father on his release from Marseille exactly four years earlier, he returned to the Château de l'Aubraie.

Clemenceau now appears to suffer a loss of orientation or, at least, this is where a modern psychologist could point to the start of a prolonged 'identity crisis', a depression, that continued with varying degrees of severity until, some eight years later, war and the eventual overthrow of the Emperor propelled him into national politics.

Overthrowing the Emperor might have been an unconscious attempt at deposing the father (even if his expressed admiration for Benjamin remained constant); his effort had been rewarded with two and a half months in an empty cell.

He did not stay at L'Aubraie for long – two or three weeks at the most. By June he was back in Paris at rue de Bac, a well-to-do corner of the seventh arrondissement, and this time he had a room-mate, J. A. Lafont.

Jean-Anne Antoine Lafont was from the south of France and had been active for some time among republican circles in Paris. Georges Wormser, Clemenceau's *chef de cabinet* after the Great War, identified Lafont as the best friend that Clemenceau made in his youth, and the only one with whom he kept in contact. Clemenceau was twenty, Lafont was in his late thirties, so he was old enough to have provided a substitute to the febrile advice Clemenceau had been accustomed to get from his father.

In fact, Paris is all of a sudden bristling with father-figures. Clemenceau's externship was at the Hôpital de la Pitié which at that time, it just so happened, was right next door to the Sainte-Pélagie gaol where Taule was still serving his sentence. Sainte-Pélagie was designed for political prisoners and its inmates were not submitted to the same rigorous regime of activity and confinement as at Mazas; indeed, it was another stalking ground within the republican network, not entirely unlike Arago's flat or Delestre's studio.

Republicans were gathering around two figures at Sainte-Pélagie in June 1862. One was rich and respectable, the other was poor and contemptible. The rich one was a man in his late twenties who had formed a partnership in a chemical firm in Alsace with a brother-in-law. His name was Auguste Scheurer-Kestner, a rather typical member of the kind of industrial dynasties that had been growing in northern and eastern France over the last two hundred odd years. In addition to chemicals, he was interested in pamphlets and German printing presses, not popular products among the governing classes – this is what put him in gaol. The poor man made a profession of being poor and a revolutionary. He tried to keep it a secret, but his elder brother had in fact been a very famous university professor, an economist of the liberal cause, honoured by every government since Waterloo. The younger brother had tried to overthrow every government since Waterloo, including the Second Republic. He knew prisons well, since he had spent most of his adult life in them. His name was Auguste Blanqui.

Clemenceau was fascinated with Blanqui; he said he was drawn to him by the shock of black rays which emanated from the emaciated prisoner's face. One of the few times Clemenceau used the word 'soul' without contempt was when he spoke of Blanqui's 'high and strict lesson of an unalterable soul' – a striking phrase, hinting at 'will power', pure intellect pitted against a blind and inexorably mechanical system.

There was friction between the two. Predictably, Blanqui had a plot. Clemenceau was entrusted with the smuggling of a printing press across the Franco–Belgian border. This was no problem in itself. Clemenceau, accompanied with his room-mate Lafont, set off for Brussels where they introduced themselves to an exiled French medical doctor, Watteau, who provided him with the press. A printing press is not a small machine and it must have taken a certain amount of ingenuity to get it through the French customs. They took it to rue de Bac where, two days later, the police arrived. Clemenceau kept them at the door, dazzling them with an oil lamp held at eye level, while Lafont successfully managed to hide the incriminating object. But one prison sentence was enough. The press ended at the bottom of the Seine.

The issue that finally separated Clemenceau from Blanqui was over another of Clemenceau's older friends, Charles Delescluze. Clemenceau had met him at the Café de Cluny. Delescluze's credentials as defender of the people were almost as good as Blanqui's: he applied his ideas – though most of his commentators agreed they were few in number – with admirable rigidity; he had a sturdy court record, even if he did pass his sentences in exile rather than prison; and in his photographs he had the same earnestly lost look as Blanqui. They were men of a kind and it is not very surprising that Clemenceau was attracted to them both. But the similarity had bred a bitter rivalry. When Blanqui heard that Clemenceau was seeing Delescluze he abruptly broke off all contact with him.

It was during this time that Clemenceau began to develop close ties with Scheurer-Kestner, Etienne Arago and particularly Gustave Jourdan, a man he had first met at Delestre's.

Jourdan had begun his career as a public prosecutor [*procureur du roi*] in the French island colony of Réunion during the reign of Louis-Philippe. The Revolution of 1848 had brought him back to France where he developed his own particular brand of republican philosophy, later published in a book, linking the notion of freedom to work. After marrying a wealthy Parisian widow he settled down to a life of cafés and art studios. Late in his life Clemenceau described Jourdan as the most eloquent man he had ever known. Jourdan said of Clemenceau, 'You will replace for me the brother and the son I do not have.' His were the only personal letters Clemenceau did not destroy in his last years.

Some time in the autumn or winter of 1862 Clemenceau moved out of Lafont's apartment to lodgings of his own, ostensibly for a little peace and quiet for study. He had reason enough for alarm. An internship at a Paris hospital depended on one's performance in a competitive exam, a *concours*. Clemenceau had so far managed to place himself as an extern – his duties would have been limited to the dressing of wounds – at La Pitié by a *concours* that he had taken in his first month in Paris where he had managed to come tenth out of 330 candidates. In October 1862 he sat with thirty-three other externs for the full internship. He came thirty-third and, as a result, lost his position at La Pitié.

He was moved to Bicêtre, an infamous seventeenth-century establishment for two thousand mad and old men in the southern outskirts of the city. The patients were kept in large open dormitories and the same humanist doctrine, enshrined in the 'right to work', was applied here as at Mazas. It was another opportunity for Clemenceau to test his principles, another chance to moralise the masses. In February 1863 he told Scheurer-Kestner that he felt obliged 'to moderate some of the theories I have on the influence of the environment'.

Clemenceau's calling for medicine, which had not been strong to begin with, was now at its nadir. There were roughly six or seven kilometres between his new apartment at rue Saint-Sulpice and Bicêtre; he must have trudged them on foot. In July 1863 he was suspended for absenteeism and by August he had been moved back, as an extern, to La Pitié. He took the *concours* again that October, but he never made it to the internship.

Was this because he was so politically active? Hardly. Beyond his bizarre involvement with Blanqui his political activities after Mazas were limited. On his return to Paris in June 1862 he had helped set up a new journal, *Le Matin*, with basically the same team as the now defunct *Le Travail*. Pierre Denis became its director. Clemenceau contributed only one short article. In August the paper folded. Almost two years later, in April 1864, the same group founded *Les Ecoles de France*, which was even shorter-lived than the previous two papers. The editor-in-chief this time was Charles Longuet, whose principal claim to fame lay in his future marriage to one of Karl Marx's daughters. Clemenceau contributed nothing. The first number of *Les Ecoles* reported that Clemenceau had been elected president of the Society of Medical Students. The society never met.

Backwards, sidewards, forwards, everywhere; he was breathing in empty space. The will to control, to impose meaning, was at odds with the direction life presently seemed to be taking. This was an uncomfortable way of experiencing freedom.

He was not to be the world's finest doctor. His science was the old romantic's, the philosopher's science. It was not at all clear that he had a future in politics. His journalism was hardly a shower of glory. He could be an intellectual, a writer – Jourdan provided the model. He was still enamoured of science, the old humanist science. And he read a great deal, primarily philosophy and histories of the French Revolution. 'We are dwarfs by the side of our fathers,' he wrote after completing one of Charles-Louis Chassin's books on the Revolution. Chassin was a romantic from Nantes and had been active in 1848; another father-figure, yes.

VI

FREUD WROTE somewhere that most men spend their lives in pursuit of fame, wealth and the love of women. Since Clemenceau had little immediate prospect of achieving the former two, he plunged into the latter with the same gusto that had marked most of his earlier pursuits. The enterprise lasted about as long.

From his correspondence one gathers that in June 1863, one month before he was suspended from Bicêtre, Clemenceau was in Geneva. No reasons are given Perhaps this was another clandestine operation in pursuit of printing presses, or he might have just gone there for the fresh air and the jam. But he returned via Alsace to visit his friend Auguste Scheurer-Kestner, who was now back managing the family business in Thann.

Alsace was one of the most successful industrial regions in the country: it had shot ahead of its domestic competitors in productivity, mechanisation and quality of output during the Napoleonic Wars, and it experienced a second burst of activity in the 1840's – revolution was good for Alsatian business and, until its annexation into the German Reich in 1871, this was among the most active centres of liberal agitation in France. Its principal product was cotton and its principal industrial city was Mulhouse in the department of Haut-Rhin, where poor soil and a large population rendered success in manufacture a matter of survival.

Thann was near Mulhouse and the Kestners' chemical factory was typical of the derivative industries that grew up along the eastern escarpment of the Vosges, feeding on and goading the increasingly varied production demands of the makers of Alsatian cotton *percales* and chintzes, the muslins and the light cotton calico that not even the crisis of the American war could abate. The firm had been set up by Philippe Charles Kestner during the expansive years of the First Empire. He formed a partnership with his son Charles who, in turn, formed a partnership with his sons-in-law Auguste Scheurer, Camille Risler and Victor Chauffour so that, within three generations, a complex family and business network of Kestners, Scheurers, Rislers and Chauffours had crystallised around the factory. This was also typical, as could be seen in the mimicking lives of the Kœchlins, Blechs, Webers, Méquillet-Noblets, Gros-Romans – rich men, big families, who could cover their costs through their own savings and, if that wasn't sufficient, through personal links to the merchants of Strasbourg – the Saglios, the Humanns and the Ratisbonnes.

What was not so typical, thought Clemenceau, was the daughter, Charles Kestner's daughter, Hortense. Hortense had brown eyes that addressed you directly, too directly for a man of science and Bicêtre on leave without permit. When the conversation broke, in a secret second of silence, the student would lean back in his chair and just watch: she gathered her black hair loosely back into a single thick tress which lent her face high culture and compassion, the nose of Andromeda that, if it put the edge on penetrating eyes, hid the soul or what for Clemenceau was the creative source, the initial intention, of life. How easily it excited his sense of mission, the sensation that he should treat her as the enchained Greek goddess she appeared to be, towards whom he alone had the duty and the right of rescue.

That, unfortunately, was not an opinion shared by the others, neither his friend Auguste, the parents, the cousins or, it would seem from the screaming silence from her side in the written correspondence, Hortense herself.

The atmosphere was tangibly courteous. It must have appeared incongruous to Georges Clemenceau for whom directness of language was the badge of virtue: all of a sudden he found himself in a household of republicans who could not, would not, speak their minds. It was the antithesis of L'Aubraie, of Delestre's, of Arago's formal circles even. It was as if it were only the abstract principles of his education that protected him, as though it were only by some common understanding of reason and grace that his presence at Thann was tolerated at all. But the message was clear; he was not wanted.

He was in every way an outsider to Alsace's industrial elite, not that this in itself would have barricaded friendship. After all, it was Scheurer-Kestner who brought him there and who also proved to have a patient, sympathetic ear in the months that followed. Alsatians were proud, but they did not in general isolate themselves.

Clemenceau's behaviour – the frenzied gestures, the excited little speeches, the attitude that propelled the assumption to every corner of the room that of course, of course, you must agree with me – offended the old as much as it intimidated the young. The family, said Scheurer-Kestner in a journal that he wrote some thirty years later, 'found him abrupt, which he was, and odd, which he was not'. So Hortense sits in an easy chair with a length of white needlework under her chin, while her mother leans forward to say three words and then moves back, shifts a cushion fractionally, and, with this, dissociates herself from her flippant guest. Another joke, another comment, it had no effect.

Clemenceau was twenty-three, so he was young. Hortense was twenty-four, she was old. In another age it hardly would have mattered. But in this time and place the issue was convention. She was not an old maid, yet. Yes, she was beautiful and she played the piano well. Proposals? There had been several. But she was not married. The parents were worried. She was scared. They were then confronted with this bubbly youth – thirty-third in his last medical exam, the extern at Bicêtre. Impossible.

Thus was born the will to conquer. The more impossible the prospect, the more exciting was the thought of winning – positively erotic. It took Clemenceau six months to fall in love, or to make the proper distress calls that simulated love. He had met her in June; he began to write in November or December, one cannot be certain, but it appears to be towards the end of the year. By January, for sure, he was in a frenzy.

It was an affair of letters and imagined speeches delivered in the solitude of his flat or made by way of Arago's circle. This was the link, the last frail vein between them. For once the silence of Mademoiselle Kestner – his term of address – and of her parents had been affirmed, he was forced to turn to proxies, older men, the father figures who could use the weight of their authority to force a way of access. '*Ce brave Clemenceau,*' wrote Etienne Arago to Scheurer-Kestner in the first fortnight of January 1864, wanted only 'a *yes* or a *no* from the father, mother or daughter. You love and appreciate Clemenceau as I do, which is why I address myself directly to you in these circumstances.'

In other circumstances, one would have called this politics. There was the constellation of micro-powers, one agent acting on, for or against the other – Arago to Scheurer-Kestner, Scheurer-Kestner to the brother-in-law, Victor Chauffour, to the parents, to the daughter. There was the object, Hortense Kestner, the urge for action, the risk of loss of face. The fact that she was unavailable and did not answer made the matter more political and more of a risk than it otherwise might have been.

Her denial created complexity. Clemenceau had chosen the impossible. And the goal became marriage.

And then the woman's silence created words, words, an intensely uneven ebb and flow of written words, for the strength of the man *was* words; with his sense of pride challenged, words were mustered into action, pained words: 'Ah, why can't I think of the words to make you understand what I feel?' he wrote to Scheurer-Kestner, 'I told you the other day of all the great speeches I make when you are not here. It's different now. Every day I plan great feats of eloquence, then when I try to write it all down, everything freezes up. If I haven't been able to make you feel what it is in my heart, it is the fault of words, my poor friend, and not of feelings.'

In the spring and early summer of 1864 Clemenceau was pacing floors, his speeches addressed to walls and his writing reduced to love letters that never reached their source. No response, no *yes* or *no*; the reply he only imagined, there, lying on the table for more than an hour, unopened, fingered, left lying. He took several trips to Mulhouse where he would meet, in an inn or a tavern, Scheurer-Kestner. He never got to Thann. Finally, in September, against all advice, he wrote to Hortense Kestner with a formal proposal of marriage. She refused.

It was under these conditions that he wrote his medical thesis. He felt at the time, and for a long time afterwards, as though he were being buried alive. Burial, earth and a sudden flaring forth of life, of self-directed energy; it was a sentiment – no philosophy – Clemenceau expressed in his thesis and it would constantly recur in his speech, in his writing and in his conversation. He was touched to the core by a sentiment of fate which nestled uncomfortably beside his better-known individualism, creating a tension within him that he projected on all those about him. Defiantly conscious of his being, he also knew that at any moment he might cease to be. 'The truth,' he once wrote, 'is that there is only one sort of resignation to propose to man, the submission of his being to the inevitable laws that moulded it of soil to surrender it to clay. The only illegitimate revolt is against the higher fate which, having made us surge to consciousness, surrenders us to an earlier non-being.' The conflict at times could be profoundly moving, one could feel the rare sense of relief and respect that one sometimes experiences in the company of an artist whose gifts speak not at you but through you – a sense of being a part of the work with the stroke of humanity tweaking you on. Or it was havoc, the ravages of war which pulled you down, him down; not a hope, not a stalk or blade of life left erect, he could destroy.

This affair typified it. In his words there was a generosity that seemed compelling enough to carry the whole of mankind; but they were words addressed to a vacuum. He didn't even know the girl. Just an object of conquest. 'You are the living contradiction,' screamed Jaurès in the Chamber of Deputies forty years down the road, 'you are necessarily the civil war!' The charge could have been levelled at him in 1864. Clemenceau sensed it. His friends knew it. Scheurer-Kestner, referring to the affair, actually said it in his journal: 'The contrast between Clemenceau's head and heart shows up in every line. As a man he remained what he had been as a student. I have always found him to have the same heart he had then. But experience did not ripen him, and after hurting himself because of his lack of common sense, he ended up hurting all others around him without realising it.'

'Here I pass my time,' said Clemenceau in a long letter written, that spring, to Scheurer-Kestner after one of his trips to Mulhouse, 'weighing each of your words, interpreting each one according to my mood. Invariably, the conclusion is that I am very much afraid. Then I tell myself it is mad to hope – the dread of learning what I fear overcomes my wish to know the truth. I float back and forth between these two feelings.'

Dread and hope, fate and will, anger and love had converged into an intense personal event, an occasion, that seemed almost invented to satisfy the multiple contradictions living within him, though not one sign lay ahead as to how this might be achieved. The pain sprang forth from all that and that, as if he had deliberately created it for himself, using each contradiction to lay out its course, a carefully staged tragedy, put on at first with his father in mind but gradually surrendering to the solitude of his own existence in a growing political capital and to the dismal realisation that, in the crowd, his was only one understanding, one petty act, from the prison, to Bicêtre, to the bourgeois woman in an Alsatian drawing room. The anger was sharply defined, and then it would fade into a vague sense of helplessness, a burial – an anger against the silence of women, or against the gagged savage male isolated by his own silly codes of honour, or the ridiculous situation of it all, a social injustice; it was tangible, it was lost in a babble of eloquent words. One vision dissolved into another. The order of things lost its sense.

At this moment, here, the whole experience of Paris came together, scrambled and entangled, it did not cohere: poor quarters and rich quarters, eros and the wish to die, to give up, the individual urge to create and the urge to please the other, the altruistic urge, the drive of the reformer, the reason of science, the passion of art, the failure, the despair, life.

CHAPTER THREE

New York

I

'YOU KNOW why I go,' he wrote, 'What more do you need to know? What am I going to do? I know nothing. I am going, that's all. Chance will do the rest; perhaps a surgeon in the federal army, perhaps something else, perhaps nothing.'

Clemenceau had last met Scheurer-Kestner in January 1865 and had written the note a few weeks later, in Paris on 10 February.

The decision to leave for America had been sealed at that meeting, a funeral for Colonel Charras in Basel. Charras had been a part of the family to which Clemenceau had proffered his hopes months before, a husband to one of Hortense Kestner's sisters; he had lived in Switzerland since 1851, a good republican hero who, if he hadn't made a mark as a writer, a speaker, a politician, at least had the good sense to die with an aura of suffering about him, in exile.

The coffin was borne through the streets of Basel by six Swiss officers. Behind marched a small group of men, a delegation representing 'French youth', carrying the funeral ornaments – a 'civic crown' of oak and laurel and a broken sword signifying 'the brutal force of the coup d'état'. They were followed by 'long files of veterans of the Republic, whose plenteous tears rolled down their grey beards and flooded these proud faces'. A sizeable crowd stretched along both sides of the procession.

Then there were the speeches, republican speeches. Chauffour-Kestner, Edgar Quinet, Etienne Arago and the historian from Nantes, Charles-Louis Chassin, had words of respect and praise to deliver. 'He has given me two orders,' said Chauffour-Kestner, 'two missions, which I shall carry out religiously with you. He has ordered me, in consecrating this tomb, to invite no minister of any faith whatsoever.' His second order was that his body be returned to France only when France was politically free.

Old ambiguities stalked Chauffour-Kestner's phrases. Republicanism and anticlericalism were partners in politics. But private lives were at times constrained to perform untidy roles, to live the hypocrisy born of necessity, a necessity that made all those Jacobin virtues of the Revolution a praiseworthy quality in others but, at home, slightly inconvenient. The Kestners' Alsace was republican all right, but it was also, and it had always been, one of the strongholds of Catholicism – a fact which must have anguished some souls in the trip across the Rhine and down to the funeral in Basel; the contradiction was bound to have crossed the minds of one or two persons, watching the body of an emigrant son-in-law lowered into the Protestant soil of Switzerland.

It was a place for decision. It was January. If there was no priest present and not the train of attendants, the vicar, the choirboys in white and red, there was at least the solemnity of black-robed women, weeping, and the men upright, some in top hats, the others bareheaded, gazing into empty spaces, not talking – a scene to compare with Courbet's *Burial at Ornans* (which Clemenceau would say was the one painting in the Louvre he would take home if offered): mourners filled the foreground, they were silent, their clothes in tones of black, ochre, the white of the spats and the two crumpled kerchiefs in grey gloved hands, blended with the cliffed hills behind them and the horizontal grey and white streaks of the sky touching just above, closing all and everyone in.

Burial was a levelling. It brought together in an instant a full variety of lives and characters, all the emotions, and made them look small beside a nature that was imposing, and half hidden. Clemenceau knew that. To understand man, he used to say, you have to study and link him with the inanimate elements of nature. That is where his decisions were born. It was the source. Two years later in New York, without work and without the support of his family, the theme of burial still loomed up in his writing: 'I expect nothing. I hope for nothing and desire nothing. I am in quest of a cemetery where I might bury myself alive. Paris would be as good as any other place.'

Burial was the withdrawal which always accompanied decision. 'Where I go,' he said in his letter of 10 February. 'What I think, what I suffer, what I do, all that is only a concern between me and me. I find great charm (I do not know what blend of pride and bitterness) in closing myself up in myself and opening myself to no one.'

Burial shut the world into itself, a material world without gods and not too much to expect of human pity either. But it was not without hope. You could see it in the gravedigger at the centre of Courbet's painting, self-disciplined, kneeling at the edge of the open pit, a hand on his left thigh, his head turned upward.

America was the hope. All Europe, Lafayette had said, looked up to America. Through tinted spectacles, he might have added, with a mouth wide open ready for the sweets to drop. The French in particular had been

enjoying a two-hundred-year-old fantasy of naked noble savages basking
in a world, as Chateaubriand described it, of magnolia, maple, caribou,
crimson-tinged woodpeckers and cardinals where even burial, such as that
of Atala, had colour and enchantment. America offered its innocence to
the victims of European avarice, material power, manipulation – cuckolds
in search of regeneration. It was in America that the Chevalier des Grieux
had found a moment's happiness with Manon Lescaut after the violence
and the games of honour of eighteenth-century Paris – a savage simplicity,
their author wrote, and not one that should be treated romantically. 'Every
woman who emigrates to Canada,' Michelet had remarked, 'is considered
purified of every fault and of every misfortune by the baptism of the sea.'
America made the pursuit of human happiness possible, you could look
up from the grave.

This was an old dream; it was contradicted by another. If America was
a retreat, it was a retreat that required travel. The discovery of America
and the voyages it took to achieve it introduced a note of anguish into a
European world already tormented by centuries of movement. 'When I set
myself at times to consider the various agitations of men, and the perils,
and the pains,' Blaise Pascal had written in the middle of the seventeenth
century, 'I have often said that the whole of men's misfortune comes from
just one thing, which is to not know how to stay at rest in one room.' It
was not the kind of advice that had much of a following, even in his day.
A generation later it was vigorously attacked as counter to the essential
interests of man, an 'animal of action,' and, as Paul Hazard showed, the
taste for travel spread from the persecuted and adventurous in search
of rewarding work and fortune to the principal thinkers of Europe, to
the salons and drawing-rooms of the well-to-do. 'Si vous êtes curieux, allez
voyager . . .'

France contributed very little to the population and settlement of
America (though through the eighteenth and nineteenth centuries there
was massive movement within her frontiers). The idea of America –
knowledge of its existence – had a rather more substantial impact on
French society than its potential as a flood basin for unwanted numbers.
The French knew how to control their population. They were less good at
controlling ideas; that teasing invitation to travel gave rise to a new type
of intellectual game. Travel provided comparisons that could be used to
question the value of established religion, of customs and morals.

But if America had for a long time represented to Frenchmen a place
for primitive fantasy and a place to travel, it was not until well into the
nineteenth century that it became a place for the study of government.
Since the seventeenth century England had been the model, not America.
The French Revolution, if anything, magnified this interest: How do
you establish liberal government that is simultaneously stable? Seven
constitutions in less than twenty-five years had put a few people off

the idea of radical popular revolution, and for years England with its 'bloodless' revolution of 1688, its common law, its constitutional monarchy, remained an ideal in the French liberal mind. The picture of the imperturbable English gentleman handing out his parliamentary laws according to need, not ideology, was a very difficult one to abandon.

It never was entirely. But Alexis de Tocqueville in his famous book published in three volumes in the late 1830s, *De la démocratie en Amérique*, transferred the English Revolution backward over time and forward across the Atlantic Ocean. He also spoke of democracy – not sovereignty, not natural right, not the superior legislator of Rousseau's text, but of a major historical movement: 'A great democratic revolution is operating among us.' The English had got there first not, as François Guizot and his friends were arguing, by the Glorious Revolution of 1688 – England's genteel dress rehearsal for 1789 – but by the emigration of Englishmen to America. The germ of democracy was sown with the foundation of the English colonies in America: it was England without the aristocracy.

There were lessons to be learned over there.

Lessons? Clemenceau's motives for going to America were clearly personal and emotional. His failure to win as much as a kind letter from Hortense Kestner had sent him into a depression from which America seemed to offer the one way out. His correspondence of this period is full of immediate 'projects' and 'programmes', but he continually sidesteps the reasons for his actions.

Depression would bring out the old humanist in Clemenceau. This caused problems. Ever respectful of the logical reason of science, Clemenceau remained incapable of abandoning the instinctive passions of the artist. '*Ma chère Madame,*' he wrote in a revealing letter to Gustave Jourdan's wife nearly two years after first setting foot in New York,

> *Eh bien non*, it will still not be today that I am going to write to you that famous letter, so frequently promised, in which I will give you reasons. The *reason* for which I abstain from *reasons* is that here I am again with one foot in the air and I still don't know to what side the wind will turn me ... You are going to see that I am more reasonable and more sensible than you suppose. I admit that I have been dreamy and temperamental like all the people whose nervous system is a little too excitable and excited, but experience corrects me a little every day of this default. You give me a very sharp scolding for my mania for roaming about the world. However, whatever you might believe, I can assure you that it is against my taste. I would like to live peacefully and regularly in a little spot. This was my feeling before leaving Paris, and the more I go, the more I

find refuge in the hope of imprisoning myself some day in a calm and regular life.

The most striking aspect of the letter is that he should have considered a calm and regular life in *'un petit coin'*, 'a little spot', as the reasonable solution, while he regarded travelling as a symptom of mania. Again, he finds hope in imprisonment, as if such a closing up of himself were to give him the autonomy he so ardently sought. 'Nobody is less ambitious than me,' this extraordinary statement for Clemenceau is made in the same letter, 'but I would like to be independent so as to need no one (*my friends excepted*) and to be able to scorn everyone at my pleasure (*with the exception of the above mentioned*) – that's my ideal' (his emphasis).

This was not the Clemenceau the public would later get to know, not the confident *veni, vidi, vici* he would exclaim in his eighties:

ME [J. MARTET]: I would like to know why you left in '65 for America.

CLEMENCEAU: Oh! Oh! Big question! Because I had just finished my medical thesis. I felt that democracy was about to have its hour at home. I said to my father: 'I should like to go and see how it functions over there.' He said to me: 'Go.' I went, I saw . . .

ME: And?

CLEMENCEAU: And nothing. Democracy is democracy. It's nothing remarkable. But in the first place it is the inevitable end of human experience. And, secondly, democracy, aristocracy, plutocracy . . . all those 'cracies are unending. There is only one good 'cracy: that's theocracy. Provided there is a *theos*.

Democracy on its way in France, the inevitability of the movement, the cynicism over its seamy side – it sounds like a wittier de Tocqueville. But the picture of Clemenceau sailing gallantly off to the New World to discover democracy is incomplete at best. What we have of his private correspondence at the time points to a young man who is frightened ('What am I going to? I know nothing'), insecure, ('I am going, that's all, chance will do the rest') and apparently incapable of communicating feelings with his parents (a letter from Gustave Jourdan addressed to Clemenceau on his arrival in New York suggests as much: 'It is good to hold on to the petticoats of one's mother and to the affection of one's father and I thank you for having shown me so simply the feelings which you can have never too strongly . . . [But] there is one point where I am not altogether of your opinion. You say, "You can be assured that I haven't written home a word about all this . . ." And why not? A word from the heart does good, and it doesn't take an effort of sublime virtue not to say it to the one who doesn't dare ask for it, but who expects it').

Clemenceau had a generous heart, but virtue for him lay in suppressing it. A tension thus began to develop between the private and the public man. In private, there is a Pascalian yearning for peace, '*un petit coin*' – a man, one might say, of another age. But in public, he was a man of movement, of action – the man of the nineteenth century. With the public Clemenceau, matters of the heart were not open for discussion.

One suspects this modern 'animal of action' might have silently winked with Pascal, whom he liked to quote: 'The heart has reasons which reason knows not of.'

II

CLEMENCEAU DELAYED his departure for two reasons. He had first to write and then defend his medical thesis – it seems he had not even begun to write until January 1865. He sat for the defence on 13 May. Apart from his director, Charles Robin, the jury showed little interest in the 'generation of anatomic elements'. Only Robin had read the thesis. The others were more concerned with the practical side of curing patients; an embarrassing question from Pierre Potain on scarlet fever might have ended the session and the doctorate there and then had it not been for Professor Robin's astute intervention at the critical moment. Clemenceau received his diploma, 'in the name of the Emperor', three weeks later.

The second reason was the bond he felt with his father. In the same letter to Scheurer-Kestner where he outlined his decision to part for America, he wrote, 'I leave behind me only one regret, it is that of my father. One evening I said to you that he would forgive me and you replied that I would never forgive myself. If you are my friend, then hope that day never arrives.' Whatever Scheurer-Kestner had said to him on that unspecified evening it was cold comfort to a young man in search of his own autonomy. 'Finally,' he added, 'once this last rift has been accomplished, I will be free from all attachments (who can say whether this is good or bad) and I will go whichever way the wind blows me.'

What he wanted was his freedom, but once faced with its realisation he felt a regret, and regret gave spring to confusion. He could not leave his father, and his father could not let go either. Paris had given him an education in politics, but not freedom. America at least had the advantage of being at the other side of an ocean.

Still he delayed. He remained in France for almost two months after receiving his diploma. Finally, on 25 July, he left. But not for America. He left for England. With his father.

*

England, the other model for good government, the older model, was the proper place for French republican farewells for it was not only a haven from Napoleon's police state but a country in transition. The rumblings of political change that were to lead to the Great Reform Bill of 1867 could already be heard. An odd country, England – in 1867 Walter Bagehot would publish his *English Constitution*, hallowed text for a few generations of English schoolboys: 'A Republic,' he said, 'has insinuated itself beneath the folds of a Monarchy.'

This was hardly the kind of government most French observers in the eighteenth century had had in mind, the clockwork government of checks and balances: a pinch of monarchy here, a tablespoon of aristocracy there and a few drops of democracy to keep the whole thing going. The two Clemenceaus would never have accepted that. Their England was a reforming England, being swept along by the ineluctable flood of democracy. It was an urban England, an ugly England, an England in which wealth harboured poverty. That was the England the young Clemenceau remembered.

As in his first trip to Paris, his father introduced Clemenceau, on arriving in London, to some of the major political thinkers, including Herbert Spencer and John Stuart Mill. Both were well known in France, and Mill actually spent his last years there.

Herbert Spencer was a British version of Comte, eclectic in his methodology and an evolutionist in theory. The greatest difference between Spencer and Comte was that Spencer glorified the *laissez-faire* individualism of his own day, whereas Comte rejected the competitive society, seeing it as a mere transition between the medieval community and the solidarity of the coming scientific community. This affected their respective views of biology. For Comte, knowledge of biology was essential because of the light it threw on the origin of society – biology defined the given physical quality of life upon which human society was built. For Spencer, biology defined not only the basis of the first human society, it provided the dynamic model of all societies that proceeded from it; hence the 'Social Darwinist' in Spencer, his extreme individualism and his employment of the biological metaphor.

Clemenceau has often been called, and criticised as, a Social Darwinist. He certainly picked up some of the language of Social Darwinism – 'the struggle for life', 'the survival of the fittest' (which Darwin borrowed from Spencer) – during his visit to England and his stay in the United States. It is also true that Laurent Pichat and Henri Lefort, associates of Clemenceau during his student days, published one of the first synopses of Darwin's *Origin of Species* in their *La Réforme littéraire*, a paper with which Clemenceau was undoubtedly familiar. But the language was window-dressing to an already well-constructed ideological edifice. Clemenceau's ideology was the ideology of the Revolution, that he had garnered from his father, and the ideology of Comte, which he had learned in Paris.

It seems likely that Benjamin Clemenceau and his son visited Spencer and Mill because they were the leading figures embroiled in the ongoing cross-Channel debate about Comte. Mill had just completed a book on the subject, *Auguste Comte and Positivism*, and the younger Clemenceau somehow managed to get himself commissioned to translate the book into French for publication by Germer-Baillière, who had published his medical thesis. In return for the translation Baillière would publish a second edition of the thesis.

For Clemenceau Mill's book must have presented a challenging apprenticeship to the English language; two years later he was still referring to it as 'heavy and stuffy'. What Clemenceau recalled about his interview with Mill did not, anyway, have much to do with Comte; it was a more general discussion revolving around questions of morality, democracy and science. Morality, said Mill, is only the sum of a series of practical recipes, it is only the means of arriving at a noble end, happiness. Democracy, he said, is not government by the people but a guarantee to the people of good government: this is only possible if the people are instructed with the ideas that create good government. Science, he remarked, has no absolute truth, it is only relative. These comments would stay with Clemenceau for the rest of his life.

Some time early in August Clemenceau boarded a steamboat, the *Etna*, at Liverpool for the two-week voyage to New York. He left, alone,[1] with letters of reference in his pocket. Where and when he had said farewell to his father is unrecorded. It had certainly been painful. On 21 August he sent a letter from New York to Gustave Jourdan in Paris. We know this because of Jourdan's reply:

> A Monsieur Georges Clemenceau, D.M.
> chez M. Mataran
> 21 Bockmann [Beekman?] Street
> New-York
> Etats-Unis

[1] Some insist Clemenceau travelled with a student friend, Gustave Dourlen, but an analysis of correspondence shows that Dourlen did not arrive in New York until a year later. The French-language newspaper, *Le Courrier des Etats-Unis* (New York Public Library, Annex, Film *ZY) reports the *Etna* arriving in New York on 15 August.

Paris, ce 10 septembre 1865

Mon cher Georges,

Your letter, sent on the 21 August, arrived on the 3rd of this month. I
was waiting with impatience for what I wanted to believe you thought.
I saw your father on his return from London. I saw him twice. I found
him rather gay and busy, not beaten down. It is true he is reserved
and the more his feelings are dear to him the more he keeps them to
himself. I don't mean to suggest that he is going to take his side of
your leaving easily but, everything considered, it seemed to me that he
had a tendency for distractions from his distress and has found them in
farming, an easy outlet for him. May the regrets you have left behind
not divert you from your duty to look ahead . . .

He continued,

I am not at all surprised at your state of mind . . . I was very moved
by what you said about your feelings at the moment you left your father
and it pleased me, for you and for me: for you because I love to see
you that way, knowing full well that pride will take its turn; and for
me because, never having known such sorrows in so tender a reality,
I like to think about them . . .

One has to recognise a lot of sympathy, a deep affection even, in Jourdan's
remarks. At the same time one senses the awkwardness of his position,
somewhere between friend and father, now sharing a moment of intense
sadness, now reminding the boy of his duties. Love and will try to blend,
but they do not have the same consistency.

Clemenceau had been led to believe that Jourdan was going to act as
an intermediary in the financial transactions that would enable the father
to support the son in New York. This made sense since Jourdan was in
Paris, while his father was living out in the Vendée. Before he left for
England Clemenceau had gone on a shopping spree. He ordered books
– Paul Challemel, Pouchet's treatise on spontaneous generation, a book
by George Washington, a book by Carlyle, La Fontaine's fables, much
philosophy (Spinoza, Descartes, De Maistre), two volumes of Proudhon.
He ordered clothes – a black frock coat, a blue eiderdown overcoat, several
pairs of trousers including one in black satin, waistcoats, jackets, high
collars, the black silk tie. These were all loaded in trunks and sent off
to Le Havre from where they would be shipped to New York. The bills
were sent to Jourdan.

'This has led me to grouse a little,' the perplexed friend said in his letter.
'You know your weakness, and I remind you without further ceremony.
Men are made so that one might pass by their side, not over them,

aristocrat that you are.' But Jourdan would sign off '*de bien bon cœur*' all the same.

Clemenceau was apparently not communicating his sentiments or even more practical financial questions to his father or to his older friend – it was an uncomfortable triangle of relationships from which he might well have wanted to escape. But the escape had no goal, apart from a vague desire 'to discover democracy.' The political animal had not yet taken shape.

III

NEW YORK: it literally stank. One only had to take a short walk around the back of City Hall to get a full whiff of that 'sickening stench,' as contemporaries would describe it, a stench which came from the narrow streets and alleys of the Five Points quarter and the Lower East Side (that bunion in a south-east corner without which, along with the northern tail of Fort Washington and Tubby Hook, would have existed the perfect lozenge of an island, Manhattan). Smells of dead animals, decaying garbage, untreated sewage, horse manure, even human beings too crowded and unwashed, filled the air of New York. You couldn't escape it, like in Paris; it was there in front of you.

The American Civil War had brought a few benefits to civilisation. Improved sewage disposal, for one thing – the streamlining of city government, under the exigency of war, had made this possible. But it only applied to the newer sections. Below Fourteenth Street there remained a maze of gutters, open channels and pipes, some still in the wood that the Dutch had laid two hundred years earlier. When it rained, they became blocked. When it poured, the major thoroughfares like Broadway or Fifth Avenue were transformed into sluggish streams of thick brown mud, exhaling foul odours and hindering the movement of the horse-drawn streetcars, the private carriages, and the hapless pedestrian most especially.

As for the animals, New York was a city of animals. There were, of course, the horses. Because the city was located on an island, there was no open periphery where horses could be stabled, the gridiron pattern of the streets extended to the waterfront. So whole streets – Eighth, Thirteenth, Twenty-fourth, Thirty-third, Forty-third – were allocated to the stabling of horses. Forty-second and Forty-third were about as far north as the city extended, so here were the cattle-pens. They adjoined the Bull's Head Tavern, which was on the corner of Forty-fourth and Lexington. Farmers from Westchester and Connecticut would drive their beasts across the trestled Mott-Haven Bridge, through Yorkville, itself a village of herdsmen and hog dealers, to the Bull's Head. They could go no further; cattle drives through the city streets had been prohibited by Mayor Fernando Wood in the 1850's.

Pigs, fowl and dogs, however, continued to be brought into the city where they were kept by the poor. A newspaper reported, in 1863, the story of a boy being attacked and seriously injured by a wandering pig on Broome Street in the Fourteenth Ward. In 1867 the municipal government, responding to an apparent need, passed a law that forbade pigs to be loosed on the city streets.

But the worst crowding in New York City was of the human kind, the animals were only the accessory, an appurtenance, of the immigrant peasants.

Nobody knew exactly how large the population of New York was in 1865. The census for that year had been tabulated, by hand, by a single clerk who was also responsible for the entire state. Census-taking was politics in democratic America, and the politicians from rural up-state New York applied any amount of pressure to undercount the numbers in the city so as to reduce its legislative representation in Albany. The official figure for 1865 gave the city a population of three-quarters of a million. That of 1870 was closer to a million. Whatever the exact number, New York had become the receiving station of the greatest migration in the history of mankind, the transfer of thirty-five million people from the Old World to the New. No city in the world had experienced as great an influx of people as New York in the late 1860's.

No city had faced its accompanying problems. Most immigrants who passed through the processing centre of Castle Garden in the years immediately after the Civil War did not have the means to move further west than the piered shores of the Hudson: or further north, for that matter, than Fourteenth Street. Upper Manhattan was still rural – 'The high elevated and in part precipitous ridges that run through this tract,' said an official report in 1865, 'the romantic valleys and fertile meadows make this by nature one of the most charming places in the state, with unsurpassed views and landscapes up and down each of the rivers that wash it.'

Lower Manhattan, on the other hand, suffocated with humanity. If close to one half of the city's population in 1870 had been born in Europe, their mobility stopped once they had got off the ship and through the official clearing. Eighty-five per cent of New York's population lived within two miles of Union Square, and half of it was to be found in the narrow zone, one and a quarter miles long, between Canal and Fourteenth Streets. Lower Manhattan was caught unprepared for these numbers.

So it was filthy – writing in his diary of the approaching and inevitable outbreak of cholera in 1866, that prolific misanthrope and Dean of the School of Mines at Columbia College, George Templeton Strong noted, 'The new Board of Health is trying to clean the city . . . But time is too short. To purify "Mackerelville" alone is a year's work. And that district, however scrubbed and deodorized, will never be fit for human creatures to live in till its long lines of huge, many-storeyed tenement houses are razed to the ground.'

It was violent – some of the gangs of post-bellum New York were: the True Blue Americans, the Kerryonians, the Bowery Boys, the Dead Rabbits; in the Draft Riots of 1863 (known locally as the 'Colored Riots' because of their racial tone) between one and two thousand people lost their lives.

And it was riddled with disease and death – with a death rate in 1864 of forty in every thousand, New York could boast of being the most morbid large city in the Western world; two-thirds of all these deaths were the children of foreign-born parents; over eighty per cent of the admissions to Bellevue Hospital (as sure and as quick a road down to death as any) were foreign-born; about sixty per cent of all cancer deaths occurred among the foreign-born.

Even though the city was the victor and economic beneficiary of war, there was plenty to be gloomy about in post-bellum New York, especially among the older communities that could look nostalgically back at the halcyon days of Knickerbockers and of 'respectable' reformers and abolitionists. Under the banner heading, 'Crime – demoralisation', the *Courrier des Etats-Unis*, official organ of the long-established French-speaking community in New York, crowed: 'There is not one of our readers who has not been struck by the enormous growth of crimes against persons that has been occurring for some time . . . One could say all monstrosities are the order of the day and decent men are terrified of the outrages that their wives, their children and themselves can be exposed to.'

Of course there was demoralisation and violence in New York because there was no one group that could keep its interests dominant in a city like this for very long. In a sense, New York stood at the pinnacle of Western development in that it represented for old Europe the hope, the hope of a better place for 'your tired, your poor, your huddled masses yearning to breathe free.' But in reality it was an abject, foreign town for everyone who lived in it. Its combination of nationalities, languages, even the extremes of climate gave New Yorkers a feeling of detachment, the attitude that insinuated to each and every inhabitant, without a word of it pronounced, that this is not my town and nor is it yours.

Foreign in attitude, foreign in appearance, and foreign in politics. For somebody fresh out of Paris, New York must have appeared as some city out of the Orient, Shanghai or Calcutta; only perhaps more foreign still.

There was no history here, the land was anybody's, and power went to anyone with the wit, and the money, to manipulate others. As in Paris, social reform had proved ineffectual and urban government incapable of dealing with the problem of rapid growth. But, to take an example, there was nothing in Paris, including the shanties that had sprung up near the new fortifications, to compare with the whole villages of squatters that stretched from Fortieth Street up to Central Park and further. 'To Fifty-ninth Street this afternoon,' entered Strong in his diary for 22 October 1867 as if setting out on a safari,

> traversing for the first time the newly opened section of Madison Avenue between Fortieth Street and the College, a rough and ragged track, as yet, and hardly a thoroughfare, rich in mudholes, goats, pigs, geese and stramonium. Here and there Irish shanties 'come out' (like smallpox pustules), each composed of a dozen rotten boards and a piece of stove-pipe for a chimney . . .

No government, democratic or autocratic, had ever had to cope with such a large number of migrants, and few governments had been faced with so much squalor. New York in the 1860's had a small-town administration to run a growing, punishing metropolis. Policing was limited to an odd conglomerate of quasi-independent fiefdoms, firefighting was left to private initiative, garbage collection was non-existent and, naturally, social welfare was relegated to charity.

All this had the inevitable result of isolating each and every ethnic community from the other as they fended for themselves while shutting the door on 'foreigners', interlopers, wastrels and didicois. The Irish hated the blacks, the blacks hated the Irish, the Germans hated both, the French hated the English, and the English hated them all. None of the noble human qualities, like morality or honour, could bring them together because each community had its peculiar understanding of morality and honour. The English wanted temperance, the French wanted wine, the Germans preferred beer and the Irish demanded whisky. Public conduct in New York would shock most European visitors, and many Americans too. In politics as in business, dealings across cultural lines lacked protocol; New Yorkers wanted performance and did not stand on ceremony. For them, the pomp and punctilio of Europe's power brokers would have been viewed as vaguely quaint.

If anything tied them together, apart from being inhabitants of the same island, it was the code of 'smartness.' 'Smartness' was the common denominator in this city of immigrants. 'Smartness' was rewarded, it brought money and position, it made you 'respectable', whatever your origins. Dickens had described the phenomenon twenty years earlier, without perhaps fully understanding it and certainly not sympathising with it:

> Another prominent feature is the love of 'smart' dealing: which gilds over many a swindle and gross breach of trust; many a defalcation, public and private; and enables many a knave to hold his head up with the best, who well deserves a halter . . . The following dialogue I have held a hundred times: 'Is it not a very disgraceful circumstance that such a man as So-and-so should be acquiring a large property by the most infamous and odious means, and notwithstanding all the crimes of which he has been guilty, should be tolerated and abetted by your Citizens? He is a public nuisance, is he not?' 'Yes, Sir.' 'A convicted liar?' 'Yes, Sir.' 'He has been kicked, and cuffed, and caned?' 'Yes, Sir.' 'And he is utterly dishonourable, debased, and profligate?' 'Yes, Sir.' 'In the name of wonder, then, what is his merit?' 'Well, Sir, he is a smart man.'

Such a man as So-and-so was alive and promoting himself quickly through the public corridors and coffers of New York City in 1865. This was the Honorable William Marcy Tweed.

Tweed looked like a public bandit. He stood nearly six feet and weighed almost 300 pounds. His neck was stocky, his shoulders broad, his arms equally well-upholstered; but his hands were smaller than one might expect, and they sweated at the palm. His oblong head extended, upward, to a bald crown fringed with short hair of off-coloured red and, downward, to a cropped greying beard and the near ochre moustache which had withstood his years. In short, Tweed bore all the accoutrements of the Celt that he was (his grandparents had migrated in the eighteenth century from their village on the River Tweed, near Edinburgh) plus an extraordinary memory for names that put him to the front of New York politics, the 'Boss'.

Tweed was made of New York. His father had been a successful small businessman operating a chair and brush manufacture a block away from their home at the top of Cherry Hill in the Lower East Side, or the Seventh 'Irish' Ward. This, along with his leadership of the local street gang, proved a splendid education for the civic potentate he was to be.

For a little over five years, between 1865 and 1871, Tweed and his companions, 'Brains' Sweeney, 'Slippery Dick' Connolly and the 'Elegant' Oakey Hall, ruled over New York like despots of some misbegotten European principality. Tweed was never mayor. He was an exceedingly good organiser and the power he exercised was derived from the positions he held in various municipal committees and political clubs – legacy, in fact, of America's democracy.

His political career began when, having worked in a private fire brigade, he became member of the Board of Aldermen, popularly known as the

'Forty Thieves'. Here he consolidated his following in the Seventh Ward and dipped his fingers into the creamy pot of city franchises. But that was only the first course in a great feast of public plunder.

For there was always a reason for increasing the city budget. 'New York has no greater glory,' read a report of 1865,

> than the freedom with which we spend money on public institutions and for public purposes, and, in some cases, including these improvements, with a judiciousness and economy which are marvellous. We are an imperial people giving freely to the public – our imperial selves – the most magnificent and costly entertainment. Judicious expenditure for public purposes is the highest sort of economy.

One of the most imperial of expenditures was for the new county courthouse that still stands on the northern side of City Hall Park. Its original cost was estimated at $350,000. By the time the Tweed Ring had finished with it the costs were approaching $13,000,000: thermometers were billed at $7,500 each, brooms went at the bargain price of $41,190.95 apiece, three tables and forty chairs were purchased at a discount for $179,729.60.

Tweed was to die a multi-millionaire, in gaol, at the age of fifty-five. He was destroyed by one of his own, Jimmy O'Brien, a Democrat and sheriff of New York, disgruntled at an inadequate payoff for his services. In the summer of 1871 he passed on to the press evidence of fraud in the courthouse, the armouries, the padded payrolls, and more. Within four months the Tweed Ring was broken.

But the complex political machine that Tweed had helped create survived. Tammany Hall (with its roots in the eighteenth century) was still nominating Democratic candidates in the early 1960's. The system of party caucuses, the municipal committees, the clubs (the Young Men's Democratic Club, the St Patrick Mutual Alliance, the Jefferson Club, the Unique Club) that had produced a man like Tweed continued to operate. New York merely got Tweeds of a different name: the Kellys, the Crokers, the Murphys.

Something remarkable had happened in democratic New York in the 1860's. It was not quite what the learned pundits of hope and human prog-ress had expected. It was uglier than anything described in de Tocqueville, it was more fantastic than anything dreamed up by Chateaubriand, it was more savage, more confused than any romance of the abbé Prévost. New York was a real democracy. While high-minded reformers continued to talk, Tweed delivered. He gave the poor the vote – it was his agents at Castle Garden that naturalised the mass of new immigrants. He brought the unemployed food – $50,000 worth of groceries were distributed in the

Seventh Ward in the winter of 1870. He provided jobs – his public works programme, on the streets, in the courthouse, outdistanced Roosevelt's by seventy years.

Tweed had demonstrated what a well-organised political machine, the Democratic party controlled by the sachems (or party managers) of Tammany Hall, could do for the foreign poor, and most notably the Irish. It is true that the lion's share of the spoils went to the corrupt leadership of the party, and no amount of analysis can explain away the fact that these men were robbers. But money and jobs did go to the poor.

This led to a curious inversion of the social structure of New York politics. The Republican party was the party of Lincoln, the party that led the Union against the confederacy, the party of abolition, the party of reform. It was also the party of New York's elite, the educated, the rich, the Protestants. Possessed of all the hatred and prejudice that New Yorkers had of each other at this time, these Republican 'reformers' found it well nigh impossible to communicate their enlightened programmes to the poor. They hated the Catholics, they hated the life-style and the stink of the poor.

Tweed's Democratic party suffered no such illusions. These were the professional politicians; they had won their positions through manipulation and graft. If charity was graft's by-product, so much the better – they could do with the vote. One month after Tweed had been indicted for fraud, with stories of municipal corruption headlining all papers, the Seventh Ward re-elected Tweed to the state senate. Tweed was a manipulator, Tweed was a robber, but he gave the poor of New York a voice, while no one else listened, no one else bothered.

In New York political corruption and aid to the poor marched hand in hand: some lesson in democracy, some future for the Republic.

IV

CLEMENCEAU ARRIVED in New York one imagines somewhat isolated, with an idea of democracy – a great historical drama made up of great historical men – already fixed in his mind. It was a view well suited to a man whose own personal story had the smack of battle, a collision of two selves, public and private.

As American correspondent for *Le Temps* he could hurl phrases of avenging justice at anachronisms the Civil War had not entirely eliminated. 'As the year 1867 opens,' he wrote with typical gall in an untypically cold New York winter, 'it promises rather ill for the United

States. Reconstruction has not been accomplished, and the great war of the Rebellion, though it is over in the military sense, still goes on in men's minds. The hatred of the South for the North is more bitter than ever . . .' 'And, as we know,' he reminded his readers two weeks later, 'any postponement of justice is a postponement of peace.'

But a letter of the following winter shows less combativeness, a rather more self-conscious man; and his words bear a faint touch of the estranged city around him: 'I am endeavouring to be wise, honest and temperate, *respectable* as they say here. [But] between us I have up to now made little way along this difficult route. However every day I age twenty-four hours: every evening on going to bed I look at myself in the mirror and I find myself with a more thoughtful look than the night before . . . In a few months, I will be buttoning my frock-coat up to my chin and I will buy myself a walking stick, and perhaps some snow boots.' He added, 'Some day when I am in the mood, I will give you a detailed history of these two years, but one shouldn't expect too much in one go.'

As far as can be established, he never did. Clemenceau's bid for 'respectability' – frock-coat, walking stick and the snow-boots – would have been standard wear for many of the French who resided in, or visited, the United States in the last years of the Second Empire; and as one of Napoleon III's enemies he would have found himself in good company with the elite society of New York's reformers and former abolitionists.

But it wasn't just politics that drew Frenchmen to Americans. The French-speaking community in New York was not small for its time. In 1870 a *Guide du Français à New York* listed over six thousand names and addresses (along with their occupation) of people whose first language was French; most of them were merchants, shopkeepers and artisans living in what was known as the *quartier français* that extended from Greenwich Village to Washington Square, University Place and onward up the two sides of Broadway as far as Twenty-fifth or Twenty-sixth Street.

It was largely thanks to this population that French culture had become a major component of entertainment for New York's upper classes. Jacques Blau directed the prestigious French Theatre on Fourteenth Street, many of the finest hotels were staffed by the French, on White Street there was a French bookstore which also housed a library, or *cabinet de lecture*, with a collection of over five thousand titles. But perhaps the most important contribution that the French made to respectability was in the area of food and drink. French confectioners, bakers, even butchers could be found in many of the streets of Greenwich Village. The best French wines were bought at A. E. Mirabel's on Sixth Avenue; it had a particularly good selection of Bordeaux, Côtes du Rhône and Armagnac brandy. Some of the restaurants – Delmonico's, Guerin's, Charles Pfaff's – would have compared favourably with the best of Paris. There were even some famous French chefs, like 'Flotte', a Blanquist who lived in New York to escape a life sentence; he was back in Paris, for a short stay, in the spring of 1871 . . .

You saw him each evening at Pfaff's. The beard had gone but not the moustache, now thick and combed downward at each end so that it looked, face-on, like the wings of a swallow or nighthawk; the sunken cheeks and temples combined with the high cheek-bones to give him that appearance, so often noted, of a Mongolian warrior (from which the peasants of the west of France had once claimed descent). His hair was cut short and receded at the forehead. Impeccably dressed, Clemenceau in his late twenties seemed the right man for Republican New York.

His most frequent companion at dinner was Eugene Bush, a young lawyer, who had first met Clemenceau in Paris. Bush was a liberal Republican who owned an apartment next door to Clemenceau's on Twelfth Street. More important, his practice was now bringing in money – Clemenceau was going to need friends like this. Another acquaintance from his student days was William E. Marshall, an artist who had achieved some renown for his engraving of Abraham Lincoln. Through Marshall, Clemenceau was to meet a number of good painters and engravers. For example, Asher Brown, as editor of *The Crayon*, was able to open a number of doors for Clemenceau. His son, John Durand was a close friend of Clemenceau – and as a letter of 1 April 1867 indicates, another source of credit.

Art, and most especially painting, was going to become increasingly important in Clemenceau's life. He could spend hours musing over a landscape, a still life, or a portrait by some famous artist; and if he was going to develop a long-lasting friendship it would be with an artist, not the lawyers and the politicians. This attitude he inherited from his father; we find it reflected in his medical thesis – the spontaneous urge that makes life out of matter. For Clemenceau, art transcended the schematised categories of the lawyer and pedantic orator, it provided direct access to the creative impulse, individualised human will-power. The real artist was the one who exposed himself directly to his public, who laid himself open to the primal, singular energy source of life. For the artist, ideas would rush in pell-mell; the intellect withdraws its guard; a self-creative will is freed. It was in foreign New York that Clemenceau began to befriend artists.

But these were not very productive years. Baillière published a second edition of his thesis that included an abstruse introduction by his master, Charles Robin; Clemenceau carried the book's positivist approach to America. This had worried Jourdan. 'I didn't shake the least bit,' he said in his last letter from Paris,

> on hearing you say that you were going to study America in the light
> of the positivist method. Only I do believe (and Littré's book on

Comte, which you cite, is proof) that up to now this method has been
more negative than constructive. It has been used to overthrow some
presumptuous *a priori* notions; I do not see, in the areas of political and
moral sciences, what it has built.

The insight that Clemenceau might be using ideas for destructive rather
than constructive purposes indicates how well Jourdan knew his young
friend. The positivist project, at any rate, was never written. The Mill
translation, no more than a philosophical pamphlet to begin with, dragged
on until 1868. His own introduction, which he started in 1866, was never
completed. But he must have derived some pleasure from punishment
because he also had under way, against Jourdan's better advice (Jourdan
told him it would cost 'lots of time and pain for a sterile honour and
constantly disputed conclusions') a translation of Mill's gigantesque *System
of Logic*. He only abandoned this on discovering that the job had already
been done. He had a shot at a play, *Le Puritain* (of which an outline along
with thirteen lines of Alexandrine verse have been preserved).

And he began a most extraordinary dissertation on women which,
fortunately for his reputation, was never made public in his lifetime. He
got nowhere near completing it; all we have is the preface and an outline
for a seven-chapter book, to which are appended notes written on various
scraps of paper. Judging from his bibliography one would guess that it
was begun towards the end of his stay in America and that he continued
to collect notes on the subject for a long period afterwards. For instance,
A. F. W. Schimper's *Traité de paléontologie végétale*, which he cites, did not
appear until the 1870's.

The project was essentially designed to answer J. S. Mill's *On the
Subjection of Women*, published in 1869. 'Mill's book,' he jotted down on one
of his addenda, 'High thoughts but neither method nor clarity. What does
he want? Equality of rights in marriage? Agreed. Civil equality? Agreed.
Open immediately the door of politics to women? I say no. Politics changes
inasmuch as man changes.' He goes on to note that politics today – no one
knows what it will be in the future – consists of parliament *and* war, for
which women are unsuited. If women ever do manage to open the door
to politics it will be because the character of politics has changed, not
women. If, on the other hand, they somehow succeed in entering politics as
it exists today, a political condition that they have not themselves created,
'they would find themselves in the position of the blacks in America whose
conditions have had a souring effect on admission into the body politic.
Corruption and venality would grow remarkably.'

The outline then lists 'scientific' proofs of male superiority. They seem
painfully adolescent to a reader today. Some examples: a study shows that
male flowers in full bloom consume more oxygen than female flowers; the
male American black hazel-hen (of which there would have been a number

north of Twelfth Street) has a higher body temperature than the female; only men (we assume the best) become bald, a woman's head remains in the state of a child; a man avoids conscription through sickness, a woman through her physiological condition, thus the physiological woman is the equivalent of the pathological man ('*La femme est une malade,*' *dixit* Michelet). One is not encouraged by one source whose title (*Histoire philosophique et médicale de la femme considérée* . . .) extends over seven lines of print and whose author goes by the dubious name of 'Dr. Menville'.

But what appears childlike to one culture can be an unshakeable truth for another. Behind a façade of ridiculous statements hid a man and a world of science that has since faded – that foreign, eclectic world of the idéologues and positivists, of Cabanis, Comte and Littré, of Clemenceau's father, Benjamin, and his teacher, Charles Robin. They would all have agreed that social behaviour had a biological base. But they would never have agreed as to exactly how one was related to the other.

Clemenceau took the lack of consensus in his own day as a sign of imminent unity. The truth was just around the corner, just beyond the next tidal wave. Hold on. Science shall bear us out. In the meantime, take heed, watch your step. If the question is raised you can still get out, even if you do sound a little tame: 'What constitutes the originality of this work,' proclaims Clemenceau's confident self, 'is that the social side of the question that I am studying is everywhere subordinated to the biological.' Right, so behaviour is determined by biology? Not quite, retorts Clemenceau's humbler self: 'Now, one knows that the glory goes to Comte for having shown, *in a definitive manner, the subordination of biological phenomena to the sociological.* In the hierarchy of Comte's sciences, several points have been contested, but this one (see Huxley and Spencer) has remained *unattacked and unattackable.*'

Where, then, would Clemenceau have stood in the ongoing debate between Spencer and Littré, between the competitive biological model and the altruistic sociological model? Clemenceau was certainly aware of the disagreement; Mill's *Comte* discusses it, and a letter from Clemenceau to John Durand refers to it.

Perhaps the artist in Clemenceau put a pox on both houses. At any rate, he never did finish his physiological study of women.

V

TRAGEDY BROUGHT Clemenceau back to France in March 1866. Jourdan was dead. Cholera was making its rounds once more. The major ports of western Europe were invariably the first to open their gates. Jourdan had taken a trip to Brest. For three days he struggled with the fever, the cramps, the vomiting. Then he fell in a coma; he lay unstirring on a couch – quite peaceful it was said, like a convalescent. But after two days his frantic wife awoke him.

'*Ah! ma pauvre amie, quelle bizarre maladie!*' he said, and died.

This was more than the death of a friend. Jourdan was a mentor, who didn't balk at criticising some of Clemenceau's hastier conclusions. Don't, he wrote to Clemenceau just two weeks before his death, make everything a function of the senses and material organs. 'Man is more than pure organism. I would never sacrifice liberty for a materialist or providential theory.'

How could you account for progress, he went on, if the germs of creation were only born within each individual?

'Work to death,' he closed, 'and love me. Tibi.'

Jourdan was an emotional prop for Clemenceau; he played the role of father. With his death Clemenceau was forced to face his real father head on. Jourdan had also made the embarrassing question of money easier by acting as a middleman; now Clemenceau would have to send his bills directly to his father.

Clemenceau made this a short stay, probably not more than three months, including the two Atlantic crossings. Most of that time was spent in Paris with the friends he had made as a student.

The political situation was awful. Nobody talked of 'liberalisation' in 1866. Morny, the Emperor's half brother, was dead, and without him there seemed little hope of internal reform. Foreign policy was racked by uncertainties on several sides. Napoleon's curious Mexican venture was still going on, still costing money and soldiers who could have been better deployed elsewhere. In the case of Italy, an earlier diplomatic muddle, which included a brief war with Austria, had had the unexpected and, from the Emperor's viewpoint, undesirable result of uniting the whole peninsula under one crown, except for Venetia (still occupied by Austria) and Rome. In the meantime, Prussia was in the process of modernising murder and plunder under the able guidance of Count Otto von Bismarck. In June 1866 a complicated matter in southern Denmark had led to open conflict between Austria and Prussia. The war was prosecuted with such thoroughness that it was over in seven weeks. Prussia was triumphant; Austria in disarray; and Louis Napoleon, who had hoped as arbitrator in a longer struggle to win a little real estate on the Rhine's left bank, was left with the frightening prospect of having to face yet another nation state to the east.

Oddly enough it was Italy, not the expansion of Prussia, that stirred the most political debate in Paris that spring and early summer. There was a religious factor involved here that France just could not let go. Because of the Pope in Rome, Italian policy had become the litmus test of a government's loyalty to the principles of the French Revolution. Old divisions were reappearing. For whatever reason, France in the 1860's was experiencing something of a religious revival. There had never been in France as many churches, nor as many priests, as there were in the France of the Second Empire. Louis Napoleon's government spent twice as much on religion as it did on education. Not that this endeared the Emperor to many churchmen. They had been appalled by his apparently cavalier treatment of the Pope in 1859 and 1860. Now, with the promise of complete withdrawal from Rome, there was talk of the 'persecution' of the papacy, the 'betrayal' of France's divine mission as protector of the Church.

If there was something new in all this it was the attitude of the Church. Poor peasants had always tailored their religion to fit their own local beliefs – in faith healing, sorcery, the magic power of a rock, the miracle work of a fountain, the repeated name of a saint – making much of the history of the Church a running battle between the priest and his parishioners. But now the Church listened. Democracy was even spreading to this corner. Idolatry was sanctioned, shrines were dedicated, village processions encouraged. There was an outburst of miracles. With the miracles came the pilgrimages. And there was an onrush of prophecies. 'We are at the end of time,' a peasant girl claimed Christ to have told her in that choleric year of 1866. 'It is a great epoch which is opening, the third. After the Father who created us in order to know, love, and serve Him; after the Son who has saved us, now the Father and the Son to console us, send us Their triumphant Spirit, with His wife Mary. It is a great miracle.'

Miracle or not, the authority of Louis-Napoleon was on the wane and France was moving rapidly in opposite directions, towards a clerical Right and a relentlessly anti-clerical Left.

Clemenceau had returned to an uneasy Paris. His friends had either left the capital or were getting ready to leave. Eugène Carré was eking out a pittance of a living as a country doctor, Ferdinand Taule was getting prepared for the same. 'This poor fellow is out in his province,' Clemenceau was to tell Jourdan's widow. 'In six months the medical profession has brought him 60 francs. He is a fellow full of heart who I fear will never be happy.' Onimus was finishing a thesis on the 'dynamic theory of heat'. Aristide Rey, one of the closest of Jourdan's friends, had spent the year in Heidelberg. Gustave Dourlen was actually in New York when the news of Jourdan's death arrived.

Somehow, however, they managed to put a manifesto together which they published in the ephemeral *La Revue encyclopédique*:

The undersigned consider it a duty to break in actual fact with the doctrines that they reject in principle; they declare that they pledge themselves to never receive any sacrament from any religion; no priest at birth, no priest at marriage, no priest at death. They constitute under this title, '*Agis comme tu penses*' ['Act as You Think'], an association which has as its law science, as its condition solidarity, as its end justice.

It was signed by Clemenceau, Taule, Rey, Onimus, Dubois, Dourlen and Lafont and served as a memorial to their late republican friend. But the wording is like a declaration of war on that clerical half of France, which was itself gathering forces for the coming battle. For the moment the struggle was still limited to words. Louis Napoleon continued to balance on the tight rope separating them.

Clemenceau was in a hurry to get back to America with the vague plan of launching a career in journalism. He had shown, as a student, that he had a talent. Now he wanted to turn that talent into money.

VI

MONEY WAS, in fact, the central issue. Science, solidarity and justice had a feebler ring when purses were empty. Clemenceau's father was bringing in a good income from the family estates, but relations between the two men became increasingly strained. In the summer of 1867 Clemenceau got himself involved in a daft landholding scheme out in Illinois. Benjamin would have none of it and ordered his son back to France. Clemenceau refused, so Benjamin cut off his allowance.

Contrary to myth, Clemenceau's first efforts as a professional journalist were not a shining success. More than a year had passed before he had earned as much as a sou and then he was only paid by the line – not a lucrative job when the number of lines is determined by your boss. Clemenceau's employer was the liberal Paris daily, *Le Temps*, whose archives do show payments made to Dr Georges Clemenceau in the autumn of 1867. By 1868 the 'American correspondent' was earning a regular monthly salary of 150 francs a month.

But at this point the identity of the 'American correspondent' becomes rather obscure. Why didn't Clemenceau sign these articles? The story goes that Dr Georges Clemenceau, deceived by the progress of republicanism at home, went overseas to get a dose of it. Aware of the contagious effect of the modern printed page, Clemenceau decided to go into journalism and, over a five-year period, managed to publish more than ninety articles in this prestigious French newspaper. But because of his reputation as opponent of the Empire, he was obliged to remain anonymous, the 'American correspondent.'

This is odd. Delescluze published under his name. So did Rochefort. As did Lefort and Pichat. At the time, these posed a far greater threat to Louis Napoleon than Clemenceau, an unknown. What is more puzzling is how he could have managed to witness and report, amongst other events, the presidential elections of 1868 when the record shows him to have been in France or somewhere in the mid-Atlantic.

Between summer 1865 and summer 1869, Clemenceau crossed the Atlantic eight times. Letters that he wrote in 1867 to Mme Jourdan (10 March), to John Durand (1 April), to Mme Jourdan again (29 November) and to Auguste Scheurer-Kestner (27 December) show this to be the only year where he did not make the crossing. He planned a short trip to France in January 1868, but only left on 27 June as proven by two letters to Scheurer-Kestner, one written from New York a few days before his departure, and the other from the family home in Féaule, Vendée, on 27 July. On 21 November he boarded a ship at Brest for New York, but by 3 February 1869 he was once more in the Vendée. At the end of May, the same year, he sailed to New York. On 28 June he was on board another ship bound for France. The next time he was to see the United States was in 1922.

All in all, of those forty-eight months, Clemenceau spent about ten in France, four on board a boat and about thirty-four in America. The longest uninterrupted visit was the twenty-four-month period extending from June 1866 to June 1868.

VII

IN FACT the 'American correspondent' of *Le Temps* was almost undoubtedly a team of contributors – a frequent feature of French journalism at that time. Of the ninety-four 'Lettres des Etats-Unis' commonly attributed to Clemenceau well over half must have been written by others. After comparing the dates of location mentioned in Clemenceau's private correspondence with the dates of the articles we would conclude that the main body of articles written by Clemenceau in America is limited to nineteen, written between 26 December 1866 and 8 November 1867. He made only a small contribution to the articles on President Johnson's impeachment hearings of 1868. As for the articles on the presidential elections later that year, they were almost certainly not written by

Clemenceau. A study of style and ideas expressed also seems to confirm Clemenceau's rather limited contribution. With this in mind, what was Clemenceau's vision of America?

Above all else, it was French; this was an America seen through the eyes of an educated, nineteenth-century Frenchman. His republicanism forced him into seeking in America a workable alternative to Napoleonic government, just as his positivism encouraged a vision of human progress, or his romanticism the thought that the odd genius really could speak with the voice of the people. Clemenceau in America was witnessing a great event in history; to Clemenceau's mind, the American Civil War and Reconstruction were another French Revolution.

In his articles we find the obvious parallels. Edwin Stanton is described as the 'Carnot of the American war'. Thaddeus Stevens has 'the wrath of Robespierre', he 'does not throw over his staff into the enemy's ground, as Condé did, but he leaps over the barrier himself and lets anyone follow him who can'. (The image recalls the long staffs, or *sautoux*, that marshland peasants of the Vendée used to jump over the small canals which criss-crossed the region.) On several occasions he refers to the Republican party as the party of the 'great American revolution' – the party 'strong enough to carry through successfully the revolution which it had begun.'

This 'great American revolution', we discover, is nothing less than Michelet's Revolution: 'the advent of Law, the resurrection of Right, the reaction of Justice'.

Eighteen-sixty-seven, the year Clemenceau wrote most of the articles that can be genuinely attributed to him, saw an escalation of racial violence in the former Confederate states. It was the year that the Ku Klux Klan was founded in Pulaski, Tennessee. Murder, rape, intimidation – a familiar story, but no myth. There was frail shelter for those who were black and lived in the South. Clemenceau himself witnessed a lynching on a trip he made through the area that year.

The situation called into question the role of the federal government and set off one of the most serious constitutional crises in American history. Was the job of the federal government to protect the Union by tolerating this behaviour, or was it to protect the weak, to force on the South what Clemenceau called the 'political equality of the races'?

The latter could mean another war. The president, Andrew Johnson, the tailor from Tennessee, a man without a party, had after some hesitation come down on the side of amnesty. Congress, with an overwhelming majority of Republicans, took the opposite course. All through 1867 it waged a campaign for ratification of the Fourteenth Amendment, a measure intended to guarantee civil rights for blacks. In one single day, 2 March 1868, it passed the First Reconstruction Act, which replaced the civilian governments in the South with military rule, the Command of the Army Act, which deprived the president of control of the army, and the Tenure of Office Act, which deprived him of the right to dismiss civilian government officials – including members of his own cabinet. In the meantime a special House committee had been set up to gather enough evidence to impeach Mr A. Johnson.

For Clemenceau the issue was clearcut. It was a struggle between 'the president, supported by the Supreme Court and the Southern states on one side, against the Congress, supported by the people of the North on the other.' Privilege on one side, the nation on the other; personal power against the people. If the Supreme Court supported the president, it was the Court that was wrong: 'As we all know, there is never a lack of legal texts any more than of religious texts, when men seek to stifle their consciences and proclaim the necessity and the need of injustice, or to set up some bit of nonsense as their creed.' The advent of Law, the resurrection of Right and the reaction of Justice – these things could only be consummated in the people's court, Congress. Clemenceau likened Congress to the Convention of 92: 'The first duty of the Republicans when they meet will be to decide whether they must summon the president to the bar of the Senate, as *the enemy of the nation.*'

The avowed foe of popes and emperors could give no credit to the president's argument that his impeachment would undermine the central principle of the American constitution, the separation of powers. Clemenceau would have had, as the United States very nearly did have, a parliamentary democracy where the executive branch would have been entirely answerable to the legislature. 'The war between the president and Congress goes on,' he wrote, slapping his thighs,

> Contrary to all that has happened, is happening, and will happen in certain countries, the legislative power here has the upper hand. That is the peculiarity of the situation, or rather of this government. Congress may, when it pleases, take the president by the ear and lead him down from his high seat, and he can do nothing about it except to struggle and shout. [But] the Radicals are limiting themselves, for the present, to binding Andrew Johnson firmly with good brand-new laws. At each session they add a shackle to his bonds, tighten the bit in a different place, file a claw or draw a tooth, and then when he is bound up, fastened, and caught in an inextricable net of laws and decrees, more or less contradicting each other, they tie him to the stake of the constitution and take a good look at him, feeling quite sure he cannot move this time.

Clemenceau was clearly delighted at the prospect of seeing a head of state 'deposed' by act of parliament. He became increasingly sympathetic to the radical cause.

*

The Radicals were the militant left of Lincoln's Republican party that had taken shape during the wartime debates over slavery and race relations. The most extreme Radicals, led by Charles Sumner of Massachusetts and Thaddeus Stevens of Pennsylvania, argued that the Union's war aims should include not only the abolition of slavery but complete civil and political rights for blacks. It was under pressure from the Radical wing that Lincoln made his famous Emancipation Proclamation of 1863. Lincoln did not go far enough as far as the Radicals were concerned. He faced stern opposition to his wartime plans for Reconstruction in the South, and it was this opposition that his successor, Johnson, had to take up in the immediate post-war years.

One can well imagine how Clemenceau could be attracted to the American Radicals, schooled as he was in the story of the First French Republic – the war against European monarchies and aristocracies, the vetoes of the French king, his dethronement through popular revolt, his trial before the Convention, his constitutional defence and his eventual execution. It was the people, not the constitution, that had to be defended. A written constitution was a written apology of the powers that be; if those powers were unjust, the constitution would have to go. After all, Louis Napoleon ruled by constitution. Clemenceau had the same fears for America. 'We are threatened', he warned his French readers in one of his first articles, 'with seeing the nullification of all the measures taken by Congress to do justice to the blacks in the ex-Confederate states, by having them tainted with unconstitutionality.' On two occasions he spoke of the possibility of a coup d'etat, though he dismissed this as unlikely given the strength of Congress and the loyalty of the Union army.

Clemenceau's faith in the 'people' was closely tied to his sense of History. History moved forward through pressure from the 'people,' Monseigneur Tout le Monde – despite the odd setback. First, the appearance of the people: 'Public opinion is growing accustomed to the idea of deposing the president.' Their relentless progress: 'In the meantime, Congress proceeds unhesitatingly in its course towards emancipation.' The disappointment: 'Well, the reaction has come, and much stronger, to all appearances at least, than the Democrats had dared to hope.' But the truth goes marching on: 'It is certainly a triumph that the Democrats should have been obliged, in order to conquer the Radicals, to take the same position as they; that is, to condemn the rebellion of the South . . . and to accept the abolition of slavery and the equality of the blacks with the whites in civil affairs.' And, in the end, the people triumphant, a resolution of opposites: 'It is certain from now on that the political equality of the two races is only a question of time. There has been a continual growth of opinion towards this end.'

*

These were not Tweed's people. Clemenceau rarely mentioned the poor of New York. The poor voted Democrat. Clemenceau was returning to a habit he had picked up in Paris; he preferred to view the people from a distance, a habit that had its merits.

He spoke of the blacks in the South, but not of the blacks in New York. He showed some sympathy for the Indians in the West: 'The whites hunt down and drive the Indians as they formerly did the blacks in the South, and the Indians, in return, when they take prisoners, send them back to their relatives in pieces, without regard for age or sex. It is sad to be obliged to state that the first and real offenders are nearly always the white men.' He noted that the Chinese were also excluded from all political rights. 'I wonder whether it is because the Indians and Chinese are not citizens, and whether they might not become citizens on the same terms as other immigrants. I doubt it. Anglo-Saxon justice cannot go quite to that length. It had difficulty enough in extending as far as the blacks . . .' Yes, but what of the two hundred thousand Irish, or the one hundred thousand Germans on his own backdoor? Clemenceau speaks of them, like George Templeton Strong, in connection with crowds, racism and drink.

Crowds made democracy tangible, they gave public opinion visibility. There was no more dramatic way of reporting the state of a nation than describing the state of its crowds. 'But where are the people?' asked a baffled Lafayette at his mass reception on the Battery back in the 1820's. He couldn't understand: American crowds and French crowds were different; one was democratic and the other was not.

The applause of the crowd, the cheers of the crowd, the din of the crowd, the colours of the crowd, the smells of the crowd. There was nothing more infectious, nothing more impetuous, nothing more so well-heartedly elated than the crowds at New York.

The torchlight parade. The band. The bandwagon. 'If the measure of success', wrote Clemenceau four days before the New York state elections, 'is the number of torchlight processions, fireworks, cannon shots, flares, drums, clarions, and all sorts of musical instruments, racket, in short, the Democrats are surely winning, for in these respects they have left the Republicans far behind.' Noise was the principal force, not thought. 'Orator succeeded orator on the platform until midnight, no one saying anything new or even anything particularly interesting.' The themes were mainly racist. 'Any Democrat who did not manage to hint in his speech that the black is a degenerate gorilla, would be considered lacking in enthusiasm.' The crowd could appreciate that. 'The Irish mob had come to applaud, and applaud it did, occasionally giving utterance to formidable "hurrahs" which, coming from the depths of five thousand Celtic chests, made the building re-echo to the ceiling.' The meeting had been arranged by Mr John T. Hoffman, mayor (through Tweed's good graces), and Mr James T. Brady, chairman of the party and former candidate for governor on the pro-slavery ticket.

Perhaps it was just a coincidence, but only two evenings before Mr Horace Greeley, famed Republican and editor of the *New York Tribune*, had spoken in the same hall, the Great Hall of the Cooper Institute, on the evils of drink. It was, said Clemenceau, 'a meeting of parsons, religious old women and fanatical puritans'. Together they decided, 'between prayers, that morality, the Bible, Providence, as well as order and propriety, demand that every Sunday New York take on the aspect of a cemetery'.

Clemenceau hated this puritan aspect of the Republican party. It was not only stuffy, it brought religion into politics and could cost votes. 'The Germans', he said, 'are not willing to vote for men who will take away their regular glass of beer in the name of religion.'

The detachment of the Republicans from the Irish and Germans over issues of race and drink created a tension that Clemenceau, in his articles, never resolved. It lingered there, pulling at both ends, distorting Clemenceau's image of America's 'second revolution'.

At bottom, there was a very uncomfortable ambiguity about the historical role Clemenceau assigned America's Republican party. Oh yes, the Republican party had the 'glorious distinction' of spearheading the 'far-reaching revolution through which the country has passed.' And yes, 'the real mass of the people' was the 'body of the Republican party.' But – and there was the hitch – the Republican party was also 'the party of the industrial aristocracy'.

The Republicans, including the Radicals, made unorthodox Jacobins. This could be one of the reasons why Clemenceau concentrated on the national heroes of the revolution rather than the wider political forces that were at play. He could make Thaddeus Stevens look like Robespierre's elder uncle, or his own brief associate, Auguste Blanqui – 'once in a while a sardonic smile, like a grimace, flickers over his livid face . . . the fire smouldering in the depths of his piercing eyes.' But he had a harder time defining his *sans-culottes*.

There was a lot to be learnt in New York, a lot that was not learnt. Clemenceau's contributions as the 'American correspondent' are incisive and a lot of fun. But one cannot help thinking that, if he had looked a little closer at the poor of New York, if he had just glanced at New York's municipal government, he might have said more on the yawning gap between the Democratic 'crowd' at his doorstep and his own hopeful notion of the 'real mass of the people'. In this town, at any rate, democracy was hanging upside down. In this town, the crowds cheered for drink, racism and slavery; the reformists were left in search of a people.

VIII

'MEN ARE made so that one may pass by their side, not over them, aristocrat that you are.' That remark of Jourdan's caught both the sense of defiance and withdrawal which weighed so heavily on Clemenceau during his first couple of years in New York.

He had pulled at every string, every acquaintance he had made in Paris, in New York – excluding his father – to obtain a column in some paper. He was not fussy.

That acquired, he faltered. He was not interested. Or he was not ready. There were other things to do.

His first series for *Le Temps* came to an abrupt halt in early February 1867. On 1 April he wrote to John Durand, then in Paris, that he was still working on the Mill translation, but that there were some money problems he had to discuss. He owed Durand for the steamer he had taken to France the previous year, for the books he had purchased and for the settlement of an outstanding debt he had with Baillière, the publisher, who was apparently getting impatient with the translation's slow progress. Endless worries. Anyway, he couldn't pay now; he had lost the scrap of paper on which he was keeping his accounts (his life revolved around scraps of paper).

Earlier, in March, he told Mme Jourdan that he was waiting for Bush to return from a trip to Savannah so that he could decide whether he should go South or not. He was considering the possibility of practising medicine there. California was another possibility. Neither project materialised.

But, with Bush's help, he did rent a couple of rooms on Twelfth Street to use as a doctor's office. The problem here was that he never kept office hours.

The Illinois land scheme was shot down by his father.

He tried selling subscriptions for a newspaper edited by Charles Delescluze, but evidently the French-speaking market was satisfied with the politically more moderate *Courrier des Etats-Unis*, despite the lightning tour of America Henri Rochefort had made that year. Clemenceau wrote to Scheurer-Kestner that the Delescluze episode was 'the beginning and end of my commercial career'.

Nevertheless, his situation was not entirely hopeless. His education, combined with his reformist ideals, gave him an entry ticket into clubland, New York. The fact that he was French also helped.

He was often seen in the reading rooms of the Astor Library or the Cooper Union. He also attended the Republican meetings held at the

Union League Clubhouse which, at that time, was leading a vicious anti-Catholic campaign against state aid to parochial schools. Tweed and his *confrères* became the centre of the fight, for it was the Tweed Ring that had initiated school aid for Catholics and other minority religions. The real victims of the struggle were, of course, the Irish: once more, reformers held hands with the rich, leaving the poor to the Ring, the professional politicians – or as the French in New York called them, *Les politiciens*, a term of contempt which Clemenceau would carry back home.

In July he was again writing for *Le Temps*. As somebody once suggested, journalism may have served Clemenceau as a kind of pick-me-up, but alone it was no remedy. Another letter to Mme Jourdan, written in September, betrays his chagrin and concern for the future.

In November he stopped the writing and, with the Mill translation still incomplete, took off at last for his trip down South, though he got no further than Washington and Virginia. By Christmas he was back in New York, sick; of what is unknown, but he was treated with morphine, which left him slightly giddy.

With the New Year, 1868, his energies were restored and he started once again to contribute the odd article to *Le Temps*. But by this time he had found a more regular job, teaching French and horse-riding in Stamford, Connecticut.

It was his lawyer friend, Eugene Bush, who had found him the job. For the next six months, Clemenceau commuted by train between New York and Stamford to teach two days a week at Miss Aiken's Seminary for Young Ladies. He was quite a success.

He used variations on the charge-thump-and-retreat technique of instruction which so impressed one pupil, Mary Wolton, that she was still talking about it half a century later. 'Seated calmly in class explaining something,' she said in a letter to Clemenceau's son, 'you saw him suddenly leap up, slam the open door shut with his foot up as high as the handle and then, without interrupting his explanation, return to his seat as serious as a pope.'

He beamed good trust, with a play of gestures, a congenial bearing, which reflected a growing sentiment of inner confidence. Authority. He spoke with it, he imparted it. This was the first time he had experienced it. Up till then, all he had tasted of his own persuasive powers had been his brief term as president of the student medical association four years earlier, his writing and his observation of others, especially the political pulpiteers in New York. The setting in Miss Aiken's school was artificial all right. A classroom could be nothing other. The rows of wooden benches on cast-iron trestles, the hand-cut planks for desks and at the front the teacher's pew with two grammars and a French-and-English dictionary on it. He could never have known such authority in another place.

Miss Aiken's Seminary brought Clemenceau more than that. Mary Wolton had been placed in charge of a new arrival, an orphan from Springfield in western Massachusetts, Mary Plummer. In truth, she was not beautiful, but she could attract a glance, with discretion, closing her eyes now and then; it seemed at first no more than a sign of her preoccupation with the declension of the future perfect, though, with her eyelids open again, it became clear that the neatly written columns in her exercise book were not entirely in focus, peering as she was at her half-empty ink pot as if it were a person, or something special: a calculated inspiration. The neck, the nose, the eyebrows he remembered. As the slow pupil nearby hesitated on the second person singular, he doodled, he doodled on a scrap of paper torn from his own muddled notes. It became a habit and a source of amusement. Until one day a colleague remarked, 'These eyebrows look like those of Mary Plummer.' He was for the moment foiled and, perhaps out of good French manners, the doodling stopped, but not for long.

The fact that she had no parents, no brothers, no sisters was important. Here he had no complicated warren of fictive and related kin to burrow through to get him to his object; no Kestners, no Scheurers, Rislers, nor Chauffours – no plurality of resistances could stop him here in the mid-passage of his aim. The way seemed free. The politics of love was simpler. He did not even have the need to lean on father figures, another Arago or Jourdan. As teacher, he was himself the father figure and, still not thirty, he could make himself a friend.

There was an uncle, a devout and religious uncle named Horace Taylor. He was a wealthy man. He lived in a lavishly carpeted, lavishly furnished, lavishly envied flat in New York. Fifth Avenue, New York City. For the last eight years, his home had been Mary's home.

Mr Horace Taylor had no interest in political theory, still less in scientific humanism. If this young French doctor (who for some unconvincing reason earned his keep through teaching) had signed an oath while last in Paris forbidding him to take part in priestly ceremony, then let the matter rest on his conscience. Mary would get married in a church.

Clemenceau took up the challenge as if it were all he needed to confirm his newly discovered strength. If Horace Taylor could be forced to yield, what a conquest! If he did not, then let her go! So be it! It was the principle that mattered! He could be another 'martyr of History'!

And so he left New York for France, in a huff, leaving Mary Plummer with her uncle, in tears. To let the world know of his departure he had his name placed on the list of passengers that the *Courrier de France* then published. It is there: Dr Georges Clemenceau, leaving aboard the *Ville de France* for France, 27 June 1868.

The fact that he had not compromised himself boosted his morale. He had surrendered nothing. Before leaving, he wrote to Scheurer-Kestner that he was now 'the most friendly man in the world'.

He was able to conciliate his father and spent the summer with him at L'Aubraie. Whatever ill feelings he might have had regarding Mary Plummer, he had got over them that summer. As for America, he wrote in a second letter to Scheurer-Kestner that he had vague plans for returning, but only after a year or two. For the moment, he was more interested in learning German; he planned to take a trip to Germany in the autumn.

Then suddenly the project changed, for on 21 November he boarded a steamer at Brest for New York. What was it? The recent news that Hortense Kestner was engaged to marry? A trip to Germany would have taken him through Alsace, and perhaps he still had hopes there. Had Horace Taylor backed down? There is no evidence to prove it. But once in New York arrangements were made for a secular wedding, with the mayor himself, Mayor Oakey Hall, presiding. It was Mary Plummer who had paid the price – she had renounced her inheritance.

With the hurdle of the uncle's protests cleared, he returned to France, either to iron out the bureaucratic problems of getting the French state to recognise the marriage, or simply to talk with Mme Jourdan who appears at this time to have been his confidante. From Paris, he broke the happy news to Scheurer-Kestner, describing his future bride in these terms: 'Brunette, 29 teeth (3 still on their way): size – medium, etc., etc. Character – I dare not talk about it after knowing her for only two years. Ideas – still being formed. Religion – it doesn't go very deep. The parents raised a fuss about having a minister. I raised a fuss about not having one . . . they had to give in to me.' One gets the point.

Georges Clemenceau married Mary Plummer in New York on 23 June 1869. The following day the couple left for France. By July they were settling down at the Château de l'Aubraie and Clemenceau, for the first time in his life, took up a medical practice. He did his rounds on horseback, from village to village, through those sunken roadways, following the crosses and the *querus* – a country doctor in service of the peasants of the Vendée.

He must have felt he had earned the right to be, the right to breed, a right to set a family up in a peaceful '*petit coin*'.

CHAPTER FOUR

Revolution

I

THE WAR between the Germans and the French began as a result of a rude telegram – a wicked, trivial reason for a war that was in so many ways a beginning and an end. It was the first genuinely 'German' war ever fought in Europe. It was the last major dynastic war, a faint echo of the conflicts of an earlier age, a war that involved questions of royalty and succession. The style of fighting was new. It was Europe's first 'total war', a 'people's war', '*la guerre intégrale*' as Clemenceau would one day call it, a war fed by mass media and sustained by an advanced industrial technology. The issues the war raised were new. An hereditary monarch, or even an emperor, could lose territory, but a democratic nation could not – not without the profoundest consequences.

The original version of the telegram had been written by a foreign office official, Abeken, who had accompanied the Prussian King, Wilhelm I, to the baths at Ems early in July 1870. To an outsider it reads like a standard report on the King's business of the day addressed to the chancellor, Bismarck, then in Berlin. 'His Majesty', went the original note of 13 July, 'has decided not to receive Count Benedetti again, but only let him be informed through an aide-de-camp . . . His Majesty has now received from the Prince confirmation of the news which Benedetti had already received from Paris and has nothing further to communicate to the ambassador.' Count Benedetti was the French ambassador, the 'Prince' was the father of Leopold von Hohenzollern-Sigmaringen, King Wilhelm's cousin, who had been a candidate – to the distress of the French – for the vacant Spanish throne, the 'news' was that the father had formally renounced the candidature on behalf of his son. Benedetti that Wednesday morning at Ems had asked the King for guarantees that the candidature would not be renewed. The telegram stated that His Majesty had 'nothing further to communicate' because the renunciation was formal. Good news surely for the French. Abeken's telegram concluded with an authorisation to make all this public: 'His Majesty leaves it to Your

Excellency whether Benedetti's fresh demand and its rejection should not at once be communicated both to our ambassadors and to the press.' Do nations go to war on that?

Bismarck happened to be having dinner with Roon, the minister of war, and Moltke, the chief of staff, when the telegram arrived. According to his memoirs it was a rather gloomy meal with nobody showing much of an appetite. It was barely twenty-four hours since Bismarck had received the news of Leopold's renunciation, a nasty bolt from the blue. 'My first thought', he said, 'had been to hand in my resignation. I reckoned that France would consider the prince's renunciation a conciliation.' He ruefully added, 'I was very shocked because I regarded war as a necessity that we could no longer honourably escape.'

And then the telegram. Bismarck told the two generals, silent, agape, that 'Gallic presumption and susceptibility' would guarantee war.

He asked Moltke for a final assurance that the armies were ready, and then took up a pencil. Just a little editing should do the trick. A more concise, unvarnished account would do: cut out those modifiers, the euphemisms, the verbiage, the polite details. Tell it as it is! The European languages were entering a new phase! Stripped to the bones, the telegram would appear to report such a diplomatic rebuff that France could not avoid declaring war. There was no falsification, no change in the facts; it was all a matter of style:

> Ems, 13 July 1870. After the news of the renunciation of the Prince-Hereditary von Hohenzollern had been communicated to the French Imperial Government by the Spanish Royal Government, the ambassador of France demanded once more from His Majesty, at Ems, the authority to telegraph Paris that His Majesty pledged throughout the future never to give his authorisation were Hohenzollerns to present their candidature again.
>
> Thereupon, His Majesty the King refused to receive the French ambassador again and has let him know through an aide-de-camp that His Majesty has nothing further to communicate to the ambassador.

'*Se. Majestät dem Botschafter nichts weiter mitzuteilen habe*' – 'His Majesty has nothing further to communicate to the ambassador' – Abeken's very words; but the dismissal appears final.

Bismarck had his edited version sent immediately (conforming to the King's advice) 'both to our ambassadors and to the press'. Paris would have the news by midnight. The appetites of the three men at dinner made a remarkable recovery.

*

The telegram could never have had such deadly effect if French intentions had been for peace. But that was hardly the case. Since the Austrian defeat at Sadowa in July 1866 (where in a single day thirty-five thousand men managed to get killed or mutilated), French officials at every level of government had gradually come round to the view that war with Prussia was inevitable. Even the venerable deputy from Marseille, Adolphe Thiers, considered Sadowa a national catastrophe for France, and he was no warhorse. He had told the Corps législatif in April 1870 that French military hegemony in Europe could no longer be taken for granted. But he warned that if the situation were to be rectified by war it must be a just war, a war not only supported by the nation but by the civilised world. If not this, better peace: 'Yes, it must be peace. Yes, it must be a France which would refuse peace only if intolerable undertakings were to oblige her to draw her sword. And if such undertakings justified such a grand resolution as war, let her have the world as her witness, her ally, her auxiliary perhaps. It must be a France that takes her resolution herself, [but a France] that takes it after deep reflection.'

Peace or a just war. The partisans for peace were divided in the French Empire of 1870. Under the canopy of the imperial dictator countless political seeds had been whipped up and scattered to the outside winds. There were no political parties in the English sense. There was not even the kind of political machinery America had developed to unite its different elements. The one issue which united the opposition on the Left (but certainly not on the Right) was the 'tradition' of the French Revolution: it was hardly a tradition of peace, but it could be and was employed as a means of defining a 'just war'. A just war in the republican mind of 1870 was a citizens' war, a nation in arms, the *lévée en masse* of 1792, citizens defending their rights, their liberties. The greatest threat to peace, republicans argued, was the existence of large standing armies, isolated from civilian life and ready to march at a moment's notice on whatever enemy was in fashion. It was an opinion which flew in the face of the military policy of most governments that had existed in Europe since the Restoration of 1815. For these governments the principal concern had been with social order; and the way they would maintain it would be through a politically reliable army of long-serving professionals, untainted with radical vice for the simple reason that its recruits lived apart from the rabble: well-ordered barracks for a well-ordered army.

That was what confronted the Left. The issue really wasn't one of peace. If the Left was for peace it was because they were against war of a certain kind, the war of the professionals, the officers' war, the aristocrats' war, the King's war, even the Emperor's war.

But where did they stand in the case of a citizens' war? They had no single answer. It was not a situation with which they had much familiarity.

The Bonapartists were no less equivocal than their opponents. After all, they were a product of the Revolution and most particularly of the *lévée en masse*. The Emperor himself privately rather liked the idea of combining universal conscription with short-term military service – as he had shown at a military conference held at Compiègne just a few months after Sadowa – but eventually he had been forced to give priority to the political reliability of his army; it was the army that had created him, so an army of professionals it would be. At least so he thought. At times. But he was not quite sure.

The Prussian menace, the self-contradictory arguments for peace and the confusions in French military policy all came out in a parliamentary debate that took place on the last day of June 1870.

The debate began with a well prepared speech by a deputy on the far Right, the comte de la Tour. The speech dealt with the most pressing problem of all armies at that time, manpower. His statistics indicated the overwhelming superiority of the Prussian army over that of the French.

This raised once more the hoary question of recruitment. Would French interests be best served by an army of long-serving professionals (the authoritarian model of the Restoration, the July Monarchy and also of the Empire)? Or should the army be re-formed into a citizens' army based on universal short-term military service (the revolutionary model)?

Garnier-Pagès, old *quarante-huitard*, spoke for the latter. Abolish, he said, the current unjust system of recruitment – based on lottery, substitution and a five-year service (it was seven years before 1868) – and replace it with a military service of two years for all; expand the Garde Nationale Mobile (a reserve of all able-bodied men, only introduced in 1868); and, he added, negotiate a disarmament with Germany. In Germany one could observe 'a general and ardent struggle with the goal of reducing the army'. Bismarck no longer had the confidence of the people because he wanted 'to unite the nation by force, by despotism: he will not succeed!'

The minister of war, Marshal Edmond Leboeuf, responded that a four- or five-year service, at a minimum, was necessary to form the 'military spirit' in a soldier and give the army the ability to assume a rapid offensive. But to show the country and those outside that French intentions were peaceful he had accepted a reduction of ten thousand men for the class of 1870.

Thiers managed to alienate all sides by arguing simultaneously against disarmament and for Bismarck, 'a superior man and partisan of peace'.

Naturally, the debate resolved nothing. The prime minister, Emile Ollivier, bespectacled and looking a little tragic in his black coat-tails, tried to put in a good note for the day with a memorable concluding address. 'Never,' he said, 'has peace in Europe been more assured.'

The news that Prince Leopold had accepted the offer of the Spanish throne was announced three days later, on 3 July, in the *Gazette de France*. News of his subsequent withdrawal came a little over a week later, on Tuesday, 12 July. Under pressure from the press (tired of reporting failures in French foreign policy) and Bonapartist deputies (eager to reverse an earlier electoral verdict), the government that evening sent its message to Benedetti, the demand for guarantees. The telegram of the next afternoon, reporting King Wilhelm's refusal, reached Bismarck just after six in the evening. Within three hours, at nine o'clock, Bismarck's version of the telegram was in the streets of Berlin, reported in a special edition of the *Norddeutsche Allgemeine Zeitung*.

All through that evening and night the news spread via modern telegraph to Munich, to Saint-Petersburg, to London, to Florence, to Madrid, to Brussels, the Hague, Vienna, New York, even Istanbul. *'Teilen Sie dies dort unverzüglich mit!'* – 'To be communicated without delay!'

Paris awoke to the news. Through Thursday the government assured and reassured itself (within its hermetically tight chambers) that its forces were ready. Leboeuf assured his colleagues that the army was ready down to its last gaiter button. He estimated that the French would have a fifteen-day advance over the Prussians; if France doesn't immediately go to war, he said, she will lose an opportunity that will not be repeated.

At 4.40 p.m. the order went out for the general mobilisation of the Emperor's armies.

The following morning, Friday, 15 July, Ollivier went before the Corps législatif to ask for the credits of war. The Left stood opposed. Thiers repeated his earlier warning:

> We have war for a cabinet error. That curses this war . . . For there is one thing I see in our century: it is that one can no longer make war capriciously. It is necessary for nations, present at a war as witnesses in a duel, to approve of you, to support you in their esteem and in their wishes. It is necessary, in a word, to have the opinion of the world with you . . .

The war credits were promptly voted by an overwhelming majority.

In effect, the French Empire had gone to war over a piece of paper.

II

ONE WEEK later Clemenceau, still in the Vendée, was writing again to Scheurer-Kestner. He was very concerned for the safety of his friend and the family he had known in Alsace.

'Do I have to tell you my feelings before the horrible slaughter which is being prepared and which you are going to see from so near? Don't you know that my thought is constantly with you and I shiver as I rank up the numberless sorrows that could at any moment sweep down on you and your people?'

He hated the thought of this war – everything it represented:

> I am more distressed than I can put down in writing, by all that I see, by all that I hear. Whatever happens, this war shall inevitably be an awful disaster, but it doesn't seem that anyone is the slightest bit troubled. As for myself, I had never even dreamt opinion could sink so low. The great coil must be broken. It has even wound in that wretched Delescluze, who is beating his thighs to convince himself and others that 'the enemy of European liberty is in Berlin' and that we carry the Revolution in the folds of our flag.

He must have been receiving *Le Réveil*, Delescluze's republican daily. Its original uncompromising line would have suited Clemenceau.

Since their encounters at the Café de Cluny back in 1864 that 'wretched Delescluze' had been hawking his revolutionary talents around France's political exiles (including Clemenceau in New York) to raise the funds for a new radical newspaper. He finally got going in July 1868. '*Liberté, Egalité, Fraternité*,' he announced, '*voilà notre programme*.' 'If France still holds the sceptre of ideas, she owes it to the Revolution alone.' 'It is there, nowhere else, that you find the secret of those fantastic resurrections with which she has so often bedazzled Europe and which we shall not delay in saluting once more.'

For a man of republican temperament, a '*travailleur de la pensée*' (as distinct from a bourgeois man of letters), it was superb material. Its style and political colour were perfect. It even bowed to science – talk of 'resurrections' had the hint of life surging forth, the spontaneous generation of anatomic elements! And the paper got results. For a while it was the front-line weapon of the Empire's opposition. Arthur Ranc collaborated with it. Léon Gambetta defended it. Emile Ollivier attacked it.

And then the war. Clemenceau's brief remark in a letter – all that we have from him at that critical moment, with France standing in limbo between peace and war – hints slightly of trouble among the nation's republicans. Of course there were the emotion and fear that any war must engender. Only now they were amplified by the fact that it was the Empire that declared it. Whose side were you on?

Charles Delescluze took a very bold step. Only a week before, as the story of the Hohenzollern candidature was picking up in the press, he was shrugging his shoulders. It could hardly be taken seriously: 'If the cabinet at the Tuileries is vexed and humiliated, that's their problem, not ours.' On the day the Ems despatch was made public he still made the distinction between 'them' and 'us': 'It is not on M. de Bismarck that M. Ollivier ought to declare war, it is on Democracy, which is for him a source of menace and remorse.' But following the parliamentary debate of Friday, the 15th, the tone changed. Yes, he said, Democracy is the declared enemy of wars, but what does this conflict represent for *us*? France is the home of the French Revolution; Prussia is in league with the forces of reaction. Do not confuse the issue of our freedom at home with the essentiality of guarding our independence abroad. It was almost as if he were defining some natural law:

> Faithful to its race's tradition as invader, intoxicated with its easy victories of 1866, the House of Hohenzollern longs for its grandeur through the ruin of European liberty ... Eventually will come the day when France alone will pick herself up to defend herself from these attacks and we will see if Democracy is not the first to enter the combat.

Three days later, he elaborated:

> Better to have a brief adjournment of our hopes than the triumph of Prussian Cæsarism. They wanted a dynastic war, they will have a national war; and once the people, raised to a man by the bursting peals of the *Marseillaise*, have won security for French soil, then will it be time for liberty to regain what she has lost.

'Cæsarism' in France is a mishap; the Prussians have it in their blood – the war will make that clear: French victory, European liberty.

Hardly any republicans believed this in July 1870. But within months, if not all of them, at least a significant portion of them would be following the same line.

What offended Clemenceau and most other republicans at the moment of outbreak was that Delescluze seemed to be jumping the gun. This was not their war. 'Three peoples living in peace,' wrote Auguste Vacquerie in Hugo's *Le Rappel*, 'a monarch appears, and there is a war set alight!' This war was the product of 'dynastic games' which ran counter to the great principles of the French Revolution:

> Liberty, Equality, Fraternity. Liberty, which suppresses the monarchy;
> Equality, which suppresses poverty and ignorance; Fraternity, which
> suppresses war. As long as this end is not attained ... we will never
> stop saying and repeating to those who call themselves and believe
> themselves conservative ... to these troublemakers without knowing
> it, that they will never be able to count with security and confidence
> on the two principles for which they would sacrifice everything: Order
> within the interior, Peace beyond the exterior.

It was as if a Republic once established would automatically bring peace
and order, and liberty, equality and fraternity would somehow find natural
expression. How the Republic was beautiful under the Empire! – and less
than two months before the fall of the latter.

That France was going to win this war, there was no doubt. The
distinction that all republicans made between 'dynastic war' and 'national
war' allowed them to assume that, even if the Emperor's armies were
defeated, the nation, rising in arms against a common enemy, would
eventually steal the victory for democracy and a freed citizenry. The
republican concern in July was not so much over the question of victory
or defeat as it was over whose victory this would be and what would be
its political significance. 'We can expect victory,' the veteran journalist
Auguste Nefftzer wrote in *Le Temps*, 'but the political results we fear will be
illusory.' The prospect of the Emperor's victory was frightening. It would
prolong the regime for many more years and even lay the groundwork for
the imperial succession, for a Napoleon IV.

Very few appear to have grasped the importance of technology. There
was one rare case in which Hugo's son reported to his readers, on the 13th,
that at Sadowa Prussia had compensated her smaller army with the use of
the Dreyse needle-gun, which could kill at a rate of ten men a minute –
'gunpower had made the House of Hohenzollern master of Brandenburg;
the needle-gun made it master of Germany'.

But it was not the killing power of guns which made republicans
pacifists; it was the fear of an imperial victory.

III

YOU CAN still see the cottage where the Emperor surrendered. The hedge
that concealed the tiny vegetable plot is gone, replaced by a red iron
fence and two stone pillars, Provençal in style and absurdly out of keeping
with the heavy black gates they are designed to support. The garden too

has disappeared. Beyond the fence one sees only a pile of rubble where Napoleon and Bismarck had sat – it looks as if some enterprising new owner is determined to build a driveway. It is not very pretty. Rope, shovels, a sack of tools, brackets, beams, lintels lie scattered in front of the two-storey building whose windows, dark and empty, squint (as if they had something to hide) at the traffic that passes inattentively down the road from Sedan to Donchéry. Their frames and their shutters are undoubtedly the originals, but they are painted in a flaring green. The rough stone façade of the four sides of the cottage is today covered with a flat cement stucco, probably half a century old judging from the black and brown water stains that descend from the gutters to the ground on the northern and western walls. No guide, no map, no sign will tell you of this place. Two horse shoes, painted white, are welded to the fence. And the only notice is to the far side of the left stone pillar: '*Attention*', it says, '*Chien méchant*.'

The poplar trees that lined the straight road are mostly gone. In their place are heavy concrete pillboxes, their gun holes facing northwards across the Meuse to the Ardennes and the blue horizon of Belgium. But these too are dilapidated, the concrete cracked, while weeds, moss and grass grow out and over them. Cattle – Friesian and Charollais – graze nearby.

Sedan itself is a new city; modern streets, shopping arcades and many, many monuments. This seventeenth-century citadel was destroyed in another war.

It was not the most murderous battle. More had died around Metz. But it was the most significant.

They crossed the Meuse at Donchéry in the early hours of the morning in a thick fog, after shelling the right bank for nearly twenty hours. The French had sent in a team by train to demolish the bridge the evening before, but the driver was so terrified by the cannon that, having dropped off the engineers, he left at full throttle – with the equipment and the explosives.

They crossed at Bazeilles. The railway bridge was in perfect condition. On the previous day, General Lebrun had sent a detachment of infantry to blow it up, but their work was interrupted by a battalion of Jägers who threw the powder barrels into the Meuse.

The two bridges across the tributary, the Givonne, were left untouched.

By midday Sedan was surrounded by two German armies.

The fighting at Bazeilles had been vicious. For a day and a night the village had been bombarded by the German batteries placed at every crest west and south of the river, a constant line of fire that sent chimneys, roofs and walls crumbling. Though half the inhabitants had by now taken shelter in Belgium, civilian casualties were high. The scalding flame and embers kindled a bitterness that the war had not witnessed to that moment. The residents took to arms. When the Bavarians moved in, before dawn, they were met by a hail of gunfire from windows, from doors, from every corner of every street. Civilians fought beside soldiers. No neat formations, learned at manœuvres, were to be found at Bazeilles. It was house to house combat in which each side lost numbers, handful by handful, trapped and slaughtered. Who was the enemy now? If the French would not follow the basic rules of warfare, then neither would the Germans. So all through the morning the Germans conducted a series of summary executions – many men, some women, some children were lined up against walls and shot. Bazeilles marked the beginning of a new kind of war.

The cavalry charges might have been the end of another: they served no tactical purpose. General Wimpffen, who had taken over command from MacMahon, wounded early that morning, described them as *'intempestives'*, 'inopportune'. General Rozat, chevalier de Mandres, who spent eight years studying every inch of each charge, thought they might have even contributed to the chaos in the last infantry lines, turning the retreat into a rout. But, he concluded,

> The truth is that these charges re-established military honour compromised by the defeat, and these glorious episodes still shine like stars in a sombre sky. The role of the cavalry, when the ill-fated hour of reverse sounds, is confined to sacrifice. The cavaliers of Sedan, like those of Froeschwiller, were at the summit of their glorious task. That is what must be said to the young who, happier than us, have not known the sorrows of defeat . . . Waterloo, Froeschwiller and Sedan are, for the French cavalry, three glorious defeats, which force admiration from the enemy. If we are not masters of victory, which depends on the command, we are always, we, cavaliers, the masters of dying well, falling with sabre at hand, nobler than the victor himself, in a supreme and final *élan*.

He meant every word of it: in 1899 he got himself killed in a glorious charge over some foreign cabbage patch.

The cavalry was the proudest, the most honoured, the most colourful, the most devoutly respected section of the French army. Noblemen's sons joined it. Noblemen's daughters married into it. A cavalry's performance on the battlefield evinced, for many, the spirit of the nation, the empire, or, for those who still clung to it, the kingdom. It embodied all the virtues of the old order: courage, loyalty, discipline – and there was perhaps no better symbol of the erosion of that order than the demise of the cavalry which began in that campaign of 1871.

In a moment of peculiar silence, they took up formation. The bugle sang. *'Enlevez-moi ça, les chasseurs,'* shouted General Margueritte, pointing at a row of spanking new steel cannon. The Nassau riflemen must have been impressed, even awed, at the sight of five hundred horsemen as they emerged, at first at a slow trot; a curved line of greens and reds and blues, like an advancing amphitheatre, the silver breastplates, the golden helmets glittering in the September sun. Gradually the trot picked up to a canter. At about six hundred metres from the German lines – still silent – Margueritte raised his sabre: '*En avant, au galop, mes enfants! Partez! Partez!*' Sabres drawn. '*Sentez la botte, sentez la botte! . . .*' cried the officers, hunched in their saddles, ready to meet bullets now buzzing like bees – until they hit flesh; one thud, then two. '*De l'éperon, de l'éperon! . . .*' Suddenly a cannonade ripped and ripped again through their columns. Riderless horses bolted in every direction, the ornate saddle blankets flapping at their flanks; riders staggered across the uneven ground strewn with the bodies of men and animals. A few actually made it into the square formations of the Nassau riflemen.

'*Ah! les braves gens!*' exclaimed old King Wilhelm – tradition has it in French. From the heights of Frénois he was watching the afternoon charges, accompanied by Bismarck, Moltke, the whole general staff, the foreign press, General Sheridan from the United States and a host of German princes and princelings. Say he had cried out, 'Those bloody idiots!' With that honourable party present he might have put an end to a certain mad kind of war, this absurd war of glory. But not a lesson was learnt. Nobody said anything at the time. And if Zola, some twenty years later, emphasised the absurdity of the whole business in a novel, this was an isolated case – and he paid for it. *La gloire*, the spirit of Margueritte, was carried in the hearts of cavalry officers, yes, but also poets, educators, novelists, politicians, men of the Right, men of the Left, for a generation or more.

'*Allons, mon petit Galliffet,*' Ducrot shouted to the new cavalry commander now that Margueritte lay mortally, and hideously, wounded, '*encore un effort?*'

'*Tant que vous voudrez, mon général!*' he raised his képi, '*tant qu'il en restera un!*' And three more batches of adolescents were ridden into the valley of death.

The rout that afternoon should have taught something. It began at one when the right of 7th Corps, standing in two lines of trenches at the Calvaire d'Illy, was broken by a flanking movement of the German 22nd. Down the slopes they scuttled, a tangled crowd of men, horses and wagons, leaving behind a trail of guns, blue shakos, torn clothes and the wounded, that led helplessly to Sedan, its gates locked against them.

The rout continued, and intensified, till dark. The men ran for the cover that their fathers and grandfathers would have taken, the woodland. No human being had yet seen the kind of destruction the Saxon guns of

Givonne, Haybés and Daigny then wrought upon the Bois de la Garenne.
You could hear a heavy, hollow sound – it was like the deep echo of a huge
filled steel vat when hit at its base, a kind of submerged rumble. Those in
the open could see the shells coming, whistling, and leaving a thread of
white smoke across the blue sky. The explosion at impact was horrifying.
One spoke of whole trees – grand oaks, pine, tall beeches – being simply
lifted from the ground, shuddering. There was nowhere to go. It was
worse than in the open. The wounded were left where they fell. There
was no question of help. The human injury was horrible; flying shorn
metal against flesh; the details are known and recorded. It seemed the
day would never end. Men shivered in absurd shelters – cramped in the
hollows, huddled beside the torn tree trunks – waiting, waiting, waiting
for the sun to go down.

When the battle was done and the capitulation finalised, the German
occupation of Sedan began. The first troops arrived on horseback in the
early afternoon of Friday, 2 September. The skies were overcast. The city
was filthy. The remnants of Marshal MacMahon's army were gathered in
a central square and marched in columns through the main portcullis to
Torcy between two long rows of German guard and a cavalry ready for
escapees. It is said that the Germans showed respect for their prisoners
at that moment; their bands struck up French tunes. The evacuation took
the rest of Friday and most of Saturday, in thunder and torrential rain.

The site that the Germans had selected as a prison camp was the
presquîle d'Iges, a stretch of low-lying land of about one and a half
kilometres by one, surrounded on three sides by a loop in the Meuse
and cut off at its base by a canal. There was only one bridge, guarded by
two cannon. The rains had turned much of the area into a shallow lake,
and the rest consisted of fields of beet and potatoes. For over a week this
was the home for sixty-five thousand men and ten thousand horses. They
called it the Camp de Misère.

On Saturday, the Germans distributed through French noncommissioned
officers sugar, coffee and biscuits. The men cooked for themselves the
shrivelled potatoes that they found in the fields, reserving the beets for
the horses. They spent the evening gathering leaves for their own bedding
on the sodden ground. For many, the water was so deep that they simply
sat the night out on their knapsacks.

On Sunday – it was 4 September – the sun at last came out. But there
were no rations. So the men ate beets. That left the horses unfed. By
afternoon the animals were gnawing at the bark of trees, at fences, at
anything they could dig their teeth into. By evening herds of horses,
insane with hunger, were stampeding through the camp. And it began
to rain again.

Between the 2 and 10 September there were only five distributions of rations and in the clamour for food, many ended with nothing. Violence broke out. On the 7th the German command issued an order requiring the noncommissioned officers to 'use all means of repression to make themselves obeyed. Whenever it is necessary the recalcitrants will be placed in the hands of the Prussian authorities to be shot.'

Dysentery took a heavy toll. The men were reduced to the rotting meat of the dead horses. They had run out of wood so they made fires out of saddles and harnesses; the cuirassier's breastplates and helmets were used as pots.

The dead were not buried. Those who remembered spoke of the stench, the crows circling above and the distant sound of beautiful German music. The departures for the permanent camps at Mainz, Wiesbaden, Bonn and Darmstadt began on the 8th. The last prisoners were moved out on the 12th.

The historians say Bismarck was a master of 'limited war'.

IV

IN A crowd, a face, a woman's face, under the same Sunday sun that had brought damp warmth to the presqu'île d'Iges. Just as silent, the classic profile – which a young man, drawn into the war, had first seen in Thann – was casting off, as it always had, tell-tale glances in search for initiative in the other men about her. Her black hair, as before, had been hastily combed and was held in place at the top of her head with a small white ribbon. For a moment he was struck by her resemblance to the statue nearby, a feminine allegory of Strasbourg, also looking, searching – or was it simple admiration? Probably the latter. One of Hugo's mistresses had modelled for Strasbourg. He couldn't accept that. The smoothly chiselled cannon at her foot was already slightly cracked. The likeness at once faded; he returned to his first regard. The men were taller than her, and older. One of them, an earnest-looking gentleman in his mid sixties, stood motionless in freshly pressed frock-coat, waistcoat and trousers, and a high collar which, combined with the neatly trimmed white chin whiskers, made him look like a cleric, a stern preacher of the evangelical sort – this was somebody who had certainly never had a frivolous thought in his life. It was Victor Schœlcher, the hero of the campaign against slavery that achieved, like so many other noble struggles, a glorious finale in '48. The others were somewhat younger, but old enough, none the less, to have been *quarante-huitards*. The man in the blue tunic and white epaulets – uniform of the National Guard that he had purchased a couple of weeks earlier – was Charles Floquet. He had been sick in bed the previous night and had only got the news of the battle and Napoleon's capture that morning out of the newspapers. The woman was his wife, Hortense Floquet, *née* Kestner.

There was the sound of the drums. They were marching.

Eugène Pelletan's son, Camille, said that it had probably been a mistake to bring the whole family. Safety in numbers, all right: but he hadn't expected a crowd of this size. There were perhaps as many as ten thousand crammed into the square and overflowing into the quays of the right bank. It was as hot as a day in July. The red crêpe around the lamp-posts fluttered. Near the bridge, a man in a red fez had clambered up a lamp and was bellowing out the *Marseillaise*.

'It's in the code,' thought the young man, tugging at his newly cultivated moustache and recollecting Arago's remark earlier that day when the question of the Empress taking full powers had been raised, 'the wife should follow the husband.' But Floquet and Pelletan were going too far in bringing their own wives along. 'My little wife Mary' was just fine in the Vendée, thank you very much. The women should stay out of it. Revolution was a matter for men.

Keep to the front. Don't panic.

So far, so good. Things were proceeding roughly the way Ranc had said they would, and you could trust Ranc, he'd been in this sort of situation before. Calm was essential. They were all well dressed citizens. Lafont had lent him the képi and, apparently, that was all you needed to be in the National Guard today.

Considering the pressure they were getting from the crowd, pushing from every angle, they were moving in remarkably good order: the *redingotes* at the head, unarmed, mostly in black costume and wearing the képi; then the uniformed brigades from the richer districts, carrying guns; and finally ... well, there the order stopped, though some of them wore a *vareuse*, the blue blouse braided with red, issued to the volunteers of the Camp de Saint-Maur – some of these fellows also carried guns and they were neither 'respectable' nor 'bourgeois'.

It was a bit reminiscent, he thought, of the neat social divisions represented in the three estates marching down the avenue at Versailles in May 1789; only now the bourgeoisie were in front and the people behind. At least there was some sign of progress!

There was also a line of municipal cavalrymen cordoning off access to the far side of the bridge. They had just drawn sabres.

Some later said no blood was spilt on 4 September. They were wrong. It could have been a massacre. As the column approached the bridge the unarmed 'guardsmen' made way for those with guns. For a moment they all halted. Negotiations between the armed guards and the police cavalry seemed to be going on and, after a while, the cavalry moved back to let the armed guards through. They didn't have time to close ranks before three hundred or so unarmed 'guards' had managed to push their way ahead. There then ensued '*une petite mêlée*' in which a man to Floquet's left got anointed by a sabre; blood came pouring out of some point on his left side. And then that damned horse haughtily lifted its tail and let drop a steaming load of bright yellow dung, leaving another man swearing.

But from then on it was simple. Amazing, he muttered. The gridiron gates were open. Up the steps. Through the hall. And into the Assembly itself. He could shout '*Déchéance*' into the face of the president. The Corps législatif was in the hands of the people.

The Assembly, it just so happened, was virtually empty at that moment. There had been the famous midnight session in which the Empress's new prime minister, Palikao, had broken the news of Sedan; it lasted only twenty minutes. The government spent the major part of the following morning trying to prolong its life through a 'council of regency'. Adolphe Thiers in the meantime had been drumming up support for a 'committee of national defence', elected by the Corps législatif, which would carry on the business of government until peace was established (there was already the call for an immediate armistice) when the country could elect a constituent assembly. The deputies had retired to their bureaux to work out the exact formula. There were only fifteen deputies in the Chamber when the first of the crowd burst into the visitors' galleries. Palikao was at the government bench, Schneider was in the president's chair. The Assembly stenographers recorded what happened.

Amid cries of '*Vive la République! la déchéance!*' Léon Gambetta, round and triumphant, mounted the tribune. He was only thirty-two, but he already had the voice of a war leader. The cries continued for many minutes. He could not be heard.

Finally silence. 'What I demand from you, citizens, is that you feel with me the supreme gravity of the situation and that you do not interrupt me, neither with cries, neither with applause.'

There were immediate cries and applause. 'We want a Republic,' screamed one – and a Republic there already was in the streets of Marseille and Lyon. 'We must appeal', cried another, 'to national sovereignty' – that old lady had a violent history.

Gambetta's first worry was to maintain some semblance of legal procedure; he didn't want it said that the Empire had been laid low by the crowds, the Republic snatched from the deputies by violence. 'It is necessary', he bellowed out, 'that the deputies return to take their places, and that the session be held in ordinary conditions with the most absolute freedom for discussion, with the end of pronouncing the most solemn and the most indisputable declaration of destitution.'

The people were not hostile to Gambetta. But they did not listen. '*La déchéance!*' cried one man from the gallery. 'One doesn't discuss it! We want it!'

Three times Gambetta tried to restore order. Schneider, the president, made an abortive effort. Meanwhile, the deputies were gradually making their appearance. One of them shouted to Schneider: 'Cover yourself!' – a cryptic message. The president got up, put a coat on his shoulders, then took it off, and promptly sat down again. Nobody in the galleries could have understood this curious little ceremony. But the deputies did: a coat on the shoulders of a standing president meant that the session was adjourned. Quite what the return to his chair meant was left to febrile imaginations.

Gambetta made another effort. The comte de Palikao, scheming in corridors for the past ten minutes, returned to his bench. As he placed base next to bulwark there was a loud boom. The huge door directly opposite the president's platform had been broken open and the crowd outside poured in. Some of them were armed. And they were not wearing black suits.

They filled the benches reserved for the deputies. They clambered over the desks of the stenographers, who kept on scribbling. They covered the steps of the tribune from which five or six orators gave simultaneous addresses. Up the flight of stairs to the president's chair they scrambled; Schneider was looking worried. From the stairs and the platforms flew government minutes, lists of registration, papers of divers colours, torn from spoiled desks and raining upon the heads of the invaders of the benches.

The babble of speeches continued. 'The president is at his post!' – he didn't have much choice – 'it is odd that the deputies are not at theirs!' – they couldn't get in. But they could have got in earlier. 'It was as if', Jules Simon later remarked, 'they had wanted to give the invaders time to arrive.'

Schneider managed an escape. For a fourth time Gambetta appealed for order, asking those who were not of the National Guard to leave. The problem was that everyone in the crowd considered themselves members of the Guard that day.

Once more Gambetta mounted the tribune, this time with Emile, comte de Kératry, at his side. That son of Breton revolutionary nobility was a qualified enemy of the Empire.

'Get back when I ask you, and be sure we are going to proclaim *la déchéance* . . .'

'And the Republic??'

There was a piece of paper in Gambetta's hand. After a moment of silence: '*Citoyens.*' A rumble. '*Citoyens, Attendu que la patrie est en danger . . .*'

'Ssssh! shut-up!'

'. . . Whereas all necessary time has been granted to the national representation to pronounce *la déchéance*;

'Whereas we are and we constitute the valid power born of free universal suffrage;

'We declare that Louis-Napoleon Bonaparte and his dynasty have for ever ceased to reign over France.'

That was, presumably, the end of the Second Empire. One young active participant was very happy. It had been better than *Gaëtana*.

And what about the Republic? Gambetta's pronouncement was not enough to quieten the crowd. 'We want two things,' said the brave citizen who had just completed a tight-rope walk along one of the benches to the right of the assembly and now stood spreadeagled between one bench and another, '*la déchéance d'abord, la République ensuite*.'

'And especially no more bloody Empire!' came an echo from the balconies.

'It's gone! Fallen! Fallen with its chief! . . .'

'. . . The chief who doesn't even know how to die!'

It was chaotic. It was hopeless. Gambetta was smarting.

Then in came Favre, stumping down the outer passageway in a fret. (Favre always seemed to be in a fret; his hair was too long. This had frightful consequences when it came to negotiating with the Germans.) He had just heard that Blanqui, Delescluze and company had formed, or were in the process of forming, a government at the Hôtel de Ville, shrine of revolutionaries. Time was of the essence.

'Drums, *battez aux champs*!' cried a uniformed guardsman. The drums rolled out their eerie chant, an eighteenth-century blood song. It had been heard at Froeschwiller, at Saarbrücken and Spicheren, at Gravelotte and the hills, strewn in corpses, of Saint-Privat. It had rolled out in battle in the fields of Sedan. Now it was the turn of the parliamentary chamber.

'*Vive Jules Favre! Vive Gambetta!*'

'Let Favre speak!'

'Do you want,' said Favre before he had even reached the tribune, 'Do you want or do you not want a civil war?'

'No! no! no civil war! War only on Prussians!'

To which Favre replied. 'We have to constitute immediately a provisional government.'

'*A l'Hôtel de Ville! A l'Hôtel de Ville alors!*' cried several from the crowd.

Thus were Ferry, Favre and Gambetta swept along by the crowd, by the drums, and the march on the Hôtel de Ville began.

So look. It stands today much as it appeared over a century ago, an immense building overlooking the former military barracks, the church, the river and the old place de Grève. In its rooms – not the same rooms – your senses are wakened to the scale and the temper of the city beyond. A bend in the Seine and a channel between two islands take your eyes through the Latin Quarter to Bercy, Ivry and the south-east. A riverboat churns its way stubbornly against the stream. It heads perhaps to the end of the world, engendering a succession of ripples and a thousand little whirlpools that circle and entwine memories heavier than stone; a vessel of happy foreign travellers moving forward, forward as the hope of the many street warriors who, in the past, have stood there at the river's edge in prospect of the millennium. The rue François-Miron leads you northeastward, an old Roman way, site of pagan cemeteries, a road of royal entry, the capital of artisans and *commerçants*; a street torn and mutilated by the reforms of baron Haussmann. The square on the west side is filled with people talking, walking and unashamedly embracing. What the Second Empire did for this square was to open it, make it more public, more populous than it had ever been: an outdoor assembly on the days of politics, a fairground on the days of self-indulgence, a battle ground on the days of remorse.

The crowd had filled the square long before Favre and his colleagues arrived. They had been gathering since early morning. They had come down from Belleville and Ménilmontant. There were carpenters and join-ers, *les trôleurs*, from the faubourg Saint-Antoine and the marché d'Aligre. From the village of La Chapelle and the heights of Montmartre came quarrymen, market gardeners and *caberetiers*. There were the fishmongers, the grocers and the butchers from Les Halles. A number of workers from the faubourg Saint-Marceau (although part of Paris, the name was still used) were also present.

It was a poorer crowd than at the Concorde. There were more men wearing smocks. And there were more women.

People of political ambition were scattered through the crowd, mostly in small groups: men of the opposition press, of the clubs and societies that had sprung up in Paris in the last years of the Empire. Several of Blanqui's followers could have been found in that crowd, like those of Delescluze, of Pyat and Vermorel. But up to the moment that the parliamentary deputies arrived the leaders kept a low profile.

The first man of political consequence to enter the Hôtel de Ville – he was protected by national guardsmen, and the regulars gave him no trouble – was J.-B. Millière, son of a Burgundian cooper, himself a lawyer. He strove for the '*république démocratique et sociale*'. He had little faith in the *quarante-huitards*, whom he felt were as responsible as Napoleon for the republican failure the last time round. In his articles published by Rochefort he placed his faith in a 'socialism' formulated by rigorous 'scientific method'.

Inside the Hôtel de Ville the scientist and his followers drew up lists (that included the names of Blanqui and Delescluze) for a radical new government. They threw their lists from the window and measured the applause: direct democracy in action. A red flag was hoisted over the Hôtel's clock tower.

It was the news of the lists that had brought Favre scampering into the assembly of the Corps législatif. Small wonder the call to march on the Hôtel de Ville. There wasn't a moment to lose.

The deputies arrived shortly before 4 pm. Favre, Ferry and Kératry had taken the right bank, followed by a torrent of men in uniform, in their Sunday bests, and again those in the clothes of workers. Gambetta, Pelletan, Wilson and Glais-Bizoin, accompanied by another varied mass of people, had followed the left bank. The square was now crammed; there had never been so many in front of the Hôtel de Ville, the House of the People, *La Maison commune*. On seeing the deputies approach, the line of regular troops, ostensibly guards of the building, held the butts of their guns to the air.

What happened next? Accounts differ. The idea of forming a government out of the deputies of Paris had probably been first expressed when they were in consultation at the Corps législatif. But it was still only that, a vague idea, as they mounted the stairs to the first floor and encountered, in the Salle de Trône which overlooked the square, a group of men in the process of forming an alternative government. Some report the presence of Pyat and Delescluze. Perhaps there was some negotiation. Perhaps the presence of the National Guard – *'cette bourgeoisie armée,'* said Cordon, soon to be radical mayor of the 15th arrondissement – was the deciding factor. The need for unity in the face of a common enemy was on the minds of all. Floquet reported that Jules Favre 'stood up on a piece of furniture and made a little harangue which lasted barely a few minutes'. He said in substance that the situation demanded the growth of patriotism which was only possible with the Republic. He received a loud *'Vive la République!'* The deputies then disappeared into a small telegraph office next door to the prefect's bureau. At that very moment, who should appear in the Salle de Trône, with a long red scarf wrapped about him, but Henri Rochefort. He had just been released by a mob from the Sainte-Pélagie gaol. He said he wanted to be mayor of Paris. But when he was informed that Etienne Arago had just got the job (named by Gambetta and cheered by the crowd), he declined and, with a kiss on the cheeks from Jules Ferry, accepted to join the Government of National Defence.

All this – events that would leave their mark on French institutions for two generations or more – occurred in less than twenty-five minutes. At about 4.15 pm the crowd outside saw the red flag hauled down and a tricolour raised, and at 4.30 a French Republic was proclaimed. The declaration was signed by all the deputies present, read from a window sill overlooking the square (there was no balcony at the Hôtel de Ville) and was met with loud, sustained applause which could have been heard beyond the city's fortifications. France had a Republic by acclamation of the people of Paris.

The confusion of events over the next eight hours determined who would govern France, and how she would be governed.

Trochu was still in Paris, and still governor. His predecessor, Baraguey d'Hilliers, would have been out facing the horde at the Palais-Bourbon. But ever since mid-August when Trochu, under Napoleon's orders, arrived in Paris, the military administration of the capital had been virtually independent of the political government. They simply did not communicate. So the 4 September found Trochu without instructions. He decided to lie hidden, with his cavalry, in the courtyard of the Louvre and wait and see what would happen. There had been quite a bit of noise wafting its way from the Assembly. Shortly after 3 p.m. he ordered his forces out and they started, at a trot, westward down the quai des Tuileries. Halfway down they came head on to the crowd escorting Favre, Ferry and Kératry to the Hôtel de Ville. There was a moment's tension. Favre walked up to Trochu, who was on horseback. The failure of the now defunct government to communicate with the military must have been on Favre's mind. He knew that no government in Paris could survive without the support of the military and he probably told Trochu, 'We need you.' At any rate, Trochu was observed doffing his hat. He then gave orders for an about turn and the crowd, accompanied by the deputies and now the cavalry, continued onward to the Hôtel.

After the proclamation, Trochu entered the building and worked his way through a cheering mob of guardsmen and civilians. He made slow progress up Baltard's fabulously sculpted double winding staircase – the vast glass skylights above glittering in the evening sun. Eventually he reached the telegraph office where the deputies sat, virtual prisoners of the ecstatic crowd. 'It was with an immense joy that we saw the general enter the little room where we lay in refuge,' Jules Simon later wrote. 'We said to ourselves that the danger of civil war had been put off and from then on we resolved to do everything not to bring it closer again.' Trochu announced his conditions for joining the new government: that it be a resolute defender 'of the family, of property and of religion,' and the deputies quiesced – a most extraordinary pledge for republicans to swallow. 'The condition is accepted,' Favre announced most formally. So General Louis Jules Trochu, an Orleanist in the employ of the last imperial government, became the first president of the Third French Republic. Most of the deputies then left, agreeing to return to the Hôtel at 10.30

p.m. for the first formal session of the Government of National Defence; there were other accounts to be made.

They rushed to the government buildings scattered throughout the city. Crêmieux was seen scampering across the place Vendôme to the ministry of justice. But the major race was on the ministry of the interior. Whoever controlled the ministry of the interior controlled the administration of the provinces. The character of the relationship between Paris and the provinces and, one could say without much exaggeration, the character of the republican state (centralised or federal) would be determined by what happened at the ministry of the interior. Two men vied for the post, Picard and Gambetta. They arrived at the ministry at the same time.

Picard was a compromiser and a liberal of the most classical sort. In the chamber he had headed the '*gauche ouverte*'. Gambetta was a spokesman of the '*gauche fermée*': he viewed Picard's liberalism as an obstruction to the development of a genuine republican state. A dispatch to the provinces would settle the matter! (He had things in common with the Prussian chancellor.) So to all the prefects, sub-prefects, the generals, to the governor-general of Algeria and to every telegraph station in France. Gambetta dictated a circular announcing the overthrow of the Empire, the proclamation of the Republic, the formation of the Government of National Defence and the presidency of General Trochu. He signed it, 'For the Government of National Defence, the Minister of the Interior, Léon Gambetta, Paris, this 4 September 1870, six o'clock in the evening.'

Who would now dare refuse Gambetta the ministry? In the night session, Gambetta got it by one or two votes (depending on which source you choose to believe). Gambetta at the ministry of the interior was one of the most critical developments of 4 September.

What of parliament?

Schneider's antics at the president's chair that afternoon could hardly be considered an official suspension of parliament. A delegation of eight deputies, two of them Bonapartists, arrived at the Hôtel de Ville just as Trochu was leaving for his accounting at the ministry of war. They told the Paris deputies that they intended to pick up the session at the point at which it had broken off, that is, at the debate over the creation of a government committee to be named by the Corps législatif. In other words, business as usual, as if nothing had happened.

Favre told them this was impossible, it would lead to civil war, but he and Simon agreed to explain the day's developments before a session that evening if the delegates could patch one together. They did. It took place in the president's dining room in the Palais-Bourbon at eight in the evening. It was presided over by that engineer of crisis management, compromiser, intransigent, liberal, reactionary, monarchist, republican (it depended on the direction of the wind), Adolphe Thiers.

Favre repeated his story. 'We can change nothing of what has just happened,' he said, reassuringly adding, 'we are men of order and liberty, and we believe that our acceptance of this government accomplishes a patriotic mission.' Thiers responded that History would be the judge and reminded Favre and Simon of their 'immense responsibility'. Favre and Simon then left. Thiers told the small assembly, 'We must keep quiet, make our wishes and let History take care of the judging.' They then dispersed. Thiers went home to read a book.

As for the Senate, it had been virtually forgotten until about nine when an anonymous telegram arrived on Arago's desk reporting that it was going to meet within the hour to denounce the new government. Arago told his assistant mayor, Charles Floquet, to report at once to the government chamber (the telegraph office down the corridor). There, Floquet found only one member, Eugène Pelletan.

'Look at what we've just heard,' said Floquet. He quickly drafted a notice giving himself authority to close the Senate and got Pelletan to sign it.

He then rushed off to the Senate – 'accompanied by our friends,' the mayor later wrote, Messieurs Valentin, Engelhardt and the doctor, Georges Clemenceau.

The president of the Senate, Eugène Rouher, reports spending a rather lonely couple of hours in his office at the Palais de Luxembourg after an adjournment at 4.30 p.m. Every half hour or so he had been sending messenger boys to the Corps législatif for news. Every hour or so they returned to say the road was blocked, the Assembly was invaded, or, as he heard at 4.30, that the Corps législatif had been dissolved and a new government had been installed at the Hôtel de Ville. After that, there was no more news. The senators agreed to reassemble the next morning. Rouher twiddled his thumbs until six and then got in his carriage and headed over to his son-in-law's. There he packed a few of his belongings and, at dawn the next morning, took an express train for the coast and London.

Floquet, Clemenceau and friends arrived at the Palais de Luxembourg at ten o'clock. They knocked at the large main door. Nothing. They knocked again, all four of them. The boards clanked, the bolts rattled. Surely somebody would answer. Eventually an old man in a nightshirt and cap appeared. It was General de Montfort, governor of the palace. Behind him, bleary eyed, was Ferdinand Barrot, the Grand référendaire (keeper of the seals). Without allowing his formal visitors a word Barrot said, 'We yield to force and I'm going to bed.'

Somebody sniggered.

'You can see,' Floquet's face was as flat as the plain of Picardy, 'we are not a very considerable force. You can stay here as long as you like on condition that the Senate does not meet.' He then read his government order, 'The Government of National Defence gives as mission to M. Floquet, assistant to the mayor of Paris . . .'

'Well, come along then, we'll copy all this into my register.'

They all mounted the steps to de Montfort's office where they found a few other serene looking gentlemen. De Montfort copied the order into a large bound volume, turned to Floquet and shook his hand.

'I can assure you the order will be executed. But I have one favour to ask of you. Will you allow the senators into the palace to collect their clothes and whatever other belongings they may have left in their bureaux?'

'Without any doubt. But you must not let them meet.'

As Floquet, Valentin, Engelhardt and Clemenceau returned to the Hôtel de Ville, a sense of awe overcame them. They had just witnessed events that would go down as one of the great revolutionary days in history. They crossed the square in shocked silence. The night sky was overcast and a gust of wind picked up the crumpled pages of a newspaper, which hurtled across the naked cobbles, curled upwards, then lunged into a gutter. An awning flapped. A handful of drunken men sang in a corner café. Near the steps lay an abandoned placard. To it was attached paper torn from an assembly register; it carried a slogan in capital letters. A L'HOTEL DE VILLE!

So this was the Republic. The entire powers of government, municipal and national, were now concentrated in a single building. The executive was made up of deputies of one town, though three of its members, by virtue of a system which gave winners a choice of constituency, had opted for a provincial seat in the Assembly. But parliament had evaporated. Consultation was limited to the representations that still crowded the corridors and passageways of the Hôtel de Ville. As for the place of the people – for the moment the proponents of a direct democracy had won; the noise of the crowd was the vote of the people.

It was a temporary solution, born out of a desperate situation, but loaded with consequences for the future.

V

WHAT HAPPENS on the day after a revolution? The *savants*, the masters and the dissertators can all tell you what happened on 4 July 1776. But ask them what happened on the 5th. The day the severed heads of de Launay, keeper of the Bastille, and Flesselles, Prévôt des Marchands, were paraded on pikes is legendary. But what happened on 15 July 1789?

Clemenceau remembered 5 September 1870. It was the day Arago named him mayor of Montmartre.

Jules Vallès remembered 5 September 1870. He had twenty sous. His three friends had thirty between them. They came out of instinct to the Hôtel de Ville and just stood there, in the rain. He noticed a few tramps and oddballs prowling about the square, their backs sodden. One of his companions, a decorator, coughed violently. His trousers were torn. He laughed, but shivered none the less. 'The Republic does not dress him, any more than it feeds him,' wrote Vallès. 'The victory of the people, it's unemployment; it's unemployment, it's hunger – after as before, just the same! What did we have for dinner? . . . I don't know any more! A bit of bread, some cheese, a rough litre, a snack of sausage, standing, standing at a counter.'

VI

'CITIZENS,' READ the poster on the broken stone wall,

> Must France be engulfed and disappear, or shall she take up her ancient rank as advance guard of the peoples?
>
> This is the question asked today and it is our responsibility to answer it.
>
> The Enemy is at the City gates. The day perhaps is not too distant when our breasts will provide the final rampart of the Nation.
>
> Each knows his duty.
>
> We are the children of the Revolution. Let us take inspiration from the example of our fathers of 1792 and, as they did, so we shall conquer.

Long live France!
Long live the Republic!

Paris, 23 September 1870

Deputy Mayors:
J.-A. LAFONT
A. SIMONEAU

The Mayor:
G. CLEMENCEAU

Rue Capron was narrow, cobbled and it made a sharp turn so as to form two sides of a parallelogram with the corner of the boulevard and the avenue de Clichy which, for several hundred metres, marked the boundary of the 18th arrondissement, Montmartre. Les Batignolles lay on the other side of the avenue; Paris proper, *'le centre'* as the Montmartrois would say, was just across the boulevard. For more than half a century the significance of this had been more than a matter of dull municipal lines. You were in frontier country. It had only been ten years since the fencing along the southern edge of the boulevard had been pulled down. Until then, the way out of Paris was limited to the barrière Blanche and the barrière de Clichy, an imposing neoclassical affair complete with dome and pillars – a few paces past that and you had left Paris and had stepped into the provinces. It gave you a sense of importance, a feeling that something momentous could happen here, the great divide! If the people here suffered the illusion that their actions were actions committed on behalf of the whole nation, it was because they were not *in* the centre, but *near* the centre, watching it – their privilege lay in the proximity of their neighbourhood to powermongers – but, like those in the provinces, rarely able to touch it. Between the flower pot on Montmartre's side and the newspaper kiosk on the Paris side two worlds met, or tried to meet – because, despite the demolitions, there was still some distance. Montmartre was cheap. That explained the *estaminet* at the corner of rue Capron and the boulevard, where cheap wine flowed, and so did the women. The rents were cheap. The poor crossed from Paris in their thousands after Haussmann's evictions. And when the seasonal migrants from Flanders, Picardy, from the east and the north-east, finally did settle down, they chose places like Montmartre, Les Batignolles, La Villette and Belleville, not *le centre*.

Carts and wagons were pulled up carelessly against a stoned pavement so narrow as to be functionless; old rattletraps awaiting repair at a wheelwright's. His shop was opposite a building that had obviously once been a farmhouse, now shaded by the winking autumnal leaves of a misplaced acacia. Above the shop window was a sign in large yellow letters, '*Charon, Magasin de Clouterie, Lattes, Fils de Fer, et Crépins.*' And beyond the *porte-cochère* of no. 19 rue Capron, you could see where he

worked and catch the smell of his forge. To the left were the steps that
led to the apartment rented by the mayor and his assistant.

The poster had been a joint effort. There was nothing exceptional
about it. Posters like this were being plastered all over Paris. Lafont
had suggested the bit on breasts and duty – he knew the quarter better
and thought an appeal to the citizens' obligations might help in the
awesome task of governing what he considered essentially ungovernable.
'The fathers of 92' was of course Clemenceau's phrase – he could not, nor
ever would, abandon his own father-figure of the Revolution.

An unexceptional poster, but none the less one that suggests what must
have been going on in Clemenceau's mind at the moment his public life
began. Clemenceau would never have accepted Favre's formula for a
Revolution – 'it is necessary to provide the people with a symbol.' What
a sop! The Revolution might leave mere symbols to the dullards of later
generations, who see no further than the dust on old documents; but the
Revolution itself is a positive and collective act, no symbol. '*L'Ennemi aux
portes de la Cité*', that's no symbol; tens of thousands are already dead, now
the war is to be carried to the capital! '*Nos poitrines seront le dernier rempart
de la Patrie*', no symbol there; you might literally have to bare them! '*La
République*', thousands have died for it, millions demand it!

Could democracy be only *symbolic*? There can be little doubt that the
moment Clemenceau stepped into office his political convictions placed
him on the side of a direct democracy with the people actively participating
in every decision that affected them. Democracy was not, for the new
district mayor, a simple matter of 'representations' and 'semblances'. True,
he owed his position to the fact that he was known by the 'representatives'
of the people, Arago, Floquet, Schœlcher and others. He was indebted to
the parliamentarians. But he also knew Blanqui. He knew Delescluze.
He could remember the long discussions he had had with them, only
five years earlier.

Blanqui had the most extraordinary hold over people. His words were
electric. Now he was out of hiding again, speaking frequently in fact in
the clubs, theatres and dance halls of Montmartre.

'After forty years of prison,' he might say, his bent body quivering with
excitement, 'after forty years, when the cell door, ajar for an instant, shuts
again on the few days remaining me, I can no longer go back into my night
without speaking my mind. I have fought all my life for justice and for the
law against iniquity and privilege, for the oppressed majority against the
oppressive minority. Poor and captive I have lived, poor and captive will
I die. No one more than I, I think, has the right to say that the wretched
are brothers . . .'

The night of despair. The flash of hope. The will to speak. The need
to act. Clemenceau, listening, would recall his own spell in prison, his
dark mood at the moment of his first encounter with *l'Enfermé*. What an

idea he carried! A direct democracy! A democracy of cobblers, bakers and wine merchants; of butchers, cattlemen, mechanics and gardeners; of railwaymen and of wheelwrights – of the *menu peuple* of Montmartre.

There was one other event of 5 September which would give the idea a boost. The mayors had been nominated, not elected. What of the 'people'? A call went out for the election, by popular assembly in each arrondissement, of 'vigilance committees'. Montmartre had one of the most active. The initiative is generally attributed to a *'Chambre fédérale des Sociétaires ouvrières'*, a front for the famous 'International' – it sat in the same office (no. 6, place de la Corderie, in the 3rd arrondissement) and it had the same members.

But there were no artful plotters and no master plan. The success of the vigilance committees was bound up to a popular and peculiarly Parisian tradition that went back to the French Revolution. They were an imitation of the Sections of 1793–4 which effectively governed Paris during those years through the mediation of a municipal 'Commune' operating from the Hôtel de Ville. Of course, Parisian society had changed a good deal since those days, most notably in the area of organised labour; the guilds (abolished in 1790) had been replaced by mutual benefit societies, trade associations, cooperatives, etc. But such 'organisation' did not go very far. Industry was still small scale and its participants were ferociously individualistic. Like peasants, they were apprehensive of central authorities. Like guildsmen, they were the jealous guardians of their trade. When they did well, they kept to themselves, when they were in need they appealed to the mairie of their arrondissement, not the central government. Their notion of political involvement was simple: their physical presence at the moment of decision, their approval by acclamation, their disapproval by denunciation. In this sense, the spirit of the *sans culottes* was still alive in Paris.

The vigilance committees gave substance to that spirit. The Vigilance Committee of the 18th arrondissement was elected in the course of two assemblies that took place in the third week of September. By October it had forty-four members, most of them artisans or small tradesmen. They were stubbornly independent, ignoring all attempts by the municipal government, by 'central committees', or even by the International (of which, however, many were members) to take them into tow. The vast majority would have described themselves as Blanquists, which meant virtually anything you wanted provided you showed veneration for the Revolution, made a commitment to liberty and demanded, now and again, immediate cession of the powers to the *'damnés de l'histoire'*. They also exerted enormous influence in the political life of the quarter. By November two of its members, Simon Dereure, a cobbler, and Charles Victor Jaclard, a mathematics teacher and medical doctor, had got themselves elected as assistants to the mayor.

Clemenceau was not hostile to this group. Louise Michel would even refer to him as 'an overt revolutionary'. But he carried the memory of New York in him. Crowds have their smells. All right, in the name of justice and equity their voice must be heard, but their voice is not enough. For justice to rule, justice must have authority. That was at the root of Clemenceau's admiration for Stevens. Abolish authority and you not only abolish justice, you abolish society itself. 'Although partisans of total liberty,' wrote Jules Simon in *La Politique radicale*, a book that Clemenceau had undoubtedly read, 'we do not suppress authority for that would be to suppress society.' Here was the key to Clemenceau's actions. It is what made him a Jacobin and what would, within months, generate vehement criticism from the extreme Left.

In war, the combined demand for liberty and authority was all the more pressing. Self-sacrifice was imperative. Action was requisite. It was a time to go beyond your own limitations, to move out of your *'petit coin'*. The war, yes, was mad, but madder still when looked at from the confines of a private retreat. The war demanded of each citizen a public life, a home-leaving. Terrified, you floated in an unknown void; goodbye to childhood, farewell to family, country, all that was near, familiar and sacred. The intractable reason of the 'public thing' was stronger. You stretched, you fidgeted and turned to grab another 'thing' out of the gauzy emptiness, another poisoned quantity to pull you further down and away; memories, beliefs, a father's face, you had to leave them all.

VII

PARIS WAS being turned into a fortress. If you had been able to wade through the maze of unpaved alleys, huts, makeshift fences, animals and ragamuffins to the summit of the Butte Montmartre, you would have got a very good idea of what was going on in Paris that September. The top of the Solferino Tower had been taken down, out of fear that the Prussians might use it for target practice. But you could still clamber up what remained of that blue monstrosity and get a splendid view of Aubervilliers, Saint-Denis and Pierrefitte. Beyond the line of fortifications was bare country, bare because whatever had been standing there was now demolished. The villages deserted, the houses pulled down, their wretched inhabitants streaming into Paris. Wood after wood lay smouldering, wisps of smoke circling upwards. Nearer Aubervilliers a few fires burned briskly in a keen north wind. Everything had been cut, toppled or razed to give clear line of fire for the cannon at the fortified village of Saint-Denis, the forts de l'Est and d'Aubervilliers. The guns of Montmartre were manned by sailors, who seemed quite cheerful at their task; some were digging rifle pits.

It was a similar pattern right round Paris: beyond the fortifications, a desert. A barricade had been erected at Montrouge built of barrels of stone and stable litter, themselves embedded in an assortment of household garbage – old tin cans, broken ladders, carriage wheels, a couple of hats, a pair of old boots, a stove, a tree and a battered warming pan. Adding strength to the people's defences was the city wall, ten metres high and a moat more than three metres in width. A walk further along the narrow paved road that led to Sceaux and Palaiseau would have confronted you with crowds of country waggons and carts filled with everything from cradles to the kitchen boiler, and mile upon mile of desolation: the crops destroyed, the trees cut down. From porte d'Auteuil to porte Maillot you could have heard the sound of the axes at work in the bois de Boulogne, the crash of the trees. The Swiss chalets, pleasure palaces of the Second Empire, were now fields of rubble. The restaurants, the cafés, the gardens too were gone.

The fortifications at porte Maillot were fantastic, like out of some medieval epic. The walls of the fort were nearly two metres thick, pierced at regular intervals with gun holes. The immense drawbridge was supported on either side with steep earthworks covered with stakes and wire. The avenue de la Grande Armée was aligned with field artillery. The Arc de Triomphe was a miserable sight. Every road leading to it was filthy, the army of German female sweepers having left in a hurry (along with the German sewage-disposal men); the circle itself was covered with earth and sand nearly a metre thick to lessen the damage from the expected onslaught of percussion shells.

The German encirclement of Paris began on 17 September, a classic pincer movement with the Saxon Crown Prince establishing himself in positions opposite the northern forts, and the Prussian Crown Prince advancing westward across the Marne and the Seine to Versailles and on round to the Seine again near Saint-Germain-en-Laye. In a major battle for the Châtillon heights a full regiment of bell-bottomed Zouaves fled, in panic, behind the fortifications and down the streets of Montparnasse screaming, 'We have been betrayed!' – an ominous note for the first day of the siege of Paris.

Less than a year later, Jules Favre, sitting before a parliamentary commission, hinted at the mood that subsequently developed in the capital. 'To shut up two million people behind city walls,' he noted with deliberate understatement, 'was to create the most abnormal state of affairs. It was a denial, a violation of all the laws of common sense and of political economy and, to a certain point, of all laws of morality.' Ferry, on the same day, called it *'la folie du siège'*: 'that is to say, a state of mind determined by a change of custom and of life, a change radically contrary to one's habits, to one's life, to the common behaviour of our modern society. A society created for work suddenly finds itself thrown into a military life.'

The abrupt transition to military life was visible everywhere. 'The city is a queer sight,' wrote the English diarist Felix Whitehurst on Thursday, 8 September. 'Nine people out of ten are in uniform of some kind; they begin at 6 a.m. and the first noises that reach the irritated ear are the equivalents to "Tenshun", "As you were", and "Eyes right". If you walk out, all is military – a waggon full of spades, a flock of sheep, a lot of stores and orderlies riding (rapidly and very badly) with despatches; the officer of the day and his orderly, Zouaves, Turcos, National Guards from the provinces, Moblots, a regiment of cavalry two thousand strong, provincial Municipal Guards and a very fine string of wagons.'

The people of Paris expected victory. One could catch the character of the popular militia by a visit to the camp of 'Moblots' (or the Garde Nationale Mobile as they were officially known) at Saint-Maur, neighbouring the slopes of Belleville. There was a constant coming and going between the two areas; wives and children were to be seen in the mud tracks that aligned the tents; and the men were often absent, visiting the cabarets, the theatres and the women of Popincourt and Ménilmontant. The camp contained as many as perhaps twenty or even thirty thousand guardsmen under canvas. Within days of its installation, there were restaurants, a theatre, dance halls. The camp even had its own newspaper. Each dirt track had its name, as did most of the tents: 'Hôtel Splendide', 'Hôtel des Deux Mondes'; the 'Hôtel des Cocottes' had a garden, the 'Grand Hôtel' had a restaurant. On the canvas, on the tentpoles, on the signposts were pasted wicked caricatures: the King of Prussia, Bismarck, the Prussians in flight, hundreds of Moblots marching onto Berlin: the French politicans and generals were notably absent.

Four hundred thousand patriotic men to defend the capital! How could any force overcome them? They were ready for a siege. We have supplies for at least six weeks, said the officials, and the Germans will not be able to maintain an eighty kilometre front for longer than that. They will attack. Even if they breach the walls, they will stand no chance against the fighting Parisians – a street-by-street battle; you don't require a military training for that.

Rationing and a limitation on domestic services were instituted almost immediately, but at that early date it affected only the rich. 'There are also the servile labours for the mistress of the house,' wrote Madame Edgar Quinet, 'obliged to manage without domestics; one has to get up at dawn to light the fires.' 'Today,' said Whitehurst, 'we have orders not to wash much (the self-sacrifice of the natives in this respect is patriotic to an unpleasant degree). We get water from 8 till 11 a.m. The gas to be cut off next week which, as the convicts of Toulon are let loose, and we have no police, is not narcotic.' It made no difference for the inhabitants of the Butte Montmartre; they had no water nor gas.

But there was probably nothing more representative of the passions and the paradoxes of the day than what was going on at the palais d'Industrie. The palais d'Industrie, its huge façade facing the Elysée, had been built in the early 1850's as a celebration of industry, a monument to the new energies that steam, coal and iron had let loose on civilisation. It had been host to the world in the Exhibitions of 1855 and 1867. It had displayed machines that could provide clothing for the poor and new comforts for the rich, speed for the traveller and instant information for the reader. Half of it had been converted into an arms depôt. The other half was now a hospital, an 'ambulance' as all military sanitoriums were then known. 'One gathered together,' wrote Maxime Du Camp, a witness, 'the engines of destruction beside the vast halls where pity sheltered the objects of relief, which had to subdue the pains of war and carry the injury unto death. The activity was intense; both sides knew no rest; barbarism and humanity were zealous rivals.'

There was something new about this 'ambulance'. Its doctors, its nurses, its working personnel wore white armbands with a red cross. Above the large tent flanking the building on the left there also flew a white flag with a red cross. It was the first time Frenchmen had ever seen the emblem. But behind it lay a movement of international aid to both belligerents of a kind the world had never known before. From Britain, Belgium, Holland, Luxembourg, Austria, Switzerland, Italy, Spain, Portugal, Norway, Sweden and Russia, funds, materials, medicines, nurses and doctors poured into the zones of war. The United States set up their own 'ambulance' on the avenue de l'Impératrice. War in Europe could no longer be confined to the belligerents; it was the concern of all. '*La pitié, la sainte pitié*,' again said Du Camp, 'is making its voice heard.'

VIII

'*LA PITIÉ! LA sainte pitié!*' – the man was obviously a 48er and this might have been the first time in twenty years that he had ever spoken to such a large rabble of half-attentive ears. He was grabbing at old straws. '*La sainte pitié!* All we had, all we could bring to bear in our long struggle. Fanatics who wore no officer's stripes, nor plumes; just our hearts bleeding for the betrayed people, just our souls weeping, suffering, groaning, groaning in unison.'

His remarks were most inappropriate for the occasion, but they let him speak. After all, the political club was partly his creation and he had been a hero, once.

The 'Club de la Reine-Blanche', named after the dance hall in which the meetings took place, was an unqualified success. Despite an entrance of ten centimes, over a hundred persons met there every evening for a smoke, for a chat, to listen to the speeches, to applaud the good or to hurl abuse at the bad. Clemenceau was frequently seen, standing near the back of the room, occasionally volunteering his opinions; sometimes he would even come forward to the 'tribune' and make a little speech, usually an appeal for calm, unity and defiance in the face of the German dynastic enemy. Since 4 September, the clubs had become the centre of popular politics in Paris. There were several reasons for their success. The theatres, a traditional forum for politics as well as entertainment, had been closed (but even after they reopened, in October, the clubs continued to attract numbers). The cooler weather had made the streets and boulevards less attractive; the crowds of July, August and September were seeking cover. And there was the unquenchable thirst for news, a keener need than ever now that information from beyond the walls was limited to the flight of carrier pigeon. Clubs sprang up all over Paris, but most especially in the northern and eastern quarters, like little Athenian sovereign states. There was the Club des Folies-Bergère, the Club de la Cour des Miracles, the Club des Montagnards, the Club Démocratique, the Club de la Délivrance, the Club de la Révolution, even a Club des Clubs. In the 18th arrondissement alone one could count, in addition to the Club de la Reine-Blanche, the Club de l'Elysée-Montmartre, the Club Montmartre, the Club de la Chapelle, the Club de Clichy, the Club Webert, the Club du Peuple and the Club d'Égalité. Many of these clubs changed their names, while several names could stand for a single club. Their exact number is unknown, the exact extent of participation is impossible to calculate. But the number was large and participation was extensive.

Every evening they would vote for the bureau and president, though unvaryingly the same personalities won each time. In the 18th arrondissement the club bureaux were dominated by the Vigilance Committee. Théophile Ferré, a notary's clerk and one of the most articulate members of the Committee, remained president of the Club de la Salle Perot. Burlot was president of La Reine-Blanche. And one outstanding woman, Louise Michel, a teacher, a converted militant, was president of a club that called itself the 'Justice of the Peace'.

Not every speech was flavoured with phrases of human pity, though the theme was still common, especially among the older Blanquists. The principal topic of debate was the National Defence, and the principal issue was the arming of the people.

The Government of National Defence had left the details of armament to the twenty arrondissement mayors – campaigns in this war were a function of the *système D*, 'muddling through'. Keen new volunteers from the National Guard would literally scour the capital for arms on behalf of their mayors and elected commanders. One hundred thousand rifles were uncovered in the railway stations, rifles that had never got through to the Emperor's army. Imperial treachery! The minister of public works, Pierre-Frédéric Dorian, a former manufacturer of sickles and scythes from the Upper Loire, gained immediate recognition among the people of the clubs for his efforts in converting the workshops of Paris into armament factories. By the end of September his workshops were turning out 300,000 cartridges a day. The costs were covered by subscription. Guardsmen, committee members, volunteers from the clubs would go from house to house collecting money for the 'National Defence'. The repeated slogan, 'a people in arms', came to have real meaning; the contrast with the first disastrous weeks of the war, the 'imperial war', was not forgotten for a moment. Our effort, our blood, our revenge. This was accompanied by a passionate sense of possession and control: our money, our guns, our cannon.

The pressure on the mayors from the clubs and the vigilance committees to produce arms could have ludicrous consequences. Clemenceau himself was persuaded to set up a bomb factory in the basement of the mairie and in several of the neighbouring houses. He personally supervised the project. He began with 'bombes Orsini', simple petrol bombs made of iron pipes, named after the illustrious Italian anarchist who had attempted to blow up Napoleon III in 1858. But the technology of war was making its advances at the mairie of Montmartre too. By early November sophisticated percussion bombs were being churned out. By this time, according to Ernest Cresson, prefect of police throughout most of the siege, the Clemenceau munitions factory had produced twenty-three thousand bombs, six hundred of which were charged and ready for action – though he added in his parliamentary hearing that 'I was extremely tired, I was sleeping three hours at night [one begins to understand why] and it is possible that I was mistaken on the quantity.'

But Clemenceau had more than bombs on his mind. The tasks of an arrondissement mayor during the siege were unremitting. Arago, in his book on the municipal administration of Paris of the time, listed the mayors' various functions; he filled three printed pages. In normal times, he noted, the arrondissement mayor presided over marriages, signed registers and organised the electoral lists. He was also responsible for the inspection and maintenance of primary schools, he was a control on the influence of the clergy, he had to report on and, if necessary, intervene in the matters of hygiene and physical welfare of the population. Obviously the siege made such tasks more burdensome. And on top of that were his responsibilities in improving and maintaining the city's fortifications that lay within his jurisdiction, and his role in recruiting and arming the National Guard. 'A spirit of initiative was thus essential among these magistrates. And what energy, zeal and intelligence they had to have to triumph over our perfidious enemies and to resist our impatient friends!'

When Corbon, a 48er who had been named mayor of the 15th arrondissment, came before the parliamentary commission the following year, he remarked that his first concern was the formation of the National Guard. 'Consequently,' he added, 'I immediately entered the political life. I was no longer an officer of the civil state but an organiser of the public force. All the mayors found themselves in the same situation. And, more than just that, we finished up by being, each in our arrondissement, a complete government. The action of the central power was not to be felt, even in the matter of defence. Serious action was nowhere to be felt. We had to furnish everything, and especially, we had to cover the government, face-to-face with the population.'

Once more, the words betray a feeling of isolation and abandonment; a sentiment one encounters again and again in the annals of that war.

Two posters, published on 17 October 1870, and signed by Clemenceau. One announces the formation in the 18th arrondissement of two battalions of the National Guard; 'they shall have a total of 1500 men each,' and 'they shall be provided with rapid firing arms.' The other reports the reconstitution of 'the Committee of Hygiene and Health of the 18th Arrondissement'; 'we ask citizens to report: pile-ups of refuse and any stagnant water lying on public thoroughfares or waste grounds; unhealthy industries; sunken drain traps, stops, ducts of waste water, poorly maintained lavatories – in short hotbeds of infection whether small or large.'

Between recruitment and sewage maintenance existed a heap of drudgeries and troubles that fell daily into the lap of the mayor, doctor and magistrate of that stinking city quarter. He was always busy.

But the one issue outside defence into which he threw his heart was the matter of education, the education of the people, the mainstay of the Republic. Montmartre needed educating. It was, along with La Villette, Belleville, Grenelle and Les Gobelins, one of the five sinks of ignorance in Paris. Madame Quinet, loyal republican and great romantic like her husband, visited Montmartre on 14 September – 'roads built like ladders, a deserted square, a sad popular forum, boutiques, street stalls, indigents camped out in the street.' Education was the problem! 'When you see up there, this breeding ground of ignorance, this abandonment, and lower down opulent Paris, shimmering and elegant, you are startled. Oh! set up the schools and libraries . . . ! Open the lay schools for these unfortunate small Parisians of Montmartre . . . In each of them is the material for an artist, a useful citizen, who could acquire a name in science, the arts and letters.'

Clemenceau apparently agreed and wrote a circular to the *instituteurs* (the primary school teachers) of the 18th arrondissement. The *instituteurs*, he said, must respect the 'freedom of conscience' of their pupils. He reminded them that they had been given no directive to receive the clergy of their parish, that the children were under no obligation to learn the catechism, that they did not have to attend church and that the *instituteurs* 'must not apply any regrettable pressure on their [the children's] conscience'.

Most *instituteurs* placed the circular in that eternal, customary file for government notices, the waste-paper basket. He had just one answer. A letter came from the *institutrice* of a girls' school in the rue Houdon (a few paces down the steep slope from the mairie) – Louise Michel. It was the beginning of a friendship that would last several decades.

A most unlikely pair. Louise Michel is known in history as the 'Red Virgin'. Virgin she almost undoubtedly was. The conditions of her birth, birthplace, her looks, her profession, her politics threw her cruelly into the margins of society. She was born in 1830 (though she insisted throughout her adult life that it was in 1836) in an austere château – known by the villagers as the 'Tomb' – on the frontiers of Champagne and the Franche Comté. The birth was an accident anyway; her mother was a chamber maid and her father . . . it was either a count's son, Laurent Demahis, or the count himself, Etienne *ci-devant* de Mahis (the particle was integrated during the Revolution). She was brought up in the count's household, with the middling sum of love that such a household could afford her. Her two principal passions were poetry and animals. There were five dogs in the château, innumerable cats and a foal, all of them going in and out of the house as they pleased. Her poetry was so good that by the age of thirteen or fourteen she had started up a regular correspondence with Victor Hugo. Following the death of Etienne and his wife she left the château to teach in a nearby town. An agonising departure, one imagines. It was then that she was forced to abandon, against her will, the name of the count and to adopt the name of the chamber maid.

In 1857 she came to Paris. She was twenty-seven and a very devout Christian. But she was soon attending evening courses offered by Favre, Simon and Eugène Pelletan at rue Hauteville. She thus entered that narrow, narrow world of republicans where everybody knew everyone else. Her devotion to the Revolution came from Théophile Ferré whom she met in Montmartre. The Church became her enemy.

Was she so ugly? Her photographs show a most intriguing woman: a studied neglect of hair and clothes, so obvious, so apparent, that one is enticed to think she wished it would be otherwise. Seated or standing, she leaned her head forward, her shoulder shrugged, a slumped thin bosom, which added yet more emphasis to those strong features of her face which made her profile famous. At moments there was even an unsigned graciousness about her that one might have attributed to her eyes, the eyes of a Bernadette Soubirous, tragic, devoted, unsmiling and burning for some recognition of a suppressed friendship. Was it a passion? A shadow lay over her, it covered her entirely, like some terrible storm, an anger, a devastating hopelessness, a devouring, infrangible pity. It was total; indeed, so great that she could embrace a 'social class' and consider this a passion. That studied dishevelment, that public wooing of an abstraction were what made her in other people's minds (in keeping with their prejudices) an unfavoured woman, unappealing, unregarded, ugly.

It had to be religion and education that brought Louise Michel and Clemenceau together. Both had grasped the central issue of the Republic and democracy, the conquest of mass ignorance. And both had fostered their interest for personal reasons. For Clemenceau it arose from the continuing desire to achieve his father's graces. For Louise Michel it was the consequence of a conversion.

How they hated the clerics! And the Jewish and Christian financiers were not immune to their contempt. Louise Michel tells how she collected money for an ambulance at Montmartre:

> We would bring with us a tall National Guardsman who looked as if he had been drawn straight out of an engraving of '93. He would march in front, a bayonet attached to his rifle. We would be wearing long red scarfs and carrying purses made for the occasion. All three of us would set out with gloomy faces for the rich. We would begin with the churches, the National Guardsman marching down the aisle banging his gun on the flagstones, while we approached from each end of the nave and collected, beginning with the priests at the altar. The worshippers, shivering and pale with terror, would in their turn empty coins into our purses. Some of them did it with grace. All the curés gave to the collection. Then it would be the turn of a few Jewish or Christian financiers. Then the decent, worthy men – a pharmacist from the Butte offered us material. The ambulance was founded.

She added, 'We laughed a lot at the mairie of Montmartre over this expedition, which no one would have encouraged had we not placed confidence before success.'

Louise Michel, with her band of municipal women, either as members of the *Société de Secours pour les Victimes de la Guerre* or the *Société pour l'Instruction Elémentaire*, had a close working relationship with Clemenceau's mairie. It was the women's home front of 1870. Through them a clothes cooperative was set up. Clemenceau requisitioned the building and they hired seventy-five to eighty women workers, with another fifty or sixty doing piece-work in their own homes. Through them the programmes of health, food distribution and the services for refugees were executed; many a refugee child found a lodging and a home among the women of Montmartre during the months of the Paris siege.

The one activity, vital to the defence, where neither Clemenceau nor Louise Michel played a major part, was the manufacture and the flight of balloons. Nadar, the photographer, had picked the place Saint-Pierre at the foot of the Butte as the site for his reconnaissance flights. Since early September, twice a day, the Montmartrois saw Nadar in his six-year-old balloon, the *Neptune*, climb to three hundred metres or more above the square to observe the enemy advance. He would be attached to the ground by a rope. But once the enemy positions were established the operation ceased to have much meaning and the idea was put forward that balloons could be used to break the blockade.

The first flight out of Paris took place on 23 September; it was undertaken by the aeronaut, Jules Dufour, nicknamed Duruof, carrying two sacks of mail aboard the same *Neptune*. Thus began the first airmail service in history, which would spark off the first mass manufacture of aircraft, the first case of aerial warfare and, as one might expect of an investing army which had as innovative an industrialist as Alfred Krupp at their service, the first production and deployment of anti-aircraft guns.

When the siege began there were less than a dozen balloons in Paris and most of them were in such a poor state of repair as to be functionless. Furthermore there was no question of the balloons being used more than once since there was no question of a return flight. So the manufacture of balloons began. The first government contract was signed on 18 September by Duruof and Dartois. They chose, for its size and proximity to the place Saint-Pierre, the old dance hall, the Elysée-Montmartre, as the location of their factory. But it soon became clear that not even a dance hall was large enough and within three weeks the whole operation, now under Nadar's direction, had been moved to the gare du Nord. There, in parallel to Eugène Godard's huge operation at the gare d'Orléans, Nadar installed a full-fledged production line. Sixty seamstresses worked at sixty sewing machines. A battalion of sailors was employed to varnish the two sides of the percaline balloon walls. The wickerwork of the baskets was also carried out by sailors under the supervision of a master artisan basket weaver.

The first of the new series took off from the place Saint-Pierre late on a clear October morning, a south-south-easterly breeze having finally cleared the fog which had forced postponement for two days. The white balloon, carrying an American arms dealer, got off a few seconds earlier than the yellow one which, however, held the attention of a crowd thronging the square and cheering from the naked slopes of the Butte. Clemenceau was there. So was Louis Blanc, along with Victor Hugo, the poet Mathieu, and the novelist and critic, Alphonse Daudet. But the second balloon was also beginning to climb, timidly at first, then, all of a sudden, with an upward rush as if the winds themselves had become conscious of their urgent purpose. As the crowd looked up, the golden sphere turned on itself, like a planet, a huge cotton envelope filled with municipal gas, supporting beneath it, on thin tendrils of rope, the minister of the interior and the hope of all France.

IX

GAMBETTA'S INSTRUCTIONS were clear enough. 'M. Gambetta has precise instructions to make known and execute the will of the government. He will apply himself to a unity of action and, in case of division, will have a deciding vote' – Gambetta would be taskmaster. 'He will execute the decree by which the elections of the Constituant are adjourned to the time when the circumstances of the war allow a consultation of the country' – there would be no elections in the foreseeable future. 'As minister of the interior he is invested with full powers to recruit, to unite and to arm all the national forces that he deems proper for the defence of the country' – Gambetta would decide on the structure of the armed forces. 'As far as military organisation and action are concerned, the resolutions made by the delegation are to be executed by the ministry of war and of the navy' – the elderly Glais-Bizoin and Admiral Fourichon of the Tours delegation would be permitted to speak. 'The delegation will continue to represent the Government of National Defence according to the terms indicated. It will pursue diplomatic negotiations on the condition that they be referred to the ministry of foreign affairs; but it can make absolutely no decisions on this point, the Government of National Defence having alone the right to decree one' – the delegation could take no diplomatic initiative.

Gambetta came to Tours with the power to make a revolution. His position might be compared to that of war leaders of a later age, struggling in principle for a democratic liberty yet forced to resort to dictatorial methods to get at it – Clemenceau in 1917, Churchill in 1940. Yet so strong was the principle and so resolute the method that a more pertinent parallel might be a Lenin or a Stalin. And unfortunately the only positive thing

Adolf Hitler ever said about the French was in connection with Gambetta
and his government: with Gambetta, he said, 'The war was fought with a
new energy . . . French national honour was raised again by the Republic.
What a contrast to our Republic!' It is not an endearing reference.

But Gambetta couldn't look into the future, he had just one, unique
historical parallel to contemplate: the German invasion of 1792 and
Danton's resolve to repel it.

Of course, every follower of the republican ideal, every pretender,
bidder and hawker, every local demagogue trying to disguise his own
advancement under the name of the public good spoke of 1792 as
an example to be imitated. 'The French nation will show, if it has
to, before the universe and all posterity that thirty-five million free
citizens are invincible when they fight for justice, when they guarantee
the rights of man in the face of the oppression of despots.' You read it
everywhere, you heard it everywhere. The language was identical to that
of '92. What's more, it was perfectly compatible with the pacifism that
most republicans had demonstrated at the outbreak of the war. As Jules
Simon put it, what republicans wanted was 'an army of citizens invincible
at home and incapable of carrying the war abroad'.

But only Gambetta had the position and the power to turn that ideal
into a reality. Gambetta spoke like Danton, he looked like Danton, he was
exactly the same age as Danton had been in '92, he shared the same legal
background and the same talent for turning a situation to his advantage.
He was an opportunist, like Danton. He spoke with authority, he fumed
with authority, he even laughed with authority – as had Danton. Danton
had told the Assembly as the Austrian and Prussian armies advanced fast
on Paris, 'Up to now we have made the simulated war of La Fayette. We
must make a war more terrible!' When Gambetta descended from the skies
to announce to the peasants of Villiers-le-Sec that 'my very presence among
you means "courage and hope!"' he meant just that: the simulated war
of Louis-Napoleon and his generals was over, the real one had only just
begun. In government council, Danton had blocked the attempt to move
the government out of Paris to the Loire; he claimed that Paris was as
much, if not more, a symbol for revolutionary France as it was for her
monarchist enemies: an evacuation of Paris would cause a political and
military rout and open the way to the forces of the counter-revolution.
Gambetta's position was much the same. '*Toute l'armée de la Loire sur Paris!*'
were his first words to the crowd as he entered Tours. In his proclamation
that night to the 'citizens of the departments' he underlined the central
role of Paris in the national defence. 'Paris,' he said, 'has given the world a
unique spectacle: the spectacle of over two million men closed up around
the flag of the Republic.' . . . 'Behind those fortifications,' he went on, 'the
child of Paris has rediscovered, for the defence of republican institutions,
the very genius of street combat.' Paris had given France its government.

The age of tyranny was gone – thank you, Paris. 'Paris surrounded affirms more gloriously yet its immortal slogan which will also dictate that of all France: Long live the Nation! Long live the Republic one and indivisible!' In short, Gambetta conformed faithfully to Danton's holy principle, 'Paris *is* France.'

It would have to be more than a slogan that Paris dictated to France. Paris suffered with 'manly perseverance' rationing, privation and even hunger to give their brothers in the departments time to mount a new offensive: so, 'Citizens of the departments, this situation imposes on you great duties.' The first was that 'you don't let yourself be diverted by any preoccupation other than that of war, the *combat à outrance*'. And the second was that you accept 'as you would the orders of a father the command of republican authority emanating out of necessity and the law'. Gambetta had added his own southern appreciation of the law, an element of the *paterfamilias*, to the rigours of Dantonian war talk.

The legend was more important than the facts. The real possibility that Danton was a plunderer of public monies, a liar, even a traitor to his country (as a later generation of historians would try to prove) was utterly irrelevant to somebody of Gambetta's stature. Gambetta's Danton was Michelet's Danton. 'Danton was first and above all', wrote the historian, 'a male; there was in him elements of a lion, a mastiff and also a great deal of bull. His mask startled; the sublime ugliness of a distressed face lent to his word, brusque and hurled out in bursts, a sort of savage goad.' Gambetta too, corpulent and *bon vivant*, wore a mask, southern and Italian; and there was a sublime ugliness about it, an outward cruelty, that he used to tremendous effect. Behind Danton's 'violent, furious mask', said Michelet, 'one also felt a heart', and it was from that heart that the 'words of violent tenderness for France' surged forth. Gambetta embodied France with a lion's heart.

The parallel was most significant, for it was to colour the political life of the Republic for many decades. The corollary of the Danton legend was a rejection of Robespierre – 'an inquisitorial countenance, destitute, blinking, hiding his dim eyes under his spectacles', Robespierre, that 'foreign sphinx', Robespierre, the fanatic. Behind the nineteenth-century version of the conflict between Danton and Robespierre lay a fundamental opposition between action – male and physical – and ideology – female and spiritual. This was reflected in the way the two men spoke. 'Let no one say that the word counts for little in such moments,' said Michelet of Danton before the Assembly. 'Word and act, they are entirely one . . . Action is here the servant of the word; it follows tamely behind, as on the first day of the world: "*He said and the world was.*"' In Robespierre's case, words only fed on words, the vicious cycle of the fanatic: 'He was born so credulous for all that hatred and fear could counsel him to believe, so fanatic of himself and ready to believe his dreams, that conviction came to him with over-abundance . . . The prodigious respect he had for his own word ended by making him think that all proof was superfluous. His speeches could have been summarised with these words. "Robespierre can well swear to it, for Robespierre has already said it.'"

The continual references to '*la force d'âme*' and the need 'to show to the universe what is a great people who will not perish' are perhaps proof enough that Gambetta, like Michelet's Danton, never lost sight of the humanist side (universal and steeped in the classics) of republicanism. His adaptablility to the circumstances, his opportunism, was a sign of his realism: in the same way his rapid build-up of a new army established him as a man of action. When Gambetta calls on the French people to come out of the twilight, to awaken, to shed their veils, he conjures up images reminiscent of one of the Theban plays, an Antigone, a people buried alive under twenty years of political despotism and now, of necessity, responding to those already dead and exposed on the field of battle, a people condoling a brother's child or one closer in blood. It is a language mindedly 'male and physical'. This war would defend those 'virgin' citadels as yet undefiled by the enemy invader; it would exhaust to the very limit 'our political and social virility'. Danton was not sleeping.

But the Paris of 1792 was never under siege and the invading army was not Moltke's vast military machine. Ernest Renan once said that Gambetta destroyed the legend of '92. This is not true. If anything, it was Moltke's armies which destroyed the legend; their clockwork precision and their finely manufactured weapons were changing all the rules. Well might the defenders have cried, 'We must make a war more terrible!' How easily the word 'sacrifice' tripped off the tongue. What an obvious message of hope the Revolution and Danton provided. But the *guerre à outrance*, of which Gambetta now spoke, was a step into the shadows of a new era of war, a call for total exhaustion to which a nation of millions was entirely committed. The *guerre à outrance* had abolished all limits. The distinction, as old as ancient Greece, between the *polis* and the field of battle was gone; the hell of the field would be carried to the city. The distinction between the sexes would gradually fade; all would be dragooned into the action of war. Gambetta even called on the heavens to assist in the republican cause ('The sky itself will cease to be an element for our adversaries. The autumn rains will come . . .'). No scapegoats, no treacherous dynasty could then take the blame. The burden was on all.

One other Dantonian phrase from Michelet purchased new meaning in 1870. Michelet reported Danton as saying, when averted that his life was in danger: 'Me, one does not touch me, *I am the Ark*' – a religious phrase that suggests unity by contract or covenant. One sees Danton striding forth, carrying the faith of the people.

Gambetta would not have been uncomfortable with the remark. It was not that he was vain or refused to stoop to the daily torments of war. He had to believe in the sanctity of his role because the task he faced was enormous. He was bearing the ark that pledged delivery of a new Jerusalem. 'I shall return with an army,' he had told Favre before taking off for the skies, 'and if I have the glory of delivering Paris, I shall ask nothing more of destiny.' That 'glory' was the *gloire* of Corneille and Louis XIV, the will to touch God, though Gambetta's god was in the people, by the people, through the people: *la patrie*. '*En avant!*' Gambetta ordered his army on the first day of November (a sacred day in the old calendar). 'You fight for the safety and health of *la patrie* . . . holy and national war, sublime mission, for which, without ever looking back, we must sacrifice everything, entirely everything.'

Thirty-five million Frenchmen! How could they be overcome by 'an invasion of five hundred thousand men'?

The best information available to Gambetta on the opinions of these thirty-five million was in his prefects' reports. They indicated local attitudes ranging from fraternal bloodthirst through disinterest to outright hostility. It was in the occupied north-east that Gambetta found his most enthusiastic following for *la guerre à outrance*. Such solidarity was unknown outside the occupied zone. From the West and the South came warnings of civil war. The prefect at Nantes was enormously relieved when he heard of Gambetta's arrival, for that meant no elections. The elections in his view would have brought in the Bonapartists and conservatives; they would have led to violence and a revival of all the hatreds of the first Revolution. A radical left threatened the South. Between 4 and 15 September Lyon was governed by its own Committee of Public Safety under the guidance of that wandering Russian aristocrat and head of the anarchist cause, Mikhaïl Bakunin. 'Bourgeois' guardsmen soon restored order, though the city remained tense. Marseille had been under the control of a revolutionary committee since the announcement of the Empire's first lost battles on 7 August. It was also strongly influenced by Bakunin's anti-authoritarian ideas which were spread throughout the South by a 'Ligue du Midi'. However, Marseille took its lesson from the failed Lyon revolt. The city merely simmered.

But the greatest threat came from those who ploughed and sowed the land. Vast areas of France remained quite indifferent to the war. Why should they abandon their daily labours? It was not because men died that the earth should cease to bear fruit or that others should cease to reap it. Rural life went on. 'The truth is sad,' Gambetta confided in a dispatch to Favre, 'the countryside is inert, the bourgeoisie of the small towns is cowardly, the administration is perfidious and passive or desperately slow.'

The thirty-five million were not united.

X

GAMBETTA'S OWN revolution would be brought about by a complete reorganisation of what remained of the nation's military forces and a purging of the civilian administration. It was a virtual dictatorship.

Gambetta had used his post at the ministry of the interior to get the purge of the civilian administration well under way before even leaving Paris and he used his new position as minister of war to prepare the new army. For twenty years, republicans had argued in favour of a people's army. This was their chance. Gambetta's second proclamation on his arrival at Tours was addressed to the army:

> Soldiers,
>   I have left Paris to be your Minister of War [though this had hardly been the intention of Paris]. Given the situation, I am decided on abandoning the usual paths. I wish to give you young, active, capable leaders who by their intelligence and vigour will renew the prodigies of 1792. For that, I do not hesitate to break with the old administrative tradition.

For assistance in the task of building his revolutionary model army, Gambetta turned not to a general but an engineer, Charles de Freycinet. He was only forty-two. His political record had been disastrous (he had been forced to resign as prefect of Tarn-et-Garonne) but he had somehow found his way into the Committee of Armaments at Tours. There he had prepared a report recommending a number of radical reforms within the ministry of war. Gambetta took an immediate liking to the man, smiling, courteous, calculating, and within days named him chief secretary to the minister of war.[1] From a comfortable office in the centre of Tours Freycinet issued detailed orders for the transformation of the French army.

The professionals were ousted from the delegation. The war of the people brought the amateur to the forefront, who looked in righteous contempt at all that 'military science' had to offer. He was unforgiving. The Emperor's war had been the generals' war and their deeds were not very impressive. Gambetta's take-over of the Tours delegation had been made on behalf of the people. They would decide, Gambetta would decide, the tactics, the strategy, the structure of the democratic army in the face of the German dynastic oppressor.

---

[1]Gambetta formally named him '*délégué de ministre auprès du département de la Guerre et chargé de la direction des services à sa place et dans la limite devant être tracée pour lui par le ministre*'.

The new organisation had immediate impact on the higher ranks of the army. When Gambetta arrived, only one army corps existed on the Loire, the 15th under General de la Motte Rouge. He was replaced in mid-October for failing to hold on to Orléans. The new commander was General d'Aurelle de Paladines, Catholic, but a renowned disciplinarian. Chaplains were appointed in the reconstituted army at Salbris and summary court-martials were set up. A few men were shot *pour encourager les autres*.

Meanwhile, vaster plans were underfoot. Every strategic consideration revolved around Paris. The famous *plan Trochu*, developed after Gambetta's departure, envisaged an offensive northward. Contrary to many accounts, Gambetta was certainly aware of the *plan Trochu*: he had received a full report from Ranc who had taken a balloon out of Paris only a week after his own departure. Gambetta's chief problem was time: how long would it be before Paris was starved into surrender? And how long could Metz be expected to pin down Friedrich Karl's investing force? All information available to Gambetta prior to his departure indicated that supplies in the capital would run out in the middle of December. The capitulation would come before: the delegation estimated 1 December. Metz was an unknown factor. The city had been cut off long before the republicans took office. So they based their estimates on what they knew about Paris; they gave Metz six weeks.

Gambetta therefore had little more than a month to launch a successful operation on Paris. A direct march from the Loire to Paris seemed the only option available – anything else would have left too much responsibility in the hands of the generals, the professionals. Gambetta would dictate his own victory.

Two laws would provide the recruits for the nation in arms. The decree of 14 September required all male citizens aged between twenty-one and sixty to join the National Guard. Gambetta started the process with a circular instructing his prefects to enroll volunteers, bachelors and widowers without children. This measure, he informed Favre, would create 'a reservoir of almost two million men.' On 14 October, under Freycinet's initiative, the delegation decreed the creation of an auxiliary army which would consist of all those forces not already in the regular army. Freycinet had been studying the American Civil War; this law was drawn directly on Lincoln's auxiliaries and regional training camps. But unlike Lincoln, Gambetta and Freycinet had only a matter of weeks at their disposal and they had less geographical space in which to manœuvre. They had too few officers, and those they did have they did not trust. They had too few arms. French agents went hunting throughout the world. France became a dumping ground for guns and rifles, many of them rusted and beyond repair, most of them without cartridges, none of them conforming to any standard.

That was only the beginning. From about the middle of October troubling rumours about Bazaine's real intentions had been circulating in high places: he was negotiating with the enemy, he was planning to set himself up as regent and await the Emperor's return, he would not hold out for a republican victory. On the night of 21–22 October, Thiers arrived in Tours, exhausted after a tour of all the major capitals of Europe. The last leg of his journey had taken him from Italy through the Col de Mont-Cenis in a blinding early winter snow storm – an augury that nature would not, as Gambetta had supposed, always look kindly on the Republic. On the 25th Thiers announced to the delegation in council that, on evidence from varied sources, the fall of Metz was imminent. Gambetta would not believe it. But three days later confirmation from London arrived, Metz had fallen.

Throughout October deaths from dysentery, diarrhoea, typhus and smallpox had been increasing within the citadel at alarming rates. Townsfolk accused the military of consuming civilian rations. The military accused the civilians of hoarding. Troops accused officers. Officers accused troops. The horsemeat was filthy. There was no salt, no sugar, no coffee. On 20 October civilian bread rations were reduced to three hundred grams per day. The army was limited to a diet of tepid horsemeat soup. Rain pelted down on their camps, turning them into lakes. The capitulation came on 29 October.

Thus, with the exception of Vinoy's 13th Corps in Paris and a few escapees from Sedan, the whole of Napoleon's original army (or what remained of it) was now in German hands; and Friedrich Karl's Second Army was free to march on the Loire.

Gambetta was unforgiving. His proclamation the next day to the French people was an unqualified damnation, '*Le maréchal Bazaine a trahi!*'

XI

GOD IT was hard, that winter. If September had brought to Paris days like July, October trailed in its wake the sorry promise of a long and unhappy cold season. Mournful grey days edged in silver twilights, chilly starless nights, rain, fog, drizzle complemented cruelly the sense of dejection among the two million persons shut up in a fort. Their faces betrayed the experience, victims caught in another man's phoney war: the torpor, the isolation, the anger. There was a yearning to do *something*.

November was like January. December was worse. For twelve days the thermometer barely rose above freezing. There was a few days' respite before Christmas, only to be followed by a period of piercing cold that lasted a month. Temperatures plunged to lows of $-12°$ C and on only three occasions rose above zero.

Milk, eggs and butter – staple for the poor – disappeared from the markets within the first fortnight of the siege. Vegetables – no less essential – dwindled to virtually nothing by the end of November; after that, you might buy (at a price) half a carrot, a bit of beet or a leaf of cabbage. Meat rationing began on 8 October to calm the crowds that had been gathering around places such as Duval's, the huge butcher's shop in the rue Tronchet. It was in fact the first time in history that the poor were forced to eat meat and, though the quantity was small and the quality bad, this would bring a change in custom that would outlast the siege. However, bread remained the fundamental foodstuff and it was not rationed until 19 January, the eighteenth week of the siege. But the bread you bought in December was a hardened black mixture of grains to which had been added dried peas, poorly ground rice, wine-lees and bran. After panic buying on 11 December the government and wealthier citizens lived in constant fear of 'bread riots' or 'starvation riots' as Felix Whitehurst called them, something nobody had spoken of since the 1840's.

The worst privation was the shortage of fuel. Those who remembered the siege of Paris recalled, above all else, the image of long lines of shivering men and women waiting their turn to be handed two or three little pieces of green wood about as incombustible as the ice beneath their feet. The trees of the Parc Monceau were rapidly consumed; the wood frames of houses under construction were stolen; gates, fences, even the doors of private homes were hacked to pieces.

And yet, surprisingly, crimes against property were the lowest ever recorded.

The death rates were among the highest. Doctor Thomas Evans of the American ambulance made a statistical study that compared the weekly rates of mortality with rates averaged over the preceding five years. Within the first week of the siege the rates had climbed to one and a half times the normal level. By the end of October they were two and a half times. By November they were three. By the end of December they were four. And the worst was yet to come.

Death carried off *four per cent* of the total population of Paris during the three and a half months of the siege. Doctor Vacher, director-general of ambulances, was appalled at the toll. 'In the poor quarters,' he wrote in early January, 'the rate of mortality is such that the doctors of the *état civil* can hardly cope with their daily task of certifying deaths. Let no one accuse us of promoting distress: the incessant flow of hearses in the streets says more and speaks louder than we could do.' Smallpox had been ravaging the city since 1869. But by August the epidemic had died down, only to break out with a new fury with the arrival of over one hundred thousand provincial guardsmen and nearly a quarter of a million refugees from the surrounding suburbs. The worst rates were in the 10th, 11th and 18th arrondissements. By November smallpox had been overtaken by typhus, pneumonia and bronchitis.

The main burden of the relief effort fell, like the arming of the guard, on the arrondissement mayors. The central government seemed strangely absent. As Evans again remarked, 'the Revolution of 4 September put an end not only to the Imperial Government but to all systematic efforts to provision the city. If Paris was able to feed its population for five months or more, official provision is entitled to very little credit for the fact.'

Louise Michel continued to provide assistance to her mayor at the place des Abbesses. Clemenceau's knowledge of medicine was put to a test, both as administrator and supervisor; and one of Louise Michel's principal undertakings was tending to the sick. They closely collaborated in the organisation of food centres and the increasingly important task of distributing fuel. The 'ambulances' of the 18th arrondissement were the result of their combined effort. Their common position on religion and education served as a moral base in the launching of an emergency free school system for refugee children. It was the refugees (mostly suburban cultivators) that suffered worst during the siege, as Doctor Vacher was to discover: 'I do not believe it would be an exaggeration to say', he noted, 'that four fifths of the deaths arising from the prevalent epidemics are carried by the exotic part of the Parisian agglomeration.' Montmartre in the autumn and winter of 1870 had a large 'exotic' element in its population. Louise Michel lodged a half dozen refugee children in her own home.

Arago, who remained mayor of Paris until early November, tried to bring some semblance of city-wide order by holding regular meetings with the arrondissement mayors. These took place in the lavish surroundings of the council hall of the Hôtel de Ville. It was a dialogue of the deaf. The arrondissement mayors demanded 'municipal elections'. The Paris government at first said 'yes', and then withdrew. In any event, what the government and what Arago understood as 'municipal elections' had nothing in common with what the mayors of northern and eastern Paris, including Clemenceau, had in mind. The government thought it only right, indeed genuinely republican, to let the people confirm their newly nominated mayors – 'but let us win the war first.' The mayors, burdened with the daily task of recruiting, of feeding, of answering every frustrated cry for victory and relief, thought it only just that the 'municipal elections' would be not merely a vote for the local mayor but also for a central municipal council to coordinate their actions. And even in October they were calling that council a 'Commune', the people's council, a governmental body responsive to local distress. Arago and the National Defence had no intention of setting up such a municipal council: this would have created two competing governments in Paris. But they would go on talking about 'municipal elections', forever adjourning the dark day when they would actually be held and the issue of what was meant decided.

One sees Clemenceau on his way back to his mairie after one of these meetings – the journey between two worlds. It would be mid-afternoon as he climbs rue Montmartre and les Martyrs: up the final slope, alleys spawning washerwomen and half-dressed children on each side of him (where are the men?), pockets of poverty, of ugliness, of smells. There would be a good five hours of work awaiting him at the mairie, which he would have to complete in three, for this evening there is an urgent meeting of citizens at the Club de la Reine-Blanche. The major item on the agenda tonight is, as it is most evenings, rationing and requisitions. Clemenceau's constituents are against both.

They don't mince words at la Reine-Blanche. One brave orator the other evening told the audience to go out and lay their hands on 'the vegetables that the peasants are harvesting in the suburbs'. You don't need to ration. There's plenty around. Everybody knows what a hoard of foodstuffs *le citoyen* Leost-Lacombe on the rue des Dames is holding – to line his pockets in silver and gold while the honest people sitting here starve. We must immediately institute *visites domiciliaires*, house searches, not only of the wholesale and retail merchants, but of everybody. *Vider les cachettes*, empty the hidden storing places, *vider toutes les cachettes*; all food, oil, firewood, charcoal and the rest have to be collected in a common stock and distributed in equal portions to 'all defenders of *la patrie* and to their families.'

In the eyes of the national government, Clemenceau and the other arrondissement mayors were to act as liaisons between the government and the people of Paris. This was the old hierarchical, administrative view handed down by kings to emperors and on to their republican successors. And it worked very well – in the 16th arrondissement, or in the 7th or the 8th. Gambetta was applying the same principle in the provinces. But try it in the 18th! A liaison between Arago and the clubs? It was impossible. The distance was too great. Clemenceau was faced with an impossible task and he must have known it.

When he heard those speeches from the 'tribune' of la Reine-Blanche he must have been immensely moved, for the language of the Revolution was the language of his father. True, he was a public man now, he was a man of movement and of action, a man gay and busy, not beaten down, not sentimental: a political animal. But it was only in this public frame of mind, this show of altruism, that he could realise the dream of his father's dinner-table talk. For the first time in his life he could bring action to his words. No longer just a journalist, no more the speculator of human right and justice, not a teacher, not a country doctor, he now portrayed himself as a statesman with a specific democratic goal.

The pleasure he took in democratic action extended to everything he touched. It put the egoism of his private life in a secret cubicle, tucked away in a remote Vendée château, hidden, dominated. The pleasure was long-abiding. As late as December he was sending by balloon the same elated message to his wife: 'I am well in every way,' he wrote in English, 'my most ardent wish is that little wife Mary and little baby Maddie may be as well and buoyant as I am. Yes dear, buoyant I am. Buoyant we all are.' No reason for feeling otherwise. 'We have made cannons, guns, cartridges, powder, etc.. etc. We have armed and equipped the *Garde Nationale*, organised a new army.' That would surely work. 'I *guess* the Prussians will soon find they have a *hard nut to crack*, as a yankee would say. The spirit of the people has never been so good as it is now.'

Always the people. As he had argued in America, it was the people, not the laws of government, which needed defending. Faced with the enormous gap that lay between the government and the people, Clemenceau knew he would soon have to make a choice. As man of action, son of the Revolution, he resorted to his instincts. When the day of reckoning arrived he would stand by his constituents, the people.

XII

THE CRISIS broke on the last day of October.

Early that morning Arago had summoned all the mayors to the Hôtel de Ville for an emergency meeting. The news was bad. Metz had fallen. Le Bourget had been retaken by the enemy. Thiers was negotiating an armistice. Treachery! cried the revolutionaries. Posters had been plastered all over Montmartre. 'The municipality of the 18th arrondissement protests with indignation against an armistice that the government cannot accept without treason.'

The mayors made the predictable demand for immediate 'municipal elections' and Arago, still misunderstanding their intent, accepted it. As the mayors left to prepare their constituencies for elections the next day, Arago went into the next room where the government was in session to formalise the agreement. There was a large crowd outside, led by the revolutionary Belleville battalion, shouting for 'the Commune'. This was clearly not what the government wanted. But while they were discussing what to do a few shots were heard and the crowd burst into the building.

For the next twelve hours Paris had no government or, at least, no single government. Lissagaray, revolutionary historian, said that every room in the building had its own government. The Salon Jaune, where the National Defence had sat in deliberation, was taken over by Gustave Flourens, dressed in a magnificent Grecian uniform. Striding back and forth on the conference table, he addressed the Belleville battalion until the table collapsed beneath him. Victor Hugo was also somewhere in the building. So were Pyat, Delescluze and, of course, Blanqui. 'Government' lists were, like on 4 September, thrown from the windows and the applause of the crowd duly measured. Blanqui didn't want Flourens on his list, Delescluze didn't want Blanqui. Chaos.

But one member of the National Defence, the minister of finance, Ernest Picard, managed an escape and from his offices at the Louvre began organising the rescue of his colleagues. He had the assistance of General Ducrot and his 'expeditionary force' of Bretons and loyal guardsmen of the western arrondissements. By nightfall it was raining hard and most of the crowd had dispersed. There was no violence. The Hôtel de Ville was surrounded. In the early hours of the morning the rebels reached an agreement with the government that there would be immediate 'municipal elections'. The government promised no arrests. Everyone went to bed.

At daybreak the government ordered the posters, put up by the mayors the previous afternoon announcing the elections that day, to be torn down. This was followed with a declaration that there would be, instead, a plebiscite on 3 November and an election of the mayors, and only the mayors, on the 5th.

Several of the mayors returned to the Hôtel de Ville and angrily informed Arago that they would hold their elections instantly, whatever the government said. They were told they would be arrested. What happened? There were several resignations. Clemenceau's was apparently among them. In a letter dated the same day, 1 November, and signed by him with his assistants, he writes to his former friend:

> Citizen Mayor of Paris,
>   I have the honour of reminding you that we tendered our resignation this morning and that we are awaiting our successor. In view of the government's latest acts we are more than ever insistent on disengaging our responsibility and we earnestly repeat our demand for an *immediate* replacement.

Did he send it? Was he bluffing? If so, whom? Did he expect the government to change its mind once more? The letter was never made public, so it could hardly have been an appeal to his nervous constituents. But it does suggest, when considered alongside his poster of the preceding day, that he was losing patience with the National Defence.

None the less, the elections took place as the government had planned. The plebiscite of 3 November showed that the revolutionaries were clearly out of line with public opinion. Only the 20th arrondissement showed a majority of 'No's'. Of the nearly 24,000 who voted in Montmartre, 17,000, or three voters out of four, opted for the 'Yes'. When a speaker at the Reine-Blanche the following evening declared that 'the plebiscite leads to armistice, the armistice leads to peace and the peace to an Orleanist restoration', he was greeted by loud cries of dissent.

'Oh, yes!' he continued stubbornly, 'before three months are up we will be governed by Louis-Philippe II. That's what those who voted "Yes" yesterday don't understand. They've been dazed and bewildered.'

There was more jeering. Another man walked up to the tribune and said, 'I am one of the three hundred thousand idiots whom the speaker was denouncing. I voted "Yes" and I readily declare that in giving this proof of confidence in the government I had no belief and had no desire of voting for any kind of restoration.' He was cheered.

Clemenceau, standing to one side, remained quiet. He was eyeing Delescluze and Millière, who usually dominated the proceedings. They too were strangely quiet.

Several unfamiliar figures denounced the people's verdict, the plebiscite – old manoeuvre of the Empire, they said. A Pole, in spectacles and looking very nervous, tried to break the tension. 'Yes,' he said with a touch of bitterness in his voice, 'the plebiscite has obtained the great majority, perhaps it has obtained it even here – and I know very well why. It's because behind the plebiscite one had an inkling there was an armistice and peace, and behind the armistice and peace there was gruyère cheese and pats of butter.' The hall burst into laughter. There was pandemonium when another orator, without the flicker of a smile, proposed, 'If you have the Commune you'll be able to act as revolutionaries: you'll be able to send out special commissioners to stir up "the mud" in the departments.' These humourless extremists were not popular.

But there were other things to look at. Red posters (the *affiches rouges* were normally identified with the revolutionaries and the International) were being plastered up on the walls of the hall, announcing that France would be 'dishonoured' if the 18th arrondissment did not re-elect Clemenceau with Jaclard, Dereure and Lafont as his assistants.

Then, in the midst of the whole furore, a messenger appeared, like in a Greek play, and announced that the government had broken its word: it was rounding up the ringleaders of 31 October: Jaclard and Lefrançais were among those arrested. The hall again fell into a tense silence.

Clemenceau asked to speak.

This was the first major speech in his political career. Unfortunately his exact words have not been recorded. Clearly, the vast majority had little sympathy for Jacobins and Blanquists. The meeting had been an embarrassment for the revolutionaries. And Clemenceau himself must have felt that he had overstepped the mark with his poster of 31 October.

At any rate, in that speech he showed the talent of a Gambetta, the guile of an opportunist. According to G. de Molinari, editor of the *Journal des Débats* and who was present that evening, Clemenceau began by posing his candidature with the rather original opening comment that he was not soliciting votes from the electors. It might not be dishonouring France if they did not vote for him, but he asked them to look at his record. He had done his best in rationing meat, and while the best might not be worth much he was of the opinion that the problem of rationing would one day be resolved – when there was no more meat. He said he did not approve of the government but (and it was a 'but' that would win him voters at the cost of ruffling some influential colleagues) he had no pretension of trying to teach General Trochu a lesson in military science and he would recognise that the government at the Hôtel de Ville responded better than anyone else to the current state of opinion. There were a few rumblings among the 'irreconcilables', but Clemenceau had scored an enormous success.

At the elections the next day, he defeated the government candidate by more than nine thousand votes. In only three other arrondissements was the government defeated, the 19th (by Delescluze), the 20th (by Ranvier) and the 11th (by Mottu).

The *journée* of 31 October had brought a shake-up in the government. Adam, the prefect of police, had resigned, disgusted over the arrests. He was replaced by Ernest Cresson, who immediately had twenty-two men thrown into Mazas, including Blanqui, Millière, Vallès and Eudes. Within a month Pyat and Flourens were also arrested and sixteen battalion commanders were cashiered. In a further attempt to centralise 'republican authority' the offices of mayor and prefect of the Seine were combined under one man, Jules Ferry. Rochefort resigned. General Clément Thomas took over command of the National Guard in the place of Tamisier. And the government decided that its seat at the Hôtel de Ville was not healthy for body and mind, so it henceforth met in Trochu's offices at the Louvre.

The government's refusal to bend to the demand from the clubs and the radical mayors for an elected 'Commune', or municipal council, was based on a fear that this would create a rival government in Paris. National sovereignty was the central issue. The events of 31 October represented a clash between two different understandings of what national sovereignty actually meant.

On the one side were the former republican deputies in the government who saw themselves standing on the edge of anarchy. From mid-October onwards they regarded the 'national defence' as a double task to be directed simultaneously against the Prussians and against the internal threat of civil disorder. 'They hated the foreigner most, but were more fearful of the Bellevillois,' said Francisque Sarcey, theatre critic of *Le Temps*. The paradox of it was that the government was a creation not of an organised electorate but of a crowd on 4 September.

The extreme Left, who were now beginning to call themselves 'Revolutionary' or 'Republican Socialists', faced no such problem. National sovereignty, for them, was the direct and spontaneous expression of the people. Their difficulty was in defining not the institutions of a just republic, but the 'people'. In time the 'socialist' definition – developed over decades of debate, obscure writing and war in the street – would prevail over all the others: they would describe the 'people' as 'workers'. 'The revolutionary Commune', you read in *Le Combat* towards the end of the siege, 'should consist of workers; of true workers, of workers who are not property owners, but workers labouring with their hands in order to attend to their needs: of workers, finally, supporting the full weight of life's difficulties and understanding all of the aspiration of our republican slogan, all of the importance of association and solidarity.' It was very different from the older romantic vision of the 'people', that theatrical personification of every human component of the sovereign nation: 'France is a people.'

Those working hands, of which the Republican Socialists spoke, would bear not only the products of their labour but also, in the revolutionaries' view, the weapons to defend them. The right of citizens to bear arms was the most controversial of all sovereign rights. The United States had written it into the sacred text of its Constitution. But in old Europe, where civil war and international war were more easily confused, there was no such simple accord. The tendency had been to deny such a right and confine the violence of justice to a monopoly of the sovereign state. The issue had been fought out at Edgeworth Hill, Naseby and Culloden, at La Rochelle, Cholet and the barricades of Paris. It was still undecided in France under the new Republic of 1870. But for the defenders of institutions, for the Government of National Defence, the right of citizens to bear arms was the right to murder; it was an intolerable affront to freedom.

*

As for Clemenceau, he had still not solved the enigma. When, a few days after the election, he appeared before the prefect of police he expected to be arrested. Several of his more radical acquaintances were already in gaol for bearing arms. He knew the scenario. He had been through it before.

But Cresson was surprisingly obliging. 'They're claiming that you know all about these Orsini bombs and that you're actually mixed up in the business.'

Clemenceau didn't answer. It was hardly his fault that a whole house had been blown up and every building in the neighbourhood threatened with fire. He had warned the barricade committee and even sent in a supervisor. But patriotic enthusiasm had taken over, and at a most unfortunate time too.

'You know,' continued Cresson, with an understanding nod, 'in times like we're going through now bombs of this sort, even if they are designed for the enemy, present a danger for the interests of Paris. I've got to have them. I don't want to order a house search of your place or anything else that could be unpleasant for the mayor of Montmartre. I am counting on you to deliver them.'

'Oh I will,' replied Clemenceau. It was an amazing reprieve and he now had to think quickly of how he might turn it to good account. 'But first I'm going to ask you to understand me. It's true that I had helped a few workers construct these bombs and obviously they were designed to be used against the Prussians. I even agree that in present circumstances they represent something of a threat to domestic peace. I have about six hundred of these bombs left, they're carefully stacked in a cellar and I will turn them over to Dorian, as minister of public works.'

It was a calculated gesture. Dorian, the sickle manufacturer turned arms producer, had become an idol in Montmartre and north-eastern Paris: the *octobristes* had even proposed his name as president of their new revolutionary government.

'Very well,' said Cresson, 'you can deliver them to the ministry of public works. But we will also have to include the ministry of war because they're the only ones equipped to handle these preposterous objects.'

So a few days later an artillery officer turned up at the mairie with an empty horse-drawn wagon, accompanied by a delegate from M. Dorian's ministry. It took several fearful hours to load the wagon with the six hundred bombs and the rest of the afternoon to make their precarious way down through the cobbled streets to Vincennes where they were placed in a pit and destroyed. 'With every step on the way,' the officer later reported, 'I expected a formidable explosion. There was something terrible about these bombs.'

XIII

THERE WAS good news from the provinces. For a moment it looked as if the people's war was working. On 14 November a line crosser carried the news to Paris that the Army of the Loire had defeated a German force and had retaken Orléans. Good citizens exploded with joy.

Seven days earlier, a combined French force of a hundred thousand men had in fact defeated van der Tann's twenty thousand Bavarians cornered in the village of Coulmiers, a few kilometres to the west of Orléans. It had been a standard two-pronged attack with d'Aurelle de Paladines' 15th Corps moving down the Loire from Gien and the newly constituted 16th Corps under Pallières coming up the river from Blois. The victory might have come a lot earlier had Aurelle not delayed his advance for a week; poorly scheduled train connections, chaotic provisioning, bad weather – the same confusions that had cursed the imperial army – were the cause. Freycinet had telegraphed Aurelle to 'make the best we can of the situation'. The delay was to prove the undoing of Gambetta and his army, but no one saw this at the time.

Meanwhile in Paris *le plan Trochu* was proceeding in its muddled way. Trochu himself had no intention of throwing the National Guard against the German professionals, he was sceptical enough of his regulars. There was also the most basic problem of communications. A coordinated national plan was impossible. Trochu would have probably gone on waiting for the Germans to attack, for Paris to starve – for anything rather than send this undisciplined rabble into battle. 'I had no idea of strategy,' as he candidly put it the following year, 'and none of tactics.' But 31 October forced his hand. The date for the *sortie torrentielle* northwestward across the Gennevilliers peninsula and down the Seine was set for 15 November. By this time he would have a hundred thousand regulars available, organised into three army corps under the command of General Ducrot. The National Guard would be kept behind walls, acting as the city's garrison force.

Coulmiers brought a last-minute change in plan. The government decided to suspend the original operation, despite a second message from Gambetta envisioning a 'vigorous break-out towards Normandy' that might act as a 'counter-weight to the forces which Prince Friedrich Karl is bringing from Metz'. They were responding to extremist influences in the press which, intoxicated by the good news from Tours, was chanting *'Ils viennent à nous; allons à eux!'* To have ignored their demand would have been to invite another insurrection, more popular and bloodier than 31 October.

So four hundred heavy guns, fifty-four pontoon bridges, and eighty thousand men, along with their field artillery, transport and supplies were transferred from north-western Paris to the south-eastern side. Politics, *la folie du siège*, was taking precedence over military considerations. The people were determining the direction of the people's war.

Ducrot's force was now facing one of the strongest points of the German line of investment. Worse still, heavy gunfire from the forts warned the Germans of the coming offensive. Moltke brought up reinforcements to the Left Bank of the Seine. Friedrich Karl's army took up its new positions between Paris and Orléans, ready to strike in either direction. As if to give the Germans a further sign that something was about to happen, the city gates were closed on 26 November. On the morning of the 28th posters went up all over Paris announcing to citizens and spies alike that the attack was to take place the next day. Then the level of the Seine and the Marne rose a few feet, making the bridging operation impossible. The attack was postponed for a day.

News of the planned break-out was to be communicated to Gambetta by balloon.

The flight of the *Ville d'Orléans* was the most fantastic of all the seventy-two balloon flights that left Paris under siege; indeed, it was one of the most extraordinary flights in history. Freak winds blew the two-man crew and their crucial message not to Tours but to a snow covered wood in the middle of Norway. In just under fifteen hours their balloon had covered over 1,200 kilometres.

In Christiana (as Oslo was then known) the two Frenchmen were treated to a princely reception. But their message for Gambetta arrived too late.

The *sortie torrentielle* was an unmitigated disaster. Casualties reached 1914 proportions, men in scarlet and blue charging with rifles against cannon of steel. The Germans allowed a twenty-four-hour ceasefire to clear the fields of the dead.

There was chaos among the ambulances that had moved up to the Fort de Nogent and Joinville. Felix Whitehurst, who was present, complained bitterly of the 'competition system' – 'there are ten times too many ambulances and two hundred times too many to manage them . . . On the battlefield there is a rush, not to succour the suffering, but to fill ambulances.'

At that very moment the Army of the Loire suffered two devastating blows which, by the normal standards of nineteeth-century warfare, should have brought the Government of National Defence to its knees. But a Republic does not yield. The standards of warfare, the code of diplomacy – the exchange, the threat, the attack, the peace – had been set by men who were not democrats. The people's war, the democratic war would go on.

Moltke addressed a letter to Trochu in the language of an aristocratic warrior:

> It might be useful to inform Your Excellency that the Army of the Loire was defeated yesterday near Orléans and that this town is re-occupied by German troops.
>
> If, however, Your Excellency deems it fitting to prove this to himself through one of his officers, I will not fail to furnish him with a safe conduct to leave and return.

Trochu replied with a second *sortie*.

The attack was launched northward onto Le Bourget on 21 December. As in the previous *sortie*, the Prussians were given fair notice by a closing of the city gates, official proclamations, heavy gunfire from the northern forts and detailed reports in the Paris press. Reinforcements were sent in. The climate again turned its back on the Republic. For the previous week temperatures had been relatively mild. But in the evening before the attack another Arctic air mass moved into the region. And for the first time the National Guard were to join the regulars on the field of battle.

They never saw their enemy. One observer wrote: 'The French fire was quite furious, half a dozen guns flashing out at once; but it seemed wild. The Germans' was regular as the beats of a pendulum of a clock.' With the failure of the frontal attack, Trochu ordered, in a style somewhat reminiscent of seventeenth-century siege warfare, that saps and parallels be dug – in ground that had turned as hard as concrete. The army camped that night at its positions in the field, hardly even able to erect tents. The following morning they staggered back into Paris. They had suffered nearly three thousand casualties, of which almost a third were due to frostbite.

XIV

WITH THE growing rigour of winter the rational order of power scattered like a thousand leaves in the wind. The centre disappeared, shedding the uncounted little sovereign entities that the autocracy of Empire had so cunningly held in place. Every trunk, every branch, every solid attachment which had given politics its shape experienced the same loss. It was not just the Government of National Defence that suffered, nor even Gambetta's delegation out in Tours. It affected every sprig of power in Paris, and indeed the nation. The Central Committee of the Twenty Arrondissements, which had played an important part in the campaign for municipal elections at the beginning of the siege, had disappeared from the press. What little power the International had originally exerted seemed now to have gone. You read instead of clubs and local committees whose number rapidly multiplied after November. There was no consensus. Internationalists competed with Blanquists and Proudhonists. Ledru-Rollin led an important contingent of *quarante-huitards* who were represented in most of the eastern arrondissements, but they were violently hated by those who called themselves 'socialist'. There was open argument in the clubs. There was division in the National Guard – the 'popular' guard opposed the 'bourgeois' guard. The press was a cacophony of polemic, denunciation and rebellion. There was no single cause, no single principle that a political man could follow. Each day presented a different challenge. Each social and political group had its own peculiar demands.

The meetings of the arrondissement mayors had evolved like the rest. Since the elections of early November they had taken place every Monday afternoon in the Hôtel de Ville's great assembly hall overlooking the square. Arago was gone. Ferry presided over the weekly theatre of war like a general who had forgotten what side he was on. All the elements were present, from Delescluze of the 19th arrondissement to Vacherot of the 5th. Several members of the government would come in for a battering. In fact, there was probably no better place to observe the pandemonium of siege politics than at this assembly of mayors; about the only thing you could count on was the time they met.

And then that changed. On the first Monday following the assault on Le Bourget the meeting was at the last minute cancelled. The mayors were told that Jules Ferry would receive them at the ministry of the interior, place Beauvau (a safe spot next to the Elysée in the 8th arrondissement), on Wednesday, 28 December.

When at the appointed hour the mayors turned up, several accompanied by their deputies, Ferry with some dismay in his voice reminded the assembly that only the mayors had been convoked. 'It is vital,' replied the mayor of the 18th arrondissement, 'that *everyone* be present at the debate before us.'

For the next ten critical days Clemenceau's actions would place him squarely on the side of the revolutionary Left; Molinari described him at the time as 'democrat and socialist'. Of course by now there was more than one Left; there would be plenty of room for the retrospective argument that his alignment with 'purist' elements – subsequently defined – was superficial, not bound. Clemenceau's Left was Jacobin. The time and the situation brought him into collaboration with Charles Delescluze. Since his election as mayor of the 19th arrondissement in November, Delescluze had become the hero of Belleville and Montmartre. His paper, *Le Réveil*, was the harshest but also by far the most informed of the radical press. He was still occasionally seen at the Club de la Reine-Blanche, fraternising with *le doux* Millière who had been elected commander of 208th Battalion of the National Guard. That Clemenceau should find himself working on Delescluze's side was hardly surprising; he had once been a father figure for the young politician and he was still a man, calm in private and always pained by violence, who deserved respect. In fact, the distinction between the public and private Delescluze was something Clemenceau was beginning to understand.

Delescluze opened the session with a scathing indictment of Trochu and his colleagues. Jules Favre, as acting minister of the interior, was there, looking very grim, without as much as shaking a lock of that unkempt mane of his, a good deal longer and greyer now after three months of siege. Vacherot responded to Delescluze by refuting every point in his speech. And then up got Clemenceau to denounce as viciously as had Delescluze the record of 'our government of national defection'. Then Lafont. Then the mayor of the 2nd arrondissement, Tirard, rose and for the first time sided with the mayors of northern and eastern Paris. He demanded more involvement in government decisions. 'We take all the responsibility,' he said, 'and yet we are allowed no initiative. It is that right of initiative which, in the name of all my colleagues, I demand of you.'

Favre was actually very much on form that evening, delivering a masterful review of the maze of troubles he and his colleagues had been dragged through. 'What did we find on 4 September? No army, no supplies, no cannon, no rifles. Nothing prepared for the defence.' As for Trochu, 'it is true that he has not always been exempt from blame, that he has often shown himself hesitant . . . But I am confident of the final result: that he wants triumph and he wants to maintain the Republic; that he will maintain it and that he will make it triumph.'

This did little to calm the gentlemen of the 18th and 19th arrondissements. Simon Dereure said there was no more firewood in Montmartre. Delescluze repudiated every point in Favre's speech and so Vacherot repudiated Delescluze. But by then the parliamentary order had completely broken down in a 'tempest of interpellations' as the official report put it. The meeting was adjourned with Favre promising to convoke them for Saturday, or Sunday at the latest.

They met on Monday at the Hôtel de Ville. There was debate over fuel and bread. But the principal item discussed that day was rents that were falling due on 8 and 15 January. The mayors demanded, on behalf of their constituents, an extension of a moratorium already granted by a law of 15 August. The government agreed within the week to extend the moratorium 'to the end of the war'.

The question of the government's military policy did not come up again until a meeting two days later, on Wednesday, 4 January. It was another ferocious encounter, a battle of personalities as much as of principles.

Delescluze presented a motion for the resignation and court martial of generals and the creation of a 'supreme council of defence'. Then he withdrew it. Then Clemenceau made the same motion, forcing a vote and its rejection. Three of the more moderate mayors, Carnot, Vautrain and Vacherot, who had been constantly at odds with the likes of Delescluze and Clemenceau, themselves proposed the institution of a 'war council' with a fifty per cent civilian representation. Amazingly the motion passed.

Thus, from the Left to the Right of the political spectrum, as it appeared in the assembly of mayors, there was a common dismissal of the army 'professionals'. Military failure, far from discrediting the popular republican faith in citizens' armies, had actually strengthened it. According to Favre's report of the meeting, there was also a general demand among the mayors for another 'prompt *sortie*'.

Trochu, in the council of ministers the following day, of course refused to cede to the mayors' 'pretensions' and warned that their frequent meetings could lead to the establishment of the increasingly dreaded 'Commune'. Despite some disagreement, the government ended by supporting Trochu. Trochu, in return, agreed to meet with the mayors the next day.

The mayors' meeting of 6 January was an anticlimax. The unity of the mayors had already evaporated. All they asked for was that there be 'appended' to the government 'a council of war in which the civilian element would be represented.' The loud protesters of the previous meetings abstained. Delescluze and his two deputies of the 19th arrondissement promptly resigned their posts, while Trochu reported to the council of ministers that he was 'very satisfied with the meeting'.

The same day an *affiche rouge* was plastered on walls throughout Paris. It attacked the incompetence of the government with Gambetta's argument: 'We are five hundred thousand combatants and two hundred thousand Prussians hold us in their grasp!' It questioned the authenticity of the government's republicanism: 'They have refused the *levée en masse*. They have left the Bonapartists alone and have put republicans in prison.' It accused the government of all the popular suffering: 'Where there could have been abundance they have created poverty; people are dying of cold and almost of hunger: women suffer, children languish and die.' It pointed to what would happen if nothing were done: 'The continuation of this regime means capitulation.' And it concluded with what had to be done:

GENERAL REQUISITION –
FREE RATIONING –
ATTAQUE EN MASSE

The policies, the strategies, the administration of 4 September, carried
over from the Empire, are judged.

MAKE ROOM FOR THE PEOPLE!
MAKE ROOM FOR THE COMMUNE!

The *affiche rouge* was in fact a desperate attempt by the Central Committee
of the Twenty Arrondissements to reassert itself. The clubs in the 18th
arrondissement, as in other parts of northern and eastern Paris, had
been calling for an elected Commune since November. Trochu had
been perfectly right in pointing out the possibility that the mayors'
assembly might turn into a Commune: if Delescluze had successfully
imposed on the government 'the direct and permanent intervention of
the municipalities in all that concerns the defence of the capital' as he
put it in his motion of 4 January, he would have effectively created a
Commune. His failure and subsequent resignation opened a rift between
the revolutionaries and those still willing to parley with the government.
From the revolutionaries' point of view the mayors' meetings had ceased
to be useful: the Commune would have to draw its constituent elements
from another source.

This is what led to a reanimation of the virtually defunct Central
Committee of the Twenty Arrondissements. It met at no. 6 place de
la Corderie (the same locale as the International), on 5 January 1871,
which suggests that the decision had already been made to work towards
a Commune outside the framework of the mayors' meetings (there had
been declarations of its 'establishment' in the clubs back in December).
Four men, Vaillant, Leverdays, Tridon and Vallès, were designated to
draft the *affiche rouge*. Vallès has described how they spent the night of 5–6
January closeted in a tiny lodging on rue Saint-Jacques, with the sound
of Prussian cannon booming on the southern perimeter of the city: 'We
had to think of the Patrie at the same time as the Revolution . . . These
four men of letters tore at their hair with each line that they trailed out
on white sheets of paper, in constant fear of turning out either platitudes
or a ranting harangue. We felt a certain disgrace for ourselves and each
sound of the pendulum ticked painfully in our heads.'

Clemenceau had been, up to 6 January, the leading figure, with Delescluze,
in the extremists' fight within the mayors' meetings for the civilian war
council and municipal representation. It is possible that he was acting

under pressure from his constituents. Since mid-December, the clubs had fallen back to the old revolutionary practice of public denunciation: 'denunciation', said the journalist Guy Molinari, 'is a vice under the monarchy but it is a virtue under the Republic and all citizens should practise it as a social and civic duty.' Citizen Clemenceau was the first man to be denounced in the eighteenth arrondissement. He was accused at the club de la Reine-Blanche of 'realising an illegal profit of 5000 francs a day from the sale of meat and other commodities from the butchers.' A deputation of citizens was sent round to the mairie. At the following club session, on 20 December, the deputation reported that they were satisfied with Clemenceau's explanation – the municipality had in fact realised a small profit, only seven hundred francs in total, which was being used 'to lighten the sufferings of the needy'. These denunciations could be terrifying and might have had something to do with Clemenceau's public demonstration, a week later, of his revolutionary ardour.

At any rate, in the meeting of 6 January, before Trochu, he either kept quiet or was absent. His name was not to be found among the 140 signatures which followed the *affiche rouge*, though many of those who signed were very close acquaintances of his: he had known Tridon as a student, Chassin had been one of his father's closest collaborators in the republican circle at Nantes, Ferré worked with Clemenceau and Louise Michel on an almost daily basis . . . the list is long. But then Delescluze did not sign the *affiche rouge* either, so the absence of Clemencau's signature is not, in itself, enormously significant.

However the fact that he did not resign with Delescluze surely is. Clemenceau was not going to commit himself now. The rift between conciliators and revolutionaries that had developed on 6 January would be a difficult one to close. But it was not impossible. And if it were possible, Clemenceau was one of a handful of men equipped to achieve it. He had friends in the government and friends among the revolutionaries. In the last week he had demonstrated to the revolutionaries that he could fight for their cause. But he had also shown the prefect of police, back in November, that he could listen to reason. Justice, reason and authority were the bedrock of Clemenceau's Revolution.

XV

THE PEOPLE demanded an '*attaque en masse*'? The government would let them have an '*attaque en masse*'.

For three weeks German cannon on the heights of L'Hay and of

Châtillon rained shells at a rate of three or four hundred a day into the city of Paris. Bismarck had said this would weaken the population's morale. The effect, as in the case of most twentieth-century bombardments, was of course the opposite. The people became only more determined and international opinion, horrified at the spectacle of civilian casualties, swung round to the French side.

Even the beleaguered government found growing support, though not in the poorer arrondissements. 'If they continue to let us be bombarded by the Prussians,' said one orator at the Reine-Blanche, 'we'll go and bomb them at the Hôtel de Ville.' [Applause and *'Vive la Commune!'*] On the day bread was rationed to three hundred grams and the government began distributing free wine to the poor, another orator came up with a much more original idea:

> They've been bombarding the faubourg Saint-Germain since yesterday. Oh yes, and do you know who is bombing the faubourg Saint-Germain? Everybody says it's the Prussians: it's not true; it's Trochu [*sounds of astonishment, several signs of disbelief*]. It's Trochu, I tell you. And do you know why Trochu is having the faubourg Saint-Germain bombed? It's to spur the property-owners into going to the Hôtel de Ville and demand a capitulation. Then they'll say at the Hôtel de Ville, 'Don't you see, we've got to capitulate, the population itself is demanding it.' If we protest and if we march from our side onto the Hôtel de Ville then they'll attack us, they'll use the Bretons to shoot us. For these fellows have only one idea: capitulate! But then, do you know what's awaiting you if you capitulate? Once the Prussians have arrived, they'll slit the throats of every child under twelve and of every old man and woman over fifty [*motions of horror*]. As for the fit, they'll send them to hammer stone in Germany, while they'll keep for themselves the women they take a fancy to [*agitation among the* citoyennes].

It was late afternoon, 18 January. In the Hall of Mirrors at the château of Versailles a new Empire was proclaimed before an assembly of princes, counts and their retinue. The regimental bands struck up the hymn and a huge military choir chanted a pledge to a united German nation.

In Paris the *attaque en masse* was to begin that night.

The plan was similar to Trochu's abandoned project of October involving a concentration of troops on the Gennevilliers peninsula west of Paris; only now, instead of aiming the attack north-westward, the forces would push southward directly on to the German headquarters at Versailles. Junior staff had drawn up the scheme and it was only on 15 January that it was presented to the council of ministers. They accepted it not because of its chances of success (which everybody in the government regarded as nul) but because this was thought to be the only way Paris could be forced to accept the inevitable capitulation without a major rebellion. 'It will not succeed,' said Trochu in a magnificently ambivalent phrase, 'but Paris must fall standing.' Another member of the government was blunter: 'There must be a big *sortie* of the National Guard because opinion will only be appeased when there are ten thousand guardsmen dead on the ground.'

Through the late afternoon and all of the night ninety thousand troops, of whom almost half were of the Parisian National Guard, headed for their positions before the huge fort of Mont Valérien. The volunteer battalions of Crisenoy, Briancion, Langlois and Rochebrune converged in untidy unsoldierly clusters onto portes d'Asnières and Maillot, accompanied by their children, their wives, their lovers. They marched to the distant booming of the siege cannon. Proud old men limped under the weight of knapsacks bursting with camping equipment and supplies for three days, while beardless youths pushed their way up to the front. There was no order in this citizens' army. Lumbering along with the crowd were the unpainted omnibuses, the battered cabs and shopkeepers' carts which were to serve as provision wagons when the battle was engaged, as 'voluntary ambulances' when the slaughter was done. Many of the women, their heads covered, had rifles slung over their backs: some carried small packages perhaps of food or of foolish souvenirs, while others just grasped at a damp handkerchief or at the coat of their man. At the city gates they parted. It was raining.

The men's trousers and boots were already caked in mud and clinging wet snow. Beyond the city gates were the barricades. Incredibly, nobody had thought of clearing a passage. So the whole chaotic procession of soldiers and wagons had to advance single-file towards the only two bridges that crossed the river to Mont Valérien.

They fell hopelessly behind schedule. The attack was supposed to begin before dawn in the form of a three column assault along the broad ridge that stretched across the neck of the peninsula from Montretout to Malmaison. But with the first light of day only the left column under General Vinoy was in position. After a delay of more than an hour Vinoy moved forward, his men groping through thick fog and muddy meadows until they found themselves opposite a Posen regiment at Montretout.

For once, the surprise was total. Within minutes, the small German force was overcome and Vinoy and his troops advanced as far as the outskirts of Saint-Cloud. Meanwhile, troops assigned to the centre and right columns were thrown into battle as they arrived, soaked, exhausted and confused. It was nearly ten o'clock when Ducrot, commander of the right, arrived to take charge of his troops. One reporter on the scene compared, unfavourably, the general's twelve kilometre train ride into the outskirts of Paris (which had taken him all night) with a journey through the rain forests of Cochin-China. But again, the initial offensives were successful. Under the cover of yet thicker fog, Bellemare's centre column was able to mount the steep slopes of Garches at the northern edge of the La Bergerie plateau and secure a position on the heights which formed one of the critical artillery defences of German headquarters at Versailles. By eleven o'clock he was within sight and sound of the enemy stronghold at the Château de Buzenval. A hail of gunfire began.

The German Reich, on its second day, was facing the real possibility of collapse. The Kaiser and his staff, including Bismarck, had withdrawn to Marly. The Hall of Mirrors was converted into a hospital. It was one of the tensest moments in the war.

Trochu, in general command back at Mont Valérien, sent a dispatch at 10.50 a.m to Paris indicating his total ignorance of what was going on: 'A thick fog completely conceals the phases of the battle. The officers bearing orders have difficulty enough finding their troops. It is most regrettable; it has become difficult for me to centre the action as I have been doing up to now. We fight in the night.'

It was at that moment that the Germans at last managed to bring up their reinforcements, backed by heavy artillery. For more than four hours amidst the pounding of cannon, the crackle of rifle and musket fire, and the constant whirr and rattle of the *mitrailleuse*, the French held on to their positions won that morning. But Ducrot's right column arrived too late to be of any help to Bellemare so vulnerably exposed before Buzenval.

At 3.30 p.m. the German counter-offensive began.

There are conflicting reports on the performance of the National Guard up to that point. Had there been a breakthrough, no doubt the myth of 'the people in arms' would have survived the war. But as they fell back in late afternoon whatever discipline existed evaporated.

The counter-offensive was concentrated at a point between the French left and centre columns. It was a battle fought metre by metre, soldiers taking cover behind the crenellated walls of the parc de Saint-Cloud, or from the houses that stood along its northern perimeter. The crest of Montretout fell to the Germans, only to be retaken again within the hour.

Among the French troops fighting there that afternoon was Amilcare Cipriani of the 19th Regiment of the National Guard under the command of Colonel Rochebrune. Cipriani came from Italy, had joined Garibaldi's army at the age of fifteen and was on his way to becoming a great romantic revolutionary of the most classical kind. But his account of the battle of Buzenval, if spiced with an insurgent's imagination, at least gave an idea of the bitterness that developed within the ranks of citizen-soldiers at that time. 'Rochebrune,' he explained.

> quickly advanced into the thick of the battle. A battalion commanded by de Boulen stayed behind at the farm of La Fouilleuse. Two companies took up positions in the lodge of de Chayne. The rest of the regiment boldly made for the front line. We were fighting for two hours. Then Rochebrune turned to me and said, 'Go and get the battalion that is back at la Fouilleuse.' When I got there I communicated this order to Major de Boulen. 'In order to march,' he replied, 'I have to have an order from the commanding major.' 'What do you mean?' I said, 'your colonel demands it, the battle requires it and you refuse it.' 'I can't march,' he said. So I had to carry this cowardly response back to Rochebrune who, on hearing it, bit his hands with rage and cried, 'Treason everywhere!' Then, climbing the wall which protected our flank, he ordered his men to follow. But at that very moment, he fell mortally wounded.

Rochebrune's death was to become an inspiration, a cause, for the extreme Left in the tumult of the days to come. 'I have taken part in several battles,' continued Cipriani, 'but I have never seen soldiers in such distress as the brave National Guard on that day of 19 January. They were shot at in front by the Prussians, fired at from behind by Mont Valérien which flung its shells upon us, believing that it was aiming at the enemy army. Closeted up there was that notorious governor of Paris who would never surrender. On our right we were shot at by a French battery positioned at Rueil, which somehow managed to take us for Prussians.'

Other accounts also speak of French troops being caught in 'friendly fire'. Trochu himself testified that an eighth of his casualties were caused by his own men. But most of the accounts blame this, perhaps unfairly, on the poorly trained National Guard. Visibility was dreadful and fighting continued on after dark. At around nine German troops again stormed the crest of Montretout and through the sound of gunfire and shells, the peal of bugles could be heard. A full retreat had begun.

From the trenches before Mont Valérien the next morning stragglers could look through the grey mists to the plain littered with the dead, the abandoned carts and the guns. They could hear the cries of the wounded, catch the outline of men with stretchers carrying others to the small wagons that flew the fluttering red cross. Montretout and Saint-Cloud would have still been shrouded in smoke.

News of the defeat did not reach most Parisians until late on the 20th, a Friday. The sounds of the battle of the previous day could not be heard in the capital and for the first time in two weeks the booming of the siege cannon ceased. In the peculiar silence that lasted through the afternoon and evening the rumour spread that the breakthrough had been made.

So was the disappointment all the more bitter when Trochu's final dispatch along with a full official report were published on Friday evening.

Colonel Rochebrune was buried at the cemetery of Père Lachaise the next day, having been carried in a casket across the 11th arrondissement in a procession of guardsmen, mayors, their assistants, committee members and a crowd of not very well dressed *faubouriens*. Some had cried, '*La décheance!*' A few others, '*Vive la Commune!*' There was even talk of marching instead on the Hôtel de Ville. But they didn't.

Immediately after the funeral several of the clubs opened for a special meeting. The hall at La Reine-Blanche was packed. Somebody from the Committee of Vigilance for the 18th Arrondissement began with the announcement, 'We shall meet tomorrow at midday on the place de l'Hôtel de Ville!' There was lots of applause.

'A citizen has informed us', the speaker went on, 'that there will be no more bread after 4 February because of the three hundred grams a day [who cared if his reasoning was a little skewed?]; but,' he added in a none-too-friendly tone, 'as soon as the Commune has replaced and punished the traitors, domiciliary visits will be organised; all is ready, the places have been designated.' Loud cheers.

Opinion was divided as to how much support such a Commune could be expected to get, but towards the end of the meeting a citizen of the 17th arrondissement told the assembly that the republicans of Les Batignolles were planning to set off the next morning at eight o'clock for their own mairie where they would summon the mayor and his assistants to come with them to the Hôtel de Ville, dressed in their official scarfs.

It was decided that the 18th arrondissement should do the same. So off went a delegation to the place des Abbesses. Within an hour they were back to say that Clemenceau was not in his office, but that one of his assistants, Simon Dereure, had agreed to join them. The meeting finished with an agreement to meet the next day at 10 a.m. in front of the mairie and from there they would march, with arms, onto the Hôtel de Ville. '*A demain! à demain!*' they cried and adjourned with a loud '*Vive la Commune!*' It was about ten in the evening.

At that very moment Clemenceau was attending a joint session of, as the official minutes put it, 'the members of the government, the ministers, the mayors of Paris, the secretaries'. It was the second time the mayors had been summoned in twenty-four hours. On Friday afternoon they had met at the ministry of foreign affairs. Favre, looking very shaken, had told them that General Chanzy had just been defeated outside Le Mans and had been forced to retreat behind Laval. Faideherbe had been defeated at Saint-Quentin. Bourbaki's army was in the Jura – it would be impossible to wait for any success there; in a week Paris would be facing famine.

The mayors refused to accept the idea of a capitulation. Clemenceau renewed his calls for Trochu's resignation and insisted on another *sortie en masse*. Trochu, who was present, was counselled to designate a man more confident than he in the possibility of success. The government did agree to consult five of the 'most capable and energetic generals' and then to report back to the mayors the following evening.

Five generals were duly consulted, but not one of them was willing to command a new *sortie*. One of them said, 'I'll go because you demand it, but I'll only go dressed as a civilian: I do not wish to do it in uniform.'

It was Tirard who took up the mayors' cause that Saturday evening. The Prussians, he said, were embarking on a *guerre de race*, the National Guard had not been properly used, the generals were too full of contempt, but Paris's honour had to be satisfied. Trochu was indeed relieved of his military command.

But at the moment that the government was casting its vote for his replacement another of those timely messengers appeared in the hall. 'It is announced that the gates of Mazas had been forced and that Flourens had been freed,' the official minutes recorded. 'In the face of this situation all deliberation is considered null and void. The council unites around the general.'

From an Emperor's war, Paris had led the nation into a people's war; it was now marching, insistently, inexorably, on to a third phase, a war of Frenchmen against Frenchmen.

The 'forcing' of the gates of Mazas was undertaken by about seventy armed Blanquists and National Guardsmen, including Cipriani. It was no Bastille. Earlier that afternoon a few of them had conducted an initial reconnaissance of the gaol by persuading the one guardian at the entrance that they had come to see a warder one of them had known while serving time as an agitator. The guardian actually led them to the central observation tower and even showed them where they could find Flourens (who had been there since the rising of 31 October). There were only nine prison guards on duty that night. They were easily overcome. The intruders locked them up in Flourens' cell and made off with their hero to the mairie of Belleville. (According to Louise Michel, Flourens was none too cooperative; he had not yet 'seen the importance of the revolutionary movement.') At the mairie the small band consumed most of the wine set aside for the poor and they made plans for an invasion of the Hôtel de Ville the next day.

But this time the government was ready. General Vinoy, the new

1. The father, Benjamin Clemenceau   2. The mother, Emma Gautreau Clemenceau
3. Georges Clemenceau at 16, the year of his father's arrest in Nantes

4. The château de L'Aubraie

5. Professor Charles Robin, histologist, defender of the theory of spontaneous generation and supervisor of Clemenceau's medical thesis

6. Georges Clemenceau in 1862: medical student and political rebel

7. Paris in the Second Empire: a view of the Rue Royale and Place de la Concorde on a summer's day

8. Georges Clemenceau (1865), disappointed in love, leaves for New York

9. The Right Honorable William Marcy Tweed, city boss, philanthropist, crook

10. New York in the 1860's

11. A cavalry charge: H. Dupray's
Dragoons at Gravelotte, 18 August 1870

12. A silhouette of destruction: Bazeilles, outside Sedan, in September 1870

13. Georges Clemenceau, mayor of Montmartre

14. The crowd invades the Corps législatif, 4 September 1870

15. E. Betsellère's *L'Oublié* suggests some of the devastation and solitude of the winter of 1870–1871

16. Place de la Concorde in the winter of 1871

17. The 'Red Virgin', Louise Michel in 1871

18. Dolivet, National Guard, and his wife, *cantinière*

19. During the Siege, one of the Red Clubs holds a meeting in the Eglise Saint-Sulpice

20. The Hôtel de Ville, Paris, under the Commune, 2 April 1871

commander-in-chief of the armed forces, had stationed a company of Breton *gardes mobiles* behind the windows and grille fencing overlooking the square. It was a significant move. Bretons hated Parisians. They hated their presumption as spokesmen for the nation, their irreverence for the Church, even their language (a significant portion of Bretons could not even speak French). In Gambetta's army the Bretons had fought alongside Vendéens as 'Volunteers of the West' not under the tricolour but under the white banner of the Sacred Heart – '*Cœur de Jésus*,' read its motto, '*Sauvez la France*.' In Paris they had waited out the siege isolated and bitter. If they could not convert Parisians through their faith, they would attempt to do so with guns.

The crowd which gathered on the square at midday could be measured in hundreds rather than thousands. However, seen from the ground, the Hôtel de Ville, its clock-tower shrouded in mist, 'looked like a ship, its portholes open to the ocean, the human waves at first swirling beneath it, then stopping, motionless'.

Who fired first? All one can say is that there was the sound of a shot. In less than a second it was followed by a crackling of rifles; their bullets made a patter against the paving of the square and the stone walls opposite.

A man in a top hat fell. A guardsman screamed. A woman with a child in her hand seemed to trip. Another put a rifle to her shoulder, took careful aim and fired straight at the Bretons. 'Some of the National Guards,' said Louise Michel,

> later admitted to have shot not on those firing at us but on the walls, which were in fact marked with traces of the bullets. I was not among them . . . Standing before the wretched windows I could not take my gun-sights off those pale-faced savages who, without emotion, like machines, shot at us as if they were firing on a pack of wolves . . . The stories of old grandfather passed before my eyes, stories of that time when heroes fought relentlessly against heroes, the peasants of Charette, of Cathelineau, of Larochejaquelin, against the army of the Republic.

So from the very beginning of the civil disorders of 1871 there was an open breach between the poor of the city and the poor of the countryside.

Six days later the armistice was signed. Favre had to take the trip to Bismarck's residence by river; he knew he would not make it out by land alive. On 8 February, elections for a National Assembly were held. It was the revenge of the provinces.

XVI

THE DAY after the National Assembly at Bordeaux ratified the preliminary peace proposals with the German Reich, Clemenceau and
Scheurer–Kestner, both now deputies, took the train to the small health
resort of Arcachon.

It was March. Sitting opposite each other in a first-class carriage they
would periodically look out at the damp early morning mist that hid
the pine forest. Only the trees of the wayside were visible, rushing
monotonously by so as to fill the whole compartment with dapples
of grey. Both men showed a desire to talk, but they remained for the
most part silent. This day would renew a friendship that the war had
interrupted. One had administered in Paris, the other had conducted a
business in the provinces. How little each one knew of what the other had
experienced. Today there would be a recounting of tales.

By the time the train had pulled into the station the cheerless humour
of the skies had begun to break up; a splash of sunshine added contrast
to the fantastic ornamentation of the railway shed, its wooden beams, the
cast-iron brackets and the tie-rods of steel. They hired a victoria for the
short trip to the shore.

In those days Arcachon was described as 'Tahiti a few kilometres from
Bordeaux'. There were even a few who thought of it as some alien corner
of America; 'Anyone who knew Louisiana', said the anarchist, Elisée
Reclus, 'could believe themselves transported to Madisonville, to La
Passe-Christiane, to Pascagoula.' The 'Buffet chinois', next to the station,
had served as house for many a grand reception in the last years of the
Empire – a huge block of imperial masonry, five storeys high, girdled by
two open-air galleries supported by white columns and protected by the
cocked hat roof which, if it didn't carry the mind to Shanghai or Peking,
was at least outrageous enough to make the sick, the tired or those in search
of refuge believe that this spot was somewhere well beyond the reaches of
French civilisation. The 'Casino mauresque' had every handcrafted detail
and ornament that its name suggested. Along each side of every street
(their curves designed by doctors as a control on unhealthy draughts and
vapours) were the private pavilions and villas of the rich, their families,
their hordes of servants. Verandas were in full vogue, a structure the
French had borrowed from the English, the English had borrowed from
the Indians, and the Indians from who knows else. So too the bungalows.
There was pointed Gothic, there was Italianate belvedere. From roof top
to the bottom of each staircase one's eyes were teased with intricate wood
bric-à-brac, a terra cotta motif, a coat of arms, repeating arches and
pillars, a wraparound porch, a summer Victorian rose garden. Or was

it an oriental hiding place? Part Pacific, part American, part Arab, part Hindu; the town was wholly exotic.

'*Mon Dieu*,' he muttered.

Clemenceau was in a peculiar situation. Since his arrival in Bordeaux two weeks earlier he had been vigorously campaigning for the Republic and continued war against the dynastic oppressor. The same old themes were still there: if we had the leaders of 1792 we'd win; we have the means – a week ago it was the *Ville de Paris* that had berthed at Bordeaux, and a few days later the *Washington*, carrying arms from America to sustain the just war; Spain had done it, Mexico had done it; there was no refuge for an invader among a people in arms. Let the people speak (Bordeaux was a republican town): What are these restrictions to a public viewing of the Assembly debate? Why is an army of regulars surrounding the gates?

Clemenceau with Quinet, Hugo, Louis Blanc, the majority of Paris deputies along with those of Alsace and Lorraine, had kept up the struggle. But Garibaldi had gone, he had returned to Italy. Gambetta had given up, he was now living in Spain. 'Have the courage of your opinions,' said Thiers, head of government, 'either war or peace.' The provincials had voted, the demand was for peace.

The deputies of Alsace and Lorraine had walked out, not resigned. So too a few Parisian 'representatives of the people'. But not Clemenceau. None the less, the element of fight in him was gone, gone for a moment. The issue had been lost. Now he had to listen.

They arrived at the empty beach.

'How much time, how much time do you think we have?' wondered Scheurer-Kestner aloud and, without waiting for a response, gave his answer. Nobody on the political Left doubted for a moment that France would one day retrieve the two provinces. '*La revanche*', as the sentiment was to be known for decades to come, was more than a simple matter of getting back at the Germans; it was the fundamental issue of democracy. Scheurer-Kestner referred to a letter he had received from an Alsatian in exile. 'An absolute monarch, a Louis XI, or even the Tsar of all the Russias, can dispose of lands which are by law his property, but the Republic, or any power emanating directly from the nation, has only a mandate to govern it, to administer its affairs and is absolutely incapable of ceding, to whomever or whatever, something which is not theirs.' You can raze all the fortresses. You can declare the frontier regions neutral under the guarantee of a concert of powers, but the territory of a free people is not up for bids; it belongs to the people, not the state.

But time, time was the unknown element. Perhaps Alsace will allow France the time that is necessary; but there are limits, even to patriotism. The Germans were already setting up the scaffolding for the administration of the new provinces. Scheurer-Kestner's wife had been sending him detailed letters throughout the war. In November Alsatians were assured of postal services throughout 'all non-French countries, including German Alsace and Lorraine.' Ten days later Mulhouse got its first *Kreisdirektor*, or district administrator, a Doctor Schulze – 'They all seem to be doctors in that country; at any rate the Alsatians were promised that Doctor Schulze had nothing to do with the shemozzle, the *Kladderadatsch*, that reigned at that time.' In October all the French judges were fired and a new justice, in the name of the King of Prussia, was established. For a while they kept the trains going, but around Christmas they were cut off under the pretext that the rails led to Switzerland, which was prejudicial to the interests of the German army. Oh, it was not every line. A few lines to Germany were kept open. 'In early January they forced into military trains hostages taken from among the most distinguished and most popular men of the Haut-Rhin. The first of the trains left Mulhouse for Bollwiller, then there were the trains from Colmar to Bollwiller; they didn't even spare the venerable Jean Dollfuss, and Colmar had to pay its tribute by choosing Doctor Birckel, Doctor Macker and a first-rate magistrate, Maître Laurent-AthAlin.'

Five years, would five years be enough to give France time to reorganise before the Germanisation of Alsace and Lorraine had taken full root? 'Five years, five years,' said Clemenceau, 'but you're a fool. Five years! If we haven't retaken Alsace in two, or three years at the most, we will never, never retake her.' What Clemenceau neglected, shut up in Paris for five months, was something painfully obvious to the provincials, who alone were able to watch the movement and organisation of Moltke's armies on the field. 'Today,' Scheurer-Kestner remarked, 'battles are won scientifically; you need much more time for the recovery because it depends so much on the material organisation and the armament.'

'I believe,' reassured Clemenceau, 'I could count on the patriotism of my citizens for five years and I would even say "I swear on my head that they would hold out for ten years like a rock."' Brave words, but he had missed the point. Patriotism was insufficient. 'Let's say fifteen years,' retorted Scheurer-Kestner.

But then how odd it all was, how inapt, how utterly remote and irrelevant that whole story sounded in this place of silence, beauty, pleasure.

There was a sea-gull serenely balancing with one foot on an off-shore post; it was oblivious to the wind, the tide and the shock that each wave brought to its precarious cradle. Two more gulls found elation in the winds, they hovered, would make an upward spiral and launch themselves on an accelerated glide over water, the jetty, land; and then, just as suddenly, they would dive to a spot, overcrowded with their cousins, in the sand. It was a wind that smelt of pine, or more exactly, salt and pine: a 'maritime balsamic effluvium' the doctors called it – no better remedy, they claimed, for the three scourges of the day, scrofula, 'lymphatisme' and 'phtisie' (tuberculosis).

Michelet knew Arcachon, a place, he said, filled with 'the odour of life'. 'It is there that one would want to hide one's beloved sick, the tender and delicate objects for whom one fears the shock of the world.'

The air was a tonic. The hushed sea breakers created the calm of a temple. No conflict, no violence, no extraneous threat; a unity. Politics were absent, the war strangely distant. Here that other international frontier, between France and the Atlantic, was drawn across the damp sands with a tangled pathway of seaweed; it changed twice each day, and only the lap of the tide contested it.

'Oh my dear Clemenceau, how our hearts and our pulses beat in unison at that time!' Two times in his journal Scheurer-Kestner described that day as a 'beautiful day'.

At one end of the beach stood the 'Bains d'Arcachon', a two-storey canary-box on stilts. You could take as many kinds of bath as you could imagine; *bains chauds, bains froids, bains sulfureux, bains de pieds, douches* . . . You could rent a cabin and bathing costume as well. There the 'odour of life' merged with the remedy of mixed waters. If it was not disease that they conquered they at least, together, could promote an atonement of memories, a redemption.

Scheurer-Kestner came back, and back again, to the awful isolation that this war had created. At Arcachon he at last felt *le premier souffle du revoir*, the first breath of reunion. The gap to be breached was considerable. For Parisians like Clemenceau, it was Paris, and Paris alone, that had saved French honour and thus had the right to speak for the whole country. For a republican provincial like Scheurer-Kestner, Paris had abused its position and had capitulated in the name of all France. But two friends on a beach could together work out the reason. 'We had been unjust, one to the other, because we had been poorly informed.' Clemenceau, Scheurer-Kestner found to his amazement, was quite unaware of Gambetta's war. So they talked.

They talked, too, of the Assembly at Bordeaux. 'It's a tower of Babel,' said Scheurer-Kestner. 'There was the Paris we knew, and the Paris of the siege: two absolutely different Parises. There was the province of the Empire, and the province of the war: two absolutely different provinces.' It all amounted to a very peculiar National Assembly. Its most indicative feature, reflected Scheurer-Kestner, was the varied dress of its members. There was Hugo's képi which he wore throughout the sessions, throughout those long and boring republican meetings on rue Lafaurie de Monbadon – he probably slept with the damned thing on. There were a number of uniforms; Chanzy looking young and elegant, d'Aurelle de Paladines in bright regalia, Billot in an oversized tunic. Uniform did nothing for poor General Ducrot; he had the walk and the presence of a hippopotamus. Schoelcher wore the coat of a preacher. Langlois had his arm in a sling; the result of a wound, he would say, suffered at Bougival.

But he could gesticulate with both arms just as well when he stood up to speak. Grévy could be taken for a bourgeois and provincial judge in his blue jacket and tiny bowler hat. The Viscount This and the Marquis That – they all had the trousers, waistcoats and jackets of a rural nobility. 'The whole thing smelt of localism and stank of particularism; these men, coming from all four corners of France, arrived tainted with the odour of the profoundest inexperience.' That was about all you could say.

Late in the afternoon the two men took the train back to Bordeaux. They felt the release that only friendship can bring. And they felt the sadness of the new reality confronting them. The Republic seemed not only compromised, but lost.

In the night Scheurer-Kestner, restless, wrote a letter to his wife. He broke the news: '110 votes for honour; 540 for shame.'

XVII

THE FIRST thing Clemenceau knew about the troubles was a loud banging at his door. It was 6 a.m. 'Oh, lord,' he said, got up, opened the door and was greeted by Simon Dereure's cold blue face, his eyes shivering big and gloating. Clemenceau had never liked the cobbler Dereure. It was a question, he said, of 'temperament and intelligence.'

So, they were taking the cannon by force.

Dereure said he had had enormous difficulty just getting to the rue Capron; most of the streets were blocked by soldiers. Clemenceau, furious at the flagrant betrayal this represented, donned coat, trousers and boots, and headed straight out for the Butte.

The problem of the cannon had begun soon after it was announced that the Germans were going to make a formal entry into Paris. Since this had been reputedly a people's war, the people – that is, the elected officers of the Paris National Guard and their friends on the vigilance committees – decided that the cannon of Paris belonged to them. With the avowed purpose of protecting them from German hands, a newly organised 'Central Committee of the National Guard' gave orders to 'retrieve' over four hundred guns parked in a western corner of Paris and to haul them over to those citadels of popular power, the heights of Belleville and Montmartre.

The Germans made their entry into Paris and left two days later, with grace. The cannon remained in their new positions.

The conservative members of the National Assembly had little patience with the popular sovereigns of Paris. Hardly had they warmed their seats when they abolished the daily pay of 1 franc 50 for the National Guard (this was not in fact executed), had given commercial debtors forty-eight hours to pay up on all outstanding bills (deferred for the 'duration of the war') and had thrown out a petition for a further moratorium on rents. Thousands in Paris – shopkeepers, artisans, petty tradesmen – as a result faced bankruptcy, unemployment and worse. To cap it all, the National Assembly voted to have their permanent address in Versailles, not Paris. The government, however, would return to the capital.

As for Thiers himself, there was no way he could have been persuaded to yield on the issue of the guns. Their seizure had made the National Guard of Paris the most powerful military force in France (not of course counting the Germans). Sovereignty resided in the nation, the nation had elected its representatives, the representatives had designated its government. The guns belonged to the government. 'We must march on,' Thiers told his council of ministers, 'whatever the cost; the cannon must be taken before the arrival of the Assembly.' The Assembly was due to meet in Versailles on 20 March.

Thiers was being unreasonably stubborn; there was plenty of room for manœuvre. One of the principal proponents for a negotiated settlement was Clemenceau. At a meeting of the arrondissement mayors he proposed the creation of a central artillery park under the command of Victor Schœlcher, who was both an officer in the guard and a Paris deputy. Picard, the new minister of the interior, hadn't been very enthusiastic: 'We can't', he said, 'allow these cannon to go wandering about like this on the streets any longer.' Negotiations, however, were undertaken. They even had some success. On the same day that Thiers ordered seizure by force, Schœlcher and Clemenceau had visited the Butte Montmartre and persuaded the National Guard committee to turn the cannon over to the deputies of Paris; Schœlcher would get the title 'Colonel of the Artillery of the National Guard'.

Unfortunately, Thiers had his own deadline to meet.

On his way up to the Butte that Saturday morning, 18 March, Clemenceau had crossed several of the road-blocks which Dereure had mentioned. The troops had the look you might expect of people forced to their feet at three in the morning – phlegmatic and bored. Apart from a couple of men in shirtsleeves standing at a door and an anxiety-ridden mayor, the soldiers posted on the boulevard had nothing to watch.

Dawn began lifting the sluggish night rainclouds.

As he climbed the hill Clemenceau noticed a few more signs of life. Some women were up early, as usual, running a family errand or cleaning a shop-front. Small groups of men in blouses were chatting with the soldiers. There was nothing remotely resembling a road block here. It was as if a military operation in the middle of a working suburb was the most ordinary event in the world, like the setting up of a street market. The soldiers were hungry. They had been told to leave their knapsacks behind. So they would go wandering around the streets looking for a bite to eat, their abandoned rifles lying scattered across the pavement. The queues at the bakers' shops were getting quite long.

At last he reached the summit. There were more soldiers strolling aimlessly about. At the far end of the artillery park he could recognise General Lecomte, with whom he had had an encounter during the events of 22 January. Clemenceau explained how upset he was at not being consulted and he warned Lecomte that if he hung around much longer he could expect trouble. The general replied that he was waiting for horses; the capture of the cannon had been simple enough – one guardsman seriously wounded and the remainder locked up in a restaurant – but nobody had remembered to bring horses.

There was a pregnant silence and then Clemenceau, seeing no further point to the discussion, left for no. 6, rue des Rosiers.

This rue des Rosiers no longer exists today. But, then, it ran from behind the old church wall of Saint Pierre's down an increasingly steep slope in the direction of the chaussée Clignancourt. It was one of the few attractive streets of the neighbourhood. The road was pebbled and on each side of the street were stone houses with gardens; it had reminded Alphonse Daudet of 'one of those peaceful suburbs where the town straggles out and becomes diminished, eventually to die at the edge of the fields'. Number 6 had almost certainly been a farmhouse, the former yard now converted into a garden. On the morning of the 18th the building was requisitioned to serve as headquarters for the police force backing up the military operation. Clemenceau had gone there to have a word with their commander, Captain Piquot.

Piquot met him at the door and let him in. They were holding about a hundred prisoners in the garden, most of them in the uniform of the National Guard. He was told that there was a wounded man in one of the rooms. Clemenceau went in to tend to him.

It was a tiny bare room overlooking the garden. The man was laid out on a mattress, his face blanch-white. A *cantinière* of the National Guard bent over him, while on the other side knelt a very solemn Louise Michel. Hardly a word passed between them. The man had been hit in his thigh and in his stomach; there was no chance of survival. The best thing to be done was to throw out the dirty old rags, clean the wounds – 'Isn't there any water in the place?' – and get him transported to the nearest hospital. Louise Michel left first and, having cleared the building, ran down the hill shouting 'Treason! treason!' Then Clemenceau left, taking the opposite direction to get a stretcher from the mairie. The dying man stared, frightened silly, at the *cantinière*.

Clemenceau was back within fifteen minutes with the stretcher and two guardsmen. They managed to get the man out of the room through a window into the courtyard. Just then Captain Piquot arrived to report that Lecomte had refused permission to have the man transported; the sight of blood might anger the crowd. So the operation was repeated in reverse. Clemenceau left the man staring again at the *cantinière*.

On his way back down to the mairie Clemenceau noted that the crowd had grown considerably. But it was the same scenario; more rifles on the pavement, knots of soldiers and civilians chattering, women with children and rather more men of the National Guard. In the rue de Mont-Cenis a guardsman was abusing one of the soldiers for taking part in the expedition: the soldier made no reply. In the rue du Vieux-Chemin another guardsman started abusing Clemenceau.

Outside the mairie were about twenty people, members of this committee or that; men of influence, who were complaining about the government's betrayal. Dereure was among them. They accused Clemenceau of conniving with the government. But their posture was hardly threatening and they soon moved off, leaving in different directions.

So it was back to business as usual. Sabourdy, of the armaments committee, arrived a little before eight. Clemenceau sent him over to rue Lepic to deal with a landlord who had been causing some trouble. There were papers that needed arranging, a couple of letters to write. He could look out over the square. It was empty.

After a while, a few men of the National Guard strolled into the square. They were not armed. Then more groups. There was the dull sound of drums in the distance, the *rappel*. One of the guardsmen went over to the corner of the rue des Abbesses, just opposite the post office and started blowing his bugle. He should have been arrested, but this would have required assistance from the National Guard: there were armed men arriving in the square. Within minutes the square was seething. Total chaos. Guardsmen were coming from every direction, some with packs on their backs, others with their coats wide open, most of them with rifles.

Then there was the roll of drums again and down the rue Marie-Antoinette into the square marched several companies of guardsmen. Clemenceau was just figuring out where to put a report on drainage and sanitation when, glancing out the window once more, he noticed something odd. There were regular troops in the crowd. They must be some of Lecomte's men.

Sabourdy returned, a bit out of breath. He told Clemenceau that at rue Lepic he had witnessed the arrival of the long-awaited horses and that he had seen them seized, in a hail of stones and bottles, by the National Guard.

Now cannon were being hauled into the square. Sabourdy turned to Clemenceau and added, 'I've heard that Lecomte has been arrested.'

The story is told that Lecomte was arrested by the National Guard for ordering his troops to fire on the crowd. There is some truth to it, but not the entire truth.

By 8.30 whatever infantry cordon existed to hold back the crowd had disintegrated. The lines simply disappeared into a horde of men, women and children who were now approaching the summit from all angles. A company of *chasseurs* had been ordered forward to check their progress, but they did it with their rifle butts in the air in such a way that the crowd could move past on either side. Lecomte had at his disposal men such as the 136th reserves who had been billeted in Belleville. Their lieutenant told them to 'do what they liked' and then ran away. They were never ordered to fire; their second lieutenant finally 'surrendered his sword' when he realised that there were only ten of his company left. The battalion commander of the 88th ordered his men to put the ramrods into their barrels to show the crowd that their rifles were not loaded. Another commander hung his cap on the end of his rifle and shouted '*Vive la République!*'

Lecomte, seeing the crowd approach, shouted out to them to hold their distance. They kept on coming. He ordered a bugle to be blown as a warning. Then he ordered one of his commanders to read out three summations instructing the crowd to disperse. They kept on coming. Lecomte made a sign which his commanders interpreted as an order not to fire. Two of his officers later testified that he had given such an order because 'there were too many women and children.' To one of them Lecomte then handed a pistol and told him to go down the hill to the place Blanche and bring up a reserve battalion. It was there that the only serious fighting of the day took place. Their commander had ordered a cavalry unit to push back the crowd. They were met by a volley of rifle fire. One officer was killed and six men wounded.

The Butte Montmartre was eventually overrun, with Lecomte's men openly cheering the mob on. Lecomte and some of his officers were arrested.

Also arrested were the police and *gardiens de la paix* of the rue des Rosiers. They were marched down the hill to the main positions of the National Guard opposite the mairie. Captain Piquot was among them. Clemenceau left the mairie to speak to him.

'I am so awfully sorry this has happened,' he said.

'We're all right,' replied the captain. 'We're trained to deal with this sort of problem, you know.'

'Well, you're best off here. Just stay put. With any luck the Guard will forget about you.' Policemen were not very popular in the 18th arrondissement and any movement now would have attracted the attention of citizens with long memories. But Clemenceau was right. Once the focus of events had shifted to the top of the hill the police force was forgotten and he was able to invite them all to take refuge in his cellars.

Clemenceau had a number of visitors in his office. Most of them were either National Guards coming in with accusations of betrayal, or various officials from other parts of Paris wondering what on earth was going on.

It was a deeply emotional mayor that received them and, typically, the greater his emotion, the greater his effort to repress it. His outer appearance was that of a man acting without feeling, a man with little compassion for those who had suffered five months of siege and, on top of that, a series of humiliations doled out by their own national government. It must have been a source of irritation and, one imagines, a leading factor behind the hostility he received from his constituents from that day onward.

But on one occasion, by his own account, he was moved to tears. Josselin, member of the Central Committee and one of the critical figures in Clemenceau's abortive attempt at a negotiated settlement, accused Clemenceau of swindling. '*Vous nous avez roulés*', he said. Apparently Clemenceau was at a loss for words. He made some sort of gesture and Josselin continued, 'Oh yes. You negotiated with us to send us off to sleep. Don't ever hope you are going to make me believe you were not conniving with the government.'

'I was so stupefied', Clemenceau wrote a year later, 'by the profound conviction in his voice that I couldn't find a single word of response. I was dumbfounded, confused. However, my expression was such that, without me pronouncing a word and noticing a tear of rage on my cheek, he begged pardon for having insulted me and swore that he would no longer believe what he had just said.'

Tears of rage, tears of distress; these were sentimental signs appropriate for a day where events were fast overtaking what the generals, what the politicians, what the people had planned.

The announcement that Lecomte and another general were about to be shot came as an utter surprise to Clemenceau. It was Captain Mayer who brought the news. Mayer had worked closely with the mayor during the siege; he was a muddle-headed fellow, according to Clemenceau, easy to influence, but one who wouldn't hurt a mouse. On the 18th it was Mayer's battalion of the National Guard that was given charge of the prisoners at the Château Rouge, one of the most famous dance halls of Montmartre. It was on the corner of the main road leading to Clignancourt, sufficiently far from the Butte, one would have thought, to keep the prisoners out of trouble. Clemenceau personally arranged their lunch with Mayer.

Clemenceau had just booted out a committee of fifteen citizens who seemed intent on taking over the mairie.

'I mean it, monsieur. It's Lecomte and Thomas that are being dragged up the hill. And if you don't come quickly they will be shot.'

'That's impossible. Thomas is in America.'

'Well, he looks awfully like Thomas to me, monsieur.'

'Come on!'

He grabbed his mayor's scarf and they hurtled out the door.

General Clément Thomas had distinguished himself in service of the Second Republic during the bloody June days of 1848. In 1870 he had been nominated commander of the National Guard and it was under his command that the Guards were led out to slaughter at Buzenval. General Thomas was not very popular among the people of Montmartre. That afternoon he had foolishly ventured out to the place Pigalle where he was recognised and taken under guard to no. 6 rue des Rosiers. The building had been recaptured by the National Guard shortly after the fall of the Butte. For some unknown reason (perhaps out of fear of Clemenceau's intervention) an order was made, presumably by the Vigilance Committee, to transfer Lecomte to rue des Rosiers. It was a death warrant. The mixed escort of guardsmen and soldiers of his own force broke up within the howling mob that had converged on all streets leading to the summit, a crowd quite different from the one Clemenceau had seen earlier in the day. There were people from the boulevards, beggars from back alleys, prostitutes, harpies. The appearance of General Thomas on the scene only excited them further.

One of the witnesses was a commander of the National Guard, Louis Valigranne. Shortly after four he arrived at rue des Rosiers accompanied by two other guard commanders. They had come on hearing troubling rumours about the fate of the two prisoners. Once inside the courtyard Valigranne turned round to discover that his colleagues had very sensibly abandoned him. Many in the crowd were regulars, Lecomte's troops. A captain in 'Garibaldian uniform' had hoisted himself to a window ledge and was pleading the crowd not to do anything damaging to the health of the prisoners. Valigranne made his way into a little room just opposite.

Thomas was standing to his right, dressed in a dark blue overcoat, military buttons and a black felt hat in his hand. He was very pale. Valigranne knew him personally.

'I give you my word that I will demand you are protected from the insults of the crowd.' Then, turning to the man on his left, he asked, 'And who are you?'

'General Lecomte.'

There were four other officers in the room. Valigranne repeated his promise. 'I will protect you to the peril of my own life.'

There was a banging on the doors, one window pane was shattered, fists, sticks and rifle points could be seen. Valigranne left the room and, under the protection of the two sentries at the door, tried to make a little speech.

'. . . The generals are the prisoners of the people; they must be referred to a regularly constituted court . . . I plead you . . . in the name of the true Republic . . . in the name of the people's dignity . . .'

'We'll make you judge at our court martial!'

'That's not my responsibility.'

This was enough for the people. They dragged him off to the courtyard. 'Death! death!' A little man in uniform stuck a chassepot in his belly. Valigranne grabbed hold of it and was about to hit him over the head with the butt when a couple of other guardsmen came over shouting, 'But that's our brave commandant!' The rest lowered their guns, excused themselves and asked him out for a drink. Valigranne declined, and took the opportunity to get out of the building. As he went down the street he could hear the dull detonations of rifle shot.

It was very messy. Thomas, his hat still in his hand, was stood up against a wall and shot. The hat dropped but not Thomas, who continued calling his executioners cowards. They shot him again. Still he stood. He only fell after receiving a bullet in his eye. But he continued breathing and mumbling as he lay on the ground while the shooting went on in ragged volley. A coroner later reported that he had found more than forty bullets in his body. Lecomte was shot just once, in the back.

Clemenceau arrived too late. As he rushed across the Butte with Sabourdy, he had bumped into Josselin. 'It is awful! awful!' he was shouting. Then suddenly, wrote Clemenceau in a famous passage of his account of the day,

> there was a great boom and the crowd which had filled the courtyard of Number 6 rushed headlong into the street, as if they were in some sort of daze. There were *chasseurs*, regulars, National Guards, women and children. All of them were letting out the cries of wild animals, not fully aware of what was going on. I was witnessing there that pathological phenomenon that one might call blood lust. A breath of folly appeared to have blown over this crowd; children had climbed up a wall and were waving Lord knows what kinds of trophy, ragged, dishevelled women twisted their bare arms, screaming themselves hoarse and empty of all

sense. I noticed several who were crying louder than the others. There were men dancing and jostling each other about in a sort of frenetic state. It was one of those hysterical phenomena that occurred so often in the middle ages and is still to be found among human masses under the shock of some powerful emotional drive.

The return to the mairie was a run of the gauntlet. 'Without your *sang-froid*,' remarked Sabourdy once they had reached the foot of the hill, 'you would have been lost.'

XVIII

BUT WHAT had happened to Adolphe Thiers' 'usual *sang-froid*'? The accounts of the government's precipitate flight from Paris that afternoon are contradictory. Some suggest panic, others speak of calculated manœuvre by this former minister of King Louis-Philippe who was intent on avoiding mistakes of the past. 'If Louis-Philippe had left Paris in February 1848,' he told his worried ministers, 'he would have returned eight days later.'

Thiers was the first to leave. Accompanied by Pouyer-Quertier, Dufaure, de Larcy, Lambrecht and Admiral Pothuau, he departed at 3.30 p.m., under the cover of a cavalry squadron, through the porte du Point-du-Jour and the main road for Versailles. By early the next morning every minister, the majority of their staff and a chaotic fraction of the armed forces still loyal to the government had withdrawn to Versailles, the city of kings. Paris and the provinces were effectively at war.

The subsequent takeover of the government offices in Paris was unplanned, unforeseen. If ever the world had known a truly spontaneous revolution, it was in Paris on 18 March 1871.

Of that whole scattered constellation of powers, of little sovereignties – the committees, the clubs, the political press – which had spread under the isolated conditions of war, there were at least five political bodies that could have claimed the right to govern Paris. There was of course the government and the National Assembly; they drew their authority from the national elections of February. On 22 March the Assembly did actually discuss a bill introduced by the minister of the interior that would have given Paris a municipal council. But it was hardly the kind of council that the Parisians wanted; its membership would be determined by the number of arrondissements rather than by size of population and it would meet only with the approval of the prefect of the Seine.

Admiral Saisset had been nominated commander of the National Guard by the government but he held little respect among the ranks in Paris; they had elected their own commander, Garibaldi.

There were the arrondissement mayors and the Paris deputies, several of whom, like Clemenceau, held both positions. When the government left Paris, Picard, the minister of the interior formally designated the mayors and deputies as provisional administrators of the city, but again this was not what most Parisians wanted.

The ever-elusive Committee of the Twenty Arrondissements continued to exist (for a time under a different name) and one imagines that if it had been able to maintain its authority it might have been able to impose a municipal government more in line with its own revolutionary, if contradictory, principles. But after 31 October its influence in Paris politics waned. Its participation in the troubles of 22 January, though indirect, further diminished its role, which was henceforth essentially limited to electoral campaigns on behalf of its members.

The real source of political power in Paris in March 1871 was the National Guard. But the National Guard was a hydra-headed beast. Its recruitment as well as its supplies of food, uniform and arms were organised by arrondissement, not by any city-wide administration. It was only in February that an obscure journalist, Henri de La Pommeraye, and a shopkeeper from the 3rd arrondissement took the initiative to organise a central committee designed to respond to the National Guard's collective needs. After numerous local meetings, a general assembly, which drew together over two thousand delegates, set up a provisional committee that would draft the statutes of the new organisation. By early March the Central Committee of the National Guard had been elected. It had around thirty members ('membership' varied with each meeting) of whom the vast majority were unknown outside their arrondissements. From this moment onward the National Guards were referred to as the Fédérés, a term which in itself suggested the continuing emphasis on local initiative and organisation.

No one had anticipated the events of 18 March. The Central Committee had met the previous night, adjourning at 3.30 a.m. (just at the moment that Thiers' military operation began) with the agreement that they would meet again at eleven o'clock the next evening. The first most of its members knew of the operation was the sound of the drums around eight or nine in the morning and the government posters prematurely announcing the retrieval of the cannon. Barricades were already going up along the grands boulevards, at Château d'Eau and the Bastille. The crowds were gaining intensity and number. At 10 a.m. there were only ten members of the Central Committee in council at the temporary headquarters at rue Basfroi, a street in the 11th arrondissement which by now had been barricaded at both ends. By far the largest number of members were in their own arrondissement organising the 'defence'. Information was spotty and very few of the Committee's own messengers got back to headquarters to report. By early afternoon the popular movement had virtually come to a halt for want of orders. Duval, for example, had gathered together several battalions at the Panthéon and just sat there waiting to learn what he should do next. Faltot's note to the Committee fairly summarised the situation, 'I have five or six battalions in the rue de Sèvres, what should be done?'

At the moment that Thiers and his colleagues started out for Versailles not one government building had been occupied; the National Guards limited their activity to noisy demonstrations. The first to realise that the government was abandoning Paris was Paul-Antoine Brunel, a member of the Central Committee and one of the most brilliant military officers on the rebels' side. Typically, he was with his troops that day, not with the Committee. It was on his own initiative that he marched onto the barracks of Prince-Eugène, which he captured without a single shot being fired; the occupants were soldiers of the 120th Regiment who showed the same readiness to fraternise with the National Guard as Lecomte's troops that morning. By 5 p.m. Brunel had taken over the Imprimerie Nationale, which put him in control of the government's most essential line of communication with the people. He then headed for the Hôtel de Ville.

By midnight the National Guard was in full control of every major government building in Paris, while a reluctant Central Committee, whose members continually protested that 'We have no mandate as a government', was installed at the Hôtel de Ville.

In its first proclamation, dated 19 March, the Committee again emphasised the provisional nature of its authority: 'If the Central Committee of the National Guard were a government it could, out of respect for its electors, disdain from justifying itself. But since its first assertion has been to declare "that it did not pretend to take the place of those whom the breath of the people has blown over," and resting, out of plain honesty, within the limits set by its mandate, it [the Committee] remains a composite of personalities who have the right to defend themselves.'

The editor of La Vérité put it more succinctly: 'Nous sommes en pleine anarchie.'

XIX

PARIS IN February and early March was a city still living in conditions of war. To be sure, there was no sound of cannon, there were no dramatic dispatches reproduced in the papers or affixed to the walls; no calls for a new offensive, no casualty lists, no more the rumble of artillery, pontoons and military equipment being dragged through the streets on their way to the front. The sounds of early March were the sounds of peace: the hissing of a train advancing on wet rails, the clatter of pedestrians and carriages following their permanent ways. But war was present, even if war was silent: there was hunger in Paris, there was immense poverty, and there was the appalling death toll.

Hardly a soul commented on the growing number of deaths in the capital. It was as if death had become just one more uncomfortable fact that ordinary citizens had to tolerate that winter. The mortality rates had been rising since August. Did anyone really expect this to stop with the armistice? In the last weeks of January and onward into February the death rates in Paris surged from four to five times the normal average for the season. 'The intense inaction and unearthly calm are killing us', noted Felix Whitehurst in his diary on 21 February – a comment rather more literal than its author intended. Death rates were still three times the average when the troubles began in mid-March.

A major cause of the high mortality was the incredibly slow and inefficient distribution of provisions. It was more than a week after the armistice before the first train arrived, carrying amongst its cargo pheasants from England which the French government felt obliged to send back, explaining that 'These things are for the aristocracy and not for the people – it would be more prudent not to distribute them.' And of course it was the people who were the last to benefit from the reopening of the supply lines. 'Great supplies of food have arrived,' it was reported in the *Journal officiel*. There was a riot in Les Halles when the provisions from the first wagons were delivered: eggs, vegetables, butter and chickens trampled into inedible muck. Oh, the visitors to Paris were certainly impressed. 'Lots of meat I see,' would say the English gentleman as he stepped out from dinner at Bignon's. But it was not meat for the poor. It was too expensive. How could one pay for food when there were no jobs, no means of income save the pittance drawn by National Guards (which the Assembly had anyway promised to revoke)?

Death was selective. The poor of course suffered most. But it was selective in other ways, unusual in peace, common in war. The death rate among women barely doubled and it has been estimated that, had it not been for smallpox, the increase would have been a good deal less than that. It was the men who died. Death rates among men increased six times the seasonal average. The worst affected were not the very young and not the very old (the normal pattern in peacetime), but those aged between fifteen and thirty. Here the death rates were ten times greater than normal.

The principal cause of death was the terrible, terrible conditions that the National Guards had endured through the winter of 1870–71. They were exposed to the cold, they were poorly dressed, the sick were huddled among the rest in makeshift barracks – 'villages' they sometimes called them, beneath the fortifications, an area which in times of peace had its reputation for unwholesomeness.

But no one talked about death among the non combatants. No politician, no journalist, no high official commented on it. There were a few doctors – and they only commented on it once the business of war was done.

So it was more than boredom that drove the National Guards to violence that March; it was isolation and abandonment in the profoundest sense.

Paris had the look of abandonment. Several of the buildings around the Panthéon and the Invalides had been reduced to rubble by the bombardment of early January; the hospital of Salpêtrière had been seriously damaged, as had the Odéon theatre, Saint-Sulpice and the Gare d'Orléans. Paris was no longer a city of lights. Even the cafés looked gloomy, their windows and mirrors sometimes shattered or cracked, the gas lamps out of order and the makeshift replacements flickering hues of yellow and blue. The sight of avenues, their gracious tree verges cut back to stumps, like the sight of parks denuded and spoiled, evoked feelings of loss and of sadness. The waters of the Seine presented a similar forlorn spectacle, emptied of river traffic and reflecting the monotonous greys of its neglected embankments. For weeks a faint and luminous fog lay over the whole city like thin silken veils holding, as it were, the rays of the night's moon, the beam of the day's sun, in suspension and out of touch of the human movement below. Temperatures continued to hover over freezing-point.

There was of course movement. Perhaps as many as one hundred thousand Parisians left the city in the weeks following the armistice. They left by private carriage or by train, their trunks, suitcases and hatboxes neatly assembled for a porter or a valet to carry – it was not the poor who left. And when they had finally gone Paris was treated to yet another absence: you could have walked through whole streets in the 7th, the 8th and the 16th arrondissements and have heard only silence and have seen only darkness. Heavy wooden shutters hid the windows, the doors were all locked, and the odd dog barked.

There was the movement of the National Guard, often joined by regulars as on that day in February when three hundred thousand marched from the Bastille to the Seine. A man, taken as either a former imperial police officer or as a government spy, was arrested. It took the crowd over two hours to kill him. He was kicked, he was beaten, he was tied up like a packet and thrown in the river. But the winter currents brought him back to the shore. So he was kicked again and thrown back. On the third time and the fourth, when he again drifted ashore, he was stoned. He eventually drowned.

The mood of the people was savage because their conditions were savage. Trade was still blocked, shops were deserted, commercial orders were delayed indefinitely and there was no credit. Victor Schœlcher met a manufacturer one day. 'What can we do?' said the unhappy man, 'Who's going to defend us? We have no centre of action. We have no single authority capable of simply expressing our wishes.'

XX

IT WAS this lack of authority, of a *centre de ralliement* (or rallying point), that tormented Paris's elected representatives, like Schœlcher and Clemenceau, in the days that followed 18 March. On Sunday evening, 19 March, Picard, the minister of the interior who had already left Paris for Versailles, formally delegated the job of administering the city to the arrondissement mayors.

By that time the Central Committee of the National Guard was already installed at the Hôtel de Ville and was making what efforts it could to release the administrative logjam that was piling up with every hour. But the Committee continued to stress that it was not a government. One senses here the influence of Eugène Varlin, the most articulate Committee member, who had spent several years explaining in the leftist press the principles of 'anti-statist collectivism' or, as his partisans called it, 'non-authoritarian Communism', an idea that was very popular among the artisanal classes of Paris.

So Clemenceau was in no way exaggerating when, the next day, he told the Assembly in Versailles that 'There are no longer any constituted authorities in Paris besides a few tottering municipalities which, before long, will probably be incapable of containing the flood which threatens to engulf them.'

The image of a rallying point for lawful 'good citizens' was evoked by nearly all political sides in the Assembly. Clemenceau himself appealed for a *point d'appui*, or pivot, which he thought could best be realised by an elected municipal council formally approved by the Assembly. Most of the Paris deputies agreed with this. Admiral Saisset, who had only recently been nominated commander of the Paris National Guard, used a similar image when speaking of the need to group around his flag a 'kernel of conservatives, of men of family and of property.' Schœlcher also suggested that the Guards could be used to rally the forces of good and appealed to Saisset to hold a review on the Champs Elysées, a proposal sharply contested by his colleagues on the Left who thought, undoubtedly correctly, that this would be more a provocative than a conciliatory act. The problem that everyone faced was that such rallying points would only partially correspond to the political realities, which were multiple. The siege, by isolating so many local powers, had cultivated mixed loyalties that were so profoundly hostile to one another that even, for example, if the Paris deputies' campaign for a legally constituted municipal council had succeeded it is doubtful that peace would have been maintained for very long.

It was the sort of situation which would have delighted somebody like Hobbes, would have tickled that seventeenth-century irreverence for God's good order – a situation that mystified nineteenth-century logic. When the men of reason, of representation and advocates of a parliamentary conciliation went before the people's court, they were notified it would be war. When they turned to the politician's bench, to the rulers and the frock-coated gentlefolk of land, commerce and the legal order, they were told again it would be war.

The conciliators were at work from the moment the crisis began. On 19 March, Clemenceau had accompanied Tirard, Peyrat, Schœlcher and Louis Blanc to the Hôtel de Ville to present to the Central Committee their programme for peace. 'We are the only real representatives of universal suffrage,' they said. They told the members of the Committee that it would be in their interest to hand the administration over to the mayors and give the Paris deputies time to persuade the National Assembly to pass a law guaranteeing Paris its municipal liberties. 'You contest our titles?' replied Jourde for the Committee. '*Mais, messieurs*, we also have force! It is civil war that you have come to declare on us . . . It will be an appalling civil war, with fire and pillage! We are certain to conquer, but if we are beaten, we will leave nothing standing about us.'

It was Clemenceau who proposed to the Assembly a law authorising municipal elections in Paris. 'We have no desire to irritate the debate,' he said. 'Is it not possible to conciliate the two positions?' 'No! no!' they shouted back. 'Couldn't we have, with the briefest delay, elections for a municipal council?' 'No! no!' they replied. 'Permit me, *messieurs*, I am not prepared to abandon my country to civil war.' 'It is true,' shouted out

Admiral Saisset, 'civil war is imminent.' Clemenceau was shouted down and Saisset took his place at the tribune: 'We are condemned to death,' the admiral said.

The language of war was a language of simple, catchy phrases. Thiers set the tone in a proclamation that he and his colleagues drafted – not after the failed attempt to seize the cannon, but the day before. 'For some time,' it read, 'evil-intentioned men have made themselves masters of one part of the city. They have set up defences, they have mounted the Guards and, by order of some occult committee, they are forcing you to mount these defences beside them.' While not necessarily sympathising with Thiers' cause, most people sound in body and mind would have admitted that there was an extremist element within that Committee. But Thiers was not accusing the Central Committee and its friends of extremism, he was accusing them of evil. It was an appeal to that time-honoured divine function of 'just war', war that laid the imperative on the forces of good to seek out and destroy the forces of evil. 'Let the good citizens be separated from the evil,' the proclamation went on with an evangelical ardour, 'let them aid the public force instead of resisting it. They will thus hasten the return of grace within their city and render service to the Republic itself which, in the belief of France, disorder would ruin.'

During the debates within the Assembly epithets were thrown about that would make the enemy appear something not only unworthy of such pious respect, but downright inhuman; savage. The rebels were described as 'agitators', 'wretches', 'villains', or the 'bandits of Paris'. They were rarely identified. Indeed, the blacker the name the more indiscriminate its application, to the point that the 'agitators' and 'wretches' became synonymous with all Paris. 'These men who have not listened' could be understood as 'these men who oppress Paris'; however it was not 'these men' but 'Paris who has abandoned us'.

The proclamations issued by the Central Committee were not entirely innocent of such confusion either. Who did the Committee represent? Officially it maintained that its powers, provisional in nature, were derived from the vote (by acclamation) of 215 battalions of the Paris National Guard. When, however, it charged the 'fugitive Government at Versailles' with 'the most appalling of all crimes, civil war' it spoke for all Paris. When it appealed to the provinces, out of 'concord, union and love', to follow the lead of the capital, it spoke for '*la patrie*'. And then, on 22 March, it announced to an astonished public that it had just concluded what amounted to a non-aggression pact with the Prussian imperial armies (to be followed up two days later with a decree condemning anyone found shooting at Prussians to the firing-squad); the German command, it was reported, had been assured that 'the revolution accomplished in Paris by the Central Committee, being of an *essentially municipal character*, is in no way hostile to the German armies'. This act alone (which contradicted every revolutionary slogan since 31 October) underlined the ambiguous nature of the Committee's authority; by signing the pact the Committee assumed the role of a sovereign state, while its chief negotiating line suggested that it was nothing much more than a county borough. The Central Committee, it appeared, represented whatever best suited it for the occasion.

The catchy phrases of war were not designed to clarify matters. It would be a war between Paris and the provinces. Never mind the internal differences, that Belleville is not the Madeleine, Provence is neither Poitou nor Bigorre. War is a great simplifier. The enemy must be defined.

The government, proclaimed the Central Committee on 19 March, 'has slandered Paris and has assembled against it a mob from the provinces.' It was an old fear in Paris, that kings and emperors, to oppress the 'people''s rights, would turn to the 'blind forces of the provinces'. The government and the Assembly at Versailles provided ample material to encourage such fears. Almost as soon as the remnants of Vinoy's army, which had been defending Paris, arrived in Versailles, the process of weeding out native Parisian soldiers began; they were all packed off to North Africa. It was somewhat more difficult to prepare newly recruited provincials for hostilities against their capital. They arrived totally ignorant of the course of events and were anxious to get home – 'The war is finished, so why are we fighting?' was the standard sentiment among the ranks. And it was, in fact, only with the escalation of violence in April that their commitment to Versailles and its army grew.

But the mood of the majority within the Assembly was one of unmitigated loathing from the start. What Scheurer-Kestner had called the 'smell of localism and the stink of particularism' at Bordeaux had turned into a sharp and acrimonious vapour in the seats of the Versailles opera house. Not that they made much noise about it. The most remarkable feature in the first week of the sessions was the silence of the majority. When there was debate, it was largely a debate between the government and the Left. When there was a Committee report, comments were largely confined to the Committee chairman. The conservative majority was an audience, not an acting body. Their contribution to parliamentary debate was more akin to the role of the 'pit' in nineteenth-century theatre. They would jeer, they would applaud, they would not speak.

On one occasion – it was a Friday – the conciliators had invited a delegation of the arrondissement mayors and their deputies to present their case to the Assembly. They came in formal dress, wearing tricolour scarfs and the insignia of the city of Paris. This was the group to whom Picard had formally delegated authority the day after the government had fled for Versailles. 'Long live the Republic!' shouted the members of the Left. 'Long live the Republic!' the mayors replied from the stage, 'Long live France! Long live the National Assembly!'

Such a show of honours for Paris and its Republic was too much for the tongue-tied gentlemen of the Right. 'Order! order!' they blurted out. 'We can't take this!' cried the good marquis de Castellone. And promptly they all jumped to their feet and ran down to the tribune to heckle the president. The session was immediately adjourned. The government later expressed its 'deepest regrets at the reception given to the mayors.'

But the turning-point was Jules Favre's speech of the previous Tuesday. It was odd to think that it was only six months since he had marched on the Hôtel de Ville to the cheers of the Paris crowd. Today, he was not the same man.

Clemenceau had just made a second disastrous appeal for immediate elections in Paris. 'The government has been induced to launch the country into a series of events . . .' – that was a bad enough start. 'The government is the first cause for the events . . .' – that was even worse. The strength of smells on the right wing was rising. 'Oh! It's shameful,' mumbled the minister of justice.

'I didn't mean to say that. These interruptions push my words beyond my thoughts . . .'

'It is an act of accusation before the executioners, that's what your words mean,' said the minister of foreign affairs. Words went scudding past thoughts. Clemenceau stepped down from the tribune in a fluster and up got the foreign minister.

Who were the accusers? Where were the executioners?

Favre began by reading a declaration reproduced in twenty-seven Paris newspapers urging their readers to abstain from an 'illegal election' proposed for the following day. 'We do not want Paris separated from France,' it announced and, hinting at the foreign occupier, added, 'we do not want to un-make our unity when other peoples are remaking theirs.' Favre thought this was marvellous. The declaration, he said, had been 'courageously penned under the knife of the assassins' and it seemed perfectly evident to him that, if the Assembly hesitated, it might be the Germans who consummate the 'right to repress the riot'. Once more, 'Paris' became synonymous with the new enemy and a 'civil war' was already underway: 'I ask those who object to this, what do they call the current state of affairs in Paris?'

Confronted with these words of war – repeated, agitated, confused – the Assembly reacted. 'We must appeal to the provinces!' hooted the comte Gaslonde. 'Yes, let's appeal to the provinces and we'll march on Paris: let's be done with it!' piped up the admiral Saisset. He was a man of advanced years and needed a break. Favre had spoken for more than ninety minutes.

Eventually he stepped down from the tribune and was surrounded by a throng of cheering deputies. He was a hero again, but this time a war hero.

There was opposition, of course. The most eloquent, the most articulate – the members of the Left – rebuked Favre's speech. 'After the provocative speech of the minister of foreign affairs,' shouted Clemenceau from his seat, 'I declare, in the name of my colleagues of the Left as well as myself, that we withdraw our bill for a municipal council in Paris.' Langlois mounted the tribune, but could not be heard in the tumult. 'The house is burning,' he screamed, 'and you indulge in chatter.'

Tirard was the last to speak at that session. He said he would return to his mairie, even if it meant death, 'when one is prepared to die, one has the right to be heard.' There was a short silence. Paris could still be saved without violence, he said. There was still time. He deeply regretted Favre's speech and most particularly 'this antagonism one seeks to make between Paris and the provinces.'

Favre said he meant the opposite, and of course it was a false image of the country. But it gave the warmongers their chance. The 'appeal to the provinces' had gone out and France, seen from the deputies' seats, was divided into two blocks.

The next day in Paris, a miscellaneous collection of retired captains and colonels, blue-blooded gentlemen, a handful of 'respectable' shopkeepers and a retinue of commoners set out on a march from Tirard's 2nd arrondissement in the direction of the Hôtel de Ville. They called themselves *Les Amis de l'Ordre*. Their banners bore the slogans '*Pour la paix!*', '*Vive l'Assemblée!*', and '*Vive la République!*' But there were also cries, singular and unidentifiable, of '*A bas le Comité!*' '*A bas les assassins!*' As they turned into rue de la Paix the front of their column came up face to face with a line of National Guards blocking the entrance to the place Vendôme. The back of the column continued to push forward. Shooting broke out. A dozen men were killed. Many more were wounded.

That same afternoon, several of the arrondissement mairies were taken over by force. The 18th arrondissement was one of them. Clemenceau, Lafont and Jaclard were arrested. It was, in relation to the other events, a minor affair. They were freed within an hour. However, the mayor published a warning: 'We have our hearts set on avoiding a conflict, the disastrous consequences of which appal us. But we strongly protest the action that the National Guard of the 18th arrondissement has taken against freely elected republican magistrates . . .' It was another plea for conciliation, one more attempt to stem the tide of violence that others, with a sort of passive delight, had let flow between their feet. Since his return from Bordeaux Clemenceau had been working for a negotiated settlement, not out of any infirmity of purpose but because, after six months of war and seven months in office of the poor, he believed that a parliamentary form of Republic was the only 'public thing' possible.

But the word had been given: there were people of opposite convictions, in Paris and Versailles, who regarded the dozen deaths of Wednesday as unavoidable, written into History. Edouard Lockroy, writing in prison two months later, said the whole disaster could be attributed to two attitudes that developed at the critical moment: that the course of events was inevitable and that this was a historical opportunity to 'exterminate the enemies of society'. '*Je demande quatre-vingt mille têtes; après cela, nous vivrons tranquilles.*' Revolutions are like children, he went on (introducing a novel approach to the doctrine of original sin), they don't ask to be born, it's easy to avoid them, but, when they come into the world, there is always somebody to be blamed.

'History' took the blame. 'Before the Assembly', 'before History' and 'before God' Thiers swore 'to accept this mission: to defend order and to reorganise at the same time the country in a way that will bring it life . . . Be assured, this great and noble nation will not allow the triumph of the villains who want to cover it with blood, confusion and ruins!'

The war rhetoric had played out its part, like an exchange of insults before the gladiators' combat or the twirl of sabres before the duel.

Thiers appealed to God and History. He was not alone. Leaders on both sides had become convinced of their 'historical' role. Both sides predicted death. Did they know it would be, for the most part, death of the innocent, the inarticulate? Their rhetoric could hide the crime. One thinks of Creon threatening torture to a simple sentry, swearing in the name of Zeus, that if justice is not done, 'simple death will not be enough for you.'

When people hate with all that energy, it is something in themselves they are hating.

XXI

THE 'COMMUNE'. The word meant 'common' in Latin, in the sense that you might speak of the 'common good', the 'commonweal', the 'common service'. It meant a sharing, the end of separation, the eradication of wartime's isolation – a homecoming. The word also carried the implication of a deliverance from the alienation that poverty and the drudgery of menial labour had always entailed. France was divided into departments and communes, little family communities: 'The commune,' wrote Pierre Denis on 26 March on behalf of the Committee of the Twenty Arrondissements, 'is the base of any political state, just as the family is the embryo of all societies.' The 'Commune' also suggested freedom. Cities exempt from feudal obligations in twelfth-century France were known as *comugnes*. The municipal government of the *sans-culottes* of 1792 was called the 'Commune'. Solicitude and fellow-feeling, sublimity and a nostalgia for a golden past: the 'Commune' was all this. For the great leap forward, revolution, it seemed, first required a movement backwards into history several paces. 'On the aftermath of disastrous and bloody defeat,' Denis's manifesto went on, 'and following the punishment of seventy years of Empire, of Monarchy, of clerical, parliamentary, authoritarian and centralised reaction, a new era begins, bringing a return to the tradition of the ancient communes and the French Revolution.' The Commune would bring to the people 'independence, wealth, peaceful glory and love'.

It was an eight-week passion that devoured tens of thousands, especially the poor. They could see only what was good and beautiful. They obstinately ignored what was bad and ugly.

Tuesday, 28 March, was a day of consummation. Guns and carriages were arranged in rows parallel to the main entrance to the Hôtel de Ville. Behind them a wooden stage had been set up, covered with folds of scarlet cloth; on it, stood a long table provided with chairs for the three dozen members of the outgoing Central Committee, who arrived wearing the uniform of the Guard and red sashes lined in silver slung over their shoulders. The statue of Henry IV above the main gate was hidden behind red flags, while from a south-west sky an early spring sun beamed down on the assemblage, picking out details of green and blue dress and adding splashes of white to the grey silhouetted stone figures of the Hôtel's façade. There were perhaps as many as two hundred thousand present, cheering, screaming. Nobody would have heard Assi reading out the names of those elected. Bands blared out various versions of the *Marseillaise* and the *Chant du Départ*, drums rolled, cannon roared. 'In the name of the people,' shouted Ranvier, 'the Commune is proclaimed!' The crowd went mad. Battalions from Montmartre, Belleville and La Chapelle marched past in a rare moment of coordination, while strangers hugged, bearing the Committee's greeting of 'concord, union and love'. Parisians were exhausted of woe, yet hopeful.

That same day in Versailles, Louis de Saint-Pierre, deputy for La Manche, proposed that 'the National Assembly declares null and void the municipal elections, which took place in Paris on 26 March 1871 without a legal convocation of the voters, as well as all acts that have emanated and might emanate from a power that has usurped the national sovereignty.'

Seventy-five counts, dukes and marquis had signed it. It did not pass. But why worry? 'You don't need a declaration,' remarked a member from the Right. 'These elections are invalid by law!'

XXII

IT WAS, to put it mildly, a peculiar situation to be in. Whatever their differences, most supporters of the Republic by 1870 would have agreed that the vote was where the will of the people expressed itself best. And whether Jacobin, Hébertist, Revolutionary Socialist or simple parliamentarian, most of them had a vague sense that, once that will had been freely expressed, there would be peace. But national elections had created the Assembly at Versailles and municipal elections had created the Commune in Paris. Now there was civil war. Were these manipulated votes, as republicans had claimed of the Empire's plebiscites? Outside Paris and the other major cities the old political machinery of three kings and two emperors was restored, oiled and functioning; Gambetta's work was undone, Napoleon III's back in action. As Clemenceau remarked in mid-April, 'another general election would send us back an assembly worse than we've got now.' It was a calamity on both sides. 'The Assembly refuses our cities freedom, the Commune refuses us a programme, a flag or a goal that is either probable or even possible. We've said that Paris will rise to defend its rights and it has risen. Paris is morally standing. But what are they going to win with guns in their hands?' Emile Villeneuve, who had been deputy-mayor in the 17th arrondissement, was blunter. 'The Commune,' he said, 'is just a military force.'

Clemenceau's small circle of political friends had, of course, thrived in opposition to the powers that be and they certainly weren't going to let two elections, called in a moment of crisis, deter them. They had got the Parisian vote in October, and they had got it again in February. They were convinced that they were the ones who best represented the traditional republican virtues – justice, unity, peace, brotherhood. History was on their side. 'Our group' as an exuberant Allain-Targé had put it two years earlier, 'is the group which will govern the Republic.' They were as confident of that today. It was just a question of time. And of persuasion. The parliamentary Republic was never supposed to *conquer* power, to *force* its way up onto the stage. The intention had not been to direct men, and even less to subjugate them. The goal was to convince them. The victory was not to be won with guns, but with argument.

In February, Paris had sent forty-three deputies to the National Assembly. Six had resigned with the ratification of the peace preliminaries with Germany, of whom three (Gambon, Malon and Pyat) later took seats in the council of the Commune. Charles Delescluze and his journalist collaborator, Frédéric Cournet, did not resign until the end of March, when they too were elected to the Commune; but they never actually sat at Versailles. The parliamentary republicans (the term 'radical' was increasingly used) were virtually the only deputies left to represent Paris. But by April most of their leading speakers had also resigned. 'The greatest moral torment a man can suffer,' wrote Clemenceau a few weeks later, 'is to have to choose his line of conduct in some supreme crisis which demands an immediate decision, and not be able to see it clearly. In that respect, the torture of my last eight days in the National Assembly will never be surpassed.' Clemenceau resigned on 27 March.

The municipal elections in Paris of the preceding day had wiped out support for the radicals in all but the wealthiest arrondissements in the western part of the city. As for the 18th, of the 17,000 votes cast, Blanqui, who was once more in gaol, received nearly 15,000 and Simon Dereure had almost as many (voting was done by lists); Clemenceau obtained a derisory 752 votes, Jaclard and Lafont got about 500 each. Only nineteen moderates were elected to the Commune in contrast to sixty-five candidates put up by the Central Committee. The turnout had been good (except, again, in some of the western arrondissements). Paris had voted, in anger, against anyone affiliated with the provincials of Versailles.

So the parliamentarians had no parliament. A formula had to be devised. They would meet in private.

Up the flight of stairs to the landing, which served as a small vestibule where men's overcoats and top hats were left hanging, you would have paused a moment before proceeding onto the squeaking carpet that led to the huge high-ceilinged drawing room. War had had its effect here too: the place was not heated, no bouquet of flowers filled the Chinese vases, only the flame from the crystal chandeliers flickered on the faces of the dozen or so men drawn up together in straight armchairs; the floor and table lamps were unlit. Heavy curtains closed out the night air. The place befitted the anguish, the cold and masculine dignity of those forgathered, though there were objects around, unheeded signs – like the few sprigs of dried patchouli in a cup, or the three embroidered cushions – of the presence of a wife.

Their verbal battles were still in the service of eliminating great wrongs, but the wrongs had changed. Floquet told his guests that he had heard gunfire for the last three days; Passy was not too far from the first skirmishing points at Neuilly, Courbevoie and the rond-point de Bergères; the heavy artillery fire from Mont Valérien had made the windows chatter. Five Paris newspapers had been closed down by order of Raoul Rigault, councillor *près de l'ex-Préfecture de Police*, and more could be expected. But worse than all that was the sense of mounting violence in a fratricidal struggle that had no rules. There were rumours of summary executions, there was talk of reprisals, of hostage-taking.

Somehow, the gap between the two warring factions had to be bridged. Both sides had a claim to an electoral mandate or what was called in the day 'the authority of universal suffrage'. But then, as Floquet put it, the former mayors and deputies of Paris also had a mandate; they 'have done their duty and, having received only two months ago the honour of a hundred thousand votes, still have the right to represent Paris'. Everyone sitting there that evening agreed that the legality of these elections should not be made a stickling point. André Desonnaz, whose newspaper, *L'Avenir national*, was to become the mouthpiece for the group, remarked that 'at the present moment, nowhere – whether you're thinking of Paris or Versailles – is there legality in the ordinary sense of the word; there are only facts'. One shuddered at their possible consequences. 'Tomorrow, perhaps this evening, there will only be conquerors and the conquered. If Cathelineau, Vinoy or Valentin enter Paris as conquerors it would be not only the defeat of the Commune but of all citizens. It would be the defeat of all those who despise proscription and violence and the triumph of the reactionaries. It would establish the order of the last year of the Empire or, worse still, the order of the *Chambre introuvable* of 1816 – and we all know what that was. The success of the Commune, even if it were only a minor, relative success, would at least leave a chance for conciliation.'

The Commune was bad, but Versailles was worse, for the Commune had raised the great question that republicans had really not faced up till now: the authority of national universal suffrage meant the authority of reaction, monarchism, clericalism, militarism; it was the dominance of the rural vote over the urban vote. 'For the last twenty years, the rural populations, through a political mechanism, have annulled the influence of the towns and in the absence of all liberty, have oppressed the urban populations . . . For the next ten, fifteen or twenty years, up to the day that education has done its work of appeasement, one cannot count on a durable settlement. The chasm which separates the two parts in France, the urban or republican part and the rural or monarchist part, is too great to imagine it being filled in the near future.'

It was not a happy prospect for a group that was searching for an immediate ceasefire. 'History' again seemed to be set on a course for war. And once more, it was with an appeal to 'History' that these parliamentary republicans adopted their new cause of 'urban freedom', *les franchises municipales*. 'Paris wants the Republic,' said Desonnaz. 'It has wanted it since the days of the League. What is happening today is analogous to what happened nearly three hundred years ago, in 1592. Paris wants its municipal freedoms and no longer intends to be governed by Bretons and Vendéens.'

By the end of the evening, the group had put together a programme of three points that they forlornly hoped might square the circle and achieve some kind of reconciliation. Against the monarchist majority at Versailles, they demanded 'recognition of the Republic'. Against the rural vote, they demanded 'recognition of the right of Paris to govern itself'. Against militarism, they demanded that 'the security of Paris be confided in the National Guard, composed of all eligible voters'. They called their group the 'League of the Republican Union for the Rights of Paris'. Their programme appeared in the press the next day accompanied by twenty-five signatures, including, besides those of Floquet and Desonnaz, the names of Onimus, Lafont and Clemenceau – friends since student days.

XXIII

ANOTHER EARLY, albeit vague, acquaintance of Clemenceau was carving out a magnificent career for himself as a result of the war. Georges Boulanger, thirty-four, had been born in Rennes and attended the same lycée in Nantes as Clemenceau. They did not become close friends. In fact, about the only thing they had in common was that both their fathers, because of politics, had served time in the gaols of the Second Empire. The four years separating the two were, as schools go, enough to keep a distance between them; and while Clemenceau became a doctor, Boulanger chose soldiering. There was nothing, in 1871, that would have suggested that, fourteen years later, their lives would cross in the kind of conflux that fate, or the devil, arranges to spread trouble, woe and the gnashing of teeth.

Boulanger had fought in Italy, Algeria and China. When the Bonapartists governed he was a Bonapartist. When the Republic was proclaimed he became a republican. But the 'rights of Paris' were not going to stand between him and his career. In the new Army of Versailles Boulanger was promoted to colonel and received the command of the 114th regiment of the line.

Few were as eager to please their superiors as Colonel Boulanger. His opportunity came the day fighting broke out, on 2 April, near the Pont de Neuilly. It was, as Jules Simon described the engagement, 'an unforeseen accident', for neither army was anywhere near fit for combat. The National Guard of Paris, or the 'Fédérés' as they were now known, were as chaotic as ever. As for the new recruits of Versailles, they were indeed largely from rural areas; they were confused over the political issues, bewildered at the need to go on fighting after the war with Germany was over, and they wanted to go home. They opened fire on the Fédérés under the pistol points of their officers.

Boulanger's 114th was ordered in as a reinforcement. By the time they arrived the skirmish was over and the bridge had been captured. Boulanger took a few prisoners.

General Vinoy's instructions regarding the treatment of prisoners appeared in a circular two days later, though there is an indication that they had been passed on orally at an earlier date:

> To confirm my verbal instructions concerning prisoners ... I again request you to treat according to the laws of war, that is to say to execute immediately by firing-squad, all soldiers, *mobiles* or sailors taken in the ranks of the insurgents ... These men must be considered as deserters to the enemy and consequently shot on the spot. As for the others, they will be sent before the military tribunals.

Boulanger picked out five men – the supposed killer of the civil war's first victim (the chief surgeon to the Versailles army whom the Fédérés had mistaken for a general), a barber, two soldiers who had got mixed up with the wrong side and, for good measure, two National Guards – stood them in a field before all the other prisoners, and had them shot. 'I could not be more satisfied with the attitude and conduct of my regiment,' reported Boulanger back to Head Quarters. 'The promptness with which a platoon placed itself at my disposal to shoot five of the wretched murderers, whom we were holding, permit me to affirm that you can count on them [the regiment] always and everywhere.'

Boulanger's enthusiasm reached new heights the following day when, following the rout of the Commune's first (and last) expedition onto Versailles, the 114th was ordered to clear out 'General' Gustave Flourens' force from the village of Bougival. Out of the 1,400 troops under Boulanger's command, one was killed and two were wounded. The plea that Boulanger's regiment might have been acting under 'stress' runs a little thin. None the less, 'the soldiers searched the houses,' wrote the gleeful Boulanger, 'and shot every National Guard who was hidden.' The following morning Flourens and his faithful aide-de-camp, Amalcare Cipriani of Buzenval fame, were discovered by a company of *gendarmes*, denounced, it was said, by some villagers. Their commander cleft Flourens's head in two with a sabre and his body, along with Cipriani – shot but alive and blindfolded – was thrown onto a dung wagon and paraded through Versailles.

*

The rumour in Paris was spreading that the Versaillais had shot fifty, a hundred, even two hundred men in summary executions. War was up to its old tricks. Communications had been cut off. For one critical day life in the capital was as effectively blockaded as if a quilt of cold lead had descended on the city. The trains had been halted, the post was held up. 'One can't get out of Paris,' complained *L'Avenir national* on 4 April, 'and one can't get back in. Versailles for us is as far away as Calcutta.'

The next day the blockage partially cleared; the experience of the first siege was not to be repeated. But the damage had been done.

A measure was introduced into the council of the Commune that became known as the 'Law of Hostages'. It was inspired by the famous 'Law of Suspects' of 1793. 'Considering,' ran the preamble, 'that the government of Versailles tramples under foot the rights of humanity as those of war; that it is guilty of horrors that have not even befouled the invaders of French territory . . .' The text went on to declare that 'all persons accused of complicity with the government of Versailles shall be decreed accused and imprisoned; a jury of accusation shall be instituted . . ., the jury will pronounce judgment within twenty-four hours; all the accused detained by the verdict of the jury shall be the hostages of the people of Paris; for every execution of a prisoner of war or of a partisan of the legal government of the Commune will be immediately followed by the execution of three times the number of hostages . . .' Those to be executed were to be 'drawn by lot'. The bill was discussed on the night of 5 April and became law on the 6th.

'What,' asked Desonnaz in an editorial of the same day, 'does one mean by "complicity with the government of Versailles"?'

One Sunday afternoon late in April, as the violence mounted and the cruelties multiplied, Edmond Goncourt paid a visit to the offices of *Le Temps*. There he found the staff in great disarray because they couldn't agree on whose side they were on. He said it was like being in a ship's cabin out at sea. On leaving, he ran into 'some sort of half-breed. It was Doctor Clemenceau. One would have said one of those tawny doctors that Eugène Sue might have used in his novels.'

The atrocities of the new war – mild by twentieth-century standards – were something to which Victorian gentlemen were unaccustomed. Clemenceau was in the thick of it. He was probably near the point of exhaustion, an explanation of his looks that would not have entered Goncourt's rakish mind.

But the scene that Goncourt described at *Le Temps* was typical of the sort of situation in which the conciliators found themselves once civil war had broken out. They were not united. The *centre de ralliement* to which the former Paris deputies and mayors had appealed in March was never realised. *Le Temps*, which had been appealing for general re-elections since March, was, by the end of April, putting out two separate editions, one in Paris (which showed some sympathy for the Commune) and the other in Saint-Germain-en-Laye (which was solidly behind the Versailles government). One might have hoped that the considerable power that the liberal press had over public opinion in Paris would be channelled into some political party or association. That was obviously the League's hope. It had a programme and it also had good connections with the press and with politicians in Paris as well as in Versailles. Clemenceau's visit to *Le Temps* was undoubtedly part of an attempt to get the press to fall in behind the League. But the League was not alone. There were other groups with the same ambitions.

Why couldn't all these groups unite and make a joint stand for peace? There was no rational explanation. It was rather the atmosphere, the poisoned convictions and impressions – a culture, one could even have called it – that strengthened those who stood for war and weakened those calling for peace. Nobody would of course state publicly that they were against peace. The warmongers simply argued for a better peace: just over this hurdle, hang on, a few houses will be blown down, a few heads will fall, but after that you will enjoy a real peace. Heroism, courage, resolution – all these qualities seemed to belong to those in the forefront prosecuting the war. The conciliators appeared muddled, without direction and lacking in resolve and self-commitment. 'The solution,' said Clemenceau apologetically before the League on 16 April, 'is hardly heroic in appearance, but it is necessary, for the League can enter neither one camp nor the other.' Or again on 4 May, as both sides geared up for the final battle, with the Commune setting up a dictatorial 'Committee of Public Safety' and citizens fleeing the city: 'It is not only the timid who have left [as the members of the Committee assumed], the actions of the Commune have troubled the consciences of many.'

There were always private motives at work, if unconscious. Clemenceau, whom the minutes show to have been among the most important speakers at the League's daily sessions, was probably still trying to live up to his father's expectations. The list of 107 members included 'Clemenceau, père, propriétaire, 19 rue Capron' alongside 'Clemenceau, 19 rue Capron'. There is nothing to indicate that Clemenceau's father was even in Paris. But the presence of his name on a list implies that Clemenceau was speaking not just for himself, but for a father.

How difficult it was to be both neutral and heroic! Those old military 'heroes' of spring 1871 would curl their lips and wrinkle at that filthy word, 'conciliation'.

The programme! Clemenceau would return again and again to the fact that his party had a programme. The programme was proof that here, and here alone, were men of firm resolve, radical heirs of the Great Revolution. 'Our neutrality is only an *explanation*,' Clemenceau would say, 'we work, but we work for our programme.' It was on the basis of neutrality and their programme that the League refused to make any binding agreements with the other forces of conciliation within Paris. 'The freemasons' goal,' said Clemenceau referring to the other major parties, 'like the *Union syndicale*'s goal, though perfectly honourable, is not ours. It doesn't belong to us. We Radicals seek to let loose the opinion of the republican party. The freemasons have rallied to the Commune; that's their right. But we cannot allow it to be said that the acts of the Commune involve the republican party. The *chambres syndicales* act independent of us. That's their right. But we must follow our line.'

Everyone who was for peace in April followed their own line. In the important by-elections of 16 April, which involved thirty-two council seats (out of a theoretical total of ninety-two), the conciliators failed to produce a single electoral list. At the League, for instance, it was decided that, since the thirty-odd members present could not agree, campaigning would be left to individuals. The result was a massive rate of abstention. Over 90 per cent of the electorate failed to turn out in the 7th and 8th arrondissements. The abstention rate was 85 per cent in the 6th and the 10th. And this time abstention wasn't limited to the rich. Only a quarter of the electorate in the 18th, 19th and 20th arrondissements went to the polls. No amount of argument on the grounds of a departed bourgeoisie or of men gone off to battle can explain these high rates of abstention. The message was clear: Paris did not want war, the Commune had lost the support of a majority of its citizens. But because of division, obstinacy and a false sense of independence, the conciliators had failed to fill the vacuum. The members of the Commune showed awareness of their discomfort by publishing, two days *after* the elections, a programme. But it was too late and it was still too vague. 'The time for voting has passed,' remarked Arthur Arnoult, one of the more moderate councillors. The principal concern of the Commune was the prosecution of the war. So, in effect, Paris once more found itself with no representative government.

XXIV

THE LEAGUE had just one success. By the third week of April, the village of Neuilly, which had witnessed the first violence of the civil war, had been reduced to ruins. The trees had been felled, the streets torn up and bedding and furniture, robbed from what a month earlier had been elegant homes, were piled up in barricades. Many of the buildings had been turned into rubble; those that still stood had gaping holes as a result of shellfire or of soldiers and civilians battering out passageways not exposed to the constant gunfire in the streets. As always, it was the inhabitants who suffered the worst. The dead were not buried, while the living went underground; for days they lay cramped in cellars, without supplies, while an eternal rain of shot and shell fell outside.

The League first proposed a ceasefire at Neuilly on 16 April following an article in *Le Temps* which demanded negotiations for the evacuation of the inhabitants. They made steady progress until 20 April when the government at Versailles expressed the fear that, in agreeing to a ceasefire, it would in effect be recognising *ipso facto* the Fédérés as belligerents. This frightening prospect – recognition of the slightest humane traits in an enemy is always terrifying – was circumvented by an agreement that the League would itself present four envoys, two of whom would represent Versailles and two the Commune. The League thereupon designated Citizens Stupuy and Bonvalet for the Commune, and Citizens Floquet and Clemenceau for Versailles.

Clemenceau spent what must have been twenty-four hours of agony. He had been sceptical of the value of a negotiated ceasefire from the beginning. 'Thiers,' he had bitterly observed on 16 April, 'doesn't want a ceasefire. He's delighted with the bombardment. He hopes to intimidate the population and make them sick of the Commune. His greatest fancy is to see Parisians tearing themselves apart. As for the Commune, it should have thrown the blame of this criminal bombardment on Versailles. It could have been done. But then the Commune also wants to see its troops fighting every day so as to keep up their ardour.'

The Commune might have failed to make a propaganda coup out of the shelling. But Clemenceau was pretty certain what it (and the voters of the 18th arrondissement) would have to say about him if he started sitting in proxy for Versailles. There was only one way out: open negotiations, no secrets, no 'arrangements'. 'Republicans', he said on the 23rd, 'must not imitate the covert dealings of monarchic diplomacy.' The president called the question: 'Are there grounds for announcing in advance to the public the bases of negotiation by way of posters?' The 'nays' had it twenty-six to fifteen. Clemenceau's argument, though fervently republican, was not the sort of posture that would foster confidence between warring factions: it was a lesson he would learn in time. In an ensuing vote for new negotiators Clemenceau got the support of only one member and Floquet, still president, got two. The task of representing Versailles eventually went to Loiseau-Pinson and Armand Adam.

On Tuesday, 25 April, the guns fell silent. The accord limited the ceasefire to the western periphery of Paris, between porte Maillot and porte de Saint-Ouen, but in fact fighting stopped everywhere for a period of about twelve hours. By 9 a.m. a queue of carriages, carts and covered wagons laid on by the various ambulance services in the city, by several of the large stores (like Bon Marché), as well as by individuals, stretched from place de la Concorde to the Arc de Triomphe and beyond. *La France*, a conservative paper, found the spirit of the crowds on the Champs-Elysées comparable to those at the Longchamp horse races (though it noted the following day that most of these people were definitely not 'aristocrats'). The National Guards put sprigs of lilac in their barrels. Pedlars were at every corner selling wine and tobacco. A catastrophe nearly occurred because the Versaillais did not receive their orders to stop shooting until fifteen minutes after the nine o'clock deadline. Their last shell fell near the Arc de Triomphe where an enormous number of sightseers had gathered to inspect the ruins; it exploded in the *Château de l'Etoile*, an abandoned British beer shop.

The procession continued on to porte Maillot. But the fortifications there were in such a state of disrepair – the gun-holes on the ramparts blasted beyond recognition, fragments of iron railing scattered everywhere, the embankments ploughed up by shells – that the traffic had to be diverted to the porte des Ternes. Then they were held up because the National Guard refused to allow any man aged between eighteen and forty to leave Paris. One required a pass and these were distributed by members of the International at the Palais d'Industrie at the far end of the Champs-Elysées.

Getting into Paris was easier than getting out, so many of the refugees had to transport themselves and their belongings by foot. 'All along the avenue des Ternes,' it was reported in the *Echo du soir*, 'there is a procession of mattresses carried by their owners, of huge baskets borne by women crushed under the weight of their burden. Children follow nibbling pieces of bread.' These were not poor women. They wore clothes that 'though not tidy at least suggested they were well off.' But there was little wealth could do right now; they carried only what their arms and legs could bear. They moved in both directions. One lucky woman managed to get the local sewer collector to bring into Paris her jewels and silver.

The streets, outside and inside Paris, were still crammed with refugees, wagons and sightseers when the five o'clock deadline passed. The ceasefire was extended to eight.

Then a few shots were exchanged in Levallois and Neuilly, but not with nearly the same intensity as in the preceding days. On the boulevard Inkerman, where the Versaillais barricades were less than fifty metres from those of the Fédérés, there was no shooting at all, just a lot of yelling from side to side inviting the other to fire first.

But at about ten o'clock the night's silence was interrupted by dull blasts from the south west of cannon, rifle and the *mitrailleuse*. The following day Thiers announced that 'active operations' had begun. An army of over a hundred thousand men under the command of the legitimist, Marshal MacMahon, was moving on Paris. Their first objective: Fort Issy.

There was very little that the League could now do. A plan for a twenty-five-day ceasefire was announced, but the war had entered a new phase and neither side was going to climb down. The advantage was clearly with the Versaillais, but the Commune stood firm. On 2 May Clemenceau once more neatly summarised the predicament facing the League. Versailles, he said, was deaf to any appeal, while the Commune was foolishly obstinate. 'If the Commune could recognise its inferiority in the military situation, it could accept a re-election which would make it a real legal power. But we are far from that.'

Like Gambetta in October, the League pinned its last hope on an appeal to the provinces. A delegation was selected for the purpose. It included Corbon, Floquet, Villeneuve, Le Chevalier and Clemenceau. Again like Gambetta, they had to leave Paris in secrecy, though their preparations were hardly as elaborate. Clemenceau himself borrowed papers from an American and took a train to Saint-Denis. There he was stopped and questioned by a Versaillais officer. He replied, unruffled, indeed with measured charm, in English: the officer, somewhat perplexed, let him through.

From Saint-Denis he could look back at the summit of Montmartre, bathed in sunlight. 'They are going to shoot all my constituents,' he said to himself. 'But I can't, for all that, let my name bear the blame.'

XXV

FORT ISSY finally fell on 9 May. Fort Vanves fell on the 13th – though not entirely, from the Versaillais perspective, with glory: one commander reported being 'extremely dissatisfied with the manner in which duties are performed in the 114th,' Boulanger's brigade. Looting and summary executions (but not rape) invariably followed each victory. The way was open to Paris.

'*L'homme est un méchant animal,*' said Molière. He might have been more accurate if he had just said '*méchant*'; animals don't kill their own kind as do men. Estimates of the total slain in the last two weeks of May and early June 1871 range between fifteen and thirty thousand; the actual number was probably closer to the latter. More died in those few weeks than in the entire 'Reign of Terror' of 1793–4, than in 1830, than in 1848; more than in the October coup in Petrograd in 1917. If the sentiment of observers at the time was that civilisation had just stepped back into an age of barbarians (Schœlcher said that France had regressed four thousand years) there was also, in the deliberate manner in which wholesale murder was conducted – before the eyes of generals and those who could have stopped it – an augury of human crimes as yet unimaginable. On the last day of May, for instance, Goncourt entered in his diary his chilling passage:

> It is good. There was neither conciliation nor transaction. The solution has been pure force. The solution has backed souls away from cowardly compromise. The solution has renewed confidence in the army which has learnt in the blood of the *communeux* that it is still capable of fighting. Finally, the bleeding has been a bleeding white; and a bleeding like this, by killing off the combative element of a population, adjourns conscription for the new revolution. It is twenty years of rest that the old society has before it if the power dares all that it can dare at this moment.

Men queued up to die. The 'solution' was carried out in the gardens of the 16th arrondissement, in private courtyards; the parc Monceau on the second day of the Versaillais' entry was turned into a prison compound where thousands were probably executed. So too were Montparnasse, the Luxembourg Gardens, the court of the yet unfinished Opera house, the Buttes-Chaumont, La Roquette, Mazas and the Père Lachaise cemetery. Within hours of the capture of Montmartre, forty-two men, three women and four children were rounded up and forced to kneel before the same courtyard wall where Lecomte and Thomas were killed. After several hours in that position they were all shot. The Théâtre du Châtelet was used as a collecting point for prisoners before they were transferred in batches of fifty to the Caserne Lobeau, opposite the Hôtel de Ville. There, out of concern that the executioners might be hurt by bullets ricocheting from the rough stone walls, the prisoners were herded into the centre of the barracks' yard and fired on as they ran.

Adolphe Thiers entered Paris on Monday, 22 May, to visit General MacMahon at his new Head Quarters in the rue Franklin, near the Trocadéro. According to his memoirs, on his return to Versailles that evening he crossed, in what was left of the 'bois' de Boulogne, a convoy of prisoners. There were 'men and women of all ages dressed in the strangest costumes'. Their faces, he said, still had the look of 'the fury of the struggle, the despair of defeat. Ruins and hatred! That is all that civil strifes leave.' He then wrote, perhaps out of pity in the memory, what must be the closest account he ever gave of his role in the slaughter of May and June: 'I gave strictest orders that the anger of the soldiers be contained and the marshal [MacMahon], on his side, did all he could to prevent the flow of blood.' No such order, no letter, no telegram, not a single document exists to support such a claim. The sound of the executions could be heard over all Paris. Some of the killings might have been carried out, literally, in MacMahon's own back yard by, it was said, an old gendarme with a pistol. What are known are Thiers' words to the National Assembly that same Monday: 'Expiation will be complete. It will take place in the name of the law, by the law and within the law.' He repeated this two days later.

The battle itself lasted eight long days. The rabble of volunteers, peasant recruits, gendarmes and sailors, otherwise known as the Army of Versailles, entered Paris on Sunday, 21 May, after being tipped off by one of General Douay's paid agents that nobody was guarding the bastions between the porte d'Auteuil and the Point du Jour. By the following morning most of the 16th arrondissement, the 15th and half of the 7th arrondissement were occupied. The only fighting up to that point had been a brief skirmish with a handful of Dombrowski's Fédérés on a railway viaduct that paralleled the ramparts of the Point du Jour. The strategically placed Trocadéro Palace with its battery of cannon was surrendered in the night without a struggle. Most of Monday was spent manœuvring into positions ready for the assault on Montmartre the next day. The advance was deliberately slow. One of the reasons why the battle lasted so long was that the generals still had little confidence in the loyalty of their own troops: even a slight setback could have been catastrophic. In the meantime, hundreds of barricades started going up in the eastern half of Paris. The first summary executions inside the city were conducted by troops under General Cissey's command at the caserne de Babylone. One could hardly have blamed this on the 'fury' of the troops for they had seen, as yet, virtually no action.

But the 'bleeding white' began on Tuesday.

The Versaillais strategy was simple. Frontal attacks on enemy positions were to be avoided. The army would outflank them. Only the most reliable troops were to be used in the first strikes; they were usually the volunteers who came under the command of low-ranking officers charged with the detail of combat. It was not the fighting troops who were to perform the task of 'disarming' the population. The first arrivals generally treated the population very mildly, though there were exceptions; troops under the command of Colonel Boulanger and General Bocher launched a savage little war in the Montparnasse quarter and, later, in the slums of the 13th arrondissement. But in most cases the summary executions were carried out by troops that were moved into an area once the fighting was over. Two groups earned quite a distinction in the searches, the arrests and the killings: the special police detachments (under the direct command of superior officers) and the 'National Guard of Order' (Guards opposed to the Commune who had a special incentive for vengeance).

By contrast, the Commune had no strategy at all and very few troops available for combat. On paper, the National Guard of Paris numbered between a quarter and half a million. Thirty or even forty thousand men might have participated in the *sortie* of 3 April. But after that fiasco there was massive desertion. Cluseret and Gaston da Costa, in separate accounts, estimated that in the last weeks of April only six or seven thousand men could be mustered for combat outside the city walls (another indicator of the degree to which support for the Commune was slipping). More would have participated in the fighting once the Versaillais had entered Paris, but the great *levée en masse*, which had been the dream of the Jacobin Majority, certainly never took place. Delescluze's famous call for arms – 'The hour of revolutionary war has sounded . . . the people do not fear all the strategists of the monarchic school' – brought forward perhaps ten thousand, but not more.

Not a shot was to be fired, for example, from the Buttes Montmartre. A few rounds from the Moulin de la Galette were fired into the dozen or so defenders that happened to be gathered in the Montmartre cemetery on Monday afternoon. Fortunately the guns were soon silenced for the very simple reason that they were buried in earth; nobody had thought of building gun platforms.

That same Monday, Delescluze delegated to Arthur Arnoult the responsibility of organising the defence of both Les Batignolles and Montmartre. Wearing a red scarf and armed with a revolver he set off down the *boulevards extérieurs* in the direction of the gunfire. Soon he found himself confronted with a line of Versaillais. He covered his scarf and revolver with his cloak and ran to a neighbouring chemist's shop where he lay hidden for two days. He spent his next ten years studying Buddhism in Switzerland.

The task then fell on General Napoleon François La Cecilia, a former philosophy student and master of Asiatic languages. He got as far as the barricade, held by about a hundred men, on the corner of the rue du Porte-de-Saint-Ouen and avenue Clichy. It was two o'clock, Tuesday morning. After a brief discussion with the defendants, he climbed the hill to Montmartre where he spent the early morning hours – 'pale and determined' as Louise Michel described him – wandering between one empty committee office and another trying to get information on the hill's defence. Finally he bumped into Louis Henri Moreau, known as *le vieux* Moreau, of the Vigilance Committee, who told him that the men of the artillery had panicked and that most of the remaining Guards had thrown away their rifles (those who had them) and had gone home to change into civilian clothes. So La Cecilia went into hiding, and spent a subsequent ten years of teaching Chinese in London.

That morning an entire division of Versaillais was descending on Montmartre from the *north east*, having completed another flanking operation. They received a few pot shots from buildings scattered in the still rural parts of La Chapelle and Clignancourt, but the way was effectively open to the summit. Louise Michel recounts how she, *le vieux* Moreau and a few Fédérés planned on blowing up the Buttes the previous evening. The operation had apparently partly succeeded, for an omnibus full of explosives was found by the Versaillais parked at the corner of rue des Abbesses and place de la Mairie. In the meantime, Louise Michel was carrying out the defence of Montmartre virtually single-handed. She had marched from the mairie with about fifty men. By the time she got to the cemetery she had only about fifteen left. There she found another fifteen. 'We were getting fewer and fewer; we retreated onto the barricades, they were still holding.' With the red flag at their head, seven women, including Michel, took up positions at barricades on place Blanche. Dombrowski passed by on a horse. 'We are lost!' he cried. 'No!' retorted Michel. They touched hands and Dombrowski rode off to death. For a while Louise Michel and two men held on to a barricade blocking the chaussée Clignancourt, but she too eventually went into hiding.

Michel was less lucky than Arnoult and La Cecilia. She was to surrender herself in exchange for her mother, who had been taken prisoner, and was deported to New Caledonia in 1873. She remained there seven years.

Besides the exploits of Louise Michel, there were pockets of fighting in the low-lying populated areas to the south and east of the Buttes. But there was nothing which could excuse the butchery that followed.

More sinister still were the indications that counter-revolution, imported by the Versaillais, was catching. Most arrests were made on the basis of denunciations, an activity of course applauded by the revolutionary clubs, but an activity which could in a moment turn against them. This undoubtedly happened. However, what took place in May and June was not just a question of political revenge. The people were poor, they had been hungry and they were bitter – these were essential ingredients for denunciation, for getting back at a neighbour.

There was probably no gentler revolutionary in 1871 than Eugène Varlin. Lissagary recounts that after his arrest on Sunday, 28 May, on place Cadet he was dragged through the crowd filling the streets that led to the 'expiation' centre of the rue des Rosiers: 'Under the hail of blows his young pensive head was turned to hashed flesh; an eye hung from its socket. When he arrived at rue des Rosiers, the army headquarters, he no longer walked, he was carried. They sat him down in order to shoot him. Soldiers smashed his body with their rifle butts.' According to the official report: 'The crowd that had accompanied and had recognised the ex-minister delegate of the Commune, numbering three to four thousand, as well as a large amount of people from the neighbourhood of the Buttes-Montmartre, witnessed the execution, approving of it with their "bravos".' Now, who was to blame?

*

Images, a taste, a smell, rather than a consciousness of class or of a sense of playing part in some major event, were what haunted most who remembered the great upheaval of 1870–71. The analysis came later. Those who were mere infants remembered hunger. Those who were children remembered the shock of death, the sight of a body in a street, bloodstains on a sheet. For anyone over ten it was the fright of violence, the fear of dying. For a few very young men, the war and the Commune marked the beginning of a political career. For others, it was the beginning and the end.

But of all the ordeals it was that terrible week in May which impressed memories most. A succession of freak weather patterns, combined with the havoc of battle, made Paris really feel for a moment like hell on earth.

On Monday and Tuesday it was unusually warm for the season. The sun made the naked streets shimmer and created a sense of blight in the air; thin phantoms of men in red trousers slipped seemingly effortlessly from a farside corner; long minutes of breathless silence only made the sounds, when they came, more violent; a soldier's orders would echo down lanes and alleys; the Guards' *tabatière* rifles exploded like cannon.

And the fire. Nobody knows how, why or when it began; but the preceding days' heat had turned buildings to tinder. On Tuesday evening the rue de Rivoli, from place de la Concorde to the Louvre, was a tunnel of flame. Men scurried like black ants in a temper. What was the use of buckets of water? Even when the Versaillais came in with their pumps the hungry tongues of flame, panting out clouds of black flinder, proved insatiable. In a huge explosion the high dome of the Tuileries palace crumbled and disgorged fire from its centre. The city was steadily eaten. Before dawn both banks of the Seine were burning, as if the river itself had caught alight. Wednesday brought new fires, the most tragic being at the Hôtel de Ville. Its elaborate outer walls would not yield at first, but the flames chewed, chewed and chewed again at the hidden wooden beams; struts of metal buckled and glowed; the fire made quick meal of a hundred thousand books.

For nearly two days a pall of smoke hung over every district in Paris while an easterly wind carried to the richer quarters a shower of burnt paper, falling like little grey flakes of snow. On Thursday the wind turned to a gale. On Friday it rained. On Saturday it deluged.

The fighting finished on Whit Sunday. Delescluze was dead. Millière was dead. So were about three thousand Parisians. But the slaughter had only just begun.

Sunday ended with one of those evenings when, as so often happens after heavy rain, a brilliant sun appeared. Its rays first touched the grey mansard roofs, turning them to silver; then a brick, then a shutter. The long row of windows was soon a chain of a hundred gleaming diamonds. A chimney, in an instant, became a burning ruby and then, with an anger – no, a sadness – gave it up, lost it all, just a chimney pot again.

'*Je regarde le ciel du côté où je sens Paris,*' wrote Vallès. '*Il est d'un bleu cru, avec des nuées rouges. On dirait une grande blouse inondée de sang.*'

CHAPTER FIVE

Democracy

I

THE SMALL clinic in the rue des Trois Frères had been opened, under the mayor's initiative, during the siege. Its location was decided by the hazard of available space in a moment of need. A typical building on a typical street: the alternating pattern of wall and window, the identical ledges, the slatted shutters (on that side a woman leaned out to shake a blanket, on this there was the grating of a curtain being drawn) somehow lent unity, even a sense of blandness, to the surrounding urban landscape, though it would vanish the instant one glanced upward to the torn summits of brick, slate, lead and zinc silhouetted against a band of blue sky. Every century had its monument on rue des Trois Frères and, like almost anywhere else in Paris, the way each one of them blended into the lines and spaces that followed the curve of the street up the hill evoked the genius of unknown architects. One-storey buildings – former farmhouses – were set side by side six-storey apartment dwellings which themselves towered over the small hotel, the hostel for migrants.

On the balcony above *L'Eléphant blanc*, the bistro, two cats basked in the limp air of late mid-morning, their ears acock.

And there it was, between two rickety eighteenth-century store-fronts, on a door of equally unhappy condition: 'Dr Georges Clemenceau, Sundays and Wednesdays, 9 o'clock to 11'. The sign remained there for fifteen years.

A long dark corridor led you to a courtyard of about five or six square metres, opposite which was a second corridor that plunged into shadow. The entry of the latter served as a 'waiting-room' and a few chairs had been placed there for the purpose. A couple of tricolour flags, crossed, were fixed to the wall. On the right side of the courtyard, as you entered, were two doors and a window. One of the doors opened up to a kitchen, which had been converted into a secretary's office, while the other, whose window panes had been replaced with a sheet of cardboard daubed in black paint, led into the consulting room. It was sparsely furnished. Five engravings hung from the walls of peeling canary-yellow paper (decorated with pale flowers). On the desk of stained oak lay a bronze inkpot and goose's feather, a medical dictionary and a few journals. On the shelf above were some instruments – a spatula, a pair of forceps, some lancets, a few Pravaz syringes – along with a white ceramic pot of Blancard's pills (for anaemia and rickets), a bottle of Defresne's cod-liver oil and an emergency supply of valerian and camphor. The doctor had provided himself with a mahogany armchair while the patients were left with chairs with woven straw seats. A cast-iron stove was to be found in one corner of the room, its piping loosely fastened to the wall by two or three bits of wire. A curtain, held up by string, hung in such a way that only half the window looking out onto the courtyard was covered. The whole clinic was pervaded by the smell of a neighbour's cooking.

Doctors were rare in Montmartre. Democracy was never to be a guiding principle in the distribution of the nation's health care. The official figures for the year 1906 indicate that of the 3,342 doctors working in the capital, only three practised in the 18th arrondissement. The situation couldn't have been much better in the 1870's. However the numbers were only vaguely indicative of what was really going on. Many doctors were never officially registered and several weren't even qualified to practise. Clemenceau's own qualifications were dubious. Since he had never succeeded in getting an internship the only practical training he had had was in the dressing of wounds and the emptying of bedpans.

That didn't worry his patients. They started to arrive at around eight and by ten the queue had filled the 'waiting-room', the courtyard, the first corridor and stretched some way down the street.

A stranger passing by, on perceiving how terribly ordinary they all looked, might have muttered to himself, 'Nothing can have happened in this place in the last hundred years. Catastrophe? Mass murder? Not here!' and wandered onward indifferent. They certainly didn't look like revolutionaries and bandits. And, if the truth were known, the fight had gone out of them. Now the matter in hand was the daily struggle for survival, the pain, the boredom of unrelenting dull labours. The harsh reality of yesterday would be the harsh reality of tomorrow.

It was almost a relief to be a part of the queue. One spoke with quiet voices of neighbourhood rumour and scandal, of the price of foodstuffs which went up and the price of those which went down. Laughter was restrained. Most were silent.

Several were old – characters who could have appeared in Daumier's sketches, with pointed chins and noses, their faces wrinkled, the women dressed in black and cloaked in woollen shawls, the men broken by work, ruined, humiliated, whose worn-out jackets, either too large or too small, added one final touch to their obscure existence. But there were also the young, too many young.

They coughed, they spat. Every disease rehearsed in the books could be found in that queue: typhlitis, gastritis, enteritis, bronchitis. There were nephritic colics and hepatic colics, syphilitics and apoplectics. There were young women with chlorosis (the green sickness) and old men who were bilious. But it was consumption (phthisis, tuberculosis) which marked out the vast majority of the sick (as much as a third or even a half of their number), and it was consumption which killed. 'There was hardly room for laughter in that procession of human miseries,' wrote Clemenceau some years later. 'I saw there, in the space of a few years, all that can be seen of ill health, of mean suffering.'

If disease was a misfortune for the rich it was a disaster for the poor for there was nothing to cushion the blow to the family of the labouring man who fell sick. Occasionally a relative would come to the clinic and ask Clemenceau to make a house call. He would do it, though it brought him little personal fulfilment. 'These were irksome tasks, these visits to the worst quarters of the Butte, these trips, however brief, into the unhealthy cells of those foul hives into which were crammed, among miasmas emanating from all forms of rubbish, so many working families, families who would only leave the germs of death of their workshops for the infection of their appalling homes.'

There were other tasks, too. Clemenceau was not only a doctor and the queue contained not only the sick. 'There came the sick,' as Clemenceau put it, and 'there came the petitioners. Sometimes the two types came together in the same person.' Hawkers, wheedlers, fiddlers and dealers; relatives appealing for a deportee, petitioners for a friend's release, supplicants for labour, applicants for some bureaucratic post, however menial. It could get confusing. A reporter from the *Figaro*, visiting the clinic in 1879, said that Clemenceau would greet his patients in the most friendly fashion, looking rather like a jovial monk with his closely cropped greying hair, his sharp eyes and dark moustache. 'When you have seen him in his office, attentive, affable, ready and aimiable, one wonders how such a man could have ideas which frighten certain people.' None the less he was often obliged, in the four hours each week that he was available, to take more than one patient at a time. On one occasion a man came into his office and, on seeing two pale-looking characters already undressed, started stripping himself. Clemenceau turned to the third man, who looked perfectly fit but with trousers down at his ankles, and asked, 'Well, monsieur, what can I do for you?' 'I want a job at the post office,' he replied.

*

Clemenceau carried out his medical activities, marginal as they were in terms of his time and interest, during a period when the theme of the *médecin-prêtre*, the 'doctor-priest', was current, particularly within the republican elite. It formed, in fact, an integral element of the anti-clerical philosophy that developed during the first decades of the new Republic.

Like a priest, a doctor's vocation was ideally a mission and his consulting room was a confessional where he heard those accursed of disease and provided his blessing. Like a priest, a doctor was a protector of the poor and the weak, and his services were, ideally, too precious to be given a monetary value. In fact, he was a redistributor of wealth for, like the priest collecting alms from the rich, he would take as much as he could from the wealthy while providing his services free to the poor. But in the historical schema that the republicans propounded salvation lay with the doctor, not the priest, because his life work was in the service of science, not God, and his paradise was here on earth, not in heaven; his devotion was to the modern idea that sickness was a human disaster which could be cured and prevented by medicines, not divine intervention.

Clemenceau's clinic was a token to this belief. It brought him a moderate income – between June and December 1871 he earned 1,900 francs in medical fees. But, more importantly, it lent substance to his democratic republican principles (his patients were his constituents) and helped mark out the political task before him. Whether he was actually practising medicine or just writing and speaking about it, this lay philosophy was always behind his thoughts, justifying him, enkindling him. The philosophy he had developed as a medical student he had picked up from his doctor father and the positivists, and now he saw himself acting on it. A doctor served in the public interest, a priest did not.

Though not visible to the passing stranger, to those with money 'who live among themselves', there was real suffering now. The repression of the Commune had brought an uneasy, phoney peace to the people of the 18th arrondissement. After so many declarations of rights and so many broken promises the long days of work at a pittance, their sordid condition, seemed a foul reward. False intents, false hopes. A revolution unaccomplished. Would it ever be?

The peace of today was a peace sealed in oblivion. True, there was no more killing. The slaughter had ended. But as the good doctor put it, unrestrained murder had merely yielded to the numb pain of incessant exploitation; 'one no longer kills a man with a single blow, one uses him, one wears him out.'

With the violence of revolution exhausted, men returned to ruse and fraud to earn a place on the greasy pole, leaving beneath a residue of beggars whose sole social function was to obtain grace and eternal happiness for those generous beasts above them. An eternity for the winners.

In other words, the world was much the same as ever. This northern corner of Paris, forgotten, was a fair example of the kind of perpetual struggle – the social fray or *la mêlée sociale*, as Clemenceau called it – that characterised life down here on earth. It had no preordained purpose or direction. It was a choiceless absurdity which precipitated a sort of 'chlorosis' of the human race – a lack of sympathy, a shortage of meaningful action, where daily life went on in an uncaring environment; a soulless place on an indifferent planet circling in a deaf universe, watching, watching a dozen seasons pass.

'We are born of the earth and we return to the earth; that's the law of life,' reflected Clemenceau in a typical phrase. 'Plunged into matter, inert, we borrow all elements of action from it and we render it back, up to the final settlement of accounts.' Life was the loan, death the repayment. What mattered was how one spent it. Clemenceau's notion of the role of human will-power was more sophisticated than generally thought. It was a commitment to life. If you want meaning, you have to create it. If you want beauty, you have to live it. And if it is victory over the unbeatable forces of cruelty that you seek, think, do it willingly, be consciously aware of the unconscious fatality of the things which they press down on you. Clemenceau could turn again to that unconventional Catholic, Pascal, who said, 'If the universe crushes me, I have one advantage over it: for I know that it crushes me and the universe knows nothing.'

In a sense, Clemenceau's medical practice in the 18th arrondissement could be compared to that of another Pascal, Emile Zola's Doctor Pascal. Clemenceau must have known that four hours a week of consultation (much of it political) with a fragment of his constituents was not going to change the general course of biological wellbeing in the capital, let alone the universe. But like Doctor Pascal he believed that there was only one divine manifestation on this earth and that was life. And the key to life was biology. However, since knowledge of biology was incomplete, explanations and cures could only be of fleeting value. The medical practitioner would be in constant anxiety, confronted with diseases he could not cure and medicines which changed with every new hypothesis. The important thing was to have been an active participant in the one area where one really could speak of progress, the science of life.

For these scientists disease was everywhere. Indeed disease was in the nature of man and could be traced to his 'savage' origins, the brutal beast blind to science and reason and tied to his base instincts of lust, murder and destruction. Science and reason had curbed the beast within man. But put him in a crowd and he is overcome by what Taine had already identified as 'the laws of mental contagion'; he reverts to savagery. Clemenceau's own account of the Commune shows that he was at least influenced by such opinion. He speaks of the crowds of 18 March as pathological, 'letting out the cries of wild animals, not fully aware of what was going on', their 'frenetic state', a form of 'atavism' that reminded him of 'those hysterical phenomena that occurred so often in the middle ages'. After the trauma of the Commune the open violence of the poor gave way, observers thought, to a profounder form of savagery, a latent trait of morbid origin entrenched in the heart of those who laboured, a rage which could erupt whenever the occasion arose and thus a constant threat to those with wealth and property to defend.

Clemenceau had very little sympathy for the likes of Taine, who had used this theme to condemn the French Revolution, and probably never read Espinas or Tarde, who became the principal exponents of the idea in France before the appearance of Gustave Le Bon's *Psychology of Crowds* in the 1890's. In Clemenceau's case, the natural savagery and base barbarisms of man were more part of an attitude than of a systematic theory to counter Rousseau's noble primitive. It pointed to a certain contempt he felt for his fellow beings and dampened his none the less genuine sense of pity and altruism. 'One lives surrounded by filthy beasts,' he would say.

The healing process would have to begin at once. A plural democracy, led by enlightened men of science untainted by mysticism and religion, would encourage the rational and creative side of the individual; it would arm him against the savage crowd and liberate him from his own low origins. To live, to will, to choose – those were the freedoms the lay Republic offered to its thirty million citizens. Life from nothingness, choice from where there was none; it was a variant of spontaneous generation. Even if fate had designated total destruction, if every thought, every conscious act of creation were destined for annihilation, at least those who chose that freedom and had exercised that will could reach out for the one miracle surging from the desperate void: a new life.

II

BUT THERE was nothing much new about the national affairs of post-war France. The elections of February 1871 had created an assembly in which the monarchists outnumbered the republicans by roughly two to one. What a parliament it was! There were the de Tocquevilles, La Rochefoucaults, de Noailles and de Broglies. There was a Casimir-Périer and a Casenove de Pradines. Guizot was there and so was Anisson-Duperron. Even princes sat among them: d'Aumale and de Joinville. By-elections the following July did somewhat reduce the imbalance and brought in a number of men of the liberal professions committed to the Republic (including doctors whose number was three times that found in the Second Empire's Corps législatif). Clemenceau remarked glowingly at the time that 'the Republic is saved: provincial opinion has not been frightened'. Perhaps not frightened; but the work for republicans would have to begin in the lowermost roots of rural France, a work for local electoral committees in competition with the notables, the landowners, the *hobereaux* for the peasant vote. Even in the towns the task was formidable. The abstention rate was high. Interest vacillated. A painting of an electoral meeting in Paris, which hangs in the Palais de Luxembourg, shows five scruffy looking gentlemen seated at a long table looking down on a medley assembly of men and women dressed in round hats, square hats, oval hats and flat caps. Is any one of them listening? The five secretaries scribbling on a small wooden table in the foreground, all in top hats and dark grey overcoats, seem oblivious to both speaker and crowd.

Given the circumstances, Adolphe Thiers, 'President of the Republic' after August 1871, did a remarkably good job. The German occupation forces were evacuated ahead of schedule. Bismarck had asked for a five billion franc war indemnity. Obviously the Chancellor had not taken into account the evolution of banking since the occupation of 1815; it was paid off in a little over two years. The last German troops to leave French soil belonged to a Prussian regiment posted in the fortress city of Verdun – their children would see the irony of that.

On the question of military reform everyone agreed that the old authoritarian model of an army of long-serving professionals cut off from civilian life was no longer effective. Everyone, that is, except Thiers; Thiers as a young man had played a major role in the creation of the professional army. The army law of July 1872 therefore had to be a compromise. It established the principle of universal conscription: 'Every Frenchman is obligated to military service.' But the nation didn't have the means to support universal service for five years. So the drawing of lots was maintained: losers would serve five years, winners would serve one (which in practice became six months of 'basic training'). The system of buying a replacement – the 'blood tax' – was abolished. But, to make the bourgeois happy, one could avoid the five-year service by volunteering one month before call-up and, at the modest price of 1500 francs for 'clothing and equipment', serve only one year. In brief, the reform was hardly a reform at all.

*

The Germans gone, the army 'reformed' – that was enough from Monsieur Thiers. In May 1873 the monarchist assembly overthrew him. The new regime, under the presidency of Marshal MacMahon (his ancestors were Irish), described itself as the *Ordre moral*, though it neither showed order, nor much morality. Even if it had succeeded in placing the fat, hairy and lazy Henri de Bourbon, comte de Chambord, on the throne it is difficult to see how all the various factions of monarchism and Catholicism, in the assembly and across the country, could have remained united for long. There might have been another civil war. There almost certainly would have been another upheaval along the lines of 1830 or 1848.

None of this happened. The conservative majority dissolved into its own cauldron of factiousness, vendetta and acrimony. Finally, in January 1875, a republican deputy moved that 'the government of the Republic is composed of two chambers and a president'. The motion was defeated by 359 votes to 336. The next day a Catholic professor, Wallon, moved that 'the legislative power is exercised by two assemblies, the Chamber and the Senate' and that 'the president of the Republic is elected by the Senate and the Chamber'. The motion passed with 353 votes against 352.

Thus the French Republic was established by a majority of one vote. The dream of generations had become a reality because its opponents had been unable to come up with anything better.

Two houses and a president? It was not what most parliamentary republicans wanted and it was a far cry from what the proponents of 'direct democracy' had demanded. The Republic of 1792, like that of 1848, had only one house and the executive had been in the hands of a committee. A president nominated for seven years and – in the lovely phrase of the day – 'irresponsible' to parliament, smelt too much of first consuls, emperors and kings. And if universal suffrage was really the guiding principle of the regime, why have a Senate with one quarter of its members irremovable and the rest elected not by the people but by an electoral college made up of one delegate per commune, the parliamentary deputies and local council members?

It had been a compromise. '*Il faut sérier les problèmes*,' said Gambetta – 'you have to place your problems in good order.' Don't imagine you can have democracy in one fair swoop. Gambetta practised the art of the possible. The essence of Gambetta's campaign was to make the villages and hamlets republican, and this, by 1875, was already becoming a reality. Posing as friends of order who had mastered Parisian rebellion on one side and held off monarchist agitators on the other, republican candidates had made steady progress in many of the most rural parts of the country.

The charge of 'revolutionary' could exclude one from political life in the early 1870's. Across the country 'Conservative Republicans'[1] attacked the 'fraudulent conservativism' of the monarchist candidates, the 'Monarchist Revolutionaries' – the 'wild white revolutionaries'. The label stuck. In the backcountry of Provence, across the plains of Lower Languedoc, up the valley of the Rhône and the Saône into the heartland of rural Burgundy came the votes for the Republic, accompanied by a slighter echo through Flanders, Picardy and the hills of Upper Normandy.

But in the traditional heart-land of the Revolution there was silence. The abstention rate in the Paris by-elections of July 1871 – the slaughter just ended, the mass condemnations hardly begun – reached nearly 40 per cent.

How do you interpret silence? The violence of May was supposed to be a confirmation of legitimate governmental authority, a transformation of whole segments of a population into objects of calculation and control. But all it had achieved was estrangement, a withdrawal of opinion, indifference, apathy. There were no doors and windows to their souls. The exercise of authority had lost its purpose. The subjects of the sovereign had fallen mute.

'The silence of the peoples', it was said at Louis XV's funeral, 'is the lesson for kings.' 'If the silence of peoples is the lesson for kings,' pondered Henri Rochefort in the last years of the Second Empire, 'the resignation of the condemned is the lesson for the accuser.' There was censure and there was repression during those years, but the people had not been silent. Now they were: Paris presented a new problem: the government had stifled the clamours but how could it avenge silence? The état de siège in the city was suspended only in 1876. The prime minister had revived the press laws of the Empire, he had forbidden marches and processions, he had even re-established the old royalist law of lèse majesté. But what was the point if the people, anyway, said nothing? The by-elections of July 1871 had in Paris brought in the Moderates. For once, Paris was no longer the advance guard of the Republic. Many of the political men of the Extreme Left were forced either to run for a provincial constituency or to make do with a position in the emasculated Paris municipal council.

Georges Clemenceau was one of them. In the July by-elections he was a candidate in the list sponsored by Gambetta's Republican Union. He received only twenty thousand votes, seventy thousand short of what was needed to get elected; he was considered too revolutionary. He also tried to stand as a Radical in Nantes, but the local militants refused to select him; he was regarded as too entangled with the Versaillais conservatives.

[1] For a schematic presentation of French political groups and parties between 1871 and 1920 see the Appendix.

Finally at the end of the month he ran for the Paris municipal council where he got elected for Clignancourt, a Montmartre constituency, with a meagre 1659 votes; three out of every four of those eligible to vote had abstained.

Clemenceau's work within the council, where he remained for the next four and a half years, was not insignificant. In fact it tied in well with his functions as a doctor on rue des Trois Frères. He called attention to the lack of space in hospitals, the need to isolate women after childbirth, the frightful conditions of 'overcrowded' cemeteries. He tried to unknit the bureaucratic knots that prevented war indemnities from getting to the poor. He had an intense interest in child abandonment, the problem of unwed mothers and the continuing increase in infant mortality – he was one of the few people publicising this last fact, though it had been one of the major consequences of the siege. He was concerned with education. Spend your money on schools and foster homes, he said, not on rebuilding churches.

He impressed his colleagues, most of whom were Radicals like himself. From secretary he advanced to vice-president and, after Charles Floquet resigned, became himself president of the council. Paris, he said in his inaugural address of November 1875, was an 'immense laboratory' which was 'imbued with the lay spirit' and the 'traditions of the French Revolution'. He forecasted that the separation of Church and state would be the great struggle 'that characterises the end of the century.'

A month later the National Assembly at last dissolved itself and Clemenceau was running for the new Chamber of Deputies.

III

THE SERIES of by-elections, municipal elections and general council elections over the preceding four years had helped republicans establish rules of campaign management that were to be observed for at least a generation. Basically these involved three steps: the selection of the candidate by an electoral committee responsible for the constituency in question, the drafting of a programme by the committee which would appear in the group's newspaper and the candidate's *profession de foi*, to be published in the same paper.

Clemenceau was selected by the 'Radical Republican Committee of the Eighteenth Arrondissement'. Their programme, presented to the candidate in the form of a letter, was identical – virtually word for word – to the other republican programmes presented in Paris and, indeed, throughout the nation. Several of these 'letters' carried at their head 'Programme of the Radical Republic' and they could all be traced to a document drafted by the Nantes historian, Charles Louis Chassin, who himself had borrowed from Gambetta's Belleville programme of 1869.

These were the committee's instructions to the young candidate for the Eighteenth arrondissement:

> We invite you to accept and take under hand the following programme
> in accordance with our political and social demands:
>   Amnesty. Abolition of the death penalty.
>   Suppression of the *état de siège*.
> ....
>   Return of the public powers to Paris.
>   Liberty of the press; liberty of meeting and of association.
>   Obligatory, free and lay primary education; surveillance of the
> schools by municipal councillors.
> ....
>   Defence of civil society against clerical encroachment; reinstatement
> in full force of the laws, not repealed, pronouncing the expulsion of
> the Jesuits.
>   Military service obligatory for all, without privileges of any kind.
>   Election of mayors by the municipal councils; emancipation of the
> commune. Administrative decentralisation.
>   Revision of the source of tax revenue, aiming at reducing work.
>   Separation of Church and state.

The typical shopping-list style corresponded to the political realities of the day. The idea was to assimilate under a few titles and slogans a large body of political men who had in reality very little in common beyond the French language – itself a rather dubious assumption. This was democracy adopted to a country where the fastest form of travel was still in many areas limited to horse or even foot and where the most rapid type of communication between the larger towns was the telegram.

In his *profession de foi* Clemenceau welcomed the 'French bourgeoisie, inspired by its patriotism and finally returning to the tradition of 1789', for openly committing itself to the republican regime, but he warned that there was no question of sacrificing principles:

> We have no deal to propose to them, nor reward to promise them. We
> pretend no more to enrol them in the service of our policy than they have

the right to force us to serve theirs. They are Conservative Republicans. We are Radical Republicans, that is to say reformers. The Conservative Republicans ask from the Republic its minimum, we, its maximum. We, Radical Republicans, we want the Republic for its natural consequences: the great and fruitful reforms that it entails . . . The goal that we propose is the accomplishment of the great renovation of 1789, inaugurated by the French bourgeoisie and abandoned by it before its completion; it is the re-establishment of social peace by the singular development of justice and liberty: the republican peace.

The address was a warning, but it was also an overture to Conservative Republicans willing to make room for the radical programme. Clemenceau, like so many, was leaving his options open. The 'Programme of the Radical Republic' had to absorb local battles over taxation, contraband, military exemption, antagonisms caused by migrant labourers, rivalries between villages, between the *maire*, the *curé* and the *instituteur*, local disputes between cultivators suffering from crops destroyed by disease or weather, angry tenants, angry landowners or the pure bloody mindedness of brooding rural drudgeries. Clemenceau's campaign, like every other republican campaign that year, stretched beyond the immediate constituency.

'What wiser measure of order and justice than tax reform, than a fair distribution of its burden based on ability to contribute?' – Clemenceau's words, but any aggrieved taxpayer could have said them. 'What greater measure of order, of justice and of liberty, than the separation of the Churches and the state, than the defence of our civil society against the undertakings of a confessional sect which aims openly at controlling our institutions and our traditions through the infallible and sovereign will of a foreign prince?' – there were corners in Burgundy which were just as outraged as the 18th arrondissement in Paris. 'What more efficient measure of order, of justice and of reconciliation than the amnesty we demand with so much insistence only because we want a forgetting, a reciprocal forgetting?' – Clemenceau was after all standing for Montmartre.

His position in the political world was as yet very modest. He was involved in none of the major political decisions of the day. As the medieval scholastic wrote, 'We are dwarfs standing on the shoulders of giants.' Since the Revolution many giants had appeared and defended the republican cause. Clemenceau had not even reached their waistline; he was just a part of that complex republican network of electoral committees, special commissions and conferences that ensured republican discipline and brought the inarticulate for the first time into the political life of the nation.

To the charge that his programme lacked originality he later replied,

'We don't claim to have invented a new policy, we don't carry a new programme. Our programme is the old republican programme, the one inaugurated by the French Revolution.' It was the one solid commitment he kept in the rocky political career still ahead of him.

IV

IN THE legislative elections of February 1876 the 18th arrondissement gave Clemenceau 15,204 votes while his opponent won only 3,772. The *scrutin d'arrondissement* – an electoral system in which electors simply voted for one candidate within their constituency – probably worked in Clemenceau's favour though it was not a system that republicans liked. In 1871, when the *scrutin de liste* was used – the voter was presented with lists of candidates for the whole department and he could cast as many votes as there were deputies for his department – he came nowhere near success.

The new parliament opened in Versailles on 8 March. The Senate was housed in the same theatre, in the north wing of the palace, where the National Assembly had met. The Chamber of Deputies met in the south wing in a courtyard that had been converted into a huge hall with over nine hundred seats – ready to receive the Senate should a joint session be called. The acoustics were dreadful and journalists in the press gallery continued to complain for many months.

One can give no precise breakdown of political opinion within the Chamber because political parties had not yet been invented. When one spoke of 'parties' one meant temporary electoral alliances. Out of the 533 deputies about 340 were unambiguously republican while another two dozen could be regarded as monarchists converted to the cause. Within that broad category – which obviously held together only as long as the republican regime itself was in question – groups and splinter-groups formed, sometimes around a general political orientation, sometimes a particular interest; even self-survival could be the motive. There was, for example, a self-constituted 'Council of Ten' which met for dinner every Tuesday in the hope of coordinating left-wing activity within the Chamber. There even developed a curious 'group of deputies not inscribed to groups' which, as Robert de Jouvenel explained, existed 'to defend the parliamentary interests of its members'. Most of these groups were ephemeral. And matters were complicated by the fact that one could belong to more than one group at a time. Charonne, deputy for the Rhône, declared that he belonged to the Extreme Left 'for principles' and to the Republican Union for 'political conduct'. Clemenceau himself followed this line, arguing at a meeting of the 'Sixteen' held in Louis Blanc's home at the end of June that simultaneous membership was one of the best ways of defending the Republic.

The overall effect of all this was to give a few individual deputies enormous powers, through their oratory and their political connections, while the mass of them sank into silence and obscurity, the *bulletin de vote* being the sole proof of their existence.

The most exalted of the republicans was of course Gambetta. He had been stomping the country for five years now. 'Frenchmen do not travel enough,' he said, 'and what we know least is our own geography.' He had huge maps and tables made up giving the exact position of republicans throughout the country and he carried his 'missionary work', as he called it, everywhere – to the south-west in the summer of 1871, the north-east in the autumn, the west in spring 1872, the south and south-east the following autumn . . . Gambetta was the best travelled politician of his day, which is why his enemies called him 'democracy's travelling salesman', a title he readily adopted. Gambetta explained the purpose of his tours in a speech he made at Bordeaux in June 1871: 'We must prove to the peasant that it is to democracy, to the Revolution, that he owed not only his land but his rights.'

The original purpose of his 'Republican Union', organised in 1871 and backed up by his newspaper, *La République Française*, was to coordinate left-wing republicans in the National Assembly. But by the time the Chamber of Deputies first met, it had clearly changed its role and now stood as a kind of umbrella organisation to include all republicans.

The result was that Gambetta found himself faced with enemies both to the Right and Left. His age counted against him. Elderly conservative republicans took his political manœuvrings as a sign of shallowness. Gambetta, said Jules Grévy, was 'a below-average politician who floated on the surface because he was empty'. But his greatest republican enemies were the ageing *quarante-huitards* who never forgave him for stealing the limelight they thought was theirs; Gambetta called them a 'discontented, cantankerous, jealous, bewildered and timid people'.

His problems were aggravated by the fact that some of the youngest politicians in the Chamber – men like Clemenceau who had grown up under the shadow of their republican fathers – felt an intense, almost religious bond with these old revolutionaries. They too had difficulty accepting Gambetta's formula to *sérier les problèmes*, and the mildest of them would have subscribed to the declaration of Louis Blanc's 'Sixteen' to cede 'to the exigences of tactics only after having loudly proclaimed their principles and sought to make them prevail'.

But, among the young radical deputies, the Parisians formed a silent minority. Neither the loud proclamations nor the votes came from the capital any longer, they came from the Midi.

V

A MAJOR constitutional crisis caused republicans to bury their differences for a while. The Marshal had decided to exercise his 'irresponsibility'.

Life had been getting uncomfortable for the defenders of the *Ordre moral*. At least the republican divisions had enabled MacMahon to avoid a Gambetta government. Instead the task went to one of his conservative rivals, a former member of the National Defence, promoter of the Sacré Cœur (and, it was conveniently forgotten, author of the Belleville programme), Jules Simon. But when the Marshal demanded from Simon an explanation for the support he had shown, during a speech before the Chamber, for press freedoms, Simon resigned with the rest of his cabinet.

It was 16 May 1877. Most republicans were on that day in Paris attending the funeral of Ernest Picard, another ex-minister of the National Defence. Stupefied at the news, they abandoned the cortege and made haste to a nearby hotel where they declared their commitment to 'the preponderance of the power of parliament exercised by a responsible ministry'.

On 17 May a roaring crowd saw the deputies off at the gare Saint-Lazare. Gambetta made a splendid speech from the tribune of the Chamber in which he attacked every personality in the president's entourage save the Marshal himself. MacMahon, in the meantime, had called on his old friend, the duc de Broglie, to set up a 'government of combat'. On 18 May, parliament was prorogued for a month. The republican deputies withdrew to a restaurant in the Hôtel des Reservoirs (it was immediately remarked that there was something of a parallel with the Third Estate's withdrawal to a tennis court in 1789) where they prepared a manifesto denouncing the 'politics of reaction and adventures'. It carried 363 signatures. When the Chamber met a month later it passed a motion of no confidence, 363 to 158. MacMahon ordered its dissolution.

For Gambetta, it was a return to war. The battle, he said to a group of students, was 'between all that remains of the old world, the old castes, the privileged of the old regimes, between the agents of Roman theocracy and the sons of 1789'.

The enemy pulled out all the stops. Sixty-two prefects and sub-prefects were replaced within twenty-four hours of parliament's prorogation and another 484 swiftly followed suit. So did 184 magistrates, 83 mayors and 381 justices of the peace. No government, including those of the Second Empire, had ever proceeded at such a pace. In the election campaign of that summer and autumn tens of thousands of portraits of the Marshal were distributed around the country as were hundreds of thousands of pamphlets.

The elections were held on 14 October, one of those sunny republican days that augured, like before, so much hope, such a mingling of good feeling, the kind of fraternity the Republic was always supposed to embrace. The turnout was high. The republicans held on to 321 seats. The reaction was beaten. But who had won?

VI

CLEMENCEAU REMAINED peculiarly silent, not only during the crisis of the *Seize Mai*, but for many months thereafter.

Political calculation undoubtedly played a part. Even after the October elections the fear of a *coup d'état* was very real; it was not a moment propitious for brave speeches and principles; the accomplishment of the great renovation of 1789 would have to wait a while. In old age Clemenceau recalled being involved with Gambetta in a plot to launch a counter-coup from Lille. Gambetta, he said, was 'lost in mirages [and] he had got it into his head to conspire . . . I was something like his second whip'. Clemenceau managed to gather together a few deputies and senators in a café on rue du Bac where he handed out small slips of paper, numbered, with instructions on what to do on the 'day of the great day'. It all came to nothing. 'MacMahon stopped it all, fortunately. Otherwise we would obviously all have ended up in gaol.' Clemenceau presumably meant that MacMahon's abandonment of a second dissolution and the appointment of a republican government in December made further action unnecessary.

Secret gatherings of republican deputies were remarked on in the press at the time. In November, shortly before the new Chamber opened, *La République Française* reported a meeting of left-wing deputies at Camille Sée's apartment which adopted the resolution to make no communications to the press on further meetings of left-wing groups 'for the full length of the currently pending crisis'. The London *Times* also reported a meeting of deputies of the Left which was 'at times rather stormy'.

What they were referring to was a group calling itself the 'Committee of Delegates of the Lefts of the Chamber of Deputies', though it came down in history, fortunately, as the 'Committee of Eighteen'. It was almost certainly initiated by Gambetta, and its secretary was Georges Clemenceau. Asked years later what happened in this committee, Clemenceau replied, 'Nothing. As always in committees. Nothing ever happens. People descanting in a vacuum. There were as many opinions as there were deputies and nobody persuaded anybody. Each person spoke to himself and listened to himself. An utter farce.'

But the secrecy of useless speeches and wasted plans was, for the member for the Eighteenth arrondissement, the mask of something profounder and more personal. Since his election in February 1876, Clemenceau had made only one speech in parliament, and that within weeks of its opening. It was nearly three years before he made another major intervention. The most outstanding Radicals of the day were the deputies from the Midi, people like Alfred Naquet or Madier de Montjau. Among the Paris deputies, Floquet played a much more important role than Clemenceau. So too Lockroy.

Was it simply political tactics? Gambetta had certainly impressed Clemenceau immensely. Shortly after the elections he told Scheurer-Kestner, '*Mon cher*, Gambetta has been admirable! Admirable! from the beginning to the end. He's the one who organised everything.' Apparently the role of 'second whip' suited him for the time being.

One's impression is that Clemenceau was sinking once more into a period of withdrawal, a 'burial' where, as he had put it so many years before, 'the dread of learning what I fear overcomes my wish to know the truth'. 'My doctor is of your opinion,' he confided to Mme Jourdan in July 1875. 'I am simply a *névropathe*, that is to say in French, a man whose nerves are upside down. I have had to give up drinking tea, which has cost me a lot.' Under Gambetta's shadow he had found his *petit coin* and he sat there waiting for a new life to begin: the will to please had momentarily overtaken that defiant assertion of principle and personality; the silence of the crowds in Paris had found a compeer in the silence of the man.

A touch, a voice, a tender finger; was there trouble in home and hearth? For five years he had barely seen his wife. What had been a separation out of public duty had become a separation by habit.

In *Le Pot de basilic* his eldest daughter Madeleine left a record of life at the Château de l'Aubraie during these years. It was a house of women, *les douces femmes qui m'entouraient . . . les douces femmes qui m'aimaient . . .* The only male presence was Benjamin, her grandfather, who was now more or less permanently confined to the same sad, dingy little room – overlooking the inner courtyard – where he used to disappear when Georges was a boy. The bookshelves were where they had always been. Heaps of books were stuffed haphazardly into scarcer and scarcer spaces, their pages abundantly annoted in his chafed hand; it was all he ever wrote, for he conducted no correspondence. Meals continued to be served according to the hours of the *Ancien Régime*: lunch at ten, dinner at five. 'The evenings were long,' she wrote, 'and, especially in

winter, they went on forever without end.' The inhabitants moved about
noiselessly. They had a horror of sound, for the place was as resonant as
a cathedral.

One evening long after dinner, tucked up silent in the Tower of Treasure
(her isolated bedroom where she kept her dolls, Ernest Ludovic, Timothée
Ludovic and Marshal MacMahon), Madeleine heard something unusual
break into the airless, moonless calm. The clatter of horses' hoofs. The
heaving of wheels on the gravelled yard. The great iron knock of the
oaken portal hammered till its hinges squeaked. '*On y va-a-a*,' cried a
voice from Tante Bonne's wing (Madeleine's crippled maiden aunt was
another member of the family who never slept). The bolts thrown open.
The sound of many feet on the steps below approaching. Her door flung
wide. A man entered in the company of *les douces femmes qui m'aimaient*, his
face vaguely lit by an oil lamp; an unknown Mongol warrior.

'Papa!' she squealed.

Papa's rare visits to L'Aubraie were, on most occasions, for the hunting. In
September he would come for the migrating bustards. It was partridges,
hare and rabbit in October. Quail were a great favourite and the opening
of the season at Longeville-sur-mer on the Chabeaux' estate involved a
fabulous ceremony. An army of men arrived with their guns, cartridge
bags (the revolution in armaments had extended to sport) and their
dogs: English pointers, gordons, Vendéen braques. Forty to fifty people
were put up in the château, the hall was transformed into a ballroom and
gargantuan – Rabelaisian – meals were served to the guests. Clemenceau
also often hunted alone. Or he might bring along a few friends from Paris.
Pole-vaulting over the Marais canals with the *bâton sautoux* particularly
amused him because he was so much better at it than the Parisians.

And Paris was rather different. Shortly after Michel had come into the
world Clemenceau took Madeleine back with him for a winter in the
capital.

Madeleine found her father's quarters on the second floor of number
15, rue de Miromesnil, rather restrictive; the air, she said reflecting back,
could be 'measured in bushels'. Everything was polished. When they
arrived, the drivers in the courtyard, dressed in full livery, were applying
spit-and-polish to the cabs. The wooden staircase glistened. The landing
of the second floor was dominated by a tall, newly painted door – with
no bolts, no great iron knock! At the lower end of the hall, to the right
of the door, was a window tempered by the blues and reds of its stained
glass; the light thus produced was soft, mysterious and subdued. The
dining-room carpet, thick and springy, was patterned with flowers, the

parquet was waxed and there was at one end a magnificent buffet in buhl and marquetry, its corners and ledges adorned with hand-carved birds. The only object of note in the tiny living-room was a small bronze statue of two naked men fighting over a prostrate lion . . . or it might have been a tiger.

What she could remember of the neighbouring study were the books, especially the books: science, medicine, philosophical tomes, studies of ancient Greece, the Revolution, nothing on politics. A small bed protruded from the bookshelves. Her father worked in this room day and night – another confined male.

By far the most exciting room was the kitchen, filled with all sorts of curious gadgets, though there was no fireplace and no cauldron. But there was a tap and, horror, tepid water poured out of it; she was told that it had been installed because the neighbourhood's water fountain was too far away. Every morning she found warm croissants laid out for her on the kitchen table by some mysterious hand; the butter was awful, it wasn't salted.

There were no animals, no cats and there was only one maid, an Alsatian woman named Delphine.

But there was another woman. She was kind, bringing little cakes and tarts from Siraudin's, trinkets to play with or a funny book. She used a head-band to hold her black hair in place which, Madeleine thought, made her look rather severe; she was later astonished to hear people talk of 'the *beautiful* Madame Floquet'.

Hortense Floquet, *née* Kestner, had had no children. So she was constantly visiting such friends and relatives of her Kestner clan that had. Madeleine thus found as playmates the children of some of the most famous names in France.

She remembered a magnificent party given at the Floquets, who lived nearby on rue du Cirque. There was a Punch and Judy show put on by a group from the Champs-Elysées at the end of which her father took her behind the theatre box and, holding her up by her legs, told her to recite her favourite fable from La Fontaine. It was a great success. Afterwards she was passed through gentle arms from one abundantly dressed female lap to another. Later she used to think to herself what a curious event it was. Her father detested ostentation, *la parade*. How on earth could he have encouraged in his own child what he so contemptuously called 'the desire for attention', '*le désir de se faire remarquer*'? Well, she had no such thought at the time. She thought all women were kind and gentle, like *les douces femmes qui m'aimaient*, and all men knew science and were wise and strong, like her papa. What could be more natural than to recite a fable in front of people like that?

'How happy one is at that age!' her father used sometimes to say. Happy?

No, one is not happy. The fathers would at times love to put down life's burden and return to the time of negative pleasures. But with what passion even the most docile child will think of escaping his dependance and, for once, giving orders himself! ... It is tragic to struggle with oneself in the night when feelings are so fresh and when one so tiny is confronted with the forces of eternity.

It must have been hereditary.

VII

As in his New York days, Clemenceau presented an image of 'respectability' and could even be regarded, by people unfamiliar with him, as a bit of a dandy. Ernest Judet, no friend of Clemenceau, met him at the offices of *La République française* on the day of the October election victory:

At the headquarters where the victorious mobilisation of the republicans had been masterfully organised, where all the *chefs de corps* came in one after the other to take their orders, I met Clemenceau. He was nothing more than a *petit officier* in the army from which Gambetta took, without haughtiness and embarrassment, the honours due to the generalissimo. I was astonished at the impertinent arrogance of the young deputy whose dress and manners contrasted strongly with the correct and formal customs of an institution which embodied the Republic. His brusque manner, his mocking smile, his cheeky, mocking eyes, his splendid cane thrust like a weapon under his arm, his hat acock, with an affectation of provocative poses, of radical dandyism that would later constitute his 'Parisian' eccentricity – everything radiated self-satisfaction. Added to this was his shameful disdain for the house, already outmoded in his eyes, where he had first taken up arms like a sniper just falling in line for the battle. In no way would he have accepted to have been or even to have appeared the model soldier and traditional servant of good bearing and devoted self-denial.

Judet found him a recalcitrant, antagonistic character who covered his faults with dash and opulence – another odd testament to the very trait, *le désir de se faire remarquer*, that Clemenceau hated in others.

This was of course a moment when he was particularly conspiratorial. As a deputy he could hardly retreat like his father to an unseen corner of a country house. So, like Janus, he had two faces, the public man and the man in hiding. The more he hid, the more he appeared to ungenerous colleagues as precisely the person he did not want to be. Thus while others might have looked at him as an impulsive, anarchic sniper, he saw himself as the disciplined lieutenant of his commander-in-chief, Gambetta's 'second whip'.

But then what was he hiding? There probably was something unsettling in his private life; there was also the plain contrariness of his personality, so obvious in his youth – a mode of life that he had picked up from his father and duly passed on to his children.

But the anxiety of the moment had a more specific, obvious cause behind it. The recent civil war had had a terrible impact on Clemenceau. In old age he would speak of his 'crimes'; the most vivid among them remained the murder of the two generals in rue des Rosiers and the violence that followed. It had tempered his taste for revolution. 'One of my worst memories,' he told Jean Martet, 'is when I left Paris in 1871.' Clemenceau's behaviour in the 1870's must be seen in this light.

The trial of twenty-seven men accused of murdering Lecomte and Thomas took place before a military tribunal in Versailles in November 1871. Clemenceau was one of the witnesses. At his first appearance, on 8 November, he asked to be considered among the 'accused' so that he might benefit from the right to call witnesses for his defence. 'From the moment my honour is called into question,' he said, 'I demand to defend myself . . . I am made out to be a criminal and yet my conscience is clear, I have nothing to reproach myself with. I am an honest man.'

The 'charge' to which he stood accused was the implication in a government report – supported by two witnesses, Commanders Vassal and Poussargues, who had participated in the government's assault on Montmartre – that Clemenceau knew in advance of a planned uprising and not only did nothing to stop it but actually helped to provoke it. It had also been suggested that Clemenceau had ordered that the bodies of the two generals be buried in a common grave 'in the quarries'.

The president of the court refused Clemenceau's request on the grounds that these 'accusations' had 'only a political character' whereas the trial was concerned with a simple matter of murder. Vassal and Poussargues, however, repeated their charges that same afternoon. Specifically, they both stated that Clemenceau had seen Lecomte on the Butte *after* the National Guard had made the call to arms and that he had told the general 'I am answerable to the peace in the district.' This was presented as evidence that the mayor had prior knowledge of the call to arms and furthermore had control over the Guard.

Clemenceau was back at the witness stand the next day strenuously denying this and for the next two sessions the court heard his witnesses.

The president of the court got quite exasperated. The incident was closed with a brisk exchange between the president and the former mayor. 'We have heard enough witnesses on these different points. We have even perhaps heard too much.'

Clemenceau said that he still had not been acquitted.

The president then made some remarks on authority and democracy that give some insight into Versaillais attitudes at the time. He said, 'Authority has shown power. It has shown its force in the repression. It has not yielded before a population. In such a case a man counts for very little. Authority is not frightened of a man.'

'In the meantime, it is frightened of prosecuting me,' responded Clemenceau. 'Let it try, I challenge it.'

'We have not said that you are guilty. We don't need to make a pronouncement.'

'And I regret that enormously!'

'Authority founded by universal suffrage is very powerful. You know that it was for the repression and that it will be for the punishment.'

'How true!'

'A man counts for nothing before it. It acts in the fullness of its will and its aspirations; no individual challenge will make it act. The incident is closed.'

As far as Clemenceau was concerned the incident was not closed; his 'honour' was still at issue and it was incumbent on him to defend it. Shortly thereafter he sent his cartel to Poussargues. The two men met in a wood with pistols. 'I could kill you,' shouted out Clemenceau at twenty paces, 'but you are a French officer. I shall content myself with wounding you.' Poussargues received a bullet in his thigh, Clemenceau received a fortnight's sentence in the Conciergerie gaol.

As Paul de Cassagnac, the Chamber's most talented swashbuckler and pistoleer, put it, 'The duel derives its essential legitimacy from the gravity of the offence it must avenge; an offence of honour that the penal sanctions of the Code cannot punish, by their very definition. In effect, the standard for judicial actions is *interest*. The cause of the duel is *honour*.' The opposing school – and one might cite the comte d'Estève whose campaign against duelling lasted into the twentieth century – held that 'what pushes a man today onto the field, what pushes him despite himself and even his defensive honour, is the fear of prejudice, the fear that one is worthy of consideration only if one fights, or at least gives the public the impression of having fought. In a word, it is weakness.'

The old aristocracy (de Cassagnac was a journalist and a Bonapartist) looked down on duelling. Duelling had become democratic. It had been outlawed by kings because it represented a threat to their high-born retainers. But the Revolution abolished all laws on duelling; from then

on anybody could challenge a man to a duel. The practice spread to the
bourgeois political classes, the literati, the journalists, the pamphleteers.
If 1848 had brought, temporarily, democracy to France it also revolution-
ised the political duel. Virtually all the major politicians of that era were
experienced duellists: Ledru-Rollin, Lamartine, Raspail, Proudhon, Pyat,
Cousin. Thiers was an old hand at the art. So was Guizot. Louis-Napoleon,
while still in exile in England, fought it out with an illegitimate cousin
on Wimbledon Common. 'Today, in a democratised society,' moaned the
baron d'Ezpeleta, 'duelling is a nonsense.'

It was not a nonsense for Clemenceau. Nor for Gambetta, for Lockroy,
Ranc, Lissagaray, Rochefort . . . It was certainly a show and de Cassagnac
probably had good reason to complain that duels were increasingly being
faked. The comte d'Estève was probably also right to speak of the fear
and the weakness of the challenger. But then the politician *had* to give
the public the impression of having fought and doubly so if universal
suffrage, as the court martial president had implied, was not yet ready
to defend the individual.

Clemenceau was involved in several duels.

Clemenceau's one major speech to the Chamber in this period, made on
16 May 1876, was also linked to the insurrection. He wanted amnesty.
It was not a lone battle. Amnesty had been the principal issue in the
campaign of the Radicals and Extreme Left in the elections of the
preceding February.

When Clemenceau stepped up to the grand mahogany tribune he
realised that he had already lost part of his audience. He would have
seen before him the members seated, at their desks, on red leather benches
that rose in twelve tiers from the floor of the house, the government directly
in front of him, the monarchists to his right, the republicans to his left.
The design was very similar to that of the Palais-Bourbon in Paris. The
benches were divided into blocks by means of gangways. Each bench
accommodated two deputies and every block was composed of six double
seats in three tiers. The walls on either side were screened by red velvet
curtains through which members continued to pass. Behind him was an
enormous painting of the Meeting of the Estates General in 1789 and, at
its foot, the chair – one might even say throne – of the president of the
Chamber, Jules Grévy. This high podium of tribune and chair was also
occupied by the *questeurs*, who could be consulted on questions of order,
several parliamentary secretaries and a row of shorthand writers.

An usher was available to the speaker to cater to his thirst. Thiers used
to take hot broth while speaking. Gambetta took coffee. Pouyer-Quertier
would have nothing less than champagne to loosen his noble tongue. But
now that *questeur* Baze had started charging speakers for refreshments

– democracy was exerting an influence here too – the more exotic thirst-quenchers had disappeared. Clemenceau ordered red wine.

The speech lasted about an hour and a half. It reads a bit like a university professor's disquisition on the causes of this war or that, or one of those lawyer's briefs described in *Bleak House*. One imagines – at least for the first sixty minutes – several yawns, the rustle of newspapers being opened, a few deputies here and there catching up with last week's correspondence. Clemenceau must have spent many long hours preparing it (with much consultation).

He argued for a 'full, entire and immediate amnesty'. Either you forget or you do not forget. Either you accept that the insurrection was the result of fear, poverty and the current of events, or you do not accept it. Clemenceau subscribed to the accident theory of history, accidents for which the population of Paris bore no responsibility. Paris had not asked for the Empire, it had not asked for the war. It had lost its municipal freedoms and it subsequently lost the seat of the national parliament and government. It had demanded to fight the enemy and the demand was refused. 'If you examine the history of insurrections you will not find an insurrection where the premeditation had been less, where action and human will had been less, where responsibilities once pledged had been more numerous and more varied.' Paris was a victim of circumstances. The repression was appalling. 'I say that your repression has been assuredly a legal repression, in the strict sense of the word, but that it has been a repression no more legal than any mass transportation made in the name of the law. It has been an exceptional repression responding to an exceptional situation.' Clemenceau provided some figures (which in fact grossly underestimated the extent of the repression). He said it would be impossible to make a distinction between common law crimes and political crimes in this instance; 'I have consulted specialists.' Therefore a partial amnesty was out of question. As for a pardon, he noted that only 613 pardons had been granted in the last five years. Those opposed to an amnesty had invoked the laws of humanity: the insurgents, they argued, 'had not respected the great laws of humanity'. Were there any insurrections where the great laws of humanity had been respected? Governments had never needed an amnesty for they were the stronger side; but insurgents who did need it always obtained it in the end. He cited a number of historical examples: the Saint Bartholomew massacre, the seizure of the *biens nationaux* during the Revolution, the Vendéen civil war.

Clemenceau concluded: Don't wait for the next elections (due in 1880), 'this date that the monarchists have adjourned for us ... I ask you to proclaim amnesty while it is still a proof of strength and not to wait until opinion forces it from you when it will only be a proof of weakness. Don't abdicate, as it has been proposed to you; act. What can you fear? You will

always be strong if you govern with the country; you will always be weak
if you govern against it.'

A few deputies to his right had got a bit fidgety when he had started
on his historical examples. They were downright furious when he arrived
at the Vendée war. The Vendéens insurrectionists? De la Bassetière and
Bourgeois bounded to their feet. 'They didn't rise against France,' boomed
out de Baudry d'Asson, 'but against the Convention!' ('I still have ringing
in my ears the cries of de Baudry d'Asson,' said Clemenceau over fifty
years later.) But Clemenceau lost his nerve when, just as he was about
to make his concluding remarks, the marquis de Castellane called him to
question.

'Speak of the Commune!'

'Don't interrupt!' replied a republican.

'I only interrupt the orator to call him to question.'

'Monsieur de Castellane,' said Grévy from his chair, 'I pray you
keep silent. If you persist in interrupting I shall be obliged to call you
to order.'

The orator turned to the honourable member on the right; 'I shall speak,
Monsieur le marquis de Castellane, on whatever it pleases me to speak and
if you have some observations to make to me, I am ready to receive them
here or anywhere else.' There was an uproar. 'This is a provocation!' 'To
order!' 'To order!'

Grévy managed to restore the peace and Clemenceau finished his
speech.

The amnesty debate took up the whole week. Raspail's bill for a full
amnesty was rejected by 392 votes to 50; Gambetta, Spuller and Grévy
were among the fifty-nine deputies who abstained. Margue's bill for a
partial amnesty was rejected by 367 to 99; Gambetta voted against it,
Grévy and thirty-four others abstained. Allain-Targé withdrew his bill and
the two others failed, by voice vote, even to be considered in discussion.
The Versailles Chamber was in no mood for forgetting.

VIII

GAMBETTA USED to say that you had to bring good humour into public
life. 'Sad men,' he would explain, 'make bad politics.' Many republicans
were convinced that they were a much gayer, brighter lot than the men
of the Empire, whom they regarded as bloated plutocrats not unlike the

dry, old-fashioned windbags of the July Monarchy (Daumier's caricatures had had a lasting influence). It was not an image they projected into their newspapers, which were actually rather dull. But the republican politicians' lifestyle was, if taken at their own word, more cheerful than that of their predecessors: they were forever rejoicing in the company of their *convives* at the grand cafés of the boulevards, in private dinners or at some fashionable lady's *salon*. It was an image Clemenceau cultivated. He wanted to be seen as someone gay and full of movement. A photograph taken in the late 1870's shows him on horseback, dressed in top hat, an English riding-coat and boots, ready for an afternoon's canter across the Bois de Boulogne; he was not going to be taken for one of the *petits crevés* of the Second Empire who stayed in bed till twelve, breakfasted till two, smoked till four and turned up in the park at five looking as sick as wafers. He could also be very funny. When Berthe Szeps first met Clemenceau in the early 1880's her impression was of 'one long burst of laughter' – 'Clemenceau was not a "closed man" as he is sometimes judged, with his sombre and cold features; he was, on the contrary, explosive.'

This was also Scheurer-Kestner's impression when he started to invite the new deputy to the regular dinners he had been holding for key figures of the 'republican party' since 1872. 'Clemenceau used to be very amusing with his gusto and that something "frivolous" which this man, although so logical, so frequently evinced.' Scheurer-Kestner's dinners were almost as much of an institution as the formal *bureaux* and parliamentary committees which directed debate in the two houses, and they showed what enormous political influence he and his Alsatian industrial dynasty now exerted.

A dynasty it certainly was. When Jules Ferry married Eugénie Risler in autumn of 1875 Gambetta congratulated his colleague on allying himself with such an 'admirable race', the 'strong and patriotic *gens* of the Kestners'. Ferry's new uncles-in-law included, besides Scheurer-Kestner, Victor Chauffour and Charles Floquet. Through the Kestner link he could call Marcellin Pellet a cousin as well as Allain-Targé. The Kestner clan provided some balance to what Juliette Adam resentfully referred to as the republic of bachelors; Gambetta, Spuller, Ranc and Challemel-Lacour were all known to have had mistresses. A public service, even. For the Kestners, like the Ménard-Dorians or the Japys, gave the republicans 'respectability'. If the lowly bred bachelors could not prove through their civil status that they had entered the age of reason they could at least demonstrate, through the dignified gatherings of their wealthy married friends, that they were moving in the right circles.

By the end of 1878 Clemenceau had moved to a larger flat on avenue Montaigne where he lived with his wife and children. His attendance at the Scheurer-Kestners brought him into continual contact with the leading Gambettists and thus with people at the very top of republican politics. 'Some had become ministers,' noted Scheurer-Kestner in his journal, 'others were expecting to be ministers, still others belonged to republican groups who found the advance too slow, and finally there were those who, on the contrary, sought to slacken the pace.' Clemenceau belonged unquestionably to the third group; Edouard Lockroy, Georges Perin and he earned themselves the nickname 'the three musketeers'.

It was also in this period that he started to appear at Madame Aline Ménard-Dorian's salon. Scheurer-Kestner's dinners were strictly male affairs. They had begun in the private *cabinets* on the first floor of the café Riche, though, by Clemenceau's time, they were being held at Scheurer-Kestner's own home in the rue des Mathurins. The salon, on the other hand, bore the mark of women.

The number of salons in Paris grew rapidly in the first years of the Republic. The *grande dame* of the Republic was of course Juliette Adam. There was very little that would thwart Madame Adam; she even took her own initiatives in foreign policy. But competition was intense. Madame de Renneville led the salons of the Centre Right from her mansion next door to the archbishop's palace. Most of the conservative forces, however, remained ensconced in their walled *hôtels* in the faubourg Saint-Germain. Here, Madame Sallandrouze had built up a splendid reputation for anti-republican pomp and cordiality. Meanwhile, back on the rue de Surênes, Madame Arnaud de l'Ariège contended directly with Madame Adam for Gambetta's charms. Madame Aubernon's salon, which migrated annually to her summer residence, *Au Cœur Volant* in Louveciennes, was a much more eclectic affair, even if her mealtime conversations did resemble parliamentary gatherings; she used to control her guests' flourishes of oratory by ringing a silver bell.

On the great days of public debate, these ladies, along with the deputies, the senators and reporters, would pile into the trains at the gare Saint-Lazare and, once in Versailles, clamber to the visitors' galleries where they would nod, repine or pass off airs of indifference.

In contrast, Madame Ménard-Dorian's salon presented a more modest scene. Her star was still rising. She offered much promise. She was beautiful, she was young, and she was very rich. Her father, Pierre Dorian, had been one of the heroes of the siege; it was he, as minister of public works, who had organised the city's arms manufactures. Her husband, Paul Ménard, was director of the iron forges of Unieux near Saint-Etienne, the same factory where Dorian had developed his industrial skills. After the *Seize Mai* he was elected deputy for Montpellier and sat on the Extreme Left, with Clemenceau. With Aline's gentle encouragement, he purchased a plot out in the then uninhabited neighbourhood of the fortifications, just south of the porte Dauphine. Their *hôtel* was constructed in the standard neo-gothic design, imposing, its tall doors and windows giving the impression more of a church or cathedral than a private residence. But what impressed guests most was Madame's original taste in interior design. She crammed in everything: every age and every new artistic fashion was represented in her huge halls. Renaissance furniture was packed up against Directory, Louis XIV against Louis-Philippe; her Japanese prints, the Chinese porcelain and the peacock's tails stood out prominently against her scarlet papered walls (an orientalism to which Clemenceau would soon fall victim); the palm trees added an element worth enquiry. Artists, rejected and despised by more established homes, were welcome here. Her day would come.

It was odd to think that the lives of young republicans could be swayed by an institution that was so quintessentially aristocratic. 'I plead for the salons,' wrote Victor du Bled after sixty years of roaming through society's drawing-rooms, 'because they are one of the last refuges from the barbarians; by that I mean the socialist upsurge, the parliamentary tyranny, the moral disorder, the democratic courtesanship, evils known from the republics of antiquity . . .' It was as if democracy had to meet the enemy on its own turf. Certainly the most conservative circles felt threatened by their imitators – duelling had already been democratised; now it was the salons! Victor du Bled complained of a growing exoticism (of which Madame Ménard-Dorian was a fine example), the development of the *salons de pacotille*. But it was also an essential development for a democracy which excluded half the human race on account of sex. How could someone like Madame Adam be limited to household chores? 'The role of the brooding hen is doubtless very respectable,' she once said, 'but it does not suit all women and it is not absorbing as is claimed.' They had to bow to the various conventions; the more political, more 'serious' salons excluded women from their invitations; and if they didn't the men after dinner would withdraw to the *fumoir*. But beauty, money and wit could place the more exceptional women in positions of enormous power. There was an outlet.

The other major stamping ground for republicans – one that was exclusively male – was the newspaper office. Republican newspaper offices were not just places of work; they were social clubs. Edmond Goncourt, when he got bored, used to go down to the offices of *Le Temps*. Léon Daudet preferred to drop in at *Le Rappel* or *La Lanterne*. But most of the people one would meet in these places – which in appearance were quite the antithesis of the salons – were there for more than a chat and a drink. They were chasing after the newly expanding powers of the written word; if the Empire had veiled the force of the press and if the war and Commune had demonstrated its more natural state of anarchy, the first years of the Republic showed newspapers to be the life vein of a plural, democratic society. The press not only provided political power, it defined political power – in all its chaotic, muddled reality. The link between the parliamentary chambers, the Parisian dinner tables and salons on one side and the poor voters on the other was the press; not that every French citizen read the newspapers, but the people who 'knew what was going on' read them, and they influenced the vote.

Georges Clemenceau was one among hundreds to realise the significance of this. As that perfidious English columnist, Grenville-Murray, noted, 'The Frenchman who has climbed to political or financial eminence proceeds to hedge himself with a newspaper which, like a parapet, serves both to prevent him falling and to shield him from the stones that may be flung by people below.' It was, for example, considered perfectly normal for a politician, once in the seat of government, to found a newspaper to defend his interests. Charles de Freycinet started *Le Télégraphe* for this purpose. Waldeck-Rousseau organised two papers (*La Réforme de Paris* and *L'Opinion*) and didn't hesitate to draw on 'secret funds', i.e. public monies, to help finance them. Ferry organised a paper. Even the president of the Republic, Jules Grévy, had his own newspaper (appropriately named *La Paix*). Clemenceau, however, was not a '*ministrable*' – nobody was prepared to take him into a government – and his own efforts to found a newspaper were undoubtedly begun to strengthen his opposition to those that were. Clemenceau's parapet was of his own making and was intended for the throwing of stones rather than their reception.

In the 1870's Clemenceau might not have succeeded in gaining entry to the most important salons ('he has too much of a taste for the terrorists,' groused Madame Adam) but he was often seen at the most important newspaper offices. Goncourt met him at *Le Temps*, which remained the queen of the liberal press up to the First World War. Several witnesses speak of Clemenceau's presence at Gambetta's *République Française*, the headquarters of republicans during the *Seize Mai* crisis. He was also seen at the offices of *Le Rappel* which, under the able management of Auguste Vacquerie, catered to the demands and tastes of Victor Hugo and sons. Amnesty for the communards was a major issue at *Le Rappel* and its columns were frequently filled by the writings of old *quarante-huitards*, like Louis Blanc and Edgar Quinet, bitter contestants of Gambetta's dominant role in republican politics. Here, Clemenceau would also have been in frequent contact with Camille Pelletan, whose father Clemenceau had known through Arago's circle of friends in the early 1860's. Pelletan established his reputation as a journalist in 1876 with a series of articles advocating total amnesty – a typical example of coordination between the press and parliamentary deputies, in this case the radical campaign just starting up in the Chamber.

*

That radical campaign was Clemenceau's. In 1879 he at last came out of his long political hibernation, making several speeches in and out of parliament. He also started casting about for the funds and the staff for his own journal.

The only contemporary account we have is in Scheurer-Kestner's unpublished journal. It was on his return to Paris at the end of the parliamentary vacation, in late November 1879, that he was approached by Clemenceau. 'Clemenceau, under the influence of Camille Pelletan, had got it into his head to found a newspaper, in which they had the intention of defending republican ideas "a little more advanced" than those of *La République Française*.' Scheurer-Kestner was definitely the right person to be approached, given his connections and his money.

The first shareholders' meeting took place in Scheurer-Kestner's home some time in December. The paper was to be called *La Justice*. Scheurer-Kestner's statutes stipulated that Clemenceau, as political director, would receive an annual salary of 30,000 francs, while Camille Pelletan, as editor-in-chief, would receive 20,000 francs. But the nominal capital of the paper was only 300,000 francs.

Statutes for a new company, set up in 1882 with a nominal capital of 1,500,000 francs, are to be found in the Archives Nationales. Clemenceau this time gets no salary. There were seven shareholders – Clemenceau, a *rentier*, a merchant, an engineer, two medical doctors and a 'propertyholder'. One of the doctors was Gustave Dourlen, the student friend who visited Clemenceau while in New York.

Clemenceau's family appears to have played a major role in the newspaper's financing, even though no family member was listed as a shareholder. The major contribution probably came from his father – at Benjamin's death in 1897 Clemenceau received no inheritance because his share had already been ceded. His elder sister, Emma Jacquet, was also involved in the financing, as was his youngest brother, Albert, a lawyer, who actually joined the staff some years later. It is possible that other members were involved. Léon Daudet, a witness who has to be treated with care, speaks of the presence of the whole family, save Adrienne and the parents, at Madame Ménard-Dorian's salon. Paul, an engineer, married the daughter of a well-known Austrian journalist in 1886, Sophie married a lesser-known Austrian journalist in 1889. Clearly, journalism played an important part in the life of the family, so it would not be unreasonable to suppose that *La Justice* was more a family affair than a simple individual concern of Georges Clemenceau.

What part did the secretive Adrien Hébrard, director of *Le Temps*, play? The fact that *La Justice* shared the same premises as *Le Temps* surely has some significance. Hébrard's move from rue Faubourg-Montmartre to boulevard des Italiens occurred at approximately the same time as the nominal capital of *La Justice* increased fivefold . . .

Perhaps it was one of Hébrard's connections. Georges Wormser, Clemenceau's *chef de cabinet* in 1919, reports that 'from 31 March 1881 until 1883 the daily lived from the advances of Cornelius Herz.' On 2 December 1886 *La Justice* felt it worth publishing a note declaring 'M. Herz is not a partner of *La Justice*. He was a shareholder from 26 February 1883 to 15 April 1885. M. Clemenceau ceded him, on 26 February 1883, half of his freed shares, in payment for sums deposited by him. On 15 April 1885, M. Clemenceau rebought the shares of M. Herz.'

Cornelius Herz would one day be the doom of thousands; it was a connection that would cost Clemenceau dearly. In 1927 Clemenceau told Jean Martet, 'Cornelius Herz was, I must say, a done for scoundrel. Unfortunately it wasn't written on the tip of his nose. He had been introduced to me by Hébrard: which wasn't a bad sponsorship . . .' This was no casual acquaintance. Herz was a frequent guest to Clemenceau's home; in 1884, when Clemenceau visited cholera-stricken Marseille, he signed a paper leaving the responsibility of his children's education, in the case of his death, to Herz not his wife (with whom his relations were now very strained). Herz, in these years, was being lionised in many of Paris's most exclusive circles, including the Elysée Palace, for his contributions in the field of electricity and the telephone. His promotions in the Légion d'honneur (officer in 1881, commander in 1883, grand officer in 1886) were all reported in *La Justice*, though the paper, in the same note of 1886, reported that 'M. Clemenceau has never recommended M. Herz to any minister nor to anyone for any business or favour.'

There is nothing to indicate that this was not the truth. Clemenceau was an inexperienced businessman (his only venture up to that point being his vague scheme in land speculation while in America, during Dourlen's visit). Suddenly he embarks into an area known to be populated by financial brigands and marauders – that was the nature of the trade: the newspaper business was linked up to so many industries. Anyway, Herz, a dumpy little man, full of humour and a knowledge of technical things no one about him could understand, seemed the man of the moment. Did it matter that he was Jewish? Clemenceau was no racist. And if he had spent over half his life in the United States, so much the better: the Republic needed men familiar with the ways of democracy.

Clemenceau's only crime, perhaps, was his naïvety.

At any rate, the staff he managed to put together (probably through Pelletan's good offices) proved a marvel. Gustave Geffroy, a Breton to the core (even though he was born in Paris), wrote with great passion about his artistic friends, Manet, Monet, Renoir, Sisley, Carrière. He looked right for an art critic too, with a thick black beard, the face of an artisan, the eyes of a peasant. Louis Mullem, who had a strong literary sense, wrote about music. One of his leading political writers was Stephen Pichon; many of the articles signed by Clemenceau were actually written by Pichon. Charles Martel was the theatre critic. Edouard Durranc, Sutter Laumann, Alexandre Millerand, Jean Ajalbert, Georges Laguerre would all make names for themselves as writers and politicians. Two university professors made regular contributions to *La Justice*, Emile Accolas and Alphonse Aulard, the historian of the French Revolution. And Karl Marx's son-in-law, Charles Longuet, involved himself for a second time in a newspaper controlled by Clemenceau.

As for Pelletan, during his years at *Le Rappel* he had developed a talent for political caricature and satire which made him the bane of politicians of the Right and Centre. His physical appearance was disconcerting. Madame Adam said he never changed his underclothes; his trousers and jacket were tatty and smelt of the cigars he perpetually chewed. Some accident at birth had crippled one of his arms; 'he took his revenge for this injustice by hitting out at all those within his reach,' said Scheurer-Kestner, 'he is quite the nastiest man I have ever known.' He never married but lived with a virago of a mistress in an apartment near the Observatoire, where he also kept a parrot and an ape. 'Sacré Camille,' exclaimed Clemenceau, as somebody reflected on his editor's social graces, 'when he's invited to dinner he makes pipi in the soup bowl.'

Pelletan's bohemian habits sometimes caused tension between him and his director. Scheurer-Kestner was convinced that it was Pelletan who was behind the paper's combative style, but this would be to underestimate Clemenceau who, after so much silence, was out to establish his own independent line.

The political director wrote only a few articles during the paper's first ten years (although Gambetta, it must be remembered, wrote none for *La République Française*). But he was often at the office, turning up late at night in evening dress (his *nuits galantes* were spent in the company of men). Strutting up and down the naked floorboards he would spout out his views on the latest crisis, the latest scandal, the latest betrayal of republican principles. But his staff did not hold him in awe; he was rather a friend arriving with a nicely wrapped box of late-evening delicacies, words to be rolled on the tongue, savoured, words which left a taste of companionship and an appetite for more. Art, theatre, the Greeks, the latest literary trend – he didn't limit himself to politics.

'Write the way you speak, *nom de Dieu!*' Pelletan used to say, coaxing an article from his master. 'It's not the subjects which are lacking.'

'No, but the moment I sit down they all bugger off.' Clemenceau had a fear of blank paper.

The offices of *La Justice* became the centre of Clemenceau's social life.

Geffroy, Pichon and Mullem would be his friends for life. After the meeting
in the offices they would often go out to a café. On Sundays they received
each other at their homes. At Pelletan's chaotic abode there was always
a horde of writers and artists who would put *le patron* at ease. That was
what brought Clemenceau back to life. He really didn't like politicians.
He was more interested in ideas.

'Justice,' said Clemenceau, 'Justice, a little word, the greatest of them all
this side of kindness. A word that man cannot hear without feeling better.
No sleep that such a word will not break, no death that is not awoken by
it. It is a word stronger than force because it gives hope.' Here was again
that sense of generation that Clemenceau had found in his youth, another
resurrection. *La Justice* drew Clemenceau out of his shell.

'The great formula of the Revolution, Liberty, Equality, Fraternity,' it
was announced in the first issue (16 January 1880), 'which contain in
these three words all the rights of man, all the social reforms, all the
precepts of morality, can be resumed in a still briefer formula: Justice.
This single word contains the concepts of philosophers, the dreams of
poets, the efforts of nations, the heroism of martyrs, the centuries-long
lament of the poor, the demands of the precursors, the constitutions of
the politicians, the hopes of the visionaries: it is the deep cry of humanity
since the untold day when, once emerged from lower nature, it struggled,
it wept and it thought.' Clemenceau the sentimentalist, Clemenceau the
rationalist.

The leading newspaper of the Extreme Left, of the Radicals, had to
contain in its first issue an article on 'Work' ('*Le Travail*', a title that
recalled Clemenceau's student days). While monarchy, it said, was
based on favouritisms, on parasites, on diplomatic intrigues and foreign
adventure, the Republic would have to rely on the efforts of everyone. 'The
educated worker, free and associated, is the end of civil or social wars. It
belongs to the *true* Republic to make these factious antagonisms between
workers and bourgeois disappear.'

The disappearance of classes? The idea was to face some formidable
enemies. First there were the conservatives for whom it presented a
dangerous re-opening to the revolutionary Left. Then there was the
revolutionary Left itself, though insignificant at the time. The repression
of the Commune had stifled the Hébertists, the extreme Jacobins, the
revolutionaries who followed in the footsteps of the masters of 1792.
A new generation was being born, a generation which would turn to
an ideology that was essentially German in its origins. Jules Guesde
had founded France's first Marxist newspaper, *L'Egalité*, in November
1877. Its circulation was probably under a thousand at the moment *La
Justice* appeared on the streets (the latter selling at around 12,000). But

it was uncompromising, it made class war its end and purpose, it was not interested in absorption and cooperation – and it was the precursor to virtually every major left-wing movement that appeared in France in the next half-dozen decades.

IX

LA JUSTICE added the essential thrust that would push Clemenceau to the forefront of national political life. Circumstances had changed. Since the *Seize Mai* most members of the 'republican party' thought that the monarchist threat had been beaten, that the main concern now was to define the kind of Republic Frenchmen had voted for. Within the rather limited world which these politicians inhabited – the world of political dinners, salons and the Parisian opinion press – it was easy to start dividing colleagues into two competing groups: those who held power and who approached reform with caution, and those out of power who were impatient to establish the 'social and democratic Republic' that had been demanded, in various forms, since the Revolution. Logically, this implied a two-party system with Conservatives (the 'Opportunists') on one side and Radicals on the other. But those in power, conscious of how recent their victory had been, were determined to keep all republicans united. As for those out of power, the task of forming a single party of opposition presented enormous obstacles, not least of which was their own revolutionary tradition embodying two contradictory principles, one for strong centralised authority, the other for local or 'communal' liberties. There was always some ingenious formula available to unite the two. Clemenceau himself said, in 1881, that 'the real force of a country is the freedom of regional groups which, far from harming national unity, consolidates it and assures it', a position consistent with his declarations of spring 1871. But while this might have been an acknowledgement of political realities beyond the *fumoir* and the newspaper office, while it might have been an admirable goal for the country at large, it was not the sort of statement one needed to create a disciplined party of opposition.

Without such a party there was a danger of politics degenerating into personal rivalries. No republican wanted this. Sovereignty belonged to the nation, not a personality. Republican struggles were supposed to be struggles of principles, not of persons.

Principles, however, were not the happiest guests at republican dinner tables once the long battle with the monarchists was done. By 1879 the battle seemed to be over. The Senate elections in January gave republicans a majority in the upper house: within a month MacMahon had resigned.

So the dinners began losing their purpose, the camaraderie of former days faded. Scheurer-Kestner thought that the best way to inject new life into his weekly gatherings was by 'extending the political circle: our table companions, with the exception of Clemenceau, belonged to the same school'. He invited some of the younger deputies, Waldeck-Rousseau, Devès, Fallières, Brisson, Spuller, Develle, Casimir-Périer – there were future prime ministers, ministers and presidents in every one of them. But Brisson turned up only on the first invitation and then disappeared. Spuller showed up two or three times. Casimir-Périer only came intermittently. Devès was faithful. So was Fallières, though neither he nor the others were ever quite sure what they were doing there. 'Our dinners promptly became dinners for friends and not dinners for politicians. They wilted, became rarer and finished by disappearing.'

It was Clemenceau who dealt the first blow. On Friday, 28 February 1879, there were the usual guests present, among them, Clemenceau and Emile de Marcère. De Marcère, one of Clemenceau's neighbours on rue Montaigne, was a veteran journalist who had been affiliated with a number of conservative republican papers since the war: he had even launched a press agency. After the *Seize Mai* crisis he became minister of the interior where he presided over the process of freeing the press (a process which was eventually translated into the law of 1881). For the last year, however, Rochefort's *La Lanterne* had been running a series of articles on policy abuses which got especially nasty in December and January when a former employee of the Prefecture started contributing. De Marcère refused to answer the charges, protecting his agents through the claim of 'professional secrecy'. It was known that Clemenceau strongly disapproved of the minister's behaviour. But that evening both men were in high spirits, joining together in a game of baccarat.

The next day Clemenceau demonstrated to the Chamber, for the first time, his extraordinary powers in interpellating. 'The refusal to conduct an enquiry condemns the prefect of police, and the premature closing of the enquiry condemns the minister of the interior.' Clemenceau demanded a vote of censure. De Marcère demanded a vote of confidence. The Chamber simply voted an adjournment.

On Sunday morning Scheurer-Kestner went round to Clemenceau's apartment. 'My dear friend, what were you up to yesterday?' he exclaimed as the door swung open.

'What was I up to?' replied Clemenceau, with eyes wide open.

'You have done what one does not do: you have attacked Marcère, one of our best friends and, where you're concerned, one of your most fastidious friends, if not more.'

'But no! You're quite wrong!' There was yet more white in his eyes.

'I wasn't as sharp as all that!' A copy of the *Journal official* was lying on the table. Scheurer-Kestner walked over, opened it at the third page and, pointing to one of the columns, persevered. 'These are cruel words.'

Clemenceau was genuinely astonished and told his friend, 'I'll repair that tomorrow.'

But on Monday he was more aggressive than ever. De Marcère failed to get his vote of confidence and so resigned. Neither he nor Clemenceau ever turned up again at Scheurer-Kestner's dinners.

Clemenceau's attacks would always be made in public whereas Scheurer-Kestner's comments belonged to a more private sphere. That was significant. For Scheurer-Kestner, one could speak of politics in private terms, an encounter of personalities, whereas for Clemenceau there remained that enormous distance between his own public and private worlds which had so marked his youth. In politics, Clemenceau stuck to principles. His position was thus the more republican of the two; but one might admit that Scheurer-Kestner's approach, in a political system that lacked parties, was the more realistic.

De Marcère's fall signalled further breaches in the old alliance. One Sunday early in the same year, Clemenceau had an appointment to meet Gambetta, newly elected president of the Chamber, at the Palais Bourbon. According to Scheurer-Kestner it was to discuss Clemenceau's recent 'departure from *La République française*'. Clemenceau arrived on time, only to meet Gambetta, hair and cloak at full sail, running in the opposite direction. 'I don't have the time! I've got to go and see Lord Lyons,' he shouted out. Had he forgotten the appointment? Was the business he had with the British ambassador so pressing? Whatever, the incident proved, as Scheurer-Kestner described it, '*la goutte qui fit déborder la vase*', the last straw. Clemenceau was 'profoundly wounded' and, despite entreaties from both Scheurer-Kestner and Gambetta, he never forgot this slight. Apparently personal matters could affect the deputy for Montmartre.

In May he made a speech at the Cirque Fernando denouncing the new minister of public instruction, Jules Ferry. He pointed out (correctly as a matter of fact) that Ferry, since his appointment in February, had so far done nothing for education and, most specifically, had failed to take immediate action against the Catholic orders which still exercised enormous influence in this field. Why wait? After all, Clemenceau must have thought to himself, as mayor of Montmartre he had dealt with the Catholic orders within weeks of his appointment.

Ferry was another man who would take deep personal offence at political jibes. The night after the speech he wrote a long, rambling letter to Scheurer-Kestner. In it he characterised Clemenceau's act as a 'violent, hateful, outrageous attack against a man who is at this moment the object of all the reactionary hatreds'. He accused Clemenceau of 'muddle-headed rashness' (not the first person to do so), of 'demagogic impatience' and of a 'complete and harmful absence of political morality'. Clemenceau's behaviour was 'detestable' and showed him up as a member of Blanqui's 'sect'. 'As for myself,' he ominously concluded, 'it [i.e. this sect] frightened me neither on 4 September, when we barred it the way, nor on 31 October, when we chased it out of the Hôtel de Ville and I impatiently await the duel at the tribune to which its chief, now out in the open, challenges me.'

Clemenceau was in fact in touch with Blanqui and that year, as the campaign for full amnesty picked up momentum, he would not only plea for Blanqui's release from the Clairvaux prison but also support his candidature in a Bordeaux by-election (which Blanqui won but was subsequently declared ineligible). He had also kept up a correspondence with several former Communards, the most important being his old friend and collaborator at Montmartre, Louise Michel.

She wrote at least a dozen letters to '*cher citoyen* Clemenceau' during her exile in New Caledonia, mostly concerning politics and friends, including Madame Ménard-Dorian and Madame Lockroy who had, it seems, provided her with teaching materials. Clemenceau sent her money and books for her school and he obviously proved an ally in her struggle for full amnesty. He also followed up her request to help the families of others who had been deported. Louise Michel herself returned to France only in November 1880, after the general amnesty had been proclaimed. But three years later she was back in gaol for anarchist activities on the esplanade of the Invalides. Clemenceau, at the time, made regular visits to her anguished, dying mother; another press campaign got underway for the daughter's release on humanitarian grounds.

Nevertheless, despite his Communard connections, Clemenceau was not in any way part of a Blanquist 'sect' seeking to overthrow the government, as Ferry had suggested. Whatever influence the Blanquists had exercised on him was lost with the repression of 1871. 'Clemenceau never sought to take power by assault,' remarked Scheurer-Kestner. Furthermore, he 'is not a spirit capable of working with a party'. Clemenceau's actions appear to be more of systematic opposition to whatever powers that be. He might have caused the fall of several ministers, even governments, but as he noted himself, these short-lived governments always consisted of the same people. Perhaps he had some vague hope that the Radicals might be running a government of their own by the mid-1880's, but there was almost certainly no grand strategy involved here. Clemenceau was too much of a loner for that.

His programme changed little. The two major new features appearing after 1879 were constitutional reform and social legislation. Clemenceau spent a great deal of energy on the former, advocating the abolition not only of the Senate but also of the presidency of the Republic. The main aspects of his social programme were a demand for the freedom of workers to associate, stricter limitations on female and child labour, labour insurance and prison reform. But both these areas were consistent with the Belleville programme of 1869 and, even more so, with the ideal of the 'social and democratic Republic' of 1848. Clemenceau was hardly proposing anything new. He was regarded as a man of the extreme left wing not because of the novelty of his programme but because he was an uncompromising defender of old republican ideas, old republican ideas which had never been translated into action.

The question of full amnesty dragged on through 1879. It was actually de Marcère who offered the first government project, a partial amnesty which reduced the number of those still serving sentences or in exile to about a thousand. When Louis Blanc introduced another bill for full amnesty in January 1880 the number stood at about eight hundred. Gambetta was finally swung round and, in a magnificent speech on 21 June 1880, argued for the full amnesty: 'You must close the book on these ten years, you must place the tombstone of oblivion on the crimes and vestiges of the Commune; you must say to all, including those whose contradictions and discord we sometimes regret, that there is only one France and only one Republic!'

The bill became law three days before the nation celebrated, for the first time in ninety years, 14 July, the anniversary of the taking of the Bastille. 'The Christian festivals are dead,' wrote Camille Pelletan in *La Justice*, 'the festivals of Humanity are beginning to be born.' *La Marseillaise* was proclaimed the national anthem. And only a year earlier the two houses of parliament were transferred back to Paris, the capital of the republican Revolution.

X

THE 'WRECKER of ministries' did not have a powerful voice and the most striking thing about his speeches was their moderation. 'Please try and understand me, messieurs,' he said during a debate which led to the overthrow of Ferry's first government, 'I am not here to make any insinuation nor to carry any accusation against anybody ... If I had the misfortune of pronouncing a few words which could have suggested otherwise, I would be the first to withdraw them.'

It was a tone similar to that of his speeches before the National

Assembly in spring 1871. Unlike Gambetta, Clemenceau did not try to impress his audience with great feats of eloquence. Clemenceau dealt with facts; it was the way he organised and presented them that devastated his adversary. 'If you want to know the man,' wrote Camille Pelletan in 1883, 'go and listen to him at the tribune. No word resembles his. No ornaments, save from time to time a biting line, a word struck with a punch. No concern to round out a sentence, to make a phrase sing. It is raw reason. This rapid, concentrated, tight-pressed discussion doesn't need affectation and scorns all adornment. M. Clemenceau's word is naked, tempered and sharpened like a foil; his speeches resemble a fencing match; they riddle the opponent with direct lunges.'

The two principal victims were Jules Ferry and Léon Gambetta. Ferry, tall, reserved, methodical, a Lorrainer who had made his entry into politics via journalism's doorway in the last years of the Empire, was a very different character from Clemenceau. He was a party man; that is, his entire political career was guided by a desire to represent and execute the will of those who brought him to power, that small republican circle which came to prominence in the aftermath of Sedan. Ferry was faithful to people more than to ideas, though it would be unjust to call him unprincipled. He was steeped in the writings of Comte. 'I declare that I adhere to the principles of moral philosophy that I found, fifteen years ago, in the books of the founder of positivist philosophy,' he proclaimed on admission to the freemasons in the summer of 1875. Humanity, for Ferry, marched towards the light with lay education as its guide. He hated mysticism and he hated what he called 'intellectual frivolity', the sort of thing he accused Clemenceau of practising. The forward march was slow because it rested on the education of illiterate peasants. Quick changes were not possible. Jacobinism, absolutism and Bonapartism were all of the same egoistic parentage and they obstructed national unity, the altruistic 'sociability' which he hoped to develop – Ferry's 'sociability' was really a grander conception of Scheurer-Kestner's 'extending the political circle'. 'My aim,' he told Jaurès, 'is to organise humanity without God or King.' He would do it bloodlessly. After the war he abandoned 'insurrectionary' Paris to become deputy for his home country, the Vosges. It was under Ferry's administration that a free, obligatory primary education was established in France and it was also under Ferry that France's colonial empire expanded. For Ferry, the two were closely related. The 'duty' of the 'superior races', the civilised, 'possessing law, science and commerce', was to bring their knowledge and enlightenment to the 'inferior races'. As for the duty of the enlightened republican elite at home, too aggressive an approach was not conducive to 'sociability'.

There were plenty of targets for Clemenceau to lunge at here. He was

delighted at the prospect. 'Famine Ferry' had never much appealed to him;
he had not forgotten the days when Ferry was both Paris mayor and prefect
of police, the vicious debates in the municipal council that cold January,
the defeat, the sympathy he showed for Thiers' failed military assault on
Montmartre, the personal attacks and insinuations he later made in the
National Assembly.

Ferry formed his first government in late September 1880. It was the
fourth government created since MacMahon's departure in January 1879
and the only reason it lasted as long as it did (thirteen months) was
because the squabbling majority could not come up with anything better;
it ended in November 1881, within a fortnight of the opening of the new
parliament elected the previous summer. The issue which brought it down
was the establishment of a French protectorate in Tunisia and the critical
speech was Clemenceau's modest two-hour contribution. But the colonial
question would be raised again, and so would the spectre of Ferry.

Gambetta at last became prime minister. Many factors had conspired
against an earlier succession; it is quite probable that Gambetta himself
was avoiding high office. When, for example, in 1879 Jules Grévy was
elected president of the Republic Gambetta showed no bitterness at all;
his letters to Léonie Léon even suggest some relief.

Conforming to the terms of the 1875 constitution, Grévy had been
elected by the two parliamentary houses. Gambetta was then elected to
replace Grévy as president of the Chamber. The same huge mahogany
desk and chair at which Grévy had sat at Versailles was moved back
to the Palais-Bourbon when, later that year, the two houses voted to
return to Paris. At the beginning of each session, as the deputies took
up their seats in the dominantly red-coloured amphitheatre, the bugle
would sound, the drums would roll and the doorkeeper would announce
'Monsieur le Président'. Four uniformed ushers with swords buckled to
their sides would then enter the chamber followed by a short, heavy-set
man in coat-tails. Accompanied by the ushers, he would solemnly mount
the carpeted staircase to the president's chair.

In the war Gambetta had descended from the skies to speak to the
people. During the first years of the republicans' Republic Gambetta
was the only member of the Chamber who had to *descend* to the
tribune whenever he wanted to make a speech. For the bargainers and
place-hunters – people who wanted to move up in the world – Gambetta
was obviously the man to see, and the more they sought him, the more
his name became linked with the governing power. Some even argued
that it was he, not the ministries, who constituted the real government
in France. This was a line that *La Justice* followed unrepentantly. 'The
head of the majority has openly taken possession of power,' Clemenceau

wrote a couple of days after Gambetta's amnesty speech. 'M. Gambetta is *maître du pouvoir*.'

For Clemenceau and his collaborators at *La Justice* the greatest threat to republican institutions, the concentration of power in a person or a *pouvoir occulte*, was re-emerging. 'What the country has designated for power is not a man, it is a party,' wrote Pelletan in February 1881. 'Since 14 October 1877 the country has designated the republican party for power.' Gambetta 'was the uncontested head' of this party. So what did Gambetta do? 'He rushed to the shelter of the presidential chair.' Simple party representation is not enough for Gambetta; he will wait '"until the day that it pleases my country to designate me." It is certainly a personal designation that is involved here, and from a personal designation there can only emerge a personal power.'

But with no 'parties' personalities were bound to come to the fore. At any rate, the whole French recipe of groups, committees, clubs and dinner companions was finally mixed into the grimy pot of dissent with the legislative elections of August 1881. A new law added further spice to the mixture by allowing a second deputy to stand in arrondissements whose population had increased to over a hundred thousand. One more subtle turn: a candidate was eligible to stand for both constituencies. The law was applicable to Belleville and Montmartre, Gambetta's and Clemenceau's respective districts. Braleret, Gambetta's former local aide, invited Clemenceau to oppose Gambetta in Belleville, but Clemenceau said he preferred to stand for the two constituencies in Montmartre. So Braleret went to Tony Révillon, one of the leading Radicals in the Chamber. In the second constituency Gambetta was opposed by another Radical, Sigismond Lacroix ('Sigismond Krzyzanowki, *dit* Lacroix' said *La République Française*, to emphasise his Polish origins). In Montmartre, Clemenceau faced his old contender, the cobbler Simon Dereure – now running as a 'Collectivist' – and an obscure Opportunist named Vauthier.

With the two most eloquent members of the Chamber fighting for re-election on the two highest, densest, poorest hills in Paris, emerged a new kind of extra-parliamentary politics, one aimed directly at the voters. Dancing halls, theatres and schoolrooms were rented and the candidates' newspapers kept a jealous score of the number of thousands their rival attracted. Gambetta spoke at the Elysée-Ménilmontant hall and at a construction site near the fortifications (lit by electricity generated from a big steam engine, which made hearing hard). Gambetta's construction site speech was interrupted so many times ('Down with the dictator!' 'Down with Gambetta!') that, after twenty-five minutes, he had to abandon both speech and platform (he left banging his silver-knobbed cane on the table and shouting, 'You are drunken slaves!').

Clemenceau's speeches at the Cirque Fernando and the Théâtre des

Bouffes du Nord didn't lack interruptions either, but he held up better. He had had more practice at this sort of thing. He had been speaking at regular intervals at the Cirque Fernando, on boulevard de Rochechouart, since 1879. It was one of the largest auditoriums in Paris and was built to carry sound, unlike Gambetta's construction site; thus, not only could the speaker be heard by the audience but the audience could be heard by the speaker. Clemenceau would speak without notes, save a few jottings which he would leave on a table nearby, and was always prepared to answer interrupters. In a sense, the Cirque Fernando was a grander imitation of the political clubs that had sprung up during the siege and it continued the tradition of 'direct democracy' which went back to the *sans-culottes* of the 1790's. Clemenceau felt at home in Montmartre.

The results spoke for themselves. Clemenceau was elected in both constituencies with a total of 16,484 votes, less than two thousand short of the number who elected him in 1877 when he was running against a monarchist. Gambetta also won in both constituencies of Belleville but, with only 9404 votes, he had lost half his electorate.

Ferry was, at the time, still prime minister. But nobody expected his government to last even if, at the national level, the republicans had gained another million votes at the expense of the Right. At the end of October, when Gambetta was finally called upon to form his *grand ministère* he found he had no great names to join him. Ferry was too mortified. Freycinet claimed he was never invited. Challemel-Lacour was too sick. Brisson wanted to replace Gambetta as president of the Chamber. One of Gambetta's greatest disappointments was the last-minute refusal of Léon Say, the economist, to join his cabinet. 'I have failed to get the *grand ministère* together,' wrote the new premier to Léonie Léon, 'I have formed a phalanx of young men.' They were twelve in number which, in addition to the nine under-secretaries, made it a somewhat larger cabinet than its predecessors. 'For want of a *grand ministère*,' wrote Camille Pelletan in *La Justice*, 'we have *ministère nombreux*. It is not enough.'

The government lasted less than eighty days. It foundered on the issue of constitutional reform. After Gambetta had read his lengthy, though moderate (too moderate), proposals to the Chamber an *ad hoc* Committee of Thirty-Three was elected. All but one of its members were known to be hostile to Gambetta; Clemenceau was among them. After a two-hour hearing in which Gambetta defended the proposals, a rumour went about that he would resort to the use of force if the two houses, united to enact the revisions, declared their sovereignty. The charge was ridiculous, but it confirmed several legislators' suspicions about Gambetta's intentions. The Chamber debate on the committee's report, which against Gambetta's wishes recommended an open parliamentary discussion on revision, took place on a cold and gloomy day in January. Gambetta made a rousing appeal in defence of a two-house parliament and disavowed the 'wretched idea' that he was seeking a dictatorship. None the less the committee's report carried by forty votes.

Within an hour Gambetta and his ministers resigned. Although Clemenceau was an ardent opponent of a two-house legislature and despite the fact that *La Justice* had run a campaign against the government's proposals, it is significant that on this day the 'wrecker of ministers' remained silent.

Eleven months later, Gambetta was dead.

Once more the crowd gathered before the legislative palace, its steps a mass of bouquets, garlands and wreaths, its pillared façade half covered by a great black cloth swagged to one side like a theatre curtain. Senators, deputies, municipal councillors, the chiefs-of-staff, delegations from every province, representatives of the ministries, the colonies, learned societies, the masonic lodges; practically every workers' association in the country carried a banner at Gambetta's funeral. It was estimated that there were over three thousand civil servants who followed in formation. Men had climbed the trees, the walls, the statues – save that of Our Lady of Strasbourg, draped in black. A military band boomed out a dirge and the procession headed across place de la Concorde.

There was little said among the deputies as they advanced across the bridge, though Clemenceau was heard repeating '*Ah! voilà un grand malheur! oui, c'est un grand malheur!*' They turned down rue de Rivoli because the great boulevards were blocked by shopstands set up for the New Year. A life cut short, a task unfinished. Most people dreamed of the Republic, Gambetta created it.

The morning sun caught the silver markings on the hearse as its six horses turned up the boulevard Sébastopol where you would have caught a glimpse of a gleaming new Hôtel de Ville, inaugurated six months earlier. It was a sight that might have prompted a few lines from Lucretius (another man who had proposed eliminating the fear of the gods): 'Behold the infant: Like a shipwrecked sailor cast ashore by the fury of the billows, after Nature has dragged him in pain from his mother's womb.'

From there it was a march up the rue Turbigo. The red everlasting flowers, a gift from a village in Alsace, fell from one corner of the great funeral wagon on entering place du Château d'Eau, recently renamed place de la République – birth through exposure with a very bitter destiny. That was the Republic!

Then the climb into the popular quarters: Gambetta would have replaced the old paternalism of the state with a fraternity of the peoples, but he got too entangled in his own creative dynamism to succeed. Yet, had he failed? The streets of the Belleville slopes were as crowded as place de la Concorde, and the procession moved on. The people, perhaps, had too simple an idea of progress; 'Gambetta might not have known where he was going,' Clemenceau later said, 'but wherever he went, he went with fire.'

The ceremony ended with four dull speeches at the gates of the Père Lachaise cemetery. No priests were present.

XI

AT THE time of Gambetta's death Europe was entering a period of economic recession which was to last until the end of the century. Factories were closed, unemployment increased, stock markets plunged; agriculture, which had hardly benefited from the mid-century boom in the first place, faced some very hard years, setting off a stream of rural migrants towards towns where there were no jobs. Europe's governments – whether democratic, autocratic or monarchical – had to do something, though nothing in the political debates that had raged across the continent since the French Revolution gave a clear indication of exactly what. Some looked to the past, believing that the best safeguards against economic disaster were those that their forefathers had commended; others laid their eyes on the future, convinced that only a totally new society would provide the conditions for durable solutions. But for most politicians, in western Europe at any rate, the crisis implied a return to an old issue, even if it had now to be seen in a context of larger factories, larger towns, larger populations. A perennial issue, a simmering issue. Was modern industry making life generally better, or making it worse? On one side of the Channel they had called it the 'Condition of England Question'. On the other side, it was known as *la question sociale*.

Gambetta had come close to saying that there was no *question sociale*. 'Believe me,' he once told an audience, 'there is no social remedy because there is no social question. There is a series of problems to be solved, or difficulties to be overcome.' The phrase, *la question sociale*, implied a simplicity which Gambetta was unable to accept. Locality, climate, custom, sanitary conditions and economic problems were specific difficulties which could only be solved in their own terms, 'one by one and not by a single formula'. On the same grounds, Gambetta had refused to accept the idea that there was a single social class, excluded from national political life, which might one day force its entry. He preferred to speak of *ce monde qui travaille*, the new 'social strata' or *couches sociales*, which included along with manual labourers, artisans, businessmen and traders, anyone in effect who exerted some kind of professional activity. In this sense he was not very far from the thinking of the abbé Siéyès who, a hundred years earlier, had divided the world into those who performed useful work for society and those who lived by the work of others. As far as Gambetta was concerned, the Republic was open to all who worked. Yet it was not a very realistic picture when major political decisions were being made at dinner parties. Gambetta belonged to a small, self-contained elite. But as long as the economy thrived he could ignore the fact, though his loss of votes in Belleville must have indicated that something was wrong.

Clemenceau's view of society was not very different from Gambetta's in that he too rejected the idea of a single excluded social class and the possibility of a one-formula solution. But that there were large numbers of Frenchmen excluded from the democratic life he was utterly convinced. The talking and the slogans were not enough. The continuing elitist nature of politics was an obstacle to democratic liberty. The state would have to act. Unlike Gambetta, the *question sociale* was a pivotal issue for Clemenceau.

As on virtually every other occasion when the issue had been raised, it was a deteriorating situation in Paris which attracted the attention of the Chamber of Deputies in January 1884. A Moderate Republican, Langlois, initiated the debate by asking the government, again under Ferry's tutelage, what it intended to do about the economic crisis. The debate, which lasted five days, gave a very good idea of parliamentary opinion on social issues, ranging from de Mun's 'Social Catholicism' on the Right, through the economic liberalism upheld by the majority, to the state interventionists on the Left. Most contributors were imbued with a sense of History, a feeling that there were forces at work here that were beyond their control, though few had the catastrophic vision of Charles Longuet who wrote in *La Justice* of 'the transformations or the perturbations – I was going to say the deluge – which threatens the contemporary economic order.' The notion that there existed a single excluded social class waiting in the wings to take over power was also far from the thoughts of most who spoke during that week in January.

Were the people getting richer or poorer? The comte Albert de Mun, a tall handsome former army officer, who had done more than anyone else in the Chamber to get the Church involved in the lives of working people, believed the latter. Industry, he explained, was producing too many goods and demanding too much work; 'one has abused the forces of man.' It was destroying the family. One might have dreamed that overproduction would lead to a general increase in welfare but in fact it had had the

opposite effect and 'pauperism, far from declining, has only increased.'
De Mun had been working on a solution for almost ten years. 'In the
past,' he told the assembly, 'there was a mediating power in the universe:
this was the Catholic Church.' In its place – his enemies would say, in
awaiting its return – he proposed the organisation of a 'concert of states'
and 'congresses' which should be held to discuss the 'interests of labour'.
He didn't elaborate, but what he envisioned must have corresponded to
the *Œuvre des cercles catholiques d'ouvriers* which he had founded in 1875.
These were hierarchically organised workers' circles supervised, as the
original prospectus put it, by 'the devotion of the directing class to the
working class'.

De Mun's speech was a commitment to state intervention. Most of the
debate, however, was dominated by non-interventionists, republicans
who minimised the seriousness of the crisis and who were convinced that
History was on their side, that wealth was growing to the ultimate benefit
of all, provided the state didn't step in and mess things up. Clemenceau's
supporters referred to these proponents collectively as the 'economists';
their ideas were in fact heavily influenced by English economic liberalism
and the writings of the former minister of finance, Léon Say. The most
forceful case for the 'economists' was made by Ferry himself who, in a speech
spanning two days, argued that the best thing for the government to do
was nothing. 'The struggle for life is bitter,' the prime minister concluded,
shaking his long side-whiskers, 'the ruins heap up on the battlefields of
competition. One can dream of a more fraternal society, but we will not
see it, any more than our successors will see this promised land. One has
thus to resign oneself to the consequences, painful as they are, of free
competition.'

Clemenceau followed Ferry at the tribune. Of course, he said, there was a
question sociale, though it couldn't be solved *'en bloc'*. These great panaceas
of some reformers were unscientific. The problem today was that one did
not as yet – despite the fact that France was one of the most centralised
countries in the world – have enough information to gauge the extent of
the crisis. Clemenceau would ask for a 'grand commission of inquiry' on
industry and agriculture, a motion adopted by the Chamber by a margin
of eight votes.
  Much of this important, if somewhat jumbled speech (it was delivered
as always, without detailed notes) was devoted to the problem of human
liberty. Because Clemenceau was later accused of turning tail on the Left,
of abandoning his earlier principles, it is worth pondering a moment on
what he meant by human liberty at this time.

Clemenceau was as convinced as his more moderate colleagues that History, at any rate contemporary history, meant progress and that even if prices plummeted, profits diminished and real wages fell there was enough force in the democratic motor to push society onwards to greater freedoms and to higher levels of civilisation. The question facing those in power today was not so much whether this would happen as how it would happen. The government had a choice: either it legislated in favour of those who remained oppressed, or it waited for the oppressed to take matters into their own hands. 'It is a question of knowing in the end whether we are going to leave the era of revolutions or whether every twenty years we have to witness a social war . . .'

Clemenceau emphasised two areas where the state would have to play a more active role if it genuinely intended to strengthen the weak and avoid such a war. The first was in education – 'You have organised primary education on paper,' he told a scowling Ferry, 'but I tell you at this very moment from the point of view of technical training and an integral teaching, nothing has been done. You still have the old primary education, the old secondary education, the old higher education, such as had been instituted by the monarchical regimes and which you have inherited.' The second was in granting workers the same right to associate as that enjoyed by employers – and that right had to be enforced.

But this did not require expropriating a section of the economy for the pleasure of the state. State intervention, yes, but not a state-controlled economy: there were two personalities, said Clemenceau, that would ensure liberty, the legislator and the citizen: 'there is the legislator who removes a privilege, who pulls down a barrier and who legally grants a right; and then there is the citizen who, following the intellectual and political education that he has received, can serve himself, to a greater or lesser advantage, of this liberty.' One could say that Clemenceau was once again applying his early lessons of the French Revolution, with the experience of violence behind him. Robespierre had spoken of the legislator, but in Robespierre's world the legislator was all powerful, he had the right to force the citizen to be free if the situation demanded it. Clemenceau would leave the critical act of freedom to the citizen, the state could only encourage the condition which would make that act possible.

There were economic forces at play in the 1880's, forces that were creating wealth at a scale unimaginable a hundred years earlier. Clemenceau had the insight, borrowed undoubtedly from his more liberal colleagues of the Centre, that it was the citizen, not the legislator, who was behind those forces.

The legislator, he said, cannot create wealth, but he can and has to equalise it.

So here in 1884, at the height of the radical phase in his political career, in the midst of a plea for greater state involvement in social affairs, Clemenceau appeals to the individual initiative of the citizen. It was like life emerging from inert matter, the spontaneous urge to create. The passionate side of his instinct, his inward sense of the solitary being forging its place in the universe, was irrepressible.

The fact that Clemenceau believed that the bearers of progress were individuals and not classes condemned him in the eyes of a more theoretically oriented Left; by failing to give class first place, they would argue, Clemenceau would never be able to develop a theory of social movement. But then Clemenceau was not very interested in theory.

In the same speech he declared that he did not seek to organise workers into regiments, to add to an already oppressive political centralisation a system of economic centralisation, or 'to do what M. de Mun has demanded, to brigade workers in the interest of some sort of doctrine'. He compared the private, but state-supported, system of social insurance in Britain to the obligatory insurance of the German centralised state and openly rejected the latter: 'I am the declared enemy of a system of distributive justice by the state or by the commune; I solicit the intervention of the individual, of individual initiative; I want it to be exercised at all times, but in conditions where the struggle is possible and not in those of society such as it has been organised up to now.'

Clovis Hugues spoke for the Socialists during the debate, but it was hardly the place or the time to discuss their differences.

Differences there were. Since the siege and Commune Clemenceau had been aware of inconsistencies between his own political programme and the various tendencies of the revolutionary Left; heckling from the Left had become a permanent feature of his campaign addresses, almost a dramatic device. Guesde's Marxist followers were proving to be particularly mischievous. In April 1880 he had been interrupted at the Cirque Fernando by one of them who wanted to know what he thought of the resolutions of the recent Marseille 'workers' congress'; Clemenceau replied that he had no taste for 'collectivist barracks and convents'.

But in October of the same year he adopted, word for word, Guesde's 'minimum programme', an act which delighted Karl Marx, who had already been impressed by a brief personal encounter arranged by his son-in-law, Longuet, when Clemenceau had visited England in May. None the less there was continual skirmishing between Guesde's paper and La Justice and one has difficulty imagining how peace within the parliamentary Left could be maintained once the Marxists began winning seats in the Chamber. After all, Guesde was predicting the revolution by the end of the decade while Clemenceau was giving heated advice on how best to avoid it. And Clemenceau's references in his speech of 1884 to state regimentation and the brigading of workers for the sake of doctrine showed that he hadn't lost all his fears of 'barracks and convents', whether of the Right or Left.

The 'grand commission of inquiry', soon known as the Commission of Forty-four, won its narrow approval as a result of support from the extreme Right; its most vigorous opponents were from the Centre. Most of its subsequent members, however, also came from the Centre, including twenty-four who had voted against the bill. *La Justice* promptly announced the 'death of the inquiry'. In fact, this inquiry remains one of the major sources of nineteenth-century social history. Eugène Spuller, Gambetta's former aide, was elected its president, Floquet was one of its two vice-presidents, while Clemenceau was elected president of one of the eight sub-commissions. It was decided to proceed directly into an examination of the situation in Paris before opening the more general inquiry. In the meantime Clemenceau, accompanied by Richard Waddington, brother of the ambassador in London and also a member of the commission, left for England to study the procedure of British parliamentary commissions. It was during this short visit that one of the most bitter strikes of the century broke out at Anzin in the department of the Nord.

XII

THE INHABITANTS of the Nord – like those of South Wales, Lancashire, the Ruhr or the Donetz Basin – owed their livelihoods to a primeval subtropical forest which, three hundred million years ago, had stretched from what are today the British Isles to the Ukraine; a flat monotonous expanse of swamp, ponds and damp soils, where the trees did not vary. For several million years the trees dominated the landscape. For another odd million it was the turn of the swamps. Later, whole areas were covered by sea. Then the forests returned, and the swamps. Each age left its deposit. The older organic sediments were pushed downward and outward by ground pressures (pressures which produced the mountains of the South and the plains of the North). Between Hamm in central Germany and Fléchinelle in the Pas-de-Calais they took the form of a huge subterranean arc dipping, in Germany, northward to a depth and extent that is still unknown, while, in Belgium and France, they plunged downward and westward. Practically every native of Europe could trace his ancestry to men who had crossed the northern plains overlaying these deposits. They had travelled chiefly in armies. Most agricutural techniques had followed a similar route; Europe's agriculture came from Germany, not Rome. But it was only since the Middle Ages that man had started digging beneath the fertile loam to the black seams that remained of the primeval forest; he called the stuff coal.

Coal was bulky and costly to transport. Far into the nineteenth century water-power continued to be the main energy source for industry. But when the blast furnace and the steam engine finally did become the gauge of industrial might, manufacture was forced to locate around the coalfields that bordered the northern plains. So it was that Europe built its main industrial belt on an agricutural belt, along the old route of armies.

The belt's western limit was French because of past wars. It crossed the two former Burgundian provinces of Hainaut and Artois, which since late medieval times had exchanged hands between the Austrian Habsburgs, the Spanish Habsburgs, the French, the Dutch and even the English – the area had provided battlefields for practically every major armed conflict in Europe since the days of the Emperor Charles V. Under Louis XIV Artois became French while the County of Hainaut was split in two, the western half with the cities of Valenciennes, Condé and Maubeuge, going to France while the eastern half, which included Mons and Charleroi, went to the portion of the Holy Roman Empire that later became Belgium. No natural frontier determined the political map of the region, for the land was flat. No language or culture played a role, for they spoke the same *patois* on either side of the border. But when the French mining companies started bringing in cheap labour from the Borinage, on the Belgian side, the French began to detest their neighbours – '*A mort les étrangers!*' cried Zola's miners (the sentiment was perfectly authentic). '*A mort les Borains! Nous voulons être les maîtres chez nous!*'[1]

The westward dip of the coal seams determined when and how they were mined. Around Charleroi they had been digging up coal since the fourteenth century, by hand or with the help of horses. Coal was only discovered on the French side in the eighteenth century, at Anzin in 1734 – the country's first steam-engines had to be brought in to clear the pits of water and make them operable. More powerful machines, more precise engineering were required when, in the 1850's, the first pits – many of them going down a thousand metres or more – were opened in the Pas-de-Calais.

Thus geography, war and technology combined to create a peculiarly human landscape, the agitated skyline of the coal world. 'What is striking about the countryside is this character of the struggle for life,' wrote Ardouin-Dumazet when visiting the Anzin region in the 1890's. It appeared a most exclusive struggle. A regime of minerals, gouged out

[1] 'Death to strangers! Death to the Borains! We want to be the masters in our own home!' Emile Zola, *Germinal*.

from the underworld, had chased off the surface regime of animal and vegetable, leaving only man, his machines and his materials to reap a livelihood.

These men were a proud people. Small wonder miners attracted the attention of the politicians, the press, the novelists, even poets. In the 1880's coalminers made up a little over one half of 1 per cent of the economically active population in France. But they fascinated, they drew on the pity and the fears of the readers of the new mass media. In their leather helmets and coats, covered in grime, they looked like soldiers returning from the front. They were employed in large numbers and governed, it seemed, as in D.H. Lawrence's Beldover, by 'powerful underworld men who spent most of their time in darkness.' Live burial was a common theme in the literature on coalminers. Inasmuch as they influenced the debate on the *question sociale*, the images the miners projected through second- and third-hand reports were probably as important as the lives they actually led. These were images of suffering, images of struggle, images of a foreign and industrial new world.

But the ironic thing about the Anzin Coalmining Company was that it was in so many ways an anachronism. Of course it was large, monopolistic and produced a lot of coal, thus fulfilling people's expectations that industry was getting larger, more monopolistic and increasingly productive. These, however, were not the trends at Anzin.

The Company had been created in 1757 by what amounted to a treaty drawn up between the squabbling aristocratic landowners involved in the discovery of the coal seam more than twenty years earlier. Most of the shareholders and administrators were drawn from the region until the July Monarchy when capital from Paris began to seep its way in. Nevertheless, the Company's founding charter remained unchanged. It was governed by a council of six managers, a managing director and a president, all nominated for life. Among recent presidents of the Company were Joseph Périer, brother of Casimir Périer, who had been prime minister in the 1830's, and Adolphe Thiers. The current president, the duc d'Audiffret-Pasquier, was active in the monarchist cause.

In 1884 the Company hired fourteen thousand workers, making it the largest commercial employer in France. A brochure published shortly after the strike described Anzin as 'the most important colliery of France and even of the world.'

But once coal was discovered in the Pas-de-Calais, new fields started opening up. Price wars began. A boom in the early 1870's allowed the Company to sell at a better price and slightly increase production. But it did so at the cost of ignoring the need for capital renewal. The galleries, in particular, were extended with insufficient aeration and there were several accidents, owing to coal gas, with serious loss of life. The productivity of workers declined.

Conditions in the pits were probably dreadful, though this was one of the Company's best-kept secrets. It was still using pits that had been opened in the previous century while its competitors worked the latest modern technology could supply. Government inspectors rarely descended the pits. One of the few outsiders who actually did was Emile Zola who visited the Company in February 1884, just as the strike was beginning, to take notes for his new novel, *Germinal*. He descended, like Clemenceau eight months later, one of the Company's most modern pits, *la fosse Renard*. He had to take an interpreter with him, for the miners spoke *rouchi*, incomprehensible to anyone not from the region. Zola's description of the descent, in his notes and in his novel, is one of terror.

There was something very special about the 'working class' of Anzin. It was a closed family affair, for it was not just the father who worked but the whole family; one's position within the family to a great extent determined one's position in the Company's work hierarchy and most especially the physical location of one's work. Women were forbidden to work in the pits by a law of 1874, but in 1884 Anzin employed many hundreds of women, mostly working on the mechanical belts that fed the train wagons, collecting pebbles and letting only high quality coal through. It also employed a larger proportion of children than elsewhere. In 1874 the lower age-limit for the employment of children was set at twelve, so the life cycle in the pits began at twelve.

A child would start as a *galibot* with 'elderly' men, the *raccommodeurs*, who were responsible for maintaining the wooden support systems in the secondary galleries that led from the principal gallery to the coal face. At the age of sixteen he would normally become a haulier (or *hercheur*) and by eighteen he would be working on the face. Most miners were well past the peak of their earning power by the time they reached forty-five when they would try to maintain a position inside the pits as a *raccommodeur*. Retirement, despite the claims of the Company, frequently meant financial disaster.

One of the main causes of Anzin's low productivity was the high proportion of *galibots* and *raccommodeurs* to those actually working the face. The Company, with its sclerotic system of management, had been unable to adjust its workforce to the new competitive realities facing it after the mid-century. Finally, in 1883, the Company engaged a consulting engineer, a Monsieur Ledoux. He made two drastic proposals: first, workers were to be paid by the cartload of coal delivered at pithead (the price being determined by foremen) rather than by the square metre worked at the face; second, the system of *marchandage* was to be extended and improved.

Marchandage was very similar to the hated English 'butty' system, by which groups of five to six workers (often related) would bid for sections of the face to be worked for the pay-period of two weeks. Payment would be made to the group, its division determined by the group's most senior member. Such a system fitted in very well, from the Company's point of view, with the family ties that were already so strong among its workers. But it was diametrically opposed, relying as it did on competition between the groups, to the principle of collective action, which received a boost the following March when, shortly after the debate on the *question sociale*, parliament legitimised trade unions.

The strike began with the announcement of a third measure. On pay day, Saturday, 16 February 1884, yellow posters of the Company, plastered on the walls of the cashiers' offices, gave notice that 'the workers who have been extracting coal in the stalls and who have been cutting out the secondary galleries must henceforth, at the same time, be charged with the responsibility of maintaining the woodwork in these galleries, to be reimbursed by supplementary pay variable according to the difficulties of this maintenance.' This meant the suppression of a large number of *galibots* and *raccommodeurs*. Given family loyalties, it is impossible to see how a strike could have been avoided, and the Company obviously knew this.

The much-feared union movement was in fact just beginning to get underway at Anzin. Its star was Emile Basly (pronounced 'Basili'), an orphan raised by the Hospice de Valenciennes, employed by the Anzin Company as a *galibot* and fired at the age of twenty-six for his involvement in a strike in 1880. For three years he had been eking out a living from a café, Au Dix-Neuvième Siècle, which a rival company had put at his disposal on rue de Villars, just off the limits of the Anzin properties. Basly spoke of 'the hard profession of the miner who entombs himself in the bowels of the earth' – Zola used Basly as a model for both Etienne and Rasseneur – 'and in a corrupted atmosphere, whose life is only a battle to fill the strongboxes of the shareholders'. His more practical demands included an eight-hour day, the abolition of *marchandage*, the setting-up of savings and retirement accounts for all miners and a fixed daily wage. At a more ideological level, he announced that 'we have never provoked a strike' but that if the miners were forced to take action they would henceforth aim at a 'general strike, forerunner of the social revolution'. He also proposed the nationalisation of all coalmines.

On Wednesday, 20 February, Basly wrote a long circular addressed to all the deputies in Paris and to the governing authorities in the department asking the government 'if it will intervene to bring justice to these brave workers'. That same afternoon, at a meeting in Denain attended by perhaps a thousand, perhaps three thousand miners, the strike was decided.

On Thursday, 1,700 workers were missing from work at the pits of Denain. On Friday, the pits of Anzin and Saint-Waast were struck. By Saturday every pit of the Company was affected, with only about a quarter of the workforce turning up. It grew every day thereafter.

Zola, who left Paris on 23 February expecting to witness a revolt, returned a little over a week later, on 3 March, impressed by the tranquillity of the region. The workers generally stayed at home. The squares were empty, the streets were quiet. A few miners, dressed in their Sunday best, sipped beer in the cafés. Much of the machinery at the pits was closed down, though the engineers – an augury of things to come – did not join the strike. Some engines continued puffing out white steam but the skies were luminous, for there was so little smoke.

On Friday a delegation of miners led by Basly went to see the managing director, Guary. The meeting lasted nearly two hours. The delegation left with the feeling that the situation was bad, but not hopeless.

Then on Sunday a rumour spread that there were more than just *raccommodeurs* and *galibots* who were going to be laid off. And sure enough on Monday every strike organiser, along with 140 other miners, learned they had lost their jobs. The strikers' determination intensified.

In an interview granted to *Le Matin* on 4 March (as the trade union law was going through parliament), d'Audiffret-Pasquier explained the reason for the firings: 'In less than a year our workers have been convoked to nineteen meetings in which they have been demoralised by putting on trial the Company and presenting it as an arbitrary and tyrannical exploitation whereas, on the contrary, our administration is entirely paternal.' He went on, 'We could no longer tolerate these meetings, meetings that were exclusively political. You can report it: We will not yield. We are old battle horses who have seen many other battles. We reject the intervention of government in the question of the patronage of workers.'

At least the issue was now clear. The strike was certainly political and the 'entirely paternal' administration was being put in question.

The Chamber of Deputies began to get involved in the affair when, on 27 February, two of the deputies from the Nord, Giard and Girard, asked the minister of the interior, Raynal, to intervene in favour of the miners. The minister replied that current legislation completely disarmed him and that any approach to the Company's administrators, motivated by 'a spirit which was hardly republican', would 'not be very well welcomed'. The Chamber agreed by a vote of 327 to 131; there was nothing to be done.

*

What of the 'grand commission of inquiry'? Because it was dominated by Moderates and Opportunists, one couldn't expect much. But on 10 March Clemenceau began to play a role.

He proposed that the commission immediately send a delegation to Anzin to begin an inquiry into the strike and examine the workers' demands, insisting on the point that the Company's administrators were all 'Orleanists and reactionaries'. A majority opposed him with Raynal's argument: the state cannot intervene. Not to be daunted, however, Clemenceau sent a personal invitation to Basly to come to Paris, offering to pay for the trip out of his own pocket.

Basly appeared before the commission on 18 March. He demanded that its own members come to Anzin because the government's inquiry, currently underway, was totally inadequate. Clemenceau re-introduced his proposal for an immediate commission inquiry, but this, like his first proposal, was rejected after more than a week's debate.

XIII

How ODD it was to see men in their prime sieving dirt in the slag heaps for scraps of coal; they were digging muddy holes as deep as themselves to carry something home to burn. Someone found a coin that must have dated from the Revolution. Two men chatted merrily, discussing the use of bricks in their grates. *Le terri*, the slag heap: they used to call it the coal mine of the poor; when the pits were working it was only old men and old women that you'd find under the shadow of the tip, sifting for the fuel they had broken their bodies and their lives to supply others. Everyone was poor today. The cold was the thing; they were freezing.

Vieux Condé, Fresnes, Bruay, Hérin, Wallers, Fenain and Nœux: these small conurbations merged into one another, never quite town, never quite country. But during the strike one was more conscious of the country. Nature had the upper hand again. The unending plains exerted their eternal will once more, the winds swept in from the seas, a flight of gulls temporarily broke the horizon while, lower down, bare trees in the distance added touches of mauve to the greys and greens of the sleeping winter fields.

In the third fortnight of the strike an appeal was sent through the press to other unions: 'The delegates decide to address a pressing appeal to all their brothers in the mining departments to invite them to take, in the shortest delay, the measures necessary in view of the general strike.'

The general strike. It was already an article of faith among the leaders. But at Saint-Etienne the 'Central Committee of the Unions of French Miners' refused, deciding instead to make an appeal to the minister of the interior. The *Chambre syndicale de la Loire* forwarded 120 francs, which was returned as derisory. Nothing came of the appeal to the British Trades Union Congress. Could one have expected otherwise when miners in the neighbouring department refused to make a movement?

Justice, fraternity and the rights of man were poor things beside the eyes of hungry children. By the third fortnight, men were returning to the pits in fives and tens. By the fourth, in scores.

So a new acrimony was born. The strikers started taking action against the *rouffians*, those who worked. By the first week of April – the sixth week of the strike – the whole region looked like a military camp, with soldiers guarding the machinery, troops with bayonets standing before the administrators' buildings and the shops, and the slow passage of striker patrols treading shadows through the streets.

There was a violent debate on 8 April in the Chamber. Indeed, the atmosphere was not wholly unlike Versailles in 1871 when Clemenceau mounted the tribune: 'One knows that it is not against M. d'Audiffret-Pasquier and his colleagues that you are sending the troops. No, it is against the miners, who struggle in conditions of inequality. The soldier in the affair represents the state itself put at the service of the Anzin Company! The intervention of troops is contrary to the doctrine of the republican party.' So apparently was the Company: it was opposed to unions authorised by law and was conducting monarchist manœuvres by way of 'an economic struggle infinitely more dangerous for the Republic than the political struggle'. This had to be stopped. 'The French worker has to know that he has the support of the government of the Republic.'

Well, he did not get it that month. Groups of exhausted women visited the miners' homes to persuade their men to return to work. By Thursday, 17 April, the 56th day of the strike, the number of workers back at their jobs was approximately 68 per cent of the total – this is generally taken as the last day of the Anzin strike.

Clemenceau did eventually get to lead a sub-commission to Anzin for an inquiry. The delegation, which included his old student friend Germain Casse, left on 7 October for a week's tour of the mining district. They descended the *fosse Thiers*, among the most modern of the Anzin pits, but were refused access to the *fosse Saint-Louis*, where much of the violence had occurred. The secretary's record of the meeting with 'workers', in the ornate surroundings of the Anzin mairie, was one of the shortest appendices in the commission's report. No wonder: not one of these men were currently employed by the Company.

Despite its two hundred pages (containing a wealth of information on the history of the Company and details of the strike) Clemenceau concluded that the report was a failure. The state was equipped with insufficient powers. 'We estimate that national representation must have, in a Republic, the means to conquer the resistance that egoistic interests of individuals put up against it when the state wants to put under full light questions of general interest.' There were thus, in Clemenceau's political ideals, limits on how far individual initiative could be pushed. He cited the case of the United States, where Congress was armed with the power of inquiry on behalf of the public interest. In France, by contrast, state intervention was still limited to sending troops when 'agents of authority' demand the aid of armed force. 'It is necessary,' wrote the sub-commission's president, 'that the government of the Republic cease to follow the old ways of the Monarchy and the Empire.'

XIV

IN THE 1880's the monarchies and the empires outnumbered the republics. France and Switzerland were the only two in Europe. One would have to have gone to the New World to find the others: the United States and several, at least by name, in Latin America. France, diplomatically isolated since the war, hardly conformed to the norm when it came to government. There were, to be sure, politicians in Paris like Clemenceau who were convinced that History was on their side but, besides a few intellectual circles and a scattering of reformers and revolutionaries, there was no reason for the rest of the world to think the same.

Nobody, however, would have been able to deny that there was not something that was dramatically changing the structure of powers within this world. There was, in the first place, a simple biological fact that no one to this day has fully explained: the population was increasing at unprecedented rates. The world had reached its first thousand million at about the time of Waterloo. By the 1880's it was already halfway along to its second. Secondly, there were changes afoot in the distribution of economic and political forces. For the previous century the Europeans had been accumulating wealth that no other part of the world could equal. But whereas, in the world's commerce, Britain's supremacy had been virtually unchallenged, by the late 1870's there were other contenders. In 1860 half the exports of Asia, Africa and Latin America went to Britain. Now it was down to about one-quarter. In the 1850's and 60's it was Britain that built the world's first railway networks. Now other countries were showing an interest.

It was a more competitive world. It was a more jealous world. There was talk of protectionism in Europe: that was perhaps the greatest fear. 'If you were not such persistent protectionists,' the British prime minister would tell the French ambassador in the 1890's, 'you would not find us so keen to annex territories.'

It was the colonial issue that provided Clemenceau with the ammunition that would bring down three governments (two of Ferry's and one of Freycinet's) and contributed to the destruction of a fourth (Gambetta's). Clemenceau told the crowd at Cirque Fernando in October 1882, 'There has been established in Europe a state of affairs where, though pretending to maintain the peace, the powers at the first opportunity indulge themselves in veritable acts of depredation, seizing countries where they are assured of encountering no resistance. The other powers do nothing, sometimes out of fear of a general conflagration, sometimes simply because they are awaiting their own turn. That is a policy we openly repudiate.'

Clemenceau's position on colonialism ('imperialism' was a new word in the 1880's and rarely used) was tightly linked to his position on the *question sociale*. 'The eternal *question sociale*, which groans in the workshops,' he said to the Chamber in July 1885, during an extended comment on the colonial problem; 'don't you find there sufficient domain for human ambition . . .? When a statesman dares even to look into the face of such a work, when he finds nothing to advise a nation but to go off and make war in the four corners of the world, if he doesn't understand that the first condition of the progress he wishes to serve is peace, if he formulates a doctrine of war, he is perhaps a great man in the vulgar sense of the word, but he is not a democrat.'

Democracy was the underlying principle of the Republic – who could have disagreed with that? And this Republic was born in opposition to a foreign occupying force – how could the same Republic now rush off and occupy other peoples' lands, invade someone else's *'foyer national'*?

Even so, there was a republican colonialism, and many French statesmen over several generations saw no hypocrisy in it. The progress of civilisation was their main argument: 'the European nations have a superior duty of civilisation towards native peoples,' said Ferry – and, after all, wasn't it in the name of such universal progress that the revolutionary armies of the First Republic had pressed into foreign territories?

It was Gambetta, not Ferry, who spoke of a policy of *fierté nationale*, who most enthusiastically embraced the Tunisian venture and who was the keenest proponent of a combined Anglo-French expedition into Egypt;

the columns of *La République française* had been, since the early 1870's, ardently championing the colonialist cause. None the less, it was the parliamentary duel between Ferry and Clemenceau which encapsulated the disagreement between those republicans committed to expansion and those who were opposed.

Ferry argued, as he had in the discussion of the *question sociale*, that the world was becoming increasingly competitive. Germany and the United States were becoming protectionist while pouring their own goods into French markets. France would only be able to exert her position in the world by expanding her colonies. In the Tunisian debate of November 1881 he argued that France's military strength, and hence her security and position within Europe, were directly tied to the success of the colonial campaigns. 'Do nothing,' he said, 'that can be prejudicial to French interest. Do nothing that can harm the recognition we owe the army and those who lead it. Do not touch, however light your hand, these two great interests: do not touch France, and do not touch the army!'

As for those who feared that military force was perhaps not the most effective way of spreading civilisation, he remarked that 'superior races have rights over inferior races.' France could not abdicate her responsibilities: 'France must carry everywhere she can her language, her customs, her flag, her arms, her genius.'

Clemenceau opposed Ferry on every point. In the first place, France was fighting undeclared wars. In November 1881 he told Ferry, 'You have wanted to rob [parliament] of its two most precious rights: the right to consent to taxation, and the right to decide on peace and war.'

Clemenceau entirely disagreed with the strategic and military argument, constantly noting that the colonial ventures weakened the country's defences of its northern and eastern frontiers; unlike Britain, he said, France is not an island. This was not to suggest that Clemenceau was looking for a fight with Germany. 'France needs a revenge,' he said at the Cirque Fernando in May 1884, 'the revenge of liberty and justice against the Monarchy which has precipitated so much ruin. It is a hard task, begun a hundred years ago. If we accomplish it we will have done more for our country than all the victors of battle. The real revenge will be the victory of the new social order.'

As for the economics of colonialism, Clemenceau thought that the principal economic interests were private concerns, not those of the nation ('One begins with the missionaries, one continues with the soldiers and one ends with the bankers'); he believed that the colonies would be more of an expense than a benefit:

> Commercial outlets are not opened with gunfire; they are closed . . .
> So many men killed, so many millions spent, so many new expenses
> for the work, so many outlets closed . . ., You have to count the costs

of installation, the costs of depreciation, the costs of maintenance, the costs of settlement, the costs of surveillance. In a word, there is an enormous accounting to be done ... Up to now your main export to the newly acquired colonies has been the five hundred thousand million francs they have cost us.

This was the permanent problem France faced with her colonies; they never paid.

But Clemenceau's most memorable remarks on the colonial problem were surely those regarding race:

Superior races! Inferior races! it's quick enough said. For my part, I have been singularly sick of it since German scholars demonstrated scientifically that the French had to be defeated in the Franco-German war because the Frenchman was from a race inferior to the German. Since then, I'll admit, I look twice before turning back on a man or a civilisation to declare: inferior man, inferior civilisation. The Hindus, an inferior race! That great and refined civilisation lost in the night of time! That great Buddhist religion spread from India to China! That great efflorence of art, its vestiges still visible today! The Chinese, an inferior race! That civilisation of unknown origin! Confucius inferior! Truly, even today, permit me to say that when Chinese diplomats are at grips with certain European diplomats . . . [*Laughter and applause from various benches*] they cut a pretty good figure; if you consult the diplomatic records of certain peoples you'll find documents which prove that the yellow race from the standpoint of business skills – the conduct of infinitely delicate operations – is in no way inferior to those who are in too much of a hurry to proclaim their supremacy.

XV

IT WAS neither business nor the cause of civilisation that brought General Brière de l'Isle to Hanoi. Like many of his army comrades it was the opportunity of promotion that had made the colonies so attractive to him. Brière de l'Isle, a Martiniquais, had spent the major part of his professional life in the Far East, first with General Cousin de Montauban during his march on Peking, then in Cochinchina and now in Tonkin. In Cochinchina, the taking of the Kim Hoa forts had earned him a citation and the command of a battalion. He was soon lieutenant colonel, then colonel.

Thank heavens for the colonies! In the Franco-Prussian war all he had managed was to get taken prisoner at Sedan; he wasn't returned to France until the spring of 1871. He had a spell in the colonial office in Paris until he was sent out to Senegal, where he received his general's stripes.

Now he was in command of all French forces in Tonkin. These comprised, in March 1885, a total of about thirty-five thousand men.

Brière de l'Isle had his main forces based in Hanoi, at the head of the Red River delta, with advance guards at Cho Moi, Kep and Lang Son on the Chinese border. The main problem he faced was communications. Telephones were now in use, but only over short distances. Between Head Quarters and the forward troops (about 150 kilometres separated them) the system of the Franco-Prussian war prevailed: brief telegrams, letters brought in by horse and, of course, pigeon. Communications with the French capital, halfway round the world, were limited to telegrams which took from six to twelve hours to reach their destination.

The prevailing opinion in Hanoi, inasmuch as there was one, was that the French forces were over extended. Brière de l'Isle urged restraint. But General de Négrier, who had only captured Lang Son the previous January, was as keen as any soldier prying the frontiers of a new colony – out of reach, beyond the jealous clutch of his superiors, he felt not unlike the captain of some private Italian army roaming the hill country of fifteenth-century Tuscany, or a conquistador in Peru. If he could plant the flag on this hill, why not plant it on the next?

At two o'clock on a Sunday morning (22 March) de Négrier's outpost at Dong-Dang was attacked by a detachment of Chinese troops. 'To give myself a little air', he reported in a dispatch to Brière de l'Isle, he crossed the frontier and seized a line of Chinese forts. Two days later he was locked in combat with what looked like the entire Imperial Army – a terrifying sight: unending hordes of men in armour and huge exotically coloured helmets. 'All the wounded have been transferred to Lang Son', he telegraphed Hanoi. 'Our losses stand at about two hundred killed and wounded.'

Why hadn't the fool at least waited? thought Brière de l'Isle. The troops were already involved in fighting with the Black Flag pirates on the Red River. An invasion from the north was not an appealing prospect. Only two years earlier Henri Rivière's head had been paraded around Hanoi on the end of a Black Flag pike.

De Négrier began concentrating his troops around Lang Son. The attack came on Saturday, 28 March. That evening, de Brière de l'Isle telegraphed Paris:

I announce with sorrow that General de Négrier, gravely wounded, has been forced to evacuate Lang Son. The Chinese, advancing in great masses and in three columns, have attacked with an impetuosity our forward positions of Kilua. Colonel Herbinger, before this great numerical superiority and exhausted of ammunition, informs me that he has been obliged to retreat to Dong Son and Cho Moi. I am concentrating all my means of action on the outlets of Chu and of Kep. The enemy continues to increase on the Song Koi [the Red River]. Whatever happens, I hope to be able to defend the whole Delta. I ask the government to send me fresh reinforcements as soon as possible.

The situation was, in fact, not critical. De Négrier, suffering from a 'slight stomach wound' according to a later dispatch, soon recovered. Herbinger easily held on to his new positions. The Imperial Army, no match for an army battalion equipped with repeating rifles, was in flight within days; Peking recognised the new French protectorate in Tonkin on 4 April.

But the telegram was enough to sow a fury in Paris. 'DISASTER IN TONKIN' ran the banner headlines; 'NEGRIER MORTALLY WOUNDED', 'AN INVASION OF 200,000 CHINESE'.

Very few Parisians knew where China was, let alone Tonkin; by the size and mood of the crowds gathering that grey Monday morning around the kiosks on the boulevards, at the Bourse, along the river embankments and before the legislative palace, one might have thought that the yellow horde was about to lay another siege to Paris. 'It was 4 September, 1870, on a small scale,' reported the normally sober *Times* of London. 'Exclamations were heard in the streets reminding one of those fifteen years ago.'

Ferry's government was doomed. Even the members of the cabinet advised the premier to step down before the afternoon's parliamentary sitting to avoid a humiliating spectacle. He refused; there were some ambiguous constitutional issues involved and Ferry, anyway, was as determined as he had been in 1870 not to give way to pressures from the mob and the popular Paris press. In particular, he was not going to show weakness before the 'violent, hateful, outrageous' Clemenceau.

When the first deputies started arriving at the Palais-Bourbon the crowd was fairly calm. *Le Petit Journal* described it as 'a crowd avid to know, nervous, impatient, but in sum a benign and silent crowd'. There had been some demonstrations before the foreign ministry at the quai d'Orsay, Ferry's residence. The police, prepared for worse, had no difficulty in forming a passageway for those with passes to the assembly. Ferry and his ministers, however, were never seen; they had taken another route.

There had not been such a crush in the hall since Gambetta's fall. The princes of the newspapers scrambled with one another for access to the men in top hats; most deputies pushed through without comment. The

most important business of the day was conducted not in the assembly –
that was the show. Ferry's fate was decided in the *bureaux*. There was chaos
at the general meeting of the *Groupes Républicains*, where all the groups of
the Centre were represented. After two hours of debate there was a timid
suggestion to ask Ferry to resign, but Ferry – alone in the Salle Casimir –
refused to meet the group's delegates. Meanwhile, the Extreme Left held
their own meeting. Clemenceau presented an *ordre du jour* that his group
would propose at the close of the session: 'The Chamber, condemning
the ministry and resolute to vote the credits necessary to bring help to
the French soldiers engaged in the Far East, passes to the order of the
day.' Citoyen Laisant proposed to impeach all the ministers. A *bureau* of
the Right also voted for an impeachment.

Thus the political trend of the last few years was confirmed. The
Extreme Right had manœuvred with the Extreme Left to upset the
fragile and complex alliances that had been holding together the Centre.
Sensational news, the crowd and the press had played a part.

The session had to be delayed because of all the dealing going on behind
the scenes. It was a scrum in the visitors' galleries; hardly a place for
ladies to be seen, though a few stalwart salon hostesses had come along
to air their grievances. The old Marshal MacMahon was observed taking
a snooze in one of the corners reserved for senators.

Around 2.30 p.m. there was a roll of the drums and the brouhaha in the
galleries died down. A puzzled deputy from one of the rural departments
walked into the empty amphitheatre: a false alarm.

It was almost three when the drums rolled out again. 'Monsieur le
président' and in came Henri Brisson to take possession of his high chair.
The ministers filed in silently to their bench before the tribune, Ferry
looking, according to newspaper reports, lonely and melancholy; but then,
Ferry always looked lonely and melancholy. The deputies followed, in no
apparent hurry. There was absolute silence as Ferry mounted the tribune.
He read a statement that had been prepared that morning in the council
of ministers leading to a proposed bill for a further 200 million francs. 'The
speech was listened to with, perhaps, fewer interruptions than had been
the case on Saturday,' remarked *The Times*; there was deliberate control
within the opposition.

But there was an explosion as he read 'We have the honour to place
before the bureau of the Chamber . . .'

'Who has compromised our honour?' shouted out Georges Périn from
the Left.

'It's him! It's him alone! That coward!' screamed de Cassagnac from
the Right.

Then there was a pause, the reading of the bill and another crescendo of

howls, twitter and bombination when, to the astonishment of many, Ferry
announced that 'the vote of credits is not considered by the government
as implying a vote of confidence'. He was unyielding.

'*A Mazas, l'assassin! la Conciergerie!*'

There was another pause in the uproar. Clemenceau made his way
to the tribune. So, from the opposite side of the amphitheatre, did the
Bonapartist, Delafosse. Clemenceau got to the top of the steps first. The
Chamber was now in total silence; *Le Petit Journal* described it as 'a
profound silence, one of those hostile silences where the animosity comes
across more eloquently than [it would] with the most vehement rhetoric'.
Rather dramatically, Clemenceau refused the traditional glass of bordeaux
offered by an usher and launched straight into his indictment. 'Messieurs,
I do not come to respond to M. le président du conseil. I consider at the
present hour no debate can any longer be undertaken between the ministry,
at whose head he is placed, and a republican member of this Chamber.'
Correspondents described Clemenceau, as he pronounced these words,
variously as 'pale with emotion but with an assured voice', 'grave . . .,
patriotic . . ., with the design of not recriminating . . .' or 'overwhelming
in his contempt and bitterness'.

Three members on the Right (de Cassagnac and a couple of counts)
shouted out their support for the Radical leader: 'Republican or otherwise!'
'Just say Frenchmen!' 'We count for something too!'

'Let me speak, messieurs,' continued Clemenceau; 'this is no longer a
minister, these are no longer ministers whom I have before me, these are
the accused.'

'So get off the ministers' bench!' came a voice from nowhere.

The insolence of office, the pang of too great an effort to hold on, or of
too little an appreciation from others, the absurdity of the charge; whatever
the cause, Ferry laughed.

Albert de Mun was the first to publicise the fact. 'They are not laughing
in Tonkin, Monsieur le président du conseil! It is essential that all France
knows that you have just laughed!' Raoul Duval, another member on
the Right, made the same remark. Clemenceau continued amidst an
uproar. Gaillard, a Radical from the Vaucluse, shouted out that Ferry
was still laughing. Clemenceau read the proposal agreed on in the *bureau*,
stressing that he was not asking for the abandonment of the troops, 'When
a Frenchman, just one, holds up the flag before the foreigner in arms, the
representatives of the nation can haggle over neither the credits nor the
men for his defence.'

A Moderate, Alexandre Ribot, brought the brief session to a close by
telling Ferry that he had no choice but to resign. 'You owe it to the
Republic,' he said, 'and most especially you owe it to France.'

Ferry demanded that priority be given to the vote on credits. This was
refused by 308 votes to 161. Ferry stood up and announced 'the cabinet

understands the meaning of the vote' and that they would immediately present their resignations to the president of the Republic. The ministers filed out, pursued by hoots from the floor and public galleries.

Delafosse, the Bonapartist, then read out a proposal that, if adopted, would have arraigned the ministers before a court for high treason. Citizen Laisant, on the Left, seconded the motion. It was rejected by 304 votes to 161.

There was a moment – on the report of Ferry's initial refusal to accept the vote on credits as a vote of confidence – when it looked as if the crowd outside was going to invade the assembly. The jostling lessened but the yelling increased once it was known that the government had resigned. By the time the deputies appeared (the ministers had escaped through the gardens at the back of the palace) there was considerably more calm; the trams held up along the quai d'Orsay were rattling forward again; the police managed to form human corridors that allowed the legislators a way out. The extremists were hailed, the moderates were hooted.

Was it to be the democracy of crowds once more? This was certainly the end of the Opportunists' Republic and one might have smacked one's lips at the thought that a political class which had excluded the world of work and made war on the weak was now out of office. But one might also have felt the vague discomfort of something repeated, of memories evoked, of democracies impatient with legal process, of an intolerant Paris – of a place that hinted of Thucydides' Athens, not Juliette Adam's, a place where words changed their meaning, where recklessness had come to be seen as courage, prudent hesitation as cowardice, and moderation as the cloak of unmanliness: thoughts anyone might have had amid the cries of the newspaper boys. 'Le vote de la Chambre! La chute de Ferry! La chute de Ferry!'

CHAPTER SIX

Demagogy

DEMAGOGY WAS the ugly underside of democracy. Between 1885 and 1893 France, on two occasions, nearly abandoned the Republic to the demagogues – Boulanger, Rochefort, Delahaye, Déroulède. The political intrigue this involved was just the surface of profounder rogueries and vice that touched most corners of Parisian high society during those years, years that have come down in history as the *belle époque*.

The problem was that Paris was the capital of a country where the people had, as yet, very little in common. The grand principles discussed in the Chamber did not have much immediate relevance to ordinary Frenchmen. It was easier for them to identify with a person – who was this Republic? a government with no King? no Emperor? – it was more fascinating for them to be told about some sordid scandal. A cascade of legislative elections, municipal elections, department council elections and arrondissement council elections (not to mention the various by-elections) had done little to bring them closer together. The Anzin strike had shown that there was not a great deal the politicians could or would do for men who worked for a wage. As for the peasants, still the majority of the population, their principal concern was crops, while their links with Paris remained essentially those of their forefathers – taxation and the army.

You didn't have to be a cynic to regard the national politics of the era as an extension of that hallowed French tradition of communal *rixes*, where gangs of village youth, armed with wooden weapons, clashed with their neighbours on the open field. It was not so much that society outside the political grandstands was ignorant of the celebrated issues of the day (though the ignorance was widespread). The critical factor working on political structures at this time was that national disputes were being enlisted into the service of local causes, not the other way round. Clemenceau, like many of his radical colleagues, had imagined France following the English model; now that the Republic appeared established, the country, he hoped, would see a two-party system evolve with the Opportunists acting as Conservatives and the Radicals playing the part of socially conscious Liberals. But the English model demanded a disciplined clientèle that simply didn't exist in France. It was not just the multiplication of political newspapers and groups that undermined the chances of such a system developing. These newspapers and groups corresponded to a social fact: France in the last decades of the nineteenth century was a country made up of more or less isolated communities which might come together in a moment of political or economic crisis but, in more ordinary times, lived for themselves alone.

Education was designed to change all this but, as Clemenceau had pointed out to Ferry, the national educational programme existed only on paper.

Knowledge was in more than one sense the key to power. If one wanted to advance within the governing elite – they already called it *la classe politique* – it was an advantage to demonstrate access to rare information, to be an initiate, to show that one could breach the mysteries of the other person's wealth, his network of relations and influences. It was important to be principled, important to speak of reform (though always the right reform); but it was also essential to denounce the enemy on the grounds of some special knowledge: suspicions, rumours, outrage, names pronounced and repeated, figures cited, confidences received and passed on. If one couldn't share principles, if one couldn't agree on matters of policy, couldn't one at least join up against a common enemy?

The new press, so much a part of the new political regime, built its market on this. But its market was limited – until the last decade of the century provincial administrators continued to distinguish between the 'newspaper reading classes' of the towns and the rural populations, exclusively concerned with local matters. Were there inroads to be made here? How could their interest be attracted?

Clemenceau had wanted a Republic of ideas, but he had himself unwittingly contributed to the politics of personal rivalry and public shame. His bout with Ferry had sealed his reputation as the 'wrecker of ministries'. But if he remained the darling of the campaign speech halls, he created fear among those deputies ambitious for power: talk began that Clemenceau was more a destroyer than a creator. There was also the obvious political lesson in the showdown of 30 March; the idea of the game seemed no longer to win points of principle but to prove your opponent a rogue.

I

ESTIMATES OF the crowd in front of the Palais-Bourbon on 30 March ranged between fifteen hundred and ten thousand. Even if one accepted the latter figure (appearing in Rochefort's *L'Intransigeant* and thus almost certainly an exaggeration), it would hardly have been fair to regard that crowd as representative of attitudes in Paris as a whole, let alone the country. But Ferry's fall signalled the opening of an agitated campaign for the legislative elections, held six months later. One of the last acts of the Ferry government had been to reform the system of voting with the establishment of the *scrutin de liste*. Voters were presented with competing lists of candidates for their whole department. The idea, which had been argued by Gambetta (and supported by Clemenceau), was that such a system would encourage the growth of parties by forcing local electoral committees to combine for a common list. In fact, the system had exactly the opposite effect.

In Paris, where the whole department of the Seine was combined into a single constituency, the situation deteriorated into chaos. There was neither a Clemenceau list nor a Ferry list. There were simply lists, with only the vaguest indication of what kind of programme they represented. Electoral committees multiplied to a degree that made even the heady days of the Commune look like ordered political procedure. Because of Ferry's spectacular fall, everybody wanted to be 'radical'. There were twelve Radical Socialist Committees, including the 'Radical Socialist Departmental Committee' endorsed by *La Justice* and a competing 'Radical Socialist Committee' headed by Rochefort and Maujan. There were four Republican Democratic Radical Committees, two Republican Radical Socialist Alliances, two Republican Radical Liberal Alliances, a Central Republican Radical Socialist Committee, a Central Radical Socialist Progressist Committee, a Democratic Radical Committee, a Radical Committee, a Radical Group, a Permanent Elected Radical Committee, a Radical Socialist Anti-Opportunist Committee, a Republican Radical Committee, a Republican Radical Democratic Committee and a Radical Socialist Anti-Opportunist Committee

All of which goes some way to explaining why Clemenceau decided, that year, to represent the rural department of the Var.

II

ABOUT A month before the elections, Clemenceau's old acquaintance – and former rival in love – Charles Floquet made a campaign tour through his native Pyrenees. His speeches were mostly reaffirmations of the issues Radicals were stressing at that time: the separation of Church and state, constitutional revision, the vague commitment to social and economic reform, and criticism of colonial ventures. But in Perpignan he addressed a question that was going to be of increasing interest to the Radicals in the years to come; the place of the peasant in a reformist Republic. 'We're taught that the peasant doesn't care for this ideal,' he said. 'One is mistaken. The peasant, from the time he has approached the Republic and to the extent to which his education has developed, has finally understood, and will understand yet more, that this noble form of government brings to the world aspirations of universal justice that go beyond the modest horizon of his laborious and respected existence.'

Gambetta had been the first major republican to appeal to the peasant vote and he did this with the same kind of moral conviction that Floquet later expressed: the educators would arrive in the countryside, horizons would be lifted. Every time the republicans scored a victory in a rural area, they saw it as a mark of progress. Every time the conservatives won, they attributed it to backwardness. Historians a hundred years later were still describing votes for the Left as signs of a 'modern' and 'outward-looking' attitude and votes for the Right as 'archaic' and 'inward'.

In fact, there was no hard and fast rule that could explain the peasant's electoral behaviour. Clemenceau's Vendée voted for the Right. The Var, in the south of France, voted for the Left. The differing manner in which the land had been settled seems to have exercised some influence. The kind of dispersed habitat that one found in the Vendée probably encouraged Catholicism, and thus voting for the Right, because the Sunday church service was one of the few occasions when the rural population got together. In the south, on the other hand, peasants lived in compact villages built on the summits or the sides of hills. They spent their whole time together, when not at work, in circles, clubs, *chambrées*, cafés – not the sort of places that encouraged piety and respect for the hierarchy. The diocese of Fréjus (i.e. the Var) had the lowest rate of church attendance in the country. The brothers of the Ecoles Chrétiennes in Barjos got accustomed to having stones and dung flung at them. The curé of Rebouillon, outside Draguignan, used to carry a revolver under his habit.

But patterns of settlement did not explain everything. In central France there were isolated regions, such as the Sologne, where the Church was very weak while, in the tightly conglomerated villages of the east, and notably Alsace, it was very strong. Religious and political attitudes could also be the result of historical accident.

At any rate, it was largely historical accident which made the Var Clemenceau's new political home, one that would endure. His annual trips of October, and sometimes May, gave him an acquaintance with the region that he would sometimes express with a profound kind of warmth. 'The department of the Var,' he wrote in the 1890's, 'is one of the jewels of our France.' In his comments on the Var you could find the same ebullience that marked his depictions of his native Vendée: the same identity with place – especially place, yes. The background to Clemenceau's feeling for the region was a huge landscape, 'with its blue gulfs crowned by the Maures or the Estérel, dominated by the Alps, with its headlands of porphyry or red sandstone whose burning reflection ignites the sea, with its mountains peeled or frothed with black pines or cork-oaks . . .'

Clemenceau's first link with the Var was through Toulon's mayor, Henri Dutasta, a former philosophy teacher who, one year earlier, had founded *le Petit Var*, the leading radical paper of the region. Dutasta represented just the sort of combination – education, newspapers and politics – that the republicans in Paris were interested in and Clemenceau must have been delighted at the prospect of the new ties he could bring. It was Dutasta who had invited Clemenceau down to help in the local elections of 1881, and it was Dutasta who gave Clemenceau enormous publicity when he paid a second visit during the cholera epidemic of 1884.

The Var was having plenty of problems with disease at that time, and not only of a human kind. Phylloxera had devastated the vineyards and the few vines that survived suffered from mildew. Potatoes were destroyed by the late blight, silk worms were virtually wiped out by problems affecting the mulberry trees. These were all difficulties suggesting an overly intensive cultivation of the land. There were also problems with livestock. And then the problems all France faced: agricultural prices were dropping, foreign competition was stepping up.

Obviously there was fertile land here for a protest vote. But, oddly, one finds in none of Clemenceau's speeches made during his five-day campaign tour of the department in September 1885 any substantive response to these problems. Nor in those of the other Radicals on the list (even though they were mostly local men). When Clemenceau did touch on the agricultural needs of the department he expressed himself in the same general language as his 1884 speech on the *question sociale*: 'taxes more justly distributed, good credit, better equipment, a more complete technical education, the creation of a new economic order to protect you against the enterprises of the financial oligarchies . . .' The only major specific project he *ever* put forward in favour of agriculture was a protectionist tariff; it appeared in his programme of 1889 – 'thus will French agriculture, so cruelly stricken, revive.' The irony was that the tariff was bitterly opposed by most cultivators in the Var who, now more specialised than ever, were reliant on cheap foodstuffs which they were forced to buy on the market.

The Radicals managed to garner the votes in the Var in 1885, not because of a detailed programme, but because they were the best organised opposition group that existed in the department at that time. Their platform might have been vague, but they had one thing in common with the natives: they were opposed to the government in Paris.

One has to say that Clemenceau, even if he contributed little directly to the department's economic well being, had a personality that was ideally

suited to the Mediterranean tradition of conviviality, of fraternisation –
of local republican *cercles*, of cafés and agricultural syndicates. The texts
of his campaign speeches reveal little of that commanding presence which
would make him a legend in the region for generations. At Draguignan he
made his speech not in a theatre, as announced, but from a bandstand in
the middle of the town square (quite illegal at the time). Crowds would
gather at train stations and await his arrival, they would mass outside his
hotel. This was a department where transportation was still extremely
primitive; Clemenceau got a reputation of not balking at such obstacles,
even if this meant several hours' trekking on muleback. 'Nobody has ever
come to see us,' complained the mayor of a small village in the Estérel.
'I'll come,' replied Clemenceau. 'Eh bien! if you give me your word you
will have all the votes of Tanneron.' Clemenceau spent a day crossing the
valley of the Biançon, the rocky fords and the deserted woodland paths to
reach his destination. The mountain village celebrated his arrival with 'a
feast without parallel' where even the curé joined in with a canticle. At
the elections that year (1889) Clemenceau received all 128 votes of the
village, including that of the priest.

III

FOR RADICALS, who regarded election results as the unrolling chain of
Manifest Destiny, 1885 came as a real shock. They thought that if the
people had voted for the Empire in the 1860's and for the Opportunist
Republic in the 1870's then surely the 1880's was theirs.

In the Var it was. Clemenceau and his colleagues won all four seats
on the second ballot.

But Destiny fell to pieces with the national vote and Chaos made a
return. On the first ballot, the conservatives won 176 seats, against the
hundred they had held in the previous legislature, while the republicans
won only 127. 'The hour is not for quarrels,' wrote Pelletan in *La Justice*,
though he heedfully added, 'We do not want to forget the past: it must
serve us as an education for the future.' So the various republican factions
agreed to put forward a single list for each constituency. As a result, the
republicans came out of the second ballot with 383 seats, against 201 for the
conservatives – a general balance not very different from that of 1877.

These numbers however hid a jumble of ephemeral combinations and
hotchpotch alliances which made nonsense of any claim of republican
'victory'. Poor Henri Brisson, who had succeeded Ferry, had the impossible
task of putting together a government majority in the new Chamber. The

Opportunists, such as they existed, could now count on about 230 deputies whereas in the previous legislature they had numbered around 370. Like his several successors, Brisson had to choose between an alliance with the Right or an alliance with the Left. The former was still considered taboo in 1885, though, in one of the many paradoxes of the day, whenever the Left bid for the overthrow of a government their success always depended on support from the Right. Opposition politics bred the most peculiar associations, but these were not permissible for a government. Brisson was thus obliged to make overtures to the Left – so began a policy that came to be known as *la concentration républicaine*.

This was in fact a polite term for a parliamentary stalemate. Gone were the chances of major social and economic reforms; no government could last long enough to push them through. Gone were the hopes of putting republican ideals into practice. The men in power had only one obsession: keeping it. One of President Grévy's advisers, Bernard Lavergne, recorded nervously in his diary, 'We have never been more completely in the midst of intrigues.'

The elections had brought a handful of Socialists into the Chamber. They called themselves new men. Yet, among the long lists of candidates at the first ballot, could be found names from a former era. Camelinat had been one of the founders of the International and, following the Commune, had spent several years of exile in England. 'Old militant of the International, veteran combatant of the Commune, I shall strive to be in the Chamber the man of my communalist and socialist past.' Benoît Malon, 'General' Eudes, Félix Pyat, Vaillant were all in the running too. And there was of course Rochefort. The followers of Blanqui were making a come-back and the municipal council installed at the Hôtel de Ville was their stepping stone.

The old voice of the barricades echoed and hummed. Old antagonisms too. What had parliament to do with universal suffrage? Attacks on the Constitution of 1875 became venomous. The stalemate in the Chamber, the impossibility of social reform, the intrigue, the frustration would encourage the most extreme sort of thinking and lend support – sizeable support in Paris – to Rochefort's denunciations in *L'Intransigeant* of the '*saletés parlementaires*' and the '*pourriture d'Assemblée*'.

On the Right, deputies were delighted, believing this would advance their own aims; one of them even got up to the tribune, in February 1886, to announce 'we hope France will soon be rid of the Republic.' Admiral Galiber kept on telling his friend Grévy not to worry too much about finding a successor since he, Grévy, was almost certainly going to be the last president of the Republic.

It is not very surprising that the same elections which saw the return of old-guard Socialists in Paris witnessed some of the first efforts by Radicals to build a wider political base in the provinces, especially the rural areas. Clemenceau for one must have felt uncomfortable with all this anti-parliamentarian talk, even if he had denounced Ferry only a year earlier for declaring that 'the real enemies of the Republic are now on the Left'. As a deputy for the Var he could speak to France and not just Paris – a good way of avoiding the destructive entanglements he had known when acting as middleman, in 1871, between a parliamentary assembly and a revolutionary Left.

Thus, 1885 represented a significant break for Clemenceau – and for France. Clemenceau would hold on to a 'republican revision of the Constitution by a constituent Assembly' as his 1889 programme put it, but from 1886 onwards the issue was given nothing like the attention it had received in former years. Events were overtaking 'the programme of 1869', the 'old programme which has not been realised'. The destruction of the Senate was less pressing than the defence of parliament, whose enemies were increasingly strident.

History had just taken an unforeseen turn.

IV

WAS IT a political tactic? Or a more personal reason? Perhaps it had something to do with that 'spirit of the times' historians once liked to evoke. Poets and novelists took little interest in politics; this was a long period of *littérature dégagée*, said André Billy looking back half a century (and compared to the 1930's and 40's it was) – perhaps the politicians were getting bored with politics too.

One can put forward numerous hypotheses. But whatever caused it, Clemenceau, after the elections of 1885, entered another of his peculiar periods of silence. One of his opponents, the monarchist Albert Duchesne, got so frustrated with his silence in 1886 that he actually challenged Clemenceau to a duel, though it was prevented thanks to the intervention of Charles Floquet, now president of the Chamber. That year, Clemenceau only spoke in parliament on three occasions. In the first half of 1887 he remained completely silent and when he did finally chirp up, on 11 June 1887, the deputies were so surprised that there was some commotion in the assembly. 'Ah! Ah!' records the *Journal Officiel*, '*Mouvement d'Attention.*'

Clemenceau's activities in the corridors were certainly intense, as various comments by Bernard Lavergne prove. One can understand why; he was an important man to know. As Doctor Portefaix – another chatterbox and relative of Lavergne – put it just after the elections, 'Clemenceau can perfectly well make and unmake a cabinet when he wants.' Freycinet had a hunch that it was power inside government that he was after. Reflecting in his memoirs on Clemenceau's speech of December 1886 over the formation of the Goblet ministry, Freycinet said that Clemenceau appeared to believe that the Radicals were the only group capable of constituting a solid government majority.

Clemenceau was certainly being by-passed by the president of the Republic, Grévy. But why didn't he come out clean and say it? Ferry, recollecting undoubtedly Clemenceau's criticisms of Gambetta, started referring to his old enemy as a '*ministre occulte*'. One might push the parallel a little further and surmise that Clemenceau, like Gambetta, really didn't want power: the honour of a government post in those years was like the uncertain glory of an April day.

And then Clemenceau's personal life, like Gambetta's, was not a picture of Victorian concord and felicity. It was the nosy Lavergne who recorded through a second-hand source (Jézierski, director of *Le Télégraphe* and one of Ferry's collaborators) that Clemenceau 'was not winning opinion because of his escapades at the Opera (Léonide Leblanc, etc.) – the life of a *viveur*,' thus setting off a torrent of speculation among later biographers and historians. It is the only contemporary reference to Clemenceau's legendary exploits with women.

Clemenceau had plenty of enemies, but his private life was never seriously put in question; this, at a time when there was growing talk about Wilson's infidelities and when it was said that Rouvier's wife posed nude for artists at five francs a sitting. No woman ever vaunted her triumph with the famous radical leader. Not an impudent line was printed in the gutter press.

'The greatest moment of love,' Clemenceau is supposed to have once said, 'is the moment one climbs the staircase.' The statement at least has the merit of suggesting the degree of significance one should give to his love affairs. As for the actress Léonide Leblanc, she was almost fifty – Jean Ajalbert, who had just joined the staff of *La Justice*, considered the rumoured liaison 'improbable'.

Letters, letters written by the dozen, from Clemenceau's youngest brother Albert to Gustave Geffroy give a rare glimpse of life among the Clemenceaus in the 1880's and a whispered hint on what was actually happening.

Geffroy first visited L'Aubraie in September 1883 for the opening of the *chasse des Dunes* at La Tranche. Hunting was a test of skills and in the matter of jumping canals with *batons sautoux* the Parisians were no match for the Vendéens. Geffroy seriously hurt his leg. Albert also had an accident; one's impression is that he had shot himself in his foot. Thus the two young men (Geffroy was twenty-eight, Albert twenty-two) found themselves confined to L'Aubraie under the care of *les douces femmes* who lived there. 'This camaraderie which misfortune (!) has created seems to me to have already lasted several years,' wrote Albert to Geffroy on 26 October 1883. 'Should anyone ask the reasons for this friendship so quickly formed, we would reply like Montaigne, "It is because it was him, it is because it was me."' Geffroy was up and off to Paris after a few days, but Albert remained in bed for several weeks. 'You'll be walking in eight days,' said the elder brother – 'and eight days have passed and I continue to remain in bed.' 'Walk! Walk!!!' wrote Georges from Paris. 'I have blocked my ears,' Albert told Geffroy.

Albert described his place of gentle internment. 'I am in a rage and still the word is not strong enough. Everything is united against me.' No letters received. Nothing for two days. 'It is a real rage. I curse these people who come to talk with me and those who do not come.' The sound of the piano in the main hall infuriated him – one or two pieces were played and replayed over a period of weeks. 'For an hour I have been listening to these monotonous exercises, these notes twenty times restarted and nineteen times wrong, and I say to myself that once the girl has finished the mother will start at the same exercises, and I get a fancy for saying offensive things to the mother, to the children, to make them all cry, to take away forever their desire to play the piano. That's not all. My sister-in-law comes in from the garden to show me several vile flowers she has just picked and offers me comments which drive me mad: "Look at this one, it's like a little old lady; oh! that one resembles Bornelotte. Don't you think so?" No I don't think so, and I say so, and I plead to be left quiet. My sister-in-law concludes that I am in a bad mood and, after a kind response from me, leaves.'

Mary Plummer got some rough treatment in the Clemenceau household. Seven polite cards and letters in Geffroy's collection – invitations to dinner, thanks for a gift, requests for theatre tickets – reveal a person who has perhaps mastered the correct social formulæ, the proper forms of address, but who has a way of presenting them that is different from the others. Her handwriting is long and slanted; no Frenchman would ever write like that. Her stationery is unique. In America the letter 'M', decorated in flowers of pink and blue, which is on each letter-head and embossed on the back of each envelope would have been considered quite pretty, if a little quaint. In France it was decidedly bad taste. Albert stole some of the stationery to use in his correspondence with Geffroy; it was a joke, but a nasty joke. 'This letter paper resembles [Sutter] Laumann a bit, don't you think so, *ma Geff?*'

A lot of this was horseplay. Albert's correspondence with Geffroy displays the same biting wit as his brother; the letters remind one of

Clemenceau's letters to Scheurer-Kestner twenty years earlier. Only this time there is rather more on women, rather less on books.

Whatever, Albert's sense of humour seemed none too funny to Georges Clemenceau's lonely American wife. After she had been locked up in a room for a day – 'Irma by my orders has latched the hook,' reported Albert triumphantly – she suddenly made a trip to Paris in late August 1885, with no explanation to the family. Albert was bewildered. 'If you want to know a mysterious thing, let me inform you that my sister-in-law left for Paris this morning and will be back on Friday. Why? I tell you, it is a mystery; perhaps you don't even know of the trip.'

One of the reasons why Mary had been consigned to L'Aubraie in the early years of her marriage was that the tiny Paris flat on rue Miromesnil was not large enough for a family. But in 1878 Clemenceau moved to larger quarters on avenue Montaigne and, ten years later, to a still more spacious flat in the neighbouring rue Clément-Marot – though he paid the same rent, 2,800 francs a year.

Of course, space was needed for a politician of Clemenceau's standing. The three carton loads of correspondence with various Clemenceaus, which Geffroy has left us, show the intricate network of professional and private relations that furnished the props of his career.

We find Cornelius Herz extending his tentacles to both Paul and Albert Clemenceau. But Herz was also seeing Paul Déroulède, president of the League of Patriots and no friend of the family. Perhaps the Clemenceaus had an inkling that something ugly was going on, which would explain why Georges Clemenceau repurchased Herz's shares in *La Justice* in April 1885. At any rate, the paper was making no money. Two of Geffroy's letters suggest real financial problems – the staff was not getting paid.

The father, Benjamin, followed the affairs of the newspaper as best as he could. Three notes scribbled in pencil can be found in Geffroy's correspondence. But Benjamin was a very sick man. 'My father yesterday morning suffered another crisis,' wrote Albert to Geffroy in January 1884. 'I was alone with my father who suffered a lot and searched in vain for a position in which he could remain for five minutes in peace. What a day, *mon pauvre vieux* . . . On his request I slept this night in his room, idem for the next.' The next day he noted, '*Le patron* [Georges was in fact usually referred to as *le patron*, Benjamin was *le patron suprême* or *le grand patron*] *le patron* is feeling a little the way you would expect, he is very weak, but that is understandable. Tonight, the removal of the catheter and a remaking of the bed. I sleep again this evening in the paternal bedroom. This continual existence in this overheated atmosphere makes me half sick.' Georges arrived from Paris four days later. 'My father has suffered a great deal,' reported Albert.

On 25 January 1885, only days before the matter of the Herz shares was settled, Benjamin wrote a short note to Geffroy: 'I have just been quite seriously ill and I have not been able to thank you earlier for the books, papers and other odd items that you have heaped on me.' It is in the writing of a man who has suffered a stroke.

The next reference Albert makes to his father is in a long letter written to Geffroy from a hotel room in Luçon seven years later, on 15 May 1892. His father, he says, 'is in a hospital, in a small but clean room; the doctor comes to see him twice a day.' 'This hospital,' he goes on, 'is especially a hospice,' and he then describes the grounds, the nuns in their tall white caps. A dozen senile old men 'in the most curious costumes' walk about the gardens; 'those who still have use of their mental faculties gather in groups and talk; the least idiotic are employed in gardening.' He speaks of his father as 'nervous, nervous as you know him. Giving him the smallest amount of medicine is an event. He gets angry over anything, or rather over nothing.' After a week, Geffroy receives a telegram from Luçon: 'Mullem and I are returning to Paris tomorrow morning. Father much better. Albert.'

Clemenceau had been very close to his father. It would not be unreasonable to assume that it was his father's illness, rather than his 'escapades at the Opera', that was the cause of his relative silence after 1885.

Benjamin Clemenceau finally died in 1897.

V

'IF YOU want to avenge me, work,' Benjamin had cried out in 1858 as he was marched off to one of the Empire's gaols. Thirty years later the whole family was working for the political success of Georges Clemenceau and they did this through *La Justice*.

For more than a generation, an opinion press, short on objective and anonymous news reporting and long on personal commentary, had provided France with an alternative to political parties: the papers lasted longer than the ephemeral groups in and out of the Chamber. But the same press offered the essential outlet for the nineteenth-century novel (in the form of the daily *feuilleton*), its plays (the theatre critic could determine the success or failure of a performance like a Greek despot determining a man's freedom) and its plastic arts (manifestos and long interpretive essays often made up the third page of the four-page political journal). This gave literature and the arts in France a prestige that could not be found, for example, in England where the press had evolved so differently and where the link between politicians and men of letters was so much weaker. Literature in the 1880's might not have been overly concerned with political questions, but the amazing thing is the degree to which the major figures in literature and the arts and the major figures of politics all knew each other, intimately.

The list of artistic friends who passed through Georges and Paul Clemenceau's drawing rooms, who corresponded with Albert and his close companion Gustave Geffroy, reads like a roll call of the dignitaries of late nineteenth-century French culture. Among the literary acquaintances figured José-Maria Heredia, Stéphane Mallarmé, Octave Mirbeau, Alphonse and Léon Daudet, J.-K. Huysmans, Emile Zola, Edmond de Goncourt and the publisher Paul Gallimard. Among the artists were Eugène Carrière, Jean-François Raffaelli, Auguste Rodin and Edouard Manet. It was Geffroy who introduced Georges Clemenceau to Claude Monet. Geffroy had been preparing a biography on Blanqui when he had met the artist, in the same inn at Belle-Ile where *l'Enfermé* had made one of his numerous escapes. Geffroy brought Clemenceau to Giverny in 1890; it was the beginning of one of the profoundest friendships Clemenceau was to know.

Albert, in his correspondence with Geffroy, refers to the extended Clemenceau family as 'our municipal council'. Four important marriages took place after 1885, all tightening bonds with business, politics and the press. In a fabulous ceremony in Vienna's city hall, Paul, on 23 December 1886, married Sophie Szeps, the second daughter of Moritz Szeps, a correspondent of the left-wing Austrian *Neue Wiener Tagblatt*. In May 1888 Albert married Marthe Meurice, daughter of a famous lawyer who had been the executor of Victor Hugo's will. Sophie, his elder sister, married the ailing Ferdinand Bryndza, the Paris correspondent of the *Tagblatt*, in 1889, the same year that Clemenceau's nineteen-year-old daughter, Madeleine, married Numa Jacquemaire, another lawyer, twenty years older than his wife and closely linked with the affairs of *La Justice*. One finds among Geffroy's papers a rough draft, in Geffroy's hand, of guests to be invited to the latter ceremony, to be held in the mairie of the Fifth Arrondissement on 29 May. There are two columns of 'Deputies' and two columns of 'Various'. The nineteen deputies included Pelletan, Millerand, Floquet, Delcassé, Tony Révillon, Georges Périn and José-Maria de Heredia. Clovis Hugues' presence shows that some of the Socialists in the Chamber were still considered close enough to participate in a family event. More remarkable still was the presence of Alfred Naquet, who was now pushing hard the cause of the new Boulangist movement. Among the thirty-five 'various' names one finds Rodin, Raffaelli, Georges Hugo, Léon Hennique, Vacquerie and Dr Taule (of student days).

*

An ostracised wife, an unhappy son (Michel, having been dismissed from several schools, was sent off to Zurich at the age of fifteen for private tuition in 1888), the very early marriage of his daughter were perhaps the price of fame and the hectic pace of the social rounds that politics demanded.

Jean Ajalbert left a description of life in the offices of *La Justice* during this period. He found it, unlike the reports left by Geffroy and Albert, rather lonely. He had been introduced to Geffroy by Raffaelli and became a friend of Albert. Ajalbert thought the contrast in character between Albert and Georges quite striking. Albert was 'as engaging, as tender, with a vivaciousness albeit smiling, as Georges could be aggressive and disconcerting with his outbursts of anger and his incessant hostile remarks.' Ajalbert would deliver his articles to the offices at four o'clock in the afternoon. The place was usually deserted at that time; papers, notebooks and dossiers were left in heaps on the unattended tables and the subtle stink of the coal fire, stoked by minions earlier in the day, hung over the open space, reinforcing a sense of abandonment. The only decoration on the walls was a notice above Geffroy's desk: '*On est prié de ne pas parler politique.*' But then there was also the smell of tobacco. It was Mullem's pipe. For, in a distant corner, emerging from behind a pile of books, was the round figure of the assistant editor, very pleased to get something to work on for the next day's edition.

Ajalbert wouldn't return until eight o'clock in the evening when the staff gathered for the almost daily encounter with *le patron*. Clemenceau, who had his own room overlooking the main office, would come in dressed 'like a prince', an image that contrasted sharply with the shaggy silhouettes around him: Pelletan with an overcoat draped over his shoulders 'like a sparrow's scarecrow' and Mullem's face 'lost in a tangled mop, a thick moustache, the eyes shrunken under their heavy lids and a pince-nez.' Clemenceau could go on speaking for hours ... 'on Racine, whom he recited admirably and commented on long passages. Politics lay in wait, under the classical or the romantic.' Around midnight they would go out to eat at a neighbouring restaurant or they might have their meal in the office, consuming the victuals the family had brought from the Vendée. Sometimes there were private dinners to attend. An evening might be spent at Geffroy's home, or at Mullem's, or with Paul Gallimard or Paul Clemenceau.

Clemenceau, said Ajalbert, was very critical of his collaborators. 'His tone froze me. Clemenceau was hardly preoccupied with the sensibilities of others and worried little about drawing people out.' He referred to his staff in ways that shocked – '*ce cul de Mullem*'; he continued to call Ajalbert 'Enjolras' (one of Victor Hugo's characters), which Ajalbert hated. As a result, Clemenceau had no followers: 'In politics, in art, in literature, in science, the master makes the students, followed by a clientèle. But with Clemenceau everyone broke loose, from Georges Laguerre to Millerand, who could have done him honours. Who among his collaborators can remember having lunched, dined, travelled with him apart from Gustave Geffroy? He was the most distant, the most elusive, the most secret of men.'

Little was said of private lives. These evenings *were* the private lives for most. Geffroy lived with his mother and invalid sister (he remained with his sister for the rest of his life). Clemenceau said nothing on his. There was perhaps not much to say.

Nor must one imagine that visits to the opera or the theatre were always very gay. In the portraits Geffroy depicted in *La Justice*, he speaks of the balls at the Opera as 'a great modern sadness': 'In the grand foyer, perfect order is established, everybody walks in silence from one end to the other of the immense gallery. And when they have finished, they begin again.' At the concerts, women were nowhere more charming – these 'luxurious festivals given in their honour, ceremonies that they must preside over with the impassiveness of idols paved, gilded and illuminated with the fires of precious stones. It is accepted without revolt. But look at such high coldness and sadness on the faces of those who, on the appointed day, in the same lodge, hold themselves upright and resigned, under their lace and their diamonds, like a soldier under arms.'

VI

WITH SO many friends to choose from – even if they were mostly selected by his family and even if he did prove a little distant – why should Clemenceau be attracted to General Georges Boulanger? True, Clemenceau was unaware of the key role Boulanger had played in the summary executions of April and May 1871. But even then, you could not imagine a more unlikely pair. Boulanger was ambitious, ambitious to a point that distressed even the closest of his associates. He was unprincipled; monarchists and republicans were alike to him for he would countenance whoever granted him the greatest favour. He was hot-headed; his decisions were always made with an intent to impress and if they did not impress he would resort to aggression or, failing that, high-flown retreat. But the greatest difference from Clemenceau was that he did not read books. Paul Cambon made perhaps the acutest observation on this point. 'Even though he has been around the world, returning via India from his mission in the United States for the centenary of Independence, he hasn't a conversation that is very varied or nourished.' Boulanger, said Cambon, is 'a man who has read little.'

Yet Berthe Szeps, Sophie's elder sister, would write in her diary on her first visit to Paris in autumn 1885, 'Georges finds Boulanger likeable. After everything he says about him, he seems to be a charmer.' A charmer. The old photographs make his hair look black but in fact it was a chestnut brown. He waxed his blond moustache to give it a slight curl upward, revealing a mouth that observers said rarely smiled. Séverine of *Le Cri du Peuple* remembered him laughing; she said it was the laugh of a small child that finds life full of fun. Everybody noticed his eyes, which were blue. He dressed well, he greeted well, he rode his horse well. 'His whole appearance is correct,' described a popular biography published in his first year as minister of war, 'and of a superb military allure.' That same year he grew a beard which both his friends and enemies agreed made him look exactly like Napoleon III in 1852.

Boulanger had a talent, you could even say a genius, for public relations that he had been developing since the age of five when he had written to his father, 'I hope you will see me with the cross of honour and the epaulets of a marshal of France.' He had an extraordinary memory for names – he might encounter a man months after their first meeting and still recall the names of every one of his children. 'You are going to see,' said a soldier about to introduce a comrade to the new minister of war, 'the greatest theatre director that ever existed. He is a man who can do nothing, simple as it may be, without it appearing extraordinary. He has always been like this, from the day he entered the army as a second lieutenant. He has a manner of giving orders, even of wounding himself that attracts attention. Put a hundred generals together and, in the middle of all of them, he's virtually the only one you'll notice.'

He had run a magnificent, if not exactly straight, course since leaving the heap of bodies and rubble in the suburbs of Paris for his superior, General Vinoy, to admire. Like a skilled sailor who knew how to avoid bad weather or a dangerous race, how to best exploit capricious winds, Boulanger always had an eye trained on the horizon for a landmark, a sign of a major port of entry. He didn't know what wind would push him, which coast he would pass, how much time it would take. But every morning he was ready on deck, looking out yonder, hoping, waiting, turning the tiller with measured intention. In 1874 he was nominated colonel of the 133rd, an infantry regiment belonging to 7th Corps under the command of the duc d'Aumale. The duke was the fourth son of Louis-Philippe, a close ally of the Orleanist pretender and this was the age of the *Ordre moral*. Boulanger attended the military masses, he carried a gilt-edged missal under his arm and he helped the bishop of Belley distribute prizes at the local seminary. But Boulanger didn't lose touch with the common soldier from whose ranks he rose; he was a genuinely popular officer, unlike so many of the other officers who came from a different social class. In 1880 he became a brigadier general; he was only forty-three. 'I will always have been proud to have served under a commander like you,' he confided to the duke on leaving, 'and blessed be the day when I am recalled under your orders.'

But the winds had changed. It was not the duke who had taken the initiative in Boulanger's promotion but the pressure from republican civilians. Boulanger was now an ardent republican. Gambetta, who hadn't abandoned his aspirations for a republican army of citizens, was always ready to talk to an officer who had the right politics. So when Boulanger asked to meet him the request was immediately granted. Boulanger assured Gambetta of 'devotion to his person and to the Republic' and within a month had won his promotion. A year later he was representing the French Republic at the centenary celebration of the Battle of Yorktown in America and a year after that he was called by the ministry of war to act as general director of infantry in the minister's offices on rue Saint-Dominique.

It was here that Boulanger met Clemenceau. Boulanger had reached the core of the French military machine, the point where the civilian political powers plugged into the military; the position opened up a vast new network for the general to turn to good account. There were common interests at stake. Republican generals were in short supply. For sure, they existed; men like Faidherbe and Chanzy had not been forgotten. But the distinctive feature about Boulanger was that he was so active, so keen and so manifestly committed to thoroughgoing army reform. The 1872 law had essentially left the structure of Napoleon III's army of long-serving professionals, the *armée de métier*, intact. The Radicals in particular were determined to change all this. They wanted adoption of a three-year military service for everyone and they wanted the anti-republican officers ousted. Boulanger was willing to do both.

Exactly how the acquaintance was established is unknown. But it is likely that Clemenceau was introduced to Boulanger by Félix Granet. Granet was another man who was not very fussy about political principles. He had been a republican prefect when still in his twenties and had served as *chef de cabinet* to Ernest Constans, Ferry's minister of the interior. In the legislative elections of 1881 he ran for the Bouches-du-Rhône and only won his seat because Clemenceau, who was also in the running, decided to opt for Paris that year. But Granet had to pay the price, which was a switch in political affiliation from Opportunist to Radical. Granet's leading role in Ferry's downfall at least showed his eagerness for his new alignment.

Since his election Granet had been in continual contact with Boulanger. It was in fact through Granet, along with an obscure journalist by the name of Buret, that Boulanger first established his links with the press, specifically *La Lanterne*, *L'Evénement*, *La France*, *La Nation*, and *La Justice*, which soon began publishing glowing articles about the director of infantry. Clemenceau's earliest correspondence with Boulanger dates from this period.

It was perhaps not a very close relationship. Clemenceau's dealings were at first limited to calming Boulanger's nerves ('*on se fout de moi*,' wailed Boulanger) when he threatened to resign because General Thibaudin, the minister of war, had refused to accept – not surprisingly – Boulanger's candidate for a general chief of staff.

At any rate, Boulanger was soon out of range of all personal contact with Clemenceau because in February 1884, at the ripe old age of forty-seven, he was named division general and put in command of the troops occupying Tunisia. Boulanger now found himself faced with a new barrier to his ambitions in the person of Paul Cambon, the French civil resident. The appointment proved a disaster. Rivalry between Boulanger and Cambon ended only when Paris decided to recall them both. For six months Tunisia had effectively no colonial government. Opportunists and Radicals entered the fray. Several duels were fought. But *La Justice* was notably silent. Clemenceau was reported in private to call Boulanger a '*farceur*'. In December Cambon went to see Clemenceau to ask him frankly what his position was. After hearing Cambon's version of the story Clemenceau replied that he had disapproved of the general's behaviour, that he had seen Boulanger only five or six times since his return, and that the source of the problem was not in Tunis but Paris. 'Everything for the affairs of France, whether at home or abroad, goes the same way,' he concluded reflecting on the muddle.

Cambon returned to Tunis and received the Légion d'honneur in the New Year promotions. Boulanger remained in Paris and on 7 January 1886 became minister of war.

The exact nature of the wheels and deals involved in this delicate operation are again a mystery. The opportunist press was convinced that Clemenceau was behind it all and most subsequent accounts have accepted that verdict. 'It is to the friendship of M. Clemenceau that General Boulanger owes his portfolio,' warned *Le Figaro* three days after the nomination. 'The Radicals have their hands on the ministry of war. It is perhaps the gravest symptom of the situation.'

The ministry of war was on offer because of another change in government. Late in December 1885 Grévy had called on Freycinet, Gambetta's old war aide, to form a ministry. Freycinet was a staunch advocate of *la concentration républicaine*. 'My guiding principle,' he later wrote, 'was always to associate the two great shades of opinion, radical and moderate, in the establishment of the cabinet, a sort of ministerial syndicate . . .' His syndicate included, in addition to Boulanger, four Radicals, Granet, René Goblet, Jean Sarrien and Edouard Lockroy (the only really close associate of Georges Clemenceau).

As far as Boulanger was concerned, Freycinet was formal and categoric:

it was the outgoing minister of war, General Campenon, who recommended Boulanger's nomination, not Clemenceau. There is no reason not to believe it. Campenon soothed Freycinet's concern over the Tunisian episode. 'He's a *discipliné*,' said Campenon, 'and if you have a firm hand he will render you some real services. He has the advantage of knowing the administration of the [ministry of] War, having for a long time been director of infantry.'

Boulanger, at the ministry of war, carried out what he had promised. He supported the radical project for a three-year military service obligatory to all, including priests. He demoted royalist officers and even had the duc d'Aumale, his old commander, sent out of the country. He reformed the military schools. He allowed soldiers to wear beards, gave them beds instead of straw to sleep on and provided them with a new gun, the Lebel rifle, which loaded more easily and killed more effectively. A republican general was he.

VII

ON THE ninety-seventh anniversary of the fall of the Bastille the Republic celebrated the glory of its army. The Fourteenth of July had been a national holiday for eight years and there had been several military reviews since the last war. But the capital had never been offered a spectacle like this.

From early in the morning people from every quarter in Paris began gathering at the hippodrome of Longchamp. They came by carriage, by omnibus and by foot. The early arrivers crowded along the grey fences that enclosed the racecourse, guarded by a line of *sergeants de ville*. Those with carriages carefully marked out their territory, spread out blankets, chairs and tables and sat down like princes at court for the long wait. The wind carried the faint popping of the champagne bottles, a peal of laughter, the shout of a child. The men wore suits in browns and greys, their heads crowned with the inevitable top hat; the women were in satins, silks, and cotton, shirred at the waist and billowing over the bustles that assured them attention and, above all, space. Some had attached ribbons in patriotic reds, whites and blues to their hats. Others, the colours of a regiment, or was it of the horse team they had cheered on in the same place the previous week?

The unending column of rich, middling and poor streamed in from the Grande Cascade to fill the platforms and the sloping lawns until all one could see, from one end of the hippodrome to the other, was a field of humanity and an array of travelling machines: landaus, victorias, dogcarts, the vast steel spokes of the spider buggies shining, the scores of dilapidated fiacres serving as high seats with a view. Wealthy men had brought in their mistresses on plushly furbished vehicles where they sat, disdainful as duchesses of the horde of lesser mortals who had arrived on foot. After fifteen years, the woods had grown back again. You could see the tips of young trees on the hills of Saint-Cloud and Suresnes and further west, in the haze, a blue profile of Mont Valérien.

It was probably not until well after three that the first officials started filing into the stand reserved at one end of the field. The civilian contingent was dressed in the fashionable colour of the day, black. Their wan and pendulous faces, profiled in whiskers, only reinforced their stern appearance. The crowds were visibly satisfied to find the president of the Republic sicker and more aged than most had anticipated.

Beneath the row of the ruling class sat the foreign delegations. The English looked English, the Germans looked German.

A shiver of excitement ran through the crowd with the rumour that the military procession was about to begin. Shadows from the high clouds joined league, speeding across ten thousand white parasols to turn the stalls and terraces into a sea of tossing waves.

At four o'clock precisely the drums thumped, the brass brayed and the first company of red pantaloons strutted into the great arena to the 'March of Sellenick'. The bandleader twirled nimbly his staff, left, right, above; not a soldier lost step. An immense sigh surged from the stadium. Every regiment, brigade and squadron carried its colours. The uniforms were an apt visual accompaniment to the sounds of the band, now pounding like a dozen copper cauldrons bouncing down stairs. The hussars appeared in their greens and reds, the Foreign Legion in a dark blue, the Algerian tirailleurs in a hideous sky blue. There was a thunderous moan of glee . . .

It was a patriotic show and a republican show, a tribute to France, 'her flag, her arms, her genius' as Ferry might have said. You could forget for a moment that these armies were meant for fighting and that the kind of war the country had experienced almost two decades ago had not demanded heroes. There was great applause when Colonel Dominé marched into the field at the head of a contingent that had only just returned from Tonkin. Nobody blamed the soldiers for the failures and they all got credit for the successes.

The minister of war passed before his troops. His hat sported great white plumes, his tunic was decorated with a row of shining medals crossed with a purple ribbon, his pantaloons were of white cashmere and his horse was black. A swirl of excitement was released when he led over three hundred mounted staff officers at a suspended trot along the crowd periphery, ending in a magnificent half circle before the president's box. He stood immobile. The band blasted out the *Marseillaise*.

Some were not impressed. Anatole France's head throbbed. Lord Lyons thought the ministers looked threatened. Sporting figures were already aware that Tunis, the minister's horse, was a mixed breed.

As the troops filed out, Grévy, accompanied by Freycinet and General Pittié, left for the president's carriage where Boulanger and Saussier, the military governor of Paris, were awaiting him. Grévy climbed in. Saussier, grey and corpulent, joined him on his right; Boulanger, slim and glorious, sat on his left. Preceded by a company of spahis, the president and his retinue then set off for the Elysée Palace. But the crowds that stood on either side of the route cheered for the minister of war, not the president. For the minister, the journey down the Champs Elysées had only been paralleled by Cæsar in victory descending the Appian Way.

There were balls that evening throughout Paris. At the Alcazar, Paulus sang for the first time the rousing *'En rev'nant de la revue'*. Do you hear it?

VIII

THERE WAS one person who had taken special interest in the show. Otto von Bismarck had not mellowed with age; his authoritarianism, his taste for vengeance and his susceptibilities had only increased. Certainly, at seventy-three his health was better than it had been at seventy – his doctor had put him on a diet and he had lost over twenty kilos. He no longer had a taste for war. Since 1871 this, the most powerful man in Europe, had concentrated his efforts on securing peace to construct a 'solid house', the German Reich. The aim of his foreign policy was not to attack France but to isolate it. But at home he faced the most difficult parliament he had ever known in his life, a coalition of *Reichsfeinde* – the Catholic Centre, the Progressists and the Social Democrats. He was nervous. His associates noted how he screamed if handed a pipe with poorly packed tobacco or a pencil that had not been sharpened.

Boulanger proved a godsend for Bismarck; 'I could not invent Boulanger,' the chancellor later confessed, 'but he happened very conveniently for me.' Profiting from the sabre-rattling that had developed in the French and German press Bismarck decided in early 1887 to attempt a renewal of the seven-year military budget (the Septennat) which was due to expire the following year. His purpose was more to challenge the *Reichsfeinde* at home than to strengthen his hand abroad. When the Reichstag voted a budget limited to three years, Bismarck dissolved it.

There followed the most bellicose electoral campaign the Reich had yet experienced. Articles on Boulanger's readiness for a *coup d'état* and an attack on Germany were run in the press. Posters portraying black zouaves and brown turcos carrying off German peasant women were pasted to street walls. There was a stock market panic. Civil servants were instructed how to influence the voters. Unlike Marshal MacMahon's 1877 electoral campaign in France, the Reich's elections of February 1887 were a serious defeat for the German Left and Bismarck eventually obtained his Septennat, 223 votes to 40.

In fact, Boulanger in Paris was hardly a menace to anyone at this time. Publication, only weeks after the military review, of his obsequious letter of thanks to the duc d'Aumale on his promotion eight years previously – 'blessed would be the day . . . ' – had seriously damaged his reputation among republicans. *La Justice* remained silent. For six months Boulanger also thought silence the best policy and, like Clemenceau, he made no pronouncements in parliament and offered no startling new programmes. He was, however, a busy figure at the ministry of war, particularly with his newly established press bureau.

The Paris press had actually picked up Bismarck's bait, and for about a month it continued to make belligerent noises. But the government remained calm. Grévy considered war and foreign affairs his domain and war, he thought, would be a disaster for France. According to Lavergne, Boulanger's behaviour in the cabinet meetings was 'absolutely correct'; it was his popularity that troubled Grévy, not his actual attitude within the government.

Then, with the showers of April, came a new war scare. Increasing discontent in Alsace–Lorraine had encouraged the war ministry to commit certain imprudences on the frontier. Customs officials were used as intermediaries with spy rings and clandestine organisations growing within the province. Explosives had been supplied. The German authorities, under local initiative but with Bismarck's blessing, decided to act. On 20 April a French customs official, Schnaebelé, was invited to talks with his German colleague at the frontier outpost of Pagny-sur-Moselle. Almost as soon as he was across the border he was arrested and carried off to Leipzig where he was put on trial for spying.

Goblet, now prime minister, wanted an immediate ultimatum. Boulanger, still minister of war, wanted a mobilisation. But Grévy argued that nothing could be done until the German government 'had responded to our observations'. The Germans were in fact so obviously in violation of international law that after ten days Schnaebelé was released. It was Grévy who had saved the situation, not Boulanger. But Boulanger became a national hero: Boulanger had stood up to Bismarck.

The divisions within the cabinet and parliament were too great for the Goblet government to last. On 18 May, during a debate on the budget, he was overthrown by a combination of the Right, the majority of the Opportunists and several dissatisfied Radicals, including Clemenceau. It took Grévy two weeks to find a new prime minister. Neither Freycinet nor Floquet was prepared to serve because Grévy refused to reappoint Boulanger as minister of war. Finally, on a Whitsun weekend, he got an Opportunist, Rouvier, to put a government together with the tacit support of members from the Right.

Rouvier was breaking the rules: republicans, for the first time, were opposing republicans through a royalist alliance.

The radical republican committees in Paris at once launched a campaign in support of Boulanger and, implicitly, against the faint-heartedness and treachery of the bourgeois parliamentary regime. Rochefort advised his readers to vote for Boulanger in a by-election to be held on 23 May. Boulanger won thirty-nine thousand votes without even running as a candidate. There were street demonstrations and several scuffles.

On 27 May Lavergne recorded in his diary another of his third-hand tales. He had had a chat with Méline who had just had a chat with Ribot. Ribot mentioned Clemenceau's attitude about Boulanger's new popularity, 'If I told you what Clemenceau said to me about it, I would make you shudder . . .'

Clemenceau was uneasy with the developments. He had been as hostile as Rochefort to 'distant expeditions' because of the weakness they created in France's eastern frontiers. He openly attacked the Opportunists for pandering to Bismarck. But he did not want war. Above all, he did not want a war provoked by the generals. 'Although a nation might not want war,' he said in a speech made during the Chamber's spring recess, 'one man alone can undertake it despite the nation.' 'Clemenceau is going to let Boulanger go because Boulanger wants war and we are not ready,' Gévolot told Lavergne just before the vote that overturned the Goblet government.

The prospect of war was opening old wounds. It has been argued that the republican consensus was broken in 1888 because of a fear of the 'new urban masses'. Clemenceau saw nothing new in the masses that gathered in the streets of Paris that year. Not only were they reminiscent of the demonstrations of 1870–1, they were being led by the same people.

The new minister of war assigned Boulanger to a remote command in Clermont-Ferrand. A crowd of thousands saw the general off at the gare de Lyon. 'The first duty of republicans,' warned a column in La Justice the same day, 'is never to exalt to this point an individual. It is to the idea, and only the idea, that they owe their homages.'

IX

TODAY ONE dismisses the fear of crowds expressed by writers like Taine, Zola or Le Bon as the paranoid mumblings of the propertied, and in part it undoubtedly was. None the less, it was the sentiment of witnesses, articulate witnesses, who, like many others, tell us that the crowds of that time really did represent something very ugly. The historian does not have to walk down the streets of Paris of late spring 1887. These writers did. The capital had just experienced two war scares. Now there was a government openly courting the Royalists, not a particularly welcome sign for Parisians. The economic crisis had not abated either; unemployment hadn't been this high since the siege and the Commune.

You could have captured a festive mood here and there, such as on the evening of 28 May when the boulevards and the place de l'Opéra were filled, after the theatres closed, with people singing '*C'est Boulanger*': the police were brought in to disperse them. Three days later, the cavalry was used to guard the Palais-Bourbon and the approaches of the Elysée. When the prison sentences of the Alsatians at the Leipzig trials were announced a mass meeting was organised at the Cirque d'Hiver by Paul Déroulède's League of Patriots. Some of those attending might have been at one of Clemenceau's rallies a few years earlier. They would have noticed how the violence of language had increased. The hawkers and the news vendors were also more conspicuous, selling pamphlets, the latest Boulanger song, medals of the general, busts of the general. Boulanger soap was supposed to be 'refreshing for the skin', while the Boulanger pipe encouraged patriotic thoughts in moments of meditation – like the Boulanger watch chain and the Boulanger perfumes, which would give you an air of confidence and purpose as you prepared to go out for an evening's demonstration in the streets.

Three days after the pandemonium at the gare de Lyon, a vicious debate took place in the Chamber. Rouvier tried to present his new cabinet as a 'cabinet of appeasement', not a government of combat against the Right any more than against the Left; the Radicals, led by Pelletan and Clemenceau, retorted that it was a sell-out to the Royalists and the clergy. But Clemenceau had equally scolding words for Boulanger's movement. 'I rebuke entirely the demonstrations that have taken place,' he said. 'The popularity of General Boulanger has come too early to someone who has too much love for noise.' Clemenceau had been in crowds before. He'd seen violence. He had supported the rights of parliament in the past, in the face of the red clubs.

The government had serious fears of a *coup d'état* and there was particular concern that the Fourteenth of July would provide the occasion.

General Saussier met a group of officers on the evening of the 13th to plan a course of action. The national holiday was indeed noisy. The president's cortège got booed and hooted at the Grande Cascade as they entered Longchamp and for the return trip they were forced to take an alternative route. Another demonstration followed suit on the place d'Etoile. It was a good day of business for the Boulangist hawkers. But it was not the day of the revolution.

Boulanger had actually been urged by Naquet to stage a *coup*, but he had dismissed the idea because he said he hadn't the support of the generals and he couldn't tell how the Germans might react.

Nobody had foreseen Boulanger's massive popularity, least of all Boulanger. There was certainly no political group sufficiently organised to have created it. It was literally a movement of people, some well-intentioned, some greedy, some simply following their stars, all trying to by-pass a parliament in deadlock – little Machiavellis taking advantage of situations as they developed. No theory explained Boulanger. If the Radicals thought historical progress was operating in curious ways, the small nascent group of Marxists was utterly baffled. Guesde remained silent. Engels wrote to Lafargue, at *La Justice*, and blamed it all on *la revanche*. The Blanquists were keen Boulangists because it catered to their grassroot instincts: the movement was popular and it was a threat to parliament. In June 1887 committees sprang up all over Paris in support of Boulanger, but none of them had a specific programme.

The Right was just as confused as the Left. It was the fear of war and another Commune that led the baron de Mackau to approach Rouvier who got the support of the whole Right in return for the promise of Boulanger's exclusion. But what Right was this? The Union des Droites was a cover for a muddle. The Bonapartists had two candidates for Emperor; the Royalists' pretender to the throne was the comte de Paris, in exile in London.

Probably the best structured group to support Boulanger at this time was Déroulède's League of Patriots which belonged neither to the Right nor the Left. 'Republicans, Orleanists, Legitimists and Bonapartists are only the first names,' Déroulède said; 'their family name is French.' The League had been founded in 1882. By 1887 it boasted a national membership of two hundred thousand. But the vast majority of these belonged to provincial gymnastic societies – vague precursors to scouting – which had not the slightest interest in politics. The politically active element of the League was limited to Paris and its suburbs, a mixed bag of about twenty-five thousand patriotic shopkeepers, small traders and artisans. Even here, there was little unity. Many of them were supporters of Ferry and the following year, 1888, the League split into two warring camps, Ferryist and anti-Ferryist.

Adding further spice to the Boulanger mix were the general's personal connections developed over the previous years, not the least important of which were the salons of Madame Arman de Caillavet and of the comtesse de Loynes. Clemenceau, Geffroy, Pelletan and other staff members from *La Justice* were also frequent visitors here. In such ways, the narrow world of high political intrigue and the wide disorganised world of mass politics coupled and gave birth to Europe's first experience of modern political demagogy.

X

WHILE THE populist Boulangist movement was picking up steam there burst out the 'Wilson Scandal', which would bring Grévy's presidency to its knees.

Daniel Wilson had begun his career in the gambling dens of the Second Empire. In 1871 his winnings had purchased him a seat in the National Assembly and the affection of the Assembly's president, Jules Grévy. Within years he had also won the favours of Grévy's daughter, whom he married in 1879, the year Grévy was elected president of the Republic.

This opened up a vast new enterprise for Wilson, the business of connections, *les relations, les recommendations, les démarches*. If you wanted an introduction to a major figure in politics, you could go and see Wilson at the Elysée Palace. If you wanted your good works in the world to get official recognition and honour, Wilson was the man to see. By 1887 Wilson's Elysée office handled twenty-three thousand dossiers containing over two hundred thousand letters. Wilson himself granted 150 interviews a week.

But the whole business collapsed in September 1887 when the newspapers caught hold of a story – from two quarrelling prostitutes – that Wilson and his friends were trafficking government decorations.

If Grévy had made some sign of dissociating himself from his son-in-law's activities he might possibly have saved his presidency. But the already highly charged atmosphere in the Chamber and on the streets would have made this difficult. Grévy was anyway determined to defend the honour of 'dear Daniel'.

Grévy's obstinacy of course made Rouvier's position as prime minister impossible. On 19 November Clemenceau mounted the tribune to inflict one more of his historic blows. 'If there arose an international event that I can't foresee,' he asked the defenceless Rouvier, 'to whom does the country address itself? Where is the flag? Who is holding it? Who carries it? Where is the government?' The Chamber decided that it was not under Rouvier's premiership by 317 votes to 228 (with all the members of the Right, save seven, joining Clemenceau on the Extreme Left).

But Rouvier could not be dismissed because nobody wanted to be Grévy's prime minister. Grévy even called, in a desperate manœuvre, on Clemenceau. Clemenceau refused. Waldeck-Rousseau refused. Marcère refused. Even Ferry refused: for Ferry had higher ambitions.

Ferry? Ferry? Suddenly the spectre arose: Ferry might become the next president of the Republic. Clemenceau commented that it would be the end of the Republic, an opinion shared by several deputies, some quite happy with the prospect, others frightened. Jules Auffray, secretary of the Union des Droites, wrote, 'The Radicals will never accept Ferry. They will resort to violence to prevent him being elected or to overthrow him. The Republic will perish with him in civil war.'

There were, indeed, people in Paris who were ready to fight. Déroulède said the League of Patriots would descend into the streets. On 25 November, the Blanquists held a big meeting, under the auspices of the 'Central Revolutionary Committee', where 'General' Eudes announced that the 'the revolution has begun'. Political clubs reminiscent of the siege began to organise themselves. There were speeches made every night at the salle Favié, near place de la République. The 'Egaux de Montmartre' plastered the walls of the 18th arrondissement with posters appealing for support in the new struggle, 'The Republic is in danger!' Louise Michel, just out of gaol, organised the municipal women. At the Hôtel de Ville, councillors set up a Vigilance Committee. 'The Parisian guns will go off alone,' announced John Labusquière in Le Cri du Peuple. Séverine, in the same paper, explained why: 'A bas Ferry! in the name of those who have endured the pains and miseries of the siege, who have trembled with hunger on the military outposts, biting balls of bran, hardened by some sinister baker's assistant for the despised "trente sous". A bas Ferry-Famine!'

Edmond de Goncourt had forecast 'twenty years of rest' after the 'bleeding white'. He had got just sixteen.

Some curious alliances were formed to prevent Ferry from getting into office. In the first place, a reconciliation between Clemenceau and Boulanger was in order. The mathematician Charles Laisant, radical deputy for Nantes and founder of Le Petit Parisien, organised a luncheon on 27 November. Boulanger was now in Paris working on a committee for army promotions, having served his thirty-day confinement to barracks in Clermont-Ferrand. The next day, in the corridors of the Chamber,

Félix Granet and Georges Laguerre invited fellow Radicals, including Clemenceau, to a meeting that evening at the Grand Orient on rue Cadet. Clemenceau brought along his main collaborators at *La Justice*. There were a number of Radical deputies attending, a scattering of Socialists and several of the major radical newspaper directors, including Rochefort. Granet told the meeting that Ferry was negotiating with the Catholics (he was) and that the only way of preventing his victory was by keeping Grévy in office. Grévy would need a ministry. Three candidates were mentioned, Floquet, Freycinet and Clemenceau. Clemenceau, in a rather amazing *volte-face* agreed, but he insisted on the unanimous approval of those present. The meeting, not surprisingly, broke up in total confusion.

Eugène Mayer of *La Lanterne*, Laguerre, Granet and Laisant decided they needed further clarification from Clemenceau and went straight round to the offices of *La Justice* to get it. It was midnight and they were only just in time. Clemenceau announced to their astonishment that he was off to meet 'Boul-boul', who was waiting for him in a fiacre opposite number 3, rue de Rougement. '*Eh bien*, come along with me, we'll have supper with him.' Laguerre thought it would be a good idea if Rochefort could join them. An office boy was dispatched with an invitation to the offices of *L'Intransigeant*. Then off went the five men to the tiny alley off Boulevard Poissonnière. Boulanger was there all right. They rode together to place de la Madeleine and ordered dinner at the restaurant Durand. It was about one o'clock in the morning.

Rochefort was holding council with Déroulède when the invitation arrived at *L'Intransigeant*. They both left immediately for Durand's. Over dinner, it was decided that if Grévy were to be kept on as president an offer for a ministry would have to be made the next morning. An opinion had to be got from Floquet and Freycinet at once. They were pulled out of their beds but, in their dressing gowns and night caps, politely refused the offers: they both wanted to be president of the Republic. The only candidate left was Clemenceau.

But Clemenceau had no intention of committing himself, either to the formation of a government or to his peculiar accomplices. The following evening a dinner took place at Georges Laguerre's home on rue Saint-Honoré. Laguerre's principal achievement up to this point in life had been his marriage to Marguerite Durand, who had been a very popular actress at the Comédie Française. She was extremely beautiful and also very bright. At the age of twenty-three she was already running a well-reputed salon and was branching into journalism, where she would make a considerable mark. Wearing that evening a low-necked dress, she presided over a dinner for men: Rochefort, Déroulède, Naquet, Laisant, Granet, Camille Dreyfus of *La Nation*, Boulanger and Clemenceau. Nothing of any consequence happened until they all withdrew to the library. Clemenceau was detached, nervous, jittery. He explained his refusal: it was under the pressure of his friends. After that, save the odd comment, he took no more part in the discussion, showing rather more interest in Marguerite Durand, who lurked like a cat from library to dining room, to library again. The other men continued to toss faint thoughts from one to the other; Boulanger lounged in an armchair with a cigar in his hand, half-listening, half-dreaming. At 2 a.m. they at last came to a decision. Andrieux would constitute a government. Louis Andrieux had been both an enemy and a friend of Clemenceau. When prefect of police and opponent of amnesty he had been an enemy. When proponent of a single-chamber parliament he had been a friend. Andrieux hated Ferry. So he was a friend. Monsieur Malaspina, who had just arrived with Lockroy, was sent to pull Andrieux out of bed.

Parliament would have to be prorogued for a month to avoid Andrieux' overthrow the day the cabinet was presented. What if parliament refused? Would it be civil war, as with Ferry?

'I can see Augereau, but . . .' Clemenceau stopped a moment and looked straight at Boulanger: 'But what would the garrison in Paris do?'

Boulanger had to answer. 'The army? The army would stay in its barracks.'

Clemenceau, who had just started towards the door, brusquely turned on his heels and stared again at Boulanger. There was complete silence. Then he looked to Madame Laguerre. 'Why don't you offer me a slice of cold meat?' She quietly got up from her chair, put her hand on his arm and led him to the dining room. 'To think a French general is listening to what we say,' he loudly muttered.

Andrieux appeared at about 3.30 a.m., by his looks, not prepared for an evening at Madame Laguerre's. Monsieur Malaspina was a complete stranger to him and the wake-up had been a bit of a shock; as a precaution, he had hidden a revolver under his jacket. Laguerre explained what was expected of him. Andrieux replied that, despite his sympathies for the plan, it couldn't work in the face of the Opportunists and the Right. 'We will count then on your energy to do what is necessary,' said Rochefort. But Andrieux, supported by Clemenceau, would not do anything illegal.

Several variations on an Andrieux ministry were still being discussed, with Rochefort at Laguerre's desk writing down names, his coat open and his braces showing. One could anticipate the ministry being overthrown on its first day but, like Rouvier's government, it would have to stay in office to run day-to-day affairs. Then, when the inevitable day came, when the two chambers met together in Versailles as a National Assembly to decide on the future structure of government, Boulanger would appear on his horse among the crowd and would be proclaimed the leader of the French. Andrieux and Clemenceau naturally refused to take part in any such madness and the evening ended in a stalemate.

Boulanger, however, had made some progress. At midnight he had disappeared for an hour. He had an appointment with the baron de Mackau, leader of the Union des Droites. Several hypotheses have been made on how this critical link was established; it now seems certain that the first initiative came from Boulanger's side, not Mackau's. Three weeks earlier, one of Boulanger's aides, the comte Arthur Dillon, had paid a visit to the comte de Paris in London. The conditions that Boulanger accepted at the meeting with Mackau were that the Right would oppose Ferry's candidature, they would also temporarily support a government of the Left under Freycinet, Floquet or Brisson, with Boulanger as minister of war. After the election of the president, Boulanger would make an appeal to the country, a plebiscite in effect, in which he would recommend the restoration of the monarchy. In return, Boulanger would become supreme commander of the armed forces.

Grévy never found his prime minister. Huge crowds gathered at the Palais-Bourbon on 1 December, the day he was to announce his resignation. A squadron of dragoons were brought in to protect the deputies. But at the last minute, Grévy relented and the Chamber adjourned for the following day. Police charged the crowd on place de la Concorde. There was further violence outside the Hôtel de Ville and in the faubourg Montmartre. Several people were arrested, including Déroulède and Louise Michel (they were shortly released).

On 2 December, Grévy did finally resign. But the situation in Paris was now critical. The army promotions committee had been disbanded and Ferron ordered Boulanger to leave Paris. He left by train that morning. Boulevard Saint-Germain, place de la Concorde and all the major accesses to the Hôtel de Ville were blocked by noisy demonstrators. There was another cavalry charge into the crowd. The barracks of the Garde républicaine was attacked. Louise Michel had been forcibly carried by police to the outskirts of the city, but she made her way back to the centre by taking a bateau Mouche and the Panthéon–Courcelles omnibus. 'You are all imbeciles!' she told the mounted guard. The day would not have been complete without a march on the Hôtel de Ville. Basly, dressed in a top hat and a red scarf, accompanied by Camelinat, an old Communard and now deputy, crossed the bridge from the Chamber of Deputies and exhorted the crowd to follow them to the people's palace. There the municipal council had just passed a Blanquist motion to join with the deputies of the Seine 'to fend off the dangers that the Republic would face if the election of M. Ferry, by misfortune, were to take place.' Basly and Camelinat led the councillors back to the Palais-Bourbon to confer with the said deputies.

The next day the Chamber and the Senate were due to meet at Versailles to elect a new president. Military forces were posted at all the

major railway stations in Paris. The Paris garrison, a cavalry regiment
and three marine battalions were deployed to protect the approaches to
Versailles. Groups of the Right met at the Hôtel des Reservoirs where
they couldn't decide whether General Appert or General Saussier was
their man. They worked out a complicated compromise. It took three
rounds of balloting at the Théâtre des Variétés for the groups of the
Left finally to select Sadi Carnot as their candidate, thanks in great part
to an intervention by Clemenceau. Clemenceau did not say, 'Vote for the
stupidest'; but the apocryphal comment reveals something of the spirit
within the two chambers when they joined together in National Assembly
and, at six o'clock, elected Carnot president of the French Republic. Carnot
was the grandson of the great revolutionary military hero.

XI

ANDRÉ SIEGFRIED, who wrote a wonderful book about peasants, property
and politics in the West of France, remembered the year his father Jules,
cotton merchant and former mayor of Le Havre, was elected to parliament.
It was 1885. For the provincial notable the adjustment to life in Paris
was very hard. He had come as an enthusiastic defender of liberalism,
democracy, progress and prosperity – all that the Republic had promised.
He discovered cynicism, intrigue and greed. His guests at his flat, which
overlooked the rond-point des Champs-Elysées, continually chided him
for his naïvety. Even his brother Jacques, who had lived in the capital
for fifteen years, used to make fun of him, 'How little Parisian you are!'
Being a man of great promise, eloquent to an exceptional degree, he soon
got invited to Wilson's shooting gallery at the Elysée Palace. On several
Sunday mornings he visited the place, where he practised a little fencing
and got to know some of the most powerful men in the country. 'He had the
impression,' said André, 'that he had entered a den of thieves.' Within a
year of his election, Jules Siegfried was so sick – with a sort of 'neurasthenia'
– that he seriously considered resigning.

Every deputy in Paris knew that the telephone monopoly involved some
shabby operations; the names of Freycinet and Granet, in addition to
the Herz and Wilson duo, kept coming up. Those who moved within
parliament's inner circles were already aware of some unorthodox methods
in the financing of the Panama Canal Company. The laying of the new
transatlantic cable was said to be enriching a few men of influence. It was
not that the dissolute private lives of so many of the Republic's leading
statesmen were in themselves a menace to the new regime – other regimes

had survived with worse. The latest scandal about the police was nothing compared to the corruption that went on in the 'forces of order' of the July Monarchy and the Second Empire. So a municipal councillor had embezzled ten thousand francs. Ten thousand francs, was that all? The railway concessions? Well, that was an old story. The preparations for the Great Exhibition and the centenary celebrations: there was money to be made there. Vice was not invented by the Republic. But for those who had dreamed of democracy there was an assumption that, somehow, all this sordidness would disappear.

Moreover, the people remained poor. A democracy could accommodate scandal; it would have difficulty accommodating poverty. Since the great debate on the *question sociale* in 1884 the situation had certainly not improved. In 1888 several developments contributed to the impression that things were actually getting worse. The harvests were terrible. The price of bread went up. This was not 1788 and it was not 1848; nobody was going to starve. But there were food shortages. There was still widespread unemployment. Strikes were breaking out in various parts of the country. One of the worst was in Paris where construction workers, led by a man named Boulé, took to the streets to demand a wage increase. They were joined by the hairdressers. Then the soft-drink sellers. There were several collisions between police and demonstrators. The employment agencies had to be closed.

The time, in other words, was ripe – as the time is always ripe – for a general on horseback to appear, for a saviour to redeem the sufferers. The turn of the republican play had fallen on an unreceptive audience; the actors, if they had not forgotten their lines, found their magic lacking, the applause half-hearted. Old inspirations were lost in an inferno of ordinariness and contention.

The idea of directly appealing to voters for support for Boulanger was initiated by a Bonapartist journalist, Georges Thiébaud. By-elections were to take place in seven departments on 26 February 1888. Thiébaud distributed ballot papers in Boulanger's name and a significant proportion of the votes went to the general. 'All this proves,' Thiébaud explained to a reporter, 'that the country is in a state of mind which is very favourable to a policy of union and of national concentration. This policy will be made despite the Chamber, against the Chamber, if it does not take care.'

The by-elections showed that, in the country at large, Boulanger was getting his support from conservative voters rather than from the Left, thus confirming the aptness of his approach to the Royalists the preceding November. In December he had secretly left his command in Clermont–Ferrand to confer again with Mackau in Paris. Early in the

New Year he had visited Prince Jerome Bonaparte in Switzerland. None of this, however, was made public at the time. One's impression from the newspapers, whose distribution remained limited to urban areas, would have been that this was a republican general eager to by-pass the obstructive politicking of parliament.

By law, an officer on active duty was forbidden to present his candidature in an election. Boulanger denied all knowledge of Thiébaud's activities, but correspondence proved the contrary. Then, on 16 March, *La Justice* published an official report showing that Boulanger had, without authorisation, left his command post at least three times. Carnot, the next week, ordered that the general be put on the inactive list. This freed Boulanger for a campaign which very nearly destroyed the principal institutions of the Third Republic.

The Boulangists in Paris – Rochefort, Laguerre, Déroulède, Laisant, along with several other journalists and deputies – immediately responded to the general's dismissal by setting up a Republican Committtee of National Protest. The campaign was launched with a two-word slogan, 'Dissolution, Revision' – dissolution of parliament and revision of the constitution.

The new electoral system, the *scrutin de liste*, had unwittingly aided Boulangist strategy. Whenever a vacancy occurred in parliament an entire department had to be consulted. Furthermore, a candidate could stand simultaneously for several constituencies. Thus the way was open for a permanent plebiscite on a single individual. Boulanger would give the campaign a national dimension by resigning every time he won a seat and running again in the next by-elections.

How did he generate his support? Most of the money came from the Royalists who saw Boulanger as the last hope for a restoration. As for the organisation, the Committee of National Protest – nearly all of whose members were former Radicals – coordinated action at national level. In June a parallel organisation was set up, the League of Republican Action, under Laguerre's presidency. But the groundwork in the provinces was again left largely to the Royalists and Bonapartists.

By their scale and the extent to which they relied on the new popular press the Boulangist campaigns of 1888 and 1889 belonged to the twentieth century. But they also employed old techniques to attract the vote from a population which had roots embedded in the past. Peasants didn't read newspapers, but for centuries they had purchased the images of saints and heroes. Portraits of Boulanger, effigies of Boulanger, playing cards with Boulanger's profile in the place of the King, were carried in their thousands into the remotest corners of the constituencies concerned. Boulangist images were deliberately confused with those of Bonaparte, Louis XIV and Vercingetorix. And didn't Joan of Arc ride a horse?

Maxime Lecomte remembered how the railway stations in the Nord were congested with great packets of posters, song-sheets, booklets and the like during the two by-elections of 1888. Jules Isaac recalled the general's visit to the industrial region of Valenciennes. The most astonishing feature was that his carriage was not pulled by horses, but by men, 'men as I had rarely seen, miners with rough faces, coarsely engraved by too hard a labour. The mines of Anzin, nearby, had emptied out onto the main road leading to the town these thousands of workers who served as escorts, as bodyguards and as troops for the good-looking "Monsieur" in the carriage.'

Boulanger did well in the Nord. But it wasn't just the miners who supported him. Roubaix voted for him. The working-class areas of Douai voted for him. The Nord was ideal country for a Boulangist campaign because it was industrial, urban and, paradoxically, a haven for Catholicism and conservative politics. In the by-elections of 15 April 1888, 173,000 citizens voted for Boulanger while less than 76,000 voted for the Opportunist opponent. Nearly three-quarters of those endorsing the general had formerly voted for the Right.

XII

HOW COULD you stop him? Two plans developed. One was legalistic and parliamentarian; this was Clemenceau's plan. The other was entirely illegal and authoritarian; this was the government's plan. It was the government's plan which finally stopped Boulanger.

For ten years constitutional reform – yes, 'reform' rather than 'revision' – had been one of the main planks of Clemenceau's radical programme. At the beginning of the Boulangist movement Clemenceau still blamed 'this plebiscite campaign' on the Constitution of 1875 which had created a two-house parliament unresponsive to the demands and hopes of the population. The idea was that once the Radicals came into office and carried out all the reforms the country demanded then agitators like Boulanger would be silenced.

But the first thing Sadi Carnot did as president of the Republic was to call on Charles Floquet to form a government of Radicals. It of course confirmed the worst fears. Reforms were not possible because the government lacked a majority. Troubles in the street had to be repressed and one was faced, for the first time, with the embarrassing sight of a Radical government using force against strikers. Boulanger at once became the strikers' friend.

So the Radicals were no longer on the offensive. The Republic had to be defended. To this end Clemenceau attempted, in the first place, to organise a parliamentary alliance that cut across the old divisions and, secondly, he once more pressed into service his extraordinary talents of oratory.

Clemenceau's great republican alliance was to be initiated by a 'Society of the Rights of Man and of the Citizen' which met in the Freemasons' Grand Orient on 23 May 1888 – the same place where Clemenceau's Radicals had proclaimed their programme in 1885. The Society's manifesto, probably written by Lissagaray, the socialist historian of the Commune, fell back on the one point of unity republicans had repeatedly evoked during the Second Empire, the French Revolution. 'Sons of the Revolution,' it read,

> admirers, not of a single period of this Revolution, but of the whole step forward of a free people, people who had posed all the problems and who would have resolved them all had they not been stopped, we are determined to use all means to prevent the Cæsarean reaction from setting our country back a third time . . . Revision alone is insufficient . . . One must pursue the total development of the Republic, that is to say, the progressive realisation of all the reforms, constitutional, political and social, that it contains. In the face of the attempts at dictatorship which threaten us, we must set the demand for the Rights of Man and of the Citizen, proclaimed by the Revolution.

'The realisation of all the reforms the Republic contains': one finds here that positivist image of life emerging ineluctably from matter, an image so favoured by Clemenceau. You find here too that principle which he had endorsed as a student: the Revolution was not something you could separate into nice bits and nasty bits, it had to be swallowed whole.

A return to the sources, a touch of the past; you could even say proof of something lacking. The Radicals were thrown back on their own devices. It was not enough.

Of the hundreds present that May, only three played a leading role, Jules Joffrin (a 'Possibilist', that is a Socialist who had broken with the Guesdist dogma of class struggle in favour of parliamentary reform), Arthur Ranc (now an Opportunist) and Clemenceau. A hostile press soon labelled them the 'three Anabaptists'. The Guesdists were appalled at Joffrin's 'treachery' and the Blanquists would never support him because they had all gone over to the Boulangist camp. So Joffrin had no party. As for Ranc, the majority of Opportunists had always considered him an outsider. So Ranc had no party. Clemenceau himself played little part in the society after the initial meeting and by the end of 1888 it fell to pieces

over the issue of electoral reform. Clemenceau's first riposte to Boulanger
had failed.

There remained his oratory. Clemenceau got his opportunity on 4 June
1888 when Boulanger took his seat in the Chamber. Boulanger mounted
the tribune to read a prepared statement proclaiming his victories as a sign
that the country was disgusted with parliamentarianism, which was never
the 'exact expression of self-government', and he demanded a revision of
the constitution. He read the statement very badly and the Chamber was
overcome with uncontrollable fits of laughter. Floquet said, 'At your age,
General Boulanger, Napoleon was dead.' Basly, thinking no doubt of the
support his mining comrades at Anzin had given Boulanger, reproached
the general for failing to develop a serious social programme. But the
greatest speech of the day was of course Clemenceau's.

Clemenceau made an impassioned defence of the parliamentary system;
it was another of those classical statements, with a ring of universality
about it, a fitting tribute to the ideal of the Republic and the Revolution.
'Glory to the countries where one speaks out, shame to the countries
where one says nothing! If it is the regime of discussion that you think
you sully under the name of parliamentarianism, know this, it is on the
representative regime itself, it is on the Republic that you wish to lay your
hands.' Boulanger's motion for constitutional revision failed by a vote of
377 to 186.

But parliamentary defeat was unimportant to Boulanger because
Boulanger was working outside parliament. Clemenceau's power of
speech could overthrow a government responsible to parliament but it
would not stop Boulanger. After a triumphal tour through conservative
Brittany Boulanger was back in the Chamber on 12 July demanding the
second part of his two-point programme, parliament's dismissal. New
insults were exchanged between Boulanger and Floquet and the two men
eventually decided to fight it out with swords.

The duel took place in comte Dillon's garden a couple of days later,
with Clemenceau and Périn acting as Floquet's seconds, and Laguerre
and Laisant as Boulanger's. Boulanger began the battle lunging at his
elderly opponent with great majestic sweeps, like a ballet dancer. Floquet,
short and very fat, simply held out his sword and remained steady. It
was the right tactic. Boulanger was skewered in the neck and for a while
it appeared he was going to die, if not of his wounds at least of shame.

But amazingly Boulanger's name did not suffer and, within a month,
he was scoring magnificent electoral successes in the Nord once more, in
the Somme and in Charente-Inférieure. More damage was probably done
to parliament because the press took a very dim view of a swashbuckling
prime minister supported by deputies in a period of crisis like this.

*

On 23 December an obscure Paris Radical deputy named Hude died. Under the rules of the *scrutin de liste* this opened up the whole department of the Seine for election.

The government decreed that it would take place on 27 January 1889, hoping this would be insufficient time for the Boulangists to organise themselves. Unfortunately the Boulangists were already organised. In Paris, it was not the conservative vote they were after but the traditional radical and socialist vote. The League of Patriots was called into action, Rochefort's press ran a scurrilous campaign, Laguerre's League and Vergoin's and Le Hérissé's Federation pulled out all the stops, the Blanquists set to work in the arrondissement committees – everything was prepared. The comte de Paris helped by telling Royalists to abstain (which was an underhand way of advising them to vote for Boulanger); the royalist press openly campaigned for Boulanger.

As for the republicans, all they could come up with was a man named Jacques, president of the general council of the Seine. 'He's a real nonentity, a veritable dolt,' mocked Paul de Cassagnac. 'Such men are precious. They make the convergence of forces possible, without wounding anybody's pride.' A lot of republicans would have agreed. When the electoral committee met to discuss its programme under Clemenceau's presidency, Jacques made a few feeble attempts at contributing. 'Shut up,' said Clemenceau, 'this is none of your business.'

On the eve of the election Clemenceau visited his old constituency of Montmartre with one of his English friends. The walls, the pavements, even the traffic – foot and on wheels – were plastered with Jacques posters and Boulanger posters. But clearly the Boulanger posters were dominant. And so were the Boulanger votes.

The Paris by-election was a terrible defeat for republicanism. Boulanger was elected on the first ballot with 244,070 votes to 162,520 for Jacques and 16,766 for the socialist candidate Boulé, leader of the construction workers' strike the previous summer. It has been calculated that over 150,000 of the ballots cast for Boulanger came from former supporters of the Extreme Left, both socialist and radical.

That evening Paris was in another of its turmoils. There were calls for Boulanger, who sat most of the evening out at Durand's, to march on the Elysée. But Boulanger was waiting for a greater occasion, the legislative elections that autumn.

There was only one way of dealing with a movement like this, the authoritarian solution: Boulanger had to be outlawed. It ran against the grain of parliamentary procedure and no Radical could ever have advocated it. In a speech made on 31 January, Clemenceau admitted the magnitude of the republican loss; it was Clemenceau's last major public utterance on the affair. Two week's later Floquet's government was overturned when, after succesfully abolishing the *scrutin de liste*, it made another half-hearted attempt at 'republican constitutional revision'. Parliament had had enough. Tirard was brought back into office with Ernest Constans as his minister of the interior. Constans, having just completed three years as governor general in Indochina, had none of the qualms that his radical colleagues suffered. Indeed, a few months earlier he had come close to supporting Boulanger. But as a member of the government he found himself on the other side of the barricade and he swiftly dragged Laguerre, Naquet and Déroulède into court for running a secret society, the League of Patriots – a ludicrous charge for an organisation that had been patronised by many leading republicans, including Ferry and Gambetta, at its foundation eight years earlier. Boulanger realised that he was the next on Constans's list and, on 1 April, he fled to Brussels. That summer, the Senate, acting as a high court, sentenced Boulanger, Rochefort and Dillon to deportation – a fairly safe measure since all three men were already out of the country.

Throughout the trials and the passage of various anti-Boulangist laws, *La Justice* maintained a judicious silence, broken occasionally by open endorsement. The Senate's role in the destruction of Boulangism earned Clemenceau's praise; he compared it to the great Revolutionary Tribunal of 1793, a rather remarkable image for an institution that he had for years considered as the principal obstacle to 'the will of the Chamber and of universal suffrage'.

Boulanger shot himself on his mistress's grave in 1891 – 'Here lies General Boulanger,' riposted Clemenceau, 'who died as he had lived, a second lieutenant.' But time would show that Boulangism had also found victims from a somewhat higher rank.

XIII

A PLAY written by Victor Sardou, put on by the Comédie Française and starring Coquelin, brought out some of the most cherished beliefs of the period, and some of its worst zealotry too. *Thermidor* was about the French Revolution. It made martyrs of Danton's followers, it damned Robespierre. Even its defenders admitted that it was not a very good play and thought it better suited to the boulevard theatres than the hallowed premises of the Salle Richelieu. But somehow it had got past the censors and had its première on Friday, 23 January 1891. The audience seemed fairly happy with the first three acts, but during the fourth some ugly noises emerged from the pit. The following day a few Paris newspapers announced that the 'youth of the Schools' would be organising a demonstration to stop its second performance which was to take place the following Monday. Jean Ajalbert, a sprightly youth of thirty-one, was prominent among them. Sure enough, there was enough of a racket within the audience the second night to ruin the show. On Tuesday, the minister of the interior – still Ernest Constans – suspended the play. The audience that evening was so angry with the substitute performance, *Tartuffe*, that it too had to be interrupted after the second act.

The Frenchman's love of mixing politics with theatre and opera had not abated with the Republic. *Les Français au Tonkin*, shown at the Théâtre du Château-d'Eau, had been interrupted by catcalls at the time of Ferry's fall. Wagner's *Lohengrin* had to be stopped simply because it was German. At Nîmes, a performance of Meyerbeer's *Les Huguenots* had recently been suspended because of local Protestant pressures. But the Comédie Française had been largely free of this sort of difficulty, even when it had put on plays dealing with issues as sensitive as the French Revolution. François Ponsard's *Charlotte Corday*, for instance, had been regularly performed with no trouble. It seemed one could scorn Marat on the stage and get away with it.

Robespierre was another matter. When Clemenceau had appealed to the 'sons of the French Revolution' at the Grand Orient in May 1888 he was invoking one of the most sacred political creeds of his generation: the Revolution, the 'whole step forward of a free people', the Rights of Man, the 'total development of the Republic'. He was saluting the struggle of the century, that was personal, that was universal. To call it an ideology would be to stress too much ideology's strict order of things. It was a sentiment, it was the passion of childhood, of origins, of growth, something almost biological. There was reason in it, but there was more than reason. It was not an abstraction. It was not always consistent. Clemenceau could at times accept his father's hero, Robespierre, whilst at other times he would despise him. But that was a family matter. A public attack on Robespierre was, for Clemenceau, an attack on the Revolution. It was a way of declaring one's faith, of telling the world which side you were on. Accept the principles of the Revolution but reject its violence? 'People who talk like that are simpletons,' Clemenceau had written as a student. He had not changed his mind in thirty years. 'Idealist, humanitarian, dreaming of "a better future", he sacrificed the present for a theoretical and somewhat undecided future,' said Ajalbert of his director. Charles Benoist thought 'M. Clemenceau is a theologian of a theology without God.' Clemenceau had adopted and nurtured the French Revolution in the way some people would adopt a child or others a work of art, or God. It was a force within him, waiting to get out. Since it guided his actions, he was convinced it would guide the action of others.

It was not the kind of sentiment which promoted conciliation. But then the Revolution was not a conciliation; it was the replacement of the sovereignty of the King by the sovereignty of the people, the substitution of the rule of self-interest with the rule for the common good. There were no compromises to be made. Robespierre was simply following the logic of revolution to its bitter end. The justification of Terror was unity, an uncompromising unity in the face of the enemies of popular sovereignty. When the members of the Convention proclaimed the right of all men to self-government, they joined to the Rights of Man the belief that the elect, whether a majority or not, were not only licensed, they were morally obliged to repress dissent in the name of a general will, for which they were the custodians. The idea Robespierre represented was that it was legitimate to use methods, which might be considered abominable in another context, for the regeneration of a society not fully conscious of what was good for it. Robespierre was a proponent of continual regeneration. And so, in a way, was Clemenceau.

He had not planned to intervene in the Chamber debate that had been set for that Thursday, 29 January. Since the general elections of October 1889 he had made only three major speeches; a play hardly seemed to merit a fourth.

The initial issue raised by Joseph Reinach's interpellation was the 'liberty of dramatic art' ('And the liberty of booing?' interjected Clemenceau at one point). Henry Fouquier and Joseph Reinach argued for the government that they did not want 'our Théâtre-Français' turned into a 'school for politics in our pay'; keep 'state doctrine' out of the theatre, they said. For anyone with the slightest respect for the freedom of expression, Fouquier's and Reinach's argument was foolproof and if they hadn't embarked on their own historical commentary the day would undoubtedly have been theirs.

Fouquier should have kept quiet. Instead he made the fatal error of saying that the play's problems arose from a mistaken 'romantic' political interpretation which refused to admit that 'if the Revolution, in bloc, is a great thing, the men who played out the drama were actors of most unequal merit.' The word 'bloc' stuck in Clemenceau's throat but for the moment he said nothing. 'The Revolution is a great act,' continued Fouquier, 'I refuse to admit it is a religion.' With that, the Chamber slid little by little, bit by bit, with one poisoned phrase currying the other, into a heated turmoil, the likes of which had not been witnessed since Boulanger's days. This was no longer a debate about a play; it was an inquisition on the French Revolution.

Joseph Reinach made the sincerest plea that he was as much a partisan of the Revolution as anyone in the Chamber. But he refused to confuse 'men of heart, incomparable patriots' with the 'men who lumbered this country, for long months, with the most fearful and the most odious of tyrannies!' There was loud applause from the Centre and the Right, there was a lot of noise on the Left. 'The reaction is applauding you, Monsieur Reinach,' one member of the Left shouted out.

A few other deputies spoke, or rather tried to, but they were all drowned out in noise. When Clemenceau asked to speak, the president, although fully aware that his request was out of turn, let the Radical mount the tribune for he knew, in that turmoil, that Clemenceau was the only person in the Chamber capable of drawing on the ears of the deputies.

'Messieurs, a play has been performed at the Comédie Française that is evidently against the French Revolution. It is time to set aside all the *tartufferies* . . .' There were probably very few who heard his first remarks and the text is rather repetitive. 'Assuredly no one has dared openly to make an apology for the Monarchy against the Republic.' That set his theme: it was a matter of monarchists against republicans. 'They have made a detour and they are hiding behind Danton. For three days all our monarchists have been vying with one another for the succession of Danton.' Clemenceau was now off the hook as far as his pending defence of Robespierre was concerned. He had to defend Robespierre; look at who were applauding Danton.

'But here comes Monsieur Joseph Reinach who mounts this tribune to undertake the great work of dissecting, in his fashion, the French Revolution. He dissects conscientiously and, his task done, seriously tells us: I accept this, I reject that!' The French Revolution was not, then, a matter for analysis, rather, it required a leap of faith: 'Messieurs, whether we like it or not, whether it pleases us or whether it shocks us, the Revolution is a bloc . . .' There were howls of protest from the Right, a surge of applause from the Left. 'Indivisible!' shouted out the Socialist Alexandre Millerand. For the first time in years, the Chamber was neatly split in two.

'. . . a bloc from which one can separate nothing . . .' Further howls, renewed applause. '. . . because historical truth will not permit it.' In this, Clemenceau was being true to Michelet.

But a speech from the tribune would have been incomplete without some reference to current affairs. He took the case of the legal actions against the Boulangists. Clemenceau said he was surprised to learn that Reinach was not for the revolutionary tribunal. 'You have a short memory. It is not very long since we set up together a revolutionary tribunal . . .' Repeated applause from the Left and a few benches on the Right.

'You identify the high court of justice established by the Constitution of the Republic with the revolutionary tribunal established by the Law of Prairial!' exclaimed Reinach.

'Let me speak,' continued Clemenceau. 'I did not interrupt you! We set up a revolutionary tribunal together, and the worst of all. We delivered politicians to politicians, their enemies, and the sentences were assured in advance.' He added, 'I regret nothing in what I did.' Their justification was that 'we had fear for the Republic and for the *patrie* – we can say it, that is our excuse.' It was also the excuse of the Terror when the threat to the Republic was so much greater, a threat posed by 'the ancestors of these men on the Right.' Explosions of applause and protest.

Clemenceau had not done his homework. The worst of the Terror occurred months after the enemies on the frontiers had been pushed back and the civil war in the Vendée had been won. Clemenceau claimed that the 'White Terror had made more victims than the other.' The reverse was in fact the case. But Clemenceau none the less received 'a double salvo of applause from the Left'.

'And now, if you want to know why, following this unimportant event of a poor play at the Comédie Française, there has been so much emotion in Paris, and why at the present hour there is such great emotion in the Chamber, I am going to tell you.' There was nothing stopping him now. 'It is that this admirable Revolution to which we owe our being is not over . . .' The sounds of applause and of protest proved that the division within the Chamber was for once clearcut. 'We meet the same resistance. You have remained the same; we have not changed. It is thus necessary that the struggle continue until the victory is definitive.' His final words showed that he still held some admiration for Blanqui: 'I tell you loud and clear, we will not allow the French Revolution to be sullied by whatever form of speculation, we will not tolerate it; and if the Government had not done its duty, the citizens would have done theirs.' He stepped down to repeated applause from the Left.

It was not an attractive speech. Albert de Mun responded to Clemenceau's 'Revolution is a bloc' by remarking, 'you want to solidify all the history of the Revolution with that of its crimes . . . I want to know if all republicans think like you.' Freycinet, again prime minister, said he was 'surprised, I can almost say that I am offended by such a question.' He told the Chamber that 'we are the depositaries of the conquests of the Revolution; we are the resolute defenders of the Republic.' The Chamber adjourned with an '*ordre du jour pur et simple*'. *Thermidor* had to be performed in Brussels.

Clemenceau had once more demonstrated his skill at the tribune. He had, for a moment, united the Left and divided the Chamber in two – it was a rather cosy, nostalgic image many deputies would have liked to have lasted. Clemenceau had shown a passion and a sense of commitment that recalled his youth. He had shown he could relay that passion, that he could manipulate it in others. He had demonstrated, in a Blanquist sense, that he could be a leader of the people. He had just proven he could be a demagogue.

XIV

CLEMENCEAU'S 'Revolution is a bloc' was an appeal for unity on the Left, his Left, the Left of his student days, of Benjamin, of Michelet, the Left now so obviously threatened by the 'collectivist barracks and convents' schools of the Socialists. It was an appeal to pick up again the progressive banner of History, Michelet's History, to reject the socialist formula of class for a just individualism, a democracy of citizens, which Clemenceau remained convinced would ultimately prove the greater historical force. In the 1880's, and until well into the 1890's, he believed he could still persuade the Socialists to forget their wayward social dogmas and join him.

A new wave of industrial strikes created an opportunity for closing the ranks between Radicals and Socialists. Strikes fitted the image that both groups had of the progressive struggle. If they could not be regarded as an exercise in proletarian 'consciousness' – not exactly an engrossing concern for most Radicals – they could at least provide tangible evidence of dissatisfaction among those who worked in mines and factories. Here, in huge and dramatic settings, were the overwhelmed, the weak, the exploited. A genuine democracy could not exclude them. The fact that mines and factories were not the only or even the principal components of the new industrial sector or that businesses during this period (and for a long time thereafter) were actually getting smaller and not larger did not diminish the impression that turmoil on a grand scale could make in a world increasingly fascinated, through its news media, with testimonies of combat.

Strikes affected less than two per cent of business establishments in France in the 1890's. More people went on pilgrimages than strikes. The incidence of strike activity, however, had doubled in ten years and was beginning to branch out of the two traditionally strike-prone sectors, textiles and mining. Employers, especially of the larger concerns, were getting worried. Not only did they resist the specific demands of their workers (limited, for the most part, to wages and hours of work) but they even denied, despite the 1884 law, the right of unionisation. Their fears were not entirely ungrounded. Militant political groups in Paris, Lyon, the Loire, the Nord and other industrial regions considered the current wave of strikes as, to quote a police report, 'the preparation of the social revolution'. There was widespread talk of a general strike that would bring in an era almost messianic in its conception. Such talk was encouraged by the formation in Paris, in 1889, of the Second International where it was proposed that the First of May be organised as a day of international strike in support of the eight-hour workday.

The May Day movement was – like phylloxera and the Colorado beetle – an American import. Yet it catered to French memories of revolutionary 'days', of patriotic upheavals and spring's other festivities. In the season when the sap rose and blossom appeared, workers went on strike; strikes had more chance of success in spring because the demand for labour went up, the needs of winter declined. 'It has always been so,' wrote the socialist journalist Prudent Dervillier, 'that the different industrial centres of France have been covered in strikes as the apricot trees are covered in blossom.'

Demonstrations took place in about a hundred and fifty French cities on the first May Day in 1890. In 1891 they turned violent. There were clashes with police in Saint-Quentin, Charleville, Roanne, Lyon and Bordeaux. At Fourmies, a sad, grey town in a southern corner of the department of the Nord, nine people were killed, all under twenty-one; over sixty were injured.

Clemenceau spoke on the second day of questioning in the Chamber. 'Are you not struck,' he said, 'by the importance this date of the First of May has taken?' He would give it a place within the long serial of History. 'Haven't you been struck, in reading the papers, by the sight of this multitude of dispatches, sent from every point in Europe and America, reporting on what has been done and said, on the First of May, in the worker centres? It bursts in the eyes of the least clairvoyant: everywhere the world of workers is agitated, something new has surged forth, a new and formidable force has appeared, of which politicians must henceforth make a reckoning. What is it? You have to have the courage to say it, and in the very terms the promoters of the movement have adopted: it is the Fourth Estate that has arisen, that reaches out for the conquest of power.'

It was a historical view radiating Clemenceau's touch: the reference to the French Revolution, the hidden energies surging forth. Sieyès had said that the Third Estate represented everything.* Clemenceau, as he

---

* The meeting of the Estates General in Versailles in May 1789 is often taken as the beginning of the French Revolution. The Estates General consisted of the First Estate (the clergy), the Second Estate (the nobility) and the Third Estate (the commoners). Sieyès, a clergyman, argued that only the Third Estate could be considered the genuine representatives of the nation. He was one of the first members of the privileged Estates to join the Third in a 'National Assembly'.

developed his speech, appeared to be claiming the same of the Fourth. A polarisation of forces was dangerous and unnecessary: at Fourmies, he said, 'there was a terrible disproportion between the acts which preceded the shooting and the shooting itself.' He appealed across the political barriers for unity, amnesty and a determination not to repeat the bloodshed of the past: 'Alas! we have seen it flow, the blood of civil wars.'

Clemenceau's concluding remarks sound foreign today. He evoked family, country and one's sense – Michelet's sense – of pity. 'Save our children to whom we do not want to bequeath this odious heritage of civil war! Save the Republic which has extolled justice for the oppressed, as the great Revolution had promised liberty! Save the home, save the *patrie* . . .' And he turns to Constans: 'Monsieur le ministre, I ask for pity for the Republic, I ask of you pity for France. Amnesty! Let us forget. Let us prepare justice; let us make the peace, the forgetting.'

Clemenceau received a triple salvo of applause from the 'Extreme Left' and there was 'prolonged movement', but we do not know what sounds came from the Right. The Chamber refused, by 318 votes to 199, even to discuss the articles for a general amnesty.

One could criticise Clemenceau, in these years, for lack of realism. The Socialists would criticise him for a lack of theoretical rigour. One could not criticise him for a lack of sincerity.

Unfortunately, two totally incompatible views of History were emerging. One was of a more sentimental, affective kind; it was the voice of Clemenceau, an appeal to altruism. The other was more rational, more theoretical, more certain of historical laws of development; it exhibited a will to join the ranks of the weak in open battle against the powers which oppressed them; it was the voice of crusaders.

A strike at the Carmaux mines gave the two sides a chance for expression.

XV

CARMAUX WAS the sort of French settlement which would induce a traveller first to declare, 'This is a backward country'; and then, having paused and looked again, he might correct himself and say, 'Ah, no! this is an advanced country!' Perhaps. But then he would look once more and shake his head. Without a thin but high quality coal seam running through this south-western fringe of the Massif Central, Carmaux would have been like its neighbours, a settlement of poor isolated peasants, supplementing their meagre income from the land with some local trade or craft. Sons

of peasants, many of the men who worked at the Carmaux mines
were themselves peasants. The Company, however, wanted workers, not
peasants. Yet there was something quite 'preindustrial' – one is tempted to
say 'feudal' – about the Company itself. It was owned by the Reille-Solages
clan, for long the dominant political force in the department of the Tarn. If
the baron René Reille was company president the real clan chieftain was
the baron's son-in-law, the marquis Jérome-Ludovic Marie de Solages.
With his black suit, white tie and waxed moustache, he looked more like
an habitué of Proust's salons than a captain of industry. But he ruled with
a kind of bull-headed paternalism. He refused to recognise the union that
had been organised at the time of the 1883 strike and, a dyed-in-the-wool
Legitimist, he hated the Socialists.

The strike of '92 brought national attention to two other local figures.
One was Jean-Baptiste Calvignac, a trained locksmith, a man of the
'labour aristocracy', who had joined the Socialist Revolutionary Workers'
Party and had just got himself elected mayor of Carmaux. The other was
Jean Jaurès.

There was nothing in Jaurès's early life to indicate that he would one
day be France's leading Socialist. He was born in Castres, the most
southern and most prosperous part of the Tarn, to a family of textile
merchants. His father was a Royalist, his mother a devout Catholic. He
himself had been an excellent student, and in 1881 he was placed third in
the national competition for the *agrégation* in philosophy. After the *agrégation*
Jaurès taught at a lycée in Albi, the capital of the Tarn. He also contributed
to the local republican campaigns as an enthusiastic Ferryist. His speaking
abilities so impressed his colleagues that, in the 1885 elections, they asked
him to lead the republican list. He beat the baron René Reille by 110 votes
and entered the Chamber as an Opportunist and the youngest deputy in
the country. He was twenty-six years old.

The loss of his seat in the elections of 1889 to the marquis de Solages
gave him the time for further study. It was Lucien Herr, the librarian at the
Ecole normale supérieure – an immensely cultivated man who influenced
a whole generation of French historians – who opened Jaurès to the force
of socialist thought. After a year of reading and prolific writing, Jaurès
was a convinced man. In February 1890 he told the readers of *La Dépêche
de Toulouse* that the admirable thing about 'our German socialist comrades'
was that 'They are equipped with the thought of Marx and Lasalle.'
To blazes with Gallic anarchy! Jaurès read Marx in German. 'German
socialism is not a random collection of discontents and petty aspirations:
it is rooted in a doctrine, an idea, and that idea reaches the masses.'

A year later Jaurès completed his two doctoral dissertations for the
Sorbonne. His principal thesis, in French, *De la réalité du monde sensible*,
dealt with the problem of metaphysics and History. His secondary thesis,
in Latin, *De primis Germanici socialismi lineamentis apud Lutherum, Kant,*

Fichte et Hegel, traced the origins of German socialist thought back to the Reformation. It was not entirely a coincidence that this was the same year the Pope published his encyclical *De rerum novarum*. Both authors believed in God, and both claimed that much in socialism was Christian in principle.

History, action and the evolution of man were guiding themes in Jaurès's thought. 'The human individual is the product of a terrible evolution from nature, he is the inheritor of many brutal forces.' Clemenceau could not have put it much better himself. 'But the instinctive powers are disciplined and harmonised by a high and general culture. Nature will not be suppressed or weakened, but transformed or glorified.' Clemenceau also believed in such a high culture; he called it altruism. But he was not so convinced in its inevitable victory. For Clemenceau, bestiality and egoism always had a chance of gaining the upper hand, which is why Clemenceau's thought never fitted into a tight historical schema. Jaurès, by contrast, saw human society evolving towards a more 'cultured' end. This was perfectly consistent with Marx and Hegel; it was also, as Jaurès repeatedly pointed out, a profoundly religious way of thinking. The struggle against the capitalist order was a 'just and valiant action which continues, in a way, the work of God'. Jaurès sought a philosophical *understanding* that conformed to the German idealists' sense of the verb, the act, *verstehen*: 'If man understands the veritable course of things,' he wrote, 'he aids it, he precipitates it and he is really revolutionary.' Clemenceau might have believed that life meant exploding from nothing, but he was not convinced that there was a 'veritable course of things'.

Nor were the directors of the Carmaux Mining Company. Calvignac, they thought, had a perfect right to run for political office, just as they had a perfect right to fire him, which they did on 2 August.

On 15 August the miners met in general assembly and demanded that Calvignac be rehired. To reinforce their point they marched on to the home of the director, Humblot. Windows were smashed, a door was broken open and the miners came face to face with Humblot, and the barrel of his gun. Fortunately the police intervened at this point: they had taken their time, they were locals under the mayor's orders. Nobody was hurt, but that same evening the marquis de Solages and his family left their château for Albi. The strike had begun.

It got enormous publicity in the national press. Troops were sent in: one soldier for every two strikers. Socialists of various schools – Millerand, Viviani, Duc-Quercy – came down to lend their support to the working class. So did the Radicals. Clemenceau made a brief visit. Jaurès wrote articles.

'Accept arbitration,' proposed Clemenceau in the Chamber, 'and all is finished.' Arbitration was a new idea, which implied recognition of the *personne morale*, the collective, corporate body of the adversary – in other words, the union. On 14 October the marquis de Solages resigned his parliamentary seat and, four days later, the baron René Reille said he would accept arbitration. The baron Reille, Humblot, an engineer consultant and lawyers would represent the Company; Clemenceau, Pelletan, Millerand and Calvignac represented the workers. The prime minister, Emile Loubet, acting as 'arbiter', accepted every one of the Company's demands with the exception of the case of Calvignac who was 'rehired' but then 'granted leave' for the time he remained mayor. Clemenceau and the other worker representatives protested, but after ten weeks the strike ended with no further gains.

Jaurès, typically optimistic, announced that the strike had been a great blow thrust for the freedom of workers and the cause of universal suffrage. The marquis de Solages, after all, had resigned. Furthermore, on 27 December parliament passed a law of 'conciliation and arbitration' which set up the institutional framework for the negotiation of collective disputes.

The Carmaux strike had another consequence. Jaurès decided to run for the seat left vacant by the marquis de Solages. The labour leaders at Carmaux, along with their Blanquist and Guesdist allies, opposed his candidature because they were unconvinced that the author of *De primis lineamentis* was the man best suited for workers. But Jaurès, looking rather like Gambetta – short, bearded, his huge head sitting uncomfortably on a badly dressed body – made a series of moving speeches in front of the miners. 'Jaurès! Jaurès! Jaurès!' they cried. Jaurès was their candidate all right.

Jaurès took his seat in the Chamber in January 1893. Eight months later Clemenceau lost his.

XVI

So MUCH of his being was now shattered, like the block of marble, a bust of his wife, which he had smashed with a hammer; its pieces lay strewn over the carpet like petals after a storm; love, immobilised in stone, had been reduced to a fragility and a formlessness that had no congruence with earlier hopes, ideals had vanished. Broken portraits, torn up papers and other relics of the years of happiness, the years of perseverance, the years of stalemate littered the shelves, the mantelpiece, the bureau. A corner of the room was occupied by several trunks his sister had prepared for Mary's departure. Everywhere there was rubbish and there was chaos.

The divorce was a family affair and the Clemenceaus held to this secret as they had in any other matter central to their name and influence. Divorce was legal – Naquet had made it so – but it was not something you talked about.

Others might and others did. Edmond de Goncourt had picked up the story from Ernest Daudet. 'What he knows of private lives, of the secrets of theatre people, society people, political people and business people is unbelievable.' So Clemenceau had hired a detective after one of his daughters informed him of Mary's lover; caught in the act, she was marched off to the Saint-Lazare gaol and then, divested of French citizenship, packed on a boat for New York. 'The divorce of Clemenceau,' read a brief notice in *Le Petit Var*, 'was pronounced at the request of Monsieur Clemenceau, against Madame.'

Scheurer-Kestner was surprised when Clemenceau asked to see him; they hadn't said a word to one another in fifteen years. But the old friend had provided more than sympathy during the trauma with his niece, Hortense. The bad days of youth were back again. Perhaps today they were even worse, for Clemenceau had already sensed the shame, only this time it was with the presentiment that it might go on forever. There was no America on the horizon, there was no marriage, there was no Empire to be overthrown. Scheurer-Kestner wrote in his diary, 'I told myself after listening to his recital of this drama that one must never rely on rumour in matters of quarrels between husband and wife.' That is all he wrote.

The will to live, the search for a burial. Clemenceau's double personality again forced the man to assess the two extremes and to make the bitter choice. He chose silence. He wanted to hear nothing, to see nothing. He sought a concealment. Here he so closely resembled his sick father who, when first apprised of trouble between the son and the American daughter-in-law reacted, 'We shall avoid all discussions where we might not be of the same opinion.' This divorce was a disgrace. To Mary, the invalid Benjamin wrote, 'Let us end all correspondence, henceforth useless.' For both father and son, burial was a purging, a release. Faced with the insurmountable mountain, looming and threatening, they chose the same path, underneath, in shadow.

And most of this happened the month Clemenceau made his appeal, with the Fourmies shooting, to 'save our children' from civil war, to 'save the home, save the *patrie*,' and pleaded 'pity for the Republic'. Once more in his life, Clemenceau asked for a 'forgetting'.

XVII

HATE, HATE, hate. You found it everywhere. Plots of one kind or another were continually being hatched among the deputies and their associates in the press, in business and other high places. The Moderates wrangled for a power they had lost, the Radicals for a power they had never had. The Boulangists, whose forty deputies now sat on the Right, wanted revenge, especially against the radical traitors. The Royalists cursed everyone and the rest. There were the old social hatreds which Fourmies and Carmaux had only magnified. There was the recurring hatred between generations: new faces in the Chamber – Delcassé, Joseph Reinach, Barthou, Barrès, Déroulède – put the older power brokers on the defensive. And there was a new hatred, the hatred of race, engendered by the learned discourse of sociologists, anthropologists, psychophysiologists, phrenologists and other vulgarisers, misinterpreters of the Darwin myth.

Individual will was lost, swallowed up by theories of historical and biological determinism. Without will there was no responsibility, without responsibility, no bad conscience, no remorse. There was no bar to wrongdoing, no effective reproof of evil acts, evil thoughts, evil words. The political world in France opened up to an orgy of hating. Maurice Barrès captured the tone in that seminal essay on Jew-baiting he wrote in 1890: 'hatred,' he said, 'is one of the most vigorous sentiments that our civilisation, our great cities, produce.' It was a sentiment you found even among men who sought to establish Paradise on Earth: *particularly* among men who sought Paradise on Earth.

Barrès was probably right to see the far-flung hatreds of his day as signs of vigour rather than immobility and weakness. The basis of his 'great cities' was, undeniably, the production of wealth, even if growth in the last decade had faltered and the methods of finance remained primitive. It was grounded also on a level of political participation hitherto unknown, despite widespread ignorance of the issues involved and the still limited distribution of the mass media.

This civilisation bred its contradictions, contradictions most glaringly demonstrated among its political classes. Expansion, money, inequalities: all this generated a thousand hatreds. Democracy had brought to the capital deputies who could not pay their way. Financiers and businessmen rarely became legislators; they were easily outnumbered by the great land-owners. But it was the provincial doctors and the small-town lawyers who made up the fastest growing group of men who sat in the Chamber, and many of them were without resources. 'The deputy without an individual fortune is a very poor man, very poor,' wrote one of their number in 1893.

In every legislature of the 1880's and 1890's you could find fifty or sixty deputies who had their salaries withheld because of debt.

Money problems could have been another reason for the relative silence of the radical leader. Geffroy's correspondence shows that the staff at *La Justice* were not getting paid. His relationship with Pelletan had become strained. Millerand turned to socialism; Laguerre had turned to Boulanger, and now to drink. Ajalbert had never felt a part of the team. Geffroy remained close and, through him, Clemenceau strengthened his ties with men of letters and the arts. Clemenceau was already beginning to feel that politics had been the wrong avenue. The only deputy with whom he remained on intimate terms was the warm and reliable Stephen Pichon.

But Clemenceau continued to wear his high collar, top hat, he carried a cane; he was still seen at the Opera; his flat on rue Clément-Marot was not the hovel that somebody like Spuller or Brisson was known to live in. For the political commentators and opinion-makers that was enough. If you appeared rich, you were rich. Where was the money coming from?

Clemenceau's downfall was linked to one of the most fantastic engineering schemes of the century, and one of its most spectacular financial failures too. Since the completion of the Suez Canal in 1869, a number of vague projects had been bandied around in Europe and America on how to open a sea passage between the two Americas. But it was the father of Suez, Ferdinand de Lesseps, along with the Paris geographers (geographers were rather more influential in the imperial age than they are today) who finally came up with the scheme to dig a canal through the Panama isthmus. Lesseps – in his mid-seventies – had most of France's major engineers against him, including Gustave Eiffel, and he faced mammoth problems raising capital. But having failed with the first issue of stock he finally managed, in autumn 1879, to put together a bank syndicate to guarantee a second.

The bank syndicate was made up of France's newer banks, like the Crédit Lyonnais or the Société Générale, not the old established houses, and it just so happened that many of these newer banks were directed by Jews.

Furthermore, the actual guaranteeing of share issues was something novel, primitive and frowned upon by the old banks. A bank's guarantee, for example, might simply be an individual director's guarantee. Publicity was also left to individuals, the *agent financier*, in the case of Panama a man named Lévy-Crémieux and, after his death in 1886, the baron Jacques de Reinach.

It was through this rudimentary system that Lesseps's Company managed, between December 1880 and March 1888, to enact (at enormous expense) seven issues of shares and redeemable stock.

In the meantime the actual digging in Panama turned out to be a work of Sisyphus. In 1884 most of the extraction was being done by hand and shovel. Conditions of labour were terrible and the mortality rates were among the Company's best kept secrets.

By 1885 the Company was in serious trouble. On 27 May of that year Lesseps wrote a letter to the minister of the interior, Rouvier, for the authorisation of the issue of lottery bonds; lottery bonds required an act of parliament. The roots of the political scandal were being laid.

Clemenceau's involvement with the Panama Canal Company can be traced to an encounter with Lesseps and his son Charles the following July. The Company had been warned to expect opposition to the bill from the Left and Clemenceau, known to be easily impressed with grand engineering schemes, was one of several deputies the Company decided to lobby. Clemenceau told the two Lesseps that they could rely on his cooperation.

Then the reports of trouble leaked through. It is also highly probable that Clemenceau was already aware of unhealthy dealings going on between the Company's *agent financier*, Reinach, and his old friend Doctor Herz. At any rate Clemenceau got worried, or ambitious, or both. In late 1887 he paid a visit to Charles de Lesseps, who was now for all intents and purposes running the Company. Everything was in order, the latter said; they were getting a bit behind, the canal would probably be opened in mid-1890 and expenses were somewhat higher than expected; but, then, that's why they needed the support of parliament. Clemenceau went away apparently satisfied. The bill became law in early June 1888.

The passage of the bill into law had involved some very curious manœuvres that several deputies commented on at the time. Initially the general sentiment of the Chamber seemed to be against the authorisation of lottery bonds, but after the spring recess of 1888, with the attention of the press diverted to the developing Boulanger affair, the mood of the deputies had magically changed.

The debate itself lasted two days, with supporters of the bill constantly being taunted by deputies on the Left and the Right. One critical, though frequently ignored, fact emerged from this debate: if the Company had not signed a contract with Gustave Eiffel the previous December – shortly after Clemenceau's second visit to Charles de Lesseps – it could never have got the support of parliament. 'This convention,' explained Rondeleux, one of the bill's chief opponents, 'is really the pivot of the new combination . . . Without this Eiffel treaty it is quite evident that they would never have dared present the demand they have submitted to you.' Rondeleux and his allies didn't have all the details at the tip of their fingers. But Eiffel had in fact been bought out at a fantastic price: thirty-three million francs.

21. J.-F. Raffaëlli, *Georges Clemenceau at a public meeting, Cirque Fernando (1885)* – The whole team of *La Justice* can be seen behind Clemenceau. To the left of his head, the bearded face of Albert Clemenceau; two figures further left, the moustachioed Paul Clemenceau and Georges's infant son, Michel. Gustave Geffroy stands with his left hand on the banisters

22. The man on horseback was a common image of political saviours: Marshal MacMahon leads his troops

23. Gambetta speaks

24. One of the founding fathers of the Republic, one of Clemenceau's great rivals: Jules Ferry

25. The new Chamber of Deputies opens at Versailles, 5 March 1876

26. Boulevard des Italiens on election night, 14 October 1877: readers learn of the defeat of MacMahon's 'government of combat'

AU BON DIABLE

GRAND MAGASIN DE CONFECTION

pour Hommes, Jeunes Gens et Enfants

VÊTEMENTS SUR MESURE

MAISON VENDANT LE MEILLEUR MARCHÉ DE TOUTE LA VILLE

Papier de Pliage illustré, BREVAL & FILS, Boulevard Montparnasse, 97, Paris

27. This lithograph was used in a major advertising campaign for men's clothing in the winter season, 1881–82. One can see why Clemenceau mocked the magnificent Gambetta as being the only man in the Chamber who had to *descend* to speak at the tribune

28. General Boulanger leads 'Marianne', the *patrie*, the
troops and the phantoms of Alsace and Lorraine – a
popular lithograph of 1887

29. E. Detaille's *Distribution of the flags at Longchamp, 14 July 1880* is a paean to the republican and
military enthusiasms of the 1880's

30. Edouard Drumont, journalist, antisemite

31. *Clemenceau, le pas du commandité*: an antisemitic cartoon implying that Clemenceau is the Jews' paid puppet

32. The marquis de Morès, entrepreneur, gangster, antisemite

33. Emile Zola in court, February 1898. Georges Clemenceau is seated to his left

34. Albert Clemenceau pleads

35. Alfred Dreyfus sketched by a reporter on his arrival at Quiberon after four years of confinement on Devil's Island

36. Captain Dreyfus at Rennes. The sketch is signed: 'To my friend Joseph Reinach, G. Clemenceau'

37. The office of the minister of the interior, place Beauvau, on the eve of the legislative election, 5 May 1906. Next to Clemenceau stands Albert Sarraut, an under-secretary of state

38. The arrival of the coffins at Pit No. 2, Courrières, March 1906

39. Jean Jaurès, from the tribune, interpellates the minister of the interior, Georges Clemenceau – June 1906

Clemenceau didn't say a word during the debate. He was perhaps preoccupied with Boulanger's gains in the provinces; everybody was preoccupied with Boulanger's gains. In fact, the day the Chamber voted the Panama bill, the legality of two by-elections in which Boulanger had run was contested.

The new radical government of Charles Floquet was also preoccupied with the Boulanger affair, so much so that Floquet accepted 750,000 francs from Panama which he later testified were put into the Nord campaign against Boulanger that summer. Jacques de Reinach acted as intermediary between Floquet and the Company, represented by an official named Cottu. The negotiations included a meeting between Clemenceau and Cottu, though the money was not at that time mentioned. Floquet, however, did receive the 750,000 francs. Rouvier accepted vast sums. So did Baïhaut, the minister of public works. On the day of the vote, the government proclaimed its neutrality – a major potential 'enemy' of the Company had been bought out.

The lottery bond bill finally became law on 8 June 1888 and the bonds were issued on 26 June. It was a serious failure. The Company had hoped to raise 720 million francs, it brought in only 255. The end of the Company was within sight.

The subsequent scandal might have been the sign of a general political malaise, the effect of uncontrollable social, political and economic expansion: the product of a new wealth that had outgrown old institutions. But it was also the result of personal intrigue and Clemenceau found himself in the thick of it.

On 10 July, just two weeks after the issue, Fontane, a Company official, received a telegram from Germany. It read:

> Your friend is trying to cheat. He has to pay or break and, if he breaks,
> his friends will break with him. I will smash all rather than be robbed
> one centime. Look to it, for there is not much time,
> Cornelius Herz

'Your friend' was the Company's *agent financier*, the baron Jacques de Reinach.

Two days later Georges Clemenceau and Arthur Ranc paid a visit to Freycinet who was at that time minister of war. They asked him to use his influence with the Company to calm matters down. Freycinet went the same night to see Charles de Lesseps to persuade him to give money to Reinach.

Clemenceau visited the younger Lesseps a few days later and found him in a 'nervous and irritable state'. Lesseps went raging on about Reinach extorting money from him; Clemenceau was so shocked by the outburst that he decided the best thing to do was – as he later explained to a parliamentary commission – 'to get away as quickly as possible'.

On 17 July, Charles de Lesseps handed five million francs over to Reinach and the following day Reinach started paying off Doctor Herz in Germany. But Herz wanted more.

In September, Clemenceau, accompanied by the prime minister Floquet, once again visited Charles de Lesseps and persuaded him to hand over more money to Reinach. Further sums were passed on to Herz. All in all, Reinach paid Herz twelve million francs.

Herz's relationship with the baron went back to the late 1870's. They had together dabbled in practically every major business venture that had hit the front pages since that time. But in the mid-1880's something went sour. Correspondence found later in Reinach's home showed that since November 1885 – the critical year for Panama, the year of general elections and, oddly enough, the year Clemenceau bought back Herz's shares in *La Justice* – Herz had been demanding money from Reinach. Through 1886, the correspondence remained polite, but in 1887 they became more threatening. On 28 August 1887, for example, Herz commented, 'Your refusal to pay [half a million francs] would be my ruin, would be yours, be absolutely convinced of it,' and he cheerfully signed off. 'Remember your testament. An eye for an eye, a tooth for a tooth. *A vous.*'

What was it that made this experienced banker, ennobled by the King of Italy, whose reputation was established throughout western and central Europe and who had dealt with some of the roughest customers in the world – what was it that made Reinach shiver in his boots whenever a note or a telegram arrived from his old partner? Why was it that the most powerful politicians in the country were willing so to demean themselves for the sake of Herz and – perhaps unknowingly – his blackmail? Clemenceau said in his testimony that a scandal, revealed at the time of the Boulanger affair, would have meant the end of the Republic. Possibly. But this was surely not the baron's concern.

No one has ever been able to unfathom the terrible secret Herz held at Reinach's head. All that we can be sure of is that Reinach kept on paying his extortioner until the night he died.

As for Clemenceau's relationship with Herz, no more is known than what has already been related. Herz was not merely a personal friend, he was a family friend. The business side of the relationship was more an affair of the brothers than it was of Georges. Did money exchange hands? Beyond the sale and repurchase of shares in *La Justice* (where Clemenceau admitted Herz had lost 200,000 francs) nobody has ever proven it. No tell-tale fingerprints, no smoking guns.

This extraordinarily complicated network of relations, into which Panama allows a few privileged glimpses, will almost certainly never be unravelled. But the impression is that everybody, not just Clemenceau, knew each other. If there was a financial crisis looming on the horizon, the prime minister would stroll over to the home of a leading banker or a company director. When there was a military crisis, party leaders would be knocking at the doors of generals. When the whole Republic appeared threatened, a dinner would be held by some fabulous socialite. Want to discuss literature? The leading figures could be brought together in a drawing room. Perhaps a little art? The Impressionists could come along too. Clemenceau's world was a diverse world, an untidy world and a very, very small world. It represented a genuine attempt – honest, dishonest, neutral and nasty – by leaders in all fields to respond to the multiple demands of a democracy of millions. We can say it was an inadequate world, an undeveloped world; we are not in a position to condemn it.

But there is perhaps one relationship that deserves some attention, because it has never been noticed before. A letter written by Albert Clemenceau to Gustave Geffroy on 26 January 1888 – two months after Clemenceau's second visit to Lesseps, one month after Gustave Eiffel's signature with the Company, days before the lottery bond bill was presented to parliament – reveals that the Clemenceau family had developed a friendship with Eiffel, 'pivot', as Rondeleux said, of the Company's 'new combination'. Geffroy wanted to visit the unfinished Tower, which would not be opened to the public for another year. Albert, writing in a hurry, says that he is unable to accompany his friend because he has to plead at court. But,

> You have a sure way of entering and seeing. For that, you must go to the Champ de Mars entrance where Eiffel's *offices* are located. Once there you declare that you want to go into these *offices*, and you go in. You then ask if Monsieur Eiffel is there; in his absence, his son-in-law [sons-in-law filled many a powerful office in those days], Monsieur Salle; in his absence, an employee. You say to whoever you are talking to: 1° that you are editor of *La Justice*, then that you are my friend, and you will show him your card and mine, which is enclosed. Without any doubt, you will be given more information than you need and you'll be able to clamber along the red ladders. [Emphasis in original.]

Albert added, 'I would not like to learn that my friend has broken a paw. *Se méfier. A toi toute amitié.* A. Clemenceau.' Is there anything in this beyond the danger of a broken paw?

XVIII

THE UNIVERSAL Company of the Inter-Oceanic Canal of Panama was dissolved by a Paris court in February 1889 and a liquidator was appointed; but it was another three and a half years before the scandal came to public attention. This was partly due to legal hitches in preparing a case against the directors. However there was a more fundamental cause for delay. A political scandal demands a political interest and in 1889 that interest was in Boulanger, not Panama. Only after the Boulangists had been thoroughly defeated, only when their choler had been rekindled, their desire for revenge ignited was there sufficient reason to make a political case out of Panama. That moment arrived after the summer recess of 1892 as parliament reassembled in preparation for the general elections of the following year.

Panama presented undreamt of opportunities for a party desperate for a popular cause. Its revelation meant new life for the Boulangists, who now discovered another enemy, the Jew, and another hero, Edouard Drumont. What delighted the Boulangists about Drumont was the way he managed to portray the Jew as the author of all evils. In his best-selling *La France juive* (1886) every major problem connected with the *question sociale* – poverty, unemployment, the insecurity of tradesmen and artisans, social foment, even the decline of Christianity – was attributed to the Jew. Drumont could appeal to conservative Catholics and Socialist Revolutionaries alike with his rallying cry of patriotism and justice – just as the Boulangists had done. 'A patriot is not to be improvised,' he wrote, 'it is in one's blood, one's marrow.'

Blanquists and Communards within the Boulangist movement saw vast revolutionary potential in Drumont's message and adopted it into their electoral programme in 1890; even Louise Michel was temporarily drawn into the movement. Anti-semitic papers sprung up in various parts of the country. None, however, were to enjoy the success that was reserved for Drumont's *La Libre Parole* during the revelations of Panama.

The series of articles, '*Les dessous de Panama*', began on 6 September and ran for a little over a week. They were signed by 'Micros', in fact Félix Martin, a provincial banker deeply involved in the affair. He named ministers, deputies and provided long details on the parliamentary vote of April 1888 and the operations of the banking syndicate, 'the Jewish band and the gang of shady servants'. *La Libre Parole* was soon selling over a hundred thousand copies daily.

*

Among those most affected by the revelations was of course the baron Jacques de Reinach, who had the bright idea that if he provided further information to the paper his own name could be kept in the clear. So this anti-semitic paper now turned to a Jew for its principal source; not the only irony – its financial manager was Gaston Crémieux, also a Jew.

Reinach's plan backfired because at the same time another Boulangist anti-semitic paper got into the act. *La Cocarde*'s principal source was none other than Ernest Constans, the man Boulangists hated most, a Moderate and a close ally of Rouvier. Rouvier had already been implicated by *La Libre Parole*. Now it was the turn of the radicals. The main target of *La Cocarde*'s articles was the former radical prime minister, Charles Floquet. But with the revelation of Floquet's funds for the Nord campaign came the name of the baron who paid him.

Reinach became desperate.

He decided to go and see Rouvier, who was now, of all things, the minister of finance. Would Rouvier accompany him to Cornelius Herz's home? According to Louis Andrieux, former prefect of police and – since the Boulanger affair – a close associate of Clemenceau, Herz held a long list of deputies in Reinach's pay. Rouvier must have been embarrassed at Reinach's request; perhaps he thought his own name was on the list. But for whatever reason, he agreed on one condition, that they be accompanied by another witness. Reinach had no hesitation in suggesting Clemenceau. Rouvier found Clemenceau in the lobby of the Chamber and pleaded with him to join them in visiting Herz that evening. 'It is,' he told Clemenceau, 'a question of life or death.' Clemenceau was apparently convinced and agreed to meet them at Herz's home. When Rouvier and Reinach arrived, Clemenceau was already in Herz's presence. The interview, according to Clemenceau's later account to a parliamentary commission, lasted only ten minutes; Herz told Reinach he could do nothing, it was beyond his power. Reinach listened in silence then turned to Clemenceau and asked him to accompany him to Constans's home. Rouvier left and Reinach and Clemenceau took a fiacre to see Constans. During the half-hour journey, Reinach 'inspired in me so great a pity that I had not the courage to speak to him. I do not believe we exchanged three words.' Constans proved no more helpful than Herz, even denying knowledge of the affair. Clemenceau and Reinach stepped out onto the street in the same dreadful silence. Then Reinach held out his hand; 'I am lost,' he said. Clemenceau returned home by foot. 'I saw a man struck to death, but I did not know why he was lost.'

Reinach was found dead in his home the next morning. Herz was already in a club-car bound for London.

The autopsy, which was delayed for three weeks, reported that Reinach had died of a 'cerebral congestion'. Few believed this. Most thought he had poisoned himself. Some thought he had been murdered.

The day after Reinach died, on 21 November 1892, the Boulangist Jules Delahaye mounted the Chamber's tribune. He asked the deputies to fulfil 'a duty of social salubrity which is of interest to all parties', he proposed a commission of inquiry. Delahaye's speech went on for about an hour, filled with insinuations of 'consciousnesses for sale in parliament,' of 'three million distributed among a hundred and fifty members,' of 'solicitations'.

'Names! names! names!' cried the deputies. 'If you want to know them,' said Delahaye, 'vote for an inquiry.' Delahaye gave no names and he got his commission of inquiry, presided by Brisson.

Five days later, or a week after the baron's death, the commission demanded an autopsy and seizure of his papers. The government opposed the autopsy and was forced to resign. The autopsy's inconclusive report was only published on 10 December. As for the papers, they were seized, but only after they had been inspected and 'sorted' by the baron's nephew, the deputy Joseph Reinach.

An article in *Le Figaro* revealed Clemenceau's presence at the two fatal meetings on the night of Reinach's death. Clemenceau made his deposition before the commission on 15 December. In the meantime the legal inquiry proceeded apace. Arrest warrants were issued on 16 December against Charles de Lesseps, Fontane, Cottu and a former deputy named Sans-Leroy. Then on the 19th a banker called Thierrée admitted in front of a judge that he still had in his possession twenty-six cheque stubs written, in Reinach's hand, out to a number of deputies and senators, including several former ministers: Devès, Albert Grévy, Rouvier, Jules Roche, Emmanuel Arène, Antonin Proust, Dugué de la Fauconnerie . . .

The following day the Chamber met to waive the immunity of the accused deputies and drag them before the great half circle of the elected. Every row was filled; five hundred and eighty deputies, representing every corner of France, waiting, if not for the verdict, at least for an exhibition of shame, a recantation: the pride of the powerful was at stake.

Arène handled himself poorly, but Rouvier was another matter; he fumed with the same spirit the Boulangists had encountered five years earlier. 'Today one is learning, it seems, in this country – it's known everywhere else – that beside the politicians there are financiers who, sometimes, lend their help when this is necessary for the defence of the government!' One couldn't accuse the former prime minister of lacking directness. 'Yes, I didn't find in the secret funds – to call them by their name – the resources I needed and I made an appeal to the wealth of my friends.' Surely this was not news to deputies. Surely every one of them had been forced to delve outside parliament's meagre allowances. The government did not have at its disposal 'a sum sufficient to defend the Republic as it needed to be defended.' There was a lot of noise on the Right, but an honest man in that assembly would have been hard put to disagree. In silence, the Chamber voted to waive the immunities.

Already, enough had been said and done to make this one of the great parliamentary days of the Third Republic. But at seven that evening the Chamber reconvened to hear Paul Déroulède 'interpellate the government on disciplinary measures to be taken by the grand chancellor of the Legion of Honour against Monsieur Cornelius Herz, grand officer of the Order.'

Déroulède, of course, was not the slightest bit interested in Monsieur Cornelius Herz; his concern was with his friend. Cornelius Herz, said Déroulède, was a man of the French state, and when the deputies began to murmur among themselves, he added, 'I'm astonished.' It wasn't the president of the Republic to whom one pleaded pardon on the night of Reinach's death, it wasn't a judge, it wasn't the prime minister; it was Cornelius Herz. Certainly, continued Déroulède, Herz would have to have his title in the Legion of Honour revoked, but one also has to ask how he got into such a powerful position in the first place. The by now traditional combination of the Right and 'diverse benches on the left extremity' loudly applauded the speaker. 'Who amongst us came and proposed to make a place for him in our ranks? Who then was it who little by little and yet so quickly, introduced, patronised and nationalised in France this foreigner?' Déroulède's round hulk was bent over the tribune, his hand raised like Moses. 'It had to be a Frenchman, a powerful, influential, audacious Frenchman.' Now just who could he have had in mind? 'It had to be the most obliging and the most devoted of friends who would permit him to rub shoulders with ministers, with newspaper directors and, yes, I know, with General Boulanger.'

'Ah! ah!' went some deputies in the Centre.

Déroulède straightened his jacket and placed both hands on the tribune. 'Well, this obliging, this devoted, this indefatigable intermediary, so active, so dangerous, you all know him, his name is on all your lips. But not one of you, however, not one will name him, because there are three things about him you dread: his sword, his pistol, his tongue. Very well, I, I take on all three and I give him a name: it is Monsieur Clemenceau!'

There was a stir. The burden of a decade fell from his shoulders. 'That's the truth!' Then loud applause on the Right and 'diverse benches on the left extremity'.

Déroulède spent another twenty minutes giving reasons: a meeting with
Clemenceau and Herz in 1885, the offer of money, money to *La Justice*,
money to its director. 'As we await the revision of the constitution, I do
the revision of certain deputies. I revise Monsieur Clemenceau, that's all.'
Clemenceau's life has been devoted to destruction. 'How many things,
how many people you have broken! Your career is built on ruins. Here
Gambetta, there another, and then another, and always others, always
devoured by you. How Cornelius Herz must have enjoyed himself with
this continually renewed spectacle!'

He was interrupted several times by the president of the Chamber,
Charles Floquet once more; another round figure behind a pulpit.
Clemenceau asked that the orator be allowed to finish what he had to
say.

So much hate, so much to revenge, so much history to overcome.
Déroulède said he didn't have much love for the International of the
workers, but at least they were poor. What really had to be condemned was
the International of the rich, 'the coalition of egoisms and of interests which
have as their sole end the inordinate increase of luxury, the enjoyment of
fortune, the cosmopolitan speculation . . .' Déroulède had never had such
an appreciative audience. Apart from the accused, all deputies were poor
that day.

'*La parole est à Monsieur Clemenceau.*'

Clemenceau was wearing a dark blue coat. He strode to the tribune
as if he were about to overthrow another ministry: there was nothing
glum about him. Even Barrès, a Boulangist deputy at the time, found
his allure 'royal'.

The attack is easy, Clemenceau said, because it leaves its object
disarmed, unprepared, 'reduced to invoking the protest of its conscience,
its intentions'. Monsieur Déroulède, he went on, has the right to analyse,
to discuss, to dissect and to incriminate a political life. But he hasn't the
right to pour on somebody the 'most odious of calumnies', derived from
'Boulangist spite', the accusation of betraying French interests, of working
for foreigners. 'To this last accusation, there is only one response to be
made: Monsieur Paul Déroulède, you have lied!'

Clemenceau's applause came solely from the Left.

They first attempted to settle scores with pistols: six bullets at twenty-five
metres. The duel took place on the Saint-Ouen racecourse in front of
about three hundred spectators. After each shot Déroulède gave a salute.
One hysteric woman ran across the field after the third. But there were
three more to come. Nobody was hurt. Déroulède said he hadn't killed
Clemenceau, but he had killed his pistol. Clemenceau, staring down his
smoking barrel, muttered, 'It's amazing.'

XIX

BEFORE THE tourists arrived, August in Provence was the month of swallows. Without them it would have been just silence, for there were no winds; it was the hottest summer in more than fifty years. High from a mountainside north of the River Argens you might have looked across the jumbled terrain of hill and valley into the haze of the sea's horizon. That distant world melted, as in an oriental painting, into light, shade and a few basic colours; the clusters of alder and beech looked white in contrast to the bronze of the birch and willow or the dominant green of the pine, the cedar and the ilex oak. From limestone domes the ridges dropped in long vertical columns into the terraced slopes below, leaving a suggestion of blueness. A tranquil and concordant place. The only signs of human life were the white stone houses perched in small groups on the hills. Then, far off, a faint whistle and the clatter of metal wheels against metal. A thread of white steam rose from the plain. It was a train carrying a team of politicians and reporters from the national capital to the department capital, tucked between the hills of Le Malmont and Le Flayosquet, the very provincial town of Draguignan.

Clemenceau wouldn't stay there long. He, or his advisers, wanted to get out into the hills, for they expected trouble in the valley's centres. Virtually his whole campaign was to be conducted in outlying villages, mountain settlements and hamlets: if he could turn the tide where the press had, up till now carried little influence it was thought he might later be able to come back and capture the towns. So after a night at the Hotel Bertin he set out, by train once more, for Salernes.

The people of Salernes liked Clemenceau. In the 1889 elections their mayor had received him at the Cercle de Fraternité and his speech in the courtyard of the Café Sigaud had been heard by over half the town's population. A repeat performance would make a nice inauguration for the contest of '93.

Clemenceau more than lived up to expectations. Before a crowd of well over a thousand, he laid out his heart, his beliefs, his life.

'After a long trial I present myself before you.' It was more a speech for the defence he was making than a candidate's address from the hustings. 'It is the destiny of politicians – I speak of men of combat – to be exposed to all surprises, to all attacks. In the past, one murdered them; it was a golden age. Today, against them any enterprise known to be vile appears legitimate; against them lies are truth; calumny, praise; treason, loyalty.' Democracy too then had its faults and Clemenceau could hardly be blamed for developing a certain pessimism. 'Attacked from every side at once, insulted, vilified, abandoned, disowned; under the most defamatory accusations, I have not weakened; and here I am standing upright before you, ready to give you an account.' There was enormous applause, though his account had not even begun.

He traced his career back to his prison sentence in 1862 – 'I was in prison for the Republic' – to Montmartre, the Versailles assembly and his role in the early years of the Chamber. 'I fought ideas, not persons.' Let the truth on Boulanger be known: Déroulède wanted to march with his League of Patriots on the Palais-Bourbon to impose a Clemenceau–Boulanger government. 'My resistance put an end to these criminal hopes. Monsieur Déroulède has remembered that.' He said he was a defender of 'the old republican programme'. Now one was faced with a new generation of deputies whose sole concern was to reassure the world of business. 'The young have come with ideas of the old, who want nothing more of the old with ideas of the young.' The income tax had been abandoned, workers' rights had been trodden under foot, the old programme of secularising the state had been forgotten. 'We are told, "You destroy the individual." What nonsense! We protect him, we defend him, we develop him, we cultivate him.'

He spoke of Panama and of Cornelius Herz. 'What remains to be established? That there is not a trace of these millions in my life.' *La Justice* was in heavy debt. 'Shall I speak of my personal situation?' He did. 'I settled my debts of youth by a loan from a notary at Nantes. You can go there and see, the debt still exists. Where are the millions? I married my daughter without dowry. Where are the millions? Six years ago I installed myself in my current home. The furnisher and the upholsterer have been paid little by little in instalments. I have not yet finished paying them. Where are the millions? . . . Let the shame of this humiliation be on those who have made this confession necessary.'

Clemenceau's speech was reprinted in several national papers and was read aloud – for such was the tradition in Provence – in the cafés and cercles in several of the towns he did not visit. In the meantime, he followed his campaign trail as planned, up into the high country.

From Salernes he went by open wagon, accompanied by his secretary's son, Maurice Winter, to a place called Villecroze. He climbed its narrow, stinking streets to the village square where a delegation of vintners, cobblers and knife sharpeners – the village council – were standing proudly on the corner to greet him. They led him into the largest room in the mairie, its walls plastered with the laws, the appeals and reminders of official France: '*Troupeaux transhumances, arrête . . .* ', '*Jeunes gens . . .* ' (and an image of a hero on horseback) '*Adjudication de Marin . . .* ', '*Adjudication de COMBUSTIBLE . . .* ' There were a hundred-odd citizens present, all with round rimmed hats and drooping moustaches moistened with years of drink and sorrow. A call was made 'to constitute the *bureau*'. They elected the mayor as president and the deputy mayor and village secretary as assessors. Then, after a brief allocution from the mayor, Clemenceau spoke. The audience applauded and the mayor moved that the assembly vote an order of the day: 'Faced with the repeated attacks of the coalition of monarchists, the republican electors of Villecroze vote an order of the day that gives their confidence to Citizen Clemenceau and their pledge to vote for him.' It was passed with unanimity. A reception at the Cercle de l'Union Républicaine, next door to the baker's shop, followed.

In Tourtour there was a village band; all you could hear was a pounding of drums. In Claviers there was a parade of horses and wagons. In Aups he met and debated with his former ally, now one of his opponents, Maurel, who showed 'an attitude that was almost courteous.'

It seemed as if the electoral plan was working. But on the evening of the third day of his campaign Clemenceau's carriage drew into Bargemon, where the 'Friends' of the marquis de Morès were waiting for him.

As far as Clemenceau was concerned this election was a Manichean battle which pitted the defenders of the true Republic against the forces of reaction, monarchy and *la Boulange*. The real situation was of course much more complicated. His twenty-three years of public life had generated a horde of enemies ranging from far Left to extreme Right. The monarchists certainly hated him. The Guesdists, however, did not have too much respect for him either; he professed no scientific doctrine. The Blanquists thought him a traitor. The Moderates regarded him as a permanent threat to government stability. There were even Radicals who considered he had served his time, that new leadership was in order. And Clemenceau faced a particular problem in the Var where local identity was very strong and where 'foreigners' and Paris politicians had always been treated with suspicion. Panama and the Boulangist resolve for revenge managed to pull these distinct elements temporarily together.

The first attempts at an alliance against Clemenceau did not in fact come from the Boulangists but from a resentful Radical, Maurel, who had been forced to stand down for Clemenceau when the *scrutin d'arrondissement* was reintroduced in 1889. Maurel got encouragement from a group of Varois in Paris to set up a *Ligue des candidatures républicaines locales* to defeat Clemenceau in the next elections. Their principal candidate, Joseph Jourdan, local, neutral and boring, was just the sort of person who could rally the enemies without raising the awkward issues that separated them.

They would never have succeeded without Panama. Jourdan would have run a conventional campaign – speeches and articles in the local press. The Boulangists, with several seasons of antiparliamentarian buccaneering behind them, had something else in mind.

Drumont's anti-semitism and Déroulède's accusations in the Chamber set the theme of the campaign: Clemenceau was corrupt and he was working for foreigners. They had fertile lands awaiting them in the Var. Within weeks of Déroulède's attack, the *Ligue des candidatures locales* had adopted the slogan '*Le Var aux Varois*', which sounded suspiciously like Drumont's '*La France aux Français*'. Who were the foreigners the Varois resented most? There was quite a long list of candidates. Obviously one couldn't accuse Clemenceau of working for the Italians, who probably got the highest marks. But the British came in a close second because the Varois had a long memory of British incursions into their Mediterranean world; they remembered in particular the British siege of Toulon during the Revolution. Clemenceau, fortunately, happened to have a number of British friends.

In late June the director of *La Cocarde*, Edouard Ducret, announced the discovery of papers smuggled out of the British embassy proving that there were French politicians working on behalf of Her Majesty's government. Within a day a Boulangist deputy, Lucien Millevoye, was making the same charge from the tribune and was goaded into reading the documents. They were so obviously forgeries that many of the deputies, including the president of the Chamber, were overcome by giggles. Both Clemenceau and Rochefort were cited as being in British pay. Millevoye, absolutely furious at the ridicule, marched out of the Chamber and later resigned his seat, as did his companion, Déroulède.

On 1 August Clemenceau took Ducret and his accomplice, a disgruntled employee at the British embassy, to court for libel. Both were fined and sent to gaol.

Apart from delaying Clemenceau's campaign in the Var for a week, the court case revealed the extraordinary network in Paris that was working for Clemenceau's ouster. One of the principal witnesses at the trial was Ernest Judet, director of *Le Petit Journal*, the most widely distributed of all the Parisian papers. Throughout the trial and all through the campaign, despite proof to the contrary, *Le Petit Journal* continued to insist on Clemenceau's British connection. Millevoye also gave testimony. Parliamentary immunity saved him from being among the accused.

The clumsiest of all the witnesses was the marquis de Morès.

The marquis was from a family of Spanish origin which had recently been ennobled, like Reinach, by Italian royalty. His father, the duke of Villambrosa, had, with some difficulty, persuaded him to join the French army. But in 1881, at the age of twenty-three, he resigned his commission, married the daughter of a rich New York banker and headed out to make his fortune in America. In 1882 he bought forty-five thousand acres of land in Dakota Territory on which he built a lavish logwood château. He attempted to set himself up in the cattle business while simultaneously developing interests in railways, banking, meat-packaging and mining. Every one of these projects failed. His seizure of important water rights got him involved in gunfights with his neighbours, the O'Connell Gang.

After the last of his businesses in Dakota went bankrupt he left with his family for New York where, in 1886, he opened up three large wholesale meat shops, based on a cooperative scheme that was designed to free poor workers from the grips of greedy 'intermediaries'. They also went bankrupt. The marquis left for Nepal and Burma to hunt tigers with the duke d'Orléans.

Here he got the idea of building a railway line along the Red River Valley to link the new French colony of Tonkin with China. After drumming up support in France, he set out for Indochina, made arrangements with the colonial authorities and then took a leisurely trip back to France, dropping in on friends, relatives and cronies in the United States and Spain on the way. To his horror, when he arrived home he discovered that his enterprise had been taken over by others, profiting from his absence.

It was April 1889. France was in the midst of the Boulangist crisis. Morès took it to his head that it was Ernest Constans who had sabotaged his plans and he spent his summer campaigning against one of Constans's supporters who was running for a parliamentary seat in Toulouse. It was another failure.

That autumn he read a copy of La France juive and the truth suddenly dawned on him; all his failures were due to the Jews. Morès became the Boulangists' leading authority on the Jewish question.

In 1890 he ran for a seat on the Paris municipal council, calling on the electors to vote only for 'clearly revolutionary Socialists'. He again failed.

Morès decided that regular elections did not correspond to his idea of politics. So he organised a squad called 'Morès and His Friends', dressed them in purple shirts and sombreros and sent them, like his rustlers in the Bad Lands, to sow terror among Jews at their religious celebrations or among opponents who dared turn up at his antisemitic meetings. A large proportion of these 'Friends' were recruited from the butchers at the slaughterhouses of La Villette in north-eastern Paris. Morès himself took on the title, the 'King of the Market'.

In June 1892 he killed in a duel a Jewish army captain, Armand Mayer. The killing cost the antisemites a lot of support, including most Socialists. But Drumont's Libre Parole ran a campaign in his favour and, in return, Morès and His Friends became official protectors of the paper. It was a partnership that came to pieces a year later at the Clemenceau trial.

Clemenceau was able to reveal, and to get Morès to admit, that Morès's

financier in the last two years had been none other than . . . Cornelius
Herz. The admission, of course, completely destroyed the case for the
defence. It was so embarrassing that Morès felt obliged to give a full
account in *Le Figaro* where he further revealed that it was Drumont
who had actually negotiated the loan from Herz for Morès. Drumont,
mortified, challenged the marquis to a duel; it was only prevented through
arbitration. Morès, however, had lost an important friend.

He and Judet now became absolutely obsessed with the need to
humiliate Clemenceau. It was clear, after publication of the text of the
Salernes speech that Clemenceau stood a good chance of winning the
election. For Morès, there was only one solution: he had to stop him
from speaking. Accompanied with an elite corps of Friends, Morès took
a train down to the Var.

The main business in the village of Bargemon, high on the hills of Blaque
Meyanne, was the manufacture of shoes. Its artisan cobblers were more
disposed than most to the Mediterranean instincts of fraternity and
hatred of things foreign. Bargemon was one of the first villages in the
arrondissement to vote Socialist. When General Gustave Cluseret, former
delegate of war to the Commune and first elected Socialist deputy for
the Var, passed through in 1889 the cobblers had laid on an enormous
welcome. Once installed in the Chamber, Cluseret joined the Boulangists
and by 1893 he was writing nasty articles for *La Libre Parole*. The local
Socialists did not endorse his candidature for Toulon that year, but it
was clear that anti-foreign sentiment was strong in this place and could
be easily put to good use.

Bargemon was the first village in which Clemenceau encountered
violence. He had barely muttered a word when he was interrupted by
cries, in broken English, of 'Oh! Yes! Oh! Yes!' Clemenceau yelled to one
of the hecklers to stand up and admit that he was 'in solidarity with the
forgers of documents.' The shouting went on; it was impossible to speak.
'I will stay no longer among the accomplices of a band branded by both
the Chamber and the courts,' said Clemenceau and left. A fist fight broke
out in the audience.

Clemenceau spent the next day campaigning in the easternmost fringes
of the arrondissement and he had no problems, but when he descended
that weekend into the central valley of the Argens he was met by violence
everywhere he made an appearance. At Les Arcs he had to withdraw from
the village square to a schoolroom. At Lorgues and Le Luc, both socialist
strongholds, he couldn't finish his speeches.

That was the weekend his old colleague in Paris, Edouard Lockroy, was
shot at as he mounted the steps in a theatre. His heavy coat apparently
saved him, but he was out of action for the remainder of the campaign.

The assailant was an unemployed coachman and member of the Guesdist Workers' Party.

Clemenceau still did not consider Socialists his enemies. During the campaign he continued to describe his programme as 'radical and socialist' and he always emphasised that he was fighting the 'reaction'. His biggest success of the campaign was the night he spent at La Garde Freinet which, surrounded by the cork-oak forests of Les Maures, had a tradition of left-wing militancy dating back to the great rising of December 1851. There he was treated to a banquet, a fireworks display, drinks with the cork-workers at the Cercle des Travailleurs and a splendid send-off, after a much applauded speech, the next morning. Salernes was also a centre of socialist committees and societies. But most Socialists in the arrondissement were, like their shoemaker candidate for 1893, Blanquists and Blanquists at the time were still smitten with *la Boulange*.

The hate campaign that the Boulangists directed was of course quite chaotic and its alliances could never expect to outlive the election. But in a society that still had no organised political parties, their efforts proved enough to overcome their enemy. They were not lacking in experience. What happened in the arrondissement of Draguignan that late summer showed a striking parallel with the Boulangist by-elections of 1888. 'The mob,' wrote a correspondent for *Le Paris*, 'is today showing its rage with image, word and pen; they are taking up again, and propagating, the legend of English gold . . .' For several days the platforms of the railway station at Draguignan were crammed with copies, supplements and bulletins sent down from Paris by *Le Petit Journal*. The paper's famous cartoon of Clemenceau juggling on the Opera stage with sacks of pounds sterling, accompanied with the inscription 'Aoh! Yes!', was sent free to practically every elector in the arrondissement. The postal service had to hire special aids to help carry the mass of materials into the rural areas. Wagons overloaded with free newspapers, posters and circulars were seen crisscrossing the country roads. There were some streets in Draguignan where one was literally wading in papers. Scattered among them would have been copies of a circular from the marquis de Morès; he had had them printed up at his own expense (or was it Cornelius Herz's?) by a Paris printer, Lombardin: 'I have not come to the Var to busy myself with politics, I come to support no candidate, I come in the name of no one. I have come simply to strike you [Clemenceau] in the face.' Morès mixed violence with a vague appeal for sympathy. 'Defeated in my personal struggle, I expect nothing from life, to which I do not anyway feel attached. I will struggle, a lost child, for the social cause.' As a correspondent in *La Lanterne* commented, with the campaign for the first ballot drawing to a feverish end, 'Lost children from every corner of France and from every party have come to assemble in a mob against one single man.'

The last day of that campaign was the worst of all. Clemenceau's supporters had organised a meeting under a huge tent in Draguignan. There were probably over two thousand present. The mayor of the town opened the session, though he was constantly interrupted by a famous photographer, Félix Anthelme, who, it seems, had come down from Paris for that specific purpose. A number of bravos were called out as Clemenceau stepped up to the podium. He stood motionless, waiting for silence. Then, just as he was about to begin, the heckling began. Fighting broke out in several corners, chairs were overthrown, the mayor stood up, the assessors sat down and the police ordered a general evacuation. Clemenceau withdrew to his hotel where he held a private meeting that evening.

All the same *La Justice* was able to hail the elections of Sunday, 20 August, as a victory, a 'crushing defeat for the document forgers'. Clemenceau won 6,679 votes to Jourdan's 4,705. Maurel, the Radical, got 1,034 and the Socialist shoemaker mayor of Flayosc, Vincent, picked up 1,717. But Clemenceau did not have a clear majority, so a run-off had to be held two weeks later.

Summer heat and thuggery had worn him down. To cap it all, that weekend he caught dysentery and for several crucial days he was confined to his hotel room. He wrote a couple of articles exposing the unconventional procedures of the opposition, which were published anonymously in *La Justice* (Geffroy's papers prove his authorship). One of the editors of the paper, Bermont, continued the rural tour, reading extracts from Clemenceau's previous speeches. The villagers of Tanneron showed they remembered their deputy by treating Bermont to a feast, after which the curé and mayor joined in a georgic rendition of the Marseillaise. Clemenceau himself only managed three days of campaigning. At Bagnols his carriage was stoned.

The four-week ordeal ended at Comps, the main village of the poorest and most isolated canton in the department. Life was hard, hard, hard on this Alpine plateau. But a small group of peasants, dressed in their Sunday bests, gave Clemenceau a rousing applause.

At the last moment, Jean Jaurès intervened, appealing to his fellow Socialists to vote for the man who had supported the Carmaux strikers. The miners themselves published a letter of appreciation. 'Among the republicans and Socialists of this department,' wrote Calvignac on their behalf, 'you will not find one disposed to play the game for the reaction, which we have been able to defeat at Carmaux thanks to your aid.' But it was too late. The Socialists of the Var had no such feeling of fellowship. Vincent recommended his followers to vote for Jourdan.

*

The final results of the second ballot gave Jourdan a majority of just under nine hundred votes out of the eighteen thousand cast. A breakdown of these votes would show that Clemenceau had won in the countryside, he had lost in the towns.

'I assure you,' he wrote to the comte d'Aunay three days after the election, 'I take this whole adventure in complete tranquillity. There is in me no desire to recriminate, to curse, to get indignant.' He spent a few days with Geffroy and Octave Mirbeau the novelist, relaxing. It was hardly a time for recrimination, more a moment of sorrow. Or delayed sorrow. To his friend Charles Edmond Chojecki he was later to write, 'I am unrecognised in my home, betrayed by my friends, dropped by my party, ignored by my electors, suspected by my country. *La Justice* has closed its offices, its creditors banging at my door. I am riddled with debts and I have nothing, nothing, nothing.' This cragged landscape, this relentless sun, this simple, persuadable, this sometime unforgiving people, this south-eastern province had pushed one man down and down.

The successful Jourdan naturally lived up to his mandate, an unpretentious, uninfluential parliamentarian; a Moderate. As for the marquis de Morès, that November he left for Algeria where he developed a new theory which saw the world caught in a struggle between the British Empire, gold and the Jews on the one hand and the 'agricultural and silver powers' on the other. Morès decided to strike out for silver and agriculture by cutting the British Empire in two, straight through its centre, Africa. His quest ended in July 1896 when his caravan of six was ambushed by a band of Tuaregs in a lost district of the southern Sahara. A glorious memorial service was held for him in Marseille and the funeral was organised by the enemies of parliamentary democracy at Notre Dame de Paris. Maurice Barrès gave the funeral oration. 'Morès was a Socialist,' he declared. 'He was at the same time a Nationalist.'

Thus Clemenceau's defeat might be regarded as a tragedy, a comedy and the beginning of a frightening new era.

CHAPTER SEVEN

Justice

I

HOW COULD anyone hate the Jews? No people in Europe could trace their history back further; few had contributed so much to religion, jurisprudence and learning. Bossuet, Louis XIV's religious adviser and not a man noted for his tolerance, wrote that the Jews were of 'primordial influence in the spiritual progress of humanity' and described them as the 'guardians of divine secrets.' He believed that the separation between Jews and Christians was only temporary, that because their origins were the same, their destiny would be the same. Two hundred years later most French Jews and many French gentiles held a similar view. Jews and gentiles, said the History watchers, followed the same path and their end would be identical, though neither were perfect. 'Our history and that of Israel are not of the same order,' asserted the Catholic polemicist and novelist Léon Bloy, 'but they are secretly the same history; the same calling, the same wavering faith, the same atonement offered, the same promises still unfulfilled, the same anticipation of that fulfilment.' As in the history of social classes and the history of nations, once Jews and gentiles joined the same route it was thought that all would dissolve into a common humanity; there would be no more Jews and gentiles. The historian Théodore Reinach – brother of Joseph and nephew of Jacques – in his contribution, 'the Jews', to the *Grande Encyclopédie* (1894), said that Judaism had been transformed by a wave of humanism bringing all religions together; the Jewish sentiment is losing its keenness, he noted, 'and will without doubt finish by disappearing completely.'

Perhaps it was as the 'guardians of divine secrets' that the Jews had for several thousand years held on to a certain vision of justice which, with the development of democracy, became an ideal for all Western peoples. 'If Christ preached charity, Jehovah willed Justice,' wrote the young lawyer and literary critic Léon Blum in the 1890's. The Hebrew word *zedakah* meant both 'charity' and 'justice'. Since antiquity Jews were under the obligation – not the request, not the condolence, not a fellow concern, but the obligation – to reduce inequalities and repair the iniquities of blind fortune. A Jew's duty was to contribute to common funds in proportion to his means; a network of Jewish philanthropic organisations in Paris and the provinces proved that the commitment was still in force. The Jews had abolished slavery in the days of the Pharisees and they had never accepted the legal implication that anointment placed kings beyond the law. Equality before the law was an unassailable Jewish axiom. It was no mere coincidence that the text of the Declaration of the Rights of Man was so frequently presented, in the mass-produced images of the nineteenth century, in the form of two Mosaic tablets. Eugène-Melchior de Vogüé, another devout Catholic, grasped the parallel between Judaism and the ideology of the French Revolution. In response to the anti-semitic taunts of his colleagues, one of his characters, a parliamentary deputy, replies, 'Yes, I am a Jew; but not he who has enslaved you under the weight of gold, your only real master. I am he who retrieves from the depth of the centuries our old cry of justice, the cry of deliverance for your oppressed brothers as well as my own. I am the Jew whose hand engraved on your walls the three fateful words, the three words you have perjured for a hundred years, and where you, quite senseless, have been unable to read the death sentence of your Babylon.'

But that was fiction. In life, the Jews would not answer the antisemites, for the Jews were committed to peace. 'Whatever we do, whatever we say, we are sure to provoke recriminations and discontent,' said Hippolyte Prague, one of the leading Jewish editorialists of the era. Prague advised his readers 'not to stir up hatreds, not to reawaken passions.' Théodore Reinach followed a similar line, telling a gathering of the Society of Jewish Studies, just after the appearance of *La France Juive*, that Drumont got from the French Jewish community the reception he merited, the 'silence of disdain'.

The 'silence of disdain' was more than a simple matter of caution, though that is all a later generation would see in it. Nor was it the silence of defeat, like the silence one found in that miserable Paris which survived the Commune. The silence of disdain, the silence of the Jews, confirmed a genuine doctrine of peace, a doctrine of survival; and two thousand years of history had shown that it worked. Nobody knew what happened to the Canaanites, the Hittites, the Moabites, Zidonians and Babylonians. But nobody had forgotten the Jews. In the Mishnah, the codified Jewish oral law prepared by the scholars of Jabneh, one could read, 'Three things sustain the existence of the world, Justice, truth and peace.'

The Jews made a virtue out of the fact that they were a people without a state. They did not beat their swords into ploughshares – throughout much of Europe they had been forbidden to own land. Instead, they turned them to pens and passed the message down through generations that the function of their scholarship was to use the Law to promote peace.

Many of the great scholars of late nineteenth-century France were Jews.

But they were also doctors, lawyers, deputies; they made their livelihoods in teaching, in healing, in the arts, in republican politics, in the defence of the nation and in the wealth of the nation. In fact there were only two professional pursuits not open to Jews, diplomacy and the elitist Cour des Comptes.

This participation in French society at large was relatively new. Jews were declared citizens with the French Revolution, but it was only with the economic boom of the 1830's that the real process of assimilation began. (The new immigrants from Alsace, Lorraine and Eastern Europe were as yet unassimilated.)

Many admired the way the Jews adapted so quickly, Clemenceau was among them. Leading Catholics praised them. And they were indeed worthy of praise – or simply the forgetting which they so ardently sought. 'If there are still Jews,' Zola told the antisemites in May 1896, 'it is your fault.'

Yet success offered another package of recrimination to the men dowered with hatred. Hatred has privilege in neither place nor time. There is no people, no nation, no group of men, ethnic or religious, which is immune to it. But in an age when, as Barrès had said, the vigour of a civilisation was measured by hatred, it was doubly easy to hate whole categories of people. The Jews were hated for their riches, and they were hated for their poverty. They were hated when they clung to their religion, and they were hated when they rejected it. They were hated for being too French, and they were hated for not being French enough.

So when a Jewish captain, falsely accused of treason, was publicly degraded at place Fontenay on a chilly January day, there were plenty of people, ordinary people, clinging to the fences, scuffling for a place with a view and ready to cry with the journalists, the novelists and the politicians, 'Death to the Jews!'

II

THERE WAS one renowned non-Jew eager, at this moment, to beat his sword into pen, and that was Georges Clemenceau. The humiliating defeat of 1893 had completed his disenchantment with parliamentary politics that had begun a decade earlier and it allowed him to pursue a fancy which had been nagging him since his youth – that really he was not a politician at all, but a man of letters. What was parliamentary politics? A house of cards, said Clemenceau shortly after his defeat; 'One builds, the other blows and then one starts all over again.' 'Writers made the Revolution,' he told an audience at Draguignan thirteen years later. 'What a mistake it would be to think that political action is confined to parliament and cabinet.'

The change was not easy. The electoral defeat came when he was fifty-two years old. He was recently divorced. His two daughters had married and he was having serious problems with his son. His father was dying. The creditors were rushing in.

Clemenceau decided within days of the defeat that he would write a daily article for La Justice. Up until then he had been an energetic director, but he had rarely written. The paper was entirely revamped. The price was lowered from ten to five centimes and the staff was reduced. Pelletan, who had shown little support for his director during these last months, wrote his final article on 2 October. Clemenceau's series began the following day with an article entitled 'En Avant'. A worried artist friend, Jean-François Raffaeli, remarked in a letter to Geffroy that week: 'Do you think Clemenceau is right in launching out into journalism?'

Clemenceau's search into this new domain went well beyond political commentary; he was looking for an artistic outlet. He wrote of course about the government, parliament and the opposition. Several of his articles dealt with foreign policy and there were many more on his past experience as deputy, such as the strikes at Anzin and Carmaux. But he also wrote about the hungry, about abandoned children, prostitutes, prisoners, peasants. Unlike that other political journalist, Jaurès, Clemenceau did not embark on a class analysis because he was not interested in class. What social class did the people who had queued outside his Montmartre clinic belong to? the Vendéen poacher? the beggar on the Champ de Mars? the anarchist guillotined at La Roquette? Many of the characters Clemenceau sketched were fictional. But was this any more of a fiction than the History one forced into the collective strategies of class struggle? Clemenceau filled his articles with descriptions of landscapes and of people.

There is in his writing echoes of his youth and, more specifically, the ideal of his father, what Victor Hugo had called le beau social, the social aesthetic. 'The modern ideal finds its pattern in art and its means in science' – Hugo's formula, combining the disciplines, remained Clemenceau's, despite the rifts that had developed over the last decades. Clemenceau is the republican médecin-prêtre, prescribing medicines he knows probably will not work, but recommending them none the less, showing his presence, demonstrating his sympathy – his pity – for those that suffer. Writing, like any other form of action, was not justified for Clemenceau by its success or its failures, but by the motive behind it. 'At least we will have been this miracle,' said Clemenceau introducing his first collection of articles in book form, 'this miracle of conscience and of will, which surges from the dark earthly womb to oppose, in an instant of changing life, the dismal immutability of the eternal absolute.' The image of a spontaneous generation was still with him.

So was his faith in individual will. One is put in mind of the analysis of art and the artist made by Otto Rank, one of the few twentieth-century psychologists to grapple with the problem of will. Rank scandalised his more deterministic Freudian colleagues by going back to what the German romantics called 'acceptance of the universe', what he himself termed 'willing yes to the must'. There are two personalities in an artist, argued Rank, one striving for fame, the other holding in contempt all acclaim; one seeking to eternalise himself, the other searching for an ordinary life. It is the sort of internal conflict that could be totally destructive were it not also the source of the creative dynamic. The effort at creation forces the artist to withdraw from the world, fame and success allow a 'return of the artist to life'.

Writing for Clemenceau certainly represented a form of withdrawal after years in public office. At the same time it offered a 'return to life'. Clemenceau maintained a circle of friends, but none of them were politicians, most were writers and artists. He played a very active part in the literary world, attending dinners, visiting the artists' retreats, even making speeches. He gave, for example, a major address at Edmond de Goncourt's banquet held at the Grand Hôtel in March 1895. He did not end his evening visits to the offices of *La Justice* either, though, as Geffroy noted, 'the premises were less and less spacious.' There he would frequently discuss the article he planned to write the following morning.

But the writing he did alone, even if his secretary Winter, was assigned the task of preparing 'dossiers'. From 1896 he worked in his small rented flat in the rue Franklin near the Trocadero, which remained his home for the rest of his life. Besides a man-servant and a cook, he lived alone, save for a short period in the early 1900's when his divorced daughter and her two children came to stay. Rue Franklin did not look like the home of a great statesman; it had more the appearance of a temporary residence of a minor official. He kept chickens in the garden.

Clemenceau wrote in the early hours of the morning at an enormous walnut horseshoe desk that took up most of the space in his office. He used a goose-quill pen and blotted his scribblings with sand. He did not write fluently. Among his papers are numerous rough copies with whole lines crossed out, phrases added, words altered here and there. Scissors and paste formed an essential part of Clemenceau's writing equipment and the fantastic shapes of his final manuscript pages could be considered works of art in themselves. He even returned printers' proofs for second copies, so cluttered the first would be with corrections.

His output, none the less, was prodigious. Geffroy estimated that if all Clemenceau's articles were collected together they would fill over a hundred volumes – fifteen were in fact published. In addition to the daily article for *La Justice* he contributed regularly to *La Dépêche de Toulouse, Le Journal, L'Echo de Paris* and *L'Illustration*. He also produced a long novel and a play.

Among the various topics Clemenceau covered was a short series of articles devoted to the Jews, not of France but of Eastern Europe – 'emaciated Jews . . . Mongols, Kalmoucks, red, blond or black, with powerful jaws.' They were based on impressions he had drawn from his annual visits to Carlsbad, today Karlovy Vary, set in the western hills of Czechoslovakia, but at that time a bourgeois watering place within the Austrian Empire.

They are travels and tales that bear some resemblance to Daniel Defoe's accounts of northern Scotland, or Boswell's, or to Montesquieu on Persia. They are funny, exotic, irreverent – and, some have argued, antisemitic.

'The Polish Jew is, unquestionably, after the Sprudel, the principal curiosity of Carlsbad,' proclaimed Clemenceau in the first of the articles, appearing in *Le Journal* in late summer 1895. It was the physical appearance of the orthodox Jews which above all astonished (Clemenceau had obviously not recently visited the 4th arrondissement in Paris): the long frock coats dangling at the heels, the skull-caps, the black silk hats, the uncut beards and the long cork-screw curls which danced before the ears. Clemenceau described these Jews as 'sordid beings with a gleaming look' who had come to Carlsbad 'to cure themselves from the ills of the Asiatic.'

Frenchmen who travelled east of the Rhine were frequently exposed to this kind of shock. Léon Bloy, on a trip to Denmark, was overcome with horror when he visited the Jewish market in Hamburg. Victor Joze, a novelist of the Zola school, saw only ugliness in the ghettoes of Poland. There was perhaps a link with Clemenceau here, for Joze's novel, *La Tribu d'Isidore* (1897), was illustrated by the same artist who produced the lithographs for Clemenceau's essays when they appeared in a book (*Au Pied du Sinaï*) a year later – Henri de Toulouse-Lautrec. The shock these writers expressed was not necessarily proof of antisemitic sentiments, for one found it also among the French Jews – for example, Bernard Lazare, a contributor to *La Justice*.

Clemenceau was unambiguous about the cause of shock; it was poverty and superstition, not race. He makes fun of the notion of race and its scholarly defenders. He attacks the reigning obsession with the shape of heads, faces and noses. Voltaire mocked the Jews not for their race, but for their religion. So did Clemenceau. The eighteenth-century *idéologue* and the champion of a plural and lay society beam forth when Clemenceau writes of the Jews.

Nowhere is Clemenceau's attitude, on the eve of the Dreyfus Affair, stated more clearly than in his story of Schlomé Fuss, Schlomé Sellner, Schlomé the Fighter. It is a commentary on justice, on religion, on the army and the rights of one man.

Schlomé Fuss was a poor tailor living in Busk. Clemenceau had visited the village of Busk, on the eastern extreme of Austrian occupied Galicia, just a few kilometres from the border with Russian occupied Galicia. 'All wood and mud,' he remarked in a separate article. The trip had provided a graphic idea of what the historians meant when they spoke of 'Napoleon bogged down in the mud of Poland.' Perhaps it was this which inspired Clemenceau to give his tale a historical setting, that of Busk in 1848, the year revolutions broke out in most of Europe.

Even the Jews of Busk felt the effects of 1848; 'they were, that year, honoured with three successive conscriptions by His Majesty the Emperor.' The Jews were pacifists and they had managed to work out an agreement with the authorities by which their community would pay for substitutes – a system not unlike the French 'blood tax' of yore. But three conscriptions in one year! They managed to pay up for the first and the second. They even succeeded in finding replacements for soldiers demanded on the third; but they fell one man short. One man in the community would have to serve the Emperor. There were no rich Jews in Busk. 'But doesn't one find, down to the deepest poverty, moneyed oligarchies ready to appropriate all that can be monopolised of inferior life?' The Sanhedrin of Busk decided unanimously to place in a bonnet only the names of the poorest of the poor. It was Schomé Fuss who was thus selected to serve.

The police came for him in the middle of the night. Clemenceau noted a parallel between his hero and Voltaire's Candide, dragged off to serve the Bulgarians. But there was one difference: Schlomé had a wife and six children.

It was a miracle they survived. The Jewish obligation to those in need had helped.

After two years the revolutionaries were defeated, the rebels routed; the war was over. Two years of murder, rape and plunder had made Schlomé a rich man. He returned to Busk. He received a hero's welcome, he was wooed by the influential, he was praised by the pious. As in the past, he regularly attended the synagogue. 'Schlomé is a good Jew,' they all whispered; 'he has remained faithful to his God.' But he never thanked the holy men who had taken care of his wife and children. 'Schlomé is a good Jew,' they began to mutter, 'but he is an ungrateful Jew.'

Then came Yom Kippur, the day of the Great Pardon. Schlomé turned up at the synagogue, as usual, in his uniform, with a prayer shawl thrown over his shoulders. But when the moment came for the rabbi to mount the tabernacle, Schlomé, to the astonishment of all, stepped up and barred his way. There was an uproar and several physically menaced the soldier for his sacrilegious act. But Schlomé drew his sabre and soon dominated the assembly.

In silence he himself mounted the tabernacle – it was a scene Clemenceau had no difficulty in imagining – and standing magnificently, with the point of his sabre touching the ground, he said, 'You are not worthy to read in the Holy Book the word of God . . . You have sold me as formerly Benjamin was sold by his brothers.'

After a futile attempt to call on the police, who were now on Schlomé's side, the assembly was obliged to heel to the will of the man with the sword. He demanded that every member of the Sanhedrin go, the following day, on their knees before his wife to beg forgiveness, and he demanded a fine to pay for the upkeep of his family for the two years he still had to serve in the Emperor's army.

Once his military service was completed, Schlomé again returned to Busk. He grew back his long side locks and his beard and he donned the clothes of an orthodox Jew. He supported his wife, he took care of his children; he settled down to the life of a poor tailor. No stranger, on seeing him today, would ever be able to guess why he is known as Schlomé Sellner, Schlomé the Fighter.

Schlomé is an individual who stood up for his rights. But what was the source of injustice? The Jews? the police? the Austrian military? the state? All can be seen as unjust, but each element has equally some good quality. Even the army, though initially the reason why Schlomé was torn from his family, in the end gives him the means of demanding redress. It is an *engrenage*, a whole system of gears. There is no simple villain, no simple hero. Save in one heroic act, an act which, under its own impulsion, creates a moral universe and defines the forces of good and evil. After that, Schlomé, like Candide once more, withdraws to cultivate his garden. The story is pessimistic, and it is optimistic. It is very much a story of Clemenceau.

But the extraordinary thing about it is that, within a year of its publication, its author was faced with the drama of a real-life Schlomé – perhaps not as heroic, certainly twice as complicated and three times more human.

III

LA JUSTICE was, typically, two days behind the major Paris papers in reporting the arrest, in October 1894, of an army officer for high treason. However, it sang the same tune. 'No doubt remains on the abominable

crime he has committed,' it declared in breaking the story. For a week it
ran a series of articles on the personality of the accused. It repeated all
the canards of the day. He was a captain attached to the General Staff,
not popular with his colleagues, he mixed with women of ill-repute and
he had been selling top secrets to Italy. But the paper did not dwell on
the fact that he was Jewish; he was simply the 'miserable Dreyfus'.

Clemenceau contributed a leading article, 'High Treason', within days
of the revelation. He attacked the government for 'impeding disclosure
of the truth' when 'it is well known that the government is in possession
of decisive documents and that the guilty man [sic] has confessed'.
He accused General Mercier, the minister of war, of 'having tried to
conceal the treason of his subordinate.' Dreyfus he considered guilty
of the greatest of all crimes. 'The chastisement will come. It must be
inexorable.' Clemenceau opposed the death penalty, but he said that,
were it not for his principles, 'I would especially demand it in the case
of Captain Dreyfus.'

These sentiments were universal. From the Extreme Left to the
Extreme Right, every newspaper in Paris attacked the government, and
Mercier in particular. They virtually all called for Dreyfus's death.

After the court martial and sentence, Clemenceau again expressed his
contempt for this man, this traitor, who seemed to possess no emotion, no
human quality, no expression of regret – and a man 'brought up in the
religion of the flag' at that. Were it not for Article 5 of the constitution of
1848, which abolished the death penalty for 'political offences', 'Dreyfus
would be shot tommorow.' A day later in parliament – it was Christmas
Day – Jaurès said that if Dreyfus could have been put to death he should
have been put to death.

The only redeeming feature in *La Justice* at this time was its continuing
refusal, faced with the hysteria of the other papers, to condemn Dreyfus
as a Jew. More than that, *La Justice* pointed out the dangers inherent in
the equation of traitor and Jew. In November it published an article by
Bernard Lazare, author of a new book, *L'Antisémitisme, son histoire et ses
causes*. Lazare, in his article, said that up till now it had been thought
that 'the army was small' which followed the likes of Edouard Drumont.
The Dreyfus case had proved this wrong. An 'antisemitic state of mind'
was widespread: 'While the crowd would have rejected with horror such
an accusation [of treason] if it had concerned a Christian soldier, it greets
it with hardly any astonishment when it involves an Israelite soldier.'

This is a dangerous moment for Jews, he went on; they are 'entering
into death: it is a race in agony.' He meant that it was a time when Jews
were abandoning their isolation, spreading out and dissolving into the
larger society. The danger was that the Jews will 'find as an obstacle
to their disintegration the same forces which reproach them for their
particularism.' He thought it unlikely that Jews would ever again, in the

'civilised West', be physically separated from others as they had been in the ghettos of the past or in Russia today. But a 'new moral ghetto' was gradually being reconstructed. Jews were no longer being chained into their quarters but 'there is being created around them a hostile atmosphere, an atmosphere of mistrust, of latent hatred, of prejudices unavowed yet all the more powerful, a ghetto far more terrible than the one into which one could escape through revolt or exile.'

The implication was that there would be no escape possible from this new 'anti-semitic state of mind'. Yet despite it all Lazare had confidence in the more distant future. 'Antisemitism can only last a while,' he contended, 'as is the case for a certain narrow and sectarian patriotism.' The new moral ghetto would disappear with the end of 'national egoism'.

The fact that *La Justice* published the article would suggest that the editor-in-chief went along, at least in part, with the analysis. All the same, Clemenceau, more than twenty years older than Lazare and a few years the wiser, was probably not as sanguine.

IV

ALFRED DREYFUS admitted he had problems. 'My somewhat haughty reserve, my sharp tongue and judgements, my lack of indulgence have done me no good at all today,' he wrote to his wife after his first month of solitary confinement at the Cherche-Midi military gaol. 'I am neither subtle, nor cunning, nor a flatterer.' None of his fellow officers came forward to defend him, nor did any of his teachers. Later, among his most enthusiastic supporters, many criticised him for his stiffness, his lack of humour, his almost pathological concern to place reason before sentiment. Maître Labori was one day to say that you had to distinguish between 'the man and the cause'. 'From the magistracy of the hero and the magistracy of the martyr, he has lamentably extricated himself,' commented Charles Péguy. Clemenceau was to describe him as a *marchand de crayons*, a pencil merchant.

His physical appearance didn't help. He was gangly, awkward. His pince-nez spectacles only highlighted the long straight profile that fell from the forehead to the tip of his nose, his mouth hidden by a narrow, well-trimmed moustache. He rarely smiled. His eyes were perpetually fixed on the middle distance.

But then Dreyfus was not born to be a hero. He was timid as a child, the youngest of seven children born to a textile manufacturer in Mulhouse. The Dreyfuses were rich, but it was a wealth gained in a generation. The

grandparents were typical of the poor Ashkenazim to be found in rural
Alsace in the early years of the century. Boarding school – the springboard
for upwardly mobile sons – filled Alfred Dreyfus with a kind of horror.

It could well have been the unsettling experience of school, combined
with a nostalgia for a home, which prompted Dreyfus to choose a career
in the army. The army had provided a haven for aristocrats seeking to
escape a new society founded on wealth not birth and for Catholics who
rejected the lay values of the Republic. As Albert de Mun had argued in
the 1880's, the army acted as a counter weight to the chaos of democracy;
it instilled principles of hierarchy, obedience and order. You knew where
you stood in the army. It was one huge family.

It was also a proving ground where assimilated Jews could demonstrate
their loyalty to the nation. Dreyfus was a great patriot. 'I have never
forgotten,' he wrote to his wife in his third year at Devil's Island, 'that
above men, above their passions, above their errors, there is the *patrie*.
It is to it that the task of acting as my supreme judge belongs.' Dreyfus
adopted wholeheartedly the army's sense of honour. 'Above all deaths
there is honour . . . I will not allow my body to yield until honour has
been rendered to me.'

Despite the fitful start Dreyfus had turned out to be a brilliant
student, though it was not the sort of brilliance somebody like Péguy
could appreciate. Nor Clemenceau. Dreyfus was a mathematician and
an engineer. He embodied the new technique of science as it developed
after Pasteur. There was nothing romantic or literary about his perception
of the universe. In his journal, Dreyfus describes the dimensions of his cell
to the nearest centimetre, complete with diagrams. He investigates the
mechanism of the iron contraption, the *double boucle*, which held him to his
bed every night for two months. He despairs for lack of books. 'Nothing to
read, nothing to read.' But he informs us that he practised a lot of science;
'not having the necessary books available, I was obliged to reconstitute
the elements of integral and differential calculus.' When Dreyfus in court
answers the charge that he shows no emotion, he sounds like Pasteur
defending one of his theories: 'I am stupefied. I believe in reason. I
believed that reason in such affairs – where the impulses of the heart
can bring no explanation, no alleviation – had to be the only guide for
the judge.'

Ecole polytechnique, Ecole de guerre. At the age of thirty-four he
was captain and *stagiaire*, or probationer, with the General Staff. There
were several hundred Jewish officers in France. But no Jew had ever got
this high so fast. 'All in life seemed to smile on me.' Dreyfus believed his
century was the age of light; he could never accept that in the 1890's a
man could be convicted and imprisoned on false charges. 'Justice, justice!
Are we in the nineteenth century or do we have to go back a few hundred
years? Is it possible that innocence can go unrecognised in the century of

light and truth?' Why should he speak of his Jewishness? He was a citizen
of France. At his degradation the crowd screamed for the death of the
Jews. He mentioned not a word of it in his memoirs. The Jew baiters had
prepared another reception for him at La Rochelle. 'I wanted to escape
from the hands of my guards and offer myself, chest bared, to those for
whom I was a just object of indignation and say, "Don't insult me; my
soul, which you cannot know, is clear of all blemish. But if you believe me
guilty, here, take my body, I deliver it to you without regret."' This was a
frequent image in Dreyfus's writings: he carried the body of a traitor and
the soul of an innocent man; his duty was to assure that the body did not
yield before the soul's innocence had been proved.

V

THE ACCUSATION against Dreyfus was based on a piece of paper, the *bordereau*, which had been picked up in the German embassy by a charwoman
working for French counter-espionage. It was undated and contained
references, such as a departure on manœuvres, that could never have been
written by Dreyfus. But there was a vague similarity in the handwriting.
Five writing experts were consulted. Three said the handwriting belonged
to Dreyfus, two said it was somebody else's. But of the two who reported in
favour of Dreyfus one was attached to the Bank of France – untrustworthy,
it was thought, he might be under the influence of the Jews.

Dreyfus's lawyer, Maître Edgar Demange, was only allowed to consult
the evidence after the initial judicial inquiry had been completed. He told
the family that evening, 'If Captain Dreyfus was not a Jew he would not
be at Cherche-Midi. It is an abomination. I have never seen such a
dossier.'

What neither he nor Dreyfus knew was that a secret dossier, already
filled with forgeries, had been prepared to assure conviction.

There were no evil men in the Dreyfus affair. There was stupidity, there
was procedure, bureaucratic dog-headedness, matters of personal honour
to be defended, the name of the army was at stake and the names of not
a few politicians were called into question. There were a handful of petty
crooks but, apart from the really guilty man, Commandant Esterhazy,
the crooks played a secondary role. Joseph Reinach, whose seven volumes
on the affair form the basis of all subsequent studies, commented that
'since it [the affair] had been extraordinary, one wanted it to be more

extraordinary yet.' Men were drawn into the affair that one could have
never have imagined interested in the fate of a Jewish army captain, guilty
or not. One extraordinary revelation followed another. Governments were
overthrown. The regime was threatened.

The popular press was again the critical element. Without its stories,
its caricatures, its truths, its fabulations, there could have been no Dreyfus
affair. The press had brought the war in 1870 and had confirmed the peace
of 1871. It had made democracy possible and demagogy probable; it had
become a substitute for political parties. It had made Gambetta hero of
the new Republic and had created its earliest menace, Boulanger. It had
made Panama an affair of the state. It had ruined Clemenceau. It was
the press that put Dreyfus on trial.

The political situation was as unstable as ever and the parliamentary
factions more complicated than ever – one could be Union progressiste,
Gauche progressiste, Gauche démocratique, Radical Socialist, Revolutionary Socialist, or just Socialist. In the first year of the 1893 legislature,
four governments had been set up. Mercier had come to the ministry of
war with Casimier-Périer's cabinet of December 1893; he had been kept
on by Charles Dupuy. But his future was a bit bleak.

So when in late September 1894 the *bordereau* was placed in his hands,
he decided he was going to make a political coup. He wanted a rapid
arrest and conviction.

France's counter-espionage unit – the so-called Section de Statistique,
directly under the charge of the General Staff – involved six people: a
terminally ill director, four officer assistants and an archivist. Under the
constant pressure for results, created by the lynch-mob atmosphere in the
newspapers, it would have been very hard for this small group of dedicated
men not to deliver someone up to the courts martial. No doubt, when
the similarity between the handwriting of the *bordereau* and a couple of
old forms Dreyfus had filled out was discovered, they were genuinely
convinced they had found their spy. Mercier brought in a seventh man, the
commandant marquis du Paty de Clam, who had dabbled in graphology
and was a relative of the minister, to make the arrest and conduct the
subsequent interrogations. But Dreyfus, in the first interview, did not
quiver as much as was expected, he did not shoot himself when offered
a revolver and, worst of all, he continually proclaimed his innocence.

Once the arrest was made, it was difficult, though still possible, to turn
back. No additional hard evidence could be found.

The fudging of documents began in December, the second month of
Dreyfus's detention.

By that time the press was howling. The story of the arrest was possibly
leaked by one of the members of the Section de Statistique, concerned that
the prize catch might be released for want of evidence. A bit of publicity
would tie the minister's hands. Mercier walked straight into the trap. He

told a reporter for *Le Figaro* that the stories of Dreyfus selling documents to the Italians were false, that he could give no details, but that the man's 'guilt was absolute, certain.'

Now there was no backing out. It would be, in effect, a trial between the minister of war and Dreyfus. Because the government was obliged to support its minister it would also be the government against Dreyfus. And since the minister of war also represented the army it would be the army against Dreyfus. Dreyfus's prospects did not look very good.

The trial was held *in camera*. The secret dossier was handed over to the seven military judges after they had withdrawn to deliberate. They returned a unanimous verdict of guilt.

The chances of a retrial were virtually nil. The voice of authority was undoubting, unshakeable, a good deal more convincing than the facts. Ministers, presidents and governments would change, but their confidence in the verdict remained the same. *La chose jugée*, it was an article of faith. High, low, middling officers bowed their heads to 'the judged thing' as republicans had bent their knees to 'the public thing'. It was a religious principle. It was not something that one shared, it was something that one felt. 'When an officer has a secret in his head, he doesn't even confide it to his cap,' said Commandant Henry at the court martial, challenged by Dreyfus to produce evidence. The litany was repeated throughout the ranks and echoed beyond into the corners of civilian society.

No legal system, civil or military, could easily rectify such a monumental blunder. There were too many interests involved. Revision would cast doubt on the army, the government, the journalists and a host of very important people.

VI

DREYFUS HAD promised his wife, Lucie, not to die. 'I cry, I cry and then I start to cry again,' wrote Lucie to Alfred on 25 December. 'Live for me, I beseech you, my dear friend; gather your forces, struggle, let us struggle together until the discovery of the guilty man.' He made the compact two days before his public degradation; the family's hope was that the search for the guilty man would continue.

In fact it did, but not under du Paty de Clam's supervision. The director of the Section de Statistique, incapacitated by a creeping paralysis, eventually resigned in July 1895. He was replaced by the young and very energetic Lieutenant-Colonel Picquart. The office continued to receive a mass of papers from the charwoman working in the German embassy. In

March 1896 a *petit bleu* – the *petits bleus* were small notes driven under pneumatic pressure through a network of tubes that covered all Paris – revealed that a Commandant Esterhazy of the 74th Infantry Regiment stationed in Rouen was in direct relations with the German military attaché. In August Picquart finally acquired two letters that Esterhazy had addressed to the ministry of war. He compared the writing to the *bordereau*. The handwriting was not similar; it was identical.

Picquart had more than his cap to confide in, though it is amazing – as is the case with so many other insiders at this stage of the affair – how long it did take him to talk. It was only after he was faced with a serious accusation from the Section de Statistique of tampering with evidence that he took leave of his post in Tunisia and, in July 1897, consulted with his lawyer and friend, Maître Louis Leblois. After some hesitation, Leblois decided to pass Picquart's evidence on to one of the earliest and most notable doubters of Dreyfus's guilt, the vice-president of the Senate, Auguste Scheurer-Kestner.

Picquart had given Leblois the strictest instructions not to inform the Dreyfus family of his discoveries. Between Alfred, Lucie and the elder brother, Mathieu, there existed – as Alfred's grandson Jean-Louis Lévy later put it – a *pacte sacré* that no bureaucracy could break. But two years of superhuman effort had produced little. 'Silence, a silence of death, hovered over us,' said Mathieu. Among the rare early recruits to their cause figured Bernard Lazare, who had already prepared a pamphlet in defence of Dreyfus in June 1895. But here was another case of hesitation, not due to Lazare but to a cautious Demange and Mathieu; the pamphlet was only published in November 1896. Scheurer-Kestner was among the hundreds of people Mathieu had visited in 1895, but at that time the senator was convinced, like most others, of Dreyfus's guilt.

Early in November 1897 the break came. A banker by the name of de Castro, on his evening stroll down the boulevards, casually purchased one of the reproductions of the *bordereau* that the Dreyfus family had been distributing throughout the city (the reproduction included, alongside, examples of Alfred's writing). De Castro was taken aback. He immediately recognised the handwriting of one of his former clients, Commandant Esterhazy – not the kind of client one would easily forget. He collected together a few of his client's letters and got in touch with Mathieu. Mathieu at last had the name of the guilty man.

Scheurer-Kestner had been in contact with the family since July, when Leblois had presented him with Picquart's evidence. But he was gagged by the same interdiction that lay on Leblois. All he could say to the Dreyfus family, in his calm tone, was that he had *evidence*.

Mathieu didn't hang around for a horse cab. He ran, the fastest he had ever run in his life, directly to Scheurer-Kestner's home and before he had even crossed the doormat cried out, 'I am going to tell you the name of the traitor.' He took a gulp of breath. 'It's Esterhazy.'

'Yes,' said the old senator, 'that's him.'

The denunciation of Esterhazy, written and signed by Mathieu, appeared in the press on 16 November. A judicial inquiry was opened the next day.

Esterhazy's court martial began on 10 January 1898 . . . and ended with an acquittal on 11 January, the seven judges apparently convinced that the accused was the victim of a vast frame-up, and the *bordereau* – again a central piece of evidence – an elaborate bit of tracing fabricated by the prisoner on Devil's Island. There were cries in the courtroom, 'Long live the Army!' 'Long live France!' 'Death to the Jews!' 'Death to the syndicate!' It was a hard journey through the noisy crowd in the adjoining street. Mathieu saw Picquart's tall silhouette disappear into an angry shuffling of faces, shoulders, arms and feet.

Alfred Dreyfus, of course, knew nothing of all this. 'Happy the dead!' he wrote in his diary on 6 September 1895. A special law had to be passed to shut him up in the sixteen-square-metre hut on the smallest of what were then inappropriately called the Iles de Salut, a former leper colony. The governor, eager to please his superiors, ordered the mute prison guards to note every gesture Dreyfus made, night and day. Once dead the minister of colonies had left instructions that the body should be embalmed and shipped back to France – there were fears that the 'syndicate' would never accept a mere death certificate.

But Dreyfus lived.

VII

'OH THAT fellow,' said Clemenceau rather nonchalantly as he bumped into Ranc in front of Dupont the printers, 'we all like his talent, but we've insisted that he leave us in peace with his Dreyfus affair.' Ranc had just mumbled something incomprehensible about Bernard Lazare.

'What!' All of a sudden Ranc went as stiff as a winter twig, 'you don't know then that Dreyfus is innocent?'

'What are you telling me?'

'The truth.' The old *quarante-huitard* looked at Clemenceau straight in the eyes. 'The truth. Scheurer-Kestner has the proof. Go and see him, he'll show you.'

'If that is so, it is the greatest crime of the century.'

Two days later Clemenceau was staring at a copy of the *bordereau* and a sample of Esterhazy's writing.

VIII

ON THE very evening of Esterhazy's acquittal, a meeting took place in the offices of *L'Aurore*. There is no record of exactly who attended. A row of men in dark coats mumbled to one another in serious tones. The tables had been pushed to the sides of the room where the usual piles of paper had been piled yet higher. The same cloistral ambience of chaos pervaded the place, partially obscured for the moment because night had fallen and the lighting was poor. Yet one might have noted a few differences from Clemenceau's former cramped offices. On one of the tables sat an enormous black typewriter. In a corner was a telephone.

Most of the staff of *L'Aurore* must have been present that evening. There were some familiar figures from *La Justice*, which had closed its doors the previous October: Geffroy, Mullem and Guinaudeau, along with their former director, Clemenceau. Ernest Vaughan was their new boss. He had launched *L'Aurore* a few months earlier after he had fallen out with his brother-in-law, Rochefort, at *L'Intransigeant*. A number of Rochefort's collaborators had left with Vaughan, as much attracted by what the new paper promised – the title *L'Aurore* signalled light, its subtitle (*littéraire, artistique, sociale*) suggested a cultural rather than political commitment – as they were disgusted with the rag of the old warhorse.

The audience also included 'some visitors'. Was one of them Joseph Reinach, who reported the meeting? Reinach was still piqued at Clemenceau's earlier parliamentary attack over the liberty of the theatre; he would never put it behind him. And Scheurer-Kestner? He had strongly disapproved of the meeting, he wanted to give the country 'time to reflect'. But he was an interested party.

Before them all, in fully fashioned coat and trousers, stood Emile Zola, tense, hesitant and a bit tired; he was not a public speaker. Tonight he was to read a 'Letter to M. Félix Faure, President of the Republic'.

*

The mumbling stopped and Zola read. 'What a blot of mud on your name' – he had always delighted in mud – 'this abominable Dreyfus affair!' He was insistent: 'France has on her cheek this stain.'

The main lines of the Affair were all there, in black and white, more black than white. 'In the beginning,' he said, 'there was only carelessness and unintelligence.' Zola traced the story back to du Paty de Clam's preliminary investigation, conducted 'as in a fifteenth-century chronicle amidst mystery' and based on 'a single infantile charge, this imbecile *bordereau*.' It developed biologically. Couple 'unintelligence' with the 'religious passions of the milieu' then introduce a little *'esprit de corps'* and you have the essential ingredients of a judicial error; 'the egg is here.' The combination had hatched high crime. If the first court martial was unintelligent, the second – Esterhazy's – was 'inevitably criminal'. Scoundrels had got off clean, honest men were sullied.

Such a silence had fallen in the room. Such thought. Such calculation. It was an instant for each individual present to work out his tactics. A moment of reservation. Nobody could have remained insensitive to Zola's conclusion.

'I accuse Lieutenant-Colonel du Paty de Clam of having been the diabolic workman of the judicial error, unconscious I would like to believe, and of then defending his ill-fated work, for three years, through the most preposterous and delinquent machinations.

'I accuse General Mercier of allowing himself to become an accomplice, at least through a weakness of spirit, to one of the great iniquities of the century.

'I accuse General Billot . . .

'I accuse General de Boisdeffre and General Gonse . . .

'I accuse the bureaux of War . . .

'I accuse the first court martial . . .'

Scheurer-Kestner thought the piece ill-timed. Reinach grumbled that it had too many adjectives. Historians have been criticising it ever since. In fact it was a fabulous piece of journalism, beautifully written, and it contained no lies.

At any rate, the assembly applauded and the paper's major figures gathered round the speaker to develop a course of action. But Zola, if proud, was exhausted and he would not stay. The moment he was out the door Clemenceau was hit by another of those irrepressible urges – rising up from the void – to crack a joke, the obvious joke, half-kind, half-wicked. 'Well, you see, the child walks all alone.' Reinach was very offended: Clemenceau, he thought, is going to be an incurable dilettante until the day he dies.

He wasn't short of ideas for all that. 'A Letter to the President of the Republic'? It's not exactly an eye-catcher; we'll call it *J'accuse* . . . They worked on a plan for posters that would be plastered all over the city. They called in several hundred newsboys to bawl out in their little voices the headline. They printed up three hundred thousand copies.

The following afternoon *J'accuse* exploded in the streets of Paris like a bomb. The news-stands were assaulted. The pavements, whole roads, were blocked with people who had simply stopped in their tracks to read. Two hundred thousand copies had been sold within an hour. The cafés by evening had turned into maelstroms of chatterers and screamers. It was the most sensational news story of the century.

Six weeks earlier Méline, the prime minister, had reassured the Chamber with the remark that there was no Dreyfus affair. He was right in December, for in January the Affair had only just begun.

IX

IF THERE was a philosophy behind *J'accuse* it was a very basic one: it was the struggle of life against the forces of death. The crowd was crying for 'Death to the Jews', and there should be no mistake about it; the majority were for death. The policy of silence, of oblivion, of the refusal to accept the truth was a policy that went in the way of death. It was the operation of the death wish in history. When the General Staff and the politicians sought to 'limit the damages' they were bowing to the very principle of destruction. 'What the nation is dying of is obscurity,' Zola later said at his trial. The note he scribbled a few days before his own death in 1902 simply repeated his message of January 1898: 'France saved from death by education.' Why should a famous writer sacrifice his wealth, his name, for an unknown Jew? He borrowed the words from the senator, old and reputed, who was putting himself equally at risk: 'I would not have been able to live.' The greatest crime, wrote Zola in *J'accuse*, was the encouragement the handling of the affair had given to the forces of death.

Zola was dramatic. He had to be dramatic. Bernard Lazare had wanted the Jews to rise up to defend 'their absolute right to live.' But even the Jews remained silent. The only sound came from those who were calling for their deaths. Between that 'absolute right' and the politics of its defence lay a yawning gulf and it required a leap – a brutal, violent act of rupture – to cross it. 'The act that I accomplish here,' said Zola, 'is only a revolutionary means of hastening the explosion of truth and justice.'

Zola and Clemenceau shared the same heritage; their writing lives, after all, began with the same student newspaper, *Le Travail*. Both used a language of science, indeed regarded themselves as scientific. Both saw life as brutal and mean, and both abhorred violence. 'Brutal force,' said Clemenceau, 'is an avowal of the failure of intelligence.' The combination of pessimism and optimism that was characteristic of Clemenceau could also be found in Zola. And so could Clemenceau's sense of life emerging from unconscious matter, his private and public battle with disorder, with death. 'Zola was right,' he remarked in an article on Dreyfus, 'these are cannibals, they want the death of this man.' Their campaign had only one message, 'the cry of death with its normal retinue of outrages.' To combat it required an act that would jolt spirits, shake delusions, give consciousness to reason: 'We have justice on our walls, in our dogmas, in our institutions, in our laws, in our books, in our poems, in our songs, in our plays. It is absent only in our hearts.'

So consciousness was the issue. Zola's revolution was not the product of class struggle or of an existing political movement. Zola had no support from Guesde's 'proletarians' and no support, either from the Left or the Right, from the parliamentarians. The upheaval of January found its origins in a powerful individual will.

Its impact was immediate. The day after the publication of *J'accuse* a *Protestation* appeared in the top right-hand column of *L'Aurore*: 'The undersigned, protesting against the violation of judicial procedures in the trial of 1894 and against the mysteries which surrounded the Esterhazy affair, persist in demanding the retrial.' There followed the names of Emile Zola; Anatole France, of the Académie française; Duclaux, director of the Institut Pasteur, member of the Académies des sciences . . . and several dozen others. The next day the *Protestation* appeared again with a list of writers, university professors, scientists and researchers. A *Deuxième protestation* was added with signatures from the same milieu and the two *protestations* continued to fill columns in *L'Aurore* for over a week.

The lists are known in history as the 'Manifesto of the intellectuals' and it is often regarded as the beginnings of the modern 'intellectual', engaged and outspoken.

For sure, a new political grouping had arisen with the publication of *J'accuse*. The university became a centre for the campaign for a retrial. The salons were all of a sudden politicised. Mme Straus and Mme de Caillavet were both active Dreyfusard sympathisers. If the Jewish establishment retained its 'silence of disdain', most Jewish writers and university teachers – Robert Dreyfus, Daniel Halévy, Fernand Gregh,

Léon Blum, Paul Grunebaum-Ballin, Marcel Schwob, Israël Lavaillant –
became within months committed Dreyfusards. Painters, poets, scientists
– people who had never made a political comment in their lives up to
now – joined the forces of truth and justice.

Clemenceau, writing almost daily in *L'Aurore*, regarded this movement
as revolutionary. On 18 January he wrote, 'it is rare that, in movements of
public opinion, men of pure intellectual labour show up on the first row.'
'Men of intellectual labour', 'men of thought'; within days he was referring
to them as 'intellectuals'.

He hadn't invented the term. Maupassant and Barrès had spoken of
'intellectuals' in the 1880's. But Clemenceau gave the word a currency
it had never had before. Barrès developed the word 'intellectual' as an
insult; it was an insult Clemenceau liked. For Clemenceau a new force had
surged into political awareness, a force capable of making a revolution,
Clemenceau's eternal revolution of truth, the Revolution of 1789. 'Is it
not a sign, all these *intellectuals*, from all the corners of the horizon, who
gather to an idea and unshakeably hold on to it?' he asked a week after
the first *Protestation*. [Emphasis in original.]

It might have been a beginning. But it would be wrong to consider
Clemenceau's 'intellectuals' as a class, in the style of a radical intelligentsia,
enrolled in a collective plot against the state. A revolution certainly
required the involvement of society's best minds, these 'great monks in
revolt for whom the right to live implied the right to think'. Clemenceau
attacked leading members of the Jewish community because they remained
silent. He also argued that once one had spoken out, there should be
no turning back. He became terribly critical of Scheurer-Kestner and
Picquart in December 1897 when they appeared to be withdrawing into
silence once more. 'Social life doesn't lack roads all nicely laid out where,
if you follow the common run of the herd, you can meet peace of mind
and enjoy protection through those constituted for crushing the weak by
the strong. But if you have rejected this vulgar route, if you have proudly
worked at building your own way, do you do it only to back off at the
first thorns of destiny?' The image was not of a man in a crowd, but of
a man in a forest, hacking his way out in solitude; don't look behind you,
don't expect any support. Clemenceau's intellectuals were isolated figures.
'Poets, thinkers, writers, don't let yourselves be regimented. Know how to
remain yourselves. It is the highest service that you might be granted to
render to the country.'

Clemenceau was faithful to his model. He had broken all links with
political parties. He made virtually no political alliances; his kindest
words were for Urbain Gohier, a columnist like himself; the main partner
in his campaign was his younger brother, the lawyer Albert. It was only
in the summer of 1898 that he developed his contacts with the other major
figures of the movement (Jaurès, Reinach, Mathieu Dreyfus) and it is

particularly noteworthy what little he had to do with the refounding, that February, of a League for the Rights of Man – ten years earlier he had been its leading force. Clemenceau was not frequently seen at salons; *la vie mondaine*, if it ever existed, was over for Clemenceau. He was rarely seen at the theatre. Lucien Herr made the odd visit to rue Franklin. At the height of the crisis there were daily encounters at *L'Aurore* and sometimes, according to Mathieu Dreyfus, an 'improvised dinner', but these political involvements were limited to *L'Aurore*. Correspondence shows that Clemenceau maintained a close tie with Geffroy. Octave Mirbeau became a good friend and his relations with Claude Monet flourished. Mirbeau and Monet were both active Dreyfusards and the current upheaval was not the sort of topic one easily avoided. However, Clemenceau seemed decidedly more interested in their art than in their political opinions. Brief, scattered evidence points to a man who had chosen his 'own way' long before the Affair broke out and who, by and large, stuck to it. He was a man of letters, an intellectual.

'I am alone, even among my friends,' he wrote to Admiral Maxse. 'These great monks in revolt . . .'; one thinks of Clemenceau. He wrote, and he wrote, and he wrote.

X

ZOLA'S *J'ACCUSE* had another less positive effect. In Clemenceau's former hometown of Nantes, old bastion of republicanism in that western rural ocean of conservatism, dockers joined in a demonstration organised by the Catholic circles, and marched down the streets to the rallying cry, 'Death to the Jews!' A crowd of three thousand gathered in front of the city's main army barracks from which emerged, to loud applause, the defenders of France dressed in splendid uniform. The barracks were not very far from the narrow cobbled lanes of the city centre, where artisans and shopkeepers were concentrated. 'Death to the Jews! Death to Zola! Death to Dreyfus!' Soon the crowd was pouring into the alleys like excited ants. Meyer's, the tailor's shop, had its windows smashed. The awning of Peyrère, the hatmaker's, was torn from end to end. A greengrocer's shop was sacked. Newsstands were overturned and the papers, still tied in packets, were put to flame. For nearly an hour they tried to force the door of the synagogue; it would not give. 'Long live the army! Death to the Jews! Death to Zola!' Somebody announced that the city's postmaster was named Dreyfus; they screamed for his resignation. 'Death to the Jews! Death to Dreyfus!' Two days later the shops and bazaars belonging to the chosen race, or said to belong to them, remained shut as another fraternal horde descended on the streets. The dragoons charged a crowd in front of the cathedral.

It was not an isolated incident. In Bordeaux, city of the Girondins, the symbolic foes of terror, shops were pillaged and the guards brought in. At Rennes, where some had argued the Great Revolution had begun, several hundred people, armed with sticks, swarmed to the houses of a Jewish professor, Victor Basch, and his colleague Andrade, who had had the temerity to write an open letter of protest to General Mercier. Marseille, which had given its name to the national anthem, was the site of a joyful demonstration in front of the Cercle militaire, followed by several days of window smashing; the grilles of the synagogue were torn from their sockets. At Saint-Malo Dreyfus was burnt in effigy on the public square. Zola, Scheurer-Kestner and Reinach were hanged in Moulins, Montpellier, Marmande and Angoulême. The whole province of Lorraine, led by Nancy, Epinal and Bar-le-Duc, celebrated an old tradition; Jews were howled at and hounded in the smallest villages; their shops were sacked. Grenoble, Le Havre, Orléans, Besançon, Châlons and many other centres of civilisation were trawled through the same experience.

Paris, of course, was not in the least bit immune. Jules Guérin, spiritual heir of the marquis de Morès, organised festivities with his patrols of 'golden youth'. 'As of this evening,' he declared, somewhat prematurely, in *Le Figaro* on 19 January, 'MM. Reinach and Bernard Lazare are our hostages.' Hostage-taking was Paris's tradition. 'The Revolution is beginning!' exclaimed the Socialist deputy Thiébaud as a fist-fight broke out in the Chamber.

But the worst of the violence of January and February was in Algeria. The French colonists of Algeria had been among the staunchest supporters of the Republic – during the Empire. They had voted for the republican opposition during Napoleon III's reign and they had voted for Gambetta's party after he fell. They loved their country, they loved their army, and they hated the Jews. There was not a single Jewish shop left untouched in Algiers during the looting of the last week of January, and they did not stop at murder. Not a town was unaffected. Not a day went by in the remainder of that year without some antisemitic incident being reported, a wave of violence which continued for a long time thereafter.

'Antisemitic young people, they exist then?' Zola had asked in his 'Letter to Youth' the previous December. Yes, Monsieur, they did. Clemenceau entitled his article of 27 January, 'Death to the Jews': 'The anti-Jewish riots, in which Europeans and natives have fraternised in murder, fire or pillage, show under what a thin veneer of civilisation our barbarism hides.'

XI

As A PHILOSOPHER of our own times has put it, one of the chief problems facing a democracy is that, with no control on the written word and free speech an article of faith, *anything* can be said about *anything*. 'We can say any truth and any falsehood,' writes George Steiner. 'We can affirm and negate in the same breath. We can construe material impossibility at will; in the Hegelian dialectic man "falls up". Thus language itself possesses and is possessed by the dynamics of fiction.' Yet no man will ever run a mile in three-quarters of a minute and it is inconceivable that anyone will live beyond the age of five hundred. These boundary-conditions are basic to life, but they do not exist in language.

It is no triviality to observe that both Zola and Clemenceau, the defenders of life, initially saw the Affair in terms of fiction and drama. In a democracy of letters, where the word-mongers created, recomposed and interpreted everything they saw around them, where they were encouraged to demolish accepted wisdoms and build on doubts, fiction was lord. 'Ah! what a spectacle,' wrote Zola in December 1897. For Clemenceau in February this was still a 'great drama', a 'poignant drama'. The 'sign' of revolution in the Affair lay in the fact that it had captured the imagination of hundreds of writers. But the fiction was beginning to revolve around truths; the events through their very extravagance, were pointing out limits, drawing the lines, showing up the intractable roots of certain principles, laying down the boundary-conditions of living democracy. The government took Zola to court.

Proust remembered, at the Palais de Justice, the smell of coffee emanating from the flasks carried in by visitors who crammed into the back of the courtroom to listen, growl, hoot and applaud; polite ladies, soldiers in uniform, soldiers in civilian dress (brought in by a royalist lawyer, Jules Auffray), reporters, agitators, writers . . . and Proust. From early in the morning until the court rose at night they stuck to their seats, attentive, then rushed to the nearest restaurant, across the river, to continue the trial and their pleasures with friends.

Zola remembered the play of lights, an afternoon's winter sun bouncing colours off the panelled walls, the gas lamps lit as the sessions dragged on till evening . . . and the tension.

Civilisation knew how to arrange its battlefields. On the one side, twelve honest men – merchants and shopkeepers, or, in Reinach's phrase, *petites gens* – sat undistractable, ready to be converted to the reasoning of lawyers. On the other, in the dock, the two figures who were the cause of the contest. Zola spent all fifteen sessions leaning his chin on his cane, a silver chain dangling from his pince-nez glasses. Witnesses described him as pale, worn-out and nervous; he later said he was 'smitten with cramps and forced to stir myself'. The managing director of *L'Aurore*, Perrenx, in his Sunday best, looked as if he had spent the previous night in the company of a chamber-pot. Their lawyers, no less than five, sat behind them. Fernand Labori had been brought in by Leblois to defend Zola. Unlike Demange, Dreyfus's lawyer, Maître Labori defended principles rather than persons. He was only thirty-five, but he had already proven his spurs at the Panama trials and, the previous January, had represented Lucie Dreyfus, who had joined Mathieu as plaintiff at the Esterhazy court martial. As for Perrenx's representatives, they appeared to Reinach as 'two models of the same man, Vendéens of the Kalmuck type, with energetic features and penetrating, burning eyes, vowed to battle' – the Clemenceau brothers. Albert Clemenceau, a couple of years older than Labori, was also a man committed to causes. This case represented a major break in his career and he came well prepared. Georges had no legal qualifications whatever, but he had managed to obtain authorisation from the president of the court to plead with his brother for his managing director, as long as he asked no questions. His pleading was thus effectively limited to his penetrating eyes, remarks whispered to his brother and client, and a summary which he would make at the end of the trial.

The president of the court, Delegorgue, a rotund gentleman who obviously delighted in the attention he was getting, sat at the head of the room, in prominence, in the centre of three rows of assistants, clerks and scribblers, all in gowns. Above their heads hung a large crucifix, which served to remind transgressors that in the beginning there was unity and God.

Teams surrounded the principal figures. The government was represented. The army was represented. A council of defence was organised around Labori which included Reinach, Leblois, Ludovic Trarieux, Léon Blum and many others. They planned to call on nearly two hundred witnesses ranging from those immediately involved in the two courts martial to commentators, experts, politicians, professors and well-known personalities. Beyond there were the crowds; the crowd in the courtroom and the greater crowd outside. Mathieu Dreyfus described the scene as one of 'prodigious battle'. But it was more than that, it was war.

The government's strategy was unchanged, it sought to 'limit the damages'. It hadn't wanted the trial in the first place but its hand had been forced by deputies worried that if no action were taken they would lose their seats in the elections the coming May. So the policy of doing nothing had to be modified; the government would have to do a little. From the entire letter, the ministry of war selected a single sentence on which to base its lawsuit against *L'Aurore*, the one where Zola had accused the court martial of acquitting Esterhazy, under orders, despite full knowledge that the man was guilty.

The first action the prosecution took, at the opening of the trial, was to demand the court president to limit the debate to the ministry's charge. 'One doesn't have the right to put indirectly into question *la chose jugée*,' remarked the advocate-general in his plea. 'They want to provoke a revolutionary retrial.' Labori and Albert Clemenceau opposed the request but the court ruled in favour of the prosecution. The defence made no appeal; they wanted to force the military witnesses before the bar and on this they had the support of the court president.

Lucie Dreyfus, in black, came trembling before the court, the first witness. 'What do you think of Emile Zola's good faith?' asked Labori. 'The question shall not be posed,' interrupted Delegorgue, mindful of the court's first ruling – Lucie Dreyfus couldn't possibly have anything to say on the Esterhazy case. An uproar ensued during which Zola screamed out for the same right as that 'granted murderers and robbers', the right to call witnesses. 'You are aware of Article 52 of the law of 1881,' grunted the president. 'I don't know the law and I don't want to know it,' retorted Zola, slamming down his cane. The hubbub endured five long minutes. When silence was finally restored, the court made a second ruling, 'The president is correct to refuse the questions to *la dame* Dreyfus solicited by the defence.' Lucie Dreyfus, looking greyer than ever, asked if she could step down. The request was granted. '*La question ne sera pas posée*' became the watchword for Delegorgue and the bench.

There was intense excitement when, on the second day of the proceedings, the defenders of France arrived, with great pomp, at the gates of the Palais de Justice. A general with an ostrich-plumed hat would step out from his carriage, receive the salute of his men and stride swiftly up the stairs and into the court. It always worked. The spectacle of authority impressed the crowds, it impressed reporters and it impressed the jury.

But the trial did not begin well for the prosecution and nearly turned to catastrophe when, in the second week, General de Pellieux gave testimony. De Pellieux, who had headed the initial investigation into Esterhazy, was obviously unaware that the evidence against Dreyfus had been fiddled. He began by warning of the dangers of discrediting commanders in the presence of their soldiers: 'They want to lead your sons to butchery, messieurs les jurés!' For a moment the shadows of war hung over the courtroom. He had hit a sensitive nerve and he got the attention and respect he wanted.

Encouraged, he asked to return to the witness stand the next day. After a few preliminary remarks he paused, straightened out his jacket, twitched his moustache, then pushed his chest forward and his shoulders back as though about to launch a cavalry charge. 'You want the light!' he called out. 'Let's get on with it then!' The ministry of war possessed a document that was devastating, 'the absolute proof of Dreyfus's guilt! And I've seen this proof.'

Most of the officers present thought this revelation was marvellous; at last their side was going to get the boost it needed. But in one corner of the room one might have observed Commandant Henry's scarlet face turning a paler shade of crimson. The last thing the prosecution wanted in court was their fiddled documentary 'evidence'.

Labori, in his response, said that such a document was of no value whatsoever until it had been openly debated by both parties in court. General Gonse, sensing disaster, appealed to *la raison d'état*; the document could not be divulged. De Pellieux sent out an aide-de-camp to request General de Boisdeffre's immediate presence: 'There are other pieces, General de Boisdeffre will tell you about them.'

The following day the chief of staff was once again before the bar evoking, like de Pellieux, the prospects of war, but refusing to say a word on the supposed proof of Dreyfus's guilt held by the ministry of war. 'I do not have the right; I repeat, messieurs les jurés, I do not have the right.'

It was an emotional moment for the twelve *petites gens*, most of whom had lived through the last war and none were too eager to send their sons off on the next. 'You are the jury, you are the Nation,' said de Boisdeffre. They could believe it. 'If the Nation does not have confidence in the commanders of its Army . . .' Now here was a bitter choice, a personal choice and no longer a simple matter of justice. Our sons, our sons. Remember the marches, remember the hunger, remember the smell, the pain, the humiliation. Down the rooms and corridors of their memories de Boisdeffre had let loose the dogs of war and in an empty space they heard an echo of anguish, a recoil from the past, the rumble of an uncertain, troubled future. They would not let it happen. They had made up their minds, and five more days of witnesses for the defence would not budge them.

After Zola had spoken and Labori had made his closing argument, Georges Clemenceau, at the end of the trial, was allowed to make his summary. It was his first politically oriented address since the Var campaign five years earlier. For fifteen days the president had imposed silence on him, as the court had imposed silence on the debate, as the generals and the government had imposed silence on the evidence. The anxiety of the jurors was one more instance of muteness, of a blocked awareness – a dread of goodness and justice – acquired through the unconscious process of imitation. The government copied the generals, the jurors copied the government and the generals. Each man involved was becoming increasingly shut-up in himself – confronted with freedom, he chose suppression; faced with the chance of communication, he opted for silence. The policy of silence was a policy of estrangement, of alienation, of the withdrawal of all feeling. The most significant feature of Clemenceau's summary was his attack on 'the philosophy of this *huis clos*', the closed court hearing. The secret would have to end; it was necessary to start communicating again.

'Documents, whose revelation they say would be harmful to national defence, and these pieces, which they have refused to show M. Scheurer-Kestner, which they have refused to show the Chamber, rove the high streets in the pockets of M. Esterhazy.' These pieces have to be submitted to Dreyfus and his lawyer, they have to be discussed in court. 'And if you declare that, because this man is a Jew he doesn't have the right to be judged like the rest, then one day they'll say the same of a Protestant, or a free-thinker. They've said it already. Where will you stop?'

Clemenceau answered the charge that Dreyfus's defenders were insulting the army by stressing again the need for an opening, the need for communication. 'No, we are not insulting the army. We honour it and invite it to respect the law.' The law today is the law of civilian society, not of the military *huis clos*. 'The principle of civilian society is law, liberty and justice; the principle of military society is discipline, orders and obedience.' There is always a danger, because the army possesses the force, of military society encroaching on civilian society. But in a republic the whole purpose of the army is to defend the principles of civilian society. 'A reconciliation has to be made between the two institutions.' But Clemenceau's 'reconciliation' was not a simple exchange of compliments between two uncomprehending parties, it was the victory of one principle over another. It was an old struggle revived. When he said 'the professional army no longer exists' he was reviving memories of the fight with the Second Empire and demonstrating a concern that the current military leadership was too isolated from the society it was supposed to defend. 'The universal army, the army of everybody, will have to be penetrated by the ideas of everybody, the universal ideas of law.' That, in a democracy, was communication – a 'reconciliation'.

Clemenceau knew something about the fear of war. For twenty-five years of Empire (Clemenceau was not a mathematician) Frenchmen gave their confidence to the commanders of the army; that didn't prevent war, or defeat. He also knew something of crowds. 'A great cry comes up thus from the crowd: "Traitor, double-dealer, scoundrel, renegade, agent of the Jews!" And these are Frenchmen, messieurs, who believe they are serving France.' Such mass behaviour was for Clemenceau a 'treason of the French spirit', the 'spirit of tolerance and of justice'.

Then, with the momentum that had built up in his voice, there came one of those wonderful pauses. He glanced over the heads at the judges' bench, at the wall above them. You knew he was about to drop a gem.

'Messieurs, when the hour of injuries is passed, when they have finished outraging us, we will have to reply. And what will be their objection then? *La chose jugée*?' He pointed at the crucifix. 'Take a good look, messieurs. You see this Christ on a cross. There it is, *la-voilà, la chose jugée*.' Clemenceau did not have much time for the Christians, but he never insulted Christ.

He turned to the jury. 'They have put it over the head of the judge so that he not be troubled by its sight.'

And he pointed again. 'They should have placed the image at the other end of the room, so that before pronouncing sentence the judge would have before his eyes the example of judicial error which our civilisation regards as the shame of humanity.'

When the commotion died down Clemenceau told the court, 'I respect Christ certainly more than many of those who preach massacre in the name of a religion of love.'

There followed a passionate plea to the jury not to leave the decision in the hands of the politicians, 'men invested with the public powers'. 'Having some power, they want more and they fall into the usual confusion of personal interests, or group interest, with the general interest.' This vicious circle had to be broken. 'Truth,' he said, 'has no party, it is the property of all.' And one should make no compromise. 'Give us, give to the French who expect it, the truth, the whole truth.' Don't listen to the argument of *la raison d'état*. '*La raison d'état* is to be understood in the context of Louis XIV, of Napoleon, of men who hold the people in their hands and the government at their good pleasure. In a democracy, *la raison d'état* is only a contradiction, a vestige of the past.' And don't let your fears get the better of you; 'An inner Bastille,' he warned, 'has remained deep down in ourselves.'

The jury listened patiently. Then it withdrew and in thirty-five minutes delivered its verdict, guilty. Delegorgue sentenced Zola to one year in gaol and Perrenx to four months. Both were fined three thousand francs. Officers embraced each other. The crowd was exalted. 'Long live the Army!' 'Death to Zola!' 'Death to the Jews!' Clemenceau later said that if the jury had ruled otherwise he and his colleagues would never have got out of the court alive. The walls of the 'inner Bastille' had held.

XII

'WE ARE living in a time,' wrote the editorialist of *L'Univers israélite*, 'when the day is called night and night is called day.' Could it have been otherwise? What politician, with elections in the offing, would admit that his past policies had all been wrong? What general would tell his troops that his strategy was mistaken? What patriot would argue that his country had got it wrong?

The truth might creep out if the electorate questioned the politician, if the politician questioned the general. A challenge could clear the way. But stubborn conflict could equally give birth to lies. Clemenceau, Zola, Reinach, Jaurès – all the major Dreyfusards – argued that their struggle for life was also a battle of the forces of modernity against archaism and outworn tradition. Yet they themselves had never completely abandoned old habits, and what they claimed to be of a bygone era was sometimes an idea with a future. *La raison d'état* was 'a vestige of the past'? It still had some years before it. And the man who said this was, three days after Zola's conviction, out on the field to fight a duel with pistols.

Admittedly, his opponent was someone whose understanding of the world was largely limited to bullets. *La Libre Parole* had kept up a slanderous campaign throughout the trial, but Clemenceau had waited until it was over before sending in his cartel. Three bullets at twenty paces. Edouard Drumont, who with age was looking increasingly like an Eastern European *schnorrer*, was a veteran dueller and knew how to miss. So no one was hurt. A week later Picquart and Henry battled it out with swords. Henry suffered a shoulder wound.

Lies or mistakes? The Dreyfusards had said at the trial that talk of war was an idle menace: that year France very nearly went to war, not with Germany, but Britain. The Affair had been widely covered in the British press and in none too friendly a manner. Zola's trial was described as a *coup d'état*: 'the Third Republic no longer exists.' Then in September, far away, down in the Lower Sudan at a place called Fashoda, Herbert Kitchener's Anglo-Egyptian army of thirty thousand, marching southward, ran into a band of Senegalese *tirailleurs* under the command of Captain Marchand, advancing eastward. Marchand had claimed Fashoda for the French; Kitchener claimed it was British. The press on both sides of the Channel clamoured for war and they would undoubtedly have got it had not the French foreign minister, Delcassé, backed down at the last moment.

Britain became home for Zola for eleven months. In the meantime, Clemenceau continued his daily articles. There was no lack of materials. In July a new minister of war decided to set the matter straight, once and for all, by reading to the Chamber the 'devastating' evidence of Dreyfus's guilt. Picquart, in a letter to the prime minister, said the documents were forgeries and was promptly arrested. But in August Commandant Henry, confronted with proof, confessed to forgery and after a day in prison killed himself – 'I am going to bathe in the Seine,' *le sang*, he wrote to his wife the instant he slit his throat. Now it was the turn of Esterhazy – 'white as the snows of Bavaria'

(Clemenceau) – to seek a home in England. Picquart of course remained in gaol.

In the following autumn and winter there were further nationalist and antisemitic demonstrations, the president died in the arms of his mistress ('Félix Faure has just died,' wrote Clemenceau, 'that doesn't make one man less in France'), and Dupuy set up his fifth government. The legislative elections of May 1898 had shown that the deputies' tactic of silence, even hostility to Dreyfus, worked. 'They are going to have their little elections nice and peacefully,' wrote Clemenceau. 'One mustn't trouble them. Are they of the opposition? Are they of the government? There is no way of saying. They are deputies and want to be deputies: that's the whole concern.' Reinach lost his seat for the Basses-Alpes. Jaurès, though careful not to say a word on the Affair during his campaign, lost his seat for the Tarn. Déroulède and Cassagnac were re-elected and Drumont entered the Chamber as deputy for Algiers. But this was no revolution. The Chamber elected in 1898 was almost identical to that of 1893. The vast majority of the electorate were uninterested in the fate of Dreyfus.

But the attitude of voters was only one side of the coin. The new democracy relied of course on voters, but it also required the distribution of information. There was no television, there was no radio. Besides the campaign speeches, the only direct source of national news was the printed press carried by train, wagon and donkey; Catholic groups in the countryside had begun to take to bicycles. In these primitive circumstances it is not surprising that voters appeared 'indifferent': they were ignorant of national issues. The scandal of the Dreyfus Affair was that the little information that was diffused preached violence and intolerance and was antisemitic.

Were Clemenceau's numerous references to antisemitism exaggerated? It is now fashionable to argue that the Dreyfus Affair was an affair of the elite, that the antisemitism associated with it was not very widespread. Small doubt that the crowds Clemenceau encountered in Paris – 'some tricolour ribbons tied to the ends of a few umbrellas, some curés stirring up the curious on the public way . . .' – like those that were reported in virtually every major city and town in the country, no more represented urban populations than mass strikers represented the working classes. But they always claimed they did. And they were frequently violent. True, the murder of Jews was limited to Algeria. But the violence against Jewish property was widespread.

These antisemites needed an answer. For Clemenceau it was a question of 'bringing to the country this mental revolution necessary for the installation of the great reforms of general justice.' The struggle would go on.

XIII

THE FIRST vague hints Alfred Dreyfus got of the Dreyfus Affair were from a couple of letters his wife wrote in September 1897 which he had received in November. They spoke of an 'immense hope' – 'we are moving in the right direction.' Two months passed with no news. Surveillance was increased. The diary had been abandoned more than a year earlier, for he could not concentrate. He suffered from chronic fever and vomited continually; his nerves were frayed. Then another letter: 'It breaks my heart not to be able to tell you all that has impassioned me, all that has given me so much hope.' What could it be? There was further silence, further restraints on his movements.

In November 1898 he received a brief telegram from the governor of the islands informing him that the Court of Appeal had accepted a request for a revision of the judgement and that he should soon expect an invitation 'to produce your means of defence'.

At the end of December he was shown an indictment prepared for the Court of Appeal and learned, for the first time, of his brother's charge against Esterhazy, of the acquittal, the forgeries and of Henry's suicide. In early January 1899 he was interrogated by a local judge. This was followed by several more voiceless months.

It was an early Monday afternoon, 5 June, when a senior guard came to his hut and handed him a note: 'The Court quashes and annuls the verdict rendered on 22 December 1894 against Alfred Dreyfus by the First Court Martial of the military government of Paris and sends the accused before the Court Martial of Rennes.' On Friday he was on a boat for France.

Dreyfus's physical condition was appalling. Those who saw him that July and August were struck most by his thinness and the stiff manner in which he walked, stood and spoke. Many were uncomprehending. As Maurice Paléologue listened to Dreyfus trot out his 'pathetic phrases', he thought back to the degradation ceremony five years earlier and wondered, 'Why do they sound as false to my ear today when *I know* that what they say is true? Why is this man incapable of all communicative warmth?' Reinach said that what the Dreyfusards needed was an actor, what they got was a soldier; a soldier, moreover, who had lost several teeth, so that when he spoke there was a distracting whistle in his words. He had also lost the habit of speech. Mathieu closed his eyes when Dreyfus entered the courtroom. On opening them he saw a man sitting upright in a chair, a pallid complexion with sudden flushes of red, his hat on his knees and, what shocked most of all, legs without muscles, lost in a captain's trousers. Victor Basch thought of a painting by Giotto of Lazarus risen from the dead, a Lazarus who, in the place of bandages, was wrapped in a uniform 'that he did not appear to fill'. Dreyfus, in court and out, refused to speak of his ordeal. His face seemed to say – you will write, yes, you will have to write of me, but you do not know, and you shall never know, where I have been. In his first statement to the court he remarked, 'I do not know how it is that I am not dead.'

Clemenceau appears to have met Alfred Dreyfus only once – a brief encounter in 1903. He was not present at the trial in Rennes and subsequent events created a barrier to friendly relations, though there was some correspondence. Their personalities were, at any rate, worlds apart and one can well imagine Clemenceau repeating Reinach's remark that the problem with Dreyfus was that he was a soldier. Comments like this are to be found in his articles. But Clemenceau gave a sympathetic portrait of Dreyfus during the trial and reproached reporters who harped on his stiffness. 'I read in the papers that his voice is harsh and that he doesn't give the impression of friendliness. What does this matter? The mind seems precise, the language clear. There are no commonplaces. The influence of the milieu explains a lot.' Clemenceau was thus one of the few people at the time to attribute Dreyfus's odd manner to what seems today such an obvious explanation. Undoubtedly he was influenced by Mathieu, who developed a particularly close relationship with Clemenceau once the process for revision got underway in October 1898.

They had not had a moment of peace. No self-correcting legal mechanism functioned to save Dreyfus. When it looked as if the criminal chamber of the Court of Appeal was about to revoke the 1894 verdict, the Chamber of Deputies had actually passed a law transferring jurisdiction to all three constitutive chambers of the Court, united in special session – the government and deputies were sure this would be a deathblow to revision. So, like in the Boulanger affair, Clemenceau found himself again forced to defend the Senate to counter the 'cowardice' of the Chamber. In his articles of February and March 1899 he implicitly accepts the bicameral parliament as set up in 1875.

The United Appeal Court, however, did not live up to the Chamber's expectations; it was this combined body of forty-nine judges, dressed in scarlet and ermine, that finally quashed Dreyfus's conviction and ordered a retrial. Clemenceau was there on the day of the ruling, 3 June 1899. 'Victory!' he declared, 'the crime has been laid low, the lie conquered, justice triumphs.'

*

He couldn't have been further wrong. It would require a new government – founded on political alliances quite different from those practised by the Mélines, the Brissons, the Freycinets and the Dupuys – to set the stage for Dreyfus's eventual liberation.

The day after the Appeal Court's ruling, the annual Grand Prix horse race was held at the stadium of Longchamp where Boulanger had bewitched the crowds twelve years before. The Grand Prix was an affair limited essentially to the champagne cork poppers. Protocol dictated the presence of President Loubet as an official mark of encouragement to the horse-raisers of France. On advancing to the stand he was met by cries of 'Down with Loubet!' 'Down with Dreyfus!' and, by a certain logic, 'Down with Panama!' 'Resign!' All of a sudden a peevish aristocrat, armed with a cane, emerged from the crowd and started flailing out at the president. Loubet lost his hat and, regaining his balance, turned to make his excuses to the countess Tornielli who was accompanying him. As the guards rushed him and his lady to safety, a brawl broke out with the police involving about a hundred men, all wearing the white carnation of royalty and the blue cornflower of the antisemites.

The story made a scandal in the Dreyfusard press, which campaigned for a demonstration of Republican solidarity the following Sunday in the same stadium. It was a steaming hot summer's day. Clemenceau had a good, heavy lunch with his director, Vaughan, at the *Aurore* offices and then set out by foot for Longchamp, his top hat cocked on the side of his head, a cane resting on his shoulder, the pommel in his pocket. It was a day of celebration. Once more a crowd poured in through the entry at the Grande Cascade. 'Never were there so many pretty women,' wrote Clemenceau that evening, 'never were there so many extravagant dresses.' People came in from the *faubourgs*, cradle of revolutionaries. 'It has been a long time since republicans last demonstrated with such togetherness.' A memory of former times. Another Fourth of September.

On Monday there was a frightful row in the Chamber. The deputies wanted to know why the government deployed so many police to protect the president from republicans while it had done virtually nothing in the face of the Royalists the previous week. The prime minister made an embarrassing speech and resigned.

This was not just the end of Dupuy's fifth ministry, it was the end of a whole line of governments. The old formulas no longer worked. Loubet couldn't find anyone to serve him, a situation not unlike that faced by Grévy twelve years earlier. The Radicals wouldn't serve because most of them, as anti-Dreyfusards, did not want to take responsibility for the Rennes court martial. Clemenceau was called to the Elysée, though there was no question of him participating in a government without a parliamentary seat. But the government that was finally set up certainly had his approval.

It was an odd combination. The new prime minister was René Waldeck-Rousseau, a former lawyer from Nantes, whom Clemenceau had got to know at Scheurer-Kestner's dinners in the 1870's – 'the friend, the favourite student of Gambetta,' recollected Clemenceau the day the cabinet was announced, 'one of the most authoritative representatives of the politics called Opportunist.' But this Opportunist had defended Dreyfus in the Senate. The minister of commerce was Alexandre Millerand, one of Clemenceau's collaborators at *La Justice* – 'a Revolutionary Socialist who forcefully asserts the rights of labouring democracy with a view to the organisation of social justice that has been so slow in coming.' Millerand was the first Socialist ever to participate in a French government. The minister of war was none other than General Galliffet, veteran massacrer of 1871, 'a soldier from the school of gallant *sabreurs*'.* Galliffet had been a very outspoken opponent of Boulanger and he had recently, in bored retirement, been making noises in favour of Dreyfus. In the past that would not have been enough to conciliate Clemenceau with a Versaillais. But the interests of Dreyfus now came first. In a most uncharacteristic remark he said that Galliffet had 'the right to repent' and, for expiation, could serve in 'the combat against injustice'. A more general comment on the cabinet shows how optimistic Clemenceau was at this point in time: 'It is to maintain France in its old tradition of thought, of power, the republican France of justice, of law and of liberty that these three men have come from opposite corners of the horizon, abdicating for a moment all passions of the past . . .'

Zola had returned to France on 5 June. Picquart had been freed four days later. The retrial in Rennes was set for August and the government was in the hands of men sympathetic to Dreyfus. Clemenceau left, content, for a three-week holiday in Carlsbad.

XIV

THE OFFICIAL reason for the choice of Rennes was that it was the Head Quarters of 10th Corps, it had a court martial and Dreyfus, disembarked at Brest, could be transported there without much delay. The real reason was that Rennes, the old provincial capital of Brittany, was a very long way from Paris.

There was nothing picturesque about the town. Its buildings and

* Sabreur means both a swordsman and a fighting cock. During the Dreyfus Affair it became a pejorative term for a soldier.

monuments were constructed in the local stone, grey granite. Place Sainte-Anne, not far from the centre, was dominated by an animal hide market which exhaled odours of rotting flesh into the shops and homes of the neighbouring districts. The waters of the Canal d'Ille-et-Rance were described in a local paper as 'black and putrid' and must have contributed to the notorious filth of the River Vilaine. You could admire the skills of the local washerwomen who at the rinsing-boards next to the pont Saint-Martin, turned linen to white; but then the doctors did publicly worry that, snowy as their sheets appeared, they were not free of germs and might be the source of several recent typhoid epidemics. The open drains of the rue de Nantes were something to be avoided, though anyone who kept his eyes on the road was exposing himself to another menace, for the residents still emptied the contents of their 'intimate vases' from the windows.

Few workers lived in Rennes. A significant part of the town's seventy thousand inhabitants consisted of soldiers, magistrates, ecclesiastics and university professors. In other words, there existed a sizeable middle class, very conservative, whose first idea as the heat and smells of summer rose in intensity was to get out into the country.

'The first impression of the tourist when he disembarks at Rennes is sadness, the immense sadness he feels as he leaves the station to confront a huge field of manœuvres, generally deserted,' wrote a reporter for *Le Petit Marseillais* who arrived in late July 1899. By that time Rennes was beginning to look like an enormous complex of military barracks. The town was divided into sections, regularly patrolled by horse guards. In Rennes, you would not be greeted by the sounds of traffic but of galloping hoofs, rifle butts banged on the cobbles, the rattle of swords, the short sharp orders of a second lieutenant. It was as good enough explanation as any for the poor business done by the electric tramways – probably the only town in France where they were not filled to bursting-point. But the reporter from *Le Petit Marseillais* took this as a sign of the population's resistance to innovation.

There was violence. Around a hundred teenagers attacked Victor Basch's house with stones on 14 July and then went on to attack the Auberge des Trois Marches, which had been hosting a republican banquet. But during the trial there would be few disturbances because the army and *gendarmerie* came out in full force.

Clemenceau was back in Paris in the third week of July with a serious bout of bronchitis that continued to trouble him for a month. It 'tears at my chest night and day', he wrote to Labori on 11 August. Bodily ailment was perhaps not his only reason for not turning up at Rennes. In his youth Clemenceau had preferred to observe crowds at a distance, and nothing in his life since suggested any change. His experience of the

Commune had not exactly encouraged it. He might have visited mines, he had often addressed large and popular audiences, he had administered medicine to the poor, but he never milled with the crowd. Boulanger had horrified him. Zola's trial had been no pleasure party either – and Zola also refused to go to Rennes. Crowds remained a disagreeable memory. Three days before the trial opened Clemenceau published an article comparing the atmosphere in Rennes to a Roman holiday: 'We no longer have prisoners-of-war to nourish these sports. That leaves us, like the Roman emperors, with heretics for the teeth of the big game. The Christianised Jews of Rome filled the circus with their blood and the Jews will cater very nicely to our own murderous emotions.'

Jaurès went to Rennes, though he kept a low profile. Reinach stayed behind in Paris. There was a general feeling that 'murderous emotions' needed no encouragement.

However, the leading Dreyfusards were in a very combative mood as the trial began. They set up headquarters in Rennes at the Auberge des Trois Marches, which had a bit of a country atmosphere, convivial and with a certain thrill. Séverine described their evening meals as the 'banquet of Girondins' – Girondins who were expecting victory, not their execution. After the first day of hearings, highlighted by Dreyfus's testimony, the court, 'in the interest of national defence', went into closed session to examine the secret dossier, now so voluminous that it had to be carried in a huge wicker basket by two soldiers. The examination took four days and established nothing against the accused. Open hearings began again with the first witnesses on Saturday, 12 August, when Mercier was supposed to produce his 'irrefutable evidence' of Dreyfus's guilt.

The night before, Clemenceau wrote a long letter to Labori outlining the tactic he would like to see pursued. Dreyfus was represented by both Labori and Demange. The tension between the two lawyers had, if anything, increased since Zola's trial and it was significant that Clemenceau should choose to write to Labori, more concerned with the Dreyfusard cause than Demange, who was closer to the family. 'I am so much in favour of a *resolute offensive*,' he emphasised, 'that I regard the case lost if the contrary is done.' He explained – in terms which showed how far even Clemenceau was from the idea of an objective legal hearing – that their goal was not to convert the seven military judges to their views but to win over 'public opinion'. It would have to be a 'battle without mercy . . . Dreyfus is here only a symbolic protagonist.'

The 'resolute offensive' might well have worked. Mercier, on Saturday, made an utter fool of himself before the press, before the world. The prosecution had clearly nothing on which to build a case.

But the defence then suffered a serious reverse. Early Monday morning, Labori, on his way to court, received a bullet in his back.

Picquart and a cousin, who were accompanying him, were sure he was dead and took off in pursuit of a man touting a revolver; they soon lost him in the lanes of the old district that stretched along the riverside. A violent storm burst, breaking days of oppressive heat, soaking away all traces of the crime, save Labori who lay crumpled on a bridge.

Miraculously, the bullet had missed his spinal column by millimetres and had touched no vital organ. After what Basch termed a 'terrible' night, Labori was on the mend. The surgeon decided not to extract the bullet, which immediately led to rumours in the antisemitic press that the assassination attempt had been faked.

But this hardly would have been in the interests of the defence. The trial continued without the leading defence representative. Mercier was cross-examined by Demange, who was little concerned about 'public opinion' and rather more interested in the attitude of the judges. He was a good traditional lawyer.

Labori was not back in court until 22 August. He had not changed. Clemenceau in Paris had not changed. But the attitude of many Dreyfusards had; they no longer wanted to offend. The government started exerting pressure: it spoke more of moderation, more of a need to 'liquidate' tensions, less of justice. So Clemenceau turned on the government, and particularly on Galliffet, who had the gall to decorate, at the height of the trial, one of the chief suspects in the tampering of evidence. 'The crime continues, the impunity of the forgers has not been stopped, they sail on above the laws.'

In court, Labori became even more aggressive. There were some ugly clashes with the president of the court. When the long-awaited witness, du Paty de Clam, refused to present himself on the pretext of 'night diarrhoea', the relationship got vicious. 'Send the doctors!' shouted out Labori. 'The sickness is known,' retorted the president, 'it is publicly acknowledged.' So du Paty stayed at home.

Clemenceau in his articles always supported Labori, thus remaining faithful to his letter and showing the world that the trial, at heart, was a press campaign. But he and Labori were becoming increasingly isolated. The Dreyfus family closed ranks with Demange. Reinach became openly critical of Labori's behaviour. The government warned that his antics in court were actually damaging the defence.

The climax came when Labori appealed to the German Kaiser to order Schwarzkoppen, the German military attaché, to testify on Dreyfus's innocence. For the antisemites, this was proof of an international Jewish conspiracy. For the majority of Dreyfusards it was a serious error of judgement. But not for Clemenceau. In the last two weeks he had been hinting that the best evidence of Dreyfus's innocence was in Germany and he debunked the theory that truth was a function of nationality with the remark: 'two and two make five in France for the sole reason that they make four on the other side of the frontier.'

Tension within the Dreyfusard camp was reaching breaking point. It is impossible to establish exactly what happened in the last few days of the trial. One is left with a number of contradictory accounts. But one gets the impression that nearly all the major figures were paralysed with the dilemma of the need for both attack and compromise. Did Mathieu ask Labori to quit or did he ask him to stay? Jaurès's role is most ambiguous. The government was convinced that Labori's presence guaranteed a conviction and put out the word that, if he left, Dreyfus could expect an acquittal by a majority of one vote. As for Clemenceau, his position had always been clear, but he showed no willingness to push it to the point of an irreparable rift. In the end he chose silence.

On the morning the defence was to give its summing-up, Bernard Lazare, Victor Basch and Jaurès visited Labori. Jaurès said, 'Mathieu Dreyfus is going to ask you to renounce your plea' and, according to Labori, added that the government had assured acquittal if he stepped down. At court, Mathieu simply handed Labori two notes, one from the editor of *Le Figaro*, reminding Labori that the duty of lawyers was to plea 'usefully', the other from Reinach addressed to Mathieu. Reinach said that Clemenceau had left him at four o'clock that morning refusing to write to Labori on the grounds that it was Mathieu's duty to ask Labori to stay or quit, not his. 'When Clemenceau does not want to do something, you know there is no way of constraining him.' Labori, on reading this, refused to plead. Mathieu again hesitated.

Demange spoke for five hours. The seven judges retired and, after an hour and a half, returned with their verdict: guilty with attenuating circumstances. The president then condemned Dreyfus to ten years of prison and a second public degradation. For Dreyfus, it was a death sentence.

XV

'ALL THOSE who have read my articles have understood that this news could cause me no surprise,' wrote Clemenceau for his column the next day. The philosophy of the *huis clos* had prevailed, the 'impenetrable spirit' of men persuaded that 'they were going to pronounce less on the accused than on the institution of which they were a part.' Clemenceau wanted the case to be brought back to the civilian Court of Appeal. 'We want justice by the law and we will have it.'

Dreyfus in gaol asked to see his children. They had never been told of the case; Lucie's story had been that their father had gone off on a long voyage. For Mathieu, the request, which would have to be granted in the dismal surroundings of his cell, could only be interpreted as a man's dying wish. Alfred Dreyfus was not going to live through another trial.

That afternoon Mathieu left for Paris and the following morning visited Reinach at his home. Bernard Lazare had arrived just before him. 'He will not live six months if he stays in prison,' Mathieu told Reinach. Reinach said the only answer was a presidential pardon, but it would have to be given immediately, within forty-eight hours of the conviction, to demonstrate the government's total rejection of 'this iniquitous judgement'. Mathieu agreed and left immediately with Bernard Lazare for rue Franklin to let Clemenceau know of Dreyfus's terrible condition. Clemenceau received Mathieu in a state of great emotion. Mathieu explained that his brother would die if an immediate pardon were not granted. 'My heart says, yes' – Clemenceau saw two years of struggle curl up in the air like smoke – 'my reason says, no.' Mathieu pleaded with him to ask Waldeck-Rousseau to intervene. 'I will make, for you, this great sacrifice to my reason if it is necessary,' Clemenceau replied with tears in his eyes. 'But if it is not necessary, please spare me.'

A meeting took place that afternoon at *L'Aurore*, with Jaurès present, and there was another meeting in the evening in the office of the director of *Le Radical*. Victor Simond arrived in the middle of this second meeting with the news that the government was willing to pardon Dreyfus on the condition that Dreyfus withdrew his appeal. But that was an admission of guilt! It was a technical point, explained Millerand to Mathieu and Reinach later that evening at the ministry of commerce; a pardon cannot be granted in a case which is still pending. Mathieu insisted that he could do nothing without the assent of his friends, Clemenceau and Jaurès. 'All right,' said Millerand, 'I'll telephone them and tell them to come straight round to the ministry.'

Jaurès came accompanied with his party paper's editor, Gérault-Richard. Clemenceau was the last to arrive. Millerand gave a long legal explanation why Dreyfus should abandon his appeal and accept a pardon. Then Mathieu spoke: 'You know my feelings, I'll do nothing without your accord. If it is yes, I will accept; if it is no, I will refuse.' Reinach argued for an acceptance of an immediate pardon, saying that it was both the legal and humane thing to do. Clemenceau countered with the argument that acceptance of the pardon would make a continued struggle impossible and that, though Dreyfus might win his liberty, the country would gain 'no moral benefit'. But he added, 'I must not be accused of being without heart. This morning I cried on seeing Mathieu.'

'That proves that you cannot cry twice in the same day,' responded Reinach sourly.

Jaurès never did seem to make up his mind. At this particular moment he seems to have accepted Clemenceau's argument.

Gérault-Richard made a case for accepting an immediate pardon: 'public opinion' would read this as a response of civilian power to military justice.

Millerand returned with the legal argument, which now swayed Jaurès to the side of the pardon.

Clemenceau turned to Mathieu, 'You have the majority, you can accept.'

'No,' replied Mathieu. 'I also need your consent. I will not separate myself from you. If you persist in your opinion, I will refuse.'

Clemenceau rose from his chair and began pacing the thick ministerial carpet. The heavy clock on the mantelpiece continued to tick. The clatter of the night traffic outside could be heard. A voice on the street. The creak of the carpet. The clock. The window. A pause.

'All right, if I were the brother, I would accept.'

So Dreyfus was freed. But justice had not been done.

On the day that Dreyfus was pardoned, 19 September 1899, Scheurer-Kestner died in his home near Biarritz. He had suffered for several months. What was his last thought? His enormous family, Dreyfus, Alsace, *la revanche*?

CHAPTER EIGHT

Government

I

IN CLEMENCEAU'S novel, *Les Plus Forts*, the girl marries the greediest man, not the noblest; the victor in the strike is the ruthless manager, not the harrowed worker. In his play, *Le Voile du bonheur*, a contented blind man, having regained sight and taken a look around him – at the thieving servant, the mocking son, the faithless wife – decides he would be better off blind.

Clemenceau was approaching sixty. The world had become a smaller place, a richer place, but not necessarily a better place. More people had the vote and more people could read and write. But poverty had not disappeared, nor had the prospect of war. The eighteenth-century promise that scientific knowledge would bring peace, harmony and prosperity remained unfulfilled, though plenty of politicians, on the Left and Right, were convinced it was only just out of their reach.

But how far could a man reach? Distances, peripheries . . . every corner of the planet had been viewed and marked out by some European; you could buy in a shop a cheap coloured map showing all seven continents and all seven seas. Yet the world could still stop at one's doorstep. Were the windows of the house just mirrors of one's own life? It was hard not to avoid the lingering suspicion that those who grumbled about conditions outside had more serious problems within. Freud had recently said as much, and he was a man of this *belle époque*, an age of complaint. But it was not something French republicans liked to admit. Their science had taught them that private realities should never impinge on their public duties and their vision of their country's future. What went on at home was regarded as irrelevant to what one said in parliament or wrote in a newspaper. A man like Jaurès could defend the lay Republic, attack the Church, and at the same time allow his daughter to receive a strict Catholic education. Clemenceau was merciless in the way he separated his public life from the private sphere. Late in life he destroyed most of his private correspondence, not so much because he wanted to hide something; he simply considered these 'useless papers' to be of no concern to historians. There would be no memoirs. 'I don't think,' wrote Jean Ajalbert in his 1931 biography of

Clemenceau, 'one will ever collect together the necessary documentation
to compose *La Vie amoureuse de Georges Clemenceau*.' Sixty years later, one
has to conclude he was right.

But it would be wrong to ignore the coincidences between what he said
in public and what little we know happened in private. His marriage had
failed; his parliamentary career he regarded as something of the past. He
was more than ever committed to his writing yet, as the new century
dawned, his articles, like his correspondence, expressed a profound sense
of disenchantment, even bitterness. 'My poor child,' he wrote to Lady
Edward Cecil in December 1899, 'you ask me to speak of France. I haven't
the courage to do it. I struggle inch by inch, day by day. The weakness of
those in my camp is even more harmful than the audacity of our enemies.
The government has devised to amnesty Mercier and the whole criminal
band before they have given an account to justice and I have been the *only
one* to campaign against this infamy. Mercier is going to be elected *senator*
in a month. This candidature, I hope, will make the amnesty impossible.'
[His emphasis]

Mercier won his election and total amnesty was voted by parliament at
virtually the same time. 'It is a collapse of morals such as has never been
seen in the history of a people reputed to be masters of their destiny.'

Lying, treachery, the grossest violations of justice seemed to suffer no
penalty. Dreyfus, on the other hand, remained formally guilty until the
Criminal Chamber agreed to review the Rennes verdict in March 1904.
He was only reinstated as captain in July 1906, when the United Appeal
Court finally annulled the verdict. Most of the world had forgotten him by
this time. There was barely a murmur from the former anti-Dreyfusards.
Mercier gave a rather courageous speech in the Senate, only to be hooted
down. Rochefort and Drumont made rude noises in the press, but nobody
now read their newspapers. As for the old Dreyfusards, the majority
regarded the rehabilitation as preordained. The Appeal Court's ruling,
said Reinach, proclaimed 'that it was day when the sun was already high
on the horizon'. An enticing image, indeed. It was comforting to think
that the emergence of the forces of enlightenment was as inevitable as day
follows night. Perhaps the gloomy moments of struggle and temporary
defeat were simply a prelude to some grand human triumph. *L'Universe
israélite* certainly thought as much when it announced that the twelve-year
saga had 'had particularly fortunate results for our coreligionists, for in
giving birth to the Dreyfus Affair, antisemitism has died.'

That was never Clemenceau's view. He called the last of his seven
volumes of articles on Dreyfus *La Honte* (*Shame*) because of the amnesty
law of 1900 – 'the confiscation of all the rights which constitute, in civil
terms, man in society.' In a way it was ironic, for he had been one of the first
persons to appeal for an amnesty, in 1897, as one might have expected from
the man who had campaigned for a 'forgetting' following the Commune or

the industrial strikes of the 1880's and early 90's. But since then he had
been drawn into a combat which he would not relinquish. It was so easy
to say, 'We want peace.' From a distance Waldeck-Rousseau's insistence
to 'liquidate' the Affair seemed reasonable, generous, free-handed. The
problem was that principles had been sacrificed.

Clemenceau thought that the Dreyfus Affair was also a lesson lost. He
was almost certainly mistaken in identifying the basic issue in the Affair
as one of religious prejudice; with the twentieth century almost behind
us we look, rather, at the Affair as the first flicker of the prejudice of
race. Clemenceau was fighting with old enemies, most of them dead,
and failed to see the greater threat posed by the new foes of liberty. But
the republicans' war with the Church would soon reach a climax and
Clemenceau's position would prove less dogged than his words during
the Affair might have suggested.

More significant in the long run was his interpretation of a failed
struggle – that Dreyfus's personal vindication had not brought with it
more assurance of civil equality – for it represented a departure from the
general republican vision of historical progress. For Clemenceau there was
no process involved, no guarantee that justice and democracy would come
out on top, nor that they would endure if established. The only eternal
law in his eyes was the law of the jungle, the repression of the weak by
the strong – *that* one could always count on: and it took a colossal effort
of enlightened will to resist it. History, if left to impersonal forces, would
in all probability end in victory for the forces of evil and repression, not
of good.

'Social progress,' said Clemenceau, 'can only be the result of individual
progress, from which I conclude that the work that dominates all others
is, first and foremost, individual education.' Seated alone at his horseshoe
desk with shelves of books, unclassified, about him – the quill, the sand,
the scissors, the paste – he could well think of life as an individual assault
on encroaching chaos. All those articles, the impromptu meetings, the total
hostility of parliament and government. He came to regard the Affair as the
'combat of a small troup of desperate people against all the usurpations of
the earth and the sky combined'.

After the pardon and the amnesty, initiated by a government ostensibly
of the Left and passed through a parliament dominated by Radicals, he
was prepared to reject those little cells of political power, the petty
hierarchies and alliances, and present himself as the lonely intellectual
with the ghosts of millions shaking their heads at him. When Maître Labori
published an article in October 1901 advocating a broadening of Socialism
into a great party 'capable of offering a shelter to all republicans truly
preoccupied with the development of democracy,' Clemenceau replied,
nice idea, but it will not work: he had tried it himself. If you want
to avoid disillusionment, he cautioned, you have to recognise that 'all

groups of ideas end up constituting themselves – like the greatest of all, the Christian Church – into groups of interest'.

Thus generosity could be converted into a cover for selfishness and violence. No law of History prevented this. 'The French Revolution,' he noted in his opening article of his new paper, *Le Bloc*, 'announced peace and human fraternity; it ended with imperial dictatorship, conquests beyond measure and the inevitable collapse.' Since there were no guarantees, no solid promise of equality and liberty, it would be folly to talk of peace. Equality and liberty were values to be defended, not left to historical forces. 'In the current state of Europe, the force of arms cannot be neglected. All weakness, with or without aggression, will be the prey of the strongest.'

Clemenceau's contempt for political parties and government had never been greater. As he put it a number of times, the Affair had demonstrated the inability of 'party men' and the 'hateful race of government men' to adapt to the new situation and follow Zola's 'magnificent example'.

It was this refusal to meddle in party politics which had attracted Charles Péguy to Clemenceau's thinking. Péguy was another writer who had doubts about progress. In 1903 he dedicated an entire edition of his *Cahiers de quinzaine* to him, reproducing a long speech Clemenceau had made on lay education, the 'Discours pour la liberté', and several articles that had appeared in *Le Bloc*. Péguy even offered to purchase all unsold back issues of the paper (there was no shortage of supply). Clemenceau's passions, his rather poetic way of conducting his battles, his old combination of art and reason, seemed to fill the emptiness of a mechanical age. Reason had value, but reason without spirit was nothing. Corresponding to the *raison d'état* of the Right, Péguy saw a *raison d'état* of the Left emerging in the name of a supposedly objective human science; there was the voice of Bergson ringing in his ears; there was the disappointment with former Dreyfusards making political capital out of the Affair. Péguy broke all relations with Jaurès – who with his *Histoire socialiste de la Révolution française* was now something of a mandarin in the historical sciences – and became one of the most enthusiastic writers behind the 'lonely Socrates' of rue Franklin. Clemenceau, he thought, was that rare man capable of resisting the general degradation of the initial 'mystic' of an idea into the 'politics' of the parliamentarians.

By anyone's standard the 1902 election campaign accelerated the process. It was one of the longest in the history of the Third Republic and also one of the most vicious.

Clemenceau's comments in *Le Bloc* on the preparations, which began as early as February 1901, were as sarcastic as his pronouncements on the 1898 campaign. He certainly showed no ambition to join in the fray. The press would mutter the terrible phrase 'the Committees are organising themselves' and at once 'the awkward competitors – seized with a violent love for the popular – travel backwards and forwards across the arrondissements with their hands open and their hearts overflowing with sympathy for the "poor people who have been abused."'

In June 1901 the Radicals met in congress at Paris to set up the first formal political party in the history of France; the pressure was now on the Socialists to do likewise. The preceding month, Clemenceau had described parties as 'a good and an evil'. He was thinking more in terms of the loose political associations of his own earlier career. Without parties, he said, no efficient action was possible, there could be no civilisation, 'and humanity would remain in a state of dust'. Problems, he thought, began to arise when the written or spoken word is translated into an acceptable slogan for the group: 'There develops from this' – the style was reminiscent of his medical thesis – 'a collective power to the detriment of superior individualities, who are forced to descend to the average of the whole, to the profit of lesser individualities, who furnish the mass with the spiritual drive behind the mechanical effect of progress.' Perhaps he was thinking of Voltaire's remark that intelligent men, assembled in a group, only pronounce stupidities. There was also an elitism in Clemenceau's comments and even a certain parallel with the Marxist notion of a revolutionary 'spearhead'. But the essential point was that Clemenceau did not always welcome the 'mechanical effect of progress' because its direction was unpredictable and its end could be a horror.

All in all, Clemenceau's still prolific pen suggested a man with intentions not to get directly involved in the political life of the nation. He would do better as an independent commentator, a logical position for a politician who had established his reputation as a 'wrecker of ministers': he could continue to criticise the powers that be. But his fate, like his vision of History, was not sealed. Within a few years he himself would be party to those powers, exercising the highest offices in government.

II

CLEMENCEAU'S WRITING career was precarious at best. He resigned from *L'Aurore* following a row with Urbain Gohier whose enthusiasm for Dreyfus was only matched by his phobia for the army. Clemenceau had always argued like Zola that the defence of Dreyfus was not an attack on the army but on its delinquent commanders. Gohier, on the other hand, would have liked to have seen the campaign turned into a general assault on 'militarism'. Nevertheless, up until the pardon Clemenceau had been very supportive of Gohier; it was only when Gohier started arguing in his column that he had been running the campaign solo – a rather bold position to take in *L'Aurore* – that Clemenceau felt obliged to make the break. He told his literary friend Georg Brandes that he would continue his campaign in 'a great provincial journal' (*La Dépêche de Toulouse*) and that he was hoping soon to start writing for another Paris paper.

It proved a hard task. Most of the Parisian press had been anti-Dreyfusard and even those who were not had little interest in prolonging the campaign. So in January 1901 Clemenceau took the drastic step of setting up his own newspaper again, *Le Bloc* (a reference to his famous statement in the Chamber, '*La Révolution est un bloc*') edited by himself, written by himself and, after the first few months, even managed by himself. The 'administrative offices' of the paper were officially at his printers, Alcan Lévy, but one imagines that the essential activities – writing and editing – were carried out at his home. The details of its financing are unknown, but brother Albert certainly played a significant role; one doubts that the advertisements for coats and ladies' high fashion brought in much of an income. Clemenceau had editorial assistance from his secretary, Etienne Winter, and in the summer months Geffroy contributed articles. Otherwise, the paper – fifteen to twenty pages every Sunday – was entirely the product of his own labours. It was a small format newspaper suitably arranged to fit into a politician's coat pocket; it was probably not read by many others – a few intellectuals, local officials, high civil servants, people who liked to keep up with the old Radical's independent opinions.

The last number of *Le Bloc* appeared in March 1902. In the meantime, *L'Aurore* was running into serious financial difficulties despite its high quality staff and the support it got from the League of the Rights of Man. The paper actually went into liquidation in June 1903 and was only saved through the intervention of Victor Simiond and Louis Leblois, the lawyer who had given Picquart's crucial evidence on Esterhazy to Scheurer-Kestner back in 1897. Leblois, like Picquart, was a staunch Dreyfusard to the end and consequently had immense admiration for Clemenceau. He also happened to be very rich. Engaging Clemenceau as editor of *L'Aurore* might not have been the best business decision he had made – the paper faced bankruptcy again in 1904 – but it did guarantee a forceful line in the leading articles. *L'Aurore* was Clemenceau's instrument from 1903 to 1906.

But by this time the pull of active politics had become irresistible. Clemenceau had not been forgotten by the mayors, officials and radical militants who had organised his three electoral campaigns in the Var in the 1880's and 90's. A delegation of them had arrived at rue Franklin in 1898 to persuade him to run again; they received a firm 'no'. They were back on his doorstep in 1902.

Radicals were on the defensive in the Var. After Clemenceau's ouster in 1893 the Socialists had made rapid advances, especially in the small bourgs of the central valley. Var peasants had not the slightest interest in Dreyfus but were deeply concerned with dead vines, unmarketable olives, catchpenny foreigners and the declining population of their tight-knit, centrally settled communities. This had provided the entry ticket to a very doctrinal version of socialism. Early in 1902 the majority of local Socialists broke from the 'slavish' moderates and reformers to found the Revolutionary Socialist Federation of the Var, led by Maurice Allard, the deputy for Draguignan; it turned out to be one of the most significant Guesdist organisations in the country.

Clemenceau, however, still had a following, despite the fiasco of 1893. If he were to turn up in the Var he'd draw a crowd and the local Radicals were well aware of the fact.

He had given absolutely no indication that he might yield to their appeals. Quite the contrary, his articles of 1901 showed he had every intention of staying clear of the next scramble for parliamentary seats coming up in May 1902. But in early 1902 one of the 'unmovables' of the Senate, nominated in 1875, died. Under the terms of the constitution, his replacement would have to represent a department and be elected, in the normal manner, for a seven-year renewable term by local government officials. The department to be represented was selected by lot and the lot fell on the Var. As far as Clemenceau's backers were concerned this was a golden opportunity – even the 1893 campaign had demonstrated strong support for their candidate among municipal and arrondissement councillors.

Clemenceau's views on the Senate had changed. It was the Senate that had prosecuted the Boulangists in 1889 and it was again the Senate that provided the impetus within parliament for Dreyfus's retrial. The historical predictions of republicans in 1875 had been proven wrong; it was clear that some versions of direct democracy could actually pose a threat to individual liberties. Only fools and demagogues could now argue that '*Roi Peuple*' did not require some countervailing force. 'For a part of my life when I was nearer theory than reality,' confessed Clemenceau in 1911, 'I had faith in a single chamber, the direct expression of popular feeling. I used to think the people were always reasonable. I have revised my views. Events have taught me that you have to give the people the time for reflection. The time for reflection, that's the Senate.'

This was also the opinion he expressed to the mayor of Draguignan's delegation in 1902. His condemnation of the Senate, he said, had been 'an error of youth'; but he did not want to stand for the empty seat. The small group returned to their hotel. Family and friends remained at rue

Franklin to discuss the proposal further. Albert, Madeleine, Geffroy and Winter thought Clemenceau was making a mistake and told him so, but he remained adamant: he was now committed to writing, not politicking. Winter then left to call on Clemenceau's publisher, Pierre-Victor Stock, who came round to the flat that afternoon.

Clemenceau had been out on one of his long walks and entered his office with his dog. He was looking as alert as ever, a bit red around the temples, and stubborn. Stock said something about the Var and Clemenceau went straight into a tirade about the articles he had to write, the proposals he had received; this week's work for *Le Bloc* had not yet been finished, there was the editorial for *La Dépêche* and a theatre director had just promised to make a play out of his novel *Les Plus Forts*. Stock, always polite, listened patiently, adding his own comments here and there. The interview lasted more than two hours.

In the end it was Stock's observations that won the day: *Le Bloc* will soon be out of circulation because there isn't any money there; you've already asked subscribers to pay up for two years in advance, which is not a very encouraging sign. Nobody cares about Dreyfus anymore and *La Dépêche* is going to drop you unless you have some other cause for celebrity. As for the theatre director . . . theatre directors' promises should never be taken too seriously. On the other hand, go back into politics and you'll be a minister, even prime minister, for sure. And senators earn a salary of nine thousand francs.

Early the following morning the delegation at Hôtel Cusset received a telephone call from Clemenceau. 'I'm running.'

III

'THERE WILL be only two candidates,' a Jesuit preacher wrote in a printed sermon shortly before the 1902 general elections, 'Barrabas and Jesus Christ.' Clemenceau's election to the Senate in early April had gone smoothly enough. Out of 478 electors, Clemenceau won 344 votes, the Republican Moderate received 122 and the Socialist got one. But the legislative election held three weeks later was war and the forces of Barrabas were determined to win.

Anticlericalism was looking more and more like an irrational left-wing backlash to the lunacy of antisemitism. The Jesuits, with their links to top military men, and the Assumptionists, with their constant braying in the press, had provided the fuel; Clemenceau and other republican columnists added the matches; and Waldeck-Rousseau's government, in a misbegotten attempt to douse the flames, in fact fanned them when it introduced legislation defining the position of monks and nuns in French society.

Barrabas won the elections of 1902 all right, but the results – based on the *scrutin d'arrondissement* – were thoroughly misleading. The Radicals, with over two hundred seats, now constituted the largest political group in the Chamber. A loose coalition with the various socialist factions and leftward-leaning Moderates, known perversely as the *Bloc des gauches* (it resembled more a flaky pastry) gave the government a majority of about 330 seats out of a total of 591. Two rounds of elections, in late April and early May, had mobilised a larger proportion of registered voters (about eighty per cent) than any election since the *Seize Mai* crisis. Yet out of the nine million voters participating, only two hundred thousand separated the Left's majority from the supporters of the Right. The real victim of the election was the Centre. Waldeck-Rousseau, ill and a Moderate to the end, resigned almost immediately afterwards.

His successor, Emile Combes, was just the sort of candidate needed to bring the clerical conflict to a head. Combes was not against religion; he frequently criticised positivism as an inadequate moral philosophy and spoke of man's need for a spiritual rejuvenation. His heroes were Michelet and Lamartine, not Comte. Joseph Caillaux characterised him best when he said that Combes was more a Gallican than a *laïque* (a defender of lay principles); what he wanted to create was a 'Church of France' which catered to the educational needs of the country by providing an army of liberal priests obedient to the Republic rather than to Rome.

Combes' penchant for regimentation would soon exasperate the keenest anticlericals, including Clemenceau. But for the moment he was assured of a parliamentary majority and used this to turn Waldeck-Rousseau's association law into a weapon of dissolution. He refused authorisation to all the monastic orders save five (which were engaged in missionary work in the colonies), pronounced their properties to be confiscated and their chapels closed. He then proceeded to launch an offensive against their three thousand schools, threatening to have them all shut down and their personnel forbidden to teach elsewhere.

There were riots in Brittany. Large numbers of Frenchmen in curious outfits – top hats combined with sporting flannels, motoring caps with morning coats – were seen crossing the frontier to Belgium or the sea to the Channel Islands. As Teilhard de Chardin later explained, monks were unaware of the fashions of the world and took what disguises their well-wishers offered them.

Clemenceau the following October, in his first major speech in the senate, defended Combes' actions on the grounds that monks and nuns owed their allegiance to a foreign authority, the Pope, and thus forfeited the protection of common law. He presented a similar argument in a speech made a year later, when he explained that democracy made swiftest progress in countries that were free from the influence of Rome; he even included in his list Russia, which was making democratic noises at this time. Old dogmas died hard and Clemenceau could show himself, no less than his contemporaries, slave to the ideologies of his youth. In the late 1920's, with another war and several European revolutions behind him, he would still be saying that the greatest threat to liberty in the world was the Catholic Church, not the Bolsheviks.

Combes' laws were in fact of limited effect. Many monks simply became priests and carried on their work as before. Most of the Church primary schools could not be closed down because in many villages there was no alternative school. Ten years were allowed to implement the laws and by 1914 the country had something else to think about. The huge funds that the sale of monastic properties was supposed to release to the state evaporated in lawyers' fees and local graft.

It was the issue that was significant, not the effect of the laws. In the course of the debates on the closures one of those principles emerged which had so often prickled Clemenceau's instincts for denunciation. At their 1903 congress the Radical Party had approved a proposal for the establishment of a state monopoly of education. There was no way Clemenceau could accept this. In 1884 he had rejected the 'barracks and convent' model of social justice proposed by the collectivists; he was not going to take it from the Radicals now. In the same speech he had said that a healthy democracy depended on the active participation of two personalities, the legislator and the citizen, one reinforcing the other; he was not prepared to place all power in the hands of the legislator now.

He got his chance when the government presented a bill outlawing the nonauthorised orders from teaching. Though obviously designed to limit the influence of Catholic schools, the original bill confirmed the right of individuals and corporations to run their own schools. But the bill came before the Senate with the Thézard amendment, which required all schools to be authorised by decree. In the light of the way the authorisations required in the 1901 associations law had been used to dissolve all religious orders, this was clearly an attempt to set up a state monopoly in education.

So it was now in the Senate, in the richly ornate chamber of the Palais de Luxembourg, that Clemenceau rose once more to defy the will of the majority. 'I reject the omnipotence of the secular state,' he said, 'because I see it as a tyranny.' The current bill would simply transfer the spiritual power of the Pope to the state; 'It is a civil, secular catholicism, with a university clergy.' The venerable senators burst into laughter. 'Yes! we have guillotined the King, long live the State-King! We have dethroned the Pope, long live the State-Pope! We have chased out God, as these men of the Right say, long live the State-God! *Messieurs*, I am not of this monarchy, I am not of this pontificate.' Frock-coated gentlemen on the Left, the Right and the Centre howled with delight. 'The state, I know it well, it has a long history, full of murder and blood. All the crimes that have been accomplished in the world, the massacres, the wars, the breaches of sworn faith, the stakes, the punishments, the tortures, all have been justified in the interest of the state, the *raison d'état*.' There were nods of agreement on 'diverse benches'. Here were his philosophies on the social question, the Boulanger question, Dreyfus and the Church all knocked into one. Twenty years earlier he had said, 'I am the declared enemy of a system of distributive justice by the state or by the commune.' He was still impenitent defender of the individual.

The Senate threw out the amendment.

Clemenceau naturally played a leading role in the fall of Combes' government. For three years the ministry of war had been in the hands of General Louis André, freemason, republican and committed Dreyfusard. Convinced that the Jesuits were exercising an influence in army promotions, he organised a vast system of *fiches*, or note cards, which recorded officers' attendance at mass. These were collected at freemason headquarters in Paris, the Grand Orient, and then passed on to the ministry. When the inevitable disgruntled employee sold a batch of *fiches* (he had over twenty-five thousand to choose from) to a couple of right-wing deputies there was a cry of indignation from all political corners. Clemenceau in *L'Aurore* denounced André as a 'plumed cephalopode' and his methods as Jesuitical. Nationalist deputy Syveton punched the minister in the face (and then committed suicide – 'new masonic crime!' proclaimed Jules Lemaître). André was forced to resign.

To make matters worse, an international congress of Socialists in Amsterdam obliged their French colleagues to stop supporting 'bourgeois' governments. The *Bloc des gauches* was losing its flakes. Clemenceau kept up his campaign against the government's great 'inquisition'. In January 1905 *le petit père* Combes resigned.

He was succeeded by none other than Maurice Rouvier of Panama fame. Rouvier, though much more moderate, carried on Combes' good works by getting a Separation Act through parliament and by starting an inventory of Church properties that competed with Bonaparte in its taste for details. The doors of churches were thrown open and darkly dressed state functionaries crept in to count: statues, pyxes, chalices, chasubles, chandeliers and candles. Churchmen ordered processions in the towns and villages. Women crawled on their knees in protest. Riots broke out. The police and the army were called in. Peasants armed with cudgels and scythes mounted the counter-offensive. Churches were barricaded with old timbers. At Montjoie, in the Ariège, the village priest brought in two Pyrenees bears to guard the gates. One of the faithful was killed in Hazebrouck. Rouvier hesitated. Clemenceau complained. The government fell.

It was Wednesday, 7 March 1906. One more ministry down. Nothing unusual about that. Nothing save the fact that Rouvier's fall opened the way to Clemenceau's first appointment in government.

IV

ON THURSDAY and Friday Armand Fallières, who had himself only recently been nominated president of the Republic, pored over the usual list of *ministrables* of the Centre and the Left; several important deputies and senators paid him a visit at his palace, a rather larger number stayed at home in the hope of a summons.

Fallières eventually came up, on Friday afternoon, with the name Jean Sarrien, a compromise which should have upset no one; as *le petit père* Combes put it, 'Sarrien's character was to have none.' (Clemenceau was briefer, '*Ça? Rien.*') Fallières told Sarrien to present him with a list of ministers the following day.

But the business of cabinet formation was delayed, on Saturday morning, by some terrible news from the northern coalfields.

'Lens, 10 March, 9 hours,' spattered out the Elysée's new telegraphic printer. 'A fire-damp explosion has just occurred at pits 2, 3 and 4 in the mines of Courrières. There are numerous victims. According to first information the catastrophe, which occurred this morning at about seven, surpasses in horror anything one can imagine . . .'

César Danglos would remember that Saturday morning in the pits for the rest of his life. He was building wooden frames in one of the dozens of galleries of the 'grande Adélaïde' three hundred metres below the surface. These tunnels and ducts, some no more than a metre high, linked up all the pits of the Company of Courrières which had, since mid-century, been colonising a huge tract of scarred moonscape just north of Lens; a human warren of pickmen, hauliers and engineers. As Danglos and his fellow workers hammered at the sides of the gallery they heard 'a detonation' – 'the sound seemed to come from far off'. They looked at each other and, for a few minutes, went on working, in silence, with a peculiar sense of foreboding biting into their limbs.

All of a sudden one of the men responsible for the horses appeared like a phantom, he was very pale, mumbling; he fainted in front of them. Then a haulage-man came back with an empty cart. 'I think it is going to be save your own skin,' he said with inappropriate calm; Danglos cottoned on, 'It's fire.'

They scrambled through alleys and holes, past collapsed timbers, walls that had crumbled; often they were turned back by noxious fumes. Horrified, they found themselves tripping over bodies and more bodies, so many bodies. They were soon without light, it was hot: for thirteen men it was the beginning of a three-week odyssey underground.

Such survival accounts were rare. Most who did live were speechless. A miner apprentice escaped and talked: 'I heard a dull noise and the flame of my lamp, which was following the normal draught of air, changed direction. I said to my comrades, "Something extraordinary must have happened in the pit."' François Cerf left a few words: 'It was a terrible noise, leaving us half deaf; then everything began to cave in around us. We ran to the gallery mouth, but we encountered "bad air" so we retreated . . .' 'A violent blast of wind, a sort of cyclone,' commented a miner who came out of the neighbouring pit. 'All those who were working next to me ran from the gallery to the well so as to get to the mouth. But they fell dead asphyxiated.'

What had happened? Four days earlier a fire had broken out in an abandoned gallery that had been used for storing old planks and beams. The engineers sealed off the area in an effort to choke the flames, a standard practice in mines. But something went wrong. One of the workers later claimed that the seals had been built in a hurry and that normal precautions were disregarded; he refused to descend the pit Saturday morning. The fire within the blocked-up gallery functioned like 'in a coal gas factory', read a later report, producing the same fuel as in street lamps; one of the seals must have leaked. The problem was aggravated by coal dust.

There were, in fact, a series of detonations which followed in swift succession from one gallery to the next, from one pit to another. The pit shafts acted like huge vertical cannon shooting the lift cages and coal carts upwards, buildings were smashed, the ironwork was torn, fire broke out on the surface.

Within minutes more than a thousand men were dead; it was one of the worst mining disasters in history. Whole families were wiped out. Villages were decimated. Down the streets of Billy-Montigny, Sallaumines and Fourquières-les-Lens, at the gates and doors of the red brick *corons* (the Company villages) of Méricourt and Noyelles, you might have glanced over the walls, across the narrow vegetable patch, past the laundry out drying, and dared take a look in the faces of the women; you would have seen, in an instant, an old tragedy repeated, an old sentiment revived, an old theme reformulated – it was the burial of a people.

*

There was no government in Paris. Former ministers were dispatched to Lens to assure an official presence during the early critical moments of the catastrophe. In the meantime Sarrien had to perform a delicate balancing act to construct a cabinet that would see republicans safely through the next general elections, due in early May. The clerical issue appeared to have strengthened the Republic's enemies. There was general consensus that the 'Bloc' needed reinforcement. But how far left could he go? In the Senate he had to consider Léon Bourgeois' 'Democratic Left' (which was Moderate) and Clemenceau's new 'Radical Socialist Left' (which was Radical). He invited both, added a Socialist (Briand), a Moderate (Poincaré), held on to a few figures from the previous cabinet and then occupied himself with the distribution of portfolios. He reckoned on keeping the ministry of the interior for himself; it was a key post which would give him authority in the new government. But Clemenceau wasn't going to play a subordinate part and insisted – to assure the government a Radical image, he said – that the interior be his. Discussions dragged on at Sarrien's home, avenue de l'Observatoire, through Saturday night.

The first bodies were brought up at three that afternoon. They were naked and rigid, like moulded plaster, only black, the lips contracted, the eyes sunken, the arms and legs shrivelled. Some remains were collected in blankets that were then tied up with straw and carried like packets to the infirmary. Carts and wagons were requisitioned in the surrounding areas and, drawn by heavy work-horses, they rolled up in queues before the pithead towers, looming in dim profile against a sky of thin, lifeless mist.

Further off, at the tall iron colliery gates now guarded by a row of mounted police, crowds of a thousand and more congregated in the cold. They wanted news, any news. Have you seen my husband? Where is my brother? My son? There were rumours that a tapping underground had been heard, that a neighing of horses had echoed up the shafts. Surely a thousand men could not be dead. The workers demanded that dynamite be used to clear the debris. The engineers replied that this would only set off another series of explosions. Then use heavy weights to unblock the broken lift cage of Pit Number 3! That would cause further collapses in the galleries, said the engineers.

Several large black automobiles, carrying men in bowler hats, made slow progress through the throng. 'Monsieur le journaliste,' cried out a woman. 'Come back and tell us! We want to know if our men are alive.' But nobody ever came back to tell. Once past the gates, they disappeared; they must have found another exit.

One of the engineers died in an effort to get to possible survivors. Another was rapidly hauled back to the surface, choking. On Monday afternoon a team of German specialists from the Westphalian pits arrived with breathing apparatus and protective clothing and masks that made them look like characters out of a Jules Verne novel. They descended to discover what they described as a 'charnel house' in a poisoned atmosphere that reached over 50°C. The bodies were already in an advanced state of decomposition. For health reasons, the authorities decided to abandon all further attempts to retrieve them. Later that week, with the report of another fire breaking out, they sealed off three of the ruined pits.

With so little news coming through, talk spread through the miners' villages of defective construction in the pits, of inadequate precautions, of the owners' greed and obsession with dividends: they were trying to save the mines, not people.

All of Sunday, discussions continued at Sarrien's home over who would be minister of the interior. Sarrien had suggested that Clemenceau take the ministry of war, but Clemenceau showed no sign of relenting. Bourgeois, Poincaré, Briand, Thomson, Ruau and Clemenceau appeared and reappeared, one by one or periodically in groups, at avenue de l'Observatoire; they all agreed that whoever held the interior would determine the 'orientation of the cabinet'. After another long meeting in the evening, Sarrien consented to take the ministry of justice and let Clemenceau have what he wanted. Sarrien might have remained prime minister but the significance of this concession escaped few observers; the new government would bear the mark of Clemenceau.

Clemenceau realised that he was coming into office with a major new crisis on his hands – and the clerical issue had not yet been cleared up. The first thing he did Monday morning was to go over to the ministry of war to discuss with Eugène Etienne, who had been asked to stay on at this post, what arrangements already existed with the army regarding the maintenance of order. Clemenceau had his own ideas, but he had to assure himself of some coordination. He was expecting trouble.

In the afternoon there were more meetings at Sarrien's home in preparation for the public announcement the following morning of the make-up of the cabinet and their official programme.

It snowed on Tuesday, the day of the burials. Only about a hundred bodies had been recovered and most of them had been burnt beyond recognition: a common grave was dug at Méricourt-Corons. Nature contrived a bizarre and ambivalent scene. Across the black country lay a thick pall of whiteness; the victims, who had been scorched to death,

were carried to their funerals with ice covering their caskets. Clouds packed
with feather crystals bore down on the plain, closing it in and creating the
impression that the ritual was being conducted within some huge padded
cell, isolated from the world beyond. It was, in a way, a tribute to the final
wishes of an inward-looking society; the miners would keep their secret,
their losses would never be known. Have you seen my husband? Where is
my son? The flakes swirled down to earth to build impenetrable screens.
The sound of church bells was reduced to a distant boom. The call to
arms could hardly be heard; the bugler simply went through the motions.
Few noticed Fernand Dubief, the former minister of the interior, placing
a crown of roses and violets on the coffins laid out by the miners.

Ceremonies took place in several villages. Some of the miners were
offended by the presence of priests. The first voices of vengeance were
heard at Billy-Montigny. 'We must no longer serve as pieces of meat at
work,' said one of the miner delegates. They refused to let the engineer
speak. 'Murderer, your place is not here. Throw him in with the bodies!'

Within days, virtually every pit in northern France was on strike.

As planned, Sarrien's government announced its programme on Tuesday
afternoon: they would continue the church inventories; there would be
no amnesty for 'antimilitarist' demonstrators; in foreign affairs Rouvier's
search for peace, consistent with the 'rights and dignity of France', would
be maintained. The first cabinet meeting was set for Thursday at the ministry of the marine; the ministers would then go to the Elysée and afterwards,
if an interpellation were called, present their programme to the Chamber.

On Wednesday, with the first news of the miners' strike, Clemenceau
convoked the prefects to the ministry of the interior, not to review the
government's position on strikers but to find an immediate solution to
the inventories crisis. His action was drastic: on Friday he signed an
order ending the whole project. 'Counting or not counting candlesticks in
church is not worth a human life,' he later told the Senate. Early Saturday
morning, 17 March, he was on a train for the North. The Republic had
just changed gear; its principal preoccupation was no longer monks but
the *question sociale*.

V

TRAVELLING WITH Clemenceau that morning was his younger brother,
Albert. Despite the years, the bond had not weakened. A wife lost, there
might be another. A child gone, you could not deny that more were

possible. But as Antigone explained to her unkind king, when both
mother and father have left this world, who can replace a brother?
Between the two there was affection, union, error forgiven; beyond them
was the inexorable. Albert had spent a childhood under the same paternal
obstinacies as Georges at L'Aubraie. He had grown up in the offices of *La
Justice* and its liberal promise still ran in his veins: a revolution unfinished.
In the contest for Dreyfus and the principle of equality before the law
he had been his brother's closest collaborator. Albert understood better
than anyone that his brother's perpetual fight with 'the hateful race of
government men', the retainers of power, was in their evasiveness, their
refusal to define and face problems. Now he was a part of the government
and they were on a train to Arras; there was no hypocrisy in that. Albert
was aware of the immense impact the events of 1870 and 1871 had had
on his brother; Georges would never advocate class war, the *grand soir*, an
overthrow of the existing order. He wanted peace, he wanted reform, he
wanted an opening for those who had been excluded. But how was this
to be achieved when men voluntarily excluded themselves? There were
new philosophies on the Left that countenanced refusal, not reception;
separation, not assimilation. And hovering over the current mission of
goodwill was Etienne's caution that if there were serious trouble in the
coalfields the government would be obliged to call in the troops; there
were simply not enough police available.

As they moved out of the hills of Paris and onto the plain the conversation turned to another minister of the interior, Gambetta, republican
warrior, founding father. Never use troops as a preventive force in strikes,
he had warned, because it is the management that gets the protection
and the worker who has to face the bayonets. Clemenceau had cited
Gambetta in his report on the Anzin strike of 1884 and again in 1898
when the Paris builders went on strike: 'Monsieur Brisson congests our
streets with soldiers against an absent enemy . . .' But today there were
thirty-two thousand men off work and only six policemen for every pit.
Soldiers would have to be used to guard the pits, but they would not be
seen on the streets; Clemenceau intended to avert the strikers and appeal
to their republican good sense.

Talk of class war was as ancient as strikes in the northern coalfields,
though the catastrophe had certainly intensified it. A socialist deputy
attending the funeral at Méricourt-Corons the previous Tuesday had told
the mourners to defend themselves 'against capitalism and the defective
way in which it has exploited its control of the mines.' The socialist *Reveil du
Nord* began running a series of articles entitled 'The Vultures of Courrières'
which set out to review the 'profits of the murderers'. But the real struggle
building up that week was within the union ranks themselves. Ever since

Guesde's party had put together a Fédération des Syndicats back in the 1880's there had been efforts to get trade unions together under some sort of national umbrella organisation. Ideology, politics, regional loyalties, isolation and indifference prevented it. There were perhaps seven or eight million industrial workers in the country in 1906: fewer than a million were unionised and only two hundred thousand belonged to the Confédération générale du travail, which since 1895 had claimed to speak for the workers of France.

The CGT renounced parliamentarianism and reform for a policy of 'direct action', the general strike, designed to galvanise workers into the overthrow of the bourgeois regime. But miners in particular had shown little interest, apart from a few villages scattered around Lens; in the North they had their own organisation – founded by the hero of Anzin, Emile Basly – which had since the 1890's elaborated a system of collective bargaining and referendums that had undeniably improved their lives, even if much was left to be done. In 1902, during the last major strike in the region, the CGT had attempted to make inroads into the miners' association and failed. The catastrophe of Courrières provided a second chance.

Clemenceau's train shunted into the station and exhaled onto the front of the platform an immense cloud of wet vapour. An early lunch was organised at the prefecture and then Clemenceau, Prefect Duréault, a government engineer, Albert and a couple of reporters from Paris climbed into a motor car and drove off to Lens. They parked at the steps of the Hôtel de Ville and Clemenceau, accompanied by Duréault, went straight to the mayor's office where Emile Basly was waiting for them.

After six years as a Paris deputy of the Extreme Left, Basly had returned to the mining region to be elected, in 1891, deputy for Lens. Within a few months he was president of the miners' union and five years later he became mayor of Lens. 'At Lens the whole municipal council is unionised,' growled one of his opponents. 'The councillors who are not miners or old miners pay up money as if they were honorary members . . .'

Clemenceau had known Basly since the Anzin strike. During his last years in the Chamber they had cooperated in the formulation of a system of arbitration. Cooperation, for the two men, was the beginning of a solution: 'I have not come to bring here words of hatred' – one could remember Clemenceau saying – 'this Fourth Estate, either you receive it with violence, or you welcome it with open arms.'

They shook hands. Clemenceau and Basly followed the same line of thought.

Their conversation was not long. Basly soon left Clemenceau alone with Evrard, secretary, and Beugnet, treasurer of the union who outlined the demands being made to the Companies. Clemenceau then mentioned the awkward matter of troops. Evrard and Beugnet raised 'vigorous' objections, but the fact that Basly was not in the room already created some ambivalence over the union's real position. The union also had something to fear from the 'turbulent elements', the rival Fédération Syndicale or 'Young Union', which represented the CGT in the region.

'I'm going over to talk to them right now,' said Clemenceau. Evrard and Beugnet were stupefied. But there was no stopping him.

When Clemenceau stepped outside he found two or three hundred men in caps scrutinising the minister's automobile. Better, he thought, go on foot; it was only a few hundred metres to the rue de Paris where the House of the People stood. Protocol demanded that ministers wear felt top hats so Clemenceau for once . . . wore a bowler tilted to one side. He was accompanied by the special commissioner, a few reporters and the miners who had gathered round the car.

There was nothing to advertise that the workers' café on the street corner was the House of the People; the sign above the lantern read '*BAL*'. At the bar were a few men sipping glasses of red wine. Benoît Broutchoux, the twenty-seven-year-old leader of the Fédération, was at that moment in Tourcoing on some mission connected with his local newspaper, *L'Action syndicale*. The strike committee was going to hold a general assembly in the ballroom in an hour, but the only member of the committee now present was Monsieur Monatte, Broutchoux' right-hand man. Nobody had expected the minister of the interior to turn up.

Monatte, with a rather astonished expression on his face, led the minister to a small room separated from the bar by a glass partition. Inside one found two bare tables and several chairs. Monatte offered Clemenceau a seat and asked if he could wait an instant while he went off to search for the other committee members. They came in one by one. After a dozen had gathered Clemenceau said he could wait no longer. 'Then let's begin,' said Monatte.

Citizen Plouvier was the first to speak: 'You've done well not to come with the troops. We reply with order. If there are no soldiers, there'll be no disorder. We had our own patrols out last night.'

'I am here,' replied Clemenceau, 'to talk with you and tell you what I want to do. I am not a partisan for the intervention of troops in strikes. The strike is a legal right which you have the means to exercise in its fullness. It is not I who will think of contesting this right as long as you remain within the law. But in your very own interest, in the interest of both the workers and the Companies, the material of the pits, their installations, have to be safeguarded, preserved.'

Plouvier said they would be preserved. Clemenceau returned that he did not have enough police for the job and that he would have to call in the troops, but they would be billeted in the pithead buildings and they would not leave them. 'You will not see bayonets. Do we agree?' Several committee members replied, 'Yes.'

When one of the committee members suggested that the Companies might provoke attacks on the pits, Clemenceau replied that the troops would provide protection against all attacks. Plouvier remarked that soldiers had been seen in the past recruiting workers for the Companies. 'I don't know if that has been seen or not,' retorted Clemenceau, 'but I do know that you won't see it this time. These soldiers are taking their orders from no one but me. Their role is a role of social protection.' And Clemenceau offered his services as arbitrator.

Troops to guard the pits, arbitration; Clemenceau presented a third point, the 'liberty of work'. It was a principle enshrined in Waldeck-Rousseau's trade union law of 1884. Clemenceau put it in simple terms. 'A strike does not last for ever. Sooner or later, one has to go back to work.' This was the dangerous moment in a strike: some want to work, others want to continue the strike; the potential for violence is enormous. 'I'll tell you right now, I will not tolerate these conflicts.' Plouvier insisted that their committee respected the liberty of work and Clemenceau used the comment to reinforce his own point. The day workers wanted to return to their jobs, his government would use the same energy to protect their right to work as it showed respect for the right to strike. 'You cannot prevent the father of a family from working, if that is his desire. You have the right to try and convince him of your ideas by reasoning, you do not have the right to impose them by threats or by violence.'

After more discussion, Monatte asked Clemenceau if he would attend their general assembly, which was now ready to begin. Clemenceau said he couldn't attend it but that he would summarise what he had just told the committee.

The hall next door was packed with miners and their women, bottles were on every table and smoke had turned the air a pale blue. Clemenceau paused a second at the door. The bandstand, the fading and half-torn posters on the wall, the atmosphere of politics in a place meant for entertainment took him back to the Club de la Reine-Blanche; and there were even a few earnest faces in the room to remind him of other men's eyes that had promised the world change. 'Long live the strike!' they all cried out. The bandstand was already taken up by members of the 'bureau', so Clemenceau walked over to a flight of steps at the side of the room which led to a high balcony. Moustachioed men, some with round-rimmed hats, some in caps, others with no headgear at all, clambered about him.

'Citizens,' he said, with both hands firmly clinging to the banisters, 'I am not here to take part in your meeting. It is not my role to discuss your demands. I am here simply to say that the government of the Republic intends to make the law respected by all.' It was not a promising start. But was anyone listening? When he spoke of the right to strike there were cheers. When he spoke of the right of work there was rather more silence.

But Clemenceau's visit had made a tremendous impression and for many ordinary workers, as for many of their leaders, his presence in the government meant a new hope, a new peace. 'I have made myself your advocate in the council of ministers,' he had said, high on the stairs. Most of those present believed him. Even Broutchoux managed to speak of a 'compagnon Clemenceau' the following day; for him the significance of the visit was in the recognition of his union.

From Lens, Clemenceau was driven to Billy-Montigny, a village which had lost over a hundred men in the catastrophe, and he saw two of the devastated pits. He had a long interview with the inspector general of mines, he attended a conference of doctors and then returned to Lens where he visited a miners' *coron*.

He was back in Paris Sunday morning to attend, at the ministry of public works, the first meeting between delegates from Basly's union, including Basly himself and representatives of the mining Companies. The meeting was a failure. At the same time, in Lens, at the House of the People, another general assembly voted the *grève à outrance* – a strike that would not end until the 'complete triumph of all our demands'. Someone reported that Company men were spreading rumours in mining villages that their proposals in Paris had been accepted. So the House of the People voted to increase the number of patrols that night 'to inform our comrades of the situation'.

It was the same night that Clemenceau's promised troops began to arrive. Fifteen trainloads of hussars, dragoons, light cavalry and infantry were disembarked at various points throughout the department of Pas-de-Calais and consigned, as Clemenceau had said they would be, to the pithead buildings with strict orders never to leave.

The date of this Sunday could hardly have escaped him. It was 18 March.

VI

BROUTCHOUX' YOUNG Union did not preach peace. There were two types of workers' association, its leader would explain, 'the one demands direct action, the other indirect action. The first is revolutionary, the second reformist.' Broutchoux, who had started his working life as a farmhand, committed himself to the first type after he had got a job in the Burgundian coal mine of Montceau-les-Mines, an excellent school for militancy. With two bouts in gaol behind him (for his role in a metallurgists' strike at Le Creusot), he set out with a few mining comrades for the coalfields of the North where they hoped to instil a little revolutionary spirit. The 1902 strike gave them their chance and Broutchoux was soon in gaol once more. By 1903 he had taken over the Young Union from the local Guesdists and was running his own newspaper.

Journalists who met him, including moderates and conservatives, found him charming and intelligent. He believed that elected officials should keep out of trade unions and hoped that strikes would increase workers' democratic sensibilities and revolutionary elan. At the top of his paper *L'Action syndicale* ran the CGT motto, 'the emancipation of workers will be the creation only of the workers themselves,' though this did not prevent Broutchoux from cooperating with people outside the working world or even from encouraging his members to run for political office. Anna Mahe who, in the paper, had described the assassination attempt on the Spanish King as 'a republican act' – 'equal to the beauty of the gesture of Brutus stabbing Caesar' – was a schoolteacher. So was Pierre Monatte. As for Citoyenne Sorgues, who was to play an important role in the coming events, she was an aristocrat. Membership in the small militant elite was determined more by the purity of one's acts than by one's class or occupation.

Everything was in the commitment. 'The formidable revolutionary effort that we are going to witness,' wrote another of Broutchoux' columnists, 'will not be a strike with arms crossed, it will be a strike with arms stretched out and fists clenched at the temples, the barracks and the prisons. It will be a general insurrection.'

The Young Union appealed to the miners with a simple slogan, 'eight hours, eight francs', inspired from the CGT's commitment, at its Bourges Congress in 1904, to the eight-hour day. For nearly two years *L'Action syndicale* had been running a campaign with the formula (not a new one; it could be traced back to the Commune): 'eight hours of work for society, eight hours for pleasure, eight hours for rest.' It announced to its readers – all three thousand of them – the glad tidings of the Bourges Congress: on 1 May 1906 all workers, not only in France but throughout the world, were going to down tools in order to establish the eight-hour day, 'even if it is not voted by parliament.' Significantly, the great day of liberation would take place less than a week before the legislative elections. The Young Union, however, had a tough job convincing the miners that the millennium really was just about to dawn.

Then came the catastrophe, opening up an unexpected chance for revolt. Why wait till May?

*

The hush of the small hours of Monday morning was thus disturbed by the clatter of military trains and the hubbub of the Federate men banging on doors and windows to give notice that nobody was going to descend the pits that day. The Companies had closed and padlocked the gates to many *corons* to prevent the patrols from entering. At Béthune six or seven hundred men smashed the fences of the *coron* of Bully and then marched on Bruay. From Liévin they marched on Lens. Patrols from Carvin and Ostricourt took the long flat rural roads into the night for Meurchin.

A train transporting workers from Saint-Pol to Bully was stopped at a railway crossing at 3.30 a.m. by a crowd of over a thousand strikers. Throughout the day other trains heading from Béthune to the mines of Lens and Liévin were halted.

But the real trouble did not come till Tuesday. Basly and his delegates were meeting again in the Hôtel de Ville at Lens to discuss what action to take: there had been calls to unite with the Young Union ('You cannot join up with nothingness,' had been Basly's comment) and it had been suggested that a referendum be conducted on whether to continue the strike. At about three in the afternoon a crowd of over a thousand began to fill the town square opposite, waving red flags and chanting the Internationale. They were led by Broutchoux and Citoyenne Sorgues who, in a fashionable white raincoat and a magnificent wide-rimmed hat, had just given a rousing address at the House of the People where she had charged Basly with betraying the workers.

Basly had prepared a reception. Two rows of mounted police stared down at the demonstrators. Stones were thrown. The police charged. In the mêlée that followed, Broutchoux managed to get himself arrested again while Citoyenne Sorgues beat a retreat to the House of the People. By five o'clock the square was beginning to look like a battle field. Basly called in the cavalry.

From then on it was open war between the two unions. 'Baslycots' started accusing the 'Broutchoutards' of acting as 'bands of ranters' and provoking a veritable invasion of troops. 'Broutchoutards' called Basly 'man of the Companies', his union the '*vieux saint dicat*' and his paper (*Le Reveil du Nord*) the '*Menteur*' or '*Endormeur du Nord*'. Patrols stepped up their good labours and *rouffions* were put on guard, bricks and stones thrown at their windows. Several more Company trains were stopped or delayed by men on the tracks.

On Thursday morning, 22 March, every mayor in the department of Pas-de-Calais received a telegram informing him that the minister of war had exercised the 'right of requisition' and that accommodations for the military had to be prepared immediately. In the meantime in Paris there was a cabinet meeting, as there was every Thursday. After the meeting

Clemenceau left for the ministry of the interior where he had a long interview with Basly, who had just come in by train from Lens. There is no record of what passed between them. Basly was always to insist that he had opposed the intervention of troops but his enemies claimed that it was he who had initiated the 'invasion'. He was back in his mayor's office that afternoon. At nightfall two infantry companies and four cavalry squadrons were brought in by train to Lens. The infantry were put up in Company buildings and a hotel in the city centre while schools, lecture halls and theatres were requisitioned in the surrounding villages for the cavalry. The following day plenty of red pantaloons could be seen on the streets. For the Broutchoutards, compagnon Clemenceau had broken his word.

There were at this time about forty-six thousand men on strike in the two departments, Pas-de-Calais and the Nord, two thousand less than at the beginning of the week. For the next four days the number of strikers continued to fall so that on the eve of the referendum, 27 March, there were less than thirty thousand refusing to work. The geographic incidence of the strike was very uneven, reflecting the divergent attitudes of workers to the various companies. At Ferfay there was a complete stoppage, while in the neighbouring village of Merles everybody was at work in one pit and over three-quarters of the workforce were operating in the other two. Bruay, right next door, had no strikers at all; its company paid the region's highest wages and it had never joined the *Syndicat Patronal*. Béthune had three-quarters of its men at work, Ostricourt had none. Amazingly, the undamaged pits of Courrières had a few hundred men still working in them.

It was this unevenness which incited the violence. The atmosphere in some of the *corons* was now close to terror, the gates at the end of each street being locked up at night, the doors of the homes bolted and shutters firmly closed. Neighbours were pitted against neighbours, and families – such a critical part of the miners' lives – were divided.

The referendum of 28 March was hardly as decisive as the Old and Young Unions were to claim. Certainly, the published results gave the impression of a 'crushing majority' for the strike: thirty-two thousand voted to continue the strike and eighteen thousand voted for work. But there were well over twenty-five thousand abstentions, so that the numbers who actively supported the strike fell distinctly in the minority. None the less the Young Union was unruffled and an appeal was immediately launched from the House of the People: 'The return to work should be considered treason.'

Two days later a lone guardsman in the underground stables still in use at Courrières was scared out of his wits when a back-door creaked open and thirteen phantoms appeared before him. What is the time? What is the date? they groaned. The guardsman remained immobile, petrified. The glass of his safety lamp shattered as he let it drop to the floor. Finally he plucked up enough courage to scream for his supervisor, who was down in an instant. These were no ghosts. They were thirteen men who had lived for twenty days on rotting horse meat, wood fibre and their own urine.

Four days later another man emerged from the tombs. His story was even more extraordinary. Alone he had survived underground for almost a month.

The fourteen survivors could not have made it to the surface if the seal, built to stifle the second fire following the catastrophe, had not been pierced a few days earlier. An inspection of the area beyond the seal on 31 March revealed the presence of four bodies where, when the seal was constructed two weeks before, only one had been recorded.

So men had been literally buried alive. How many? Rumours spread in the *corons* that the number of newly discovered bodies was enormous, that some of them were still warm.

The strike took on a new fury. The first time dynamite was used against the homes of *rouffions* was at Hénin-Liétard on the night of 3 April. A gunfight had taken place in a neighbouring *coron* three days earlier, leaving a man of twenty dead and another adolescent seriously wounded. Adolescents and children were frequently in the front line of violence. Women played a prominent part too.

The last comment Clemenceau had made to the prefect on his visit of 17 March was, 'There will perhaps be a critical hour. If this hour arrives, give me a call and I'll be back. I will, for the final time, still have something to say to the strikers.' On 18 April the prefect made his call: 'I am surrounded in the railway station at Lens with the general,' he said. 'What should I do?' Clemenceau boarded a special train in Paris at 5.30 and was in the Lens railway station at eight.

It had been a day of riot and avengement. A day also of torrential rains. In the morning the market at Liévin had been ransacked by miners, their women and many young clamouring that the merchants were charging too much. Similar incidents the previous days in Anzin, Denain, Haveluy and Trith-Saint-Léger were proof that the conflict had entered a new phase: the strikers were getting hungry.

Like most towns in this corner of the world, the centre of Lens was dominated by a church, the Hôtel de Ville and a railway station, an imposing building which, like many of the stations in the area, had become a strategic point in the defence of order (one was beginning to speak in terms of war). Not only were stations generally well guarded:

administrators preferred to hold their meetings there because they felt safer with trains and railway lines next to them than in the more isolated municipal buildings. A few hundred metres down the street from the station stood the home of the director of the Lens Coal Company, Monsieur Reumaux, and next to it, an abandoned Company office building. There were troops at the station, but not a soldier nor a policeman was left to guard either the office building or the director's house.

Having smashed the windows and doors of the office building, the mob turned on Reumaux' stables, then the house itself – to carry out what *L'Action syndicale* termed a 'social cleansing'. Reumaux' wife, who was alone, entrenched herself in the kitchen. Other strikers, in the meantime, prepared for the arrival of troops by constructing a barricade out of railway sleepers on, of all places, the nearby rue de la Bataille, tearing up the cobbles for use as missiles.

The military response was gradual. They had received orders from the prefect – following directives from the interior – to 'exhaust all resources of patience', to be 'patient beyond the bounds of the reasonable'. Fifty mounted police were sent in but were turned back under a hail of stones. Then a detachment of infantry, but they were no more successful. Shortly after 4 p.m. a squadron of dragoons was ordered to take the barricade. One of the officers, Lieutenant Lautour, was hit in the temple with a brick; he was carried, screaming, to a neighbouring house. The prefect made his call to Paris.

The station was not in fact surrounded and the barricade was eventually taken without a shot being fired. However, one could understand why feelings were tense. Several soldiers were wounded, Lautour died in hospital that night, while no casualties were reported among the barricade's defenders, save by *L'Action syndicale* which headlined that week's edition, '*Grève à outrance*, Clemenceau's police sabre the strikers', but gave no details.

At the station, Clemenceau conferred with the prefect, the military authorities and a doctor charged with the wounded soldiers. On hearing that the minister was in town, Basly walked over from the Hôtel de Ville and expressed surprise that the defence of the director's house had been so weak. He was later to develop the thesis that the whole day's troubles had been a Company plot to discredit the government. The weeks to come would reveal several curious 'plots'.

Clemenceau spent the night in Arras and took the train back to Lens early the next morning. He started his day with a tour of the damaged zone in the town centre. Smashed windows, torn-out cobbles, a barricade were crammed in the agenda. Clemenceau was shown how the entire front of the director's house had been devastated. The high civil servants, the local officials, the military men and Clemenceau walked briskly under a sky of gloom – all this April could afford in the way of light. A church tower chimed out the hour.

He visited the hospital, spoke to the wounded soldiers and stood for a moment before the body of Lieutenant Lautour. He then took a train to Douai and Denain.

Denain had also been a scene of violence. Clemenceau appeared at the window of the Hôtel de Ville and told a crowd – armed with clubs – that he could meet their delegates in the nearby station. The telephone rang. Would the minister care for a cavalry escort? Clemenceau refused, went downstairs, opened the door and plunged into the crowd, 'which did not receive me too badly.' The meeting with the delegates took place in the stationmaster's office and Clemenceau made note 'of some of their requests which seemed just.' But he refused to withdraw the troops because the wielding of clubs in the crowd suggested that their presence 'might not be entirely useless'.

Clemenceau then returned to the railway station at Lens and, with the delegates of Basly's union in one room and Company representatives in another (for they declined to look at each other in the face), he attempted to get the two sides to reach an agreement and end the strike. The effort failed.

The next day at the prefecture in Arras he tried again, pacing from one room and another with proposals and counter-proposals. Then, late in the afternoon, he was approached by the prefect's *chef du cabinet*, who was looking a bit pale. 'Monsieur le ministre,' he mumbled, 'Captain Lesage is encircled at police headquarters in Liévin and asks you the authorisation to fire on the crowd in order to get out.'

It was staggering. Clemenceau explained to the Chamber two months later: 'Gentlemen, I saw 18 March [1871] at close range, and that was a terrible day in my life. But I don't think I have ever received a stronger blow at my heart than when this person came up to ask me – me at the prefecture of Arras, not knowing what was going on at Liévin – for authorisation to shoot on unarmed men.'

What was going on that Friday fifteen kilometres to the north is sometimes known as 'the Battle of Liévin'. *Coron* No. 3, a mining village belonging to the Lens Company, had been turned into a huge fortress. Several attempts were made by dragoons to take the barricades but they were pushed back every time by a shower of bricks and stones. Meanwhile a large crowd of angry men and women marched on the town centre, tearing up lamp-posts, cutting down telegraph poles and using the wiring to hinder the charge of horsemen. It was under these conditions that Captain Lesage had asked for authorisation to shoot.

Clemenceau replied that Captain Lesage had received very clear instructions that allowed him to use arms only if the lives of his men were threatened and that he, Clemenceau, could not from the prefecture at Arras judge whether this was the case or not. It had to be left to the captain to judge the situation.

Since the telephone lines had been cut these instructions had to be carried by messenger to Liévin. Two hours of tense waiting passed before news came back. Clemenceau went before the union delegates at the prefecture and told them that he would never order troops to fire on strikers.

Finally, at around 9 p.m., it was learnt that Captain Lesage had got out of his difficulties and that General Couturier had taken the *coron*. Not a shot had been fired. Not a man had died. But the damage was immense.

Clemenceau attended the funeral of Lieutenant Lautour the following morning. He was joined by the minister of war, Eugène Etienne, who made Lautour a posthumous member of the Légion d'honneur. The two ministers then returned to Paris. The newspapers, in the meantime, had lost interest in miners and had turned their attention to the San Francisco earthquake. Soothsayers of an earlier age would have claimed that the gods were trying to say something.

The reprisals of the military and the police were not gentle. They rarely are. By the third week of April there were perhaps twenty-six thousand troops in the region, or a little more than one soldier for every two strikers. There are conflicting reports of how many strikers were actually arrested; some say ten, some say dozens, a few claim hundreds. Many who were taken into police custody were soon released because the legality of the operation was questionable. Those who were arrested were carried off to Béthune in prison vans under the surveillance of a police force that, on account of the violence, had little love for strikers. Basly later spoke of medical certificates that proved mistreatment.

By the last week of April neither the companies nor the miners could present a united front and so negotiations proceeded company by company. The miners gradually returned to work; by the time the legislative elections were held on 6 May only the most hardened districts of the Pas-de-Calais were still on strike. Basly and his aide, Arthur Lamendin, won clear majorities over the two CGT candidates, Simon *dit* Ricq and Plouvier, in the elections that Sunday; but there were less miners voting for the moderate Socialists than in the previous elections.

'It seems that a wind of madness had swept over these crowds of workers,' wrote a reporter a few days after the insurrection, 'passing from neighbourhood to neighbourhood, village to village, from one coal basin to the other.' The real loser in that madness was the Young Union which never again could claim to be a genuine spokesman of the miners. In 1908

Basly's union joined the CGT, but it was under Basly's terms with a CGT that was changing its leadership.

Basly commented in mid-May 1906 that the strike had been a 'salutary lesson' which proved the superiority of his reformist approach. Clemenceau would also speak of 'lessons'. But above all this terrible strike represented for him the same old struggle for life that he had theorised about in a medical thesis, given speeches about in the 1880's, written about during the Dreyfus Affair and was to comment again about in 1907 when interpellated by Jaurès: 'Behind the capitalist regime, which certainly has vices but has the advantage of being' – behind, he might have said, the categories, the labels, the systems, the structures – 'there is a society that wants to live and the duty of all is to let it live.'

VII

THE FIRST of May was approaching. 'After the capitalist crime of Courrières,' wrote A. Luquet in the CGT's official weekly, *La Voix du peuple*, 'there is the spontaneous awakening of workers' consciousnesses.' A two-year campaign was reaching its climax. Some of the paper's slogans evinced a certain modesty: 'The hour of realisations has struck! The Working Class will snatch from the Capitalist Class small improvements which will increase its power in the decisive work of emancipation.' Others went directly to the point: 'To work for a maximum of eight hours is to prepare for the expropriating general strike'.

During April and May, and for a long time thereafter, the whole socialist extreme Left in France was caught up in a movement of hope, visionary struggle and petty hatreds that recollected the heady days of the Commune, and the lunacies of Boulangism as well. The 'working class', sometimes blazoned with two large letters, became the new hero on a horse, an idol, emerging from the shadows of 'capitalism', a monolith bound, as the syndicalists said, sooner or later to crumble to dust. It was the CGT which held the initiative in the movement, not the political parties, though many intellectuals and journalists lent their moral support. One could find, in its thousands of brochures distributed throughout France, language that might have been composed by a Vallès, a Rochefort, a Laisant or a Naquet. They spoke of 'disgust for the regime', of a 'popular nausea' and of the 'stagnant pond of parliamentarianism'. *La radicaille* was the name of the new evil and Clemenceau was elevated to 'dictator' months before he was even prime minister.

The 'abortion of Dreyfusism' also became a theme in some of the more advanced revolutionary tracts. A series of articles published in the May issue of *Le Mouvement socialiste* – which couldn't all have been written on the night of 30 April – purported to show how Clemenceau's entry into the government represented the triumph of 'Dreyfusism', a sop to the working class to win its support for parliamentary capitalism. The demeaning alliance between capitalists and workers on behalf of bourgeois justice had to be broken.

This need to separate the working class from parliamentary politics was the essence of 'revolutionary syndicalism' and the whole campaign for the eight-hour day. 'Universal suffrage', said the general secretary of the CGT, Victor Griffuelhes, 'must be relegated to the spare-parts shop.' Proletarians had to learn to act without the support of parties and of political men.

Posters were stuck up on walls, shopwindows, in the trams, on buses and in the passageways and platforms of the new metro. When you sipped at your absinthe in the neighbourhood café you would soon have noticed the little announcements glued onto your seat, hidden on the side of the table, staring at you from the counter. 'Sixty-seven more days till the emancipation,' read the fading scrawl on the half-demolished edifice of the nearby construction site. For several weeks a thirty-three-metre red banner hung from the fourth-floor windows of the Bourse du Travail next to the place de la République with the inscription in black letters, 'After 1st May 1906 we will work only eight hours a day.' *La Voix du peuple* issued its special edition for the First of May in mid-April. Its front page was taken up by one of Grandjouan's cartoons. Muscular men with picks and shovels stand up to the capitalists fleeing with their money-boxes under their arms:

> *Debout les damnés de la terre,*
> *Debout les forçats de la faim.*
> *La Raison tonne en son cratère,*
> *C'est le commencement de la Fin.* *

But the Damned of the Earth did not respond as one man. The incidence of strike activity had been increasing since 1904, largely on account of an unfavourable trade cycle, though the fact that agitation could now be coordinated in Paris by the CGT certainly encouraged the trend. The coordination was, however, very primitive – in 1906 there were plenty of local organisations ready to jump the gun, not willing to wait for the *grand soir* of the First of May.

---

* 'Stand up damned of the earth,/ Stand up convicts of hunger./ Reason sounds in its crater,/ It is the beginning of the End.' From '*L'Internationale*' as cited in *La Voix du Peuple*. Premier Mai 1906 (Special).

*

The miners' strike in the north had been a rude lesson for everyone in the Sarrien government and they were not prepared to witness a repeat performance in the capital. Troops were to be assembled and mass demonstrations were forbidden for 1 May. In the meantime, a few more arrests were conducted in the North, including that of Pierre Monatte who directed the Young Union while Broutchoux served his two-month sentence for his march on the Hôtel de Ville. The arrest took place in the weekend of 21–22 April.

That Sunday Victor Griffuelhes, Emile Pouget (the editor of *La Voix du peuple*) and Alphonse Merrheim (an assistant) paid a surprise visit to Clemenceau. Griffuelhes explained the mission: rumours had been spreading for the last week that the government was going to make some preventive arrests in Paris and that they had the impression they were being followed. Clemenceau responded that this was the first time he had ever heard of such rumours, that no arrests were being envisaged and that if they were being tailed it was rather stupid because it would have put them on their guard.

Without being asked, Clemenceau then volunteered some remarks on the First of May. According to Griffuelhes' account published in *La Voix du Peuple* that same week Clemenceau said, 'My role is not to ignore the existence of the Confédération générale du travail on which I have an opinion different from that of all my colleagues and which I keep to myself' – subsequent events proved that his colleagues wanted the CGT outlawed whereas Clemenceau opposed this. 'I cannot ignore either that there is going to be a First of May and my role as minister of the interior is to take the measures susceptible to the assurance of order. We are not on the same side of the barricade. I have to fulfil my functions as member of the government.'

The tone is similar to his language with the miners on 17 March. The press sensationalised the interview by reporting a fiery exchange in which Clemenceau supposedly remarked, 'You are behind a barricade. I am before it. Your way of action is disorder. My duty is to make order. My role is to counter your efforts. The best for each of us is to come to terms with this.' That wicked comment has been quoted by historians ever since, but quite evidently it did not reflect Clemenceau's style with strikers. The pattern was already clear. He would recognise their union, define their rights, lay down the limits of the action they could take and warn of the consequences if these were exceeded. Faced with a syndicalist movement that openly proclaimed that 'socialism is something other than democracy' it is difficult to imagine what alternative course he could have reasonably pursued. Clemenceau did not seek class war. He wanted reform and social peace.

'At no moment,' said Griffuelhes in his account, 'did the minister declare that he was before the barricade, nor that he treated us as an element of disorder. That would have been a language little inspired by the circumstances.'

However, on 30 April Griffuelhes and one of his assistants, Albert Lévy, were arrested. They were released a week later, two days after the first round of the legislative elections.

The only public comment that Clemenceau made on the arrests and the 'plot' that was supposed to justify them was in a campaign speech in Lyon on 3 May. He argued that the Republic was menaced on two fronts, the undemocratic Right and the undemocratic Left: 'Civil war on the Right with the inventories, civil war on the Left with the strikes and the First of May; that is what the temptations of power offered us.' He pointed out that the government had avoided both. 'We stopped the effort of the reaction. We refused to make ourselves accomplices of the revolution. The concordance of the attacks from the two extremes gives me the idea that we are holding to a straight line between two aberrations.'

And that was all he said. He never spoke of a 'plot' and he would leave it to Sarrien to explain that the arrests were ordered by a judge in Béthune 'acting in the fullness and in the independence of his powers'.

Was Clemenceau responsible for the arrests? The minister must have had some knowledge of them. Having lived through the Boulangist crisis, the idea of cooperation between political extremes was hardly strange to him either. Moreover, many revolutionary syndicalists did later join the forces of the extreme Right. Roberto Michels, for example, became a fascist and Hugh Lagardelle was to be a minister in Marshal Pétain's government. Clemenceau might not have given the orders for these arrests but he surely could have seen in them no great inconvenience.

Place de la République, on the First of May, was occupied by the military and mounted municipal guards who, trotting in tight formation around that grand statue to liberty, equality and fraternity, prevented demonstrators from gathering. There were scuffles on boulevard Saint-Martin, on the sides of the Canal Saint-Martin and on rue du faubourg du Temple, where a bus was overturned. Dragoons moved on an assembly at place de la Bastille. They probably did not temper their blows, but no one has ever produced a list of casualties.

Estimates of the numbers involved vary. There were perhaps 50,000 troops in the region of Paris that day and between 100,000 and 130,000 strikers – the largest strike the capital had yet known. The regions most affected in the provinces were in the North, where the textile workers were very active, around Lyon, with its heavy concentration of artisanal trades, and in the South where, as in Paris, construction workers played an important role. The demands of the strikers were as varied as ever. A few stayed out until they got total satisfaction, more returned with some points gained, and the majority obtained nothing at all. The strike of May 1906 is generally regarded as a failure.

This did not prevent the conservative press from sounding the alarm that the country was on the brink of chaos. 'Monsieur Thiers said the Republic will surely finish in blood and imbecility,' wrote Clemenceau's old antisemitic rival Arthur Meyer in *Le Gaulois*. 'The truth of this prophetic word is about to burst forth.' That might have been the hope of some, but it did not happen.

VIII

ALL THE same, the events of March, April and May were a challenging introduction, by anyone's standards, to the art of government. A photograph taken on the eve of the legislative elections shows the sixty-four-year-old minister of the interior seated before his heavy desk at place Beauveau. He has lost his hair, his moustache is white. He has a rather stunned look on his face. Albert Sarraut, under-secretary of state, stands beside him, studying (in what must be a deliberate pose) a batch of papers for the minister's attention; perhaps it is the latest police report.

Clemenceau was at last confronted with the riddles of power, like an artist faced with his own success, a painter or a writer plucked from his divine creative role and made human again, made mortal. 'You have seen so many ministers,' he had said to the electors in Lyon two days before, 'that for you this title has certainly lost the prestige of days gone by when power came directly from heaven.' Some anointment it had been! – in the mines. 'I am not the delegate of Providence.' Power, in the way it both provided an audience and stole the privacy of a man's ideas, implied a return to life, the end of the wilderness. Youth might be lost but age for the powerful offered a renewal; even Clemenceau's enemies spoke of him as the 'young' minister of the interior. Power brought its pleasures and constraints. Ideals had to be translated into acts, 'For it must be confessed without pretensions: Voix du Peuple, Voix de Dieu, they haven't avoided many errors. And they will make plenty of errors again.' In opposition he had been uncompromising, now it was his turn to be the object of scorn. 'I accept this misfortune with philosophy and, quite frankly, with a sense of pride, believe me.'

He was hardly responsible for the events. The unfavourable trade cycle was not his invention. The First of May had been planned two years earlier and the election date decided long before he was in office. But for many on the extreme Left he had become a class enemy. Images of Clemenceau repressing the workers with blood lust in his eye were already appearing.

'Count your wounded, we'll count ours,' he had said when Basly called to complain of the treatment the arrested strikers were getting. Well, he would explain, the casualties were all on the side of the soldiers.

At the elections the Radicals made greater gains than in 1902, while the Right lost another sixty seats. The Socialists were among those who benefited from the shift to the Left; the newly constituted party, the Section Française de l'Internationale Ouvrière (SFIO), won fifty-nine seats and was determined that nobody was going to ignore the fact.

As soon as parliament reassembled, in June, their leader, Jean Jaurès, demanded to interpellate the government on its general policy and 'notably on the action that it has taken against the working class'.

Jaurès and Clemenceau could hardly have been more unalike, whether it was in their physical appearance, their temperament, even the way they spoke. Jaurès was stocky, some now said massive, while Clemenceau was slim, a figure kneaded in nerve and muscle. Jaurès was a rationalist and a scholar; Clemenceau was more of a romantic. Jaurès spoke in deep resonant tones, his sentences were long, deliberate and if they were lyrical in style they were often theoretical in content. His best performances were in the open air where, with the inspiration of the man on the Mount, he could convert crowds to his vision of a better, juster world. Clemenceau's voice, on the other hand, was rather high-pitched, his words were incisive, incurably insolent and served up with a sarcasm that few opponents knew how to counter. He was ideally suited for the Chamber.

For the next three years the talents of the two men so coloured the course of the Chamber debates that the period has been called 'the second golden age of French parliamentary eloquence' (the first being the Revolution). But golden ages were never meant to be repeated and this one would certainly be the last, for it relied on a political oratory – the grand speeches from the tribune with full coverage in the front pages of the press – that radio and, later, television would render obsolete.

Jaurès came into the debates seriously handicapped by the decision of the Second International in Amsterdam, two years earlier, to refuse all collaboration with 'bourgeois governments'. But Jaurès was still capable of sending out peace feelers. 'I bring here no hostile intentions and want to remain, inasmuch as it depends on me, within the precise limits of what appears to me to be the truth,' he said in his opening statement. His aim was rather to present 'the very difficult and complex outline of what might be socialist organisation'. Jaurès would lean on the tribune, wag a finger and pronounce those words with an insistence that gave off a vaguely hot smell. He had spent four to five months preparing the speech and it took him two days to deliver it.

His first comments were devoted to the strikes of that spring. There were too many troops in the Pas-de-Calais, 'There is no longer room in this region for the world of work, there is only room for armed force.' The First of May represented the 'combined movement of the working class' and its object, the eight-hour day, 'is of interest rather to civilisation'. The problem had to be placed within a world view, the grander perspective. He took Clemenceau and his allies to task for their pessimistic approach to History: 'It's not your adversaries on the Right, it's not the men of theocracy who are proclaiming the bankruptcy of science and human intelligence, it's yourselves.' They were democrats who had failed to appreciate 'the laws known and noted of human nature'.

Those laws, if anyone was not already aware, predicted the 'general expropriation of capitalist property' though 'it was impossible to say with certitude how', whether 'it would be with indemnity or without indemnity'. He cited, among others, Marx and Engels, Kautsky and Liebknecht. The French Revolution had started the process with indemnity and it was evident – after a careful perusal of the texts of Liebknecht – that 'expropriation did not necessarily signify spoliation'. It could be done peacefully if only Clemenceau and the Radicals would stop ignoring the rules of 'social transformation' and 'social revolution'.

Several Socialists, of differing persuasions, followed Jaurès to the tribune. Basly made a long speech on the strike in Pas-de-Calais which in fact put Clemenceau in a rather positive light. He concluded by demanding the *déchéance* of the Companies and the expropriation of the mines by the state. Edouard Vaillant, old Communard and former Blanquist, now safely under the wing of Marxian orthodoxy, gave a long account of the 'veritable capitalist massacre of Courrières', of the First of May, the civil servants' strike and the 'anti-worker and anti-socialist action of the government'. He then proceeded into a still longer class analysis which, in the *Journal officiel*, covers four pages of three columns each. Jaurès interjected periodically with a '*Très bien!*' Deputy Gayraud on the Right remarked, 'This theory is a bit old.' Vaillant's main theme was that there was an increasing concentration of capital as demonstrated by the population censuses which indicated businesses were getting larger.

After Vaillant, Clemenceau stepped up to the tribune.

'I want first,' he said, 'to render full homage to the noble passion of social justice that animates so magnificently Monsieur Jaurès's eloquence.' It put him in mind of the ancient Greeks. 'To the strings of his lyre Amphion, modestly, raised the walls of Thebes. To the voice of Monsieur Jaurès a far greater miracle is accomplished: he speaks and all the historical organisation of human societies suddenly crumbles': everything, the whole complicated human fray, 'all that is reduced to dust, all that flies away in smoke'. But, he said, look upward, follow that smoke and you will see in sumptuous clouds 'enchanted palaces where all human misery has been banished'. Alas, he continued, 'I, vacillating mortal, I labour miserably in the plain and even in the deepest valley.' Clemenceau got his applause from the Centre and the Left, but not the extreme Left.

So he was accused of repressing the working class, of resorting to the tactics of the most reactionary governments known in the time of the Republic. 'I have repressed the working class!'; for an instant you could see the whites of his Asiatic eyes, and he took a little time for breath. 'Where then have I met it, this working class?'

The extreme Left broke into pandemonium. Jaurès shook his head impatiently and moaned 'Oh!' Jules Coutant exclaimed, *'Monsieur le ministre,* once more you are mocking the working class!'

But for Clemenceau the question before the Chamber involved not so much the working class as those who claimed to speak and act on behalf of the working class. When Coutant again interrupted him, claiming that Clemenceau was sending troops where there were not even strikes, Clemenceau replied, 'Monsieur Coutant, you are afflicted with the disease of Monsieur Jaurès: you have caught hemiopia; you see only half the phenomena. You see the phenomenon "repression", you do not see the phenomenon "repressed".' Clemenceau said troops had been sent nowhere without reason. 'But where there had been violent demonstrations it was necessary to repress.' And he elaborated: 'In my eyes those who act against the working class are those who encourage it in this mad idea that everywhere where there is a worker who does not respect the law there is the working class.'

He was also accused of forgetting the principles of the French Revolution and, worse, of overlooking the ideas of his own heroes. It was not the sort of charge Clemenceau took lightly. The Revolution, he said, was about justice and the nobility of the individual; he and his supporters were as faithful to its principles today as they had been in the past. 'You pretend to fabricate directly the future; we fabricate the man who will fabricate the future.'

Clemenceau still emphasised education, not an education by words as practised by 'the pedagogues', but an education by acts. 'We enlighten man, we exalt him, and we attenuate him in evil, and we fortify him in good, and we liberate him, and we justify him and, raised from the bestial regime of force, we lead him towards a better and better approximation of higher justice. And each day, it is with a little more impartiality, a little more nobility, goodness, beauty, a new power on himself and the exterior world. It is our ideal to magnify man, the reality rather than the dream, while you enclose yourselves, and the whole of man with you, in a narrow domain of anonymous collective absolutism. We put our ideal in the beauty of individualism . . .' It was not a doctrine, more an attitude: 'It is the development of this society of the French Revolution, in justice and by liberty, which is all our programme, and this programme we rigorously oppose to your dogmatic and authoritarian conceptions.'

The basic weakness of Jaurès's theories, according to Clemenceau, was that they failed to distinguish between the two things that make up social organisation, man and his setting. 'It appears much simpler theoretically to reform the setting.' Clemenceau turned his gaze on Jaurès. 'I do not know the product of your wakeful nights. But I can tell you that when you have given us the setting of the new society, you will still have to introduce a new man to live in it.' This man does not exist today, perhaps he will tomorrow. But even then he will have his own mind, his own intelligence, and he will not be very concerned about 'the route that you claim to trace out for him.'

In his conclusion Clemenceau showed he could also send out peace feelers: 'Either one makes reforms or one heads directly into revolution. We have made reforms; we want to continue them. Are you ready to help us? Let us work. If you want to work with us, there is our hand outstretched for you and your electors. If not, let each man follow his fate. Without you, we will attempt to be equal to the task. We will carry boldly the responsibilities of the day and, for the rest, we will place it with confidence before the enlightened justice of the Chamber and of the republican nation.'

When Jaurès climbed once more the red carpeted steps he seemed slightly baffled. 'Messieurs, I rise to this tribune all bristling with arrows that an able and still young hand has let fly at me.' He said that he was willing to cooperate on reforms and that he did not consider the Republic sterile on that count. But he continued to criticise Clemenceau for his failure to understand the processes of historical development. 'It is you, Monsieur le ministre, you, man of science, who are singularly foreign to the idea of development. I do not know of a philosophy of History more contrary to the idea of development than the one you have outlined at this tribune to combat us.' He also continued to insist that Clemenceau was resorting to reactionary methods by using the support of the Right to attack socialism.

'You are not socialism all alone', retorted Clemenceau from the government bench – for Clemenceau still considered himself a socialist, and one of his colleagues in the government was an Independent Socialist.

'Don't play with words,' shouted down Jaurès. 'There is a Socialist party here.'

'There are Socialists outside that party,' replied Clemenceau. 'You are not the good God.' The deputies laughed.

'And you, Monsieur le ministre, you are not even the devil.' There was more laughter.

'You don't know anything.'

That, perhaps, was the heart of the debate.

IX

IN THE autumn of 1906 Clemenceau was once again on a campaign trail that took him through the small country towns and villages of the Var and of his native Vendée. It was a visit to a people with whom he felt closely akin. Though his critics often claimed he was out of touch with the common man, he had probably had more contact with working people than any of his predecessors at the ministry of the interior – and he never lost his sympathy for them. But Clemenceau did not feel at home in large urban crowds. His sentiments lay further out, where the tramlines ended, the street noise stopped, where the country began. He was drawn to those who worked the land, its fabled men, its super-men, its ogres, its giants; to the rural folk and especially the rebel peasants of his own bocages. 'I cannot claim all their finer qualities,' he said in a speech at La Roche-sur-Yon, 'but I can't deny picking up some features of their character, their instinctive independent spirit, their critical sense, their headstrong obstinacy and contentiousness, and these have brought on me some of the harshest hostilities I have known in my journey through life.' He spoke a lot of that journey through life, a lot of himself. For he was not campaigning for the next legislative elections, or for the Senate; he was campaigning for himself, for his own candidature – though it was never formally announced – for the post of prime minister.

Sarrien was ill or, at least, that was the story he gave to the press when he announced his resignation a week after Clemenceau's return to Paris. He told President Fallières, who had just got back from his own bucolic wanderings (an inspection of the grape harvest on his Gascon estate), that Clemenceau was the obvious successor. Jaurès, in an editorial, agreed; for once the country would have a premier who was not just a mediator between feuding political groups but was actually leader of the majority party, the Radicals, in the Chamber.

Majority leader as head of government? This broke all traditions. While it had been a principle of Britain's unwritten constitution for more than a hundred years, until Clemenceau became prime minister it was unknown in France. The reason was partly because, in a strictly technical sense, the office of 'prime minister' did not yet exist. The 'president of the council of ministers' was more a chairman among equals than somebody who held a special function over and above his colleagues. He had his own ministry to run, usually justice or the interior, he had no independent office and had no staff besides that on hand at his ministry. But then the council of ministers had nothing remotely parallel to today's mammoth Gallic weekly encounters of fifty or sixty cabinet members around a long table equipped with microphones. The council of ministers in Clemenceau's day was a rather intimate affair. Up until the war, it never had more than twelve members (the number assembled under Clemenceau, Ferry and Gambetta). It met three times a week, in the morning, on Tuesdays, Thursdays and Saturdays. The undersecretaries of state – there were only four in Clemenceau's ministry – did not attend.

Thus the council of ministers maintained the simplicity of earlier regimes. The staffing of the various ministries, on the other hand, had evolved into a system that somehow managed to combine all the selective traditions of high bureaucracy with the crudest forms of republican patronage. Thus the style of recruitment of departmental staff, *les cabinets ministériels*, might be placed somewhere between Richelieu's royal hierarchies and Boss Tweed's New York. Democracy in its initial phase, it seems, gave patronage a tremendous boost, for it broke down the old systems of advancement. Clemenceau himself was a great practitioner of patronage and many of his most bitter personal feuds, for example with Delcassé or with Combes, could be traced to the failure of such high-ranking politicians to give his protégés government jobs.

And one must keep in mind that, where it was a question of political power, Clemenceau was never working alone; there was always the family network, the press network, the culture network and the business network behind him. 'The instant the newspaper criers announce a ministerial crisis, sometimes on the eve, before the ministerial candidates have stirred themselves,' wrote the administrative specialist Henri Chardon in 1908, 'there are people who start up their campaign. They feverishly consult the register of their relations. Politicians, bureaucrats, old school mates, table companions, residents of the neighbouring flat, people from one corner of the world, wives from another, all are exploited.'

Clemenceau was invited to the Elysée and asked to form a ministry on a Sunday morning, 21 October 1906. He spent the rest of the day being driven from one ministerial candidate's home to another in a large black automobile that he had recently acquired – already a sign that he was going to take rather more energetic direction than Sarrien, who did not drive and had merely summoned the candidates to his own home.

Six of Sarrien's ministers were to remain in office, but two of the leading moderates in the former government, Léon Bourgeois at foreign affairs and

Raymond Poincaré in finance, though approached, refused to continue to serve under Clemenceau.

Clemenceau's ministry signalled a definite shift to the Left. He created a new ministry of labour to be directed by the Independent Socialist René Viviani. Aristide Briand, whom Clemenceau had called a 'sociolo-papalin' during the debate on the separation bill in 1905, stayed on at the ministry of public instruction. This ministry was also responsible for religious affairs, and keeping Briand in charge indicated that Clemenceau intended to pursue a moderate policy regarding the Church despite his hostile declarations whilst in opposition. As minister of finance he named Joseph Caillaux, who had spent the last year working on the details of an income tax bill, a reform Clemenceau had been advocating for years. Clemenceau kept the ministry of the interior. Foreign affairs went to Stephen Pichon, the only parliamentary follower of the 1880's who had remained faithful to him after the Panama scandal. His old collaborator at *La Justice*, Camille Pelletan, was still deputy in the Chamber – he had served briefly, and disastrously, as minister of the navy in Rouvier's last government – but he was now, though a Radical, one of Clemenceau's most vicious opponents.

His most unexpected appointment was Georges Picquart as minister of war. Clemenceau's admiration for Picquart during the Dreyfus Affair had been enormous; 'Dreyfus is a victim, but Picquart is a hero,' he had remarked at the time. When Clemenceau became prime minister – only three months after Dreyfus and Picquart were reinstated into the army – he must have taken pleasure in the thought that it was in his power to play the ultimate act of the Affair, placing the man who had put his civic duties before his military duties at the army's head. It was drama to the end. Picquart, the story goes, was at that moment in Vienna about to attend a performance of *Tristan* under the direction of Gustav Mahler when a telegram arrived addressed to Berthe Zuckerkandl-Szeps: 'Please announce to General Picquart that I have named him minister of war – and that he leaves today.' The curtain had not yet risen and he left without hearing a note.

As for Clemenceau's staff at the ministry of the interior, old school mates and table companions might not have filled the top slots, but he did surround himself with people who had served him well in the past. Etienne Winter, his personal secretary, became *directeur du cabinet*, abandoning his job as director of the Institution of the Young Blind. A man who was going to be a critical aide to Clemenceau in later years, was named the under secretary of state's attaché, George Mandel. He was only twenty-one at the time but had already impressed Clemenceau through earlier contacts at *L'Aurore* (involving a favour Waldeck-Rousseau, when still in government, had done Clemenceau). One also notes that it was during Clemenceau's first ministry that Gustave Geffroy was nominated director of the national tapestry manufacturers of Les Gobelins, a rather extraordinary promotion for an art critic. But it was a sound one. Under Geffroy's administration, Les Gobelins experienced one of the most innovative periods of its centuries-long history.

Many domestic and international commentators expected Clemenceau's ministry to be rather short-lived. It was not, however, the view of the British ambassador, Sir Francis Bertie, who wrote in November, 'Clemenceau has selected as colleagues those on whom he can rely to carry out his own view. He is quite capable of being his own minister of foreign affairs and also superintending the war department. His management of the strikes showed that he is full of resource, and since he took in hand the church inventories question it has ceased to be a burning issue. As to M. Pichon, I understand that he entirely concurs in Clemenceau's views and is a capable man with common sense, and not impulsive.' Short-lived or not, there was little mistake about who was going to be running this government.

X

THE PROGRAMME that Clemenceau laid before the Chamber was ambitious, and he admitted it was so. Governments at that time had a life expectancy of eight or nine months; Clemenceau would be lucky if he realised just one or two of the items listed. But, as he said in his brief introductory address, the programme indicated the path he wanted to take so that 'everyone can assume his proper responsibility in the eyes of the country, our judge'. There would be retirement funds for labourers, a ten-hour workday, trade unions would have more rights, the Western railway lines would be nationalised (they were bankrupt), civil servants would see their professional situation enshrined in a national statute and the current chaotic system of indirect taxation would be replaced by a fairer income tax and, if need be, one on capital too. The army would be strengthened, so would the navy 'to face up to all eventualities'. After the votes were cast and counted Clemenceau knew he had the confidence of the Left and the Centre. The Socialists, who had voted against the installation of Sarrien's government, could hardly oppose these good words, so they merely abstained.

Clemenceau managed to remain in office for nearly three years, making him one of the Third Republic's exceptional survivors. It had its costs. One could draw up a long catalogue of inconsistencies between what the man in thirty-six years of opposition had demanded and what the man in government finally did. Clemenceau never denied this. In fact he was rather proud of it. 'We are in incoherence,' he remarked after Briand had accepted a particularly compromising amendment to one of his Church laws. 'It is true, we are into it up to our necks. I did not put myself there. I was put there: I am there, I will remain there.' Briand walked out of the Chamber on hearing these words, but five minutes later he and Clemenceau returned to the government bench, arm in arm; Clemenceau placed more stock in the harmony of his cabinet than in the coherence of his policies.

He was tolerant with his colleagues. He and Caillaux might one day be mortal enemies. This son of a conservative republican, this financial wizard, this solitary 'Balzacian dandy', whose head looked a bit like that of a tax inspector, had much in common with Clemenceau – similar social and cultural origins, the same independent spirit, the same refusal to bow to the powers that be – and enough petty differences to spark a hundred hatreds. But in government together they were not simply polite to one another, they were positively friends. 'Believe, my dear president, in my intense and profound affection,' Caillaux signed off in his correspondence. Clemenceau would return an 'affectionate shake of the hand'.

Pichon was always a friend. Yet one would find in Clemenceau's foreign policy some of the greatest contrasts between earlier words and later deeds. Could anyone have foreseen that the man who had opposed Gambetta on Egypt and Ferry on Tunisia and Indochina would one day be sending troops into Morocco? When the crisis came, in the summer of 1907, Clemenceau was cautious in his instructions to Pichon. 'I continue to fear entanglements,' he wrote. Don't get 'tied up in knots,' he repeatedly warned. Clemenceau was not a colonialist and his relations remained tense with the Radicals enlisted in the colonial cause, but his basic concern now was that if France did not move into Morocco, Germany would. The diplomatic environment had changed. Russia had been defeated in a brief war with Japan and there had been a revolution in Saint Petersburg. Germany's military strength continued to grow. There might be an Entente Cordiale with Britain, but British politicians were very wary of any open military commitment on the continent; Campbell-Bannerman, the prime minister, told Clemenceau that he did not think English opinion would accept it. So the Russian alliance had to be reinforced. This obliged Clemenceau to turn a blind eye on another of his liberal principles (though even in opposition he had written that 'the Russian alliance must remain without any doubt the basis of operation for our foreign policy.'). Before he even became prime minister – in fact, within the first week of being named minister of the interior – Clemenceau stated in a meeting with the Russian ambassador that international politics overrode his liberal sympathies; he would not oppose the new loans to Russia and he would do all that he could to maintain the good relations between the two countries.

Defiance of German *Machtpolitik* was perhaps the one invariable feature of Clemenceau's foreign policy. Yet Franco-German relations were never better than during Clemenceau's first ministry. Germany's earlier attempt to challenge French hegemony in North Africa, inaugurated in 1905 by the Kaiser's visit to Morocco, backfired when, at the subsequent international conference in Algeçiras, it was Germany that was isolated, not France. After Austria annexed the Balkan province of Bosnia in 1908, the Germans decided it was time to make their peace with the French and proposed an agreement over Morocco. Clemenceau's government jumped at the occasion and the agreement was signed in February 1909. Harold Nicolson, who was ambassador to Saint Petersburg at the time, remarked that the rapprochement signalled the beginning of the end of Anglo-French-Russian cooperation. It was the height of ironies that a situation like this could develop when Clemenceau, such an anglophile, was premier.

XI

As TIME wore on the Radicals divided and the Socialists became increasingly hostile. Clemenceau's room for manœuvre narrowed. But the trouble he faced at home derived not so much from the justifiable inconsistencies of his foreign policy, of his religious politics, or even from the difficult campaign he had to wage in favour of Caillaux' income tax (which he finally got through the Chamber but never managed to get past the Senate).

It was the social problem that gave him his greatest challenge, it was the 'working class'. '*Vous êtes la guerre civile!*' stormed Jaurès. 'Government of Assassins,' headlined *L'Humanité*. Clemenceau was 'dictator', a 'cop', 'Emperor of spies'. He was portrayed with a death's head, with the bloodied hands of a murderer. The extreme Left and the syndicalists learned to hate him and the tales they told have been repeated with relish by historians.

But the question Clemenceau posed after the strikes of May 1906 has still to be answered. 'Where then have I met it, this working class?'

Few would have grasped it, but there was a geographical question in there. Since the most pressing issue of the day was the competition between nations, contemporary observers almost invariably placed their analyses within the context of nations. The government's statistics were national. The analyses were national. In the articles, the books and political

debates on industrial growth and social class, the question 'where?' –
where was industry growing? where did the new industrial society live?
– was rarely posed.

Yet the regional lay-out of industry was one of the most crucial
determinants of France's fivefold increase in commodity output in
one century and it also happened to be one of the few factors which
never changed. The major industrial regions were always in the same
place. What change did occur took the form of a gradual concentration
around old poles of attraction, the North, the East, Paris and the Rhône.
But at any moment in Clemenceau's long lifetime one could have looked
across the vast rural spaces and found isolated industrial communities –
mines, factories, textile workshops, brickmakers' yards, mills, quarries –
that contributed a significant part to the nation's growth. They were there
at his birth and they were still there at his death.

These long industrial traditions were not unique to small spots in
the countryside. One could find the same phenomenon in the main
concentrations of population. There were 'industrial villages' in eastern
Paris that went back to the Middle Ages. The industrial belt around the
capital, which grew so fast in the second half of the nineteenth century, did
not spring out of nothing. Lyon and its complicated network of suburbs
and towns, which stretched northward and southward along the Saône
and the Rhône, had a long history of industrial activity. Such communities
were not immune to social tensions: conflict, in fact, partly defined their
existence and a remarkable feature was that when trouble did break out
it would frequently occur in the same place, the same quarter, the same
street, decade after decade.

The one thing French industrial communities had in common was
their capacity to accommodate the new technologies and manufacturing
procedures of the period. That is what allowed them to survive.

The way in which these new technologies were adapted is something
that is still poorly understood. Edouard Vaillant, in the long class analysis
he made in the Chamber in June 1906, argued that mechanisation involved
a concentration of wealth. It certainly did. But it also involved its dispersal.
Vaillant's proof of economic concentration lay in the growing size of
businesses. But one could use the same population censuses as Vaillant
had at his disposal to suggest that there was an opposite trend. The
average number of workers per *patron* in the industrial sector in 1896
was 4.6; it was 4.5 in 1901 and 4.4 in 1906. It was 3.2 in 1911 – and
under 3 in 1990! Averages can of course be misleading. The reality was
that in all industrial regions very large concerns, big from the day they
were founded, existed side by side with smaller firms. It was more than
a matter of coexistence. The large capital-intensive industries would turn
to the smaller labour-intensive industries for the supply of parts, tools and
precision instruments (the new automobile industry was a good example

of this). And the more durable the goods that were brought on the market, the greater the opportunity for installation, repair and general service – domain of the small labour-intensive industries: innovation was propagated through a proliferation of small shops. In some areas, technology directly contributed to the growth and dispersion of small-scale industries: electrical power freed industry from the need to locate near the sources of energy; the sewingmachine gave new life to production at home. In other areas, new technology was a product of small business: the first automobiles were built in artisanal shops.

Where did that place the 'working class'? The majority of workers evidently did not earn their living in the large factories or in the pits of the mining companies, nor was that to be the destiny of their sons and daughters. Perhaps life was no better for the men and women who worked in the smaller businesses, but it was certainly more independent. And because the economy that brought them work was regional in character, their principal concerns were regional.

As a result there was an enormous discrepancy between what the national political spokesmen for the working class said in public and what their supposed followers actually did. If the speeches and pamphlets of France's labour leaders were among the most violent in Europe, the country's workers were among the most pacific. Compared to Britain, Belgium or Germany, strikes were less frequent, they were shorter and they were smaller. The vast majority of workers never went on strike. They had their own local culture, traditions, many had their own language, a patois incomprehensible to outsiders. The regional nature of economic growth, if anything, reinforced this. Calls for a general strike could thus only work on a city-wide basis, never across the whole nation and never across a whole industry. Miners in the Loire would have nothing to do with miners in the Nord, who didn't, in their turn, show too much interest in the miners of Carmaux. It can be shown that the First of May strikes of 1906 – exceptional in so many ways – followed local rather than national lines. The national unions were so poorly financed that strikers depended on local support, in the bars, in the streets, in the neighbouring factories and workshops. Sympathy strikes were virtually unknown, even across different branches of the same company.

This preoccupation with local matters obviously affected the kind of demands workers made. While Spanish and Russian workers took to the streets to demand a change in the political regime, as Belgian, German and Italian workers struggled for voting rights and a more liberal style of government, their French brethren concentrated on an increase in wages. Money could be understood anywhere. Sixty-three per cent of the strikes in France in the first decade of the century concerned questions of pay, 25 per cent involved various problems in the conditions of work – waiters demanded the right to wear moustaches, bus conductors demanded less rudeness from their clientele – and only 16 per cent were over working hours. It was quite the reverse of what the CGT had been campaigning for.

Not surprisingly the CGT leaders, though they talked a lot about the general strike, were very wary to push it to the point of action. The problem they had with Clemenceau is that he kept on laying down the challenge.

By the time Clemenceau became prime minister the number of strikes was already on the ebb. The great surge that had started in 1904 had peaked in the May movement of 1906. It is possible that Clemenceau's tough stand had something to do with this; more likely, the syndicalists had simply reached their limit. But the less their success, the more violent their language.

In August 1906 delegates at the CGT congress voted what is known in history as the Charter of Amiens, which excluded its adherents from all alliances, even temporary, with political parties. The majority declared that the aim of syndicalist action was not to gain the odd material benefit for the working class but rather the suppression of capitalism, achieved through a strike that would lead to the Revolution.

Clemenceau's attitude regarding the general strike was very clear and could not be described as reactionary. Back in 1901 he had published an article on the subject in *Le Bloc*. He had written it at the end of a 108-day strike at Montceau-les-Mines. The most significant feature of the struggle had been the failure of the miners' call for a general strike. Clemenceau had noted how the Socialists had got caught in their own rhetoric and concluded that 'the passive insurrection of the general strike would seem to have a sure effect in theory, but everybody understands that the more the field of action is widened the more difficult it is to achieve agreement.' The chief source of friction would always be between those who wanted to strike and those who wanted to work.

He could well have said this at the end of his three years in office, for his position never changed. Clemenceau was very much aware of the local nature of social conflict, of the tension between workers and of the huge gulf which separated them from their national leaders. He was also committed to reform. He never denied the right to strike. He never wanted to outlaw the unions; when half the Chamber demanded the abolition of the CGT he defended its right to exist. He remained ready to negotiate, to offer the 'armistices and provisional treaties' – one notes enormous efforts at conciliation made at the outset of most major strikes. But when there was violence, he repressed it.

His approach was always the same. Consider the difficult case of the civil servants. Were they workers like the rest? Did they have the right to form unions and go on strike? It was a burning issue before the war.

The newspapers expended much printers' ink on the subject. The visitors' gallery was always filled to capacity whenever the Chamber debated the matter. Postal workers and primary school teachers were the most vocal contenders for union rights and it was their growing influence over other civil servants that led Sarrien's government, and then Clemenceau's, to propose a *statut des fonctionnaires* which would once and for all end the ambiguities and give every civil servant a clear guideline of his rights and restrictions. Unfortunately, like the bureaucracy it was designed to serve, the bill became cumbersome and unseemly as it waltzed between one parliamentary committee and another. In the end, the *statut des fonctionnaires* turned out to be more a cause of frustration than a solution.

Clemenceau never questioned the right of civil servants to form professional associations but he refused to recognise a minority demand for affiliation with the CGT. He argued, not unreasonably, that servants of the state could not be allowed to join an organisation that openly proclaimed its intention to destroy the state. None the less, he was ready to discuss his position with those who wanted to join. Thus, in February 1907, when a group of primary school teachers from Paris and Lyon declared their intention to seek affiliation with the CGT, he invited a delegation to the ministry. Clemenceau said that a teachers' union was a fine idea but that membership of the CGT was not. In April he published an open letter laying out all the advantages civil servants had over workers in the private sector – security, fixed wages, pensions – adding that the prohibition on a CGT affiliation was a small price to pay. But the postal and teachers' unions insisted, publishing their aims in a manifesto. As a result, the secretary of the teachers' union and five postmen lost their jobs.

It would have been a minor affair had not the Socialists and a group of dissident Radicals, including old friend Camille Pelletan, decided to unite around the issue and use it as a challenge to the government. It was the first clear break that the Socialists made with the government Radicals, it was the first time Jaurès directly accused Clemenceau of being a reactionary. Pelletan commented that the country was under a government more oppressive than the Empire.

In March 1909 the postmen in Paris went on strike over a personnel problem involving the under-secretary of state at the ministry of posts and telegrams. Clemenceau started negotiating again, actually inviting a delegation of strikers to his flat on rue Franklin. The conservative press was furious, but the strikers returned to work. However, two months later it was all blown up into a national political issue once again, with Socialists joining dissident Radicals in a challenge to the government. The government won with an easy majority. In the meantime, the postal union called public meetings in Paris, Lyon, Rouen and several other large towns and another strike broke out. It was most widespread in Paris; in the rest of the country there was only a random following. The CGT called for

a general strike, a sure sign that that support was abating, and within a
week everyone was back at work.

XII

THE TWO other major strike movements during Clemenceau's first
ministry were exceptional by anyone's standards.

The first, and by far the more serious, involved the small winegrowers
of Lower Languedoc. Politics in this region revolved around a resentment
of Paris that was rooted in a peculiar mixture of local myths and memories.
Even today one gets the impression that people here have still not forgiven
Simon de Montfort and Louis VIII for the massacres of Béziers and
Montségur, the destruction of Occitania's troubadour civilisation and its
annexation to France.

This had also been another old industrial region. But in the nineteenth
century, with the development of railways, Languedoc switched to the
production of wine because vineyards turned out to be cheaper than
textile factories. That itself was an old game. For centuries one could
follow the cycle by which local resources were transferred from agriculture
to industry and back to agriculture again. The changeovers had never been
peaceful. Nor were they this time. In the 1870's and 1880's phylloxera
devastated the region and the crisis was of course blamed on Paris. The
diseased vines were grubbed up and replaced with American vinestocks
that had higher yields; so now the problem was overproduction, though
the locals said it was fraud and blamed it all on Paris again. Wine prices
fell between 1904 and 1906 to about a fifth of their normal level. The value
of land tumbled.

Socialist leaders had long spoken about the transformation of peasants
into proletarians. Languedoc was the only area in rural France where this
had an element of truth. The winegrowers, with their tiny plots, had
become dependent on middlemen (who bore the brunt of the accusations
of fraud). There was a larger proportion of landless labourers in the
agricultural population than in any other part of the country. The poverty
was terrible and was getting worse. Proud smallholders donned masks and
went begging.

On Sundays, in March and April 1907, they could have heard at
the mass meetings called in villages and small towns by the Comités
de Défense Viticole a message of hope delivered by Marcelin Albert, a

former actor who had bought a small vineyard at Argeliers, had settled down there and opened a bar. They called him the 'Redeemer'. Town squares were filled and so were the streets leading into them, people climbed trees, walls and roofs to catch a glimpse of him, the crowds ranging between a quarter and half a million. *Curés* proclaimed that the movement harbingered the Second Coming. Monarchists declared it was the end of the Republic. Socialists argued that it was the collapse of capitalism. Placards in the crowd read 'Death to Clemenceau' and a movement got under way to stop paying taxes to the French colonisers. Many of the local elected officials tried to benefit from the movement, egging it on, promising their support; the most notable of these was Dr Ferroul, the bearded Socialist mayor of Narbonne.

Clemenceau's response was the same as always: first negotiate. He ordered the prefects to open up a dialogue with the demonstrators and legislation was prepared to control fraud in wines.

But tensions over the tax issue and various acts of violence led to the mass resignations of municipal councils, to the point that about a third of the communes of the Aude, Hérault and Pyrénées-Orientales had no administration at all. Clemenceau was obliged to send the troops in. Out of fear of mutiny, the locally recruited 17th infantry regiment was moved from its barracks at Béziers to an out-of-the-way coastal town, Agde. Crowds besieged the sub-prefecture of Narbonne and the prefecture of Perpignan. Three members of the Argeliers Comité de Défense Viticole were arrested along with Dr Ferroul. Albert went into hiding.

By 20 June the whole region was in a state of insurrection. Crowds marched on Agde, broke down the door of the barracks and, joined by about three hundred soldiers, then took the road west for Narbonne 'to kill the cavalrymen'. The mutineers stopped at Béziers where they were housed and fed by sympathetic inhabitants. In the meantime the Hôtel de Ville at Perpignan was attacked and partially burnt down and a gunfight broke out in the streets of Narbonne, leaving four demonstrators dead and many wounded on both sides.

The Socialists led a storm of protest in the Chamber. Jaurès accused the prime minister of first encouraging the movement and then repressing it and concluded with the most famous indictment ever made of Clemenceau. 'You are the living contradiction . . .' You, he said, 'by your contradictory suddennesses, by the mixture of your brutalities and your weaknesses, you have now refused yourself words of appeasement and measures of wisdom.' You, he accused, have lost 'the liberty of action to bring to this people a word of appeasement. This liberty you no longer have; you are necessarily the civil war.'

Humanity was on the side of Jaurès that day and he received applause not only from the extreme Left, but also from some in the Centre and almost all of the Right. That combination of Left and Right had once been used by Clemenceau. But the government held with a confidence vote of 328 to 227.

Two days later the fugitive Albert, with a suitcase in his hand, turned up at the ministry of the interior and asked if he could see the prime minister. The request was granted. Albert, a diminutive figure, was shown to a rather low easy-chair and Clemenceau, standing, delivered a long lecture on the disastrous effects of the movement. Albert burst into tears, saying that he had never intended to cause harm or incite violence. Clemenceau told Albert that he would have to return home to his village and surrender to the police – but first, please, tell your friends to disperse and place a bit more trust in the government which is doing everything it can to solve these dreadful economic problems. Do you have enough money for the return train? No. Clemenceau handed Albert a hundred francs.

Albert, in a chauffeur driven motor car with an open roof, was followed by a horde of reporters through the streets of Paris to the station; as many as could remained with him on the train down to Languedoc. There he told his supporters of his meeting with Clemenceau, not forgetting the detail of the hundred francs. It was the end of the 'Redeemer' and the movement collapsed.

Before the month was out, the government promulgated its new law on fraud, setting the French wine industry on a course of classifications and controls that have made it the envy of the world. Prefects were given orders to show lenience in the collection of taxes that year. As for the 17th Regiment, it was transferred to southern Tunisia; but most of the troops were near the end of their service and there were no individual convictions. The trouble was over. Wine prices were better for the 1907 crop and they continued to climb for the rest of the decade. The Second Coming had not materialised and capitalism remained the order of the day.

It is possible that Clemenceau's carrot and stick – and particularly his carrot – did incite conflict. Aristide Briand, who succeeded Clemenceau as prime minister and is generally considered more conciliatory, had to deal with higher strike rates than Clemenceau's ministry. The Popular Front of 1936, another conciliatory regime, also witnessed a wave of intense strike activity. But it is difficult to conceive how any government committed to social reform and peace, so often at odds in practice, could have proceeded otherwise. At any rate, with the second major strike movement of his ministry, where he came into a head-on conflict with the CGT, Clemenceau played the same blend of rigour and moderation that had marked his earlier actions. For the CGT he showed little mercy, for the actual strikers he was rather more compromising.

The troubles began in the gravel pits that stretched along the sides of the Seine a few kilometres upstream from Paris. Boating marinas and pleasure parks have replaced most of these pits today. But in those days you could have found tens of thousands of men earning a living by dragging the river bed, collecting the slag – often up to their knees in water – or piloting the tugs and barges that brought Paris the sands it needed for its buildings, its monuments and, most especially, its new underground railway. They were unskilled labourers, at the bottom of the wage scale, their hours were long and their first concern was probably not the date of the next Revolution; they simply wanted to be a bit better off, a bit more respected, a bit more like others. They had begun to take action to improve their lot and, because their demands were limited, had won. So they organised a union. This attracted the experts in Paris.

The building industry in Paris had been in a state of constant turmoil since the strike of May 1906. Builders provided the main battalions of the May movement, their strike had lasted the longest, but they had nothing to show for it, not a sou. In spite of this – and perhaps because of this – their Fédération was the most militant branch of the CGT.

A new strike broke out in May 1908 in the gravel pits of Seine-et-Oise, under the auspices of the workers' own recently organised local union. Every quarry in the area was drawn into the combat. This time, the workers demanded a twenty per cent increase in pay, fewer hours, overtime, the abolition of piece rates and recognition of their union. The employers responded by setting up their special association under the stone-hearted directorship of the brothers Picketty. Lines hardened. Divisions developed. Some hungry workers went back to work. Strikers conducted a *chasse aux renards*, or 'fox hunt'. There was violence at the Charvet docks and at Villeneuve-Triage. At the Ablon locks, a band of pistol-packing men waylaid a tug and its barge. Four *renards* were taken by force from the Grousselle quarries and carried off to strike headquarters in the ballroom of the Café du Progrès, at Vigneux. Police had to force their way into the building to free the four men. Did they have a warrant? Nobody thought of asking. On the morning of 2 June police came under attack twice by strikers hunting *renards*. One of the police was seriously wounded; there was a lot of emotion in the police station when somebody looked out the window and saw the aggressor walking past with a group of strikers. They decided on an arrest. The aggressor decided it was a nice time to take a drink. The ballroom of the Café du Progrès, and strike headquarters, was on private premises and the police did not have a warrant. But they went ahead anyway. Both sides were flailing pistols. In the mêlée that ensued, two strikers were shot dead. Was it legitimate defence? The strikers spoke of a planned massacre, the police of being harried by marauding bands of club-bearing workers. They were all frightened, angry men.

But the syndicalist and socialist press had no difficulty in finding who was really responsible. It was not the strikers, it was not the police, not the prefect, not the company management, not even the brothers Picketty.

It was Clemenceau-le-rouge, Clemenceau-le-tueur. Maurice Allard in *L'Humanité* wrote that 'the Clemenceau ministry cannot live without corpses. It needs them.' *La Voix du peuple* ran the headline, 'Yet another Clemencist crime'. The CGT plastered all over Paris posters denouncing the 'government of assassins'.

The CGT had just committed its first tactical error – for after such denunciation it was obliged to take action, and the action it had been talking about for the last six years had been the general strike. Only the previous April, in an article published in *L'Action directe*, General Secretary Griffuelhes had reminded his troops of its instructive values: 'The strike, wielded in the hands of a working class strengthened by its struggles, thanks to powerful and active unions, can do more than the whole content of libraries; it educates, it mobilises for war, it drives and it creates.'

The education and creative drive were to begin with the two funerals at Villeneuve-le-Roi. They were attended by over four thousand, of which fewer than a thousand were locals, the rest being brought in by train from Paris. Not even the union leaders denied that many carried Browning revolvers. To the cries of 'Down with the capitalists!' windows were smashed, lampposts torn up, private gardens destroyed, cars attacked. Then, on 6 June, the Fédération du Bâtiment held a grand meeting in Paris for the declaration of the general strike.

But they hesitated. It was finally decided that the date of the strike would be set only after Clemenceau-le-tueur had responded to an interpellation due in the Chamber on 11 June. It was somehow hoped that he would admit his errors and the strike could then, with some relief, be called off.

Clemenceau had, of course, no such thing in mind and he delivered one of the severest speeches of his career, defending the police and harshly criticising the violence of the strikers. He ended by asking the Chamber 'if it wants to create with us the legal order for reforms as opposed to revolution. That is the programme which the government presents it'; and the Chamber responded with a confidence vote of 429 to 63. It was a gauntlet thrown in the face of the CGT.

Among the many documents that Clemenceau consulted in preparing this speech – a dossier which has been preserved at the Archives Nationales – was a report presented to him by the prefecture of police on 9 June. It outlined the difficulties the CGT would encounter if forced to carry out its threat of a general strike. It painted a picture of labouring groups in Paris, of little sovereign entities, of competition, jealousies and personal rivalries, reminiscent of the red clubs of the Commune and the radical clubs of Boulanger's day. The lack of a strong centre was, in fact, one of the main reasons for the violent talk of revolutionary syndicalism; it was the child of olden Parisian anarchies and rhetoric, something Clemenceau understood only too well.

So Clemenceau called the CGT's bluff. At the same time, out of sight of publicity, he ordered that negotiations be undertaken, through the mediation of the prefect, to bring the gravel pits strikes to an end. The two sides met in the mairie of Villeneuve-Saint-Georges and were at the point of settlement when Ricordeau, delegate of the Fédération du Bâtiment, intervened.

The sabotaging of the talks was strongly resented, not only by the locals, but within the Fédération itself, and an attempt was made to replace Ricordeau with the more moderate Poignat. But it was too late. The employers' position hardened. Brothers Picketty threatened a lock out. The *chasses aux renards* started up again. Some strikers set fire to material at the Lavollay quarry and five arrests were made, including that of Ricordeau and of a mysterious character by the name of Luc Métivier. He claimed he was general secretary of the biscuit-makers' confederation; in fact he was a police spy – and had actually had a private interview with the prime minister on 20 May. When this was revealed years later, Clemenceau claimed that Métivier's 'services' to the Sûreté Générale had been most irregular.

Provoked or not, the arrests forced the CGT leaders to call a general strike. On the morning of 30 June the working class – about three thousand recruits of the Fédération du Bâtiment, along with most of the CGT leaders – boarded trains at the gare de Lyon and headed down to Villeneuve-Saint-Georges. There they were joined by a few locals in a mass meeting on the main street. Some revolver shots went off (the CGT later claimed that it was Clemenceau's agents at work again). The dragoons charged. Barricades went up. Bayonets were drawn. Gun muzzles were bared. The troops fired blanks. The demonstrators fired pistols. The troops retorted with bullets. Seventy soldiers were wounded. Four demonstrators were killed.

Charles Maurras in his new daily, *L'Action française*, compared the 'old man' of the government to the sinister figure of Thiers during the Commune. So did Camille Pelletan in *La Dépêche de Toulouse*, a paper to which Clemenceau used regularly to contribute. *L'Humanité* spoke of Clemenceau as 'the man with the death's head'. *La Voix du peuple* claimed he had planned it all 'machiavelically'.

Arrest warrants were released. But the arrests were delayed. The seven of the principal leaders of the CGT, including Griffuelhes, were not taken into custody until dawn on 1 August. This gave them time to announce another general strike for Monday, 3 August.

It was effectively the end of revolutionary syndicalism. The strike was a total fiasco and the CGT had lost its leaders. At its Marseille congress in October there was a distinctive swing to reformist policies.

When Griffuelhes and his comrades were released, without charges, a few days later, they discovered they had lost their following. The next year Léon Jouhaux, a moderate, was elected general secretary, a position he was to hold for thirty-eight years. Clemenceau's hard line with the CGT was clearly a success. In February 1909 he asked the Chamber for an amnesty for all those still facing charges. It was immediately voted.

As for the strikers of Seine-et-Oise, they were all back at work by 4 August 1908 having won some material gains, though less than had been offered at the mayor's office in May. They were probably the real victims of this political affair. But the blame could hardly be placed on Clemenceau.

There were strikes under later governments that were just as brutal as those that occurred during Clemenceau's time in office. Under Briand there was an extensive railway strike in 1910. Under Ernest Monis there was a winegrowers' revolt in Champagne country, during which the whole department of the Marne was occupied by soldiers. But none of these strikes could be compared to the violence experienced in southern Wales in 1910 and 1911, to the fighting that occurred during strikes of British dockers and railway workers in 1911, or to the battles that took place in the Ruhr mines in 1912. Generally speaking, the French were not particularly violent at this time.

The incidence of strikes declined dramatically under Clemenceau's premiership. In 1909 there were 20 per cent fewer strikes and 64 per cent fewer strikers than there had been in 1906. The figures are even more dramatic if one takes the year 1908, his last full year in office. This was not just the product of repression. Arbitration and collective bargaining became the order of the day. Indeed, a very good argument could be made that arbitration began in earnest in France under Clemenceau. Collective bargaining spread to every major industrial sector except metallurgy. Unions that had formerly rejected it as against the principle of class war, openly espoused it by 1909.

But many politicians were unforgiving. Clemenceau summed up his dilemma before the Chamber on 12 July 1909, during another mammoth debate on the general policies of his government. 'If we are generous,' he said, 'we are weak, we have capitulated. If we repress, we are brutal, we are savages. And if we mix conciliation with repression, we are incoherent.' It was the predicament every man in government had to confront. Clemenceau's problem was that he did it with eloquence and with success, and was hated for it. Generations of the political Left would remember him as Clemenceau-le-rouge, Clemenceau-le-tueur.

XIII

WHILE HE bargained with the postmen, teachers, masons, bricklayers and gravel-pit diggers, another hatred was brewing in the political ranks. In March 1909 the Chamber had set up a committee of inquiry into certain discrepancies that had appeared in the naval budget. It was chaired by Théophile Delcassé.

Delcassé was a very powerful man. During his seven years at the ministry of foreign affairs he had filled all the major diplomatic posts with his own men – Barrère at Rome, the two Cambon brothers at London and Berlin, Jusserand at Washington – and had befriended a number of members of parliament. Clemenceau was not one of them. Delcassé was an old Opportunist and was temperamentally quite the opposite of Clemenceau. Furthermore, at the outset of his term at the ministry, in the 1890's, he had refused to appoint Clemenceau's dear old friend, the comte d'Aunay, to an ambassadorial post. For a long time, their resentments just simmered. Clemenceau could never attack Delcassé while he was minister because on foreign policy they basically agreed: in the face of German military growth, Delcassé wanted to strengthen ties with Russia, Italy and Britain. But their style was different. Delcassé was a master of what a later generation would call 'brinkmanship' and on two occasions – with Britain over Fashoda in 1898 and with Germany over Morocco in 1905 – had brought France to a point of war. Clemenceau, working through Pichon, proved to be far more conciliatory.

Once Delcassé had resigned over the Moroccan affair (in June 1905), Clemenceau became much more openly critical, publishing a series of articles in L'Aurore on the 'dangerous' Delcassé and his more 'courageous' prime minister, Rouvier. He even seems to have envisaged publishing the articles in book form, as he had done in the case of the Dreyfus Affair, but had to abandon the project as too hazardous when he himself entered the government in 1906.

Delcassé made no secret of the fact that he intended to use his position on the naval committee to create difficulties for Clemenceau. It was set up at precisely the moment Clemenceau was receiving strong conservative criticism for negotiating with the postal strikers.

The great paradox of Clemenceau's first ministry, in the light of his second (he came to office in 1917), was not only its conciliatory attitude towards Germany but also the fact that, during its term, French military strength probably weakened. A law of 1905 had reduced military service from three to two years. It came into effect just as Clemenceau became prime minister. To be fair to those recruited under the old law he decided

to release *all* conscripts after two years of service. The result was that for
the next couple of years the French army was seriously undermanned. At
the same time, the navy was suffering from an ongoing dispute between
officers over how the fleet should be equipped; the old school believed in big
battleships, the new school wanted submarines and cruisers. Clemenceau's
own understanding of naval forces was summed up in an interview he had
with the journalist Wickham Steed in which he argued that all Britain
could do in the case of war, if it continued to concentrate on sea-power,
would be to make 'a nice hole in the water'. French naval confidence was
not helped when in early 1907 a battleship accidentally blew up, killing
several men.

Delcassé came to the Chamber well prepared, taking advantage of the fact
that parliament remained in session after the holiday of 14 July. The debate
on the government's general policies had ended on the 15th with a vote
of confidence of 331 to 147, and 176 deputies, most of them government
supporters, promptly jumped on a boat for Scandinavia to attend a peace
congress, convinced that Clemenceau would remain in office until at least
the next elections.

Delcassé's speech, delivered only five days later, was an indictment of
Clemenceau's handling of naval affairs both as premier and as president
of a Senate naval committee in 1904 and 1905. Clemenceau replied that
Delcassé, who had been minister at the time, was hardly qualified to speak
about the state of the nation's defence.

Delcassé's face turned white, his lips pursed, his hands fell flat on the
podium: 'You have heard what he has said: on matters of the navy I do not
have the qualifications to speak!' This cheered up a lot of men on the Right
and Centre – there was a feast of hatreds here; old indignities, old wounds,
long-suppressed urges to get even. 'Thank you, Monsieur le président du
conseil, you have made me twenty-four years younger, you have taken me
back to that famous session of March 1885 in which were exploited, in a
manner as efficient as it was inglorious, the false dispatch and the false
disaster of Lang Son.' Delcassé was now getting applause from Left, Right
and Centre. 'Ah, I don't have the qualifications to speak of the navy!'

'I did not say that,' retorted Clemenceau.

'Oh, you said it! I didn't get your exact words, but that was certainly
their sense.'

'I was speaking of preparation for national defence.'

'I'll come to that, Monsieur le président du conseil.' He never did. His
fury pressed him into a ramping crescendo. You could hear a Déroulède
in this voice. 'For three years I have kept quiet, I have said nothing . . .'
Back he came again to 1885: 'I don't have the qualifications to speak of
the navy! I saw the moment coming when Monsieur le président du conseil

was going to cry at me like he did twenty-five years ago at his predecessor Jules Ferry: "Go, we no longer know you, we do not want to discuss with you the great interests of the nation." He held his tongue. Monsieur le président du conseil had the feeling, this time, that his lethal curse would lack its effect, that, whatever happened, I would not bend . . .'

Clemenceau complained that Delcassé was wasting the Chamber's time by harping on personal ill-feelings. Several members on the Right and the extreme Left cried out, 'You were the one who started it!' Deputy Louis Dumont of the Drôme: 'This is your usual method!'

'Messieurs,' insisted Clemenceau, 'don't be in too much of a hurry to run to the aid of Monsieur Delcassé.' He wasn't going to let the Chamber think he had lost his ability to throw lethal curses, and he wasn't going to let anyone forget Monsieur Delcassé's own record on national defence. 'You led us to the gates of war and you had made no military preparation.' There were stirrings at every point on the great half circle. 'You know it, everyone knows it, all Europe knows it, that at that very moment the ministers of war and of the navy, when asked, replied that we were not ready.' There was a disgruntled clatter. 'I know for myself that at that time I was running a campaign in the press which brought me the unanimous thanks of all patriots, and I also know that, in the foreign policy we've pursued, we have won the right to look at our adversaries with pride, that I have never humiliated France: and I say, Monsieur Delcassé humiliated it.'

Now there was total chaos. Deputies howled and banged and ranted, 'The vote! The vote!'

The session was suspended. The votes were counted. 176 supported the government, 212 sent it packing.

Clemenceau walked swiftly out of the Chamber, followed by all his ministers.

The extreme Left, the Centre and the Right cheered.

Jules Delahaye, veteran nationalist, sounded out the anti-Dreyfusard salute, 'Long live France! Long live the navy!'

The marquis de Pomeren shouted, 'Justice is done!'

So ended the second longest government of the Third Republic. It had lasted just over a thousand days.

XIV

OUTSIDE THE legislative palace there lay a city that had not changed much since Ferry's days. In spite of the tramways, the métro and the automobiles, Paris remained a walkers' town. Thiers' fortifications, crammed with makeshift huts and vegetable gardens, set limits to growth; an energetic man could reach every major site in the capital by foot. Clemenceau was a walker. Jaurès was a walker. Humble or famous, all Parisians were walkers. On a sunny day, you might have descended a deserted side-street on your way to a park. The windows of the houses, in summer, were always open so you would catch the echo from invisible rooms of clattering plates, the gurgle of wine and water, the sucking of fingers, the orders from mother, the retort of the son; the sounds of the French at lunch.

From a distance, the throng of walkers in the park, with their parasols, wide hats and bustles, might have had the look of swarming butterflies, all drawn to something in one corner; an enormous mechanically operated barrel-organ, thumping out the melody of a popular march. Its nameboard, painted in browns and yellows and greens, would list the fantastic collection of instruments that the Frères Liminaire had assembled: four bass trombones, nine accompaniments, thirteen violins, ten flageolets, ten trumpets, two drums, a pair of cymbals. You too, like the others, could be drawn under its spell, working your way through the milling gay faces, broad smiles, top hats and the flutter of light spangled ribbons of silk and of gauze. Only the old men sat it out, on a nearby bench, to struggle with their grubbiness and the odours of age. An elderly lady stood in a corner proud and alone. And there was one young mother not like the rest, unaware of the music and untouched by the carnival spirit that pervaded the air. But, lifting her face, she too smiled, took her child in her arms, carried him forward to the mechanical band and there, to the beat of the drum and the clash of the cymbals, turned and turned and turned and turned . . . the sun threw its light on the back of her neck, on the twist of her hair, her forehead, her back, her face again and her eyes full of tears.

In the second arrondissement, not far from the Bourse, the newpapermen were still plying their trade. Every day at noon and every evening after six they filled the cafés and café-restaurants of rue Montmartre to hobnob with old colleagues or chatter with the young. The politicians walked here to maintain their links with the press. There were also people who came to the rue Montmartre just to catch a glimpse of the most famous newsmakers – and the doorman at *L'Humanité* would have thought nothing about the tall, trimly dressed young man who asked him to point out the *patron*, Jean Jaurès, as he stepped from the offices for a dinner with friends: Why yes, Monsieur, that's him. At the Café du Croissant, Jaurès always sat in the same place, right by the window, at a long table, between his companions. He would take his work with him. His briefcase was always stuffed with papers, and on top of the briefcase there would be another pile of notes.

Jaurés was studying plans for a general strike, a general strike not across a whole industry or even the nation, but across the entire continent of Europe, a general strike against war, a strike for peace.

Outside the window a tyre burst, or that is what witnesses said it sounded like. Oddly, it burst again, and immediately the mirror opposite shattered. There was a second of silence and then all hell broke loose.

'Somebody's shot at the mirror!' 'Who?' 'Where?' 'It came from the street.'

Everybody stood up. Everybody except Jaurès, who remained calm, seated; he bent down to pick something up.

'They've shot Jaurès!'

The news flashed across Paris like lightning. Within minutes there were criers on the streets. In the cinemas, films were interrupted, musicians stopped playing and the announcement projected on the silver screens. Crowds filled the boulevards. 'Jaurès assassinated!' 'Jaurès dead!'

Some patriots celebrated openly. But no one could seriously question the sincerity of his effort or the nobility of his ideal. The problem lay more in the illusion. Jean Jaurès had died tragically on the last day of July, 1914, for an international proletariat that did not exist, and it never had.

CHAPTER NINE

War

IN THE FIRST week of September the signs could still be found, in Paris, of the excitement that had swept the city a month earlier, of that outrage at German aggression, of the confidence of every patriot and the assurance that the soldiers would soon be back home. 'Managers and employees under the flags! Long live France!' was stuck to a shop window: the class war had apparently ended. 'Closed on account of the mobilisation': it was as if the owner was just off for his August holiday. Familiar placards on the ground floor of a few bourgeois homes had gone through a change: 'The concierge is in the stairway', it used to read; an unskilled hand had scratched the last three words out and scribbled 'on the front'. 'Sleep in peace', you saw on a door in rue Miromesnil, 'the mattress-maker is on the frontier' – and for sure he expected to be soon across it.

But the notices were looking a bit tattered now. And many of the streets were empty. The shutters of the apartments were closed. The metro had slowed down. The buses were not running. Several hundred taxis had been requisitioned by the military governor, General Joseph Gallieni (old hero of Bazeilles in the Sedan campaign).

The government was in Bordeaux and so were many of the leading newspapermen, including Clemenceau, whose *Homme libre*, founded one year before, was running his daily comments on the events . . . or at least, what little he could gather on the events.

For there was very little news available. Whereas the Franco-Prussian War had spawned a hundred new newspapers, the outbreak of hostilities in 1914 had had the opposite effect: the authorities decided that this time the German High Command would not be turning to the French press for the latest movements of the Republic's armed forces. There would be no Vallès and no Rochefort in this war. Several of the major national papers – like *L'Aurore*, *La Petite République*, *Gil Blas*, *La Cocarde* – disappeared simply because the print shops and the editors' offices were emptied of personnel. Most of those that survived reduced their length to just two pages, pages that were filled with distortions, *le bourrage de crâne*, 'brainwashing'.

Late in August an official bulletin had haplessly announced, 'Situation unchanged from the Somme to the Vosges.' The Somme? Some tried to read this as 'Situation unchanged on the summit [*le sommet*] of the Vosges'. After all, reports up until then were saying that the French were in Alsace and hinted that they were fighting it out with the Germans in brave little Belgium. But the Somme indeed it was. On 30 August a German 'Taube' puttered across the blue skies, unopposed and dropped five bombs on rue Albany and quai Valmy along with a huge flag reading, '*Les Allemands seront à Paris dans trois jours*'. By the first days of September the press was reproducing large maps of Paris designed to prove that 'Fortress Paris' was the best defended city in Europe: so it would be another siege!

Within a week around half a million Parisians, or a sixth of the city's population, had fled south or west. Their departure was partly offset by a huge influx of refugees, mostly from Belgium. Many of them arrived with just the clothes they were wearing, some with a small suitcase, others pushing a pram. They were herded into the Cirque d'Hiver where an army of volunteer women tended to their immediate needs. The Parisians, in these early days, welcomed them all.

That sinister war was not so far distant. The eternal tokens were already on show. Every war, it seemed, had its crowds. Every major battle, it appeared, found a civilian response in the capital. But the 'sun of the Marne' was not like the sun of the Fourth of September. This time, no one was calling for '*la déchéance!*' There was no parliament in session to hear the citizens' pleas, there was no government present to overthrow. You walked the streets for news. You stood in queues for the two o'clock bulletin. In the night of Saturday to Sunday, 5–6 September, you lay awake listening to the convoys of lorries and of taxis as they rumbled eastward down the boulevards, shaking the walls, the sound reverberating in the head and smothering whatever secret dream of virtue, concord and restfulness was left to you. Paris, that Sunday morning, had a rather provincial look. The Tuileries were virtually empty. There was a throng around place de la Concorde. But the main movement was towards porte de Vincennes, beyond the two tall columns of Saint Louis and of Philip Augustus. Along the major thoroughfares you encountered requisitioned wagons and rows of horses held at the bridle by silent soldiers. Down the middle of the road strode the pedestrians, their heads held high, brandishing their hats flippantly. The thin clear air above them carried the promise of an uncertain autumn and, with it, the odd vague, volcanic burst of modern cannon.

Perhaps it was the sun of the Marne which made people think, when looking back at the weeks that had preceded the crisis, that the days were always shining. But in fact there had been rain and clouds throughout most of June and July 1914. The daily weather bulletins in the newspapers still reveal the lie: 'Paris region: overcast weather; some bright intervals in the morning and around 4 p.m.; showers at various times in the day; temperature a bit low.' It was so overcast on 22 July that even at 9 a.m. 'one could see a little thanks only to the glimmer from the shops and cafés which had turned on their lamps as if the night were approaching'. The Eiffel Tower was hidden in mist down to its first storey. It rained so hard on 15 June that part of boulevard Haussmann, near the Printemps department store, caved in. Rue Boétie also collapsed into a hole of about ten metres deep and almost fifty metres wide, thus destroying virtually the whole of place Saint-Philippe-du-Roule. The flames from the broken gas line reached the second floor of the neighbouring Crédit Lyonnais. Two days later, they were still digging out the bodies.

It was one of the major stories of June, interrupted only by the report of an assassination in Sarajevo.

On 28 June *L'Homme libre* had noted on page three that the regular Austrian military manœuvres in Bosnia were over and that the inspector of the army, 'feldzeugmestre François-Ferdinand', had expressed complete satisfaction with the proceedings. Most other papers ignored the event. But the murder by a Serbian fanatic of the feldzeugmestre and his morganatic wife was on every headline the next day, for Franz Ferdinand was also heir to the Austrian imperial throne and it would have been hard to overlook the gravity of the act: one more damned problem in the Balkans, sighed the average reader, before turning to the reports on the fantastic performance of the baron de Rothschild's horse, Sardanapale, at the Grand Prix.

Nobody thought it was war. Clemenceau continued his series of articles on proportional representation ('this scandalous enterprise against universal suffrage') and only on 1 July commented on the assassination which he described, typically, as an example of the animal in human nature – 'there will probably always be more beast than angel in our terrestrial condition.' He said the Balkans were particularly subject to 'savage encounters', praised Franz Ferdinand for his courage (though criticising him for being too 'intoxicated with medieval catholicism') and concluded with the reassurance that the Austrian Emperor, Franz Josef, was a 'guarantee to peace; after him, it's the unknown'. Jaurès, in *L'Humanité*, warned the Bosnians not to try and attach themselves to a Greater Serbia for such a state would only be the vassal of Tsarism. *Le Petit Parisien* continued its daily reporting of poisonings, shootings and adulteries in Paris and the provinces. The French press in general showed some interest in the nationalist demonstrations, subsequent to Franz Ferdinand's assassination, in the Balkans and across Austria and Germany, but by the second week of July the whole story was back to page three, or had disappeared entirely.

It would be difficult to imagine a less warlike nation than that of France in July 1914. However, as the country prepared to celebrate another Fourteenth of July – which coincided, happily, with a brief break in the cloudy weather – two issues related to war were brought to national attention. Clemenceau was involved in both of them.

The first concerned a Senate debate on the state of the armed forces. Some old ghosts put in an appearance. When Clemenceau remarked, 'Forty years ago the same situation presented itself,' he was evoking memories of the famous debate on the army in the Corps législatif of 30 June 1870. 'At that time,' he admitted, 'the Chambers did not want to hear the truth. Today, thanks to a democratic regime, you have a parliament,' though he was none too convinced that these democratic senators were any more interested in the truth. The tragedy of 1870 haunted Clemenceau. 'I saw Monsieur Thiers booed by an assembly of patriots in the process of conducting us to Sedan' – Clemenceau must have been in the visitors' gallery at the time. 'I do not want to see History repeat itself,' he told the new socialist prime minister, René Viviani, amid a chorus of protest. Yet Clemenceau was totally unaware of the most uncanny parallel with the debate of June 1870. He, like all others present – and like the participants of the 1870 debate – had absolutely no awareness that the country was only two weeks from the brink of war. There was not a single reference made, either in the two days of discussion (13 and 14 July 1914) or in the article Clemenceau published on 15 July, to the developing crisis in the Balkans.

But History was not repeating itself. The debate in the Corps législatif had been over manpower. The problem of manpower had now, by and large, been resolved (though it would become a critical issue as the death rolls came in): France had a nationally conscripted army and, only the previous year, military service had been extended from two to three years. The old polemic which opposed the authoritarian model of long-serving professionals to the revolutionary model of universal short-term service was also, by now, outdated, though there remained a fair proportion of military and political leaders who thought that republican ardour – *l'attaque à outrance* – could win a battle. Clemenceau, the Senate debate would show, was not one of them.

The question before the Senate that July was one of *matériel*, the industrial dimension of war. Charles Humbert of the Senate army committee had been preparing a report for months on the state of French armaments. He finally presented it to the Senate on what was supposed to be the last session before the summer recess, due to begin on Bastille Day. His speech lasted an hour and a half; his report was devastating, though Viviani's government could not be blamed for it had only been in office for one month. Apart from the much-vaunted 75, all French heavy artillery was based on models dating from the Franco-Prussian War. The shells were housed in hangars that were protected only by tiled roofs. Petrol depots were virtually nonexistent in such major frontier towns as Verdun and Toul.

Messimy, the minister of war, said that the minister of finance had given him the formal order to reduce expenses.

'Isn't there a president of the council to whom the minister of war can always appeal?' asked Clemenceau.

'I am obliged to tell you what the situation is,' replied Messimy.

'The truth is that we are neither defended nor governed!' There was loud applause from the Left.

'But the equipment factor,' continued Messimy as if he had not heard the remark, 'certainly has repercussions on the morale of the troops: everyone knows that the inferiority of our artillery in 1870 had a considerable effect on the morale of our army . . .' There were numerous interruptions. The History lesson was coming across poorly.

'Not only on morale,' said Clemenceau.

'For six centuries we had the same explosive,' went on Messimy, indifferent. 'The old cannon powder, discovered at the beginning of the thirteenth century . . .'

'Carry on, buy crossbows,' responded the venerable senator from the Var.

That stifled Messimy's History lesson. He paused, took a good look at the high ceiling and then blamed the whole problem on 'ministerial instability'.

Clemenceau was very concerned with the issue of morale, but it seemed to him that some people in the government had got their priorities wrong: 'What happens to the morale of an army which sees that the cannon of the enemy reach them while their own cannon cannot touch the enemy army? . . . I saw myself what happened in 1870. We are better equipped in this regard than we were then. The means factor determines the morale factor. You have reversed the problem. For you it is the morale factor which would determine the offensive factor. It cannot go on like this. Make a sign, Monsieur le Président du Conseil, tell us that you will be convoking parliament in a few days . . .' Clemenceau was casting doubts on the merits of the old revolutionary theory of *la levée en masse, l'attaque à outrance*. Parliament was convoked the next day, Bastille Day – the first time this had happened since the national holiday was proclaimed in 1880.

The issue debated in the Senate that day was not so much the state of French armaments as the role parliament had to play in the defence of the nation. 'Parliament has to intervene in an effective manner,' said Clemenceau. The Senate was presented with a choice between two motions. One, from the vice-president of the Senate army committee, Boudenoot, instructed the committee to collaborate with the government in a report that would analyse Humbert's allegations. The other, Clemenceau's, instructed the committee to conduct its own inquiry.

Clemenceau explained that his motion 'demanded the direct and formal intervention of parliament [while] Monsieur le Président du Conseil wants parliament to subordinate its action to Monsieur le Ministre de la Guerre'.

Clemenceau got the applause but Boudenoot's motion won the vote after Viviani assured the assembly that there would never be a repeat of the 1870 debacle and that France was 'capable of honouring its history faced with whatever destiny is presented before her.'

The quality of arms, the role of parliament and the authority of government would dominate Clemenceau's thinking over the next four years.

It had been a busy Bastille Day for politicians. While the Senate was debating the state of French armaments, the Socialists were gathering in another corner of the capital in a *Congrès extraordinaire* to discuss the 'struggle against war'.

The special congress was not in any way a reaction to events in the Balkans; it was the spin-off of a campaign that had been running since 1913 against the new three-year military service, a campaign which, at moments, had all the fever of another Dreyfus Affair. Socialist successes in the legislative elections of April and early May 1914 had, if anything, intensified the debate. How should the French respond to the German army laws of 1912 and 1913 which had raised German forces from 645,000 to over 800,000? One socialist proposal – in the hallowed tradition of the *levée en masse* of 1792 and the National Guard of 1870–71 – was the formation of citizen militias. This had provoked Clemenceau to comment, in an article of 8 June 1914, that, in a confrontation between militiamen and the solid formations of the German army, Europe's fate would be decided by 'the sovereign argument of iron'. The other proposal came directly from Jaurès in the form of a resolution, at the congress, recommending an international general strike if governments started declaring war.

The response of the extreme nationalist press was vicious. Léon Daudet, in *L'Action Française*, came as close as one could to advocating Jaurès's assassination. But this kind of nationalism, directed as much against internal enemies as against Germans, was not representative of opinion as a whole and had no influence in governing circles. Most of the press was incredulous. Maxime Vuillaume wrote in *L'Aurore*, 'The resolutions of the socialist congress should frighten no one. They are, in our opinion, pure form. Nobody believes that a general strike can, at a given moment, and especially at the time of a declaration of war between two or several peoples, be simultaneous. The current state of Europe forbids all hope on this matter.' 'The only thing wrong with the general strike in the case of war,' wrote the editorialist of *La Lanterne*, 'is that it cannot be realised.'

The strike resolution started off another debate – the last – between

Clemenceau in *L'Homme libre* and Jaurès in *L'Humanité*. Clemenceau reproached Jaurès for his utter 'ignorance of human nature'. 'Here are two people ready to throw themselves on one another . . .' A 'long historical education' has taught them to be prepared to sacrifice their lives. Then along comes 'M. Jaurès, animated, more than anyone can be, by a professor's spirit,' to announce that 'his study of history brings him to this conclusion that, if all the students of the class (the word is here in season) only obey the sign of the pedagogue, there will be at once a coordinated gymnastic movement at which all the people of the planet will marvel.' One cannot turn the other cheek in this world, continued Clemenceau. And recalling his comments of the 1880's on 'convents and barracks' socialism he taunted, 'To the convent, to the silence of cloisters, noble heroes of this idea that is so little new. Your place is not in the tormented life of men . . . Disappear from the living world. Go and bury yourselves in the shadow of cells.'

Within the fortnight Jaurès was dead and the Germans were marching into Belgium. 'A miserable fool assassinated Jaurès,' commented Clemenceau. 'Whatever opinion one might have of his doctrines, he honoured his country with his talent.'

The war was a total surprise. It had been far from the mind of a crowd that swelled, on a patriotic Fourteenth, in the stands of Longchamp at the sight of the Republican Guard, the three engineering regiments, the two brigades of dragoons and the cuirassiers. Like every year, nobody thought for a moment that this was an army designed for killing people. The military cyclists were a novelty. The procession of ambulance dogs interested a lot of spectators – 'They are beautiful creatures,' remarked *Le Petit Parisien*, 'but, although French soldiers, they are, it appears, of German and Belgian origin.' On every corner of every street couples danced that evening the waltz, the polka or the tango to the sound of bands, pianos, organs; even a phonograph, with its huge horn, competed with the noise from the sill of a first-floor window.

There was not a sign of alarm on the frontiers. On 16 July a small French military biplane was blown off course and forced to land just north of Mulhouse in German Alsace. After a pleasant lunch with the district governor, the crew returned to France.

Poor Joseph Caillaux' wife went on trial at the Palais de Justice in the last week of July for shooting dead the director of *Le Figaro*, Gaston Calmette. The hearing was full of salacious details about Caillaux' private life and was infinitely more interesting than the story about 'Austro-Serbian difficulties' tucked away on page three. There, an anonymous reporter in Belgrade announced that an Austrian note was about to be sent to the Serbian government which, 'from reliable sources', was not going to be 'very conciliatory'. The story only reached the headlines on Saturday, 26 July. Austria declared war on Serbia the following Wednesday, the same day Madame Caillaux was acquitted. Most papers devoted more space to Madame Caillaux. But within seven days virtually the whole continent of Europe was at war.

A war that surpassed all understanding, all efforts to describe, to plan. Indeed, there was not a single military plan in that war which was carried off successfully.

'With the men gone, who will finish the harvest?' 'Will they be back, at least, to pick the grapes?' The Third Republic's army was an army of peasants. The hero of Reymond Escholier's *Le Sel de la Terre* fingers through the squad lists in the office of his company: 'And this is what he saw, bracketed implacably to each combatant's name, this simple word, large as the earth: "*cultivateur*".' The label applied to something between 75 and 80 per cent of the combatants from one end of the war to the other. They were men who had not been exposed to the prides and the prejudices of the city, to its organised labour, to its propaganda: they accepted the war as their fate, like a storm of hail, one of God's mysterious acts – and so did their women. 'Honour to the women,' wrote the curé de Gets in Haute-Savoie. But the harvests were not gay and the grape gathering of October had lost all its usual delight. 'The grape harvests have not suffered,' noted an *instituteur* from the Gard, but they 'do not in any way resemble those of previous years: no bursts of laughter, no dirty jokes, no dancing in the shadow of trees to the sound of the clarinet or the oboe: all is silent. One talks of the war, one reads the newspapers aloud at mealtimes . . .'

And the men marched. They wore the newly designed uniform that Messimy had presented, with the help of two smart male models, to the Chamber's army committee on 1 July. The dark blue jacket now had tails that reached the calf. The red pantaloons would be maintained because the rural economy in southern France depended on them: 'We have to save the Southern madder which no longer finds any buyers.' When it was remarked in November that more than half the casualties among infantry were due to head wounds Colonel Pénélon proposed replacing the képi with metal helmets; 'My friend,' replied General Joffre, 'we will not have the time to manufacture them for I will have wrung the Boches within two months.'

Past the level-crossing keepers' little red houses, their cellars filled with petrol tins of water, past the open fields of wheat and of barley dabbed in poppy, cornflower and bull-daisy, past windmills with their swinging sails that drove off thought and reason, the soldiers marched in file down tiny rural tracks, their throats parched, their stomachs empty and their feet in absolute agony. 'We are ordered: "Go there." And we go there. We are ordered: "Attack." And we attack. During the battle, at least, we know that we are fighting. But after that? Often it is a fusillade nearby, the shells tumbling in an avalanche announcing the imminence of the storm. And once we have fought, the movements begin again, the roving marches, the advances, the retreats, the halts, the formations, the manœuvres . . .' So Maurice Genevoix remembered his first months of war. '*On se fout de nous*,' groaned the soldiers. 'They repeat, throwing their packs over their shoulders with an aggressive movement, "March, slave!" And it is not funny.' 'One's intellect is numb,' said Charles Delvert. 'Never have I felt myself so empty of thoughts,' remembered Gabriel Chevallier. 'What are we?' echoed Genevoix. 'Frenchmen, who have been asked by the country to defend it, or simply brutes of combat?'

Action was generally brief and fragmentary. No combatant was aware that he was participating in what the newspapers later called the 'Battle of the Marne'. For years, the soldiers referred to the events as the 'attacks of Provins', but even that was misleading. Three quarters of the men never used their rifles. Their involvement took the form of small, individual experiences within an enclosed reality of a dozen or so horrifying metres that defied all description. 'It is probable that as long as I live, unless I finish my days in madness, I will never forget 10 September 1914.' But Marc Bloch, the historian, writing in a hospital only six months later, added: 'My memories of this day are not however very exact. In particular, they do not link up well. They form a broken series of images, a living reality, but weakly coordinated, like a cinema reel torn and ripped where one might, without anyone noticing, reverse the order of certain pictures.' His company lost a third of its number, time seemed very long; he remembered the sight on a slope of a dead corporal who had knocked over a cooking pot in his fall, leaving a pile of potatoes spread out just above him. Machine-gun bullets buzzed past branches like a swarm of wasps. Heavy explosions shook the air, followed by a singing sound as black shrapnel flew and fell, in slow motion. Horses panicked. 'How much time did we remain in this fold of terrain? How many minutes or how many hours? I know nothing.' The smoke of fuse shells was ochre, that of percussion shells was black. Maurice Genevoix' account (written in 1915) of 6–12 September does not include a single reference to the 'Battle of the Marne'.

'But how poorly one remembers and how unfaithful!' simply writes Jean Guéhenno.

Some of the most suggestive description of what had happened on the Marne was left by reporters who visited the battlefields in the days that followed the German retreat. Emile Henriot arrived in the village of Vareddes on 14 September. People were coming and going in a daze, prostrate. 'All looters will be shot' was chalked on the doors. As he passed to the flatlands above the village he found horses, dead, rigid and bloated, their hoofs in the air. Scattered about the shelled terrain beyond were thick rounds of cinder, giving off an odd sweet smell; it was where the Germans had burned their dead during the three days of combat. Further off lay a field of poppies. But on approaching, the young reporter discovered to his horror that these were not poppies; they were the red pantaloons of the soldiers lying in rows where they had fallen, under fire from the Maxim.

It would be a siege, not this time of Paris, but of Belgium, France and Alsace.

Sophocles had once observed – in the obscenest crime where Créon orders Polynices' body to be left exposed while condemning Antigone to be buried alive – the reversal of the cosmology of life and death:

> Take her away quickly!
> Wall her up in the tomb, you have your orders
> Abandon her there, alone, and let her choose –
> Death or a buried life with a good roof for shelter.

Créon, it is said, had inverted light and shadow, day and night. So did this war. 'Death and the sun', wrote La Rochefoucauld, 'cannot look each other in the face.' They did in Flanders, Picardy and Champagne.

The days matured and turned more melancholy, the skies began to reflect the colour of the grey chalky clays, the evenings closed in early. The French, like the British, had not been prepared for trench warfare. It was considered rather cowardly. Many, during the long marches, had thrown out their shovels and trowels as unnecessary dead weight. But dig in they had to for, just as the Germans failed to take the sea ports, so the Allies managed to fasten onto only a tiny corner of Belgium. Those lacking equipment scraped at the soil with their hands and their nails.

The winds carried to the plains a shrinking cold air, and it was wet. More rain fell in northern France in December 1914 than in any December since 1876. The soldiers began decking themselves in the blankets, the coats, the shawls, even the women's hats that they had 'borrowed' from abandoned rural wardrobes and bedrooms. Unwashed, unshaved, they took on that look which gave them their name, the *poilu*, the 'shaggy one' – a civilian term that the troops were slow to adopt: in the seventeenth century a *poilu* was a 'beggar'.

A new landscape was born. Barbed wire crossed the beetfields and new wicker-lined ditches curved along waterways and embankments. 'One lived', said P. Paraf, 'in a sort of concubinage with the earth.' If the countryside for an Englishman had been a garden, for a Frenchman

it was a farm. The soldiers might have been quick to rob and vandalise
the homes the refugees had left, but when they were forced to trample
over fields of lucern and dig trenches across fields planted in wheat they
became indignant. 'That beautiful rye,' they might exclaim, 'it's all the
same a pity.' They knew the value of a soil martyred by both enemy
and friend, a soil that was no longer worked, no longer producing: 'Ah!
mon lieutenant, if I could carry that earth back home that would do me
well!' They listened to the animals. They even hunted. Some have argued
that the trenches actually revived old instincts and gave the peasants a
sensitivity they had only feebly developed back home, for nobody had
worked the land at this level. But the experience was unreal, the landscape
at most times unseeable: the siege-works created intolerable constraints
that limited one's view to two mud walls and a strip of sky. On the map
the system, stretching by November from Nieuport on the Belgian coast
to Pfetterhausen and the 'trouée de Porrentruy' on the Swiss frontier, took
on the form of a drunken S, a reflection of the two summer offensives, the
French drive into Alsace and the German push through the north. On the
ground it was a foul sewer, reeking of urine and unburied mortality.

The new landscape demanded new names. Hills became 'crests' or
'counter-crests', ravines became 'advances' ('*cheminements*'), woods became
'covers'. Most got numbers (based on altitude), some got letters (based on
shape). But the soldiers never accepted the official denominations for the
trenches, the S', the S'', the R-line, the A1 and the B2. They would call their
section of the front 'Misery' trench, 'Bad Luck', 'Despair' or 'Disgrace', that
they had approached by night through the communication trench 'of the
Deserters', 'of Spite', the 'International', the 'Couloir de Languedoc'. Some
of the major intersections earned an urban designation, like 'Place de
l'Opéra'. But the French naming of trenches was nothing like as inventive
as the British – Charing Cross Road, Willow Avenue, Hyde Park Corner,
Marble Arch – probably because the vast majority of French troops did
not come from cities. And it was the small British Expeditionary Force
of 1914, virtually wiped out by December, which gave the towns and
villages of northern France and Belgium the 'Tommy' names that were
to stick throughout the war – Poperinghe became 'Pop', Vlamertinghe
'Vlam', Albert 'Bert', Etaples 'Eatables' . . .

Appearance and perceptions of the coalfields also changed. You
might still see on the long horizon the dark pyramidal forms of the
slag-heaps, but now the soft flecks of cloud that drifted across them
were no longer attributed to accidents of weather, they were regarded
as signs of bombardment. And if in a town like Béthune the miners
still trudged to the pits in the early hours of the morning, today they
would be accompanied by the London double-decker buses, with muddied
advertisements of Bass's Beer and Crosse and Blackwell, taking men in
khaki to war.

II

THE RHETORIC of that war carries a distant, foreign note today. 'All to duty until death, and even beyond . . .' The voice was not recorded, the gestures were not filmed. Clemenceau's words were intended for print, not for sight or sound. 'All to duty through the power of an example that will make the dead surge from the native earth.' Such talk of death even appears sacrilegious to later generations raised on a literature of soldiers who actually had to fight and die. 'It is no longer the time to love life when those of tomorrow's France will demand of us the glory to have lived for something more than a simple encounter with living without reason for living.' The soldiers enjoyed no glory and we, today, know it.

But when Clemenceau speaks of death, what death does he mean, what glory, what reason for living? Clemenceau in 'The Great Duty', published on 28 August 1914, like in many of his other articles of that period, was evoking once more the image of death as soulless, indifferent matter – the earth – and a life emerging spontaneously from it. 'France,' he wrote on 2 September as the government left for Bordeaux and the armies lined up at the Marne, 'France is a history, it is a life, it is a thought that has taken its place in the world; and the piece of earth from where this history, this life, this thought has shone, we cannot sacrifice it without laying down the tombstone on ourselves, on our children and on the generations which would be born to them.' This is Michelet's Danton, it is Clemenceau's Gambetta. It is also the living light that Monet gave to earth, water and stone. It is the *médecin-prêtre*. It is the fight against the dictators and the demagogues, it is the unending struggle for justice. It is a solitary man bending to grab a fistful of soil and shaking it defiantly in the face of his enemy.

When an official communiqué announced at the end of August that the fate of France hung on the result of a single battle between Maubeuge and the Donon, Clemenceau scoffed, 'France's fate can depend neither on this battle nor on those that follow.' One senses in his phrases shades of 1940: 'The observation that France is lost if her soldiers encounter defeat in one battle is the remark of a poor man who cannot weigh his words.'

In fact, Clemenceau's appeals for sacrifice were not a glorification of death at all. They were a play on the memory of Gambetta's call to the French people to come out of the twilight; they were a return to the theme of a resurrection. Only this time Clemenceau would speak of a 'rehabilitation': 'rehabilitation through the union of all French energies into a common movement of inflexible discipline in the service of the nation, rehabilitation through sacrifice and, since the events demand it, rehabilitation through blood'. France had not wanted this war, Germany had profited from French divisions and weaknesses, but forty million Frenchmen would give the invaders a singular response. That Gambettist battle cry also finds an echo in Clemenceau's preference for 'action' over 'literature'. On 30 August he criticised the speechmaking in Paris, the 'pieces of literature, without any result other than the useless sounds of words, at a time when all France is awaiting action'. This again recalls the old theme of 'action' as espoused by Michelet's Danton, male and physical, the ark of delivery, as opposed to the 'ideology' of the female Robespierre.

III

WICKEDLY, THE war would bring a certain, immediate rehabilitation both within Clemenceau's private life and in his political relations.

The first involved his son Michel. Clemenceau had been on poor terms with him ever since Michel's unstable schooldays. 'The greatest troubles I have had in my life have come from my children,' Clemenceau would confess in private. After his agricultural studies in Zurich Michel had left for Hungary, perhaps using connections of Aunt Sophie and her late Hungarian husband. There he had found a wife, but no permanent work, just a series of jobs, one more embarrassing to his father than the other: his work in the military supplies corps had looked dubious while his father was prime minister and Picquart minister of war; and his subsequent participation in aircraft and automobile contracts ended with his partner being landed in gaol. Whether relations with his father at this point were completely cut off, as Georges Gatineau suggests, is one of the imponderables of history. Sophie Bryndza, Clemenceau's sister, was certainly a great fence mender. Her correspondence with Geffroy shows that she stayed at Michel's home in the Vendée, they visited L'Aubraie together, they went, in Paris, to the theatre together and she made efforts to keep Michel within Geffroy's important circle. It is a bit difficult to imagine how Clemenceau could remain aloof from all this. But the relationship between father and son was probably not very happy.

That changed with the mobilisation of August 1914. Sophie noted in a letter to Geffroy: 'Michel arrived on his way to war. He saw his father again and both threw themselves into each other's arms and we were all so happy! Never have I seen my brother so moved.' But, she immediately added, 'less than fifteen days later my poor nephew was wounded by a bullet in the leg.'

One can imagine these moments of bonded bliss: witnessing a son, a brother and various nephews departing for war could hardly have been a pleasure party. 'My life is made only of anguish and the perpetual wait for news, which has been lacking more than once,' remarked Sophie in the same letter (of October 1914). 'I have seven of mine in this horrible war.' Three of the nephews were in hospital within two months of the outbreak of hostilities. Clemenceau's grandson, René Jacquemaire, went to a training camp at Verdun. 'He writes to me,' reports Sophie, 'that they will be departing *au feu* shortly with his comrades of the class of 1914. He appears to be enchanted. They are all like that these young, and the others as well, for that matter.'

Some of Clemenceau's rare letters suggest his feelings were no different from those of his sister. 'I live very tensely,' he tells Claude Monet on 11 August. There is the same anxiety for news: '*Ecris-moi, écris-moi, écris-moi,*' he writes to his '*cher petit frère*' Albert, who was serving in the training corps of the General Staff at Troyes.

In the second week of August Admiral Maxse's younger daughter, Lady Cecil, wrote to Clemenceau asking him if he could help find a position for her son as an interpreter in the French army. Clemenceau used to visit the Maxses annually in their home in England. But he couldn't do anything for the son. 'Our best language teachers can't even find jobs,' he said in his reply. George Cecil therefore joined the British Expeditionary Force. When his letters stopped arriving his mother came over to Paris. Clemenceau explained to Albert what had happened: 'He was commanding one of the rearguard sections in retreat. A bullet in the head killed him. The soldier next to him said he didn't even speak to him, seeing that he had not made a movement. The unhappy mother came to Paris to make her enquiry, and that is what she learned.'

What Clemenceau, friends and kin had experienced was repeated countless times throughout Europe. Families drew closer together out of the extremes of distress.

As for Clemenceau's political relations, the outbreak of war did lead to a very brief reconciliation between him and the president of the Republic, Raymond Poincaré.

There was a history here, too. 'M. Poincaré,' Clemenceau had written back in 1902, 'was for a long time one of the young prodigies of the new Republic. Like most young prodigies, he has done nothing prodigious, even though age begins to grey his temples.' Clemenceau's scorn for this patriotic lawyer from Lorraine had its roots in Poincaré's refusal to take a stand in the Dreyfus Affair. Poincaré's 'moderate' opinions and his affiliation with the right circles (particularly Waldeck-Rousseau's) had won him a ministerial post at the age of thirty-three, despite the fact that he had no personal following. In his mid-forties he had become minister

of finance under Sarrien but, not surprisingly, he had turned down
Clemenceau's offer to continue serving in Clemenceau's first ministry.
'Clemenceau detests me,' he later wrote in his memoirs. It was a long,
mutually sustained sentiment of gentle loathing.

Raymond Poincaré's one obsession was to restore to the presidency the
powers he believed the constitution of 1875 had intended for the office.
He got his chance when he was elected president in 1913 – in the face
of bitter opposition from Clemenceau. 1914 made him the guardian of a
reunited nation. The day after Germany declared war on France, Poincaré
delivered his famous message to the two chambers: 'With the outbreak of
war, France will be heroically defended by all her sons, of whom none will
shatter, before the enemy, the sacred union . . .' A Sacred Union, no less.
Clemenceau was impressed enough to add a post script to his article of 5
August: 'I have just left the Senate where we were read a very beautiful
manifesto from the president of the Republic, which resumes in strong and
concise terms what needed to be said. The high assembly greeted it with a
standing ovation.'

Poincaré was so moved by this rare flicker of praise that he wrote a
note to Clemenceau asking him to call at the Elysée. Better yet, in their
hour-long conversation Clemenceau actually let slip the phrase '*mon cher
ami*'. (Poincaré, perhaps overcome with emotion, failed to note in his diary
that he had at that moment offered Clemenceau the ministry of justice –
if Reinach is to be believed; Clemenceau refused, demanding either the
premiership or the ministry of war, or failing that the prefecture of the
invaded department of the Nord.)

The Sacred Union finally materialised after Poincaré ordered Viviani
to 'enlarge' his cabinet. The enlargement was duly made on 26 August. It
brought in, from the extreme Left, Jules Guesde as minister of state and
Marcel Sembat as minister of public works. The Right was represented
by Delcassé at foreign affairs once more and Alexandre Ribot as minister
of finance. The two former Socialists, Aristide Briand and Alexandre
Millerand, got jobs as keeper of the seals and minister of war respectively.
Poincaré wanted Albert de Mun and Denys Cochin from the Catholic
Right to be included, but de Mun was shortly to die and Viviani insisted
that Cochin was inappropriate.

With so many of his political enemies in the ministry it was hardly
surprising that Clemenceau refused to join it when approached by
Poincaré again on the 26th. In fact he was so incensed by the list that
he paid a special call on the Elysée the next day. Poincaré's entry for 27
August: 'Between two sittings of the council of ministers, I received a surly
visit from Monsieur Clemenceau. He is once again lost to his fury. After
a few weeks here we are again on the same bad terms as we were before
the war.' Clemenceau told him that he had engaged a cabinet of 'nullities'.
Poincaré watched the performance 'with stupéfaction' as 'this irritated old

man relieved his anxieties and vomited over me a flood of injuries'. They were well and truly back to the bad old days.

IV

FOR CLEMENCEAU, it was back again to the solitary struggle for truth and justice as well. 'We have the right to demand to be told everywhere and always the truth,' he had written on 21 August as the effects of censorship began to make themselves felt.

Clemenceau had founded *L'Homme libre* – the title borrowed from a paper published during the Commune – in May 1913, three months after Poincaré had been elected president. He realised that, like under Grévy, he had not the slightest chance of ever being called to office. So *L'Homme libre* would play the same function as had *La Justice*. Indeed, the formula was so similar – the *patron*'s editorial dominating the first page accompanied by a few items of information – that *L'Homme libre* had a rather old-fashioned look for 1913. The physical setting of the offices on rue Taitbout were as humble as those of rue Faubourg-Montmartre; the *patron* had one office and everybody else had the other. There were the same late evening discussions of the world and the cosmos before Clemenceau would leave for rue Franklin to compose the next day's article. The staff included Gustave Geffroy, Emile Buré, Henri Duvernois and Georges Wormser. 'The house', said Francisque Varenne, director of the affiliated *Journal du Var*, 'is quite closed and not just anybody can penetrate it.' It is rather amazing that the formula still worked; the extraordinary energy of the seventy-two-year-old director is the explanation, though even he showed signs of flagging in the first months of 1914 – apparently as the result of insomnia.

The evening discussions were dominated by François-Albert, who would soon leave, and Georges Mandel. Mandel was on his way to becoming for Clemenceau what Eugene Spuller had been for Gambetta, a faithful follower who shared all of Clemenceau's views, adopted all his quarrels and developed all his discontents. 'Mandel,' said Clemenceau, 'has no ideas, but he will defend them until death.' He did not have a strong sense of philosophy, art or science, which put him at a disadvantage in the discussions with his rival, François-Albert. Georges Wormser, another colleague, remembered Clemenceau exhorting, 'Mandel, go and see the museums!' Wormser remarked, 'Mandel went and saw the museums but remained Mandel.'

Yet he possessed an impressive intelligence and had a passion, a Jewish passion, for the Republic. At his *bar mitzvah* (the coming of age) he read an evocation of oppressed Alsace and the need to reconquer it. He inspired fellow pupils in his private boarding school with long speeches pronounced in a courtyard on the ensuing Dreyfus Affair, which were based for the most part on Clemenceau's editorials he had learned by heart the night before. His great ambition was to become a journalist working for Clemenceau, an ambition fulfilled within months of leaving school. But Clemenceau was not impressed with his style, and he never would be. Mandel had some disastrous experiences in the *Journal du Var* and he never wrote an article for *L'Homme libre*. His talent was in political counselling. After Clemenceau's fall from power in 1909, he would make daily visits to rue Franklin and report on what he had seen and heard in the corridors of the Chamber.

L'Homme libre lost three-quarters of its staff with the mobilisation of August. Mandel, short and pale (Clemenceau used to call him *le gringalet* or 'shrimp'), had already been turned down for military service on account of 'thoracic deficiency and a generally bad state of health'. But he was determined to combat the invader and spent the whole of autumn 1914 trying to persuade a recruiting board in Paris to revise his case. As a result he was unable to accompany *L'Homme libre* when it moved house in early September to be near the government in Bordeaux. Mandel lost his day-to-day contact with Clemenceau. But it would soon be re-established.

The Bordeaux 'offices' were a very modest affair. Clemenceau rented a tiny flat at No. 13 cours Saint-Jean, with his eldest daughter Madeleine Jacquemaire, who had always been an active aide in her father's journalism. Ministers, ambassadors and senior civil servants would visit Clemenceau in his bedroom. A few blocks away he rented another room to house the newspaper's staff, that is, two people, one of whom was his grandson who, every day, had to travel with articles in his briefcase to the printers in Toulouse.

One of Clemenceau's losses due to the mobilisation was his private secretary, Etienne Winter. He was replaced by a young Vendéen, Léon Martin. Martin, in a letter written to a friend in the last days of September, gave some indication of what it was like to work for Clemenceau: 'Ouf! I am exhausted, fagged out, clobbered, dead-beat. I've worked, scraped, marched, trotted all day.' He did not like his new location. 'Nothing, absolutely nothing good,' he wrote. 'From time to time a recognisable mug from the boulevards. People I've met twenty times in the antechambers of the ministries. In the midst of these Parisian dregs drift the flotsam of the capital's great sewers, carried here by the current.'

With memories of February 1871, Clemenceau could not have been too happy in Bordeaux either. It was, he said in an article of 11 September, 'a renewal of the "war in the provinces" as at the time of Gambetta and Freycinet, the same struggle against the same German invasion'. However, he added, in 1871 Paris and the provinces were divided; Gambetta had been forced to fight a war on two fronts, today Clemenceau evoked a war on just one.

But his articles were to open another. One of the greatest held secrets of the general staff was what happened to the tens of thousands of wounded during the first two bloody months of war. Clemenceau found out in Bordeaux' railway station. He saw the wagons in which the casualties were crammed, some seated, their hands clinging to the wooden struts of the rolling doors and the compartment sides, others lying on beds of straw. These wagons had made curious trips. On their way out to the front they had carried horses; on their way back they carried wounded men. The men were inadequately cleaned; their eyes were glazed, a few were murmuring. Clemenceau learned that many of them had contracted tetanus. He wrote a damning article on 28 September.

The reaction of the military authorities was prompt. They seized every copy of *L'Homme libre* and brought the matter to the attention of the council of ministers. Jean Malvy, minister of the interior, ordered an immediate suspension of the paper until 7 October. Clemenceau responded by changing the paper's name to *L'Homme enchaîné*, but somebody at the Toulouse printers got confused; while the paper carried the new title, the running head on page two onwards still read *L'Homme libre*. So *L'Homme enchaîné* was impounded too.

It was only in November, with two editions, one in Paris and one in Bordeaux, that *L'Homme enchaîné* returned to regular daily publication. The work of the censors was indicated by white blanks; that left a lot of blanks. Sometimes a whole article was suppressed. The Bordeaux censors were more lenient than those in Paris, so that one could often read in the Bordeaux edition what could not be read in the Paris one. The existence of the two editions brought Clemenceau frequently back to the capital.

There was talk among soldiers of *la guerre-habitude*. A certain normalcy came to mark the massacre.

Finally it was decided that the government would return to Paris on 10 December, parliament would be called in a special session at the end of the month and would reopen for regular sessions in mid-January 1915.

Clemenceau and Léon Martin took a night train to Paris on 8 December, arriving at seven the next morning. But almost immediately Edmond the chauffeur was driving them in a heavy, aged limousine through Neuilly, Nanterre and Pontoise to Clemenceau's new country home at Bernouville,

near Gisors, in the department of the Eure. Clemenceau had purchased
the old half-timbered long house, so typical of the region, when he was
prime minister, in 1908. Right in the middle of the drive stood one of those
round pigeon houses, in red bricks and an oddly conical roof. The property
was within seventy kilometres of Paris and it was only twenty kilometres
from Giverny, Claude Monet's home. 'No objections, *mon enfant*; we have
well earned this, both of us,' said Clemenceau when Martin complained
that he had a lot of work to do in Paris. Geffroy would join them and they
would 'make a detour through Giverny.'

At Bernouville, Clemenceau had built his own imitation of Monet's
gardens. He had planted white poplars, Spanish broom and cotoneasters.
In the ponds he had introduced trout and sturgeon, like in Monet's *Jardin
d'eau*. There were swans on the canal. But that December he had come to
contemplate his winter flowers, their tendrils pushing upward and outward
from the cold Norman soil.

V

FRANCE HAD lost, by December, about three hundred thousand men killed
and another six hundred thousand wounded or missing – the casualty figures in this war would always be limited to approximations. Germany, on
two fronts, had thrown away over a million men and there were so few left
of the original British force of a hundred and sixty thousand regulars that
it was almost wholly taken over by the voluntary, part-time Territorials.

The new French horizon blue uniforms, which blended better with the
landscape, were first seen among the reinforcements that arrived in late
autumn 1914. By the New Year the red pantaloons had disappeared. The
introduction of metal helmets was much slower. At first they were limited
to men of the artillery; it was only in the autumn of 1915 that they were
distributed to the infantry. But, then, British troops did not receive them
until 1916.

There was little talk of *la patrie* at the front. Few were concerned about
the future of Lorraine and Alsace. The *ch'ti mi* [pronounced 'shtee mee'
(= *chez moi*)] regiments – those made up of men whose homes had been
overrun by the German onslaught in the North – had a specific sense of
mission; but most fought out of commitment to a friend exposed to danger,
out of revenge for a death, out of fear of the authorities behind, out of
habit. After the first enthusiasm of August, the deception of the retreat,
the exhaustion of renewed advance and combat, came the long winter of

resignation, *le cafard*, a sadness that the soldiers' fathers had once felt around Metz or along the Loire, only this time it incorporated a complete stalemate anchored into an environment of utter destruction. 'The men have completely lost the habit of marching with packs on their backs,' noted Lieutenant Charles de Gaulle when he returned to Champagne in October 1914, following a brief bout in hospital. 'What is this war if not a war of extermination?' he wrote to his mother two months later.

Modris Ecksteins has spoken of the soldier's 'journey to the interior', a 'resignation and lassitude, this inexhaustible docility', a 'retreat, away from an external work, which on the surface was left intact, inward into a private world of spirit'. It involved a rejection not only of the soldier's immediate environment but also of every incomprehending agent beyond his own trench comrades – the bureaucrats, the politicians, the journalists, the war profiteers, what the British called the 'home front', what the French rather more accurately termed *'l'arrière'*. It was not a rebellion. It was a psychological phenomenon. There developed new superstitions, new wonders and new miracles. In this, nature played a capital role because the ash-grey landscape seemed to have forgotten the seasons. The sight of a flower could move a man to tears. The song of a bird could be taken as a harbinger. Combat too could lead, once the danger had passed, to an almost mystical sense of elation, to a feeling that one had not merely survived but had been reborn. Resurrection is a frequent theme in soldiers' literature. But it was not something that one could talk about on leave or write about in letters. Who would understand?

The French Grand Quartier Général (GQG) at Chantilly was hardly designed to understand. In the luxurious setting of a grand hotel and a Renaissance castle surrounded by moats, a forest and the most famous racecourse in France besides Longchamp, its small army of staff officers, their guards, escorts and dispatch riders came to epitomise the life of the 'château generals'. Much of the criticism from the troops on one side and the politicians on the other would be unfair; but there was none the less truth to the fundamental complaint that tens of thousands were being sent to their deaths by men out of sound of the guns and out of sight of the trenches.

The soldiers' isolation was aggravated by a press stifled by the censors. 'The prevailing opinion in the trenches', said again Marc Bloch, 'was that anything might be true except what was printed.' Newspaper readers were told that the trenches were really quite comfortable and that the troops were enjoying themselves. 'Gaiety reigns in the trenches!' wrote Maurice Barrès, champion – at least in the first year of the war – of the *bourrage de crâne*. He heaped praise on the youth that willingly received 'good wounds' and gave of its blood so 'lightly' under the humming shells of the 75, 'valiant and charming collaborators'.

The politicians' speeches were not much of an improvement. On 22

December parliament met for the first time since August. Three empty seats in the Chamber of Deputies were draped in black to mark the members who had fallen on the field of honour. Regular sessions were resumed on 12 January.

VI

CLEMENCEAU WAS also a journalist capable of writing, 'They are quietly gay, with the firm resolution of spending a good night on straw, having amply satisfied an appetite of a man of twenty.' But that was after he had visited the front in late September 1915, as the second offensive in Champagne got underway. He was referring to a hutment behind the lines where he had come upon a small group of soldiers he had previously noticed limping along one of the approach roads. 'The poor wretches no longer limped. I wanted to embrace them.'

Communication between this elderly statesman with a walking stick, his hands in grey mittens, and the teenage soldiers must have been awfully hard. Because the war proved a watershed in so many areas, laying the groundwork to new creeds and attitudes, their meeting assumed the guise of an encounter between two centuries, two cultures. Henri Barbusse, in the same campaign, described these civilian visitors as 'trench tourists' – 'two characters with overcoats and walking sticks; another dressed as a huntsman, adorned with a fluffy hat and binoculars'. Barbusse said soldiers had no truck with civilians: 'the division neat and cut – and truly unremitting, this one – exists within the crowd of a nation, between those who profit and those who suffer . . .'

Clemenceau was at least aware of – and was honest enough to report – a silence that, in a grim way, might have recalled Paris after the massacres of the Commune. In the long files of men marching to the front, he finds 'a silence'. 'The universal trait is that these men do not speak. No curses from the cart drivers, nor cries, nor recriminations at some unexpected bump. They move to the side to give us place at the continued sound of a horn, which is itself discreet.' In a bombed-out church, converted into a first-aid centre for *les petits blessés*, he encounters the same silence: 'Always these impassive faces that one would say are closed to human emotions.' After being held up by shellfire, he eventually descends a communications trench; it is an awkward moment. 'What can one say when the work into which this man has thrown himself is of such scope that he has given everything, brought everything, laying down the greatest stakes of his life?' In the 'couloir de Languedoc' he encounters more men where 'the word is imprisoned by walls of earth . . . These men are not talkers.' But he is relieved by 'smiles of kindness for the intruders that we are'.

Clemenceau had as his guide Sergeant Poissonnier. Sergeant Poissonnier was also silent: 'If I don't dare pose questions, Poissonnier, from his side, has nothing to ask me . . ., I am outside his field of vision.' Throughout the tour of the trench Clemenceau had the impression that the sergeant had 'only one idea: to get rid of us'. Finally 'we were two hundred paces from the sheds of Souain when the signal was given for a separation which brought him perhaps something of a relief'. They shook hands 'in silence'.

Clemenceau claimed that he did not want to 'present the trench as a place of delights' – a most notable comment, given the tone of the press in 1915. 'I did not go to seek, out there, material for literature.' He found the men 'ragged, ruffled, covered in mud, sober in words'. But in an instant, when the cannon quietened and even the slippery chalk cuttings took on an air of peace and innocence, he would glance at a face and see nothing more than 'a little smile'. Clemenceau said this smile was a contented smile, a smile that spoke of 'his tranquil exaltation of being what he is'. 'Friend reader,' he would write, 'I bring you the smile of the trenches of Champagne, which is also that of Artois and Argonne.'

Clemenceau's whole war effort was based, one might argue, on what he could read into that smile. It was 'tranquil', it reflected the quietness of a 'serene will' and a 'single idea', it was the 'smile of a youngster [*un gosse*] who savours the actions of life', it was 'the encouragement coming from the person one wanted to encourage'; better than a 'smile of confidence', it was a 'smile of security'.

Was this a soldier's thought? It was especially Clemenceau's. Running through all that he wrote and said was the old theme of his youth, a Pascalian absurdity: 'What it matters to them if they know that the higher law of things is in the impassive indifference of the universe where neither suns, nor planets, nor atoms are stopped in their course of renewal by cries of pain . . . They [the soldiers] certainly did not choose their lot, but they accepted it . . . They have asked nothing of others because they found everything in themselves . . .' And Clemenceau combined this with the same unrelenting will: 'We gave everything, yesterday, the war wanted, we give today everything it demands, to give tomorrow still everything it will exact.'

That kind of dogged spirit was not well received by the censors whose aim, proclaimed in scores of circulars and instructions preserved today in a Nanterre library, was 'to tranquillise' public opinion. Censorship was blind and bureaucratic. Ostensibly it came under the authority of the war ministry's Bureau de presse, housed in the Invalides. But the prime minister, the ministry of war, the ministry of the marine, GQG, the local commanders and prefects all intervened, each one of them having their own opinion on where the ugly old lady 'Anastasie' should next apply her scissors. Within days, her knotty hands had spread beyond the simple function of concealing the movement of armies.

The long and short of it was that anything could be censored. 'Provided,' wrote Alfred Capus in *Le Figaro*, 'one speaks in one's writings neither of the authority, nor of the government, nor of politics, nor of professions in credit, nor of companies of credit, nor of the wounded, nor of German atrocities, nor of the postal service, one can freely print everything, under the inspection of two or three censors'. It was less the tone of a particular article that caught Anastasie's eye than the reputation of this or that newspaper. The favourite targets were *Le Canard enchaîné*, which had its origins in the trenches, *L'Œuvre* of Gustave Téry, which by 1916 had succeeded in replacing the old radical Parisian press and, from the outset of the war, *L'Homme libre/L'Homme enchaîné*.

Clemenceau might have had, as an ideal, an army with a serene smile; he did not, however, seek to tranquillise the population. He was incensed when, in June 1915, Millerand told a deputy that he found the country in a state of 'heroic serenity'. This was no good, Clemenceau explained to the Senate army committee, the country has to be warned of problems in the command, of weaknesses in the artillery, of contradictions in government policy. In his long battle against the scandalous state of the military health service he remarked, 'The government has suppressed the difficulty by suppressing my newspaper.' Clemenceau's image of France as a nation at war was not one of heroic serenity; it was François Rude's Marseillaise, 'to which I always come back' – the outraged Marianne, a 'great infuriated goddess'.

Clemenceau's articles on military health care were censored. So too were his articles on food shortages in the army, on the lack of straw and cover, on *embusqués* (shirkers), on the Dardanelles, his criticisms of Poincaré, of Joffre, of Viviani. At first he took these cuts with good humour. 'They wanted to suppress me,' he wrote to Albert on 26 September 1914, 'then they didn't do it. Then they voted for my suppression because the paper had not been sent to the censors, then General Bailloud wrote that it had been sent, etc. What I cannot in the slightest way imagine is the state of mind of people who fill their time with such inanities.' But his correspondence with Albert indicates mounting frustration. 'This morning the whole of my article is blank,' he writes on 4 January 1915. 'The title was, "The Union of Inadequates", [showing] the frightful disorder of the administration.' And again on 10 June 1915: 'They suppressed this morning a passage of my article where I dared maintain that the country can have the right to some *explanations*. This makes me furious. I don't find enough words to describe these people.' (His emphasis)

VII

BY TRADITION and constitution, the country's right to explanation was exercised through parliament. But parliament, on the second day of the war, had ceded full powers to the government and then adjourned *sine die*. There was hope that some degree of normality would be restored when parliament reconvened in January. 'To the ministry, the decision, the execution,' wrote Clemenceau early that month, 'to parliament the care of judging. Full liberty to each in its domain.' Parliament would remain in session, without a break, until the end of the war. Yet its right to explanation – the 'interpellation' – had been seriously curtailed: the government could always avoid awkward questions by evoking that hallowed formula of war, 'reasons of security'.

So the task of questioning the government fell on the parliamentary committees, more discreet than the open sessions, and particularly on the four 'grand committees'; the Chamber committees of the army and of foreign affairs, and their two counterparts in the Senate. Because of the personalities involved, the Senate army committee became the most important of the four.

Within the first week of the opening of parliament Clemenceau managed to get elected to both the Senate's army committee and its foreign affairs committee. Presiding over the two committees was the venerable Charles de Freycinet, Gambetta's right-hand man in 1870. But he did not want to continue; he was nearly ninety and would speak of being 'a trifle tired'. He never attended any meetings and in November 1915 he eventually resigned (on receiving an appointment in Briand's first war ministry!). That was when Clemenceau was elected president of the two Senate 'grand committees'.

Henry Bérenger, a highly vocal member, claimed that the army committee resembled Robespierre's Committee of Public Safety. 'No,' responded Clemenceau with some apparent regret, 'we do not have the power to act.' All the same, ministers were terrified of the Senate army committee.

Detailed minutes of its meetings have survived. There were thirty-six members (as opposed to twenty-seven before the war), though it was normal for about a dozen to be absent. It would meet two or three times a week, sometimes more, and conducted itself like a small parliamentary assembly, complete with debates, speeches and partisan manœuvres. At the end of June 1915, for example, Clemenceau delivered two speeches which could be compared, in style, to some of his greatest displays of oratory before the war. Declarations and resolutions were communicated to the president of the Republic, the prime minister and the *bureaux de groupes* of the Senate – for despite the 'Sacred Union' party politics had not disappeared with the war. Brief reports of the committee meetings were even communicated to the press; the censorship of these reports created scandal among the members.

The purpose of the committee was criticism. After it had been suggested that the committee should 'collaborate' with the government, Paul Doumer – no friend of Clemenceau – remarked, 'There is parliamentary control on government action, parliamentary observations and objurgations of government, but a collaboration, in the real sense of the word, is impossible because we do not have at our disposal a power of execution.' That lack of executive power was lived with increasing frustration as the war dragged on, for the general conviction was that the stalemate could be avoided. Paul Doumer blamed it on 'human error'. Charles Humbert thought the problem lay in the lack of heavy artillery. Clemenceau always insisted on the lack of unity in the command.

Mistakes were in fact being made, serious military mistakes. On 9 May 1915, along a front of six kilometres in Artois, General Pétain at the head of 33rd Corps actually broke through the German front – the problem was that reinforcements were too distant to exploit this. The huge loss of life in the Champagne offensive of that same spring was largely due to the clear superiority of German artillery.

A hundred thousand deaths, Clemenceau would say, 'naturally for nothing, for the communiqué'.

But the committee was not in a hurry to bring the problems before the full Senate even though the means existed to do so. The constitution of 1875 outlined a procedure for *comités secrets*, or secret parliamentary sessions, which was designed to overcome the threat to national security that open deliberations posed. All the committee members recognised that this was impossible right now. The idea of a secret session was popular with neither the Senate nor the country as a whole. There were jealousies. 'The Senate', cautioned Henry Chéron as late as March 1916, 'wouldn't hesitate to smash us if we asked for the secret session.' So for eighteen months the committee simply limited itself to hostile resolutions.

All this involved manœuvring and political alignments that were as complicated as in times of peace. There were many personal questions, accompanied by the usual loves and hates and intrigues. The committee itself was divided roughly between moderates like Henry Bérenger, Henry Chéron and Paul Strauss who tended to advocate more dialogue with the government and advised against secret sessions, and the more aggressive members like Charles Humbert, Paul Doumer and Jules Jeanneney who wanted to denounce the government 'from the tribune'. As president, Clemenceau often remained quiet and was wary even to act as spokesman outside the committee: he preferred to delegate this responsibility to others.

The political questions didn't go away either. Clemenceau's tense relationship with the SFIO, which was referred to within his circle as the 'Unified Socialist Party', continued into the war. Most members of the committee were suspicious of the party's sudden abandonment of 'internationalism' for the 'Sacred Union' in August 1914; it was one of the underlying causes of mistrust in Viviani's government. But the committee was again divided on how to treat with the Socialists. The moderates placed priority on preserving the Sacred Union while the more aggressive members were willing to lose socialist support for a more energetic war effort. Clemenceau himself evidently did not put much stock in the Sacred Union. 'They have just thrown out over two hundred generals, some of whom are excellent,' he remarked in May 1915. 'Do you think they observe the Sacred Union in the army?' It was clear from an early date that the Socialists and the Senate army committee were heading for a clash.

Old wartime memories played a part here. Clemenceau could remember the effect the German advance in 1870 had had on the extreme Left in Paris. 'I see the peril, there is no time to lose,' nodded Paul Doumer approvingly. 'Imagine what would happen if a cannon 380 fired on Paris!' Related to this was the old image that France's centralised, bureaucratic state was a mere cover to seething chaos and anarchy below: in 1870 the cover had been lifted. Clemenceau once recollected, 'What struck me profoundly, at Bordeaux in particular in [1871], was this dissociation of all political and social bonds, because the master had disappeared. There was the dust of the French, there was no longer France.'

In the committee there was a feeling that the bureaucracy itself might turn France to dust. The fear most frequently expressed by all the members was what Henry Bérenger described as 'a bureaucratic dispersion perfectly likely to hinder the best intentions', an irrational, directionless maze of petty sovereigns – les ronds de cuir – always pointing the blame at their neighbours'.

Frequently one spoke in the committee of a 'duality of power', of a 'state within a state', of 'Chantilly versus Paris'. But it was observed that not even Chantilly was commanded. In June 1915 Clemenceau announced, 'The government has just put together a sort of war council which has put the commander-in-chief under guard. This is the worst solution. One can limit the area of command, but one needs a chief who is responsible.' Clemenceau refrained from personal attacks on Joffre. Indeed, contrary to the legend the committee minutes prove that Clemenceau rather liked him. He was a *'brave homme'*, a *'bon type'*, but not a *'chef de guerre'*.

This war required a particular kind of leadership. The historians have variously described it as an industrial war, a technological war even a 'democratic war'. For Clemenceau it was a bureaucratic war, a nightmare.

One of the most mindless affairs of the bureaucratic war was the French response to German gas attacks. At Langermarck, just north of Ypres, on an April afternoon in 1915, No. 35 Pioneer Regiment, containing some of Germany's leading chemists (including two future Nobel prizewinners), opened 5,500 heavy steel cylinders of chlorine on the two French divisions opposite. 'The valleys down which the gas descended were as yellow as the Egyptian desert while the tops of the ridges remained in their spring green.' Many of the troops fled in panic but the number of fatal casualties was actually quite small. The Germans had little protective equipment and their advance was soon halted by the combined action of French and Canadian troops. A few days later the British sector was attacked: there was the same panic, the same indecisive result. 'It was a new device in warfare,' commented a witness, 'and thoroughly illustrative of the Prussian idea of playing the game.'

The Hague Convention of 1907 had outlawed the use of gas in warfare and many British and French officials remained opposed to its use even after the German attacks. Churchill would be a leading advocate of riposte in Britain. In France, it was Clemenceau.

'From blades, to rifles, to cannon, to mines, to bombs, we will fight as the other fights,' he wrote in an article. 'He invents new devices. We shall do the same. He hurls flaming liquid on our men. We shall do the same on his. He attempts to asphyxiate us. In turn, we shall smoke him out. And if his barbaric ingenuity discovers new ways of massacring Frenchmen, we shall let him see that we can find new procedures for massacring Germans. There is, anyway, no choice.'

There was hesitation at first for understandable humanitarian reasons, but the affair soon turned into an administrative inferno.

The government attempted to hide the news of gas attacks. One of the worst took place in October 1915 between La Pompelle and Rosnes in Champagne where, the committee learned, one thousand men had died – and died horribly. Bérenger read a long letter from a witness. 'Men were dying in the autos [ambulances] before even arriving in Epernay,' it said,

> Some were in appalling agony; at the autopsy they found nothing in the lungs but clots of blackish blood and dark spots on their hands.

The men had taken off their masks. These would not have protected
them anyway because it was a new gas ... Everything is organised
in an intelligent fashion among the Germans, no stupid improvisation.
They are scientists ... Here it's a *rond de cuir parisien* who decides ...

The protection of French troops was inadequate and developed at a
snail's pace. At first Command recommended that wetted handkerchiefs
be held to the face; urine, it was discovered, partly countered the effects
of acid. Masks were introduced without method and with little attention
to research. It was only in April 1916 that effective masks, the T and the
TN, were issued.

Research into gas weapons was conducted in the greatest confusion.
'Our scientists are not backward, but they work dispersed,' said Paul
Doumer. 'The Academy of Sciences, the special commission presided
over by Monsieur Weiss, a service of studies which operates at the office
of the undersecretary of state for artillery and munitions, and finally the
ministry of public instruction ... such are the organs involved in the
question of asphyxiating gases.' Cazeneuve, the committee's specialist
on gas, reported that Monsieur Weiss's commission had sixty members
'but it has achieved nothing because it didn't have a unit for execution.'
Cazeneuve was relieved to discover that, in November 1915, General Ozil
had been put in charge of reorganising 'the service'; he created one section
for study and research and another for execution and production. In
December, however, Bérenger was reporting that Ozil's new Direction du
matériel chimique de guerre was a 'veritable administrative mushroom',
extremely expensive, with no results to show for itself: *'Jusqu'ici nous nous
trouvons devant le néant.'*[1]

The manufacture and distribution of gas weapons was equally chaotic.
The main factory charged with producing gas shells was in Aubervilliers,
outside Paris. But at the end of 1915 production was still being run on
a trial-and-error basis; experiments were conducted on pigs and sheep
at the camp de Mailly. Furthermore, the committee discovered that the
shells that had been produced were all marked 'reserved'. So they weren't
planning to use them?

The French first released chlorine gas from cylinders on German troops
in December 1915, eight months after the initial German attacks. The first
gas shells were employed by the French only the following August.

Gas was the most terrifying weapon of the war. Memories of gas attacks
would haunt survivors for the rest of their lives; not even Hitler's troops
used gas. These weapons were the product of a sophisticated industrial war

---

[1] 'To date, we find ourselves faced with nothing.'

machine that had lost the last link with human values. 'Is it through the superiority of our arms that we will attain the final decision?' Clemenceau wrote in November 1915. 'Certainly not, for the advantage of the German industrialisation of war allows for a manufacture of rifles, cannon and munitions at a scale infinitely superior to what is possible for us to realise. So what then? *Eh bien*, there are the men, the French, the soldiers, the *poilus*, call them what you like . . .' Or this question, the preceding July: 'As powerful as it may be, what is the most marvellous machine worth if man is not at the lever?'

Or this, still one month earlier – the phrases hammered out in repetition, so reminiscent of the Dreyfus Affair, a link between Zola in 1898 and Churchill in 1940:

> We shall conquer because it is our will to conquer, our will to the very end, whatever may happen. We shall conquer because the total sacrifices, by which our perseverance to conquer will be sustained, is inexhaustible. We shall conquer because we have no other choice but conquer. We shall conquer because, even if we have committed great errors, we are worthy of redeeming them . . . You can never conquer because all your servitudes, scientifically constructed simply turn you into automatons.

VIII

FLEURY-DEVANT-Douaumont was a village of five hundred inhabitants in 1914. Today it is an indistinct corner of a vast forest. Its former streets are now marked out by woodland paths, all neatly posted as in some western American National Park and illuminated by shafts of light that pierce a rustling cover of autumnal leaves. The narrow tracks rise and fall in a chill September mist as if they were ribbons floating on ocean waves: with your eyes you can follow that ground-swell of hillocks and ridges until it disappears into a shaded mass of spruce, ash and pine. The soil, carpeted in moss, is fragile. This small mound was the grocer's store. A cane or a pair of crutches would sink an inch into the earth with the next step forward. That tuft of ground over there, between the two tall beeches, was the baker's shop. A wooden post tells you are walking down rue Saint-Nicolas, which then turns into rue de l'Eglise, a hole and a scattering of stone. Here was the mairie, and this tiny isolated chapel is built on the site of a medieval church. You pause. You are alone. It is so silent. The sun brings a little warmth to the clearing. A bird takes flight. You look again through the woods at the unimaginable. Scenes of churned-up soil drawn from flickering black-and-white newsreels come to mind: these hillocks, these undulations, hidden in a forest, are not nature's gift, they are the spoliation of man. 'If the earth could speak,' said Clemenceau when he visited the battlefields of the Marne in September 1915, 'it would tell us of these great resurgences of history that still throb within it and that we embalm coldly in pages without life.' It is the old, repeated sin of historians. 'In reading the accounts of the war,' wrote Jean Guéhenno on the fiftieth anniversary of the Armistice, 'a simple reporting of the events is always enough to awaken in me the same fury.' How can one begin to describe Verdun?

Go there. You have to see it.

As president of the army committee, Clemenceau paid three visits to the Verdun region during the campaign, which lasted through most of 1916. The battle began with the launching of a German offensive from the hills north of the citadel on 21 February. Within four days the strategic Fort Douaumont had fallen: it would take the French eight months to retrieve it, at a cost of over three hundred thousand men, killed, missing or wounded. 'The forces of France will bleed to death whether we reach our goal or not,' declared Falkenhayn in formulating his plan of attack the previous December. Operation Gericht (or 'Judgment') had not, however, counted on having German casualties just as high.

Clemenceau's reports to the committee and in *L'Homme enchaîné* give little inkling of the horrifying spectacle he must have witnessed during his three brief visits. He was there in May, as the Second Army under Nivelle and Mangin prepared their first disastrous counter-offensive on Douaumont; in October, on the eve of the final 'successful' assault on what remained of the fort; and in the New Year, after the main fighting was over. An inspection of artillery deployed in the area, including two spanking new 400 millimetre railway guns brought in to demolish the casemates of Douaumont (they were built in concrete three metres thick), led Clemenceau to remark, 'Verdun is a beautiful thing to see' – surely not the opinion of infantry holed out in the Thiaumont Ridge and the salient of Fleury.

Verdun, was it a beautiful thing?

Paul Fussell has said that description in every war is ironic because every war is worse than expected; a realistic assessment of the damages and ghastliness of the whole business is impossible, so one resorts to irony. Clemenceau knew how to use irony. On his third trip to Verdun, in the freezing winter of 1916–17, he climbed the shell-pocked hills:

> I went to Fort Douaumont. Considering the season and the state of the
> terrain, the voyage is laborious. The bodies have still not been picked

up. The craters are full of frozen water. Men and commanders, including
generals, sleep on bare earth under the fire of enemy artillery. The morale
of everyone is excellent.

At least it was a suitable response to Bérenger who, after Clemenceau's
long October report, with its descriptions of Forts Moulainville and
Souville ('or rather the butte of mud which is all that remains today of
Souville'), made the damning remark that 'the observations of Monsieur
le Président have greatly interested us for their lively and picturesque
character'.

Here were two dozen or so men sitting around a well polished
table at the Palais de Luxembourg, trying to discuss intelligently the
indescribable. Even if it had been possible, full reportage was hardly
encouraged. Clemenceau was still hampered in his newspaper accounts
by the censors. So his newspaper comments on Verdun were limited to
the vaguest kinds of remark, generally allusive. The myth of Cadmus was,
of course, a favourite: 'The little men in blue helmets surge forth – one
does not know how – from the earth as formerly did soldiers born from
the teeth of a dragon.'

The survivors couldn't describe Verdun. How much more difficult the
task must have been for the politicians who visited it. Clemenceau, in his
reports of 1916 on Verdun and other sectors of the front, concentrated on
the three areas where the committee could have some practical influence:
the condition of the men, their relationship with the officers and the
problems of command.

Clemenceau's impressions of the conditions of the soldiers were mostly
positive. 'I have returned from this trip to the front with one less weight
on my heart,' he reported after a visit in January 1916. The men usually got
hot food, even if the rice wasn't always up to scratch; their quarters to the
rear weren't so bad, though there was a lack of tables, chairs and light; and
he thought the trenches were, given the situation, well constructed. The
soldiers at last had warm clothes to wear and they apparently sent their
laundry back to their wives and women to wash (an overlooked feature
of the 'home front'). His most scathing comments were reserved, as at
the outset of the war, for the medical services, fettered by bureaucracy.
At the Hôpital des Buttes, near Verdun, he had witnessed screaming men
arrive only to be confronted with a questionnaire on their *état civil*: Date
of birth? Place of birth? Are you married? Relatives? – 'cruel procedures,'
said Clemenceau, 'which will have to be modified'. But in general French
troops were better housed, he thought, than the British.

On two occasions, in January and May 1916, he spoke of British
conditions as 'mediocre'. The British had fine uniforms, they had 'great

physical and moral *élan*', but they couldn't build trenches and didn't seem to have the first idea of how to prepare for an offensive. The trenches that they had recently taken over from the French had certainly not been improved and had probably, he thought, deteriorated. In May, just six weeks before Kitchener's 'Pals' went over the top, he noted ominously, 'our allies are ready in nothing, on nothing and for nothing.' The Somme proved an expensive lesson: twenty thousand dead on the first day, and another forty thousand wounded or missing. Clemenceau considered the lesson learnt. When he returned from his trip in October he reported that the British army had been completely transformed; it was a colossal force (*'Nos alliés font tout en grand'*) and it was thoroughly professional.

The visits seem to have mellowed Clemenceau's criticisms of the officer corps. At Commercy, south of Verdun, he said that officers wore the same uniforms as the troops and accompanied them to the trenches; 'it is a pure legend to say the contrary.' He spoke of the 'fraternal relations' between men and officers and of social classes being brought together. At Fort Souville in October he met a young general, Boulorge, 'who seemed to me a commander of the hour, sharing the dangers of his soldiers and living their life'.

Obviously the president of the army committee met a lot of generals. His assessment of their character and competence was, again, mostly positive. He first encountered Philippe Pétain in May. Pétain had been appointed by Joffre to command operations at Verdun within days of the German attack. But just before Clemenceau's visit, Joffre had done an about-turn and 'promoted' Pétain to a general command post at Bar-le-Duc, about fifty kilometres away from the combat zone. Joffre thought Pétain spent too much time on the defensive and had called in General Nivelle, of the old *attaque-à-outrance* school, to replace him. Clemenceau also showed concern about Pétain's intentions; he noted that he had built fifty bridges across the Meuse which suggested that he was ready to withdraw all troops from the right bank. Pétain, he said, 'is a man whose opinion cannot be changed. He has a didactic spirit, rather uncompromising, which will not be easily influenced.' But Clemenceau would never draw himself too deeply into matters of strategy. That was not his job, he would argue. And he thought Pétain was qualified for his. 'It is best to leave him to his own inspirations that events have proven to be excellent.' He considered his replacement by Nivelle, 'a simple and modest man', an error; 'It is regrettable that our *poilus* know that General Pétain, in whom they have absolute faith, is no longer at Verdun.'

All the same, Clemenceau 'received the best impressions' from Nivelle. As for Mangin, Clemenceau had described him, on his visit to Commercy in January 1916, as 'a commander with much resolution, much drive' – after the first May counter-offensives, the troops called him 'the butcher'.

*

These reports from the front, little essays on society at war, concealed the fury which ran through the whole committee that Verdun had even happened. 'The affair of Verdun has torn the veils,' said Clemenceau during one heated discussion in May. The cry that France was neither governed nor commanded grew louder.

The prime minister, Aristide Briand, became the chief focus of discontent. Curiously, nearly all the committee's auditions of Briand – a major political figure after the war – have disappeared from the Senate archives. But there is enough evidence in the committee's minutes to reconstruct the developing crisis.

What is certain is that the German offensive in February need not have been a total surprise and French defences could have been far better prepared. After long fruitless efforts to persuade GQG to permit parliamentary visits to the front – Paul Strauss in March 1915 had spoken of an 'iron curtain' separating the army zone from the rest of France – a delegation (which did not include Clemenceau) was finally allowed to make a tour of 'fortified places' in August 1915. Their first stop was Verdun. They were astonished at what they found. All the major forts had been stripped of their heavy guns and they were now only manned by skeleton crews. Joffre, haunted by the memory of Bazaine cut off at Metz in 1870, had in fact decided that this war would be fought in the open; he needed the guns for the Champagne offensive. The ruling wisdom at Chantilly was that 'strongholds, destined to be invested, no longer have a role to play'.

The delegation also discovered that supply lines to Verdun were utterly inadequate; a few well aimed shells would cut off the whole region from the rest of the world. They recommended reinforcement of the forts to restore them to their former strength and rapid construction of an extra railway line. In December the Chamber army committee came to the same conclusions, provoking from Joffre the comment that their report was 'calculated to disturb profoundly the spirit of discipline in the army'.

'If last August we had brought to the tribune the observations we had made at Verdun, perhaps the affair set off on 21 February would never have occurred,' snorted Charles Humbert during a discussion the following May.

So it had all been predicted. The German offensive followed precisely the course the committee had outlined the previous August. Douaumont fell without a fight. The first German troops to enter discovered, to their amazement, that the fort was virtually unmanned. A bit of afternoon gunning from Crown Prince Wilhelm's long-barrelled naval cannon had turned the steel tracks of the Verdun–Sainte-Ménéhould railway into gruesome-looking snarling reptiles. Verdun was cut off.

Or almost cut off. There remained a narrow-gauged line running across the plain to Bar-le-Duc and the country road that paralleled it. It was Pétain who organised the long convoys of rattling, solid tyred lorries to carry men and supplies, day and night, into Verdun. It was Barrès who called the road the *Voie sacrée*.

'A new Sedan is developing out there,' wailed one committee member. 'Criminal negligence,' muttered another '*Cette incurie*,' repeated a third.

The moderates of the committee at once lost the initiative; henceforth the critical question was no longer whether they should interpellate the government in secret session but when.

Briand's government was essentially a reshuffled version of Viviani's. Viviani was still there (as keeper of the seals), so were Guesde, Sembat and Thomas. Louis de Freycinet and Léon Bourgeois had left the Senate army committee to serve as ministers. Emile Combes was also a new member. It was an uncomfortable ragbag collection. Abel Ferry, an ousted under-secretary of state, commented, 'To govern France you have to be, currently, either a revolutionary Socialist or an octogenarian.' Briand even asked Clemenceau to join but, as with Viviani, Clemenceau said he would accept only the premiership or the ministry of war.

Briand's style particularly annoyed the committee. He had a rather unconcerned air, a cigarette hanging from his mouth, his hands in his pockets. Unlike Poincaré, he never read reports or consulted dossiers, preferring instead simply to listen carefully to whoever addressed him and then spontaneously react. He was a master at turning the question back at his opponent. Abel Ferry, who had joined the Chamber army committee after leaving the government, described Briand as a '*digestif*': 'he "drinks" the knowledge of his inquisitors'.

IX

IT WAS through the Chamber army committee, and particularly Ferry, that the Senate army committee eventually got what it had been seeking for eighteen months, a secret session.

Ferry was an unusual character. His uncle Jules had left him, in his will, 'all my books and all my arms', had exhorted him to 'defend in all circumstances the name of his father and his uncle' and instructed 'that he serve his country and that he love it more than his life . . .' War broke out just weeks after Abel Ferry had been asked to join Viviani's government, at the age of thirty-three, as undersecretary of state for foreign affairs. He promptly tendered his resignation, arguing that the duty of men of his age was to fight. His colleagues refused the resignation, but at the same time allowed him to join up with the 166th Infantry Regiment.

So for the next year and a half Ferry found himself moving back and forth between the council of ministers and the trenches. He was involved in some of the worst fighting in Champagne in 1915, an experience which led him to draft a memorandum to the whole council. He opened with a statement which became his war cry, 'There is a need to penetrate above the experience of below' (*'Il y a lieu de faire pénétrer en haut l'expérience d'en bas'*). This was a war of details, he noted, of 'little victories', of section commanders and company commanders. It was a war that staff officers ignored entirely because they had failed to develop the necessary liaison between combatants and GQG. Like Clemenceau, Ferry recommended that all staff officers be required to spend time with the troops. 'The soul of 1793 is below,' he concluded, 'bureaucracy is above. That is the danger.'

Ferry fought in Belgium and in Lorraine. 'My moral authority,' he wrote to his wife from the trenches at Les Courtes-Chausses in the Woëvre, 'comes to me for what I am, the only civilian who knows something about the war.' Ferry's diary shows increasing frustration with the failure of the government to reform the generals of Chantilly. The moment he lost the government post he became a leading critic within the Chamber.

The Chamber's army committee was very different from its counterpart in the Senate. It had been elected before the war and was made up largely of opponents to the three-year service of 1913. Ferry said 'a few hot heads, like Accambray, or antipatriots like Raffin-Dugens, brushed aside the more balanced elements. General Pedoya presided over it, mumbling, spluttering, muddling up letters and dossiers.'

All this changed when Ferry entered the committee in early 1916, accompanied by another irrepressible critic and *grand blessé de guerre*, Sergeant André Maginot.

So the Senate army committee now had an ally and the calls within it for a secret session consequently grew louder. 'Finally the time has come,' said Paul Doumer in mid-May, 'to quit our usual *tran-tran* of reports and discussions with the government behind closed doors.' But Clemenceau was strangely silent on this matter and would only remark at the end of a meeting, 'I am engaged in political action outside the committee.' He even noted, 'I am not upset to see the Chamber take these questions up first.'

Precisely what this 'political action' involved is uncertain. But within a month the Chamber was in fact holding its first secret session. The day the interpellation was demanded, just before the session opened, Ferry was going over his notes at home when the telephone rang. The gruff voice at the other end of the line made him feel as if it were he who was about to be interpellated.

'I am Monsieur Clemenceau. I want to see you immediately. Can you come over?'

'I don't have the time.'

'Then I'll come over to you.'

'Clemenceau in my home!' noted Ferry in his diary. 'It was a private upheaval. I had been brought up in the hatred of Clemenceau, the insulter and the "overthrower" of my own people. I knew that he held all the strings that moved the supporters of the secret session: Chappedelaine, Meunier-Surcouf, Maginot, Albert Favre. Cabinet satellites swung in orbit between him and me, but as for me, I refused to see him.'

Too late. There was a bang at the door and Clemenceau entered with hat and cane, in battle array. Ferry received him coolly. Clemenceau spoke in his 'brutal and romantic manner'.

'We have to act immediately. I've just been visited by an officer from GQG. Joffre is totally disheartened. Castelnau wants to take him to Verdun to mount the morale of the major generals. But there's no way of pulling him out of it. Those people are losing France.'

Then he left. Ferry could not understand the purpose of the visit. 'Was it to have a look at my face?' The encounter was, in fact, the beginning of an important collaboration.

Joffre had reason to be upset. Mangin's offensive against Douaumont had ended in the massacre of his own troops. Fort Vaux, which had also, under Joffre's orders, been stripped of its guns, fell after terrifying fighting at close quarters with machine guns, grenades and flame-throwers. Morale among the French troops was low. Reports of 'indiscipline' were coming through. And at the moment Clemenceau had visited Ferry the Germans were launching another offensive; there was every indication that Verdun was about to fall.

As for the Chamber's secret session, it did not go very well for Ferry and his friends. Maginot, after debunking GQG's arithmetic on casualties and presenting a superb criticism of the high command's strategy of 'nibbling' ('We are the ones being nibbled!'), made the mistake of reading some of Gallieni's descriptions of Joffre, found after Gallieni's death. It caused a sensation. Briand claimed the documents were false, which caused an even greater sensation, and this time the shame was on Maginot.

The war minister's defence of the high command's conduct at Verdun was very weak. When he remarked that disciplinary action was being taken against some generals, there was an outcry. 'The names! the names!', recalling the Panama scandal of 1893.

However Briand, with exquisite deftness, again turned the situation round. He appealed to the 'Sacred Union'. His melodious voice created a certain mystique. It was as if the deputies, said Ferry, were sitting in the grotto of Lourdes.

Only ninety-seven deputies voted against the motion of confidence. The 'ninety-seven', or the 'minority', was to be repeated in Ferry's circle like republicans of yore spoke of '*Les Cinq*' in the first Corps législatif or the '363' of the *Seize Mai*.

The German advance had led itself into the narrow salient at Fleury-devant-Douaumont and had been unable to bring up its heavy guns in support. Their new 'Green Cross Gas' (from the mark on the shells), or phosgene, had not inflicted the casualties expected among French artillery men. French guns were more accurate than the Germans'. Nivelle issued his dramatic order of the day, '*Ils ne passeront pas.*'

Mangin threw waves of battalions on to Thiaumont and Fleury. From the air, all that one could see of this village was a white smear in the mud. The only recognisable object found on its site was a silver chalice from the church. Casualties had been horrendous. But the Germans did not pass.

On 1 July, after seven days of preparatory bombardment, which could be heard in Paris, Dover and Rye, the long awaited Allied offensive on the Somme began. Kitchener's 'Pals' had joined the war.

A secret session opened in the Senate four days later. It began with a speech from the minister of the interior, Louis Malvy. This was the same minister who had initiated proceedings against *L'Homme libre* back in September 1914. Today he had come to deliver a report on the situation in the war factories.

'Have you learned, Monsieur le ministre, outside the police reports' – Clemenceau had risen from his bench and was reaching for a few crumpled notes in his jacket pocket – 'that workers, good workers, moved by their conscience and by the duty of patriotism, were complaining about being prevented from giving the full yield of their work? That's the question that needs to be asked.'

'I reply at once that I have not learned of this.'

'Then I will give you, whenever you wish, the name of the officer that you called up from Bourges in order to report to him about the case.'

This was the old Clemenceau. Knowledge was used like ammunition, aimed with precision and fired to create maximum destruction. Malvy was certainly hurt by the first salvo, but he received repeated applause when afterwards he said he had won the confidence of the working class and the unions 'to make all the sacrifices that are necessary for the national defence.' Clemenceau would pick up the theme, and his quarrel with Malvy, one year later.

More than three days were spent discussing the effectiveness of French artillery. Stephen Pichon, Clemenceau's protégé and now member of the army committee, made a long speech on the Balkans, Greece and Salonika. Clemenceau himself spoke for four hours.

But Briand, in the end, scored an even greater success than in the Chamber. Only six senators voted against him, Clemenceau, Pichon, Debierre, Murat and Guinguand. 'Who is Guinguand?' muttered Clemenceau as he left the palace. It was one day, his secretary remembered, when Clemenceau did not smile.

In fact, he was ill. Laryngitis? Diabetic bronchitis? 'Call it what you like, laryngitis, pleurisy, general decomposition . . . The words explain nothing. All that I can tell you is that I cough.' But it did not impose on his time. In August he took a short trip to the Vendée with Gustave Geffroy. Sophie wrote to Geffroy just prior to the departure; her brother, she said, 'is fortunately much better.' The committee minutes show that he missed only one meeting, that of 17 August, presided by Paul Doumer.

Outside the Palais de Luxembourg, as the debate entered its third day, it had started to rain. It was the day Clemenceau spoke. By the fourth day it was deluging, the gutters of rue de Tournon and rue de Condé became little rivers and the awnings of the cafés flapped violently. The same rains fell on Verdun. They turned the hills into quicksands. Men, stumbling in the night in search of their companies, were sucked down and drowned.

The Somme offensive dragged on until November. The official British history of the war identified eight phases of the battle, but the soldiers certainly didn't notice. 'Over all our night activities the various German lights tossed their wild incoherence,' wrote the sensitive Edmund Blunden. 'Three blue lights it was half-humorously said, were the signal for peace; as time went on the definition was revised – four black lights.'

The British lost over four hundred thousand, killed, missing and wounded, on the Somme. French casualties approached two hundred thousand. The German losses are still a matter of debate.

By December, a hundred and sixty thousand Frenchmen had died or were missing at Verdun and another two hundred thousand were wounded. Contemporary German lists admitted to over a hundred thousand in killed and missing. Total casualties for this one ten-month 'battle' stood at something like three quarters of a million in dead and wounded. 'Verdun,' said Werner Beumelburg, 'transformed men's souls.'

In June and July, Brusilov, the new commander of the Russian South-Western Army, had inflicted shattering defeats on Austria-Hungary. So at the end of August, Rumania, convinced that the Austro–Hungarian army had ceased to exist, at last declared war on the side of the Allies and marched into Transylvania. It was promptly stopped by an Austro-German force under the command of Falkenhayn, recently transferred after the failure of the summer Verdun offensive. Falkenhayn's troops entered Bucharest in December. Greece, divided to the point of civil war between a king who liked the Germans and a republican prime minister who preferred the Allies, began edging towards the German camp. In Athens, a small contingent of French troops was massacred.

Thus the war entered its third winter. A long war without victory exacted political victims. In London, David Lloyd George – former radical and pacifist, the scourge of dukes and millionaires but currently hero of the press barons – replaced Herbert Asquith as prime minister and organised a special four-man 'war cabinet' to streamline the direction of Britain's war effort.

In Paris, another secret session in the Chamber ended on 7 December with a confidence vote of 344 to 160; the opposition had increased by two-thirds. Briand saw the threat and completely remodelled his ministry. Guesde and Sembat were ousted, leaving Thomas as the only member of the SFIO still serving. The octogenarians, like Méline and de Freycinet, also lost their posts. Briand even created his own version of a war cabinet, the five-member Comité de guerre, but, unlike its British counterpart, it did not have the power of decision, which was left with the whole council of ministers.

There was also a shake-up in high command. On 13 December Joffre was made technical adviser to the Comité de guerre while Nivelle, popular with the politicians because of the recapture of Douaumont and with the Allies because of his fluent English, was named commander-in-chief of the Armies of the North and North East. But this poorly defined arrangement didn't last two weeks. On 26 December Joffre resigned; the following day he was promoted 'Marshal of France' and he promptly marched out of history and into obscurity. With Joffre gone, it was no longer possible to keep on General Roques at the ministry of war. He was replaced by General Lyautey, recalled from Morocco.

When the Senate army committee met on 13 December they were in a deep quandary. They had just registered with the Senate a request for an interpellation, signed by most of the committee members, on the high command, on artillery manufacture and on the general conduct of the war. Now there was a new government and a new high command. Clemenceau had been told by the Senate president that the interpellation was still valid, but most agreed that Briand would use the changes as an excuse for delaying it. It was not a cheerful prospect.

'If we do not obtain a government and a command which prepares the campaign of 1917, our account is done,' warned Doumer. 'France will go to peace through exhaustion.' Humbert remarked that the reshuffling of ministers had not seriously modified the government. 'The president of the council, not having changed, will continue to manifest in the conduct of the war the same mentality, the same character.'

Clemenceau thought that the government would probably in the next day or so make a declaration before the Senate 'to which it would be very easy to attach our interpellation that we would resume by saying: "You refuse to make peace, so, make war!"'

They agreed to withdraw their first interpellation and register another with the *bureau du groupe* of the Democratic Left. Bérenger said that to avoid *a faux pas* – Briand might still refuse the interpellation on the grounds that the government had changed – they should address the interpellation 'uniquely to the president of the council, who can be interrogated on the direction of the war . . .' Briand thus became, out of a matter of strategy, a personal target.

Clemenceau noted explicitly that he did not want to intervene in the debate and he charged Humbert to speak of artillery, Jeanneney to treat the question of command and Doumer to discuss the 'general situation'.

Gaston Monnerville, writing in the 1960's, says that Clemenceau 'was on the eve of being submitted to a previously planned surgical operation.' He had been operated on the prostate in 1912 and it is possible that there were complications. His uncharacteristic appeals made that December to the Senate for the Assembly's 'indulgence' suggest that he was not feeling well. But no other evidence available – such as Geffroy's correspondence, where there would surely be a mention – even hints at surgery. In January he was clambering up the hills to Fort Douaumont.

The interpellation, held in secret session, began on 19 December and lasted for five days. All the speakers were members of either the army committee or the foreign affairs committee. Their opposition to Briand had an element of 'nibbling' about it; Gaston Menier discussed aeroplanes and aircraft gunnery, de Monis delved into Greek affairs, Doumer presented a mass of statistics on recruits and artillery. The general tenor of the criticism was, as Doumer put it, 'You have given neither order, nor command, nor means of manufacture.'

According to plan, Briand himself became the target of attack. Briand, said Bérenger, 'did not have the mentality of war which is needed at the present instant'. And speaking for his colleagues he went on, 'We think that the war must be less spoken than lived and acted. We want a government of war which makes war. We want a government of war which knows war.' Everybody recognises Briand's talents as an orator, Bérenger went on, and he has a 'genius for making deals'; but peacetime procedures are not going to give the success we need now. 'Are you this government of war?'

Briand responded, in style, like a one-man army rushing to the counter-attack whenever the possibility of breach appeared. He was well aware of the jealousies within the Senate and he knew that the majority would probably vote against the two 'grand committees'. His strategy was not to allow the criticisms to accumulate. So after each major speaker, he strode up to the tribune and delivered his riposte. It was an unusual procedure for a prime minister.

He said he had unprecedented responsibilities: 'There has never been, in any era or in any country of the world, a government that has had to face up to such a terrible task, on which has weighed so many difficulties, which has been so impeded in its work as this one.'

Given the conditions, 1916, he thought, had been 'more than encouraging'; Verdun had been saved, 'the Somme offensive has given confidence to our men because it has shown them that France possesses an artillery', on the Italian front the Austrians had retreated, Rumania had joined the Allies ('And the Germans are in Bucharest,' tagged on Clemenceau).

Briand got most of the applause, especially from the Right. His repeated sallies to the tribune disoriented his opponents; the applause they received was confined to a corner of the Left.

On the fourth day, after Jeanneney's long and densely argued speech on the high command, Briand asked to close the session. Then, a moment of astonishment: Clemenceau said he wanted to speak. Had he changed his mind or had he planned this from the outset? 'You think, Monsieur le Président du Conseil, we have finished with all the explanations demanded of you. What do you know? I have a question . . .' The duel was set for the following afternoon.

X

SO THE great issues of the war, the sacrifice of the nation's youth and the eternal defence of the Republic and its institutions were reduced to a trial between two men. Clemenceau was sarcastic and biting, more a bulldog than a tiger. Briand was svelte, his words allusive, his appearance serene, almost smiling – a cat. Their dispute brought a deadly nearness of contact, a strange closeness that hinted of hate, of love, of both.

'Where are we going? Where are you leading us?' After two years of war there was economic disorder, diplomatic disorder and disorder in military organisation and in the high command.

'Disorder?' answered Briand. 'No, but real difficulties, for sure, that you would have encountered yourself, Monsieur Clemenceau, and which you would not have overcome with sarcasm.' The question came naturally, 'Would you have done better?'

'Too easy an argument. I have not established a parallel between us.' Indeed, Clemenceau sincerely believed, and had noted in his introductory remarks, that this debate was not a matter of personalities.

'Allow me! We are, Monsieur Clemenceau, at an hour when the country has the right to exact from a man like you more than simple gestures of demolition.'

'What does that mean?'

'You have got to bring something else.' There was loud applause.

'The real "gesture of demolition" is in the failure to make cannon. It's you who are demolishing everything. You have left disorder in the army.'

Briand stuck impenitently to his demonstration that it was Clemenceau who was the demolisher, the source of disorder: 'When you said, "Your methods of war are bad; it is because of them that the Germans are still in France . . ."'

'Yes!' Clemenceau was as persistent with his.

'It is the most terrible reproach one can make of a government.'

'It's the truth!'

'Well, it needs to be explained, to be supported on something other . . .'

'It was Monsieur Doumer who said it.'

'. . . than a picturesque recital of the facts. I, at any rate, I cannot accept this without discussion.'

The Senate had been discussing it for five days and the matter would only be resolved by the vote. The government got 194 votes, the opposition 60.

It would not be Clemenceau who would overthrow Briand, but Lyautey, his minister of war. In March 1917, as France prepared for another great offensive, Lyautey refused to reveal to the Chamber, in secret session, several technical details for 'reasons of security'. He was probably right, but it was no longer a formula one could evoke before parliament. Lyautey resigned and, three days later, the whole government resigned. Verdun could lay claim to a few more casualties.

XI

YET THE war demanded still more. The advancing spring imposed the advancement of another offensive, another year's instalments of sleet, rain, remorseless heat, and the daily unseasonable thud and crackle of artillery and small arms. God's seasons, however, came late while man's plans were inexorable, mechanical, drawn insensibly into the wheels of unalterable timetables.

There was compelling reason for an immediate combined Allied operation in France. On the Italian front men were immobilised because of the snows; on the Russian front they were immobilised because of a revolution; and Germany, under its own domestic stress, began a campaign of unlimited submarine warfare, seriously limiting Britain's long-term ability to wage war.

As for the poor troops, their attitude puzzled administrators at that time. Some argued that the change in high command, with Robert Nivelle at its head, brought a new optimism, while others said it had the opposite effect. Certainly, the trench newspapers revealed no secrets. You would always find sadness there; *le cafard* haunted all armies. A contributor to *Sans tabac* reflected in March 1917 on the sadness one felt as the *vaguemestre* read out the names of men who had received parcels, a sadness at the silence when no one replied. 'Was it the effect of these worrying phrases or of the cold fog which continued to scourge the landscape? I felt overwhelmed with a singular sadness, a sadness where men, things and thoughts seemed coloured in grey.'

In *L'Argonnaute* one might discover how sadness could give way to indifference: 'The danger, the waiting, the obsessive idea of death have hardened our soul and it is indifference which has become the inhuman armour that protects us from too human sentiments. The less suffering, the better. So-and-so is dead? *Pauvre diable!* And one thinks no longer about it a minute later.'

On progresse offered, for the First of April, a dash of resentment: 'Military stupidity and the immensity of the waves are the only two things which can give an idea of infinity.'

Spring 1917 was the season of the 'Verdun method'. Nivelle, a gunner, had developed at Verdun the technique of the 'creeping barrage' which, in theory at least, was a boiling, roaring curtain of exploding shells which proceeded about a hundred metres in front of the attacking infantry. The technique seemed to have worked within the limited combat zone of Verdun: Nivelle was now talking of applying it to the whole western

52. Clemenceau and Monet at Giverny

53. Clemenceau, bowed in grief, witnesses the burial of Claude Monet. The coffin is covered in a multicoloured cloak

50. Aerial view of Versailles as the plenipotentiaries leave after signing the treaty, 28 June 1919

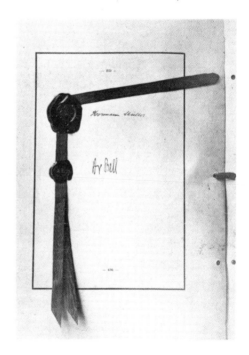

51. The last page of the Peace Treaty – the signatures and seals of the two German delegates

48. Open war: French infantry in their rifle pits, April 1918

49. The catharsis of peace: Clemenceau announces the proclamation of armistice to the Chamber of Deputies, 11 November 1918

44. Joseph Caillaux

45. Aristide Briand speaks

46. *Below:* Louis Malvy, minister of the interior, 1914–1917

47. Bolo Pasha, entrepreneur, spy, is executed, April, 1918

41. Clemenceau visits the battlefield of Maurepas in the Somme, 10 October 1916. The officer wearing a képi at the rear is Clemenceau's son, Michel. Captain Delorme leads the way

42. *Corvée*, or fatigue duty, at a 'rest camp' behind the Chemin des Dames, at the time of the mutinies of 1917

43. A stretch of the Chemin des Dames, west of Hurtebise, still intact in late May 1917

40. The Senate Army Committee takes a break, May 1916. To the left of Clemenceau (presiding over the committee) sits the prime minister, Aristide Briand, and his minister of war, General Roques. In the foreground stand Charles Humbert, Milliès-Lacroix and Gervais

54. Belébat, Clemenceau's last Vendée home

55. Clemenceau at Belébat: 'I have flowers which grow in the sand and nourish themselves with I don't know what. It is a mystery'

56. Clemenceau catches a rose, New York, 22 November 1922

front. The operation would consist of a two-pronged attack on the upper half of the front's drunken S – Nivelle called the zone variously a 'pocket' or a 'square' – with the British moving in south-east from Arras and the main French forces attacking north-eastwards from Soissons and Reims. At the heart of the operation was Nivelle's vision of a *'ruée formidable'*, a tremendous onrush of troops coming wave after wave, unending, unstoppable.

Most of Nivelle's subordinates were sceptical. Pétain considered the operation pure folly. Lyautey, while still minister of war, regarded it as the sort of plan dreamed up by the 'army of the Duchess of Gerolstein'. His successor, Paul Painlevé, expressed his doubts openly to the government, to Nivelle and to his subordinates; he said it all had an uncanny resemblance to the tactics of 1915. When, in May, the members of the Senate army committee finally got hold of Nivelle's directives, they claimed that they were identical to the military 'decree relative to the conduct of grand units' of September 1913, one of the classic statements of the pre-war school of *attaque à outrance.*

But Nivelle, tall, with eyes which addressed one directly and irradiated self-confidence, could sweep any doubter aside. Lloyd George, when he first met Nivelle in the gare du Nord in January, was so impressed with the performance that he asked the general to come immediately over to London to speak to his war cabinet. 'Nivelle has proved himself to be a Man at Verdun,' Lloyd George explained to a lovely lady friend; 'and when you get a Man against one who has not proved himself [he was referring of course to Haig], why, you back the Man!' For the next three months British army command was, under Lloyd George's instructions, effectively subordinated to Nivelle, a situation which nearly led to Haig's resignation. Hearings in the Senate army committee show that the British government's enthusiasm for Nivelle's offensive was the major reason why the operation was allowed to go ahead; after the heavy losses of Verdun, France was in no mood to upset her ally.

So divisions and divisions were moved into the points of attack, new weapons were tested, practice manœuvres were conducted, roads were built, new gun emplacements were constructed, huge ammunition dumps were set up; all under the jealous eyes of German binoculars viewing from their high positions on the Aisne, from their balloons, from their aircraft.

In order to spread Nivelle's enthusiasm down to the lowest ranks in the army, copies of his plans and directives were distributed to regional commanders, corps commanders, colonels and captains. The humblest officers on the front carried in their pockets and satchels copies of Nivelle's plan of attack. In February, following a minor trench raid, the Germans recovered a set of such documents from the body of a French officer. Within a week, the German high command had decided on a strategic withdrawal.

*

The Allies first became aware of the German movement through the strange sight of red rose-like fires on the eastward horizon at evening, distant conflagrations in the towns and the villages behind the German front: calculated mass destruction was being undertaken in the German rear prior to their retreat to the Siegfried Stellung, or what the Allies were to call the Hindenburg Line. The actual retreat began on 15 March and was completed by the 19th. Through this single manœuvre the Germans had reduced their front line by 140 kilometres. The 'pocket' – and object of Nivelle's offensive – had been emptied and flattened.

The French newspapers in March all cried victory. The beginning of the Liberation! *'Nos Alliés Anglais enlèvent Bapaume!'* *L'Homme enchaîné* announced the news that all its readers had been waiting for since 1914, *'Ils ne sont plus à Noyon!'*

But Clemenceau, in his column, remained cautious: 'Since this movement is not the effect of a general offensive from our front and because Hindenburg yields to other means of persuasion than that of our artillery, it would without doubt be premature to believe that the Boches are in the process of evacuating France.'

Nivelle meanwhile confidently informed the minister, 'Had I been charged to direct the movements of the German army so as to make them conform to my designs I would not have given it any other orders than those it received from Marshal Hindenburg.' The offensive, virtually unaltered, was set for April.

There was little rejoicing in the 'liberated' zone between Arras and Soissons. 'In the evacuated territories there are no towns or villages, it might be said, that have any houses fit to receive inhabitants,' wrote Paul Fauchille in a government report later that year. 'The principal localities, Bapaume, Ham, Chauny, Péronne, are hardly more than a collection of ruins.' The Germans had used Russian prisoners-of-war to saw down the trees, about a metre from the ground, of orchards, woodlands and copses. Wells and water sources were poisoned with arsenic. There was not an animal left alive. Starting in mid-February able-bodied men and women aged between fifteen and sixty, including the mayors, the doctors and pharmacists, were rounded up and deported by train to Germany. Beds and cupboards were smashed with shovels and mallets, china and glass were pulverised, mattresses were emptied of their wool and torn down to their springs, prams were broken, sewing-machines were shattered. 'We have orders,' said a neatly dressed boy in field grey to a resident of Frétoy-le-Château, 'to leave you nothing but your eyes with which to cry.'

A new hatred for the enemy was born among French troops, along with a new expectation of what the offensive could bring. 'Let's go to their homes, burn, devastate, rape as they do in ours,' wrote one corporal in a letter recorded by postal control; if he could not 'destroy this filthy race' he would at least 'kill as many of them as possible.'

'Ah! the monsters,' sighed a private, 'they have cut down the fruit trees!'

XII

THE TROOPS were moved up to their positions at night, only hours before the assault was launched. Heavy cannon, placed at intervals of twenty-one metres, loosed off volleys of steel over their heads, shrapnel shells rang out, burning momentarily in reds and yellows, sparks of mortars soared then sank, while the 75's and 77's kept up their steady accompaniment of castanets, though these seemed to lessen as the naval guns – 200's and 300's – spoke from hidden woods in daylight bursts, vibrating the long approach trenches like cymbals.

Slowly, weighed down by haversacks and flasks that tapped against the metal plates of their rifle butts, the infantry went up the line, that interminable boyau which a freezing rain had turned to wasteland. The planking was sparse, some said non-existent, so they tramped in water, greenweedy and ratty. The straps of the sacks cut, tore and numbed the shoulders, pushing the head forward and pressing the folds of horizon blue into bruised flesh.

These were the elite corps of Charles Mangin's Sixth Army; Blondlat's 2nd Colonial Corps, Marchand's 10th Colonial Division, the 15th, the 2nd Colonial Regiment of Brest, the 5th, the 6th.

The black battalions, the Senegalese, marched with them. They were unaccustomed to the cold. As night diluted into the river mist of dawn they fumbled with frozen hands to fix bayonets and, without success, prepared to carry their rifles into the battlefield under their arms like umbrellas.

The east began to unveil itself. The men, facing north, would catch the first glimpses of a line of hills dusted, like a Christmas log, in snow and looking quite deserted. Out of sight, but winding along the crest, was a narrow road called the Chemin des Dames.

People had been constructing roads in this region for two thousand years, mostly for the purpose of carrying armies. The major thoroughfares, appearing on the map like interlacing spokes centred on Reims, Soissons and Laon, were built by Romans to put down obstreperous Gauls. Franks and Merovingians battled it out here, so did feudal lords; Joan of Arc once passed by. But the Chemin des Dames was a more recent construction, a private way built for the two daughters of Louis XV so that, from their château in the Forêt de Vauclair they could ride in their carriage to Soissons and Paris, avoiding the muddy tracks of the Aisne and the Ailette. From the ridge one could look down steep escarpments to the meandering river, to marshes, plateaux and the steeples of Soissons. Many of the slopes were pierced with natural caverns, known to the local inhabitants as *creutes* or *boves*, some of them veritable underground labyrinths that had been enlarged by the medieval quarrymen who supplied the stone for cathedrals.

In 1917 the Chemin des Dames formed the southern rim of the Hindenburg Line and was held by three armies of the Imperial Crown Prince. It was on the capture of these formidable positions that the whole Nivelle offensive depended.

Mangin's orders to his army were as true to his own style of command as they were to the spirit of Nivelle's GQG. The attack, he signalled, 'will take the form of a brutal and continuous assault, cut only by short pauses strictly necessary for placing the units back in relative order'. He laid down the distance that the assault waves were to maintain behind the artillery barrage – seventy to eighty metres behind the percussion shell, 150 metres behind the heavier fuse shells – and the exact speed at which the troops, with '*un seul élan*', were to proceed – one hundred metres in three minutes. The machine-gun nests? 'The enemy organisations which might remain shall be overtaken by the waves of assault and will find themselves submerged, at the mercy of the reserves.' On the eve of the attack he told a subordinate that they would be taking their aperitif the next day in Laon.

This was in conformity with Nivelle's timetables: at H-hour + 3 they would be in the village of Bauconville, north of the Chemin des Dames; at H + 6 they would be passing through the village of Montbérault; and at H + 7 they would be south of Montchalons and a few kilometres from Laon – a timetable decided by haggling over the telephone between GQG and the local commanders. Cavalry held behind Soissons was to be brought in to add speed and four thousand beds were prepared which would be transported to Laon in anticipation of the wounded. Painlevé would later explain to the Senate army committee that at this rate of advance 'the troops went quicker than they would have been able to go if there had not been an enemy in front of them'; and he added, 'the enemy appeared here as a force of attraction and not as a force of repulsion'.

*

Snow had delayed the initial British offensive to the north by twenty-four hours. But on Monday, 9 April, at 5.30 a.m. they attacked on a twenty-four kilometre front between Arras and Vimy. In squalling snow and sleet two Canadian divisions, supported by tanks, took Vimy Ridge. But Horne's First Army came to a virtual halt outside Lens, Gough's Fifth could not withstand the German counter-attack, and the attempt to take Saint-Quentin had to be abandoned. The northern pinch on the empty pocket had run into a wall of concrete – which put all the more pressure for success on the pinch in the south.

It was weather again which forced Nivelle to postpone the French attack for forty-eight hours, but when the whistles blew at 6 a.m. on Monday, 16 April, it was a morning as gloomy and vast as any of the preceding week, with low grey clouds that tendered to the men a natural snare of rain and sleet.

The Germans sent up yellow flares which flickered in the half light, the French barrage gave off savage flashes from great earth geysers, smelling of hot oil and petrol; a sickening, thick, pharmaceutical odour.

The first assault wave embarked from a place called Soupir. It was pinned down by German machine-gun fire at the foot of a cliff in the quarry of Les Grinons. Blondlat's 2nd Colonial Corps headed straight up the slopes of the Valley Foulon towards Hurtebise and the Forêt de Vauclair. Rain and snow had turned the terrain into a slippery obstacle course and progress was not helped by the twenty-kilo haversacks the men still had on their backs. But up they went, clawing and grasping. They were led by General Jean-Baptiste Marchand, bane of the British at Fashoda. He was already wounded. Up and up they scrambled. They could not, of course, maintain the prescribed one hundred metres every three minutes, so the barrage, fired by gunners in fog, disappeared into the mists over the top of the hill. Still further up, their lungs heaving. There was not much shelling now. An occasional bomb came coiling downwards and burst in whorls of blackened smoke. A few machine guns puttered.

And they were there, at the crest. A great, colourless emptiness extended before them, like a Russian steppe of clay, snow and stone. Then through the sleet they could see ghostly shadows. They were the trees of the Forêt de Vauclair.

In a second they knew it was finished. They saw, they heard, they understood that their assault wave had been drawn into a trap. A flood of bullets came wheezing from unnoticed corners, from hidden concrete shelters, caves and covered holes. 'In the confusion,' wrote a week later an anonymous contributor to the trench paper, *Grenadia*, 'there are no young initiates to stick out their chests to the hail of bullets; there are

only fragile beings whose instinct of conservation flattens them against
the soil, for one has never needed to pronounce beautiful phrases in order
to know how to die.'

Some rolled themselves into human balls, others lay flat, a few simply
sat down. The Senegalese ran for the forest or back to the crest, where
they collided into the next assault wave coming over the top. Nobody knew
where they were. They were caught in the madding crowd of the dead and
the dying, surrounded by smoke and lights and gunfire coming from every
corner of the world. There was no land, there was no sky. Just cloud and
fog and noise.

Where was the enemy?

'The battle began at six,' said soldier-deputy Jean Ybarnegary, 'and it
was lost by seven.' Indeed, after only fifty minutes, Mangin called off his
main assault.

But it was not the end of the battle. A small parliamentary delegation
had gathered at an observation post outside the village of Roucy. 'In
the morning, at daybreak, from the height of a freezing hill, I saw the
formidable Battle of the Aisne get under way, its panorama unfolded
before my eyes.' In fact Clemenceau would not have been able to see a
quarter of the battle, his field of vision being essentially limited to the
action of Mazel's Fifth Army to Mangin's right on the eastern escarpment
of Hurtebise, the Plateau de Californie, the low-lying marshland area
around La Temple-au-Choléra and the nearby road running parallel to
the Aisne between Pontavert and Guignicourt. Clemenceau was joined
by other members of the two parliamentary army committees, Abel Ferry,
Paul Doumer, Albert Favre, J. L. Breton, Renaudel and Aubriot.

There was something anachronistic about these seven men, mostly in
civilian dress, who had come to watch a battle; one thinks of Bismarck,
King Wilhelm and the German princes watching from the heights of
Frénois the Battle of Sedan.

'The whole plain exploded in a collision of thunder,' Clemenceau
told his readers in *L'Homme enchaîné* three days later. 'It was the most
beautiful emotion in my life. A great festival, in fact . . .' But, although
the triumphant headlines on this page listed the villages seized, the booty
taken and the prisoners captured, Clemenceau did at least manage to
warn the reader 'not to try and anticipate the outcome; our failures in
foresight have condemned us to day-to-day victories'. And he concluded
with a remark that would be at the core of his political thinking over the
coming months: 'The firm patience of the rear is the first condition of the
soldier's heroism.'

He was almost certainly unaware of the extent of the massacre that was
being played out before him. Les Grinons and the Foulon Valley were on

the other side of the heights of the Bois de Neuville. His reference to the whole plain exploding in thunder was perhaps an unwitting record of the fate of Commandant Bossut's squadron of primitive tanks which was blown to pieces that morning on the road to Guignicourt. After Painlevé had presented the committee, on 9 May, with the first official casualty figures, Clemenceau – evidently shocked – responded, 'When I saw General Micheler [group commander of the Fifth, Sixth and Tenth Armies] he said to me nothing of the kind.'

With the abandonment of the main frontal assault, the attack shifted to the extreme wings north of Soissons and north and north-east of Reims. These would be the sites of bloody combats that would continue, at varying pace, until the end of April; a second series of attacks was launched in early May. But long before May the mood of the troops had changed.

Ten thousand wounded? The first day of the offensive alone brought in over ninety thousand. Casualties, their eyelids red, their eyes burning, their bodies covered with huge ugly blisters, were laid out in the snow by the roadside, the same roads that other troops pushed down on their way to the front. The wounded didn't have to say anything. You could read it in their faces: We have seen it all, the mines, the shells, the gas, the trees thrown over, the earth torn asunder, the wounded, the annihilating breath of machine guns; and, worst of all, the fog, the mists, that hid us for hours – counting like centuries – from the sun, the light of day.

Then the structure of command began to fall apart. Mangin blamed the division commanders, Nivelle blamed Mangin, Micheler blamed Nivelle. In an effort to disabuse GQG of its reputed isolation at Chantilly, Nivelle had moved his general staff first to Beauvais and then, shortly before the offensive, to the Château of Compiègne – a palace for emperors – less than twenty kilometres distant from operations. Telephone calls went out to the regional commanders and to the ministry of war, letters and telegrams were exchanged and a rapid visit to the three army group Head Quarters was arranged. This was a far cry from Joffre's aloof manner of handling disasters, as in the campaigns of 1915 when the casualties were in fact far worse. Joffre would have closed his apartment doors and ordered a large meal. Nivelle, instead, ordered out the staff car. His authority was crumbling.

The government didn't want to be held responsible. On the evening the offensive was launched Painlevé, at the ministry of war, heard the telephone ring. Assuming it was Nivelle, he refused to answer; he had no authoritative witness present and he didn't want to give GQG the opportunity of accusing the civilian authorities of meddling in military affairs. So he sent an officer to take the call. After five attempts to get through to the minister, Nivelle left a message; 'Tell the minister that I am going to stop Mangin's offensive all along the line.' There could be no argument, the decision was his.

For the next four weeks there followed an extraordinarily complicated series of plots and manœuvres between GQG, the regional commanders, deputies, senators, the Comité de Guerre, the war ministry ... Each general had his defenders in government and parliament. The major politicians had their servers and stooges in the army. Clemenceau had allies in Mangin, Mordacq and Micheler. Nivelle was defended by Maginot, Bourgeois, Lacaze and, most astonishing of all, Malvy, the minister of the interior. Painlevé backed Pétain. Ribot, the aged prime minister, managed to back both Nivelle and Pétain. The president of the Republic was even drawn into the combat. Having heard the pleas of a soldier-deputy whose army corps was about to be sent on one of the countless assaults on Craonne and Vauclair, Poincaré called GQG and demanded a postponement. Then the British intervened; Lloyd George appealed to the French to extend their attacks still further.

After long hours of discussion, the government finally came to a compromise arrangement on 29 April by which Pétain was named general chief-of-staff to the ministry of war. Nivelle kept his title, but effectively command had now shifted to the more cautious Pétain. Mangin was removed from the Sixth Army after a fuming encounter with Painlevé, which ended with Mangin storming out of the minister's office, slamming the door and threatening to call on Clemenceau.

Clemenceau did in fact follow this up with a series of articles on the ludicrous arrangements that had evolved in the army – 'cet engribouillis de tohu-bohu' – and he demanded, as he had many times already, a 'unity of command'. A step was made in that direction on 15 May when Pétain was named commander of the North and North-East Armies and Nivelle was retired to Paris.

XIII

AFTER 'PERFORMING their duties' in the trenches, fit men were brought back to the 'rest camps' in the rear. Some of these were squalid, especially around Soissons, a town that had already taken a knocking. 'The camp in the woods is perfectly organised to take care of itself,' recorded one rueful soldier for La Chéchia. 'Drinking water is ordinarily five hundred metres from the camp and can be procured easily – but without abuse, for example from 5.15 hours to 6.22 and from 20.30 to 24.00. It is most convenient.

Showers are in the neighbouring villages. However, on the ground, water is everywhere. This is the only water which is not strictly regulated.' Men found themselves assigned to the cellars of bombed-out houses, holes where there was a persistent odour of pipe smoke, wine and unchanged socks. Flies gathered at points on the walls in thick black layers that would spread out with a buzz as you passed. Somewhere to lie down? It took some deciding; the place was liberally scattered with ammoniacal emanations.

And it was here that you waited – though 'waiting' was spent doing drills and exercises – for the next call forward.

Painlevé, writing in 1919, remembered how the mood of letters from the front, received through postal control, changed during the week of 22–30 April. The first letters still reflected the hopes that existed on the eve of the attack: 'We are advancing', 'We have pushed', 'The Boches have suffered fantastic losses.' But later the impression changed and there came discouragement: 'It's finished and we will never have them since we did not have them this time'; 'They will not pass, but we will never pass'; 'It will only finish when we are all killed.'

A cry of pain rang out in the armies, an increasingly voluble groan of exasperation, whipped on by fear and the oppression of that long night of waiting.

Painlevé, in his first report on 'collective indiscipline' to the Senate army committee, said there were troubles even before the April offensive. There were sounds of mutiny, for example, during the Verdun campaign. On the first day of the attack on the Chemin des Dames, 16 April, six men, including a corporal, abandoned their posts prior to an assault on Le Choléra Farm; five of them were condemned to death, though their sentences were commuted. The next day, at Aubérive, seventeen men disappeared at the moment of attack; twelve of them received death sentences, but these were also commuted. On 29 April, two hundred soldiers of the 20th Infantry Regiment abandoned barracks at their rest camp of Mourmelon-le-Grand and fled to the surrounding woods after it was announced that they were being called up for an attack on Le Téton. Within days, most of them had returned, in dribbles. A few death sentences were pronounced but none, it seems, were carried out.

The really serious troubles developed in the last week of May and came to their climax in early June. Almost all of them occurred in and around Soissons or in the triangular area north-west of Reims that separated the River Aisne from the Vesle; sectors held by the Sixth and the Tenth Armies. The men were being ordered into yet another assault on the Chemin des Dames, the so-called 'Battle of the Ailette'. It was a strike: in masses, they refused to go. Whole companies, battalions and regiments vanished into the forests.

Those bands of mutineers, wandering the roads in the dark hours of the morning between Soissons and Mercin and Pernant and Saconin – flickering torches in their hands – were reminiscent of the miners' night patrols of the Pas-de-Calais in 1906. They sang, they shouted vague political slogans, they even waylaid trains like the strikers.

There were instances of elected committees – soldiers' councils – being set up in imitation of the Russians, whose 'February Revolution' (in March) had been getting wide coverage in the French press. Speakers addressed troops from military lorries. They invoked the absence of leave, the bad food; sometimes they referred to the Socialist International Congress in Stockholm for peace, to the government's refusal to negotiate with the Germans; the government wanted war, they said, it was the puppet of the arms suppliers, capitalist interests, the *buveurs de sang*. They would march on Paris; rumour had it that the capital had been delivered to fire and blood, that the troops' wives were being murdered by Annamites.

But the commonest type of 'collective indiscipline' was a simple refusal to participate in any further assaults. 'We will defend the trenches, but we won't attack.' 'If we refused to march,' it was stated in a letter recorded by postal control, 'it was not to bring a revolution; on the contrary, we wanted to attract the attention of the government, to let it understand that we were men and not beasts led to slaughter, that we wanted what was due to us.' Under the pressure of their comrades, some stayed in the camps or fled to the woods. Under pressure from their officers, others marched on to the thundering front; but when they marched they bleated like sheep, and there was nothing their officers could do to stop them.

How widespread were the mutinies? Estimates vary enormously. Mutinies were not something one talked about after the war. Today we have the official records, the police reports, the judgments of the *conseils de guerre* and a major academic study of the affair.

But so little is remembered of the torn emotions of those who witnessed these events first hand. Just a hint, here and there. In 1968 Jean Guéhenno met an old friend, a general then, a captain in 1917 when he was serving at the Chemin des Dames. Two battalions of his regiment had refused to go up the line, the third, the one he commanded, had obeyed and followed him . . . As the old general spoke his face changed, tears rolled from his eyes, he beat his breast; 'Yes, it was I. I made them a little speech and they marched. We set off. The other two battalions watched us go and started making fun of us. And I, I was twenty-three years old and I was an *instituteur*. I had six hundred men. I lost three hundred and three. Don't talk to me any longer of that! I don't want to think of it any more. Do you hear?'

Guy Pedroncini has studied the military archives. He places the total number involved at around forty thousand, a relatively small proportion of the whole army. But because of their distribution, he also calculates that two-thirds of the army were 'more or less agitated'. Only a tenth of the divisions were seriously affected by demands for immediate peace, and most of these were in the area around the Chemin des Dames. These are Pedroncini's statistics: 25,000 judgments were made, 629 men were condemned to death between 16 April 1917 and 31 January 1918 and, of these, 75 were actually executed, though '23 cases remain questionable.' This is his conclusion: 'It seems to us possible, in the absence of all solid evidence, and faced with the documents that the archives provide, to dismiss the idea that summary executions took place with deliberate purpose.' 1,381 men were condemned to five years of hard labour.

Is that the last word? One's impression is that the pain, the revolt and the punishment have vanished, like the tens of thousands of mutineers, into the forests, into the mists of time.

But we do know that GQG, already in upheaval, was worried. Painlevé, after reading its reports of early June, concluded that there were only two divisions between Paris and the front that could be relied on. General Maistre, Mangin's replacement, announced that if the Germans launched a full offensive he would be incapable of resisting. 'I do not know a more horrible sensation for a commander than suddenly to learn that his army is breaking up,' recalled General Bernard Serrigny, Pétain's subordinate at Compiègne. He had seen the 'initial disaster of Verdun', he would soon witness the Italian rout at Caporetto. 'But there had never been anything like 20 May! We seemed absolutely powerless. From every section of the front the news arrived of regiments refusing to man the trenches. The slightest German attack would have sufficed to tumble down our house of cards and bring the enemy to Paris.'

Amazingly, the Germans had little inkling of their enemy's troubles.

XIV

THE SENATE army committee was formally notified of the troubles only on 11 June when Painlevé, in a thin, squeaky voice, delivered a report 'on regrettable events . . .' 'On the mutinies,' interrupted Clemenceau, 'let's call the things by their name.'

'Messieurs,' the minister of war continued, 'I ask you that nothing that we say goes outside these four walls . . .'

'We have been informed already,' remarked Bérenger.

'Everybody knows about it,' added Clemenceau; 'great secret spreads down the boulevard.'

'The details that are told are anyway exaggerated,' said Strauss.

Clemenceau had probably got wind of the mutinies at a very early stage because it was the 24th Infantry Division, commanded by his great ally in the army, General Mordacq, which experienced one of the first cases of 'collective indiscipline', that at Aubérive on 17 April. Mordacq had warned him even before the offensive. 'I don't know how my men hold up. They are extremely tired. They had been given forty days of rest and eight days later the order to march arrives: we will have to march.' But when Painlevé presented his report, Clemenceau admitted that the committee was informed 'only in a vague fashion'. After Painlevé had enumerated just a few of the facts, the committee members were quite evidently shocked. 'There has never been a graver situation,' said Bérenger. Clemenceau: 'It puts the existence of France at peril. If the army disappears . . .' He couldn't finish his phrase.

There had been changes within the committee since December's secret session. They were the same people. But the centre of animation had shifted. Charles Humbert's rotund and previously ebullient presence had become clamlike, evasive and mysteriously silent. In three months he muttered only two sentences. The once moderate Henry Bérenger, on the other hand, had turned hawkish, pressing the others to be uncompromising with the government and particularly its minister of the interior, Malvy. He outdid even Doumer and Clemenceau. There was, he kept on repeating, a 'defeatist' organisation spreading its action through the whole of France: 'That is a national question, thus a question for the government; the very existence of the country is at issue.' Bérenger's new militancy derived from his presidency of two important subcommittees set up at the beginning of the year, the *Sous-commission de la main d'œuvre* (subcommittee of labour) and the *Sous-commission des faits de guerre* (subcommittee of facts of war). The first provided him with information on the war factories, the unions and their links with the front; the latter was the army committee's main research tool on military operations. Bérenger had, in effect, replaced Humbert as the committee's chief source of facts.

Jeanneney, vice-president of the *Commission de contrôle des effectifs* (committee of recruitment control), remained an important critic. Doumer's remarks were always biting. Strauss, by contrast, had become self-appointed spokesman for the government. Clemenceau, as before, maintained a certain presidential distance within the committee; he rarely presented himself as the main critic of the government and was, on occasion, most conciliatory. Nor did he ever mutter a word of hate or vindictiveness. Contrary to what some of his detractors would claim, both at the time and later, Clemenceau was not a man of hate; he was a man of passion. Poincaré in his memoirs says that Clemenceau burst into tears on more than one occasion during the committee meetings. The minutes suggest as much.

In addition to the shifting balance of personalities and the intensive pressures of the moment, one notes a change in the committee's attitude towards the high command. They are no longer as critical. They are more likely to play the generals off against the government. Part of this was due to tension that was developing with the Chamber and especially the Socialists who had become overtly anti-militaristic.

Even at the height of the Dreyfus Affair, Clemenceau used to repeat that he was not against the army. Nor were his colleagues in the committee now; their principal concern was how to strengthen the nation's defence. But independent of this was the extraordinary effect of Nivelle's character. As in the case of Lloyd George's war cabinet, the committee members liked Nivelle, they liked his presence, his manners, his absolute confidence, even if they were highly critical of his methods. Afterwards they would say that the offensive had been poorly prepared. But they never made a personal attack on Nivelle. Bérenger said that Nivelle showed 'grandeur in the conception but weakness in the execution'.

Clemenceau portrayed Nivelle as a rather tragic figure. He reported, in front of Painlevé, that after Poincaré's demand for a postponement of operations and 'on the acknowledgement of generals who were present and have since spoken to me, General Nivelle was thrown into inexpressible distress when he discovered he had been repudiated by the Head of State. He had tears in his eyes and said: "I am betrayed by my subordinates, I have learned this through the Head of State. Such a situation is inadmissible. I shall resign."'

The committee's *bête noire* was not this or that general; it was bureaucracy. Paul Doumer wondered if the Chemin des Dames was not simply a repetition of the bureaucratic, inexecutable plans of 1915. 'It is not the commanders which command, it is the bureaux,' he told Painlevé, who had just given a lengthy account of the April offensive. 'Didn't you get worried about this novel you've just read us? I don't know who – I think it was Napoleon – said that in a war you couldn't foresee anything after the first battle. The authors of this novel foresaw all the successive battles.' Bureaucratic confusion was the principal explanation, they argued, for the mutinies too.

Red flags? Where on earth did they come from? 'I don't know anything at the moment,' replied Painlevé. Pacifist tracts? 'It's the printers who have to be dealt with first,' said the minister. And the author? 'He is not always known while the printer must be.' Bérenger was on the edge of his seat: 'He's not known? In times of war?' After the commotion had died down, Painlevé, very ruffled, squeaked, 'What can I do! I don't control the police?'

The implication was obvious. As soon as Painlevé had left the room, Bérenger remarked that the control of pacifist propaganda was, indeed, the responsibility of the Sûreté Générale, under the orders of the minister of the interior, not the minister of war. 'But if we ask for explanations only from this Monsieur Malvy the discussion will get nowhere.' So it was decided to hear Malvy in the company of the prime minister and the minister of war. Bérenger was fearful that the British and the Americans would start modifying their war plans if defeatism in France got out of hand: 'Wouldn't it be better for us to take care of our own affairs? So, let's put the three responsible ministers on brief notice to explain themselves on the criminal propaganda that has already wrought too much devastation in the interior and on the front.'

Thus, in a single session, the committee moved into that tricky area of mass human behaviour which has baffled historians and sociologists on so many occasions: was the revolt the product of plot or of spontaneous rebellion?

The committee never actually committed itself though its leading figures, Doumer and Bérenger, clearly favoured the former thesis. Doumer would always emphasise the simultaneous nature of the events, while Bérenger always underlined the link between the front and the war factories, 'hearths of pacifist, antimilitarist, antipatriotic propaganda and anarchy'. The centres of 'propaganda and anarchy' were always the same factories, in the Rhone, the gunpowder factory of Bergerac and the munitions works of Bourges. The organisations responsible were always the same, the 'Comité de défense syndicaliste', which had been encouraging strikes throughout the country, and the 'Comité pour la reprise des relations internationales', which had been printing pacifist pamphlets, as well as the faithfully radical Fédération des Métaux and the Fédération des Syndicats d'Instituteurs. It was always the same people involved, Merrheim, Bourderon, Boudhoux, Monatte, Péricat, Mauritius – *minoritaires* within the CGT (and names already familiar to one former minister of the interior).

The committee liked the CGT's secretary-general, Léon Jouhaux, they considered him a great patriot, and when somebody such as Strauss said 'one should not incriminate the proletariat', they all evoked Jouhaux' name. Pacifism and defeatism, they argued, had nothing to do with the proletariat.

The positions of the GQG and that of the army committee were obviously getting closer together. Doumer and Bérenger would cite early warnings from Nivelle and Pétain about the harmful effects of pacifist propaganda to bolster their own positions. Paul Strauss cautioned the committee that the generals 'throw all the responsibility back onto the interior'. The prime minister, Ribot, would go even further, sounding the alert during one hearing: 'The commanders of the army! But if you listen to them there'll no longer be any press, no longer anything!' The tables had turned since the days when Viviani was prime minister.

Where exactly did Clemenceau stand? He had always been for a 'unity of command' and was as exasperated as Bérenger and Doumer with the spiralling chaos within the country's various administrations. He also, however, had a mistrust of censorship: white blanks still appeared in his articles. He had not abandoned the constitutional hierarchy that he had outlined back in January 1915: civilian power had to be placed higher than military power. He stood for war to the end, a victorious war, yet he remained haunted by the memory of civil war. He was as much a defender of democracy as any of the major politicians, but he could also remember that between democracy and demagogy there was only a vaguely defined line. War had made the boundary more hazy than ever. Where were the demagogues? and where the democrats?

As the debate on pacifism, mutiny and the April offensive was proceeding in the committee, Clemenceau published a series of articles on Russia. Russia was of course a very interesting place in June and July 1917. But Clemenceau's prime concern was not with Russia. He wrote about Russia because the censors would not let him write about France. Replace the word 'Russia' with 'France' and you get a very clear statement of his own national policy during this great crisis.

He quoted President Wilson's message to the Russian provisional government, 'The day has come to vanquish or to abdicate.' This, he said, was Russia's choice. There was a danger of being caught up in the illusion of 'the most beautiful formulas of human idealism'. 'Theories can be the joy of great dreamers. But what the people expect from thinkers are the consequences of action.' In fact, Russia had no choice at all. 'It is war and *war entirely* against the last hordes whose effort it is to establish by arms, on all the continents, the supremacy of organised violence. That is why today the word *pacifism* has no other sense than that of submission to the master of brutality.' He urged Russians not to resign themselves to the 'aesthetes of demagogy'. 'Your revolution tells us that the time has come for a *fortified* justice, as our Pascal once said. In this case, show us that you are capable of force against the enterprises of the foreign dominator.' [Clemenceau's emphasis.]

How could one have made peace with Germany in 1917? On 12 December 1916, Germany had announced to the world her plans for peace. Belgium, Holland and Denmark would become economic vassals, defended militarily by the Reich; Luxemburg would be annexed. In France, Toul, Verdun, Belfort, Briey, the northern coalfields and the whole coastal zone as far as the mouth of the Somme would be annexed. At no moment was there any question of Germany negotiating on Alsace-Lorraine. When Chancellor Bethmann-Hollweg started talking about a compromise peace he lost his job and Germany, in July, was effectively taken over by the military. The German Socialists spoke of peace? Even if they were sincere, they had no political power. When Russia did finally sue for peace at Brest-Litovsk in 1918, she discovered what 'peace without victory' meant: she lost 34 per cent of the former Empire's population (around 55 million people), 32 per cent of her agricultural land, a large portion of her heavy industry, 73 per cent of her iron-ore output and 89 per cent of her coal.

There were no elections in 1917 and no one took an opinion poll. But the scanty evidence that does exist suggests that Frenchmen on the whole were not very interested in making peace at this time. The heads of trade unions might speak of an ideal of peace, but most workers who went on strike were simply trying to make ends meet. The Instituteurs' Federation might have wanted to send delegates to Stockholm, but it had little following among teachers. It was a few sectors of organised labour, at the top, which wanted immediate peace.

And there *was* trouble in the army. Guy Pedroncini, in his analysis of the mutinies, notes that only 10 per cent of the French army divisions were touched by the political sentiment that 'peace was the only solution', a 'minority of units'. But one in ten divisions is surely a significant proportion of an army at war, especially if they are all at one of the most critical points on the front.

XV

LOUIS MALVY, Paul Painlevé and Alexandre Ribot were ushered into the committee room on a Saturday afternoon, 16 June. Twenty-five dark-coated men were seated, waiting for them; they were looking very grim. Clemenceau had just shown them an example of the *papillons*, or posters, that were glued in large numbers to the sides of the leave trains. 'Enough men killed! Peace!' it read. Then he pulled out of his brief case a few pacifist brochures; one of them recommended that the best way to hasten the end of the war was to shoot officers. Clemenceau noted that 'none of the brochures have been seized.' The committee, he said, had asked the minister of war for reports on pacifism but because the documents were held by Sûreté Générale, the request had been refused.

At forty-two Malvy was young for the man who had been the minister of the interior throughout the war years and his well-groomed moustache and black hair made him look even younger. He had entered the Chamber in 1906 and, like most Radical Socialists, had built up a career on the basis of connections and compromise; he knew newspaper editors, businessmen and union leaders and was on friendly terms with many of the most influential men in the Chamber, from the Centre through to the extreme Left. His connections were in fact so good that wartime governments could not dispense with him. He was the Sacred Union incarnate; fire Malvy, it was whispered in high circles, and the Sacred Union would fall apart.

One of the first decisions Malvy had to make after the outbreak of war was what to do with the Carnet B. The Carnet B was a list of names maintained by Sûreté Générale. It had been started in the 1880's as a list of suspected spies but, with the development of antimilitarism after 1900 and especially the threat of a general strike against war, the list had grown to include all figures who might try to sabotage a mobilisation. In 1914 the Carnet B included about 2,500 names of which only about seven hundred were suspected spies. The rest were registered 'for other motives'. Before reaching a decision Malvy consulted a number of people in politics, the press and the unions. Among them was Clemenceau.

'You probably think that the Carnet B ought to be put into operation?' asked Malvy. 'I do not believe one can do otherwise,' replied Clemenceau. Contrary to legend, he did not advise Malvy to gaol everyone on the list because it was being constantly revised and there were many different types of individual on it: 'In this list,' Clemenceau later commented, 'people enter and leave like in a ministry.'

After further consultations Malvy decided to do nothing.

The army committee's hearing began with Painlevé reviewing the state of morale within the armies. The main crisis, he said, seemed to have passed, but the situation was still very serious, particularly in the railway stations. Bérenger then made a summary of what he had been able to gather on pacifist propaganda; he complained that important documents were being withheld and especially, in violation of earlier agreements, he had received nothing on the 'moral state of wage earners now on strike'. He concluded with three questions: Why is the ministry of the interior stalling on documents? Why in the last three years has there developed 'syndicalist anarchy'? And are there two contradictory policy goals within the government, one for peace with victory and the other for a lenient treatment of the 'anarchists'?

Malvy answered by reading various circulars that he had sent to the prefects demanding greater surveillance of pacifist activities. It was not a very satisfactory performance.

In the exchanges that followed Malvy was accused of arresting 'poor devils', simply the carriers of brochures, while leaving the most influential men – like Sébastien Faure, author of *Our Conditions of Peace* – at liberty. Clemenceau pleaded for more information.

'The custom is not to communicate police reports,' Ribot sagely pointed out. 'You know this, Monsieur le Président, you were once head of government: these reports are not ordinarily communicated.'

'It is not ordinary either for the Germans to be at Saint-Quentin,' cracked Clemenceau. There was the rub. He remarked in a later hearing, 'Monsieur Malvy, who is a young man, has told himself that in order to keep a few Socialists you have to humour such or such an anarchist; that I think is his whole thinking.' In times of peace, the position might be justified. 'You can be more or less brutal, more or less soft: it's not important. But this situation no longer stands today.' France needs time. 'It is a very bad policy to let everything go, under the pretext that in discovering A one might irritate B on whom depends, through the mediation of C or D, the unleashing of a strike.'

At Malvy's hearing Ribot appeared to be of the same sentiment; he bent to the will of the committee: 'In principle I am for the widest possible communication [of documents]. As to why a propaganda that was inoffensive at the beginning of the war should become dangerous, I would simply reply that the terrain has changed. It is like individuals who become infected, having resisted a microbe for a long time; their organism has weakened.'

This was the beginning of the end for Malvy. De Selves laid down the conditions by which documents would be communicated. Malvy remained totally silent.

There then started what can only be called the 'war of the dossiers' – for Malvy refused to deliver. Immediately after the hearing the committee set up a delegation, headed by de Selves and including Jeanneney, Bérenger and Strauss, that was to appear at the ministry of the interior and demand the documents promised. They tried on Sunday. Malvy was busy. They tried on Monday. Malvy delayed, then finally announced to the delegation, 'No, I cannot communicate the documents that you have asked me.'

When all this was brought again before the committee, Bérenger threatened to resign and bring the matter before the full Senate in an interpellation. Now it was Clemenceau's turn to be conciliatory (to

Doumer's disappointment): he said he was willing to meet the prime minister in the Senate the next day and discuss the affair. But Ribot never turned up. After another angry committee session, an *ordre du jour*, demanding delivery of the promised documents without delay, was adopted.

The dispute dragged on for more than a month. The most ludicrous aspect of it was that many of the documents requested through the ministry of the interior came into the hands of the committee through the ministries of war and of foreign affairs. Clemenceau even admitted to having a few well-placed friends within Sûreté Générale. For the committee this was one more sign of the chaos in Malvy's administration.

In the meantime the Chamber met in secret session to discuss the disastrous April offensive. Diagne, a black deputy, described the massacre of the Senegalese. Ybarnegary gave a furious account of his own experience, making an unprecedented attack against Nivelle's 'petty spirit and immense pride'. He demanded penalties. Then a socialist deputy mounted the tribune, Pierre Laval, in a white bow tie, a mop of brown hair playing mischief with his eyebrows, and a file of documents under his arm.

Laval explained to the Chamber that a military victory was impossible and that 'there is in France a weariness of war and a pressure for peace.' With the aid of his documents he revealed to a hushed assembly the development of the mutinies and he asked the deputies how they could expect to continue the war with the armies in revolt. 'The way', he said, 'to give hope to the troops and confidence to the workers, whether you like it or not, is Stockholm. Stockholm is the star of the North.'

It was not only the generals who were put in question: the Senate (and by association, its army committee) also came under heavy criticism. It was another socialist deputy, Pierre Renaudel, who screamed, 'The Senate is for a *repression à outrance*. We need another style of politics.'

The Chamber had never gone this far before. The Senate army committee, though not formally apprised of the session, saw in this a challenge. For its president, the day had come to vanquish or to abdicate; the Socialists in the Chamber had apparently chosen to abdicate. There could be no bargaining now.

First the committee came to the support of the generals, and particularly Nivelle. 'The victors of Douaumont, Vaux and Bézonvaux cannot be treated like this,' cried Doumer. Bérenger claimed that vile murderers had more rights of defence than generals in the Republic's army. Clemenceau wrote an article arguing that there was a 'collective responsibility' for the offensive and ridiculed the spectacle of Painlevé at the Chamber tribune criticising a military operation over which he had himself presided. And he told his readers not to forget that 'with Monsieur Painlevé, as master of the operations he damns, we have Monsieur Malvy, member of the "Comité de Guerre".' Henceforth Clemenceau always used italics and inverted commas when writing of the 'Comité de Guerre'.

Then a bombshell arrived from an unexpected quarter. On 7 July, while Malvy was defending himself, in a public session, at the tribune of the Chamber against Clemenceau's attacks, a socialist deputy felt a sudden urge to make a verbal swipe at Maurice Barrès, royalist and nationalist. He accused him of helping an Austrian Jesuit escape from France. Barrès, totally ignoring the deputy, turned his guns on Malvy. 'Since my colleague has permitted me to speak' – he stressed every word – 'let me use the occasion to ask Monsieur le Ministre what measures he intends to take against the rag *Le Bonnet rouge*.'

There was complete silence. *Le Bonnet rouge* was one of the most infamous pacifist journals of the day. What was going on? What did Malvy have to do with *Le Bonnet rouge*?

What did Barrès know? Probably not much. But Malvy was taken aback and it was Ribot who answered, blurting out, 'A cheque has been seized at the frontier on somebody belonging to a newspaper that I shall not name ... Nothing, no consideration whatever, will prevent us from doing our duty.' A cheque? A man on the frontier? One of the major scandals of the war had just begun.

It was the business manager of *Le Bonnet rouge*, Emile-Joseph Duval, who was detained on the Swiss frontier with a cheque for 150,857 francs in his pocket. He said he was liquidating a Mediterranean resort. Why was the cheque then signed by a German? Duval was allowed to go free, but the cheque was taken. A few days later Duval turned up at the ministry of the interior and Malvy's *chef de cabinet* handed the cheque back to him.

The reason for returning it went back to Malvy's consultations, at the outbreak of the war, over the Carnet B. After meeting with Clemenceau, Malvy had interviewed the director of *Le Bonnet rouge*, Miquel Almereyda, an unhappy character who had been born in Béziers, abandoned by his parents, had spent his youth in and out of gaol but had finally found his vocation in journalism and syndicalism. His real name was Eugène Vigo, but he preferred the pen-name, an anagram for '*y a la merde*' – a clue to his philosophy of life. His paper, founded in 1913, had earned him a prominent place in the Carnet B. Malvy interviewed him in 1914 because he wanted assurance that the pacifists would cause no problems if the Carnet B were ignored. He was even willing to pay for that assurance; *Le Bonnet rouge* started to receive substantial subsidies from the government. These were ended in March 1916 because the pacifism of the paper was now notorious and, for the ministry, it was too hot a potato to handle.

Most papers would have folded as a result, but *Le Bonnet rouge* survived, and survived well. The source of its funds was Duval, a man rolling in money. But what was his source? A certain Herr Marx in Switzerland, a German agent. Unwilling to antagonise the pacifists, Malvy's ministry had turned a blind eye on the payment, even to the point of returning money seized by subordinates. Ribot's blundering statement had made the matter public.

It was the Senate's turn to have a secret session on the April offensive. Throughout July the committee prepared itself. Bérenger amassed data on the various plans, on the generals, on the complex network that linked high command to the local commanders, on the role of the government. Doumer became increasingly sympathetic to the generals' cause. Strauss evoked the 'doctrine of government'. And Humbert continued to remain oddly silent.

There was also much discussion about pacifism. On the day before the secret session began, Clemenceau proposed to the committee that the question of the government's attitude regarding pacifist propaganda be discussed after the debate on the offensive in a public, open session, 'since nothing we have to say on this question is secret.' Clemenceau said that he intended to show that the government's policy on pacifism had not succeeded, as Malvy had claimed in front of the Chamber. He would demand 'energetically' that the government change its attitude towards 'criminal propagandists'.

Clemenceau's speech in the Senate on Sunday afternoon, 22 July, is one of the major events of the Great War, like the shooting of the archduke, like Falkenhayn's memorandum on Verdun in December 1915, like President Wilson's reading to Congress of his Fourteen Points in 1918. It completely altered the pattern of war politics in France. His old grey figure shook with emotion as he spoke, his Asiatic eyes glaring from brows more bushy than ever.

'I am nothing at all,' he said, 'I am an old man at the end of his political life. I knew that the war would come. I warned my fellow citizens. I didn't believe I would see it. It came!' He then turned to the matter at hand: 'We are at war. There is somewhere, out in Verdun, an immense shell hole, huge as half of this Assembly, in which two men are buried, one locked in to the other, the Frenchman with his teeth in the Boche. They are, in their hole, a symbol of this war. Behind them; it is the civilised world which is there. The life of the whole world is playing itself out: everything that man wanted, everything that he tried to attain is going be torn from him . . . It's the greatest event in the life of the world. From it we derive joy, from it we derive pain.'

And then he described the whole Malvy 'affair', and described it with wit: the consultations on the Carnet B, Almereyda, Sûreté Générale, the laxity and complicity of the ministry of the interior.

'It is easy to repress,' said Malvy when it came his turn to speak, 'it is easy to forbid.' Malvy stood at the tribune, reported one witness, with his face glazed in a yellow sweat.

'It is very difficult,' responded Clemenceau from his bench, 'you need a heart to do it.'

'You have reproached me for not bringing you enough heads: I bring you results and it is on these results that I demand that the High Assembly judge me.'

'No, no,' Clemenceau waved his hands, 'I reproach you for having betrayed your country!'

XVI

'I CAN still hear that speech,' wrote Jean Martet thirteen years later. 'Whoever heard it will be hearing it for the rest of his life. What a speech! Neither was it composed, nor reasoned, nor even, apparently, meditated, prepared: but it was played, lived, admirably. The words were thrown out in armfuls.'

Half France heard that speech. It was reproduced in full on the front page of *L'Homme enchaîné* and when this sold out another edition was issued. Then it went through the printing presses of the publishers Plon and was circulated as a pamphlet, 'Anti-patriotism Before the Senate'. Other newspapers joined in the chorus. The noisiest – and the most dishonest – was *L'Action française*, not exactly an ally of Georges Clemenceau ('the dolt deemed a Cæsar', 'the sinister gaffer of *L'Homme enchaîné*'). Léon Daudet claimed that Malvy was actively working for the German government; Clemenceau, in his column, rebuked Daudet for extravagance. But he kept up a steady campaign against the 'defeatists', the advocates of a 'blank peace', against 'abandonment' – or 'in good French, one should say "treason".' Accusations that he had become the generals' man hardly concerned him. 'When the high command cries for help, I come. I come because to refuse to hear the voice of the French army, to lend one's ear to the liberalism of Almereyda and his friends, is to put oneself at the service of Germany and to betray.' Clemenceau regarded his speech of 22 July as one of the greatest victories of his life.

Malvy did not attend the following morning's meeting of the Comité de guerre; he was 'suffering', said Poincaré. Ten days later he took a fortnight's holiday, leaving the ministry to his old friend and former prime minister, René Viviani.

On the day he left Almereyda was arrested. On the day he returned, 18 August, Almereyda was found dead at the foot of his cell bed, strangled by his own shoe laces. The official verdict was suicide, but Clemenceau was not the only newspaperman to remark that this seemed a very curious method of inflicting self-slaughter.

Malvy's position became quite untenable. The old prime minister, Ribot, told Poincaré that he didn't think he could appear in the Chamber with Malvy at his side. Poincaré counselled him to reconstitute his cabinet and even consider making an offer to Clemenceau: 'Never!' he replied with a grave shake of his wrinkled head. 'I will offer him nothing.' Malvy continued to hang on for a few days, but his situation was hopeless. He resigned on 31 August. The whole government stood down one week later.

'Will we have or will we not have a government?' wondered Clemenceau in *L'Homme enchaîné*. 'That's the crisis, the real crisis; crisis of character, crisis of will. For three years we have been waiting for its solution.' Poincaré was getting a little tetchy too: 'And what about the war? Ah! if only Clemenceau were less impulsive and less light-minded.'

For that narrow Parisian society of reporters, deputies, wives, friends and cronies the new political obsessions did in fact create a certain amnesia; one could so easily forget that only a few dozen kilometres to the east tens of thousands were dying in ugly battlefields (or 'battle-bogs' as Wyndham Lewis more accurately described them). The neighbouring sights and sounds of the city had an anaesthetic effect. Paris was back to normal: all scandal and noise. The circulation of buses, cars and horse drawn vehicles was now as dense as it had been before the war. The women looked rather attractive in the new mode of high leather boots and slim, low-cut dresses. Theatres were attended. Prices may have gone up, but the restaurants were doing a thriving business – though you had to be a bit careful with whom you ate: 'Scandals are everywhere,' said Abel Ferry (just back from an inspection of the front). 'You don't know with whom you can have lunch, nor whose hand you can shake. The scum of France, which has poured all over the interior zone, slavers on the heroism of the front.'

So after three years of war, it was back to the old-fashioned business of politics. Most of the rumours and stories were piped out of the same source, the same bottomless barrel that had been used to prime scandals in the decades before the war: money, or rather the lack of it. In 1917 it was just as much a mystery how poorly paid politicians and newspapermen financed their ambitious enterprises as it had been in 1885. There was always a sordid tale waiting to be revealed here.

One could start with poor Senator Charles Humbert. Humbert, for Ferry, was 'the man most representative of this corrupt age.' He had been sitting so reticent in the Senate army committee because his newspaper, *Le Journal*, was enmeshed in the most terrible money problems. Poincaré had warned Clemenceau in 1916 of the curious shareholders the paper had acquired – the son of a famous publicity agent who had purchased the paper with 'Swiss' funds; a former dentist, turned champagne importer, who carried the Egyptian title 'Pasha' and who had, on behalf of Humbert, bought the paper back again with funds from 'New York'. It was only in September 1917 that the full nature of the affair was disclosed: the paper was being financed by the Germans. The Swiss funds were supplied by Herr A. Marx, Duval's German associate, and the New York funds came from the Deutsche Bank. Humbert was caught in the middle. He responded to the September revelations by attacking all and sundry. Clemenceau wrote a letter to Humbert asking him to stop attending the army committee; he replied saying that he had every intention of continuing as normal. According to a reporter from *Le Matin* (a paper sympathetic to Briand and Malvy), Humbert turned up one afternoon in October for a committee session. Clemenceau asked, 'What are you doing here?' 'I have come to take my seat,' replied Humbert with the calmest look on his face. 'You are not serious.' 'On the contrary, I am perfectly serious.' 'It's not possible; go away.' 'I will only leave with a kick in the arse and no one will dare do that.' 'Are you sure?' 'Very sure.' 'Well, we'll see.' The committee minutes show that Humbert did stop attending in October.

As in the Wilson 'decorations' scandal of the 1880's, the Boulanger scandal and the Panama scandal, all the major figures in the scandals of 1917 seemed to know one another. Bolo 'Pasha' kept the widest company of all of them. He hobnobbed with deputies, he knew the King of Spain, Barthou and Briand. Poincaré received him at the Elysée. Abel Ferry remembered having dinner with him. Clemenceau never seems to have shaken his hand, but this was pure chance. Scandal, none the less, was knocking at his door. His youngest brother Albert was accused of acting as counsel for an Austrian spy, Oskar von Rosenberg; Paul Clemenceau was said to be attempting a separate peace with Austria through his wife and Berthe Zuckerkandl-Szeps. But Clemenceau by this time had broken off relations with Paul and the accusations against Albert proved tenuous.

The man most deeply implicated in the circle of scandals was Clemenceau's former minister of finance, Joseph Caillaux. Caillaux had two things against him. The first (and for Clemenceau by far the more important) was having negotiated as prime minister in 1911 a treaty with Germany over Morocco which, time proved, was not a step in the direction of peace but only a stop-gap measure. The second was his wife, Henriette, who had suffered enormously during the trial of July 1914. At the time, Caillaux had given Almereyda 37,000 francs and *Le Bonnet Rouge* thus became the only Parisian paper to come out in open support of his wife. When war broke out, Caillaux' friend Malvy advised him to leave Paris. Caillaux joined the army where he appears to have been 'put on quarantine' by his superior officers. After two months service he left the army, and the ministry of war then shipped him and his wife, with their faithful servant, out to Brazil.

Caillaux spent a large part of the war abroad, dining out in plushy restaurants with anyone who had a kind word to say about his wife or a sign of respect for himself; he was a lonely man who wanted company. Unbeknown to Caillaux, many of these 'friends' were German agents.

While he was in Paris, Caillaux would pay visits to some of his other faithful friends, like Bolo Pasha, whom he had got to know when he was prime minister. He wrote admiring letters to Almereyda. 'My dear friend,' he wrote in February 1917, 'your articles are so good. Why don't you send them to all the deputies and senators? I will help you out if that involves costs. *Bien à vous.*'

The 'Caillaux affair' was an offshoot of the scandals related to Humbert and Bolo Pasha. Much of the press coverage was hysterical. There was, however, a serious, political element in this affair that was lacking in the stories revolving around Bolo Pasha, Humbert or Almereyda; for Caillaux, since 1911, had developed the reputation as someone ready and willing to negotiate with Germany.

The revelations that autumn seemed to confirm this. He also happened to have a strong following among Socialists and Radical Socialists in the Chamber. What would happen if Caillaux and his friends came into power? It was a nightmare scenario for Clemenceau: the tone of his articles against Caillaux in October conformed perfectly to his earlier campaigns against pacifism and defeatism. Clemenceau did not want France to be led into a 'blank peace'. France had a choice: either vanquish or abdicate. He had little time for the abdicators.

An even more dangerous man than Caillaux, in Clemenceau's eyes, was Aristide Briand, whom he called the orchestral conductor of the defeatists.

It so happened that with the 'Caillaux affair' there developed a 'Briand affair'. When Albert Thomas, the socialist munitions minister, went on mission to Russia in July, he was presented with documents dating from the last months of the Tsarist regime showing that the Russians had promised Briand, then prime minister, that they would let France annex the left bank of the Rhine. It was later claimed that Briand had even promised Russia Sweden.

The revelations caused a scandal among the Socialists, who subscribed to a policy of peace without annexation. Briand knew that if he was ever going to return to office he would need the support of the Socialists. So he made a deft about-turn and, after acting as war leader when prime minister, he now set out to become the nation's peace leader, actively seeking a negotiated settlement with Germany. But a meeting in Switzerland was eventually called off after the French government flatly refused to let Briand go.

On 15 October, Clemenceau published an article on 'the secret of a German manœuvre in view of an ignominious separate peace', without actually mentioning Briand by name. This led to a secret session in the Chamber the following day where bitter words were exchanged between Briand and the government over how and why the negotiations had been aborted; the government won an easy majority. But the Socialists now formed a block in dogged opposition to the war effort; they complained that 'the minister of foreign affairs had allowed an important occasion to pass for the engagement of talks for peace'. Ferry, of the opposite opinion, called the session 'a battle of prime ministers on France's back.' Complex manœuvring began again; nobody expected the current government to last.

The withdrawal of the Socialists from the Sacred Union thus preceded the installation of Clemenceau's second ministry by several months. The main cause of the break was not Clemenceau but this growing conviction that a peace could be negotiated. They all believed, like Laval, that Stockholm was the star of the north. With their faith in the reasonable nature of man and the assurance that every nation was tired of this war, they thought an international congress of Socialists would help usher in the new era. After all, the process had already begun in Russia, a noble model for the future. The government's refusal to supply passports only made them more stubborn.

Ribot, at the time of his resignation in early September, had hoped to set up a new cabinet; it would be basically the same one, less Malvy. But the task proved impossible because the Socialists refused to cooperate. When eventually Painlevé presented a government to the Chamber, the Socialists abstained. The Sacred Union, however, had died a long time before this.

'And what about the war?' Well, the war went on without the politicians.

Pétain had introduced a number of measures designed to improve the morale of the troops. But it was not the improvements in the conditions of leave, the better medical service or the marginally more comfortable bivouacs which brought an end to the military rebellion. The mutinies had been the product of the disastrous Nivelle offensive; there would be nothing like that again. Pétain's maxim, 'lavish with steel, stingy with blood', became the order of the day. It was, for instance, a tactic employed on 24 October to take Fort de la Malmaison at the western entrance – what was left of it – of the Chemin des Dames. Such successful, limited assaults did more than anything else to lift morale. Clemenceau, after several days on the front, reported to the army committee on 7 November, 'The men are closer to the officers and the officers are closer to the men than they ever have been; never have I noted such accord on the front.'

Yet 24 October had been a sad day for Italy. After a brief but intensive bombardment, combined German and Austrian forces launched an attack at Caporetto. Within twelve hours a million Italian soldiers were in retreat; forty thousand were killed, ninety thousand were wounded and 350,000 were taken prisoner.

The only point on the western front where the Allies were on the offensive was in the British sector of Flanders and Belgium. Haig believed that the flat lands deprived the Germans of defensive positions that had proved so effective in the earlier campaigns of that year: he would compel the Germans to pull back from Belgium. The official history called the effort the Third Battle of Ypres, an apt description of the kind of anonymous, meaningless horror the troops experienced. It dragged from damp August through to wet November. The last phase opened on 12 October with the drive onto the ridge of Passchendaele – 'the very name,' thought Wyndham Lewis, 'with its suggestion of *splashiness* and *passion* at once, was subtly appropriate . . . The moment I saw the name on the trench-map, intuitively I knew what was going to happen.' On the first day of the attack, the British front line was a mile and a quarter from the village. On 24 October they were still a mile from Passchendaele. The Canadians finally took the village on 6 November but they failed to get complete control of the ridge. That was achieved on 10 November at a cost of three thousand killed and seven thousand wounded. Casualties for the entire campaign exceeded 300,000.

Paris, during all this, continued to be preoccupied with politics; little was heard there about Passchendaele. Ferry described Painlevé at the tribune as a '*roseau pensant*', Pascal's 'thinking reed'; he tried to please the Left, he tried to please the Right – nobody listened to his speeches. The Socialists wanted to reinstate a Viviani ministry. To open the way, Marcel Sembat led an interpellation in the Chamber on 13 November. Painlevé

lost the confidence vote which followed. It was the first time in the war
that parliament had overthrown a government.

XVII

ALL THROUGH October and early November self-prospective prime ministers and ministers had been calling in at the Elysée to put on a good
face in front of the president and denounce the other contenders. Barthou
thought of himself as a fine war premier: he had a good rapport with the
Socialists and he told Poincaré he wouldn't let the scandals go too far;
this was not the time to attack Caillaux. Briand turned up several times.
He wanted to reinforce censorship; Clemenceau's article had infuriated
him. The Socialists were very active. Their most promising candidate for
a ministerial post was the former munitions minister Albert Thomas who
got on with the politicians of the Centre. Clemenceau himself refrained
from criticising Thomas. There was talk that Thomas even had ambitions
of becoming prime minister. However Lasies, a Radical, told Poincaré that
there were only four men who could be seriously considered for the post,
Viviani, Briand, Barthou and Clemenceau. Barthou? He would be another
roseau pensant. Briand? He was unacceptable because of his dealings with the
Germans. Barthou actually admitted that the essential choice was between
Viviani and Clemenceau. So what about Viviani? Poincaré regarded him
as the candidate of the 'defeatists and the hushers up'; if he became premier
France would soon sue for peace, which was, Poincaré estimated, secretly
the desire of roughly a third of the Chamber. The president was left with
no choice at all.

The one man who never came to see Poincaré was, of course,
Clemenceau. Never quite the diplomat when it came to personal advancement, he maintained a steady attack in *L'Homme enchaîné* against the
president, whom he regarded as indecisive, a man buried in administrative
and legal details – *la paperasse* – that exposed him unnecessarily to political
manipulation. So Clemenceau sat in his flat at rue Franklin where he too
received a retinue of deputies and senators, now convinced that he was
the only man capable of leading France to victory. There they found him
behind his horseshoe desk, in a dark coat, a high starched collar and a
curious forage-cap, which he turned up at the rim and ear-flaps, creating
the vague effect of a fleur-de-lys ensconced on his head.

Those closest to him thought his public stand against Poincaré was
not the most effective way of opening up the route to office. 'If in similar
circumstances, Monsieur Guizot or Monsieur Thiers . . .' 'Give me a bit

of peace, Mandel! You judge all that as a *politicien*!' His secretary, Jean Martet, said the same. 'In today's article you have again taken issue with Monsieur Poincaré. You reproach him for not willing to know and not knowing how to will.' 'Well yes. Because it's true. One mustn't say it?' 'I don't know whether one should say it or not. But I do know that in saying it you take all desire away from M. Poincaré to confide power in you.'

'So what?'

The 'so what?' was at the heart of the matter. Clemenceau had always had an ambiguous attitude towards power and fame, and this had never been more true than in 1917. He still had the ambition of the artist that had been hiding within him since youth; the man would have liked to have been a writer, a painter, a scientist of the old school. There abided within him all the contradictions of the artist; he wanted to isolate himself and at the same time he wanted to be read, to be seen, to be recognised. Circumstances, acquaintances and a certain passion for argument and oratory had pushed him into politics.

It was an odd domain for an artist. The art of war? 'I tell you, I don't have much belief in the art of war. Show me the slightest scrap of a design. The rest is literature.' The art of government? Clemenceau approached government with an artist's perception, not the calculating eye of the *politicien*.

'For the love of God,' exclaimed Martet, 'make a sign!'

'No, Martet. I will not make that sign. Take good note. I will not make it for this reason, that far from seeking power, like all these brave fellows ... I fear it. I have an atrocious fear! I would give anything to escape it! In the first place, just look at me, see how I am all buggered up: seventy-six years old, rotten with diabetes ... How do you think I am going to hold up? Secundo, I am not very sure, at the point we've reached, how we are ever going to pull out of it ...' As prime minister, he would make virtually the same statement in public, from the tribune, to the newspapers, in front of the president: 'I fear'. When Clemenceau spoke of 'courage' he always accompanied this with a comment on fear. An artist lives both simultaneously. For what is courage if it is not accompanied by the word 'fear'?

On the morning after Painlevé's government fell, the president of the Senate came round to the Elysée for a chat with Poincaré. Clemenceau was an awfully risky venture, he thought. But, he was swift to add, all the other major candidates were ready to sue for peace. Dubost didn't like Clemenceau. He shrugged his shoulders. '*Il faut laisser pisser les mérinos*',*

---

* Literally, 'Let the merinos piss', which means roughly, 'Let them all work it out for themselves.'

he said; you have to interview everyone. The Senate president was followed by Chamber president, Paul Deschanel; he didn't want to give an opinion (he never did). Then along came Léon Bourgeois; he wouldn't vouch for the Chamber, but he said the public was behind Clemenceau. Poincaré reached for the telephone. Clemenceau was round in a moment.

Poincaré found him plumper and deafer than ever; the last time he had seen him must have been in 1914. Clemenceau had just rattled off another insulting article, but, because of the president's invitation, he cancelled publication and asked Camille Picard, deputy for the Vosges, to write a column. Picard's article appeared the following morning – '*Pourquoi nous tiendrons*'. Clemenceau's long career as a newspaper columnist ended that day.

His conversation with Poincaré was long and cordial. But Poincaré made no offer; he had to let the merinos piss.

There was virtually a queue outside. Viviani had been pulled out of bed with flu. He warned that Clemenceau would have all the Socialists against him and, of course, 'the working class'. Briand dropped in. A Clemenceau ministry, he said, was 'full of hazards'. Than along came old Ribot, obviously relenting his earlier refusal: Take Clemenceau, he advised. Albert Thomas admitted that efforts had been made to bring the Socialists and Clemenceau closer together but he thought their opposition was inevitable; there would be strikes and 'dangerous movements'. He wanted a government that included Viviani, Barthou and himself, with Poincaré presiding over the Comité de guerre – in other words, a presidential government that was quite contrary to the constitution of the Third Republic. Poincaré, to his credit, declined. Sembat, being of the same party, had the same idea. But he was infinitely more hostile to Clemenceau. Poincaré thought it was time for another conversation with Clemenceau.

As an officer left with his message, Franklin-Bouillon turned up, uninvited. 'A Clemenceau ministry,' he said, 'that means civil war.' Inevitably, somebody was going to repeat Jaurès's rhetoric of 1906 and why not Franklin-Bouillon? 'You'll be laid bare,' he warned Poincaré. Poincaré paused for a moment. Then he replied: 'One will not however be able to reproach me for having made a personal choice. One has to anyway choose between Caillaux and Clemenceau. My choice is made.'

There had never been any question of Caillaux forming a government. But a Viviani government would have included a number of Caillaux' friends.

Clemenceau arrived out of breath and sniffling with a cold. Poincaré made a rather pompous presidential address, outlining the premier's duties. Clemenceau told Poincaré he would be presenting him with his cabinet the next day and concluded, 'I will never take any decision without coming to chat with you first.'

A ministry within twenty-four hours? According to Abel Ferry's notes, the stillborn Viviani ministry had been in gestation since June or July. The origins of the Clemenceau ministry can, in fact, be traced back even further. The man responsible for this was his personal assistant, Georges Mandel.

Since Clemenceau's return to Paris in the late autumn of 1914 Mandel had renewed his daily contacts with *le patron*, outlining in detail the various intrigues in the Chamber, identifying those who might be useful, those who were unfriendly, those who were neutral. Mandel had a truly photographic mind; he was a walking archive. Ask him what he knew about some obscure deputy who had shaken Clemenceau's hand sixteen months ago and he would tell you, precisely, frigidly, without a second's hesitation, where the man was born, when he joined the Chamber, who his friends were . . . 'He had a questionable relationship,' he might say, 'with one of the journalists of the gutter press for the last seven and a half years, he made a doubtful deal in the stock market seventeen years ago, the private secretary of the sanitary subcommittee's president was not very fond of him.' Mandel never filed his papers. They just piled up on his desk. That letter of June from the undersecretary of armaments? His hand would go straight to it. He collected cuttings from the *Journal officiel*, from the newspapers, magazines, parliamentary reports. This was why there was always a pair of scissors contorting his left jacket pocket. What man was best equipped to identify, select and prepare the candidates for government? What man could foretell hidden dangers? Who could place his finger on unnoticed opportunity? Who was the new evangelist? The all-present, the all-knowing, the diabolic Mandel.

Mandel first needed an inner circle of trustworthy associates. Léon Martin, Clemenceau's private secretary, had gone off to war in February 1915. 'Our good collaborator and friend, Léon Martin, from Champ-Saint-Père (Vendée), has just been gloriously wounded by the enemy,' one read at the foot of *L'Homme enchaîné* on the second day of the Nivelle offensive. Though wounded in the chest, he survived.

Martin was replaced by Jean Martet who became one of Mandel's triumvirate. The other was Georges Wormser, who had gone to school with Martet and had been on the staff of *L'Homme libre*. At the time of the Nivelle offensive he was in the army, working for the general staff at Compiègne. In May, as the mutinies reached crisis point, he was suddenly recalled to serve on the military staff at the ministry of war, then under Painlevé. On his arrival in Paris he learned through Martet that his transfer had been the work of Mandel.

Wormser was invited to dinner at Mandel's home, a flat jammed with books on avenue Mozart. 'We are at the turning-point of the war,' Mandel informed Wormser. 'Everything is going badly, even very badly. Either we are going to be forced to peace or we will struggle, and struggle desperately. To struggle there is only, in the political domain, Monsieur Clemenceau. But will the defeatists and the funks let him do it?' Clemenceau had the ideas, Clemenceau because of his Senate committee had good connections in the army, but Clemenceau 'ignores the details and the mechanism of administration.' Wormser's job was to study how an army was administered. The constitution of the Clemenceau ministry was under way.

Extensive efforts were made to get the Socialists to cooperate, chiefly through Albert Thomas and Pierre Laval. The leadership of the party was obviously opposed, but in politics public statements do not always correspond to the realities behind scene. Throughout Clemenceau's two years in office, Mandel would maintain ties with the Socialist party.

There were some members of the party who wanted more than that. According to Abel Ferry, Albert Thomas deeply regretted not being able to join Clemenceau's government. At the time of the government crisis of November, help came from an unexpected quarter. Just over on mission in Paris was the British munitions minister, Winston Churchill. Churchill liked Thomas and was ready to put in a favourable word to Clemenceau. 'I was with Clemenceau for half an hour on the morning when he was forming his Ministry,' said Churchill in an article first published in 1930. Churchill thought he had impressed Clemenceau with his appeal for a 'cross-channel combination'. But he later discovered that 'Thomas, supported by the Socialists, had declared that Clemenceau as Premier "was a danger to national defence". This of course was mortal.'[1]

Another 'failed minister' was Abel Ferry himself, but this was because of the candidate's own reluctance, induced in all likelihood by his dead uncle's will. On the evening and morning that the ministry was being set up Ferry was at the front. Clemenceau telephoned him: 'Your name has already been communicated to the papers. The decree has been signed and published in the *Officiel*. It'll be a stab in the back if you refuse.' But Ferry did refuse: 'I shall serve you better outside. I am for you, but I cannot and nor do I wish to be with you; I have fought too much with Briand and Painlevé, I would look like an *arriviste*.' Clemenceau, recorded

---

[1] Winston S. Churchill, *Great Contemporaries* (London: Thornton Butterworth, 1937), p. 310. 'Clemenceau' first published in *Strand*, December 1930. There are some problems with the story. According to Martin Gilbert, Churchill only left London on Sunday, 18 November, by which time Clemenceau's ministry had already been formed. Churchill also states that Thomas had 'only a day or two before he lost office in the ministerial earthquake'. Thomas had in fact resigned with Ribot's government in September and had no post in Painlevé's short-lived ministry. Martin Gilbert, *Winston S. Churchill* (London: Heinemann, 1975), vol. IV, p. 55.

Ferry, understood that 'I was thinking of the past.' Ancestral honour would not allow Ferry to forget 1885. 'It remains for me to excuse myself, Monsieur, for having called you so late and for so little,' replied Clemenceau. A quarter of an hour later the newspapers were told that Abrami had taken Ferry's place.

But Ferry would be acting almost as if he were a minister. He would be sent on missions for the government and he would spend much of his time on reports. 'My destiny in this war,' he would write, 'is to make reports.'

As promised, Clemenceau presented Poincaré with his ministers within twenty-four hours. He would be his own minister of war. Foreign affairs went, as in 1906, to Stephen Pichon. There was an unusual number of members who were not parliamentarians (two ministers out of eleven and two undersecretaries of state out of nine). The industrialist and highly competent technician, Louis Loucheur was kept on at the ministry of armaments – Wormser said the appointment was entirely of Mandel's making. Most of the parliamentarians were Radicals or Radical Socialists; Louis Nail at justice, Victor Boret at agriculture, Laferre at education. Edouard Ignace, Lockroy's former secretary, took what would be a key post in the conclusion of the 'affairs', the undersecretary of state for military justice. Jules Pams, whom Clemenceau had supported against Poincaré in the presidential race of 1913, was named minister of the interior. And then there was Albert Favre, close to Ferry and one of the 'ninety-seven'. 'Albert Favre? What on earth could he do at the interior, the poor fellow?' Clemenceau asked Martet several years later. Favre had been appointed under-secretary of state at the interior. 'You want to know why I took Albert Favre? It was yet another coup of Mandel's! He brought me like that, these heaps of people . . . The funniest thing is that Albert Favre had been in the opposition before entering my cabinet. Once he had entered it he remained in the opposition.'

The cabinet was united for all that. 'This government, it's Clemenceau at all the ministries!' announced the *Canard enchaîné* on 28 November over one of H. P. Gassier's most famous cartoons: the minister of war, the minister of justice, the minister of the navy, the minister of public instruction, the minister of foreign affairs . . . all with the familiar moustachioed profile of Georges Clemenceau.

Clemenceau made a little speech in front of the president. They were embarking on a 'patriotic task', they were all 'firm republicans', there would never be 'intrigues among us'. He would abolish most censorship. He would only hold one council of ministers a week ('A good way of keeping me out,' thought Poincaré). He wasn't partisan of the Comité de guerre, but he wouldn't abolish it because it was *à la mode*. Finally he once more assured Poincaré, with a grin, 'I will often come and chat with you. You'll see me coming at all times.' The president of the Republic was nervous.

The same day *L'Homme enchaîné* reverted to its former title, *L'Homme libre*.

CHAPTER TEN

Total War

ON SUNDAY night, 18 November 1917, Clemenceau sat at his bedside table and, with his quill, wrote on the back of five sheets of Senate stationery his declaration to the Chamber. This was going to be his first appearance in the lower house in more than eight years. Some occasion! Head of government at seventy-six! 1906: the worst strike. 1917: the worst war. '*Nous nous présentons devant vous dans l'insigne pensée d'une défense intégrale . . .*' No! no! not 'total defence'. He scratched out '*défense*' and scrawled in the word '*guerre*'. It would be 'total war'.

The following morning he read his text to the council of ministers. 'A very patriotic piece,' thought Poincaré, 'a little taut in form, written in the style of one of his good articles.'

The Chamber session did not take place until Tuesday. It had never been so packed. Every aisle was filled. People even crammed into the space in front of the tribune. And there, in a prominent place in front of the assembly's main entrance, a photograph (taken at 3.40 p.m.) shows Mandel standing, his arms crossed, as proud as a general.

Clemenceau began:

> We present ourselves before you with the unique thought of a total war
> . . . These Frenchmen whom we were forced to throw into battle, they
> have rights over us. They want none of our thoughts to be diverted from
> them, they want none of our acts to be foreign to them. We owe them
> everything, with no reservation. All for France bleeding on its glory, all
> for the apotheosis of law triumphant.
>
> One duty, one simple duty: to remain with the soldier, to live,
> to suffer, to fight with him. To abdicate all that is not of the
> nation. Rights of the front, duty of the rear, today let it all be
> the same. Let every zone be a zone of the army. If there must
> be men who uncover in their souls old seeds of hatred, cast them
> aside . . .

To love is not to say it, it is to prove it. This proof, it is our will to attempt to achieve it. For this proof we ask you to aid us. Can there be a more beautiful programme for government?

There have been faults. Let us only think on how to repair them.

Alas! there have also been crimes, crimes against France which call for prompt chastisement ... Weakness would be complicity. We will be without weakness, as without violence. All the guilty to the court martial. The soldier in the court, in solidarity with the soldier at combat. No more pacifist campaigns, no more German intrigues.

Neither treason, nor demi-treason: war. Nothing but war. Our armies shall not be caught between two lines of fire. Justice comes through. The country shall know that it is defended ...

The speech was frequently interrupted by applause. A few noises emanated from the benches of the Socialist party. Clemenceau did not in fact read his prepared text very well. Wormser said he faltered. Martet said he was 'searching for his words and not achieving that impression of profound and unshakable will which the Chamber had expected and feared in him'. 'It is very difficult for a foreigner with only a superficial knowledge of the language and only an indirect sensing of the atmosphere, to judge such oratical performances,' thought Churchill, sitting in the diplomats' box.

But the eleven interpellations which followed had Churchill moving towards the edge of his seat. When Clemenceau rose to the tribune to respond, he put all papers aside and just stood there, his hands on the podium, his back slightly bent, his bald head shining in the intense lighting; he would not remain immobile for long. Churchill said, 'Clemenceau reproduced more than any other French Parliamentarian I have heard, the debating method of the House of Commons.' It was not a harangue, not an address to the multitude. 'The essence and foundation of House of Commons debating is formal conversation.' Churchill thought Clemenceau was rather English. 'The set speech ... has never succeeded much in our small wisely built chamber.' What impressed the British visitor was the 'human touch' Clemenceau had with his audience, his conversational style, and his total authority. 'He ranged from one side of the tribune to the other, without a note or a book of reference or a scrap of paper, barking out sharp, staccato sentences as the thought broke upon his mind. He looked like a wild animal pacing to and fro behind bars, growling and glaring; and all around him was an assembly which would have done anything to avoid having him there, but having put him there, felt they must obey.' Churchill thought Clemenceau's profile made a far better symbol of France than a 'barnyard fowl'.

418 deputies gave the 'wild animal' their confidence, 65 voted against, of which 64 were Socialists. 25 Socialists abstained as did fifteen Radicals, among them, Malvy and Caillaux.

I

THE FRENCH war effort was henceforth directed from three rooms in the old *hôtel* on rue Saint-Dominique where the Republic lodged its ministry of war.

Painlevé's enormous office was converted into the secretary's office. 'We lived all three, Mandel, Martet and myself, from November 1917 until October 1919, in the same large room,' recorded Wormser. If they were sick they would be treated on the spot, though there was not much chance of catching a chill: winter, spring, summer and autumn Mandel had the fire stoked with logs. 'Martet and myself suffered from the excessive heat which reigned in our room': no one argued with Mandel, even over his oddest caprices. All three men were this or that side of thirty and were totally devoted to Clemenceau, *le patron*; 'we felt for our chief an admiration that was almost religious . . . Never was there such a communion of work and thought.'

A door in the triumvirate's office led into a smaller room, which Painlevé had used to house his secretary. Today it was the office of the *président du conseil*.

Clemenceau didn't need space. He understood the principle well: more space simply meant more chaos. Unlike Mandel, Clemenceau tried to file his records. But he had no system. He would slip the papers into large envelopes on which he would write some vague title and then promptly lose the envelopes. Little dramas would ensue when he insisted he had handed them over to the triumvirate and he would never be able to admit that one or two of them might still be lying on his own table. While he was out for lunch there would be a rapid search on the cluttered desktop or in his drawers. When he returned the missing document would be presented to him with the explanation that it had indeed been in their archives but wrongly filed. 'Was he really duped?' said Wormser. 'He played the game and accepted our excuses.' What he carried off, unconsciously, to lunch in his pocket created a more serious problem. Sometimes a copy was available, or Mandel might have taken notes.

Otherwise the document would have to be reproduced on the basis of Mandel's marvellous memory.

Clemenceau detested the telephone. All the direct lines to the Elyseé and the other ministries went into the triumvirate's office, not his. He would open the door without notice: 'Still on the telephone! Oh, this Mandel!'

There was another door which would open when Clemenceau pressed a concealed button on his desk. It led directly into the *cabinet militaire*, administered by General Mordacq and his assistant, General Alby. Mandel and company had nothing to do with military problems.

The physical arrangement of these three rooms in the ministry of war gives a very clear idea of how France was now governed. To one side of the premier's office was the civilian administration, on the other side it was the military; the link, the essential link between them, was the premier himself.

II

WHEN CLEMENCEAU visited Romigny in early November to ask Mordacq to be his *chef du cabinet militaire*, one of the first things he discussed was what would soon be called in his government the 'legal affairs'. Clemenceau said, 'If we can finish with the defeatists in the interior, we will also finish with the German.' The morale in the army, still not totally recovered from the mutinies of that spring, was his first concern. Pedroncini provides evidence that a few words from the Chamber's tribune could produce an effect. 86 per cent of the Seventh Army expressed discontent in October at the lack of action taken over the scandals being reported from Paris. One month later, after Clemenceau came to power with his promise that 'the country shall know that it is defended,' the figure dropped to 20 per cent.

Clemenceau had spent his entire life defending justice. It is often argued that the 'legal affairs' prove that he had abandoned his old calling, that he had adopted the logic of his enemies, that he had become custodian of the *raison d'état*. But, as he had warned Malvy in July, these were unusual times; what is justice in times of peace cannot apply when a country is invaded and men by the thousand are getting killed. He made similar statements in the army committee. The 'defenders of the army' in 1898 were the defenders of an elite group of officers poorly integrated into the life of the nation. In 1917 the situation was different. The remarkable feature of works critical of Clemenceau in this period is that they delve into the judicial details, they appraise the courts, they analyse the acts and write as if this were a normal time in history; they forget Caporetto, Passchendaele, Champagne and Verdun; they forget the front and the army of 1917. The real working class today, Clemenceau kept on repeating, is out at the front. The army of 1917 was, in Clemenceau's mind, like the army of 1792; it was Gambetta's army, the people's army. These men had priority over all else, he said in his opening government declaration. Clemenceau saw himself as a link between two separate worlds. That was why he was so popular with the troops.

In fact, once in power, Clemenceau played down the importance of the scandals, in part because several arrests had already been made before he even took office. Almereyda was dead. Duval was arrested in September and three of his associates, Marion, Landau and Goldsky were gaoled in October. Bolo was also placed under custody at this time.

Two days after Clemenceau's opening declaration, Malvy himself proposed that the Chamber set up a committee to examine the charges against him and, if it found grounds, to send him before the Senate which would be constituted as a High Court. The Chamber granted his wish and Malvy went before the High Court in January 1918. The case dragged on until August when he was finally acquitted of the charge of 'intelligence with the enemy' but was found guilty of failing to oppose defeatist propaganda; he was sentenced to five years banishment from the Republic. Shortly afterwards Malvy was escorted across the frontier to Spain.

Clemenceau always claimed that the legal procedures involved here lay outside his province and indeed, from a constitutional point of view the judicial branch was supposed to be independent of the executive. But as the Dreyfus Affair had demonstrated, government, in practice, exercised an enormous influence over the courts (as in France it still does). The government could certainly not dictate its will, yet it could and did provide evidence. The role of the undersecretary of state of military justice, Edouard Ignace, seems to have been critical though, as always in these sorts of tales from the judiciary, the smoking gun has never been found. Poincaré's memoirs show that Ignace expended a great deal of the council of ministers' time discussing Caillaux' case. We have it on the authority of General Mordacq that every evening at seven Ignace had a meeting with Clemenceau. But exactly what Clemenceau contributed to the discussions is unknown.

Anyway, like Malvy, Caillaux didn't wait for the outcome of the judicial procedure against him (the charge was 'intelligence with the enemy'). In a long and most moving speech, with Clemenceau sitting opposite in the government's bench, he asked the Chamber to lift his immunity.

'You remember,' he turned to Clemenceau, 'the tragic sessions when you were accused, some twenty-five years ago, of treason. You remember the speeches of passion, the violent interjections of Déroulède on greeting your words. Do you want to bring the injustice of that time back to life today?'

Martet was watching Clemenceau's slant eyes; he thought 'something was going to happen.' When he later asked Clemenceau what was on his mind, Clemenceau replied, 'I was thinking that there was France, that's all.'

Caillaux' voice was hoarse. 'I have clean hands, I do. Look at my fortune, look at anything.' It was an echo from Clemenceau's own speech at Salernes. Did Clemenceau himself recognise it? 'Imprudence again, they tell me! But imprudence is almost inseparable from action.' Certainly, Caillaux was not the only politician to have been a poor judge of character. He concluded, 'It is sweet to suffer for one's ideas' – words Clemenceau had used in his youth.

Some years later Clemenceau would admit, 'I never detested him.' He had told André Paisant's Chamber committee, charged with the affair, that as minister in his last government Caillaux was one of those rare people with whom he never had an argument. But Clemenceau was not going to dwell on their similarities. He rose to the tribune and said that as the 'head of military justice' he was the only person in the Assembly who did not have the right to respond to Monsieur Caillaux. Caillaux' immunity was lifted by 418 votes to 2.

He was arrested one early morning in January 1918, in his dressing gown; his wife was still in the bathtub. Police escorted him to La Santé gaol, which was to remain his residence for the following two years. Legal defence was provided by Pascal Ceccaldi, but – with yet another echo from the past – he also received counsel from old Maître Demange, Dreyfus's former lawyer. His trials before the courts martial and the High Court went on until the Senate declared him guilty in April 1920 of 'correspondence with subjects known to the enemy' but, admitting 'attenuating circumstances', had him freed.

Humbert was eventually arrested in February 1918. Bolo was shot at Vincennes on 17 April. Despite a personal plea from his mother, who visited Clemenceau at rue Franklin, Duval was shot on 17 July. The case of *Le Journal* was heard by a court martial in May 1919. Clemenceau actually intervened in favour of Humbert, writing a letter to his defence, Moro Giafferi. The letter was used to great effect in the court and Humbert was acquitted. But one of his associates got five years and Alphonse Lenoir (Humbert's main link with Bolo and the Deutsche Bank) was condemned to death. Drugged with morphine and tied, unconscious, to the firing post, he was shot in September 1919.

The syndicalists leaders and 'anarchists', such as Merrheim, were untouched. But one has to conclude that war is very hazardouś to the course of justice.

III

THE MILITARY situation was grave and demanded a forceful hand. Clemenceau's first task was to breach the gulf which separated soldiers from civilians and confront the enemy with a united and determined nation.

Clemenceau's revolution of November and December bears all the traits of Gambetta's revolution of 1870. To all intents and purposes he was, like Gambetta, minister of the interior and minister of war. As the British ambassador wrote home on 9 December, 'It is practically a one man ministry.' 'Clemenceau is a dictator: there is not a single minister in his ministry,' recorded Abel Ferry in his notes. 'Pams submits to him, even in the nomination of sub-prefects, and receives from Mandel, every evening, instructions from his master.'

Clemenceau however discovered that he had to call more than one meeting of the council of ministers a week; sometimes there were as many as three. The Comité de Guerre was reduced from ten to six members and did not meet until his third week in office. Poincaré's own prospects of making a contribution looked limited in the light of Clemenceau's publicly proclaimed philosophy, in one of his earlier articles, that 'there are two useless organs: the prostate and the presidency of the Republic.' The promised chats were infrequent. 'Still nothing from Clemenceau,' Poincaré noted on 26 November. 'Still nothing from Clemenceau,' he wrote on the 27th. 'Still no news from Clemenceau or from any minister,' he entered on the 28th. That was the day he learned that Clemenceau had placed the army of Italy under his command without consulting anyone, which got Pétain upset. For the 29th: 'Still nothing . . . Charming job I have.' When the chats did occur they would last about half an hour. He would report 'with great volubility and no less great disorder. At several moments he loses the thread of his ideas and suddenly cries out, "What was I saying? Let's see, let's see, I'm exhausted." He speaks very loudly, like a deaf man. He also speaks very quickly, touching on everything, asking my advice on nothing and not allowing me to say a word.' He was always friendly. 'Well, *bon courage*,' Poincaré might finally mutter as his premier left. 'Oh! courage I don't lack.' 'Well then, good health.' 'Yes, that wish is rather more necessary. I would like the Chamber to give me a little rest . . . I'm a pessimist like all critical spirits. But I'm confident.

Without doubt we're going to be hammered in at a few points, but we'll hold, we'll hold, we'll hold.' Soon, Poincaré took to writing long letters. 'This little handwriting that sent me mad,' commented Clemenceau. 'All in a fine, tight, small handwriting; one should never put at the head of a country a man whose heart is stuffed with dossiers. It's too dangerous.'

As for parliament, Clemenceau abolished secret sessions. If the representatives of the people wanted to criticise him, then let them criticise him publicly; if they didn't want him to stay then he would go, he had never asked for the job. Clemenceau reserved Wednesdays for the reception of parliamentarians; but whenever their questions were related to the ministry of war, he sent them to Mordacq who would receive them on Mondays and Fridays. Mordacq claimed that the vast majority came for recommendations. After February the number of appointments was rapidly reduced. Relations with the Senate and Chamber army committees, on the other hand, were always given a high priority; both Mordacq and Clemenceau thought they could make a real contribution to the war. This was where Ferry, as member of the Chamber army committee, played a critical role.

The press was Mandel's department. In his initial conversation with Poincaré, Clemenceau had indicated a desire to free the press from censorship; he said he had been active in its establishment in 1914 but that he felt that it had been abused. He expressed the same will in his statements to parliament: 'Republicans must not fear freedom of the press.' But in practice it was impossible to abolish censorship in time of war. 'Freedom of the press' was limited to the freedom to express political opinions – provided they were not 'defeatist'. Censorship was a very sensitive subject for Clemenceau and he refused to talk about it, leaving total responsibility in Mandel's hands. The cutting, under Mandel's supervision, was far less extensive than in the past and never were whole articles cut, as Clemenceau had experienced in his former *Homme enchaîné*.

Clemenceau personally supervised the direction of *L'Homme libre* and would not let Mandel meddle with it. Every afternoon the new director, Nicolas Pietri, a Corsican, came to visit him; Pietri became one of Clemenceau's closest friends during the war. But *L'Homme libre* did not have a sufficiently wide circulation to get Clemenceau's views across to the public, and a new link was established with *Le Petit Parisien*, whose political editor, Gatineau, was received twice daily at Clemenceau's office. Relations with *Le Matin* were improved by an almost daily contact with its parliamentary editor, Talabard. *Le Temps* and *L'Echo de Paris* also had easy access to the premier. Thus the old republican tradition that tied politics so closely to the life of the opinion press was resuscitated under the Clemenceau regime.

*

But the essential area of concern was of course the army. There is no evidence that Clemenceau ever said, 'War is too serious a matter to be left to the generals.' He had a great respect for good republican generals and never tried to impose his own ideas of strategy on them. What appalled him in this war was not so much the behaviour of this general or that, but the blind military bureaucracy which seemed to dominate all of them. Mordacq, commenting on his arrival at rue Saint-Dominique, repeated the war cry of the army committee: 'On the front the bureaux were more in command than ever.' One of the problems was that commanders refused to take orders over the telephone; they stuck to the old formula of the written *bordereau* (which had figured so prominently in the Dreyfus Affair). This resulted in enormous delays. Mordacq directed that every order had to be executed within a limit of three days. This had a considerable effect and Mordacq discovered that he had even managed to impress the British 'who are particularly slow.'

One issue which drew Clemenceau's special attention was the age of the men in command. He might have been in his late seventies, but Clemenceau wanted young generals. Already a law in April had lowered the age of retirement. In December, Clemenceau lowered again the maximum age for those on active service on the front and then, unlike his predecessors in April, enforced the decision. There was vigorous opposition from GQG and the question remained a source of tension for three or four months.

Another source of difficulty with GQG was Clemenceau's decision to reintegrate the disgraced generals of the April offensive, Nivelle, Mangin and Mazel. Mazel was given an interior command, the 4th Region, at Le Mans. Nivelle was posted in Algeria. But his most controversial nomination was that of 'butcher' Mangin, who got the command of an army corps on the front. Pétain was furious. Clemenceau recognised that the man had certain weaknesses; 'he considered that obedience was not made for him', he was a 'hammerer'. But Clemenceau thought that the 'hammerers' did have a contribution to make as long as they were supervised: '[Hammering] is what he did in his African campaigns where he had nothing better to do,' explained Clemenceau some years later. 'He came back to the [French] front and figured that it was the same thing. And, from time to time it was the same thing: it was a matter of weight, of force, of push. [But] from time to time you had to see further.'

It was precisely this attitude – a balancing of various schools of military strategy rather than favouring one over the others – which defined his relationship with the two most important generals in the French army, Foch and Pétain.

*

Ferdinand Foch was a man, like Joffre and Gallieni, of the Pyrenees, the sixth son in a Catholic family that was tied by marriage to the aristocracy; and in Foch's family they still made the distinction between the 'robe' and the 'sword' – they were linked to both. He himself married a Breton lady, '*issue d'une famille de robe*,' as one of his biographers records. He maintained a sizeable manor with a sizeable name, Trofeunteuniou, near Morlaix in the north of Brittany, 'a haven for the happy days of respite'. He was schooled in a Jesuit college at Metz. But as an army professor at the Ecole de Guerre in the 1890's, the time of the Dreyfus Affair, he distinguished himself from his less loyal colleagues with a personal slogan, 'Faithfulness to the Republic, Respect for the government, Obedience to the law'.

Churchill wrote that Clemenceau and Foch represented two different Frances, Clemenceau 'an apparition of the French Revolution at its sublime moment,' and Foch 'another France – ancient, aristocratic; the France whose grace and culture, whose etiquette and ceremonial has bestowed its gifts around the world.' Conflict between the two was inevitable, but for a long time remained muffled. It was Clemenceau as prime minister, under the urging of Picquart, who named Foch director of the Ecole de Guerre in 1908. 'I have a Jesuit brother,' a worried Foch said at their first encounter. '*Je m'en fous*', replied Clemenceau.

The basic message of Foch's teaching was in his idea of 'moral force'. 'Death soon hits armies without an object, nations without an ideal,' he said in a lecture delivered in 1903. 'A goal clearly perceived, a common thought, the same holy anger of all, a supreme effort together, there resides the . . . power that we must prepare in our national army to "boot the enemy out of France".' Foch and Clemenceau were on common grounds here.

The Somme had brought Foch temporary disgrace, but the fall of Nivelle, the following year, had meant the rise of Foch; he was named chief of general staff. Clemenceau revealed his feelings about him and Pétain, the commander-in-chief, in his first hearing as premier before the Senate army committee, in December 1917. He said that Foch 'counterbalanced exactly the good and the bad qualities of Pétain; they complete one another by not being the same, as two different bells might ring out in harmony, allowing one to arrive at a reasoned judgement.' Pétain was cautious and often fell into deep pessimism, a man of defence; Foch was more disposed to the military initiative, an optimist, a man of the offensive. Clemenceau's natural inclination was towards Foch. 'I am very attached to Foch,' he told the committee. 'First he has the supreme quality in my eyes: there is nothing that will discourage him. He stops at nothing . . . In addition, he has a certain measured audacity as I'll show you.' Clemenceau told the story of Foch defending the Channel ports on the Yser in October 1914. 'Since he was told "we can no longer hold!" he replied, "We can no longer hold? Very well! I'm attacking." That's the man! I am very much attached to him.' Pétain, Clemenceau later told Martet, 'was always full of good sense. Too full of good sense. He lacked a grain of folly.'

But in the long winter of 1917–1918 Clemenceau opted for good sense. He told the Senate committee that Russia's collapse would allow the Germans to transfer forty divisions to the western front (in fact they transferred over sixty). There was no question of France launching a general offensive again. 'The whole problem for us is to hold everywhere at all cost, not to bend at any point. If we momentarily lose bits of territory, we'll lose them. Then things will happen as at Verdun. We will do what we have to do.' The Americans were coming. There were currently 120,000 U.S. troops in France. In May he forecast 350,000, of which 250,000 would be ready for combat duty. The following May, he said, there would be 'a million American soldiers on the first line and a million on the second line: I think that will settle the question.' 'In 1919!' exclaimed a committee member. 'Messieurs,' Clemenceau replied, 'I tell you the things as they are. The German plan is to make peace in 1918; that of the French is to make it in 1919.'

Three days earlier, on 11 December, a meeting of the Comité de guerre had taken place which had been attended by the presidents of the two chambers, Deschanel and Dubost. The presidents had insisted on being present because there were parliamentarians complaining of the lack of a general plan for an offensive (it was a change from July!). At the meeting, Dubost was particularly aggressive. He said you couldn't win a war with partial offensives and turning to Pétain he announced, 'I cannot hide from you that I am completely opposed to your methods.' Pétain said he was ready to resign and 'return silently into the ranks.' Clemenceau then intervened: 'There is no question of that. I am the only one responsible here. I am not for the offensive because we do not have the means. We have to hold, we have to last.' He gave Pétain his total support: 'I do not want to risk the result of the war on an offensive today. General Pétain is under my orders; I cover him entirely. I insist that he be aware of this. That said, I thank Monsieur le président du Sénat for having so clearly posed the question. It wasn't without purpose.'

Poincaré muttered a few words. 'I also thank Messieurs Dubost and Deschanel.' The two men rose from their seats in silence. At the door Dubost looked back at the six members of the committee and repeated, 'At any rate, I have insisted, and I shall continue to insist, on disclaiming my moral responsibility.'

Once they were gone Poincaré said that sentimentally he was for another offensive, but the statistics on France's manpower forced him to admit this was impossible; Pétain's evidence could not be questioned. Then, looking across the room, he noticed Clemenceau; tears were welling up in his eyes. 'Monsieur le président,' said the prime minister, 'I have the pleasure of feeling a complete agreement with you. It is comforting. We will hold, we will hold. If the Chamber overthrows me, it will take its responsibility. Evidently, I cannot force the country to fight despite itself; but between you and me, we will hold.'

IV

TO HOLD demanded coordination, a single direction and goal for all forces facing Germany – what Clemenceau had insisted on since the outset of the war, a unity of command.

In November 1917 this was still a fantasy. The two major Allies on the western front, the French and the British, followed conflicting strategies. The French were on the defensive; the British were on the offensive. The first aim of the French under Pétain was to liberate Alsace Lorraine; the first aim of the British was the drive through Flanders and Belgium. Even their priorities were different. The French concentrated their efforts on the western front; the British turned to the Orient, considering the western front a stalemate. Finally, the structure of command was different. The complex French arrangements formulated at the time of Nivelle's disgrace had, amazingly, managed to sort themselves out by autumn and there existed a fair degree of harmony between the military authorities and the government, even if the relationship of Pétain to Foch was not entirely clear. On the British side, there was continual tension between the government and the army and between the generals themselves. The only thing it seems they could agree on was their total rejection of French plans for a 'unity of command'.

It has to be said that the earlier attempts in 1917 at a unity of command were not shining models of success. Nivelle's brief command of the Allied armies resulted in unacceptably high casualties for both the British and the French. And then there was Salonika. The British had never been keen on the Salonika expedition and the French had increasingly come to regard it as a drain on their resources. The problem was that they were now established in this malarial infested north-eastern port of Greece, along with Serbs, Indians, Indo-Chinese and Italians. Withdrawal was out of the question. Clemenceau, presenting a report on the area to the Senate army committee in December said, 'When you have read it you will see how one can take a train, travel a long distance and end up where you started!' The unhappy task of coordinating the Allies fell to General Sarrail. A small offensive had been launched under his command in May and ended in 'a complete fiasco' as Lloyd George put it in a letter to Ribot in June. Salonika became a source of great tension between the British and the French. In December, Clemenceau was still describing the situation as a 'lamentable state of affairs'. To calm Lloyd George, he replaced Sarrail with General Guillaumat.

But quite obviously this was not going to win the British over to the cause of the unity of command. British officials were hinting to Painlevé in October that they regarded the French parliament and army as having given up on the war; a British Flanders offensive, they suggested, was the Allies' only chance. The French viewed this as serving no purpose in the light of what was going on in Russia. Better, they thought, for the British to extend their portion of the front and for the two Allies to build up their defences in preparation for the inevitable German push the following spring.

Clemenceau held that it would need the aid of German cannon to create a unity of command. Effectively, every step in the direction of Allied unity was preceded by some major military disaster. Britain was dragged screaming into unity; at no point did she ever take the initiative.

The first catastrophe was Caporetto. The news of the Italian retreat did not reach London until Sunday, 28 October. Lloyd George set off for Italy immediately and, at the same time, the British and the French ordered the transfer of six divisions each to the Italian front (the British later cancelled the transfer of one of their divisions because it was needed in their campaign in Flanders). This proved sufficient to halt the German advance, but now, as in Salonika, the Allies were faced with the problem of command. In the first week of November the prime ministers of Britain, France and Italy met in the resort town of Rapallo and set up what would soon become known as the Supreme War Council. The first arrangements were extremely complicated and said to be the brainchild of Lloyd George who was simply seeking an alternative to the French plan for a unity of command. Its combination of political and military representation also gave him some leverage over his own generals who were then troubling him. Even this arrangement nearly failed to materialise because of a disagreement over where the Supreme War Council should sit. The French wanted Paris, the British wanted Versailles. Lloyd George argued that Versailles would be a more symbolic seat for coordinating the eventual Allied victory; it was here that the Second Reich had been founded. But he made no secret of his real reason: to escape the influence of the French government.

Clemenceau, who wanted an unambiguous single command system, did not like the arrangements at all. But since he had inherited them from his predecessor there was little he could do. The choice of Versailles particularly galled his republican sensibilities; it was 'childishness'; it was 'ridiculous' – 'we spent millions renting the Hôtel Trianon to install all the archives.' Yet Versailles it was and Versailles it would remain, for the rest of the war and on through to the peace.

The second catastrophe was Passchandaele. The British offensive was not working. Clemenceau, whose admiration for British staying power never ceased, told the Senate army committee: 'The British have been terribly hit. All the great families have their children at the front. The main politicians have had their sons mown down in such circumstances that they cannot work out what could have happened.' Yet even so cruelly beaten, 'the British are not disposed to come to any agreement over the unity of command.'

So both the British and the French began to speak, rather hypocritically, of a 'unity of direction'. The problem was that a unity of direction required a government and in Clemenceau's opinion the British government in November and December, rather like the French government after the Chemin des Dames, was in a state of chaos; 'Well, I regret to say,' Clemenceau remarked, 'there is not much existing of this [British] government.' The British could not present a united front. Generals contradicted generals; Lloyd George contradicted all of them.

On 1 December the Supreme War Council finally met in Versailles. The failure of the British offensive had led to some concessions – essentially, a simplification in procedure. 'Around a beautiful table,' reported Clemenceau two weeks later, 'I saw superb officers in various uniforms preparing to accomplish their great works.' There were about two hundred men present and, from what one can gather from Clemenceau, the whole conference was organised in obedience to that classical international principle known to the French as *le système D* and to the British as 'muddling through'. 'By chance, it was I who was obliged to preside.' According to one British witness, Colonel Repington, Clemenceau made a very brief opening statement and then invited the conference to constitute itself in different committees – allowing five minutes for the designation of members. Mordacq reports that Clemenceau asked the military representatives to act as a 'real interallied general staff'.

Of course this first conference achieved nothing of the kind. From the French point of view, the most frustrating element was the failure to get a formal commitment from the British to extend their line southward. Lloyd George made a promise, but that was not enough. Clemenceau threatened the British prime minister that if he did not receive a written, detailed commitment he would order his train out of Paris to be stopped. There was some last minute negotiation with the generals and the train left; but there was no commitment.

The German cannon spoke once more. In December the British launched another 'brilliant offensive' and the Germans obliged with a brilliant counter-offensive. In January, the British extended their line sixty kilometres southwards to Barisis. Even the British were now talking about 'waiting' for the big German push in the spring.

A second meeting of the Supreme War Council took place in Versailles as January turned to February. It was agreed that the British would extend their part of the front still further to the River Ailette. Support was also expressed for Foch's pet scheme, a general reserve. The only problem was that neither Pétain nor Haig were willing to provide it with troops. In the end it was the divisions sent to Italy in November that would contribute. But time was running out. Nobody had forgotten Verdun; the Germans had attacked on 21 February. How, when and where would their forces strike this time?

V

OUT IN Belgian Flanders at the hour of midnight, 31 December 1917, a young British poet stood with a few acquaintances at their camp overlooking the Ypres battlefield. It was covered, like all the battlefields that stretched from here to Switzerland, in a deep frozen snow and the air was tingling cold. They looked at the coloured lights of bombardment and heard the clatter of distant machine guns. Painfully, they tried to read a message into those luminous scribblings on the night's black sky; they concluded that there was none. 'The sole answer to unspoken but importune questions was the line of lights in the same relation to Flanders and our lives as at midnight the year before,' recalled Edmund Blunden. 'All agreed that 1917 had been a sad offender. All observed that 1918 did not look promising at its birth, or commissioned "to solve this dark enigma scrawled in blood".'

At his desk in the Elysée Palace the president of the Republic wrote, 'The year began in mist; it ends in fog.'

In another palace, at Compiègne, Pétain dictated his *ordre du jour* to the French armies: 'I salute your flags and, in addressing to you my most affectionate wishes for 1918, I express to you once more my pride in commanding you and my confidence in the future.'

Paris was shrouded in fog on New Year's Day. The *cabinet militaire* was scheduled to meet that morning. The members presented their wishes to the prime minister and then Mordacq proceeded into an analysis of the German commander-in-chief, General Ludendorff. He found him rather

Napoleonic but, all the same, German offensives had never worked; on each occasion they had simply worn themselves out. Had Mordacq not noticed that something new had happened at Caporetto? Did he know how those heavy German guns were rapidly moved up, across the ploughed-up battlefield? Ludendorff had learned a lesson from Verdun. Had the Allies? Mordacq wondered aloud if victory would be possible sooner than expected. Clemenceau stood by his earlier statement, that a French peace was a peace in 1919; but he thanked Mordacq for his optimism and added, 'Isn't this the day of wishes?'

President Woodrow Wilson presented his New Year's message to Congress one week later: Fourteen Points for liberty, Fourteen Points for democracy, Fourteen Points for peace. Clemenceau commented that the Lord Almighty had limited himself to Ten. From the beginning of the war he had made it clear that he would have much preferred to see Teddy Roosevelt in the White House than this professor of international law. Clemenceau's comments about Wilson in *L'Homme enchaîné*, until the moment of America's entry into the war, made a striking parallel to his verbal jousts with Jaurès. When Wilson made his famous speech in January 1917 about a possible 'peace without victory', Clemenceau wrote, 'The edifice is marvellous, but I see no men to inhabit it.' After the U.S. declaration of war in April, Wilson became the incarnation of modern democracy, but it was really the excellent rapport that Clemenceau developed with General Pershing, commander of the American forces, and Colonel House, Wilson's personal envoy to France, that led to his warm relations with the Americans during his first months in office. Pershing was one of the first foreigners to pay a visit to Clemenceau on becoming prime minister; Clemenceau was 'very touched'. House's regular meetings with Clemenceau began within the first week; by the third week Clemenceau was reporting to the Senate army committee, 'We are now a good pair of friends.' He later commented, 'He was the window through which the light shone on Wilson.' This was hardly a compliment to Wilson.

Clemenceau of course needed the Americans, not only to defeat the Germans but also to act as a counter-weight to his British allies. In December Clemenceau had been very much criticised by Paul Strauss for the overly intimate relations he seemed to be establishing with the Americans. Strauss thought that this would be harmful to Franco-British relations and he expressed fear that Wilson's arbitration might one day prove to be a humiliation for France. Clemenceau's answer was, as usual, the realistic one: this was the fourth year of war and France had no alternative. He noted that the British needed the Americans even more than the French and had no compunction about exploiting that friendship. Clemenceau looked straight into Strauss's eyes, 'Who can I ask for help when I am faced with British resistance, I who am supposed to be the friend of England?'

Criticism of the government was mounting on another front: predictable criticism. Though strikes declined and the troubles in the war factories had notably diminished since autumn, the Socialists attacked Clemenceau's handling of the treason scandals as a 'provocation of the working class'.

The dispute came to a head on 8 March when Emile Constant, supported by Pierre Renaudel, interpellated Clemenceau in the Chamber on 'the government responsibilities and compromises revealed by the debates in the Bolo trial'. Clemenceau denied any responsibility – the Bolo matter was for the courts to decide.

But one of the issues raised by Renaudel, that the government should suppress the vicious campaign against traitors which Léon Daudet was running in L'Action française, provoked Clemenceau to remark, 'I am, for the time being, the head of the republican government and I have, with this title, doctrines to defend at this tribune.' These he defined as the liberty of press and the waging of an unwanted war. 'I warned you on the first day. I told you that I was going to suppress political censorship. I have done it. You applauded me.' There would be no turning back. 'I will not stop these campaigns. If you want to stop them, name someone else in my place, overthrow me right now. Then you can have a censorship which will stop campaigns against individuals.' There were many interruptions from the socialist benches, but the Chamber as a whole applauded its premier.

'I am today confronted with events in preparation, of which you are all aware, which I must face, on which my whole thinking must bend, I can say every hour of the day and night.' He made an appeal: 'Help me yourselves, you my opponents!'

There were screams from the socialist benches. 'We do not have the same goal! Vive l'homme enchaîné!'

'So you said it: "We do not have the same goal." I would not have liked to believe it. A great misfortune occurred at the birth of my ministry. I was struck by the exclusion of Monsieur Renaudel and his friends before they even knew what I was thinking of saying or doing. They had decided, by virtue of a noble dogmatic science, that I was a danger for the working class and for the national defence . . .'

'Yes! And what about Draveil?' interrupted Monsieur Claussat from one of those noble benches of science.

'They have decreed,' Clemenceau repeated, 'that I was a danger for the working class and for the national defence.'

'And you have confirmed it,' cried out another Socialist.

'The working class is not your property, Messieurs.' The parliamentary minutes record loud applause from the Left and the Centre and interruptions from the Socialists.

'It has been your victim,' chimed out Monsieur Claussat.

'The hands of Monsieur Renaudel and of Monsieur Albert Thomas are no more calloused than my own. I am sorry for them both, but they are bourgeois like me.'

After riding the storm for many minutes, Clemenceau returned to his second 'doctrine', that of the war. He quoted an old Japanese saying, 'The victor is the one who can, for one extra quarter of an hour, make his opponent believe that he is not conquered.' 'That's my maxim of war. I have no other.' It was the basis of his whole policy: 'I entered the government with this idea that the morale of the country has to be maintained.'

One of the Socialists exclaimed, 'You have succeeded!' Clemenceau was even drawing in his parliamentary enemies.

'People say, "We don't want war, we want the soonest possible peace." Ah! I too want the soonest possible peace [yet] it is not in bleating peace that you can silence Prussian militarism.' There was prolonged applause. But like the movement of the tides, it gradually receded. 'Just a moment ago Monsieur Constant threw out a little word on my silence regarding foreign policy.' He must have smiled for a second. 'My foreign policy and my domestic policy, it is all one. Domestic policy? I wage war. Foreign policy? I wage war. I still wage war.'

VI

PARIS WAS kept awake that night by the rumble and clatter of a dozen squadrons of German Gothas which flew in from the Marne and the Oise. It sounded as if a score of old tractors had taken to the sky. For the majority of residents it was simply an unpleasant experience: shutters reverberated, glasses on the shelf clinked, a door banged shut. But rue Druot was bombed and so was rue Geoffroy-Marie. The suburbs of La Chapelle and Vincennes were also hit. The damage these aircraft could inflict was nothing compared to the raids of the Second World War – seven were killed in Paris and four in the suburbs – but the psychological effect of this new kind of war was considerable. Paris lost its sense of security, fears that had not been experienced since the summer months of 1914 returned; there was a new conscience of the proximity of the front and of the destructive power of modern weapons. Three nights later, Clemenceau's own ministry of war was nearly destroyed by fire caused by bombing; the German command was unaware that the premier retired to his flat at rue Franklin every night. On this occasion the casualties were high, not because of the bombing but because of panic. At Metro Bolivar sixty people were trampled to death.

It was a tense season of waiting. In February Clemenceau had admitted before the Senate army committee that they had lost precious time in their defence preparations but, with the help of Italian labour, much work had been accomplished in the last two months. Like the British, the French were constructing a three-tier defence system. Pétain's idea was that front positions could not stop a powerful enemy offensive; land would have to be ceded and the enemy met further to the rear. It was the same doctrine that had got him into trouble with Joffre during the Verdun offensive, and in the winter of 1918 he was still in the minority. Foch, on the other hand, was of the old school of 'never give an inch' and he was getting support from most of the generals in the field. Indeed, the whole rank and file of the army took a dim view of abandoning territory that had been so dearly won in blood.

Clemenceau's series of visits to the front had begun in late January under the shadow of this squabble. Matters were not helped by Dubost who, with the support of General Micheler, went on campaigning in parliament for a general offensive. Clemenceau knew this was impossible. His sympathy was for Foch but, for the time being, he lent his support to Pétain and his programme of defence-in-depth.

His original intention was first to visit the whole front, identify the weak spots and then return with specific plans for improvement. Mordacq always accompanied him as a military adviser. For the furthest points he travelled by special train. Otherwise he went by car. He visited Champagne and Lorraine in January, where he realised that not even the commanders in the field could agree on what constituted the 'weak spots'. In early February he was in Alsace where he passed by Thann – which must have evoked some old memories – and climbed a hill at Le Tanet that overlooked the whole plain of the German occupied province. At Pfetterhausen he insisted on shaking hands with the defenders of the last outpost before the Swiss frontier, an incident which upset some of the officers present because it was under the watch of a German machine gunner. A fortnight later Clemenceau was inspecting the defences on the beaches of Lettenburg and Dixmude with the Belgian General Ruquoy. On his visits to Chocques, to Béthune, Souchez, Vimy and Neuville-Saint-Waast, the British fell in love with him; no French prime minister had ever paid them this honour. He crossed fields of old torments, tanks burnt out, cannon with their barrels twisted like wire, German machine-gun belts scattered and a few dead preserved by the cold. Clemenceau's tours of the front became legendary among all the Allies. Did they have enough tobacco? It was to be a major issue for the new ministry. Tobacco was rationed in Paris so that the troops on the front could smoke.

The one sector Clemenceau did not have time to visit was that controlled by General Sir Hubert Gough's fated Fifth Army, stretching from the Flesquières salient south of Cambrai down to the juncture with Duchesne's Sixth French Army at La Fère. It had just taken up its positions from the French, thus fulfilling the agreement to extend the British share of the front. Its divisions were being reorganised, its supplies were poor (this was the same area the Germans had devastated in their retreat the year before) and both French and British commands were refusing it needed reserves: it was felt that the area was of low strategic value to the enemy. The first-line defences were poor, the second and third lines (or in British parlance, the 'battle' and 'reserve zones') were virtually nonexistent.

On 7 March Clemenceau's government learned from an informant in Strasbourg that German troops were being moved northward to the British front. On 12 March the Germans changed all their telegram codes: French intelligence had noticed that this normally happened ten days before the enemy launched a major attack. The information was duly passed on to Britain.

At last, on 13 March, Clemenceau set off for London resolved to get some concrete commitment from the Allies to the principle of a supreme command; he returned to Paris four days later empty handed. Not only was the idea rejected, but the one practical element where the Allies had reached an earlier agreement, the strategic reserve, fell to pieces because the Italians refused to release from their territory the troops which composed it. Thus, on the eve of the long-expected German offensive, the defence of the Western front was still left to the separate national military forces.

VII

GOUGH HAD realised that his was the army selected by Ludendorff the moment he discovered that the enemy in front of him had been placed under the command of General von Hutier. Von Hutier had led the devastating offensive against the Russians at Riga. A roar from hell broke out at 4 a.m. on 21 March: 6,600 guns, 3,500 mortars, long toms and gas, perfected, more toxic. Teenage recruits cuddled up to the older men and cried. Experienced soldiers felt numb and sleepy. At 9.40 Prussian and Bavarian storm-troopers moved in with hand grenades.

They advanced in fog, not in a line, but in small groups. Infiltrate, by-pass and mop up: it was all Nivelle had said he would do one year before, it was everything the Germans now achieved. They had mastered the technique, the weather was in their favour, the front before them was weak, the ground was flat.

Clemenceau was in the area on the 23rd: 'I saw Gough's army spread out like the white of an egg.' On the first day of the attack, the Germans had advanced over seven kilometres and had won control of about 250 square kilometres, an incredible accomplishment by the standards of that war. On the roads that led to Albert, Villers-Bretonneux, Roye and Ham streams of wagons, cars, long files of exhausted troops – many with their clothes torn, some maimed – passed through a new end of the world, a new war-ripped landscape. Private W. Lockey of the 'Sherwood Foresters' got left behind in the scramble for safety. He ran to catch up 'with our chaps'. 'There were three roads, one to the right and one to the left, while the other led straight ahead to the village, (or it had been once). Leading into it was a sunken road with deep dugouts at each side.' In front of them sped one of the Company runners. Suddenly 'he stopped and stood like a pillar of salt': Germans were coming out of the dugouts. Some ran back down the road, Lockey with others clambered up the embankments with machine guns spitting at them. Finally they made it to the village where they met 'some Gunners brewing tea'. They offered the frightened men 'some spuds' but just as they sat down to eat 'the cry that Jerry was entering the further end of the village fell upon our ears.' So off they clambered again into some wooded slopes. Where was the Company? Out in the open country once more, they ran into 'some of our chaps who informed us that Fritz had been knocking hell out of them ever since noon.' On they skeltered over desolate acres. 'Some of our Artillery with their limbers crossing a ploughed field on our right were hit by a shell, drivers, Gunners and all being blown to bits. As we went we passed an old Frenchman who stood waving his arms and shouting, "*Anglais Soldats no bon!*"' The roll-call that night revealed that only sixty were left out of Lockey's battalion.

The bombing of Paris intensified. It was now worse in the day than at night. And there was something very curious about it: no sight of a plane, no sound of the tractors. The first of the daylight bombs fell at seven in the morning on Saturday, 23 March. From then on, every twenty or thirty minutes a loud detonation rocked some quarter of the city. One bomb fell on the quays, another hit the side of the gare de l'Est. In rue Château-Landon a two-storey house collapsed, its roof falling on top of the ruins like a tea-cosy . . . for the trajectory of these bombs was not vertical, but oblique. The ten o'clock communiqué announced that they were thrown from high-flying aircraft. But the bombing went on, and

there was still no sign of a plane. By mid-afternoon the experts had made
their assessment: it was some enormous cannon. It took several days for
the French reconnaissance planes to discover the three gun emplacements
near Laon, on the Mont-de-Joie (the enemy had always had a wicked sense
of humour) in the forêt de Saint-Gobain, *one hundred and eighteen* kilometres
from the cathedral of Notre-Dame as the shell flies. Between 23 March and
8 April 183 projectiles fell on the capital and another 120 on the suburbs,
killing 253 people and wounding another 620. The most tragic incident
was when one of these shells exploded in the Eglise Saint-Gervais, packed
with worshippers celebrating a Good Friday mass. Both Clemenceau and
Poincaré were on the scene within an hour.

The prime minister was not to be perturbed. When one of his under-
secretaries of state at the ministry of war ordered his bureaucrats to take
cover in the cellars, Clemenceau ordered them all back to sit in their 'customary offices'. 'Eh bien, it's not going too badly,' he said to Poincaré when
he called in at the Elysée on the Friday evening, 22 March, for one of his
brief 'chats'. 'The British have rather uselessly yielded too much ground,
but they'll hold on.' There were a whole lot of rumours in the Chamber, so
he had spent the afternoon walking up and down the corridors with a smile
on his face, 'and I lifted their spirits.' Evacuate Ham? A few precautions
had to be taken. 'For a month we are going to be living on the alert.'

The next morning Clemenceau returned to the Elysée, a little less
confident; but he thought that Pétain's reserves would do the trick. Early
in the afternoon one of Pétain's liaison officers arrived to warn Poincaré
and Clemenceau that the situation was 'not only serious, but grave'. Gough
appeared to have 'lost his head'; the route to Paris seemed threatened;
Pétain was desperately trying to set up a new army at Montdidier, but
it would take him two days.

On Sunday afternoon Clemenceau was back again at the Elysée to
report that he was about to set off for Compiègne for dinner with Pétain.
The situation was 'very grave': the whole coal basin was probably going
to fall to the Germans and Paris was certainly under menace. 'You had
better envisage the departure of the government,' he said. But he didn't
want the same mistakes committed as in 1914. Clemenceau's vision was
more that of Gambetta in 1870. Poincaré would leave by car for Tours, a
government would be left in Paris and, at the last minute, Clemenceau
would join Poincaré by plane (in those days about as comfortable as
Gambetta's balloon). 'I do not see myself being separated from you,'
said Poincaré, suspicious. 'You really don't think I would like to play
a trick on you,' responded Clemenceau reassuringly; 'I speak to you as
I would speak to myself, I give you my word of honour.'

For the rest of the war, Poincaré was haunted by the idea of a president
separated and isolated from his government. It became an obsession and
the source of a bitter feud with Clemenceau. Visions of a plot? Jealousy?

The prime minister had stolen the limelight? It is not easy to establish what was on his mind. But his later suggestion that Clemenceau had in some way lost his nerve was an absurdity. The events of the next few days demonstrated the contrary.

VIII

SUNDAY'S DINNER with Pétain went very badly. Pétain was pale, his voice had fallen an octave; he was apparently suffering from the flu. The occasional bomb going off did not help the digestion. GQG had decided to move to Provins, so all the papers, desks and office equipment were being shipped out of the palace by queues of eructing lorries. The dining room was emptier and colder than ever.

This was no longer the man of Verdun. That dark pessimism had overcome his will to fight on. 'Imagine what he said to me,' Clemenceau told Poincaré the next day, 'if we are beaten we owe it to the British.' 'Beaten' didn't exist in Clemenceau's vocabulary and he found it outrageous that the French commander-in-chief could speak in such a manner. In the counterbalance between the two first generals of France Clemenceau now shifted in favour of his general chief-of-staff and for a while referred to the two men as 'Foch and the other'. The critical element here was Foch's close ties with the British. Pétain's attitude at that moment was more that of the old peasant Private Lockey had run into: '*Anglais soldats no bon!*' He was not willing to sacrifice too many of his precious reserves on the British. In his directive to the French armies that day he gave priority to 'maintaining solidly the framework of the French armies,' and he placed special emphasis on the need to prevent the reserves from being separated from the rest of the French forces. In practical terms, this meant holding them back from the British to their left. 'If possible,' he added pointedly, 'maintain a liaison with the British forces.' There it is in black and white: the British link had no priority.

During the dinner, Pétain expressed more fear of being attacked in Champagne than of losing contact with his Allies. 'What does it matter if he is attacked in Champagne?' Clemenceau exclaimed to the council of ministers the following morning. 'If we retreat in Champagne we lose Chaperon, the prefect of the Marne, and that's all.'

Clemenceau and Mordacq got into their car feeling very gloomy. 'After a conversation like that, you need to be a cat with nine lives to maintain your confidence,' Clemenceau commented. Like Foch, Mordacq had known the British during some of the hardest phases of the war; in particular, he had witnessed their response to the first German gas attacks outside Ypres in the spring of 1915. He said to Clemenceau, 'As soon as a firm hand has taken hold of them, they'll stop and they'll stand up to this German hurricane.'

That same night Lord Alfred Milner, British minister plenipotentiary, arrived in Versailles. Milner was a cool and hard negotiator. For Mordacq, who was not much attuned to the poker game of politics, Milner was 'not a cultivated man', he was 'like many British statesmen' in that he 'did not have perhaps a very lively intelligence.' For Clemenceau he was the exact opposite, 'a luminous intelligence crowned with a high culture which rounded itself off in a discrete sentimentality. Extreme sweetness, extreme firmness. A poet in his hours.' Clemenceau had told Poincaré the previous December, 'I like him a lot. He is an old friend of mine. We admired and loved the same woman. That's an indissoluble bond' – for Lord Milner was the second husband of Lady Cecil, Violette Maxse.

As Clemenceau had predicted, the German cannon were to bring the British and French another step closer to unity. He told Milner that it was absolutely essential to put pressure on Haig and Pétain to put all their reserves into the gap that was developing in Gough's sector. And he added that the Allies now had a simple choice between a unity of command or catastrophe.

Thus, following the morning's cabinet meeting, a convoy of vehicles set out for Compiègne, carrying Poincaré, Loucheur, Foch, Mordacq, Milner and Clemenceau. Haig and the new chief of imperial general staff, General Sir Henry Wilson, called to say that they were unable to attend. On their arrival, Clemenceau and his companions found Pétain in an even worse mood than he had been the night before. He said that the British Fifth Army no longer existed and he balked at sending any further reserves. The meeting was, in other words, a complete standoff. Milner said that he could make no decision at all without first discussing the matter with Haig and Wilson. After a long private interview with Clemenceau, Milner agreed on another conference the next day, with all the major commanders and political leaders present, at Doullens.

IX

DOULLENS WAS one of those Picardian gems, just behind the front and yet, from all you could see, untouched by war. 'Other Ranks' knew the place well. Its streets had echoed, for more than three years, to the tones of 'Dear Old Blighty', its taverns would roll out a song to the lost battalion. 'It's hanging on the old barbed wire./ I've seen 'em, I've seen 'em,/ Hanging on the old barbed wire.' In Doullens you could discover the smile of the trenches. Edmund Blunden like thousands of others had once passed through Doullens on the route to the Somme, to the front before Arras – or was it during a transfer back to Ypres? He described it as 'a placid town with cobbled complicated streets, withdrawing courtyards under archways, and curtains, and clocks, and mantelpiece ornaments, and roast fowl, and white and red wine. One longed to take one's ease in that miniature triumph of domesticity . . .' How strange. It must have been the same place before the war. Did you dream there a moment? The same porches, the same church, the same square. To be exact, it did betray a few of the signs of *la guerre intégrale*. There were the troops, there was that element of emptiness and silence that you found everywhere and there was, on Tuesday, 26 March, the grumble of the not so distant guns.

At eleven in the morning the black cars of authority shuddered down the back alleys, for the curving main street was filled with retreating troops. Clemenceau's car arrived first. Poincaré had got lost in Amiens. At the Hôtel de Ville the prime minister got out, looking very cheerful; he thrust out a hand to Senator Rouzé, mayor of the town. Haig had already installed himself with his commanders on the first floor where they were discussing the military situation. The building was a typical, imposing, nineteenth-century monument to the Republic, too close to the street to allow room for a square, so there was a garden instead. Haig came down the steps and, full of smiling apologies, asked the Frenchmen if they would mind if the British finished their discussion before the general conference opened. It seemed natural enough. Mordacq, Clemenceau and Poincaré, who had just arrived, took a walk in the garden. It was cold. The sky was a pure blue. Down the street in front of them – ragged but in perfect order – marched an unending column of men in khaki. Mordacq remembered the scene: 'British phlegm in every sense of the term; then at every instant, sounding so close, a violent cannonade.'

Foch arrived with his assistant, General Weygand. Clemenceau had just been talking about his dissatisfaction over Pétain's attitude and, as Foch walked over, he expressed his fear that the two Allies might be separated. Foch very quickly responded that when an enemy wants to open a hole you don't enlarge it, you try to shut it. 'You stick to your terrain, you defend it foot by foot. We did that at Ypres, we did it at Verdun.' Foch was in great form that day. 'My plan is not complicated, I shall fight . . .'

Pétain arrived looking very downbeat. He pointed up to the first floor window, 'There's somebody who's going to have to capitulate in open country within a fortnight, and very lucky we will be if we are not forced to do the same.'

Foch had only one answer, 'You are not fighting. I, I shall fight without stopping.'

Milner and Wilson turned up late. After exchanging a few pleasantries, the whole party mounted the steps for the conference on the first floor.

Clemenceau began by asking Haig what he intended to do about Amiens. Haig, who also seemed to be suffering from the flu, said there had been a complete misunderstanding here; he would hold on to the whole area north of the Somme, but the territory south of that river would now have to be considered a French affair: he had placed the remnants of Gough's army under Pétain's command. Pétain drily repeated that Gough's army no longer existed. After Haig, Pétain made a report. The faces around him were unconsoling. Foch was visibly furious. There was an occasional rude word from Wilson. Pétain explained that in the last day he had thrown twenty-four divisions into the battle, but these were not fresh troops. The reality was that it required time to build up an effective force. He had done everything to direct troops into the Amiens region, even to the point of withdrawing troops from his central and eastern sectors beyond what prudence should dictate. He turned the question to Haig, 'Have you done as much?'

It took a moment for the interpreter to translate. Haig said he had 'no more men capable of immediately entering into line'. There were more mumbles from the interpreters, another noise from Wilson and then the room fell into a complete silence.

Milner made a sign to Clemenceau; they had arrived at an agreement the night before. The two men got up from their chairs and started whispering in a corner. Clemenceau beckoned Pétain, Milner beckoned Haig. More whispering.

The result of all this was a conference note, adopted unanimously: 'General Foch is charged by the British and French governments to coordinate the action of the allied armies on the western front. He will arrive at an agreement, to this effect, with the generals-in-chief, who are invited to furnish him all necessary information.'

This was still not a supreme command, but it came very close to it.

The French were not invited to join the British for lunch, so they crossed the street into a side-alley where they found the Hôtel des Quatre-Fils-Aymon. Clemenceau was complaining of a stomach ache; he stuck to runner beans with a baked potato and yawned throughout the meal. Perhaps he didn't even notice that Foch was a little less combative than he had been in the garden. But Loucher did. He said with a grin, 'That's Foch after the paper's signed.' Foch didn't find this very funny.

X

THE IMMEDIATE effect of the Doullens conference was to provide the British forces with the 'firm hand' Mordacq had said they required. But whose hand was it? Haig said, 'Foch has brought great energy to bear on the present situation.' Haig had reason to be pleased with the new arrangements. He had never got on with Lloyd George and now, under the cover of Foch's 'coordination', he found he had more freedom to move than ever. For this reason, he played a major role in the process which led eventually, on 14 April (after the Germans had launched another offensive), to Foch being named 'commander-in-chief of the Allied armies in France'.

Gough was replaced by Henry Rawlinson on the day after Doullens, seventy-five thousand reinforcements were moved into the area, Pershing promised Foch American help and by evening the news came in that the British were holding a line before Amiens. On Thursday, Clemenceau was at Montdidier where he actually witnessed the German retreat (his car came under enemy machine-gun fire).

All through the Easter weekend discussions continued on how best to 'coordinate' the Allied effort. Winston Churchill was again in Paris. On Saturday, Clemenceau, Churchill, the Duke of Westminster and Loucheur drove out to Beauvais to see Foch at his new quarters. Foch was in better form than ever. Clemenceau threw himself into his arms. Then they all drove off to the château Dury, Haig's headquarters, where a lunch was awaiting them. They even managed to get a smile out of Pétain that evening over dinner back in Beauvais once more.

Lloyd George came to Beauvais on 3 April. In a rather self-effacing move, Mordacq and Clemenceau had worked out a formula for a coordinated command based on one used by the Allies against the French in 1814; an Austrian general had, on that occasion, been given the responsibility of the 'strategic direction' of the war. Lloyd George accepted the idea.

Clemenceau was very pleased with what he got out of the Beauvais conference, but he never accepted Foch's interpretation of it. Foch, as 'director of strategic operations', would say, 'You have to know how to lead the Allies. You do not command them. You cannot do with some as you would do with others. That is the united command: you do not give orders, you suggest.' When lives were at stake, Clemenceau answered, commanders must command, not suggest. What *brouillards d'obnubilation* had led Foch to deny himself his own authority, he wondered. Foch had been a magnificent soldier at the Marne and on the banks of the Yser, but it looked as if he was going to run his command like a board of managers. Trouble was on the horizon.

By the time of the Beauvais conference, the German offensive had ground to a halt all along the line, a wildly curving line that stretched from Arras (still held by the Allies), to Albert (lost), to Montdidier (held) and to Noyon (lost). The Germans had gained three thousand square kilometres of land, they had inflicted 160,000 casualties on the British and 80,000 on the French. Yet they had themselves lost nearly a quarter of a million men, their lines were over-extended and the supply problem they now faced was of their own making – for this was the same zone they had systematically devastated in their retreat one year earlier. But as General Fayolle said to Clemenceau on a visit to the defences before Amiens, 'It's a new war'; the men were using their rifles.

It was during one of the many meals which Clemenceau had at Beauvais that the question of a separate peace with Austria was raised. The telephone rang. It was Mandel in Paris asking for a word with Mordacq. Mordacq left the room and a few minutes later returned to whisper something in Clemenceau's ear. 'Well,' shouted Clemenceau, throwing his serviette down on the table, 'Czernin has lied! You can tell the press that, Count Czernin has lied!'

Clemenceau had never believed that a separate peace was possible. Two initiatives had been taken in 1917. In March of that year the new Emperor Karl had indicated a willingness to talk with Empress Zita's brother, Prince Sixte de Bourbon-Palme, who was serving in the Belgian army. With official French approval, Sixte and his brother Xavier left for Vienna where they had two days of conversation with the Emperor. Karl said he was willing to guarantee Belgium's independence and even return Alsace-Lorraine to France. Sixte carried back to Paris a letter written in Karl's own hand containing these proposals. The French were sceptical, but Lloyd George thought it was a chance. The problem was that Karl had very little control over Austria's destiny. Berlin in 1917 had no intention of guaranteeing Belgian independence or of handing over Alsace-Lorraine; and there could be little question about it, Austria's war effort was being run from Berlin. The proposals got nowhere.

The second and entirely distinct contact, consisted of conversations in Switzerland between an envoy of the Austrian foreign ministry, Count Nicholas Revetera, and an attaché of the French ministry of war, Commandant Armand, which had been proceeding off and on (more off than on) since August 1917.

Clemenceau, on coming to office in November, exhibited no interest at all in these two developments. Poincaré's memoirs show that every effort to familiarise him with the Bourbon-Palme dossier got the rebuff, 'I do not have the time.' Not even Mandel could win his attention. As for Commandant Armand, he was given instructions 'to listen and say nothing'.

What infuriated Clemenceau at Beauvais – Mordacq reported that he had never seen Clemenceau so angry – was a press conference given in Vienna in which Count Czernin, the Austrian minister of foreign affairs, had claimed 'Mr Clemenceau, some time before the beginning of the offensive on the western front, asked me if I were ready to enter into negotiations and on what basis.' Clemenceau had never taken such an initiative.

After Havas had reported to the world that 'Count Czernin has lied,' a series of diplomatic notes, denials and accusations were published, with each note revealing a little more of what had happened the preceding year. Matters were not helped by mistakes in translation. In the end Clemenceau, exasperated, published the whole Austrian dossier, including the text of Emperor Karl's hand-written letter. The Austrians replied that it was a false document.

The publications had two results. The first was a revival in the press of the pacifist campaign. Albert Thomas wrote a long article in *L'Humanité*, debates appeared in several papers over whether peace had been possible in 1917. Clemenceau had the correspondent for the *Manchester Guardian* expelled. The parliamentary committees were in upheaval, and Briand started making noises. But the chances of a separate peace with Austria in spring 1918 were quite evidently even less than they had been the year before. The official response from Austria was that they had never sought it. Most of what one might already call the former Austro-Hungarian Empire was under direct military rule. Karl and Zita could never have imposed their will. And even if they had come up with a programme for a separate peace, this would have caused a crisis among the Allies. A 'Congress of the Oppressed Nationalities of Austria-Hungary', with full support of the French government, was meeting in Rome at that time. Czechs were to be shipped out of Russia to the western front. And manpower from Italy, to whom promises had been made, had a greater priority for the French than the vague hint of a separate peace with the thousand-year Habsburg dynasty.

The second result was the resignation of Count Czernin. This, it has been said, was the last ministry Clemenceau ever overthrew.

XI

ALBERT BESSIÈRES was a priest and a stretcher-bearer serving in a regiment of territorials at the Chemin des Dames. He kept a notebook which gives a very vivid idea of what life was like in this sector in the last sixteen months of the war – the gas attacks, the sound of heavy artillery, the smell of powder, the song of birds, the sights of men and

nature. In the late winter of 1918 he was stationed at the western edge
of the Forêt de Saint-Gobain, near Coucy. He recorded one fearful night.
The Germans opposite had just installed huge cannon; they were probably
(though he was unaware) the guns that fired on Paris. The sun went down
behind a hill that looked like a wrecked skiff, keel up. On its slopes lay
the great oaks, sawn down to ground level, sleeping under a thin cover
of snow. You looked out across a valley and a lake, the ice of which had
been shattered here and there by shells and now, in the dusk, turned
blood red, violet and finally a sombre black. You could hear the supply
wagons jolting along the pocked road; it was a tacit moment of truce.
They had to eat over there as well as here. Bread and pinard: the force
of the armies. A convoy of donkeys clambered up towards the lines, each
one of them carrying two straw baskets filled with reels of wire, shells
and loaves of bread. '*Laissez passer le ministère Clemenceau*,' cried out the
drivers, whipping their animals onwards; 'Make way for the Clemenceau
ministry.'

Was it a wicked joke? A wishful thought? Clemenceau wasn't there
that evening, but he could have been. His trips to the front were not
all of châteaux and hotel luncheons. He visited the worst sectors, in
the worst conditions, at the worst times. 'For in the end what is
man in nature?' queried his old intellectual idol, Pascal. 'Nothing with
regard to the infinite, everything with regard to nothing, a middle
between nothing and everything.' It bore repeating on the darkest days.
Clemenceau could bring grandeur where there was only meanness and
insignificance, he could produce heroes in a world that hated heroics,
he could raise souls where there was only despair. 'Only one politician
escaped this unanimous reprobation,' wrote Jacques Meyer on the political
indifference of the front, 'and that was Clemenceau.' His basic message
had not changed in half a century, a message of life bursting tameless
from nothingness: to think is to will, to will is to act without weakness
and without hesitation. He was a light in the tempest, a guide to
the way home. 'Politics in time of war is a politics of gestures,' he
told Douglas Haig, who was a little shocked. Clemenceau had such a
great sense of theatre and it was theatre that was needed in the cruel,
perverse, murderous, unthinkable reality that men witnessed as the 'war
of movement' got underway. Outside Béthune a whole company of fusiliers
was blinded by mustard gas on the day, 10 April, Clemenceau visited the
region. 'You are the true descendants of the soldiers of Wellington,' he
told exhausted troops, on 21 April, in their billets of Poperinghe and
Cassel.

It was in that late spring that Clemenceau started wearing grey gloves,
first of cloth, later of leather; they calmed, and hid, an itching eczema.
He said to Poincaré one morning, 'I have hands like you have a heart,
too sensitive. I can't even touch a sheet of paper.'

Poincaré was always commenting on Clemenceau's strengths and weaknesses. When Dubost came round to croak about Clemenceau's defects, Poincaré would reflect on what was good about him: 'his patriotic inspiration which is so ardent, his intelligence which is so lively, his popularity which gives him such powerful means of action.' But he would agree that Clemenceau also had a side that was 'bad and perilous': 'the stylishness of rapid decisions, a fault which results in thoughtless acts that are later regretted, the contradictions, the fickleness, the fits and starts, that incurable light-mindedness of which Jules Ferry spoke, the habit of taking impressions for opinions.'

Clemenceau did everything, it seems, to encourage these old parrot-squawks of complaint. During the most serious conversation at the Elysée with Dubost over the defence of Paris, Clemenceau remarked, lifting his eyes to the ceiling, 'If I had died before this war, I would have died convinced that my country was lost. The vices of the parliamentary regime, the intrigue, the failings, the character, all led me to believe in our decadence. But this war has shown me, as it has shown the whole world, a France so beautiful, so admirable, that now I am full of confidence.' No doubt he was sincere, but such comments were grist to his enemies' mills. Dry and stubborn Dubost, who had never muttered a beautiful phrase in his life, thought it was pure sentimental bosh.

Joseph Reinach usually had something nasty to say about Clemenceau. 'I have found him these last days nervous, agitated, preoccupied with romantic gestures' – anyone who has read Reinach's books will recognise that he was not a man of the theatre. He said, 'Clemenceau is a man of Victor Hugo, as Briand is a man of Balzac' – Reinach was of course Balzac's man.

But in late May and June, it was Hugo that was needed.

XII

THE GERMAN attack, launched from their positions on the Chemin des Dames, came as a shock, if not for everyone a total surprise. So this time the pressure was on the French, though some of the most exhausted British divisions had been transferred here because the Chemin des Dames was considered, in May 1918, a quiet sector, the 'sanatorium of the West'. 'Well, we have not heard a shell for five days, nor a bomb for four days,' wrote a jolly tommy to his mate in hospital. 'We are now on virgin soil and in a beautiful part of the country.'

As in March, Ludendorff's cannon spoke and his gas bombs sang in the

early hours, shattering Duchesne's Sixth Army. Duchesne was a disciple
of Foch's never-give-an-inch school; he had placed the bulk of his troops
forward, under target, facing the heights with their backs to the River
Aisne. The storm-troopers infiltrated at dawn. Within hours they had
crossed the river at Vailly, bridges intact, and were in control of the
right bank of the River Vesle. Territory, which had cost France tens of
thousands of men the year before, fell to the enemy on the second day, 28
May: the plateaux of Vregny and of Crouy. Duchesne told Clemenceau,
on a visit that day, that he only had dust to throw at the Germans. The
general looked as if he had received a blow in the face and was very pleased
to see Clemenceau; no other *grand chef* had shown a sign of support.

Soissons fell on 30 May, the same day that the German left-wing reached
the River Marne. 'All the tombs of our dead *copains*,' wrote an anonymous
correspondent of *L'Argonnaute*, 'all these funereal fields fattened by war,
we have had to leave them in enemy hands. To lose these dead, who
thought they had acquired at the price of their blood the right to sleep in
their own land, that is the cause of deep bitterness.'

Men, their feet cracked and caked in blood, howied in pain as they
retreated down kilometres of roadway. Peasants insulted them. Enemy
shells rained down. Where were the French guns? It was 1914 all
over again.

The Germans moved up their great cannon to the edge of the Forêt de
Villers-Cotterets and from Crépy-Couvron another bombardment of Paris
began. On the heights of Montmartre at night you could see the lights in
the sky of the battle. The enemy was less than sixty kilometres distant.

Winston Churchill was again in Paris. He had come to evacuate
precious British munitions. After a meeting with Clemenceau he was
convinced that, whatever happened, the French were not going to
surrender. 'He uttered to me in his room at the Ministry of War words
he afterwards repeated in the tribune: "I will fight in front of Paris, I
will fight in Paris, I will fight behind Paris." Everyone knew this was no
idle boast.'

XIII

THE CLEMENCEAU ministry was entering its night of the soul. A whole
series of measures were taken in preparation for the evacuation of the
government, parliament, the chief administrative bodies and the treasures

of the nation. Châteaux on the Loire were rented for officials: the château de Cheverny for the president of the Republic, Les Grouets in Blois for the prime minister, Beauregard for the Senate president, Saint-Gervais for the Chamber president. The Senate was to be housed in the Hôtel de Ville at Tours while the Chamber was to get the Grand Théâtre. Records of the national budget were sent down to Angers, eighteen billion francs of treasury bonds were locked up in crypts at Clermont-Ferrand.

As in March, Poincaré was obstinate, 'I will not leave Paris.' Clemenceau replied with a variant of his 1914 theme, 'I do not want to play out the fate of France in a single battle. We have to hold out and await the Americans.' Poincaré did not want to refuse the Germans battle before Paris. Nor did Clemenceau. But he noted that reserves could not be brought in more quickly – the roads were clogged – and the Germans were close to being able to cut off important railway lines. Paris, even if not under siege, would be facing a problem of supplies. In this case the war effort would have to shift to the Loire. Returning from his trip to the front on 31 May, he told Mordacq, 'Yes, the Germans might take Paris, but that will not prevent me from making war. We will fight them on the Loire, then on the Garonne if necessary and even on the Pyrenees. If finally we are chased from the Pyrenees, we'll continue the war at sea; but make peace, never! Don't let anyone count on me for that!'

For the next three days the Supreme War Council met in Versailles and was attended in person by Lloyd George, Clemenceau and the Italian premier, Orlando. It was not a brilliant success for the 'unity of command'. The British were unwilling to shift reserves to the French front because they feared an attack in Flanders; the Chemin des Dames offensive, they thought, was a 'diversion'. There was even a hint that the British might be abandoning the continental campaign to concentrate on the Near East. Pershing agreed to supply a few divisions, but most of them went to the British front for training. Pershing also insisted on the complete autonomy of the American army. This implied that material, officers and men would be organised to satisfy the requirements of a completely independent armed force rather than the needs of the Allies. The three prime ministers finally agreed to telegram Woodrow Wilson, with a request for three hundred thousand men a month. They asked the Americans to concentrate on light materials; the British and the French would supply the heavy guns.

The politicians in Paris were active. Clemenceau was convinced that Briand was hatching a plot. There was certainly talk in the corridors of Briand forming a government, which would include General Sarrail as his minister of war. One rumour going around was that Clemenceau was tired and might be ready to collaborate with Briand. Senator Magny reported to Poincaré that he had recently met Briand, who said, 'Ah! If only they had listened to me! If only we had made peace when we were winning!'

There was certainly talk of peace. Deputy Jean Dupuy said that there was no way the war could continue if Paris fell. Painlevé said much the same; if Paris fell, it would be peace. And there was a lot of dissatisfaction with the generals.

Mordacq reported that on the morning of 31 May a delegation of Socialists visited the prime minister who, in a rare moment, completely lost his calm. 'With a well struck blow of his claws, he sent his talkers packing: the scene was most violent.' Exactly what was said is not mentioned, but it is known that the Socialists were pushing for a secret session. 'The Socialists can have a secret session for themselves if they want,' Clemenceau said when he visited the Elysée about an hour later. 'As far as I'm concerned, I shall explain myself only in public.'

On 3 June, straight out of Versailles, Clemenceau presented himself before a hostile Chamber army committee. Members began by complaining about the military command and expressing a fear that Paris would not be defended. By Clemenceau's own account, 'a certain confidence returned quite quickly as soon as it became evident that I intended to hide nothing.' But that was apparently not everyone's view. Albert Thomas, in a curious reversal of roles, was now a member of the committee. He told Poincaré later that afternoon that while Clemenceau 'did not make a bad impression,' he was too general and placed too much faith in unsure forces, 'like the Czechs of Silesia'. Thomas was no more than 'half reassured.'

Other Socialists were not even that. On Tuesday afternoon, 4 June, Clemenceau appeared before the Chamber. It was one of the stormiest sessions of his life; quite similar in tone, in fact, to the debate on the Chemin de Dames one year before. Aristide Jobert wanted to know what sanctions the government 'counted on taking with regard to the incompetents.' Frédéric Brunet questioned whether the commanders had really done their duty and demanded that, if the law be severe for soldiers who fail, 'it must be still more terrible for the commander who, by negligence or lack of foresight, can cause irretrievable defeats.'

Clemenceau was not going to repeat Painlevé's error. He covered his generals. He started by saying that the army committee had been handed information. 'We know nothing,' said Monsieur Cazassus to the applause of the Socialists. 'I ask my colleagues to listen in silence,' said Deschanel from the president's chair. 'To be the *Chambre enchaînée*,' interrupted Monsieur Claussat. 'We haven't said anything,' cried Monsieur Raffin-Dugens. Cachin and Dequise simultaneously asked for the right to speak, even though Clemenceau had only just begun. He managed to pronounce three sentences. 'You're making us live the era of Lang Son all over again!' shouted out Monsieur Bedouce.

The prime minister had been effectively shouted down. The Chamber would not allow him to speak so he left the tribune, which caused an even greater uproar.

Finally, after several of the interpellators had been heard, he returned. He said that the brief enquiries that had been completed to date did not suggest that any sanctions should be made. There was further uproar. 'If, in order to obtain approval from certain people who make hasty judgments, one is obliged to abandon the commanders who well merit their country, this is an act of cowardice of which I am incapable. Don't expect me to do it.' He reminded the assembly that when he took office he had spoken of the 'cruel hours' before them. The collapse of Russia – hailed by some members of the Chamber – had allowed the enemy to transfer over a million men to the western front. With obvious reference to Pétain's strategy, he asked, 'Is there one among you who has not understood that our lines had to, at some point, bend?' It had been painful for the British 'who had suffered heavy losses.' It had been dangerous for the French. 'I said dangerous, grave, but I said nothing more.'

'There's defeatism,' shouted out several members from the socialist benches. 'It's a defeatist proposal,' screamed Monsieur Raffin-Dugens.

Despite the interruptions, Clemenceau hammered on. 'Our men are engaged in battle, a terrible battle. They have fought one against five, without sleep, for three and four days.' The applause showed that Clemenceau had already won his own battle. 'These soldiers, these great soldiers have commanders, good commanders, great commanders, commanders worthy of them from every point or view.' The soldiers had won too. He wondered how could one ask for explanations in the middle of the 'hardest battle of the war'. 'A man exhausted, his head fallen on the map, as I have seen him, in terrible hours, are we going to ask this man for explanations so as to know if, on such and such a day, he did such and such a thing! Chase me from the tribune if that's what you want. I will not do it.'

Some of the socialist deputies were so furious they had left their benches and were on their way out. 'I beg you, *messieurs*,' said Deschanel, 'get back to your places.' 'Don't I have the right to leave?' answered one of them. 'And all this time our soldiers are giving their blood,' replied Deschanel. The assembly broke out into applause. Clemenceau turned round and, looking up at the president's chair, also applauded. But protests continued from the socialist benches.

Clemenceau was defending a national army, the army of '92, the army of winter 1870, not the army of Mercier, Boisdeffre and du Paty de Clam. 'We have an army made of our children, of our brothers, of all of our people. What could we have to say against it? The commanders also are from among us. They are our relatives, they too. They are good soldiers, they too.' The victory now depended on the Chamber. 'It is left to the living to give the finishing touches to the magnificent work to the dead.'

Clemenceau won a majority of 377 votes to 110 – thirty votes better than Briand in December 1916.

There were sanctions. For the next few days, and nights, Clemenceau spent his time travelling from one command post to another. He knew that something had gone wrong, though he was not prepared to talk about it in public. A study was conducted by his own staff, an enquiry was made. Arising from these were military decisions and political decisions. Several generals were sent back to the interior. Pétain complained about changes made within his staff, but complied. The most significant change was in the command of the Tenth Army where General Mangin, who had been in disgrace only one year beforehand, took the place of General Maistre. The most controversial decision was concerning Duchesne, who was replaced by General Degoutte.

Duchesne had in fact warned his superiors of an impending attack. During the worst days of the retreat he enjoyed the unconditional support of the prime minister. But the civilian powers were demanding heads and at this stage of the war Clemenceau was not in a position to refuse them: he had covered to the limit.

'Circumstances are such,' he told Pétain, 'that we cannot afford any trouble for the government. On the other hand, General Foch cannot be attacked. Because we have to hold a man responsible – the Chamber demands it – it will have to be Duchesne.'

'I have always covered him,' replied Pétain. 'I will still cover him. He is not guilty. Take me.'

'We're at war. We have no choice. You have to obey.'

In other words, the changes were painful and messy. But France probably ended up with a better army, an army prepared to take up the initiative. There was no stopping Mangin. On 11 June he launched his first counter-offensive. The territorial gains were insignificant. But the German advance was halted. The first hammer blow had struck.

XIV

JULY WAS the traditional month of republican festivals, fraternity and flowers. Poincaré could admire the rose bush which brought a 'delicious scent' through his windows at the Elysée. The garden was filled with birds: bullfinches, blackbirds, sparrows 'and also unfortunately crows', that had returned despite the labours of a *fonctionnaire des forêts* who had killed plenty and hung the bodies around the newly mown lawn 'to chase off the newcomers.' Ah, sighed the president, 'all these songs, all these perfumes, all this joy of nature, so near so much human suffering.'

At the Trianon Palace Hotel in Versailles the representatives of two republics and several monarchies gathered for another session of the Supreme War Council. His Britannic Majesty's servants were having more trouble than ever with the servitors of Marianne. '*Les Anglais étaient butés,*' recorded Mordacq. British public opinion appeared less united than the French and the government was divided over how best to make up for the losses of March. Ten divisions had been suppressed causing enormous dissatisfaction through all the ranks of the British army. The French, for their part, demanded that the divisions be reinstated (which they eventually were). Lloyd George did not much appreciate the changes Clemenceau had made in his own armies and took a particularly dim view of the nomination, at the head of the armies at Salonika, of General Franchey d'Esperey, 'the most defeated man of the war'.

The American General Bliss was there to add a further note of variety to the 'unity of command'. The Americans still insisted on their total autonomy, but they managed to get a smile out of their Allies by announcing that they had now successfully constituted twenty-two divisions; they expected to have thirty complete by the end of August.

Of course, it was the Fourth of July. Poincaré convoked all the members of the government, the representatives of the foreign diplomatic corps, members of the judiciary, the parliamentarians, the municipal authorities and the rest of French officialdom to sit under the statue of George Washington on place Iéna and watch a procession of Allied troops march past. Before leaving Lloyd George leaned over Clemenceau's chair: 'Did you realise, old friend, you have just forced me to attend the celebration of Britain's greatest defeat?' Clemenceau was almost serious: 'After all, do you really regret American independence? What harm has it done you? Anyway, Britain and France have had a brush or two and yet, just now, you saw with what a heart and with what respect the British saluted the French flag, and the French saluted the British flag.'

Abel Hermant, veteran journalist watching the old enemies salute one another, pondered over the thought that perhaps, 'in one century or two', the Germans might attend ceremonies for the anniversary of the Marne.

Ten days later the Allies celebrated the tricolour. In a grey drizzle, Americans, Englishmen, Scots, Belgians, Italians, Serbs, Poles and Czechs marched in turn down the Champs-Elysées to the thump of brass, drums and haunting bagpipes. Clemenceau is reported to have been very moved. Crowds cheered him on the avenue and again that afternoon at the Hotêl de Ville where there was a reception for the diplomats.

By that time the weather had cleared, though the clouds over Paris played cruel imitation of battle; jagged ranks of cumulus which the evening's sun gilted in reds and yellows, black billowing masses, fire against cotton, iron against flesh.

Night fell. And in the distance a thud and crackle. Experienced ears knew, Parisians knew, these were not fireworks.

XV

KAISER WILHELM had come to watch the beginnings of the German *Friedensturm*, the 'storm of peace'. His son, the Crown Prince, remembered that night of 14–15 July as 'a splendid summer's night'. From his observation post he could watch the whole front break out in an enormous belt of fire, vomiting shells of every calibre onto enemy lines. One got, he said, the most extraordinary impression. The black sky was spilt open with lightning flashes, showers of flame, 'a demoniac painting, an apocalyptic symphony of destruction'. At 4.40 a.m. the storm-troopers moved forward.

The immediate German goal was Reims and the heights to the south. But this time the offensive was no surprise. And this time the front lines had been evacuated.

At ten o'clock Mordacq waltzed gaily into the prime minister's office; 'Monsieur le président,' he announced, 'we have won the war. This attack on the Fourth and Fifth Armies is a strategic error . . .' Mordacq was a student of what was known at the time as the 'science of war'. Clemenceau listened carefully to his explanations, smiled ironically and said, 'Eh bien! News that comes just at the right time and will please my ministers, for I already have a few of them who are crumbling.' Several, in fact, were waiting outside.

None the less Clemenceau was convinced that the Allies were close to the moment when the tide would turn. They had just reached a numerical superiority. The Germans had 207 divisions on the western front, the Allies 191 of which 18 were American: in terms of manpower, one American division was the equivalent of two divisions for everyone else.

A turning of the tide? A more accurate image would be a buried people sallying forth from the earth – Cadmos's dragon's teeth again. An experience illustrates this.

After celebrating American independence Clemenceau and Mordacq had left for Châlons and the sector of Champagne, held by Gouraud's Fourth Army, where the next German offensive was expected. On the afternoon of 6 July they visited the 124th Infantry Division at Les Monts. They followed a winding road through the chalk hills. 'Not a movement of life,' remembered Clemenceau. 'But whoever did not see was seen, and the intruder quickly signalled. Thus, on descending, unkempt heads, concealed in the folds of the land, surged fantastically from invisible machine-gun holes. The men were powdered as if in snow by the chalk soils of Champagne.' Their faces were silent. Clemenceau had always found soldiers silent. Some were impassive. Others had a 'grave smile'. Clemenceau always found a smile somewhere. A hello? 'Sometimes nothing but flashes from burnt eyes.' Clemenceau and his party continued their slow march downwards towards the plain, watching men in blue helmets coming out of the hillsides 'to inspect the unexpected inspector and return, like automatons, into the bowels of the earth.' Once they reached the lowlands they found themselves among men who had more time to prepare a welcome. A halting voice announced, 'One Company, Two Battalion, Three Regiment. Here!' And then, recollected Clemenceau, 'a rough hand presented a small bouquet of chalk dusted flowers, majestic in its poverty, flaming in its will.' Clemenceau was absolutely overcome with emotion. He mumbled a promise that those flowers would go with him to his grave. They did.

The two German offensives of May and July had created a pocket stretching out from Noyon, across the River Aisne west of Soissons to the Forêt de Villers-Cotterets and Château-Thierry on the Marne, with the line then bending back up towards Reims. The drive on to Reims concentrated German forces on this south-eastern corner of the pocket, pushing in the direction of Epernay. Unknown to the Germans. Foch was amassing Allied forces on the western side of the pocket, at the Forêt de Villers-Cotterets.

The initiative really came from Foch, but Clemenceau played a crucial role in 'balancing' the generalissimo against Pétain, who was far more cautious. On 16 July Clemenceau was back in Champagne, his cloth hat staved in, a raincoat hanging open and wheeling in his right hand a stick – which gave everyone who accompanied him a sense of purpose.

He first visited Bertholot's Fifth Army at Montmort – battlefields in this war always had an appropriate name. Bertholot (who had only arrived from Rumania two weeks earlier) was coming under attack from all sides; his right wing was faltering, his centre was threatened. At Montmirail he visited a hard pressed General Lebrun of 3rd Corps: the Germans were making progress along the left bank of the Marne. This convinced Clemenceau that the counter-offensive couldn't wait. He and Mordacq drove straight down to Provins. Clemenceau told Pétain that he had no pretension of providing a solution, but something had to be done. By the time they had finished dinner, Pétain had decided to support Foch in his counter-offensive.

Mangin was the chief executor. The plan adopted was a mirror-image of Ludendorff's offensives: a short, concentrated artillery preparation followed by infiltration. What came out of the Forêt de Villers-Cotterets on the morning of 18 July caught the Germans completely by surprise.

Henceforth, Foch's role in the command of the Allied forces became critical. At the time of the May offensive he had transferred his Head Quarters from Sarcus, near Beauvais, to a point twenty kilometres east of Melun, thus giving him easier access to Pétain at Provins and American Head Quarters at Chaumont.

The place he had picked carried a name that could have been borrowed from a nineteenth-century musical comedy, the château Bombon (by lapsus, Poincaré called it the 'château Pomponne'). It was a vast edifice built at the time of Louis XIII in brick, with complicated gables, towering chimneys, set in the middle of a splendid park, out in a forest, near nowhere. Following the counter-offensive of 18 July, Clemenceau's visits to the château Bombon became something of a ceremony. Foch would receive the prime minister in the Grand Salon, which had been converted into his office. After business was done Foch would invite Clemenceau to tea in the dining-room next door. '*Allons?*' he asked. '*Venez à l'abreuvoir.*'*

'Yes!' mused Clemenceau in the final year of his life. 'We laughed sometimes. We do not laugh often today. Who would have said to me then that these were, for us, in a sense good times? We lived in the worst of torment. We had not always the time to groan. Or if there were sometimes groans, they disappeared at the grille of the "*abreuvoir*". We raged, but we hoped, we wanted everything. The enemy was there, and we were friends.'

XVI

IF FAILURE called for sanctions success called for honours. Clemenceau never much liked the title of 'marshal' – it contained too many reminiscences of Napoleon III's armies – and he told Poincaré that the nomination of Foch

---

* 'Shall we go? Come to the drinking trough.'

to the rank would probably be illegal. But he was won over with the argument that since France already had one living marshal Foch certainly deserved to be the second. It was decided at the same time that Pétain would receive a *croix de guerre*. In a quiet but moving scene at the château Bombon, Clemenceau read the decree to Foch on 5 August. It was only, however, on 23 August that he ceremoniously received his baton. In the meantime, another general had come up for an honour, Douglas Haig. Clemenceau decorated Haig with a *croix militaire* in front of the Hôtel de Ville at Amiens on 18 August.

As for other ranks, the scenery might have changed, but the war of movement brought the same punishments as the war of the trenches; the same distant demeanour of the dead, the same indifferences, the same horror, the same destiny, the same inability to choose one's hour, one's place. Several million men were now geared up to push eastward – though the lorries lacked parts and the horses lacked hay. Behind them the dusk, before them the dawn; behind the defeat, before the hope, the victory. Just over the horizon. Yet not so many soldiers had the time or the will to ponder on horizons, even if their world was more open. No longer the two mud walls to confine them, no longer the pock-marked landscape. Just fields, broken trees, uncut harvests, lurching telegraph poles and, all too often, fallen men in feldgrau, khaki and horizon blue lying there, innocently, like lovers on the town park lawn on a sunny afternoon.

Clemenceau's visits to the front in August, September and October brought home to him the full extent of the violence that had swept the eastern corners of France for the last four years. On 4 August he was in the region of Fère-en-Tardenois that had been retaken by the Allies. Villages like Coincy, Hartennes, Beurgneux and Grand-Rozoy had been reduced to rubble. He drove up to Soissons, whose northern fringes were still held by the Germans. Most of the town had been bombed. The enemy had systematically sacked those buildings still standing, collecting transportable valuables in *Beutesammelstelle*; the rest they destroyed and left in the streets. Pinned to a few doors were white paper notices with three words in black letters, '*Maison encore habitée*'. The public services still functioned, a few shops were open, one hotel received guests brought in by the night omnibus which linked the town centre to the gare de Vierzy. But traffic was reduced because many of the streets had been converted into trench systems and barricades. A communication trench stretched down the whole length of boulevard Jeanne d'Arc, earthworks dominated the gardens of the Hôtel de Ville and the streets neighbouring the River Aisne. Everywhere, street façades were blown in, roofs collapsed, leaving indoor staircases exposed to the air, leading nowhere.

On 11 August Clemenceau was at Montdidier. 'The town effectively no longer existed,' recorded Mordacq. He spoke of it as 'the most striking spectacle I had seen in the course of the war' – and Mordacq had been at the Chemin des Dames in 1917.

On 1 September they drove out from Soissons north-westward into the zone that the Germans had occupied after the March offensive. At Roye, Clemenceau, Mordacq and the chauffeur Brabant had lunch on the side of the road. Mordacq thought of the Scriptures, 'the abomination of desolation'. 'In the villages, there was not a single house left standing, only stones scattered here and there. There were no orchards, all the trees cut down or destroyed. In the country, everywhere shell holes, trenches in ruins, networks of wire: it was chaos.'

On Saturday, 7 September, they were in the north with Plumer's British Second Army and more abominations – Mount Kemmel, Locre, Bailleul, Neuve-Eglise. From an observation post west of Armentières they could perceive a few houses left standing and, further off on the horizon, a silhouette of Lille, which seemed 'to call for its delivery'. Great shells could be seen in the final seconds of their descent, plunging into brick, muck and ironware, to give off a puff of white dust. From such a distance they looked so innocent and in truth anyone's sensibility to the human losses would be blurred before that vast panorama of waste.

It was the personal losses which were devastating. They drove down on the Sunday morning to Chevreux, Mangin's Head Quarters, and there they learned that Abel Ferry, on a mission for the army committee to inspect machine guns at Vauxaillon, had just been terribly wounded. A shell had exploded as he approached the front line. The lieutenant accompanying him was killed on the spot. Gaston Dumesnil, deputy for Angers, suffered a ruptured femoral artery and died shortly afterwards. Ferry was hit in his thigh and his chest. He pulled out his note-book, all bloodied, and signed it. Its last words, written only hours beforehand, read, 'I now believe in the *definitive* defeat of Germany in 1919.'

Clemenceau was at his side that afternoon. Ferry was fighting to the end. 'Please excuse me for being under the influence of chloroform,' he gasped, 'but since we are in company let me express to you my gratitude. You know that I was devoted to you, body and soul. I entered politics to have a revenge on you . . .' He gasped again. 'Now . . .' He gasped. 'Now, I have a sweet revenge.'

'Yes, my friend,' Clemenceau was profoundly moved. Did he remember a small house on rue des Rosiers? Or was it a debate in the Chamber? 'You have a sweet revenge.'

Ferry was decorated that day with the Legion of Honour. 'I do not want my death to be useless,' he said after the small ceremony was over.

Ferry died one week later. His funeral was to take place on 20 September in anticipation of the delivery of the family home town, Saint-Dié, which was still under fire. Clemenceau let Madame Abel Ferry know that he would be prepared to make an address, but Madame Jules Ferry refused categorically – she still held Clemenceau responsible for the death of her husband. She even refused to attend the ceremony if Clemenceau as much as appeared in the old Paris home of Jules Ferry. Clemenceau was furious. 'The old she-ass!' he exclaimed. 'I am the head of France at war; nobody can prevent me from representing her.'

On the morning of the funeral Madame Ferry finally agreed that she would attend provided Clemenceau made no speech. But a complete reconciliation was impossible: the winds of new tragedy had, by unhappy accident, fanned the embers, still smouldering, of past bitternesses. Clemenceau arrived at ten o'clock, he bowed before the coffin, slowly shook the hand of the widow and then left, without uttering a single word.

About a fortnight after this, Mandel, Mordacq and Jeanneney joined Clemenceau for an evening at his flat. He seemed tired and disillusioned. He was having trouble with some of the politicians, Poincaré had written him a disagreeable letter, the Allies were creating difficulties, even his own ministers seemed to be abandoning him. He said that he saw at this time no politicians in France capable of assuring the peace that the country merited. There were simply no first-rate people on the offing.

Mordacq suggested that they might appear from the trenches. 'Oh no,' replied Clemenceau, 'you don't improvise in politics. To be a real head of government you have to have had long experience with parliamentary assemblies.' Clemenceau saw little hope in the Chamber that would be elected after the war was over; it could be worse and certainly would not be better than the current one.

Were there ever great men in history? Clemenceau shrugged his shoulders. There had not been too many of them, for sure. Even in some of the most moving times it was difficult to pick them out. He took, naturally, the example of the Revolution. 'The greatest men, who were they? Mirabeau, an orator of the first order, but he let himself be bought out. And Danton died a millionaire.'

XVII

POINCARÉ WANTED to be remembered as the man who protected the constitution and reinvigorated the presidency. Foch saw himself not just as the victor over Germany but also as the commander who kept the Allies together. Pétain preferred the image of a simple soldier who saved lives. Haig served King and country. Lloyd George was the guardian of British sovereignty in the world. Wilson thought of himself as the inventor of a new, more humane diplomacy. Pershing would like to be remembered as the creator of an American army. As the war approached an end, each of these men became increasingly concerned with their image. They knew they would be in the history books, but what would the historians say? Inevitably, this sort of concern caused tension. In the autumn of 1918, the personal relations between the major figures of the war became very difficult.

For Clemenceau, the hardest of these trials were with Foch and Poincaré. One of the principal issues which divided them was how to deal with the new American army.

The arrival of the Americans had given a tremendous boost to Allied morale. Physically they made such a contrast to the exhausted troops of the other armies. They all seemed tall, magnificent, clean-shaven and in good health. They sat in tight rows in their army lorries, with their feet up, singing out loud songs that lifted the mood of the whole country. Even in battle it was reported they sang. A few days after Mangin's offensive in July, Clemenceau had visited a ruined village outside Château-Thierry, bodies scattered liberally on the road and the ground beyond; then along strode a column of American soldiers, singing their heads off. The Germans, said Clemenceau, were not going to look with contempt at their new enemy for long.

Three American divisions had participated in the July offensive. By that time there were about a million 'sammies' in France, but the majority were not yet considered ready for combat. When in late June Clemenceau visited Pershing in his château at Chaumont, south of Verdun on the 'Voie sacrée', both he and the general agreed that the really critical point of influence would be felt when the Americans had organised ninety divisions . . . in April 1919. But as the numbers increased, so did Pershing's insistence on complete autonomy. As Clemenceau later put it, the problem was that the Americans wanted to improvise officers as well as soldiers, they wanted a complete army with all the material that an army demanded and they were willing to delay their action in France until they had achieved this. 'They wanted an American army,' said Clemenceau. 'They got it. Whoever saw, as I did, the terrible standstill of Thiaucourt, will witness that they can congratulate themselves for not getting one earlier.'

Clemenceau believed that this unsuccessful operation in the Argonne, beginning in late September and dragging on through October, was one of the major reasons why the United States ultimately failed to ratify the peace treaty: they wanted the victory to be theirs.

The operation formed part of a more general plan of attack that Foch had formulated on 3 September. The first American part of the operation, on the Saint-Mihiel salient south of Verdun, was very successful, though this was partially due to the fact that most of the German forces, forewarned, had withdrawn. The Germans had decided to make their stand to the north, on a bluff at Montfaucon, about ten kilometres distant from the gruesomely famous hills 304 and Le Mort Homme. On 26 September Gouraud's French Fourth Army and Pershing's Americans launched their attack northward. By the second day they had run into stiff resistance.

Montfaucon was the Chemin des Dames of the Americans. With their front line exposed to German cannon and machine guns their advance halted and the kind of chaos Mangin's Sixth Army had experienced eighteen months earlier developed in the rear.

Clemenceau saw it. On 29 September he and Mordacq drove from Clermont-en-Argonne, to Dombasle, Montezéville and Esnes, before Hill 304, where they abandoned the car and continued on foot. Every road leading forward was blocked by rolling artillery, columns of infantry, horses, munitions, lost warriors, lost souls and chuck wagons. The whole American army was paralysed; kilometre after kilometre repeated scene after scene of the most complete anarchy.

Two days later Clemenceau delivered, to the council of ministers, an indictment of what he had just witnessed. Poincaré, disturbed, said they were words spoken with 'a rather out-of-place briskness, and quite dangerous, in a meeting where discretion was generally excluded.' Clemenceau, less concerned about discretion than human lives, told his ministers that he was going immediately to visit Foch and ask him 'to take this question in hand'. Apparently he had second thoughts – or Mordacq did – for it was Mordacq alone who went to château Bombon that afternoon. Foch had just got back from a trip to the Belgian front where things were going very well. So was the offensive out of Amiens: the British were bashing through the Hindenburg Line. But he was not very happy about the Americans in the Argonne and was sending General Weygand 'to examine the situation'.

For Clemenceau this was not nearly enough. On 4 October he informed Poincaré that he was very upset with Foch: 'He doesn't command. It is not up to me what he commands. I leave him free. But he has at least to command. If he doesn't, my responsibility in the government will take effect and then I'll intervene.'

With the American army stalled at Montfaucon, Gouraud's Fourth Army, itself advancing with difficulty, became exposed on its right flank. Reports of serious losses started coming in. So on 11 October Clemenceau wrote a letter to Foch: 'The nation commands you to command.' Accompanied by Jeanneney, he carried a draft of the letter to Poincaré, who said it was too harsh and asked him to change it.

Jeanneney brought a revised version round to the Elysée the next day.
Poincaré demanded further revisions and, for the record, addressed a
long letter to Jeanneney in which he called into question Clemenceau's
right to intervene in the affair; it was a matter, he argued, between Foch
and the American government. Clemenceau wondered at what point, in
the process of creating a single command, the French government had
lost its authority over French commanders. This was not a time for
'softness, patience and persuasion', as Foch had defined his approach
to Pershing. Men were dying; it was a time for orders. Foch only
received Clemenceau's letter on 21 October, by which time Pershing
had effectively placed himself under Foch's command. Between 26 September and 20 October the American army had lost in the Argonne
54,118 men.

Henceforth a spirit of wrath and loathing separated Clemenceau and the
generalissimo. His relations with the president had got about as bad.
And it was now that the Germans began to make noises of peace.
After their first telegram to President Wilson (4 October), Poincaré
wrote another of his long epistles to Clemenceau. He was not in a
hurry for peace: 'Everybody firmly hopes that we will not cut the
hamstrings of our troops by an armistice' – an expression he had
picked up from his liaison officer, Leygues. Clemenceau replied in
two sentences: 'I can not believe that after three years of personal
government, which has been so successful, you can permit yourself
to advise me not to "cut the hamstrings of our soldiers". If you do
not withdraw your written letter for the history you wish to make for
yourself, I will have the honour of submitting to you my resignation.'
Poincaré of course refused the resignation but managed to add insult
to injury in his next letter in which he reminded Clemenceau that
on 24 and 25 March 'I had amiably protested against your idea of
leaving Paris.'
    On this occasion, Clemenceau decided to send back a long response
(written with the aid of Mordacq and Jeanneney) commenting that 'you
give yourself an easy advantage with a correspondence written for your
memoirs.' Clemenceau indicated that he was less concerned with history
and more worried about the outcome of difficult meetings he was having
with the Allies, the ongoing discussions for peace, the problems with
colleagues, administrators, the press and many other items that took up
his time.
    He concluded by asking Poincaré to stop writing to him; if he had
problems, he should give a call and Clemenceau would come straight
round to the Elysée. 'The sort of correspondence that you have instituted
can really not be maintained between us.'

XVIII

BUT WHETHER he sought it or not, Clemenceau was forging his own place in history, mainly through his spectacular performances at the tribune. Opposition was fading now. Even Briand, in an interview published in *Le Journal* in early September, seemed to have converted to Clemenceau's views: France would be victorious and would make no compromise. Clemenceau's speeches were pinned up in every village hall in the country, they were reproduced in booklets, they were distributed in posters, decorated with the Allies' flags, stacked rifles, garlands and crowned with the soldier's helmet. It was the imagery of an older century, an early mass media technique which had been used by democrats, demagogues and the two Napoleons. The language too went back a hundred years or more: florid, metaphorical, it was old-style political oratory. France had paid in blood more dearly than any other nation. After such heavy losses there was a need to dig into the past, to find those roots, to replant seeds, to place one's feet on the solid soil of home once more. And for their part, most soldiers had not forgotten their rural origins, even if their lives had changed. So they gave their hero a name that would honour a peasant grandee. *Père la Victoire.*

In the opening session of the Chamber that September, Clemenceau paid his respects to the parliamentary system: 'It is right that the government should turn back to the parliamentary assemblies from where has come its strength, its power to act with the means of forcing victory . . .'

In the opening session of the Senate he rejected another Austrian effort at a compromise peace without even mentioning Austria by name. France, according to Clemenceau, had only one enemy: 'For half a century, not a day went by without pacific France, in quest of the highest goals, being submitted to some undeserved injury from an enemy who did not forgive us for our temporary defeat.' He defined the enemy and the nature of the combat (again in terms of a buried life surging to the surface of appearances): 'For us, conquered, but surviving, with a life inaccessible to the power of arms, historical redress was due over the terror of the Hun [*le Germain*], in the noisy ostentation of his false victories. Not a day without the menace of war. Not a day without some studied brutality of tyranny.' He alluded to the Austrian initiative with repeated insistence on the single enemy: 'It is only yesterday that Germany, aghast, began to understand what kind of men stand before her . . . Insanely she had believed that victory would amnesty everything in hosannas of fire and blood.' Clemenceau then spoke of 'our countryside devastated, our towns, our villages ruined by mines and by fire, by methodic pillaging, refined cruelty . . .' The Allies were not going to forget this; there was a price, and there would be no amnesty: 'The announced victory did not come and the most terrible account of a people to a people is to be opened. It will be paid.' The Senate broke into repeated applause.

Clemenceau concluded his speech with that extraordinary rhetorical play on the opening line of the *Marseillaise*. Germany's fortunes, he said, had been reversed. After 'the Germanic denial of world civilisation' came 'the great retreat of the armies of the Kaiser before the peoples of a free conscience'. Wormser said that Clemenceau read his prepared text with a 'firm and clear voice', hammering out phrases that he had learnt by heart. 'Yes, the day announced more than a century ago by our national anthem has really arrived; the sons achieve the immense work begun by the fathers.' Clemenceau paid 'supreme homage' to the combatants. What do they want? What do we want? 'To fight, to fight victoriously, again and still more until the enemy understands that there is no transaction possible between crime and law.' They were now talking of peace? What kind of peace? 'I have heard it said that peace cannot be brought through a military decision. That is not what the German said when he unleashed into the peace of Europe the horrors of war.' Germany asked for a military decision. She is condemned to pursue it. The peace will be just and solid for all those who seek to be saved from 'the abominations of the past'. The Senate applauded. *'Allez donc, enfants de la patrie, allez achever de libérer les peuples des dernières fureurs de la force immonde! Allez à la victoire sans tache! Toute la France, toute l'humanité pensante sont avec vous.'**

It is difficult for one, living in another more peaceful age, with another language, another way of hearing public men address their audience, to appreciate the impact that such a speech could have. In autumn 1918 it lifted souls. The Austrians might not have appreciated it. But in Italy parliament voted to distribute the speech throughout the country as the 'noblest response to the last enemy pacifist manœuvre'. Edmund Gosse translated it into English.

The Austro-Hungarian Empire finally asked for an unconditional armistice on 4 November. 'France wills it, France wills it,' said Clemenceau from the tribune the next day.

Once more, the press carried the speech to its headlines. 'For everyone he is the liberator of the territory, the organiser of the victory,' noted Poincaré in his memoirs, rather bitterly. 'Alone, he personifies France. Foch has disappeared. The army has disappeared. As for me, of course, I do not exist. The four years of war, during which I presided over the state and Clemenceau devoted himself to opposing successive governments without mercy, are totally forgotten.'

---

* 'Go then, children of the nation, go and complete the liberation of the peoples from the last furies of squalid force! Go to stainless victory! All France, all thinking humanity are with you.'

Not quite. There were a number of important politicians who remembered. But for the moment they said nothing.

XIX

PEACE DESCENDED on the Allies, in almost total ignorance of what was going on across the Rhine. By early October they knew that there had been a change of government and that the Catholic liberal, Prince Max of Baden, was chancellor. They did not know that Ludendorff had recognised the defeat of his armies and was urging a rapid cessation of hostilities. They knew that material conditions within the Empire were bad: they did not know that many cities, including Berlin, were on the verge of revolution.

The hardest evidence they had of the approaching collapse of Germany was the progress of their own armies. In addition to their successes in Flanders and Picardy, rapid advance was being made in the Balkans by the 'most defeated general of the war', Franchet d'Esperey. But even in October there was no certainty that the war would soon be over. On 14 October Clemenceau charged Diagne, the black deputy who had spoken out over the 1917 offensive, to prepare a plan for the engagement of one million Senegalese troops in the spring of 1919.

The main item on the agenda of the Supreme War Council, which was to meet in Versailles on 9 October, was the armistice signed with Bulgaria. But the programme was completely disrupted by the news, a few days earlier, that Germany herself had telegrammed President Wilson 'to take in hand the cause of peace' and prepare the way for an armistice and a negotiated settlement of the war. Suddenly the Allies were faced with a new crisis of 'unity', with the first difficulty arising from the fact that the Germans had appealed to the United States, not even an Ally but an 'Associate'. The Council came to no agreement at all and in the end decided to do nothing; the matter was essentially left to Wilson and the Germans.

Rumours abounded. On 10 October Clemenceau announced to the Comité de guerre the (false) news of the abdication of the Kaiser, whom he insisted – by a slip of memory – on calling Frederick II. Mordacq's office at the ministry of war began a study of armistices signed over the last hundred years. Foch was ordered by Clemenceau to prepare a note outlining the essential conditions for an armistice. In the meantime telegrams were exchanged between Wilson and the Germans, with Wilson becoming increasingly harsh: the Germans would have to evacuate all invaded territories, proposals of peace would only be considered from representatives of the new German government as agent of the German people (unlike the Allies, Wilson was convinced that the German people were innocent) and the basis of such proposals would have to be his Fourteen Points presented to Congress on 8 January. The Germans wanted to set up a mixed committee. Wilson said there was nothing to negotiate. Finally the Germans replied on 21 October that they would submit to all the conditions Wilson had imposed in his previous notes. Wilson thereby asked the Allies, on 23 October, if they were ready to present their conditions for an armistice. Naturally, they were not.

There followed a week of frantic negotiation. First, the military commanders had to be consulted – an 'armistice' is, after all, a military affair. On the same afternoon that Wilson's note was received in Paris, Clemenceau, Foch and Pétain met at the ministry of war and agreed to present Foch's plan to the Allies. Basically, the plan called for the evacuation by the Germans of all occupied territories, including Alsace-Lorraine, and an Allied military occupation of the left bank of the Rhine and of bridge heads on the right bank. The next day, 25 October, all the commanders-in-chief (save the Belgians who couldn't get there on time) assembled at Senlis, Foch's new Head Quarters. Haig, mindful of the exhausted state of his own troops and conscious that the German army was still a substantial force, thought the terms were too hard. Haig also had an old British distrust of French aims in the Rhineland; he was not very keen on the idea of his forces contributing to the creation of a new French European Empire. So the commanders failed to reach an agreement.

The Supreme War Council was to meet in Versailles on 31 October. All the premiers, the council presidents and their foreign ministers were present; Colonel House came over from America to represent Wilson. On 29 and 30 October preliminary meetings were held in Paris. The first took place at the quai d'Orsay, the ministry of foreign affairs. National instincts obliged Lloyd George to take the unusual step of supporting Haig. House, cautioned by his master not to encourage old European imperialist aspirations, supported the British insistence on moderate conditions. Clemenceau came out of the meeting, according to Mordacq, 'pale with emotion'. He had a sad and sleepless night.

Another meeting had been set for 10.30 the next morning at the ministry of war. Clemenceau had asked House to arrive there early. Charm worked. So did the fact that the American commanders, Pershing and Bliss, were in favour of the Foch plan – they wanted to associate their troops more closely with the approaching victory. Within half an hour House had become an advocate of a military occupation of the left bank of the Rhine as well as the bridge heads. His change of heart swung the British around.

The place of the peace conference was discussed. Though the matter was not actually settled – the British suggested Brussels or Geneva – it became clear during the conversations that it would take place in either

Paris or Versailles. Clemenceau wanted to preside and the other Allies, conscious of his popularity and respectful of his age, were not opposed. What if Wilson came to Paris? 'Well, if Wilson comes, I'll preside all the same,' he told Poincaré a few days later. Poincaré had his usual legal objections, 'But he's a head of state!' Clemenceau was only a prime minister. 'Oh yes. But it is not as the head of state that he will come, but as the head of his government. It is not a matter of personal pride and questions of protocol leave me indifferent. But in a meeting of this kind, I represent France; I will not cede precedence to anyone. If Wilson comes, we'll give him an ovation. But he will not preside.'

By the time the Supreme War Council met on 31 October the main items of contention had been ironed out and the representatives of the various nations involved treated each other with perfect courtesy. Mordacq, in his smiling phrase, felt he was attending 'a meeting of diplomats and not heads of governments'.

The Allies sent their reply to Wilson on 4 November. They accepted in principle the Fourteen Points except for the second article, relative to the freedom of the seas, which Britain insisted on being left open for discussion at the peace conference. The invaded territories, they added in a note, had not only to be evacuated but 'restored', that is, 'Germany must compensate all damages suffered by the civilian populations of the Allied nations and by their properties.'

In an evening that fairly well typified the conditions of the war – drizzle, fog and cold – five German automobiles headed towards the front lines of General Debeney's First Army, which was by now on the Belgian frontier east of Saint-Quentin. They followed a road that led from Fourmies to La Capelle and crossed no man's land at about 8 p.m. on 7 November. The first sight French troops caught of them was a soft halo in the fog, created by their headlights. In front of the leading car flapped an enormous white flag; one might have noticed the German bugler was standing on the running board and calling out the cease-fire. A French guardsman signalled the convoy to halt. Captain Lhuillier of the 171st Infantry Regiment stepped forward, inspected the envoys' credentials and joined the leading car. They drove on to La Capelle.

At seven the next morning, after a long trip by train, its windows covered, Matthias Erzberger, General Winterfeldt, Count Oberndorff and Captain Vanselow found themselves in the middle of a fog-bound forest. On a parallel track another train shunted up beside them. A policeman revealed the secret: they were outside Compiègne.

The ground was so rough that duckboards had to be laid out to give access to the two trains. At nine o'clock the four German plenipotentiaries climbed up into an old restaurant wagon that had recently been converted into an office. Marshal Foch, accompanied by Admiral Sir Rosslyn Wemyss, Vice-Admiral Hope and General Weygand, was waiting for them.

The marshal gave a very cold reception. 'What is the object of your visit?'

Erzberger, like his chancellor Prince Max, a liberal Catholic, replied, 'We have come to receive the proposals of the Allied Powers, relative to the conclusion of an armistice on land, on sea, in the air, on all the fronts and in the colonies.'

'I have no proposals to make to you.'

Count Oberndorff, also a member of Prince Max's new government, interrupted, 'We want to know the conditions under which the Allies would consent to an armistice.'

The marshal said, 'I have no conditions to make.'

Erzberger was very timid, 'However President Wilson . . .'

Foch interrupted drily, 'I am here to reply to you if you ask for an armistice. Are you asking for an armistice? If you are asking for one, I can let you know the conditions by which it will be obtained.'

Erzberger and Oberndorff both replied, '*Ja.*'

All morning telephone calls were exchanged between Foch's train and the ministry of war. Clemenceau was adamant; 'conditions of peace' were an affair of government, not of the army. No suspension of arms would be accorded unless the envoys first signed an armistice. They were not there to negotiate. At midday Foch indicated that 'all was going well'; he was sending one of his dispatch riders with an important letter. It arrived at 3 p.m. Clemenceau was at that moment in conference with Stephen Pichon and the president of the Chamber army committee, René Renoult. Mordacq came into the office and handed Clemenceau the letter, saying, 'Good news, Monsieur le Président.' Clemenceau read the letter: the plenipotentiaries had accepted the Allies' conditions but had requested that they consult their government.

Clemenceau stared up at Mordacq. His eyes were full of tears. Then he put his head between his own two hands and wept silently. After a moment, he sat up straight: 'It's stupid. I'm not master of my nerves. It was stronger than I, but I saw once more 1870.' Mordacq took his hands and said, 'Monsieur le Président, there are emotions that are sacred.'

Armistice: 'a beautiful word,' wrote Clemenceau, 'a great word to write when one has lived four years in torture, in the worst kind of anxiety, and then a voice is heard crying out: it is finished! It has been written that at the announcement of the armistice I could not hold back my tears. I do not hide it. The rapid passage from the dark rage of combat to the tumults of hope can shake the foundations of human equilibrium, however assured they may appear.'

But it was not yet peace. When the German plenipotentiaries turned to consult their government, they discovered they had no government. On 9 November Prince Max resigned and the Kaiser – this time it was Wilhelm I for a fact – abdicated. Germany was a Republic and the new chancellor was the Social Democrat, Friedrich Ebert. So whom did those four envoys in forêt de Compiègne now represent? Clemenceau had another painful, sleepless night. The following day, 10 November, the envoys appeared to be particularly conciliatory. 'Too polite to be honest,' said Clemenceau. Credentials were again checked and confirmed, but the envoys were obliged to consult the new government on the terms presented by the Allies. The process went on all night. The armistice was finally signed at 5.30 the next morning and came into effect at the eleventh hour.

XX

SOMEWHERE IN the Argonne, music broke out in the German lines and, from their trenches 'like a jack-in-the-box', troops jumped out and ran towards the front line opposite. '*Kamaraden! Kamaraden!*' they cried in their broken French, '*la guerre ist fini!*' They sang. There was joy in their faces. 'My word,' wrote a French witness, 'they seem happier than us, these conquered men.' And he added: 'We are all today of the same persuasion, we are all the same men, men finally delivered.'

Somewhere in front of the British lines, tradition has it, a German machine gun at two minutes to eleven fired off a complete belt of ammunition without pause. At the sound of the bugle it stopped and a single gunner stood up beside his weapon, took off his helmet, bowed, turned and walked slowly to the rear.

With the official confirmation of a cease fire on the ground, on the sea and in the skies, Clemenceau asked the president to call the council of ministers. They met shortly after three. Poincaré told Clemenceau, 'You have reanimated the sacred flame in the hearts of all the soldiers, in the hearts of all the French.' The council, in a rare gesture, applauded. Clemenceau remained silent.

At four o'clock he slowly mounted the tribune of the Chamber and, with his gloved hands slightly trembling, he read the text of the armistice signed that morning outside Compiègne. 'Honour to our great dead who have brought us this victory,' he said. 'France has been liberated by the power of arms.' He hoped that a 'day of commemoration' would be instituted to remember the dead and the suffering of their families. There was continual applause. Then he saluted the survivors. 'Thanks to them, France, yesterday soldier of God, today soldier of humanity, will always be the soldier of the ideal.' The Chamber was boiling in noise. The visitors' gallery was delirious. Gradually the clapping subsided, the cheers quietened and the deputies rose to their feet to bellow out the *Marseillaise*.

At five, Clemenceau was standing before the Senate where he again read the armistice convention and repeated his short speech. When he had finished Henry Chéron, his old colleague in the army committee, mounted the tribune and read the 1871 protestation of Bordeaux that had been made in the name of the representatives of Alsace and Lorraine. Clemenceau was its sole survivor.

He returned to his office on rue Dominique and, from a window, waved to the crowd. '*Vive la France!*' he replied to the cheers.

Then he sank to his chair, in tears.

CHAPTER ELEVEN

Peace

CLEMENCEAU HAD an idea of peace – not so much a policy or a doctrine, more a sentiment, a profound emotional commitment. You would not find as much as a hint of it in the four hundred odd treaty articles printed on Japanese vellum and signed in the Hall of Mirrors in June 1919. A few references might be picked out of Clemenceau's speeches to parliament when he defended the treaty. He would speak of 'the ideal of France, the ideal of humanity itself'. That ideal he saw as a sort of joint effort: 'The day has come where force and law, fearfully separated, must be brought back together for the peace of the peoples in their labour. Let humanity rise and live its whole life. This peace, we want to achieve it, as we have wanted to pursue the war, with a single will that nothing must bend.'

Unity and will were the heart of the matter, but Clemenceau's idea of peace went deeper still. Few historians have understood this.

If you want to understand Clemenceau's idea of peace you have to skip over the documents, you have to avoid the details; you have to visit two oval rooms on the ground floor of the Orangerie, in the south-west corner of the garden of the Tuileries. Sit there for an hour, alone, in silence if you can, on an early Monday morning, and look at, contemplate Claude Monet's twenty-two panels of water lilies, *les Décorations des Nymphéas*. The air-conditioning quietly hums. A guardian sits motionless on her chair by the Rodin bust. Darkness, colour. That's Clemenceau's idea of peace. Get up from the seat in the centre of the second hall and take a close look at the canvas. The brush marks are absolutely chaotic. Then stand back, and see an eternity. You have entered another world, 'this inexpressible storm, this unaccountable world which reveals itself to our sensibility'. That's Clemenceau's idea of peace. Walk swiftly from one oval room to the other. You are looking at what Gustave Geffroy called 'a bouquet of flowers in homage of victorious war and conquered peace', *les Nymphéas*, a scientific term for a work of art – unity. That's Clemenceau's idea of peace. He said it was 'the apogee of sensation'. Monet had lived a 'superior moment of art, and by that even, of life'. That's Clemenceau's idea of peace. 'I take the sky [or Heaven] as witness that such an accomplishment is not ordinary.'

Monet created it; Clemenceau pushed and pushed and pushed to make him create it. Clemenceau was probably a better interpreter of Monet's *Nymphéas* than any other of his contemporaries, because Clemenceau knew Monet. An abstract painter? a forerunner of Stella, Kandinsky and Pollock? 'Monet cannot paint anything other than what he sees.' A 'kaleidoscope of attentive happiness, silent and mobile', said Proust. A 'lesson of calm given by sleeping waters', said Gaston Bachelard. That's Clemenceau's idea of peace.

I

CLEMENCEAU'S FIRST trip outside Paris after the armistice was signed was not to the regained provinces of Alsace and Lorraine, as Poincaré had wanted, it was to Claude Monet's home in Giverny. 'Dear and great friend,' Monet had written on 12 November,

> I am about to finish two decorative panels that I wish to sign on the day of Victory, and I approach you with the request to offer them to the State through your mediation.
>
> It is not much, but it is the only manner that I can take part in the Victory. I wish these two panels to be placed in the Musée des Arts Décoratifs and would be happy if they are chosen by you.
>
> I admire you and embrace you with all my heart.
>
> Claude Monet

Clemenceau telephoned Monet to let him know that he would be in Giverny on Monday, 18 November, to choose the panels.

14 November was Monet's birthday. It was one of the great feast days in the Monet household. Is it possible that in 1918 Monet postponed it for the visit of his favourite guest? The woodcock, shot especially for the birthday, would have been a trifle over-hung; for Monet used to have the bird hung fourteen days in his cellar before it was plucked, roasted and served by Paul. It was Monet, in a thick grey woollen suit, his jacket buttoned up high and his white beard overflowing, who would do the carving at the table in front of his guests – quite a novelty for French bourgeois homes. Monet said he was reviving an ancient tradition.

Was the *vert-vert*, the pistachio cake with spinach coloured icing, reserved for Clemenceau? The champagne served in a decanter?

Monday, the 18th, was a sunny, crisp autumn day. Clemenceau was accompanied by Gustave Geffroy. On ordinary days lunch would be served on the blue Creil earthenware plates decorated with Japanese designed cherry trees and fans. But every time Clemenceau came for lunch the white porcelain service, with its broad yellow borders, was brought out. The chairs were yellow, the table cloth was yellow, the walls were yellow, the two cabinets from the Pays de Caux were painted yellow. They sat surrounded, on all four walls, by three dozen framed Japanese prints, and looked out onto the famous flower garden.

Thus host and guests sat ready for a feast of over-indulgence, like revolutionaries at Le Procope, a visual carnival of food, an open proclamation by the country's finest painter on the physical pleasures of life, the practical side of living, an exultant repudiation of abstract art theory and political doctrine. Next to the decanters and the high pile of fruit stood the huge silver samovar ready for tea.

'It's humiliating for me,' said Clemenceau. 'We don't see things in at all the same way. My eye stops at the reflecting surface and goes no further. With you, it's another affair. The steel of your eyes' rays breaks through the crust of appearances and you penetrate deep substance. You decompose it into vehicles of light. Then you recompose it with a brush. While I look at a tree and see nothing but a tree, you, with your eyes half-closed, think, "How many tones of how many colours in the light's transitions within this simple twig?" And you have doubts. You don't want to accept that you have thrown yourself in the direction of infinity, that you are going to have to put up with approaching a goal you will never reach completely.'

Monet wiped a few crumbs of *vert-vert* from his beard. 'You cannot imagine how true everything you have just said is.' Monet, who hated commentary, always valued Clemenceau's words. 'It is the fear, the joy, the torment of all my days. To the very point that once I found myself by the deathbed of a woman who had always been very dear to me; and I surprised myself, staring at her tragic temple, in the act of mechanically searching out the succession, the advancing erosions of colour that death was just imposing on that immobile face.'

Who was the woman? Monet had lived many tragic moments. Looking at her face he had sought a memory, a coloured photograph of a final instant. But the image could not remain fixed and he was soon overtaken by a hidden mobile force that turned this exceptional moment into routine; he spoke of tones of blue, of yellow and of grey: 'Before getting an idea of fixing the features to which I was so profoundly attached, there was an automatic movement, quivering first to the shocks of colour, and I was drawn by reflex, despite myself, into an unconscious operation that set me off again on the daily course of my life. Just like the animal who turns its hay. Pity me, my friend.'

For the old medical student of Professor Charles Robin this was a story of resurrection.

*

Clemenceau had watched these 'decorative panels' develop. It was the year the war broke out that construction had begun on a specially designed, enormous and very ugly studio in the north-east corner of Monet's garden. He started work on the panels in 1916, the year of Verdun, though his study of water lilies went back much further – 'I have taken up again impossible things to do: water with grass that ripples in the background,' he had written to Geffroy in June 1890. He described his work as 'continual torture'. Continual torture it remained.

During the war Clemenceau would visit Giverny and witness Monet in his moods. Many of the canvases were destroyed. It was not a time to venture criticism even if, privately, Clemenceau found some of the clouds rather heavy: 'One day, what a surprise! An irruption of clouds, all of light vapours.'

One panel might be all light, another plunged into the mauve and deep violets of night. Clemenceau interpreted. The irruptions of white and pink, mixing the four elements – earth, water, air and fire – and breaking every rule of perspective, were for the political *médecin-prêtre* an image of birth itself. 'From his shaking hand shoot rockets of light transparences.' If peace was their inspiration and effect, Monet's canvases were also a battlefield of growth, of colour, of will. 'To feel, to think, to will in paint.' Clemenceau's descriptions of *Les Nymphéas* are like oriental texts on archery, texts Clemenceau knew well: 'In the ways of paint, there was nothing to stop him. The bow well strung, a fine arrow at the nock ready for the click of will.' What struck him was the 'perfect convergence' of so many different factors at that click. What could this lay republican have to say about Monet? Here were themes that had dominated his writing and speeches since the days of his medical thesis; a unity of science and art, sensation as the starting point of life and of thought, the relativity of truth in nature as opposed to the abstract absolutes of doctrine, the cycle from chaos and nothingness to brief life and order ending again in nothingness, an abiding Greek pantheism, a faith in the innate power of creation. In sum, a profoundly religious vision.

Decorative panels in the past had traditionally told a story, often a religious story. To Clemenceau's mind, *Les Nymphéas* also told a story. It was the story of 'the struggle engaged between the sun and the flower' in which sensitive petals and leaves, though covered by the dominant, mighty fronds of a willow, were at last overcome by 'the irresistible power of a universal blazing'.

The final panel crowned the drama with light victorious, the sun setting in the dried matter of a winter marsh . . . from where was reborn the enchantment of the new flowers of spring. Monet's study of the march of the sun, his depiction of nature in movement, where others saw only fixed absolutes, 'brings us the worst of scandals: that of the truth!'

*

Clemenceau must have seen several panels, but on 18 November he apparently made no choice. His armistice visit to Giverny was the beginning of an eight-year saga which ended in the donation, not of two panels to the Musée des Arts Décoratifs, but of twenty-two panels in eight compositions to the Orangerie. Clemenceau would be present at the inauguration – but by that time Monet was dead.

There had of course been the administrative delays, but compared to many artistic affairs of state, the administrative side of the Monet donation in fact went quite smoothly. The official act of donation, setting up a 'Musée Claude Monet' in two halls of the Orangerie, was finally signed on 12 April 1922. Many of Clemenceau's old political enemies had come to power and they were as eager to satisfy him on this account as they were determined to exclude him from more 'essential' matters. The real drama lay elsewhere.

Claude Monet was going blind.

The fulfilment of the contract became a battle of will.

Monet was aware, during the war years, that wisps of mist were entering his vision. Clemenceau's visits to Giverny were acts of encouragement, like his trips to the front; he would never admit the war could be lost, he refused to accept that Claude Monet could go blind. 'You will never lose your sight because all you need is an operation to restore it.' Monet, furious at his condition, was ripping into his canvases with blows from his feet.

The cataracts worsened considerably after the signature of 1922. 'I am not capable of doing anything beautiful,' he wrote to Marc Elder on 8 May. 'And I have destroyed several of my panels. Today I am almost blind and I have to renounce all work. It's hard, but that is the way it is: a sad end despite my good health!'

Clemenceau recommended Monet to Doctor Coutela, one of the best ophthalmologists in Paris. But Monet delayed. So Clemenceau wrote a short tale with a long title that he sent to his friend, *Réflexions philosophiques du très-haut sur le très bas ou l'histoire merveilleuse d'un aveugle qui ne voulait pas se laisser ouvrir les yeux*. It had certain parallels with his *Voile du bonheur*, the play about the Chinese mandarin who did not want to see. 'You have adjourned, like the weak who put everything off until *tomorrow*. The result is crisis today. To get out of it the sorcerer cries to you, "It is time." And you reply again, "Tomorrow." The clock will not wait for you. To live is to march forward.'

Monet underwent three bouts of surgery in 1923. Recovery was slow. 'Carry on, my old brother,' wrote Clemenceau in December. 'Your boat has taken again to the sea. Navigate. Here we are in fog. The important thing is to have the sun in one's heart.'

Late in 1924 Monet decided to break the contract and informed the museum director without breathing a word to Clemenceau. Clemenceau was of course infuriated. 'As old, as worn down as he may be, a man, artist or not, does not have the right to break his word of honour – especially when it is to France that this word is given.'

For several months all relations were broken off between the two old men. But eventually Monet started painting again. And Clemenceau started writing again. 17 September 1925: 'Bonsoir, Monet, work, work. It is the most beautiful thing there is in the world. I embrace you, as would have the defunct Encelades, the giant with a hundred arms.'

Claude Monet died on 5 December 1926, exhausted. A story, perhaps apocryphal, has been told that on the day of his funeral Clemenceau approached the coffin with its traditional dark shroud and, shaking his head, said, 'Oh, no, no, no, not black for Monet'; and with his grey gloved hands pulled off the cloth. A photograph of the ceremony does indeed show Clemenceau bowed, wordless in grief, watching the descent into the earth of Claude Monet's coffin, shrouded in a cloak of many colours.

II

THE REPRESENTATIVES of the Allied and Associated Powers who gathered in Paris in the winter of 1918–19 to discuss peace were closing the gates on a war that had killed over ten million. It was peace in a blast of thunder, said Clemenceau: 'A cry echoed in the air, "Sheath knives!" One could stop. But rebuild! Rebuild what? And how?' Hardly had the guns fallen silent when the Allies were faced with the problem of constructing a new world order of peace.

On summing up the arguments for and against the treaty signed at Versailles, Clemenceau told the Chamber in September 1919, 'What you are going to vote today is not even a beginning, it is the beginning of a beginning. The ideas that are there must grow, must bear fruit . . . Enter it into your heads that this treaty is a set of possibilities and that its success will depend on what you are able to get out of these possibilities.'

Since the earliest days of the conflict (and long before the events in Russia) he had seen the war in terms of a revolution, the 'great Revolution of Europe', a freeing of peoples. He repeated the theme that day in the Chamber; 'One has seen coalitions formed to defend countries; one has even seen coalitions formed for motives of aggression. But a liberating coalition which, having promised liberty to the peoples, gave it to them . . . that is new.'

The success of that revolution lay in its execution, in the will of those responsible, not the legal articles of the treaty. There would be no miracles. On the night following the treaty's signature Woodrow Wilson had said to his wife, 'Well, it is finished and, as no one is satisfied, it makes me hope we have made a just peace; but it is all in the lap of the gods.' Clemenceau was always ready to admit that the treaty was far from perfect, but he was never prepared to place it in the 'lap of the gods'. He told the Senate, 'One has to execute the treaty first, this treaty so bad, this treaty which has all the defects of which we are aware. It is the testing stone.' There could be no repose, no appeals to the laws of God or to the laws of History; the responsibility for what came afterwards lay squarely on the shoulders of man.

Not that Clemenceau, in turning his back on the gods, had abandoned his old *mystique* for *la politique*. He called, as he always had, for a regeneration, one based on the same determined will that had brought France through the war – 'All that we will, we shall continue to will. All that we seek, we shall continue to seek.'

That commitment was sacred, for it was founded on so much sacrifice, a pact with the dead. This was a theme he came back to repeatedly in the spring and summer of 1919. On the American Memorial Day, 30 May 1919, Clemenceau wrote to Wilson that, 'faithful to a noble tradition, the army of the living renders today solemn homage to the army of the dead'. Frenchmen and Americans had sealed their bond in blood. In a message to the Sorbonne on 2 August Clemenceau recalled Lincoln's observation at Gettysburg that it was actually outside one's power to honour the dead: 'We are here to honour ourselves through them, to follow them on the road of sacrifice and devotion where they have so magnificently gone before us.'

So the politics of peace had to be conducted with a singular will. But that did not mean blind stubbornness. Clemenceau stuck to a middle course or, as Harold Nicolson put it, a 'Clemenceau course, something between the meticulous nationalism of Poincaré, the rapid opportunism of Franklin-Bouillon and the (to him) pathetic communism of the extreme Left'.

It was the latter which caused the old prime minister most pain. He saw there a party formed 'in a project of compromise with the Germans'; these people were treading a 'slippery slope' and they might well finish up at its foot.

The extreme Left would accuse him of chauvinism. The Right, and even men of the Centre, accused him of weakness. Louis Marin, a moderate in parliament, argued that Clemenceau had given up too much to the Allies, he had ceded too much to the Germans: 'You have reduced us to a politics of vigilance.' Clemenceau's natural response was that no treaty could do away with the need for vigilance. 'Life is only a struggle. This struggle, you will not suppress it.'

*

It was easier to make war than to make peace. This 'terrible question' of peace was to be resolved in conditions that no man had ever encountered before. Even Clemenceau, who had been on the public stage since 1870, admitted he had never 'mixed in such conferences and discussions of this type'. Who had? The closest parallels the historians could make were with the conference of Westphalia of the 1640's and the Vienna Congress of 1814–15. The Westphalia conference had lasted five years, the Vienna Congress almost a year. The delegates at the Paris Peace Conference on the other hand were forced to solve the problems of the world in less than six months, because that is what the democracies demanded.

It was the sort of situation which led Harold Nicolson, working at the time for Britain's Foreign Secretary, Lord Balfour, to comment, 'Democratic diplomacy possesses many advantages: yet it possesses one supreme disadvantage: its representatives are obliged to reduce the standards of their own thoughts to the level of other people's feelings.'

The basic problem was that there was no international organisation that could streamline decision-making and provide a permanent forum for the diplomats and the politicians. Democracy had developed within the Western nations, but it had not yet developed across them. International democracy was at the same stage at the close of the Great War as national democracy had been seventy years earlier; it was expressed in terms of grand ideals, utopian dreams that had yet to be put into practice.

In Paris in 1919 council and committee structures had to be improvised as the conference progressed, as did the plans for discussion. The only pre-existing international organ was military, the famous 'unity of command' as embodied in the Supreme War Council. The two conference plans that the French had presented were rejected by the Allies.

Thus the Paris Peace Conference would be and could only be 'the beginning of a beginning'. After Clemenceau was elected president of the conference at the first plenary session – it was 18 January, the forty-eighth anniversary of the proclamation of the Second Reich in the Hall of Mirrors – he announced that 'the programme of this conference has been established by President Wilson. It is not the peace of greater or lesser territories that we are going to establish but of peoples.'

In fact, Wilson's programme – his Fourteen Points, Four Principles and Five Particulars – hardly provided a basis for detailed negotiation between the Allies, and Clemenceau was one of the first persons to recognise this. They were contradictory (Poland was to be 'inhabited by indisputably Polish populations, which should be assured a free and secure access to the sea'). It was impractical (the first of the Four Principles assured 'the destruction of all arbitrary power' that 'a simple organisation of peace would render certain'; Clemenceau commented, 'There are probably few examples of such a misunderstanding of political experience').

Above all, it ignored the vital problem of national interests. Clemenceau told the Chamber that a man will not renounce his history at the moment hundreds of thousands of his fellow citizens have been sacrificed in blood. 'Men conserve together their qualities and their faults. You have to take them as they are. They are what they are. They have a history as we have one. As for me, because they differ from myself on very serious questions, I think I am not obliged to do as has been proposed and break with them. That's the master difficulty: one must not break with them.'

There was one national interest in particular which haunted the diplomats that spring. It was the 'ghost of all our feasts' as Nicolson phrased it: America, protected to her east and west by oceans, to the north by ice, to the south by sun, America might impose her plan and then flee behind those barriers.

In the first phase of the conference, which lasted until March, they avoided the hardest questions of national interest and, in deference to the wishes of the American president, concentrated on the drafting of the 'Covenant of the League of Nations'. The more practical problem of setting out the terms of the preliminary peace was adjourned – to such a point that by March the idea of a 'preliminary peace' had become an absurdity and the teams of diplomats, secretaries, specialists, translators and hangers on were henceforth never sure whether they were working on 'preliminaries' to be discussed with the enemy or a final treaty which would be imposed.

The drafting of the Covenant was finally completed by a committee sitting in the Hôtel Crillon on, of all days, 13 February (Wilson had a terrible fear of the number thirteen). Their work was presented to the plenary session of the conference the next day and, immediately following this, Wilson left for America; he had urgent business back home, American senators were grumbling. Lloyd George in the meantime had returned to England on the 10th; his electorate was getting restless – there was serious industrial unrest, the conquered nations were not paying up and the Kaiser had yet to be hanged. Clemenceau had nowhere to go but Paris. Yet his departure on the 19th was very nearly permanent.

He was being driven from his home to the ministry of war. Standing on the roundabout at the foot of rue Franklin was Louis Cottin, amateur carpenter and professional anarchist, who promptly emptied his revolver into the back of the car. 'I was on the back seat when I suddenly saw a character pointing his revolver at me. I told myself, "*Il va me rater*" ["He's going to miss me"]. Off went the fire-crackers and, contrary to my prognosis, I was hit.' Three bullets had hit him in the back, one of them lodging near a lung. He got out of his car alone, looking a bit pale, and was assisted back to his favourite armchair at rue Franklin – lying down was painful. In the afternoon he was arguing with his doctors and within days he was arguing with House and Balfour about the conference. 'Dear, dear,' muttered Balfour on learning of the assassination attempt. 'I wonder what that portends.'

The old trench journal, *Le Crapouillot*, still in print, reported the incident with dismay. 'We were so happy to no longer read in the papers, "Official communiqués, details of the military operations" . . . *Heureusement! ils l'ont raté.*'

III

MUCH OF the idealism had dissolved by the time the Allied leaders returned to Paris in mid-March. Wilson himself said they now had to concentrate on the 'most difficult and urgent questions'; they were up against 'a veritable race between peace and anarchy, and the peoples were beginning to be impatient'. There was a civil war in Germany, the Bolsheviks were about to launch a coup in Hungary, private armies were roaming the lands of the Baltic. Harold Nicolson gives a picture of total panic in Paris. 'Wilsonism was leaking badly.' Gone were the days of the Covenant. 'Our eyes shifted uneasily in the direction of the most contiguous life-belt. The end of the conference became a *sauve qui peut*: we called it "security": it was almost with a panic rush that we scrambled for the boats.'

The kind of situation had developed, in other words, which would put Clemenceau in his element. He had given the Chamber a foretaste of what his position would be back in December when he had contrasted the 'new diplomacy' of Wilson, temporary hero of the Left, with his own more practical approach. 'We have struggled, we have suffered, we have fought, our men have been mown down, our towns and our villages have been devastated' – Wilson would refuse to visit these regions out of fear of losing his faith in a just peace – 'Everyone has said with reason: this must not be allowed to start again. I can well believe it, but how?'

He justified his own answer to the problem with a little geography; America was far, Germany was close. 'There was an old system which appears condemned today and to which I have no fear in saying I remain to a degree faithful right now: the nations organised their defence. It is very prosaic. They worked at having good frontiers; they armed themselves. It was a terrible burden for all the populations.'

His remarks set off the clamour from the Left that he had heard for nearly a generation. 'This system today seems condemned by some of the highest authorities,' he went on. 'I would like however to observe that if the balance, which was produced spontaneously during the war, had existed earlier, if for example Britain, America, France and Italy had agreed to say that whoever attacked one of them attacked all of them, the war would never have taken place.'

Clemenceau concluded his speech by complimenting Wilson for his '*noble candeur*', a phrase which the Americans could translate as 'noble candor' but which actually meant in French 'noble simple mindedness', like Candide. There was further noise on the Left.

Because it was practical, Clemenceau's 'old system' finally won the day. To ease procedure and speed up the decision-making the principal negotiations from March onwards took place in a Council of Four – Clemenceau, Lloyd George, Wilson and Orlando. Most of the meetings were held in the library of Wilson's new residence on the place des Etats-Unis, not far from rue Nitot where Lloyd George lived. It would be quite wrong to believe that the 'Four' were making decisions alone, though this was the view of many in the French parliament and it was also that of the president of the Republic, now feeling utterly isolated. (Poincaré had by now developed the profoundest hatred for Clemenceau. 'Heedless, violent, vain, swashbuckler, cheeky, terribly light-minded, deaf physically and intellectually, incapable of reasoning, of reflecting, of following a discussion. It's this fool that the country has made a god,' he wrote in the last volume of his memoirs, so shocking that it wasn't published until 1974.) In fact the 'Four' were usually twelve or fifteen in a room and the decisions were always collective.

Clemenceau was struck by the novelty of the business; it was just this kind of encounter that he had in mind when he spoke of the 'solidarity' of the alliance, a solidarity that seemed to grow out of the very 'tone of the conversation, of a conversation of friendship even though one might have cruel things to say to one another.' Paul Mantoux, the historian, acted as interpreter and later published two volumes on the Council's deliberations. Perusing them one finds a Clemenceau who was quite similar to the one who presided over the Senate army committee. For the most part he is silent. He does not dominate. But every now and again he throws out gems of practical wisdom.

The theme of unity pervaded every aspect of Clemenceau's thinking: '*Le traité est un bloc.*' Nobody could have doubted for a minute what he meant by the phrase. In the same way that he had argued, somewhat less persuasively thirty years earlier, that you either accept or reject the Revolution as a whole (and this peace for Clemenceau was after all a revolution), he told parliament that it must either accept or reject the treaty without amendment. That was the law of the land; he cited Article VIII of the 1875 constitution.

The theme of unity applied also to the psychological side of the peace. Clemenceau spoke of the *paix du dehors*, conquered by the sacrifice of thousands, and the *paix du dedans*, that was achieved only through continual effort, through, as he phrased it, 'drive, will, beliefs, thoughts, interests traditionally opposed and sometimes even contradictory'. The real revolution could only come with a profound change in man. But that wouldn't happen overnight. 'I take men as they are, the facts as they are: humanity will not change so soon. We have the League of Nations, which is fine; now we have to live it and that is where the difficulty comes in, it is not elsewhere.' You can have as many laws as you want, sign as many treaties as you like: words are nothing, he said, it is life which counts. 'We inscribe "fraternity" and still other things on our walls. I do not believe that since we put them there we feel any more fraternal.' Men had so recently been at the very bottom of the abyss; they were only just emerging. Would these be men of peace? Would they still have the will and the commitment to defend the peace? The treaty could not be regarded as a text of scripture 'as is furnished by *notaires* who bind the parties, under the threat of being locked up by the policeman; and we all know that in nuptial pacts the *notaire*'s texts do not always bring happiness.' The force of life in the treaty (and Clemenceau would speak of it as he would of a painting), the motor of the machine, was in the 'solidarity of the Allies', the British, the Americans, the Italians, the Belgians and all the others who came to fight beside the French in the years of turmoil. 'The alliance in the war has to be followed by the indestructible alliance in the peace.' Or as Clemenceau remarked at the opening ceremony of the conference, 'Success is possible only if we remain firmly united.'

This was the key to all his negotiations. Lloyd George was wavering. Wilson was on the point of physical collapse. Clemenceau emphasised unity.

IV

THE UNITY of the alliance had in fact become such a concern for Clemenceau that he was prepared to treat all the other items on the conference's haphazard agenda as bargaining counters to achieve this end. That was why he was so frequently criticised, particularly by Foch and Poincaré but also by many parliamentarians, for yielding on France's vital interests. Clemenceau's attitude also explains why, in the end, he got so much of what he wanted written into the treaty: the other leaders were perfectly conscious that anyone else representing France would demand a great deal more, so they were ready to bargain.

Every nation within the alliance had its own particular cause to champion. The French wanted the Rhineland, the Italians wanted Fiume, the Japanese wanted Shantung, the British were demanding astronomical reparations and the Americans continued to defend the Monroe Doctrine. Most of the leaders were moderate, but they all had their electorates to face. *'Nous vivions les morts'* – 'We were living the dead.' It was one of the few phrases of Auguste Comte that Clemenceau liked to quote. By it he meant that these national interests went back generations. Britain, he was convinced, came into the war not because Germany declared war on France but because Germany invaded Belgium. It was a long time after the sinking of the *Lusitania* when the United States joined battle. In both cases, there were old historical reasons for this.

As for the question of national frontiers one had even more reason for evoking the dead. And there was another element of Comte's thought to emerge here: the force of individual survival was egoism, the force that made life in society possible was altruism – Clemenceau at the conference would call it 'responsibility'. No court in heaven had decreed the boundaries of each state; they were formed in the age old struggle, one state against the other, each with its own appetite, each after its own needs. Similarly, at the peace conference in 1919, the national delegations might all have bowed to the principle of international justice, but each one of them demanded that their own interpretation of international justice must be executed first. For the sake of unity, these national egos had to be taken into account.

The only countervailing force was that of responsibility. There might be no court in heaven, but could there be any serious doubt about which nation had been the aggressor? Did one really need a list of statistics to know where the main destruction had occurred?

In practical terms, 'responsibility' meant reparations for that destruction. Clemenceau had no doubt about Germany's ability to pay. In an interview granted to an American reporter in February 1919 Clemenceau revealed that his principal fear of Germany in the post-war period was in the economic domain, not the military: 'The industrial life of France has been so hit that it is going to be very difficult to revive it, while Germany, having capitulated, has been able to keep its factories intact, ready to function immediately and usefully. Industrially and commercially between France and Prussia, for the moment, the victory is with the latter.'

Clemenceau later claimed that reparations were the most difficult question faced in the conference and they involved the longest debate. Lloyd George later reported that Clemenceau took no active interest in the question at all. The truth is that reparations became one of Clemenceau's bargaining counters; and the more the bargaining went on, the higher the bill for Germany.

The famous 'war guilt' clause, Article 231, which introduced the section of the treaty dealing with reparations, was only introduced at the last minute and was designed to satisfy British and French electorates that Germany had accepted the financial liability of the war. 'This is simply a matter of drafting,' remarked Clemenceau. Nobody foresaw its importance; it spoke, as Clemenceau would have wished, of 'responsibility' and contained no mention of 'guilt'.[1]

Clemenceau bargained over territory. Satisfaction on matters of French security was the essential counterclaim to the British satisfaction over reparations. Necessarily, the issue of national security involved a discussion of territory and borders, but there was never for Clemenceau any question of annexation. On this, he came into direct conflict with Poincaré and Foch. Clemenceau called Foch's attitude Napoleonic. 'The watchword of the Treaty of Versailles is *the liberation of the peoples*, the independence of nationalities, while the watchword for the policy of Marshal Foch and of Monsieur Poincaré was *annexation* of territory by the force of arms, against the will of its inhabitants.' Foch was trying 'to accomplish what Napoleon had not been able to do', and Clemenceau simply wondered why Napoleon himself, 'so fertile in victory', had never been able to realise his military dream either on the Rhine or elsewhere. Clemenceau notably opposed General Mangin's attempt to foster a separatist movement in the Rhineland once he realised that the movement had no following. He told the Senate, 'We have to protect them against Prussian despotism, but we don't have to go into their homes to bring them the revolution. At any rate, it is something I will not do.'

Once more the conference members took to 'living the dead'. Britain had no intention of promoting another Napoleonic Empire. So a formula had to be devised that simultaneously avoided the territorial aggrandisement of France and yet provided her with security.

It came with the joint treaties of guarantee of Britain and the United States against an unprovoked German attack. Lloyd George even offered to build a Channel tunnel. To protect France against that other 'ghost' – American isolationism and the menace that the agreement would not be ratified – Clemenceau added his own clause, Article 429, which would extend French occupation of the Rhineland beyond the fifteen year limit

---

[1] Article 231: 'The Allied and Associated Governments affirm and Germany accepts the responsibility of Germany and her Allies for all the loss to which the Allied and Associated Governments and their nationals have been subjected as a consequence of the war imposed upon them by the aggression of Germany and her Allies.'

and even permit the reoccupation of evacuated lands, if the guarantees for French security were not given. 'Consequently, we are ready [*parés*] and everything is foreseen,' he rather optimistically reported to a doubting Louis Barthou in the Chamber.

But Clemenceau was under no illusion: '*paré*' in this sense meant a constant readiness to parry an attack, like a boxer in the ring; it involved a human element which could never be guaranteed by legal clauses, a *texte de notaire*. And from the start he recognised the disastrous effect an American failure to ratify the treaty would have; this would not only be egotistical, Clemenceau implied it would be criminal: 'I count on America in the peace ... For my part, I would reproach myself for a crime if I associated myself in the slightest way with the criticisms that are addressed at [Wilson] – if not in this country, for I am not sure there are any – at least in his. We count, in a firm manner, on the ratification of this treaty by the United States. We need it. We will it. We hope it.'

As for territories elsewhere, they were used, like the reparations, as bargaining counters to further French security and the unity in the alliance.

In the case of eastern Europe, Clemenceau had nothing like the fear of Bolshevism that Lloyd George or even Wilson had. A month after the 'October Revolution' of 1917 he had said to the Senate army committee, 'The Russian Revolution is going to follow the course of all revolutions abandoned to themselves: it's like a runaway horse: it just goes on until it falls. In Russia they have suppressed property, debts, contracts; I don't know what remains for them to demolish; perhaps they could suppress themselves; they have reached the limits of the possible. In these conditions, the leaders of the movement cannot maintain themselves.' In 1928 Clemenceau was still saying that the Bolshevik peril was 'a passing moment' and he predicted that in ten years Russia would have a bourgeois government – perhaps he had underestimated the size of the country; there was a lot that remained to destroy. At any rate, his government gave very low priority to the Bolshevik menace. In the Tardieu Plan of January 1919 (rejected by the British and the Americans) the Russian problem was given last place on the agenda; it was to be postponed until after the settlement not only of the German problem but also of Central Europe, the Orient and the Balkans. The purpose of the *cordon sanitaire* across Eastern Europe – the term was Pichon's rather than Clemenceau's – was to contain Germany, not Russia. In the first place, Clemenceau's government did not want Germany to use the Bolshevik menace as an apology for a new *Drang nach Osten* and, secondly, it did not want Germany to raise the spectre of revolution, as she already had during the armistice negotiations, in order to improve her position with the Allies. The government sent a small force to the Crimea to satisfy the British and the Americans but, after a mutiny in the Black Sea, it withdrew it. It was the French encouragement of Czech, Rumanian and Serbian expansionism (a counter to Germany) that led directly to Béla Kun's Bolshevik coup in Hungary. To the delight of the French, an Allied mission to Budapest in April 1919 established that the new regime was no threat at all.

Clemenceau showed even less interest in the Middle East. There France acquired a new colony, or a 'mandate' as it came to be known. But it was not out of any enthusiasm on Clemenceau's part. He simply did not want to allow Britain to administer the entire region alone and he could not completely ignore the colonial lobby at home; France could not be made to look a subordinate of Britain. 'Lloyd George,' he complained, 'has converted me into a Syrian.'

The end of all these negotiations, in Clemenceau's mind, was that abroad France should appear strong, at home she should appear secure and her Allies should remain united: '*Nous sommes parés et tout est prévu.*'

V

EVERY MOVEMENT was planned, every location predetermined and a timetable had been set for the encounter between the representatives of the Allied powers and those of Germany: it was going to be theatre in the grandest style, a play performed before the eyes of three dozen nations. Even the weather seemed to have been prearranged, adding suitable atmosphere to the drama. The day before the German plenipotentiaries arrived in Versailles the skies turned grey, the winds howled; it started to snow. 'One would believe we were in mid-winter,' recorded *Le Petit Parisien*; the forecast in the Paris region for Tuesday, 29 April 1919, was fog, mists and hoar frost.

Doctor Walter Simons, chief of the administrative staff of the German delegation, wrote to his wife describing his trip by special train across Germany, Belgium and northern France. Along the Ruhr, 'everything was white with snow and sleet'. In Cologne all he saw was the fog. They crossed the Eifel Mountains in snow and in Belgium 'snow and sleet alternated with sunshine'. Northern France he described as an 'overwhelming experience': 'The greater part of the day the train was intentionally slowed down when passing through this bomb-torn, desolate country which once bore such rich fruit; past the ruins of villages and towns in which one saw almost no one, nothing but clean-up detachments at work. We crossed emergency bridges the predecessors of which were lying in the river below us. We stopped at stations between collapsed buildings, burnt-out sheds and exploded munitions trains, until we had seen all we could endure . . .'

The train eventually pulled into the provincial-looking station of Vaucresson; it was nightfall. They were not disembarked at Versailles out of fear of hostile crowds. Baron von Lersner, who headed an advance mission already installed in Versailles, climbed into the first coach and after a few minutes descended in the company of a tall slim man wearing a heavy black overcoat, a high wing-collar, a black tie and a bowler hat. He held his head high, his eyes were glazed (contrary to legend, he wore no monocle), his face was of 'an impressive pallor', on his upper lip was the barely visible wisp of a moustache. A news reporter described the moment when he shook the hand of the prefect of Seine-et-Oise, there to receive him, as 'solemn, almost tragic'. He was the first to mount the awaiting government car and, at the head of a column of requisitioned buses, automobiles and military lorries, he was driven to Versailles.

His name was Count Ulrich von der Brockdorff-Rantzau. One might well wonder why the Majority Socialist government of the new German Republic had picked such a caricature of the old Germany to head the delegation. The answer is that the Socialists had had no experience in diplomacy, a field monopolised by counts and barons. Brockdorff-Rantzau was in fact a particularly well qualified count. He had entered the diplomatic corps in his twenties and had served in Brussels, Saint Petersburg, Vienna and Budapest. During the war, as ambassador to Copenhagen, he had managed to maintain Danish 'neutrality', which in practical terms meant organising an illegal trade of German coal for foreign foodstuffs and raw materials. One of his most pertinent qualifications in the eyes of his new republican masters was that he had earned the hatred of Ludendorff for speaking out for an independent civilian diplomacy in the last months of the war.

In January 1919 he was asked to join the government and a month later he was named minister of foreign affairs, a position that he only accepted on the condition that he have a say in Germany's domestic affairs as well. The central piece of Brockdorff-Rantzau's diplomacy was the Bolshevik menace. Germany had no power, he said, so she would have to rely on moral persuasion: 'an effort must be made to convince our enemies that Germany's economic breakdown and political impotence are contrary to their own interests and that in actual fact we have common interests. The appropriate method to reach this goal is to flaunt the danger of Bolshevism.' Lloyd George and Wilson would prove vulnerable. Clemenceau would not shift an inch. As part of the moral argument Brockdorff-Rantzau would constantly appeal to a *Frieden des Rechts*, a 'peace of justice' based on Wilson's Fourteen Points and acknowledged by both sides in the Armistice Convention of 1918.

On 18 April, through a messenger at Spa in Belgium, the Allies had convoked German plenipotentiaries to Versailles 'to receive' the terms of the peace treaty. The Germans had at first balked but, after a further exchange of notes, they agreed to send the delegation. The government placed Brockdorff-Rantzau at its head because they thought Versailles, despite the tone of the convocation, would be something like the Vienna Congress of 1815 (where the count would have been ideally suited). Brockdorff-Rantzau certainly arrived in Versailles expecting to negotiate.

The whole Versailles quarter north and east of the Bassin de Neptune was closed off to the public on 22 April; the tram service was stopped and horse and motor traffic was forbidden along the entire length of the boulevard de la Reine. Wooden fences were constructed, connecting the three hotels where the German delegation, press and technical assistants were to be housed. The delegation would be assigned to the Hôtel des Reservoirs, Madame de Pompadour's old palace. Its elegant restaurant had been where Gambetta and his chief whip, Clemenceau, had assembled the '363' during the *Seize Mai* crisis; today it served a palatable meal. So if the delegates had a sense of imprisonment – the French authorities were seriously worried about the possibilities of violence – they could at least admit they were living in a very pleasant prison, overlooking the fountains of Neptune, trees and one of the grandest parks in all France.

Nor were they left entirely out of touch with the Allies. Just down the road from the Hôtel des Reservoirs stood the tall and impressive nineteenth-century Trianon Palace Hotel. Since the end of hostilities it had been the site of interallied General Head Quarters. On their second day in Versailles, Thursday, 1 May, the German plenipotentiaries were summoned to the hotel for the verification of their credentials. Brockdorff-Rantzau and his colleagues were driven the short distance, through pouring rain. The brief ceremony was held in the room next to where the Supreme War Council had held its meetings since 1917. A large portrait of Marshal Foch stared down on them and the members of the Allied committee, chaired by Jules Cambon. As each delegate was introduced Cambon and his committee gave a cold nod of the head. Cambon then spoke. 'Monsieur le comte,' he said, 'I have requested that you come here in order that you may present to me the powers of your delegation and prepare the negotiations which, I hope, will end in peace.' Ah, yes; he did speak of 'negotiations'. Papers were exchanged, there was a further nodding of heads and a clicking of heels; then the delegation set out again in the rain.

The next day financial experts of the Germans and the Allies met in the same hotel. But it was an encounter of small consequence and there was still no word of when the presentation of the treaty, or the 'preliminaries' as the entire press still called it, would take place.

In the meantime, Brockdorff-Rantzau was taken on a chauffeured excursion around Versailles. The windows of the car were hazed in a film of vapour. Through the spitting mists he could detect vague outlines of a gate, a palace, a church, a few private aristocratic hotels and wide wet avenues, all shadows of a former age, a golden city of dukes and of kings.

That weekend rays of sunshine began to pierce the clouds and the count was driven to the garden of Bagatelle; it was known he liked roses. At the same time the Allies were informed by a curt note from the Hôtel des Reservoirs that important members of the delegation would return to Germany if they were not received forthwith by Allied representatives for a discussion of the treaty.

The Germans received their reply on Monday. There would be a meeting at the Trianon Palace on Wednesday at three o'clock in the afternoon when they would be presented with the 'Conditions of Peace'. There would be no verbal discussion. Any observations that they had would have to be presented in writing, in French and English, within a delay of fifteen days. The meeting was expected to last five minutes. The day itself had been carefully chosen; Wednesday was 7 May, the fourth anniversary of the sinking of the *Lusitania*.

During the weekend an army of electricians had taken over the Trianon Palace Hotel. Telegraph apparatus was set up in the cellars, cabins were prepared for the press, lighting was arranged and mobile telephones were installed. It has been said that the room in which the encounter was to take place, with mirrors and large windows on two sides, was selected to dazzle the German plenipotentiaries as they entered from a long dark corridor. In fact the doors of the corridor were in glass and the converted restaurant was on the northern side of the hotel; its windows overlooked shaded gardens.

On Monday, a pleasant spring day, Wilson, Lloyd George and Clemenceau came to inspect the premises. There were no Italians present; their delegation had left Paris a few days earlier in a row over Fiume. The first to arrive was Clemenceau who had covered the distance from Paris to Versailles in fourteen minutes flat; he enjoyed speed and had even had the speedometer of his Rolls-Royce (a gift from George V) altered to give a false feeling of security to his more panicky passengers. Then came Wilson, followed shortly afterwards by Lloyd George.

Wilson asked immediately to see the restaurant. The first thing the visitors must have noticed were the tables, covered in the green baize of diplomacy and arranged into a large rectangle around which more than eighty people could sit. Within the rectangle had been laid a rich Savonnerie carpet taken from the private apartment of Louis XIV in the neighbouring palace. Chairs in gilt with crimson cushions were provided to seat the delegations. Wilson said they were garish. Clemenceau and Lloyd George agreed. So they were placed in rows at one end of the room for the press corps, and another set of chairs, in sober oak and basket-work, were brought in. The leaders were satisfied. Clemenceau would sit at the head of the rectangle with Lloyd George and Wilson on either side. The German delegation would be exactly opposite, with their backs to the press.

At the last moment the Italians had a change of mind. They returned to Paris in great pomp and ceremony, and on Tuesday their delegation took the trip to Versailles to inspect the converted restaurant.

The weather was now radiant. Doctor Walter Simons wrote again to his wife: 'Yesterday, and today after breakfast, I was in the Trianon part of the park, where there are some wonderful trees, cedars and sycamores of gigantic size. Old magnolias and crab-apple trees are in full bloom. The park is like a forest and is full of finches, thrushes, redstarts, turtledoves, nightingales – with an oriole and a cuckoo.' But something in the air troubled him: 'In the background of all this loveliness the shadow of fate, as if reaching out for us, grows constantly darker and comes steadily closer.'

VI

So MUCH of history is built in silence: the silence of the Paris crowds following the massacre of the Commune, the silence of the Jews during the Dreyfus riots, the silence of the miners after the catastrophe of Courrières, the silence of peasant soldiers marching to the front. But the silence that descended that Wednesday at one minute to three on the Allied delegates, secretaries and journalists in the Trianon Palace was more deliberate than these; more like the silence of an audience just before the curtain is set to rise.

There was a sudden chill of apprehension when the corner door to the garden was opened and five German reporters were escorted, by French officers, to their seats.

Clemenceau, Wilson and Lloyd George sat like statues. In front of them were fourteen empty wooden chairs. The German delegation was late.

The dominant tone in the room, despite the covers of the tables, the central carpet, the ornate chairs reserved for the press, was black and white – suits, cuffs and paper. There was only one woman present, Miss Allison, a British shorthand writer, and she wore navy blue.

Five long minutes ticked by.

Then, as if provoked by a gust of wind, the main doors flew open and in came a man dressed in black and silver livery: '*Messieurs, les plénipotentiaires allemands!*'

A very grave column of men, all in frock-coats, followed. The count, taking his seat directly opposite Clemenceau, had a face as white as alabaster, contrasting with his dark hair, smooth and neatly parted down the middle. To his right sat a copiously bearded Doctor Otto Landsberg, a lawyer and prominent member of the Reichstag; he was a bigger man than the count. To his left was the German postmaster general, Johann Giesbert, calm, his expression perfectly neutral.

The instant all were seated the conference president rose. The Germans had never heard Clemenceau speak. 'Messieurs les plénipotentiaires allemands, this is perhaps neither the time nor the place for superfluous words . . .' Doctor Simons, sitting directly behind the count, found Clemenceau strangely bourgeois in spite of his 'untamable expression'. He spoke, he later told his wife, 'in short staccato sentences which he threw out as if in a concentrated anger and disdain, and which from the very outset, for the Germans, made any reply quite futile'. The correspondent for *The Times*, seated further back, described Clemenceau's attitude as one of 'stern courtesy'; his words were uttered 'abruptly and with characteristic decision'.

'The hour has come for the heavy settling of accounts. You have asked us for peace. We are ready to accord it to you . . .' It was a short speech and was interrupted only once for the translations into English and German.

As Paul Mantoux translated the second half of the speech into English, Brockdorff-Rantzau raised his hand, as if he wanted to speak. Mantoux continued. At the same time Paul Dutasta, general secretary of the conference, got up from his seat behind Wilson and, carrying a large printed white book, entered the rectangle to place the volume on Brockdorff-Rantzau's table. The count muttered words of thanks and pushed the book to one side. The translations continued.

Eventually Clemenceau got to his feet again and said, '*La parole est à Monsieur le comte de Brockdorff-Rantzau.*'

To the horror of everyone in the room, Brockdorff-Rantzau remained seated. One could not have invented a greater affront to the Allied powers. The crouched figure of the count at his table created more of an impression on the reporters behind him than anything he said in the speech which followed; days, weeks and months would be spent searching for an explanation for this most undiplomatic behaviour. The *Times* correspondent reported that 'Count Brockdorff-Rantzau appeared to be suffering considerably.' The story circulated in the British delegation that his sufferings were so great that his legs were actually paralysed, that he was physically incapable of standing. Lloyd George offered a similar explanation in his memoirs. But Brockdorff-Rantzau himself denied it. So did his biographer. And so, most significantly, did Walter Simons in a letter to his wife written only three days after the event. He claims that the count had informed him just prior to the meeting that he would not stand; he had seen plans of the converted restaurant in the French press, which described the German delegation's table as the *banc des accusés*,* and he was not going to be seen as responding to the demand, 'The prisoner will stand up.' Nor was Clemenceau much moved by reports of the count's sufferings; in 1929 he still speaks of the 'Germanic arrogance' (*'jactance germanique'*) of Brockdorff-Rantzau.

Brockdorff-Rantzau donned a pair of horn-rimmed spectacles to read his typed speech in German. Having learned that there would be no face-to-face negotiations the German delegation had decided that some spoken comment at the time of the treaty presentation was in order. The speech had gone through several drafts which had passed between Versailles, the government in Weimar and another panel of experts in Berlin. The delegation had entered the Trianon Palace equipped with a short speech and a long speech. In the end, Brockdorff-Rantzau went for the long speech.

He began by saying that his country was 'under no illusion as to the extent of our defeat and the degree of our want of power,' but the spirit of the speech indicated that he was not here to plea; he intended to be treated on terms of absolute equality. He paused after each sentence to have his words translated into French and English. The interpreters sat behind him. 'We can't hear anything,' said Clemenceau after the first French phrase. He requested that the interpreters be brought before the president's table. With grace, they stood up and worked their way through the tables of the Serbian, Czech, Rumanian, Greek and Japanese delegations until they reached the small access to the rectangle just west of the Canadian delegation. Then, before the Big Three, they repeated the first sentence. *The Times* correspondent noted that the translations were in 'very German French and very American English'. Other sources indicate that the French was terrible but that the English was in fact good.

Phrase by phrase, the speech continued. *'Wir kennen die Macht des Haßes, die uns hier entgegentritt . . .' 'Nous connaissons la puissance de la haine que nous*

---

* In which paper? Our own survey of the French press had failed to uncover this.

rencontrons ici . . .' 'We are aware of the power of hatred that we are confronted with here . . .' Lloyd George, toying with the black ribbon of his pince-nez glasses, seemed to find the whole procedure rather amusing. Bonar Law yawned. Wilson earnestly took notes. Some said Clemenceau had a slight smile on his face, others that his complexion turned red. Did Lloyd George really snap an ivory paper knife in two? For a man whose knees were supposedly shaking out of control, Brockdorff-Rantzau made quite an impression. Even the *Times* correspondent, after noting that 'Count Rantzau has not a very pleasing voice,' admitted that his 'language was vigorous' and that 'he made his remarks in the level tone of a man who is not going to allow any discussion or questioning'.

Walter Simons thought the count's speech was delivered with a voice that was 'remarkably calm, precise and curt'. But it was difficult to listen. His eyes wandered to the big window on his right, for just outside there was a magnificent cherry tree in full bloom. He later confessed to his wife that this was the 'only reality'. Sitting there, as the translations droned on, he thought to himself, 'This cherry tree and its kind will still be blooming when the states whose representatives gathered here exist no longer.'

Still the speech went on. Germany had committed errors, especially in Belgium, but no nation was innocent. Before even studying the terms lying in front of him – in truth, these terms contained no surprises for a news-reading man – he was ready with his argument against German 'guilt'. 'The imperialism of all the European states has chronically poisoned the international situation.' The Allies were apparently still committing atrocities: 'Several hundreds of thousands of non-combatants who have died since 11 November as a result of the blockade have been killed with premeditation.' Perhaps this was where the paper knife snapped. 'How are you going to respond to him?' whispered Lloyd George to Clemenceau. Clemenceau replied, 'I am going to put my piece of paper under his nose saying, "That's what you are going to sign."'

Then came the argument of the Fourteen Points: 'We are not without protection [for] we have one you have provided yourselves: it is the right guaranteed us by the treaty on the principles of peace.' Then the Bolshevik menace: 'The collapse of the German people would bring incurable devastation to the economic life of Europe.' Brockdorff-Rantzau finished his speech by saying that 'We are going to examine the document you have presented us with good will and with the hope that all will be able to contribute to the final result of our meeting.'

'There are no other observations?' asked Clemenceau. The count replied, 'No.' Clemenceau declared, 'The session is then closed.'

The German delegation rose and filed slowly out, but not before Brockdorff-Rantzau had committed one final indignity: pausing at the door, he lit a cigarette.

VII

THE GERMAN press reacted in outrage to the terms of the 'Conditions of Peace'. *'Unerträglich! Unerfüllbar! Unannehmbar!'* ('Intolerable! Unattainable! Unacceptable!') was the president's terse formula, reiterated in every journal throughout the land. Germany was to lose over a third of her coal fields, three quarters of her iron deposits, one third of her blast furnaces and all of her merchant navy. On top of that were the reparations. Only the year before the nation had been convinced she was winning the war. For many the armistice came as a shock. Was this not an agreement between equals? Had the army really been beaten? In the National Assembly, temporarily back in Berlin, the deputies sang *Deutschland über alles*. Even the Socialists were united, save Hugo Haase, who dismayed his colleagues with the reminder that the Treaty of Brest Litovsk had been no kinder to Russia.

There was one popular hope: the Allies would be divided. An editorial in the Munich *Allgemeine Zeitung* confidently announced on 18 May, 'Lloyd George apparently already senses the labour-pains of the new times and no longer has his whole heart in this politics of power, hate and revenge, which only in Clemenceau and his accomplices finds support.'

That was also the fond dream of the delegation in Versailles, which had set immediately to work on written 'observations' on the terms presented. But they got lost in details. The German delegation contained proportionately more specialists than any other body attending the conference; the majority were doctors and *'Geheimräte'*. It was also a constantly changing assembly of specialists. When one group was no longer needed it would return to Germany to be replaced by another. Between 9 and 29 May (the fifteen-day deadline was extended by a week) the Allies were bombarded with notes contesting virtually every article in the treaty. In the process Brockdorff-Rantzau's principal diplomatic objective, emphasising the Fourteen Points and the Bolshevik menace, became blurred. The delegation also incorrectly believed that time was on its side, grossly overestimating the extent of social troubles and political divisions within the Allied countries.

None the less, the *Allgemeine Zeitung* and its kind were correct on one point: Lloyd George was hesitant. From its earliest days the new German regime was looked upon by Lloyd George as the only possible alternative to a Soviet government, and for this reason he believed it should be strengthened. In March and April British officials had been visiting Brockdorff-Rantzau to assure him that 'the British government had no intention whatever to destroy Germany' but rather 'wished for her reconstruction and prosperity'. As the German notes accumulated in May Lloyd George began to have second thoughts about the terms so painfully negotiated with the Allies; in early June he summoned virtually his whole cabinet to Paris. After two days of meetings his government issued an ultimatum, not to Germany but to the Allies, demanding that crucial elements of the treaty be revised. The American delegation was divided, but Woodrow Wilson took a stand against revision. 'The time to consider all these questions was when we were writing the treaty,' he said, and concluded, 'Well, the Lord be with us.' As for Clemenceau, he commented, 'We do not have to beg pardon for our victory.' He reminded his Allies that his whole policy at the conference had been to maintain a 'close union with Great Britain and America', and the result of this was that he had been criticised at home for being weak and inadequate. 'If I fall,' he warned, 'you will be faced with even greater differences of opinion than those which separate us today.' Slight modifications were made to the terms (on reparations and a plebiscite in Upper Silesia) then the ultimatum was turned on Germany.

Brockdorff-Rantzau resigned, Scheidemann's government fell, there was very nearly a military coup, but in the end, three hours before Allied troops were set to march, Germany gave notice that she would sign. The actual signing in the Hall of Mirrors, on 28 June, was mere ceremony.

So for the moment the revisionists and the appeasers were silenced, the Allies remained united and the principle of international responsibility was inscribed on vellum.

VIII

CLEMENCEAU FAILED to notice, or deliberately ignored, that the war had pushed the western world – Allies and enemies – into an era in which the economists were going to play a leading role in politics. Specialists of such esoteric topics as the gross national product, profit margins and the consumer price index did not strike him as the new inspirers of a unity between science and art. Yet agricultural production in France in 1919 was 60 per cent of what it had been in 1913 and industrial production was only 55 per cent. The consumer price index (1913 = 100) rose from 238 at the beginning of the year to 289 at its end. The nation was heavily in debt.

Clemenceau's own lack of expertise might have been made up by competent advisers, but unfortunately this was one area where Mandel's magic had failed to work. Clemenceau himself recognised that his minister of finance was not up to the job; Louis-Lucien Klotz, he said, was 'the only Jew in France who could not count.' Fiscal reform was delayed on the grounds that the Germans would eventually pay the French debt. In April 1919 the army still numbered 2.3 million men and complete demobilisation only took place after the treaty was signed. This itself was a source of friction, though not as serious as in the case of Britain. The real problem was the 'reinsertion' of tens of thousands of demobilised men into civilian life. Peasants could return to the land, though the future here was not as bright as it had appeared in the golden years just before the war. Thousands would join up France's growing army of civil servants. It was in the urban world of wage-earning that the greatest difficulties arose. Here a politics of despair would develop, a politics of extremes, a politics of providing hope to unemployed men in the street – politics for bored, poor soldiers with nothing to do.

Revolutionary syndicalism had been discredited during Clemenceau's first term in office, and moderate trade unionism, under the leadership of Léon Jouhaux, had appeared at that time triumphant. The pacifist campaigns during the war had pushed the SFIO into the margins. But the problem of reinsertion had created fertile soil for the new frondeurs. 'The soldier especially has *le cafard* because he well knows that he will come back too late, too old, diminished and poorly liked in the society of tomorrow,' wrote a contributor to the trench paper *La Fourragère*, in October 1918. For many a soldier returning to Belleville, Montmartre, to the working suburbs of Paris, to the mining and milling towns of the north, to the factories of the centre and the south, this prophecy was fulfilled only too soon. The wall that had separated civilian from soldier seemed to join old walls that had separated class.

Ironically, it was in the spring of 1919, in the very week that the German delegation arrived, that walls quite literally started coming down. The Chamber had voted in March to raze Thiers' old fortifications of Paris to the ground. On 16 April the Senate ratified the decision. The first brick fell on the morning of 2 May at the porte de Clignancourt, on a road which led – symbolically enough – from the artisan district of Montmartre to the factories of Saint-Ouen and Saint-Denis. The levelling of the walls created hope, the inspiration for a better life, not unlike the inspiration for peace. *Le Petit Parisien* foresaw 'more than three hundred hectares of fortifications demolished, soon to be transformed into wide roads, spacious avenues, bordered by comfortable buildings and cheap dwellings, so necessary for housing in Paris' – in the 1930's it would be, of course, a new zone of poverty and despair.

Through the winter and spring of 1919 the SFIO regained its lost following, the CGT regained its members. A new radicalism developed within their more political ranks; they had a new hero in Moscow. They said the cause of the war lay in abstract historical forces, capitalism and imperialism, and rejected the 'war-guilt thesis' – the idea that men are responsible for their acts – as bourgeois. Moderates went on the defence, extremists took up the initiative. Former *majoritaires* lost their majority. A new May Day was dawning.

The issue would be the same as in the 1890's, the same as in 1906, the eight-hour day. But the government pre-empted the movement. On 17 April it pushed through the Chamber a bill, ratified by the Senate one week later, establishing by law the eight-hour day. The SFIO met in congress. There was greater division than ever. *Minoritaires* spat on *majoritaires*. Loyalties were divided between two Internationals, a moderate one in Berne, a Bolshevik one in Moscow. In line with tradition, hopeless division gave rise to calls for a general strike, a demonstration of proletarian solidarity. The government's eight-hour bill was declared a sham; the general strike would take place on the First of May.

But the apricot trees were not flowering, the sap was virtually frozen. As Brockdorff-Rantzau had noticed on his tour of Versailles, it was the wettest, coldest, most miserable First of May in a generation.

In many of the major towns across France you could have found, nevertheless, some festivity in the air. Red flags flew from several mairies. In Ruelle, near Angoulême, workers from the local foundry formed a column and marched, with flags at their head, on the 'House of the People'; in the evening there was a concert and dance held there, courtesy of the unions. In Albi a 'fraternal lunch' was offered at the Bourse du Travail. In most major cities theatres were closed, the cinemas shut, the cafés had their heavy blinds drawn; only the public services operated – the trains, the buses, the trams – and they came to a halt for an hour. In centres like Toulon and Limoges the 'general strike' had the blessing of the municipal authorities. In truth, it was a holiday.

The movement in Paris was organised by an ephemeral body that went by the name of the Union des Syndicats de la Seine. The CGT leaders, meeting that morning in their headquarters at rue de la Grange-aux-Belles, did not approve. But they were just one group in a constellation of local encounters. As in the days of the Commune, the Boulanger crisis and the strikes of the '*belle époque*', many of the most important meetings took place in Belleville and Montmartre – at the Bellevilloise, the Excelsior cinema, in the theatres of boulevard Ornano and on rue Stephenson. The suburbs now also provided locations for several meetings.

Clemenceau and his minister of the interior, Pams, had decided that there would be no street demonstrations in Paris and to make their point brought in the police, municipal guards and regular troops to block off the place de la Concorde, the Elysée and the Palais-Bourbon.

In the morning the streets were deserted to a sky of November. Rain pelted down on the cobbles, denuded of all cars, taxis and trams. The odd pedestrian bent into the wind to cut a way to his anonymous destination; loose cartons and garbage clattered along alleys; the newspaper stands were battened down and empty: the iron shutters of the barrel organ in the park were closed, bolted and locked. But the Union des Syndicats de la Seine made a declaration that it would not back off and in the afternoon the crowds came.

The boulevards were turned into a sea of umbrellas; girls handed out lily of the valley and a few posies of red wild roses. There was a battle in front of the Bourse de Travail, they battled at the gare de l'Est, they scrapped and scrummed on the place de la République and there was a major knock-out on boulevard Magenta. Léon Jouhaux received a night stick blow in his eye, Paul Poncet, a socialist deputy of the Seine, got a beating and was treated on the spot by his fellow Socialist, Pierre Laval; a debt collector was fatally wounded in front of the gare de l'Est; and near place de l'Opéra an eighteen-year-old mechanic, Charles Lorne, was shot dead by pistol fire – though whose pistol it was would remain a mystery.

The Socialists called for a 'collective' interpellation on the events on 6 May. Since this was the same day as the last plenary session of the peace conference before the presentation of the treaty to the Germans (the following afternoon), it is hardly surprising that Clemenceau refused to attend. With only Pams at the tribune the Socialists walked out. Thus, at the motion of confidence, the government was faced with the opposition of only one vote.

After the funeral of Charles Lorne on 8 May, which *L'Humanité* claimed was attended by a hundred thousand, the movement became more divided than ever. Some of the union leaders in the Paris area organised a *comité d'entente* – though it turned out to be nothing of the kind. Alphonse Merrheim's metal workers' union signed an agreement with industrialists for a 48-eight-hour week which was immediately rejected by the *comité*. A *cartel interfédéral* met and split. Léon Jouhaux headed a delegation of fourteen trade unionists that visited Clemenceau, thus earning opprobrium from other union leaders as bourgeois traitors (Jouhaux was likened to the American trade union leader, Samuel Gompers). The SFIO contributed to further division. The scenario was familiar and everyone played their part. Faced with the total breakdown of 'working class solidarity' the extremist factions called again, in July, for a general strike. The result was obviously a fiasco. The great proletarian revolution was therefore adjourned for yet another day of apricot blossom.

IX

BUT IT would not be presided over by Georges Clemenceau. He had repeated many times, in public and private, that once he had completed his wartime duties and signed the peace he would like to retire. In the long night session of 29 December 1918 he had said in the Chamber, 'You have the right to tell me, "Pass the power into other hands." I promise you I would bow out. Never will you hear from my lips a word of recrimination.' When the day came to bow out, he would keep his word.

Clemenceau said in March 1919 before the Council of Four, as they debated the complex problem of the Sarre, 'I am old; in a few months I will have left political life for ever. My disinterest is absolute.' This was not a simple negotiating ploy; he meant it.

In November 1919 he began to look for a house in the Vendée where he planned to retire. His home in Bernouville went up for sale.

Except for one speech in Strasbourg, he played no active part in the legislative elections that year. The 'Horizon Blue Chamber', the most conservative legislative assembly in France since 1871, was hardly his creation. This parliament, dominated by moderate republicans, conservatives and Catholics, the *Bloc national*, would reject him within two months.

Clemenceau never suffered from a shortage of enemies, well distributed, on the Left, the Centre and the Right. There was Briand, who had never forgiven him. The day after the armistice Briand had recorded in his diary how deputies had queued up to see him; 'They find that, in the triumph, excessive praise has been made of Clemenceau. They speak of repairing an injustice . . .' A special law had just been passed proclaiming that Clemenceau 'merited *la patrie*'. Wilson was also hailed in the Chamber. But Poincaré was forgotten – and Poincaré was someone who never forgot.

Then, in December 1919, Clemenceau came before the Chamber. It was the first time he had appeared since the elections. He said his government would resign in three weeks, after the new president of the Republic had been elected. What he failed to mention was that he had just decided that he was going to run as a candidate.

What had caused this sudden change of heart? It is something of a mystery. According to Georges Wormser, who had recently replaced Mandel as Clemenceau's *chef de cabinet*, his decision was taken during a brief visit he had made to London that same month. Wormser found him unusually silent about the trip, though he was aware that it had been extremely successful: it was possible, he surmised, that Lloyd George had expressed deep regret at Clemenceau's apparent determination to step down and, for the sake of the Alliance, persuaded him to stay at the helm.

But Clemenceau wanted to play no part in political intrigue and he wanted especially to avoid a repetition of what he regarded as the sordid circumstances which had led to Poincaré's election to the presidency in 1913. So he kept his candidature secret until the very last moment.

On 13 January 1920 Briand and some of his deputy friends organised a 'manifestation' in the Chamber in favour of Paul Deschanel, only recently re-elected president of the Chamber and never very sympathetic to Clemenceau. Clemenceau asked that no public statement be made against Deschanel's candidature and he refused even to make an appearance in either of the two chambers in support of his own candidature; this particularly annoyed some senators. A key Catholic deputy, the abbé Wetterlé, announced at the same time that, according to Marshal Foch, Clemenceau sitting in the Elysée would be a 'political calamity'. The very Catholic marshal did not deny it.

The decisive vote came four days later, not at the constitutional meeting of the 'National Assembly' – the two chambers united in Versailles – but at a preliminary republican caucus held in a former chapel at the Palais de Luxembourg, open to all members of parliament. Painlevé, Barthou, Wetterlé and Briand arrived early to campaign in favour of Deschanel. Some key supporters of Clemenceau were absent. Clemenceau had even told Mandel, who had been elected deputy in November, 'At the Chamber you are in your home, but you have nothing to do in the Senate; I forbid you to put a foot in there.'

The final vote count was 408 to Deschanel and 389 to Clemenceau. After the result was read out the hall emptied in silence. There was no applause.

Clemenceau was at that moment at the quai d'Orsay where he had been presiding over a regular council meeting of Allied officials. He was just coming down the stairs, surrounded by a number of important looking figures, when he encountered Wormser in the company of Nicolas Pietri. Wormser handed the prime minister a slip of paper. Clemenceau was visibly shocked. After a moment he took a deep breath, 'Very well; get into the car with me.'

Wormser, Pietri and Clemenceau placed themselves in the back of the car. There was further silence. Clemenceau shook his head, 'It's finished, I do not want them to vote for me tomorrow.' The two younger men might have insisted that the meeting in the Senate that day had only been an informal consultation, but it was obvious that Clemenceau's decision was final. 'He was beautiful,' recorded Wormser, 'of an antique grandeur, like at the most terrible moments of the war.'

On 18 January 1920, as the National Assembly voted the presidency of the Republic to Paul Deschanel, Clemenceau was lunching in Giverny.

X

FOR TWO years following his resignation Clemenceau, by his own admission, never opened a newspaper. He spent virtually a year travelling, first to Egypt and the Upper Nile, where he shot an alligator, missed an antelope and nearly had his boat overturned in a stampede – set off by his own gun – of infuriated hippopotami. French nostalgia took him as far as Fashoda, renamed Kodok since Marchand's day. When he returned to Cairo in March he was utterly exhausted and, though under intensive care in Shepard's Hotel, came close to death from complications arising from his bronchial problems. This did not deter him. Six months later, shortly before his seventy-ninth birthday, he was sailing out by liner from Marseille with Pietri and an industrialist friend to study the religions of the Orient. The trip lasted six months and took him through Indonesia, Malaysia, Burma and a large part of India, including Ceylon. On his arrival in Calcutta he was so sick that his doctors recommended that he return immediately to France. But Clemenceau refused; 'Either I will die or I will visit India,' he said. He visited India (but his industrialist friend did die). At Benares he wrote to Monet saying he had discovered paradise. At Gwalior he shot two tigers.

All this hardly followed Pascal's famous formula for a tranquil life. 'Voyages form youth,' Clemenceau told General Mordacq, and indeed, Clemenceau was reliving his youth. What led him eventually to settle down were the three stabilising influences he had sought more desperately and less successfully when he was young – a home in the Vendée, his writing and, most especially, a woman.

Marguerite Baldensperger was the wife of a professor of comparative literature, Fernand Baldensperger, who in 1923, after teaching in Strasbourg, was offered a chair at the Sorbonne. The new position came at a time when the family was facing a private tragedy, for in March 1922 they had lost – 'mysteriously' was Marguerite Baldensperger's own word – the eldest of their four children, a daughter. For many years Marguerite Baldensperger dressed in mourning. Every spring brought an emotional crisis. From the moment of the death the parents lived separate lives, though apparently without much bitterness: 'After more than twenty years of marriage and following the grief which had struck them, Monsieur and Madame Baldensperger kept for each other a great friendship,' was the polite Gallic formula their son Pierre used to explain the situation. 'I had the great privilege of being understood by my husband,' recorded Madame.

In the first year of the loss she retired to a family property in the Vosges, 'Les Alouettes', near Saint-Dié and began work as an editor for a series of biographies designed for children, *Nobles vies, grandes oeuvres*.[1] The project had been conceived by her collaborator and friend of the family, Pierre Bucher, who before the war had been very active in keeping what had been called the 'French idea' alive in Alsace. Eventually, in early 1923, she found an interested publisher, Plon, and on 29 April she wrote letters from her husband's new home in Paris to a number of major figures in French literature and politics asking for their contribution to her series.

One of these letters was addressed to Georges Clemenceau. She proposed that he write a short volume on the Greek orator, Demosthenes, the implacable enemy of Macedonian expansionism. She could not have picked a better topic.

Clemenceau replied on 2 May, saying that his time was taken up by 'works' but adding, 'You will find me at home every day between nine o'clock and midday.' Marguerite Baldensperger was at rue Franklin the following morning.

She was amazed at the 'modest' conditions in which the great man lived. She crossed the same small courtyard, the same staircase, the same tiny hall that had welcomed presidents, kings and ambassadors. Soon she was sitting at the same horseshoe desk opposite Clemenceau, who was wearing his curious hat and gloves. He talked about his work – 'You have before you a man who is totally devoted to work that absorbs him and amuses him' – and he talked about his flowers. He pointed out Daumier's cartoon of Don Quixote, hanging opposite the desk, which political friends had given him on his retirement; 'there's humanity, the Sorbonne on an ass.'

He was rather surprised to learn that her husband actually taught at the Sorbonne and asked if he could meet him: 'I would like to see him, this young man, not too much of a university type I presume.'

'Young?'

'I would give him around forty-five.'

'He's fifty-two.'

'That astonishes me. Wouldn't he then be much older than you?'

'No, because I am forty.'

'And I am eighty-two. These are remarkable secrets for people meeting for the first time. Well, Madame, I charge you with a message for your husband. Tell him I congratulate him for having you as his wife.'

---

[1] Initially *Le Livre français*.

She gave him a peck on the cheek and left with 'an hour of unforgettable conversation' swimming in her head.

Four days later she was back at rue Franklin with her husband. The three talked at length about the United States and India. The professor brimmed with knowledge and self-confidence, the former prime minister added notes of good cheer: the only unhappy tone in the room, but all the more palpable for that, was that the lady wore black. Clemenceau might enquire of her age; he could not for the world bring himself to ask her why she wore black.

The occasion finally presented itself in June – it was Midsummer's Day – when Madame Baldensperger returned to give Clemenceau one of Paul Bucher's tokens of recognition from Alsace, a silver medal. The offering produced, as she recalled with that oft-repeated phrase of the Third Republic, 'moments of grand emotion'. Bucher, said Clemenceau, was a great among the greats, 'a real man that'. A copy, in French translation, of Demosthenes' speeches lay on the desk.

Yes Alsace, he mused, had played such an important role in his life; it was not just the war. And he spoke of other frontiers: his home at Saint-Vincent-sur-Jard on the shores of the Vendée. She and her husband must come and see it. Then he posed the question, 'But pardon me, Madame, of whom are you in mourning?'

She told him.

There was silence. Clemenceau played his role before this Alsatian princess as well as he had before deputies at the tribune. 'I am going to think of you often. We have to pick up the taste for life again. We have to struggle. I shall help you.' His gloved hand stretched out across the table. 'Put your hand in mine. There. I shall help you to live as you shall help me to die. That is our pact. Let us embrace.'

Quite typical it was that Clemenceau should destroy every letter Marguerite Baldensperger wrote to him ('One of your epistles flies off every day in smoke'); but Marguerite Baldensperger preserved the 628 letters he wrote to her and, after the death of the son Pierre, they were finally published in 1970.

Clemenceau's letters point to something more than an *amitié amoureuse*, particularly over the first year and particularly from the perspective of their author. 'Don't restrain yourself in the friendship that you have for me. Try a little. I try to love you less. I cannot.' So he wrote from Saint-Vincent-sur-Jard in September 1924 when his sentiments seemed to have reached a peak. 'Come, come, if you have the heart, and if you do not, I will give you one. The epistolary adieu of the Ancients was:

Vale et me ama, which means, "Keep well and love me."' It was only a few days away from a reunion; a few days, also, from his eighty-third birthday. 'I truly fear you have only reservations. Wait at least a week before expressing them. Madame, Madame, I am mad with friendship.'

It was a relationship especially of hands: 'You ask me to put *my hand* in yours. And the other, Madame, what should I do with that? Whether you take it or not, I offer you all that I have'; *'Deux mains à la plus belle'*; 'There are my two hands. Give me yours. And your two eyes. And your sweet smile. There we are. I am happy.'

With colour, flowers, a sensitivity to nature's movements, an imagination which never failed, a commitment to his pact with life, Clemenceau sustained the story till the day of his death. 'I send you all the blue of the sea. There is a lot of it.' 'Flowers, sun, waves, breeze and your thought, with all that I will succeed in living if you help me.' There was in all his letters an urge to continue and to continue writing, though this was always linked with his willed acceptance of the universe, his Pascalian sense of destiny: 'If I were at the floor of the ocean I think I would ask Neptune for pen and paper. I would be astonished if I could remain a month without writing to you and without receiving anything from you. We have promised to count one on the other ... Such a day, such a joy. Such something else, such annoyance. The universe is good enough provided we do not force it.' There was of course his age and, if he constantly emphasised that their '126 years' were unevenly distributed between them, he did enjoy describing how this 'grotty nonagenarian', this 'emaciated old pithecrope' had found new life: 'The buds begin to burst, spring spreads out in a thousand ways and my old heart itself begins to push out little hoary leaves.'

Above all there was the mutual promise of comfort, coupled with an old concept of struggle. Clemenceau's letters indicate that Marguerite Baldensperger was constantly haunted by the loss of her daughter. 'Regret is only a puerile torment of powerlessness,' he would reply. 'There is nothing that aids more than courage and will. Yet how many people know what that is?' Clemenceau still sought the answer in his pantheistic, rural soul: 'Meadows, roses, goats, chicken broods, the "memories of your dead", all that still contains force if only you are able to free yourself from it. I only ask to help you in some way in this great effort. Demand less from outside and more of oneself, that's the great secret.' But he had to admit that the effort was easier when two were involved: 'Let us think as two, if that can bring some security.' His recommendations were predictable, like an address to his colleagues on the Left: 'Stop crying. Struggle. Affront.' Yet this was not brutality; rather, he felt himself simply pushed to the frontier of what could be expressed with words: 'A pressure of the hand, a supportive look say all that can be said.'

The man in his eighties was evidently not so very different from the man in his twenties, though his Alsatian correspondent, this time, was either more subtle or more willing, and certainly less silent. And there was reason for that. She was sad, she was in mourning. Out of the darkest, the grimmest of moments Clemenceau could always pull something out which bore a smile: 'Cease to cry, great and noble heroine. You only have the right to cry when I am there to dry your tears and appease you. Tears in a smile, that is the most beautiful thing in humanity.'

This then was the context in which he wrote his account of Demosthenes and 'the defeat of the most beautiful people of history out of an insufficiency of will'. It was the summer of 1925, the year of Locarno.

He began writing at the end of June and his first draft was completed within a month. One can imagine a Michelet or a Carlyle composing this essay – loaded with emotion – about Demosthenes and the people of Athens. 'My lunch in town was exempt of surprises,' wrote Clemenceau to Marguerite Baldensperger, 'and my day was spent in Athens in the company of Demosthenes and his enemies.'

He opens his small book with a declaration: 'Men of Athens, do you recognise him?' These men are guilty. 'In a sinister way, you bear the charge of his death.' The theme is set. We already have some idea of where he is going.

The book is about a war between titans, two men, not so much personalities as the ideas they represent – 'two implacable heroisms, worthy of confronting each other under the sky'. It was the drama of 'iron against the idealism of human consciousness expressed by the organ of a people of proud thought but wavering action'. On one side there was Philip of Macedonia, a military genius, a man with no scruples. What did Macedonia bring to the world, asks Clemenceau? Philip and Alexander, and then she entered forever into the night. On the other there was Demosthenes, who put all his hope in the power of his speech, 'because his speech, it was him'. Clemenceau contrasted Demosthenes with Aeschines, a smooth talker, a man born with superior oratorical gifts, the adroit Athenian orator, a man with no principles who worked, rather, 'in the service of Philip'. Demosthenes' force was quite different. It derived from an 'unshakable resolution of a consciousness which wills and does because it believes'. Athens would also want to believe, but Athens could be seduced by 'the rhythms and sonorities of a voice'.

For years Demosthenes warned the Athenians of the dangers of Macedonian expansionism; the peace treaties with Philip worked out by 'Aeschines and his band' meant nothing. Clemenceau analysed the 'Philippics' of Demosthenes not from the point of view of oratorical technique – 'I do not have the qualifications for that' – but for their ideas or, as Clemenceau found at their base, the 'temperament' of their author; for Demosthenes was 'one of those men of war who adapt their strategy to the situation of each moment.' Demosthenes did not rely on polemics. 'He fired cannon. He fired cannon to destroy first the best concealed defences of the enemy. He fired cannon to engage his fellow citizens in the beginning battle, to thwart the treasons, to animate the weak, to give some of his stoicism to those he sent against the enemy.'

Clemenceau also came back to '*On the Crown*', Demosthenes' answer to Aeschines' political challenge, a piece of rhetoric which had given Clemenceau much misery in his school days. Now it all looked so refreshing! The debate had lasted over eight years. It sent Aeschines into exile and put Demosthenes, 'for a day, at the summits of his apotheosis'. But 'Aeschines and his band' were soon back. Alexander proved worse than Philip. Athens came under the rule of Phocion, 'honest citizen, intrepid general, but obstinate defeatist', and it was Demosthenes who was forced to flee, eventually taking poison. This spelled the end of Athenian independence and democracy.

Clemenceau might have sworn to make no political commentary but there could be little mistaking what he was writing about. The legislative elections of 1924 had brought to power the *Cartel des gauches* and with it most of Clemenceau's old political enemies. One of the first acts of Edouard Herriot's new government had been to grant an amnesty to those condemned for anti-patriotic acts during the war, including Malvy and Caillaux. Within months Caillaux was minister of finance once more. Aristide Briand was soon minister of foreign affairs, and when he became prime minister he named Malvy his minister of the interior. All it seemed that was needed to make the scenario complete was to look across the Rhine and find some new Alexander and then wait at home for the democratic government to be turned over to another General Phocion, honest, intrepid and defeatist. Clemenceau, happily, did not live to see that day. But he was haunted by its possibility.

The accession of the *Cartel des gauches* inaugurated a foreign policy designed to replace the 'old policy' of alliances and armament with one based on 'the solidarity of the people, the settling of conflicts by arbitration and collective security'. Herriot set the tone in his general proposal for 'collective security' to the League of Nations in September 1924. Adopted unanimously, this 'Geneva Protocol' was put into effect one year later, in October 1925, in a treaty signed at Locarno, Switzerland, in the presence of Aristide Briand, Austen Chamberlain (the half-brother of Neville) and Gustav Stresemann.

Clemenceau regarded Locarno as the end of the Versailles settlement. It was a treaty where 'everybody protects everybody against everybody, which in the final hour the violators of the Belgian pact will know how to accommodate in their fashion'. Against a 'piece of paper' (*'le chiffon de papier'*) France had abandoned her territorial guarantee in the Rhineland – Clause 429. The victors had become the defeated; it was now they who had to explain themselves to Germany. 'Monsieur Briand once more comes to Germany with his hands outstretched, his arms open.' It was only seven years after the victory! 'On one side France (Messieurs Briand, Caillaux, Malvy, Steeg, etc . . .) seek peace at the price of any concession and any renunciation. On the other, Germany has only one end: the cancellation of the treaty consecrated to her blame and our victory.'

In *Grandeurs et misères d'une victoire* Clemenceau would trace the origin of this disaster to the failure of the alliance and, particularly, America's sudden retreat behind her natural barricades. This he called a catastrophe. The United States refused to ratify Versailles but none the less insisted, in a separate treaty with Germany, on all the 'advantages, privileges, indemnities, reparations or rights' won in the collective negotiations with the Allies. America thus enriched herself on French and British blood – 'she lost fifty thousand men and we a million and a half.' More galling still, though she had rejected the treaty, she became arbitrator and executor of its most important clauses, the reparations.

For all that (even in this posthumous work) Clemenceau was never anti-American; he knew where a friend in need could be found. In the final analysis one had to look, as in fourth-century Athens, at character. He would write in *Grandeurs*, 'Weakness of soul or of heart, the failures of character are no less formidable in peace than in war, since they lead man just as surely to the abandonment of his dignity, of his will, of his personality, of everything that gives him value in the conflicts of peace or of war.'

That was wholly Clemenceau.

His first revisions to *Demosthenes* were completed in one week, at the beginning of August, in time for the arrival in the Vendée home of a young typist, scantily dressed in the mode of the day. 'My typist is a poem,' he wrote to Marguerite Baldensperger. 'A timid and honest girl, who I may add is stripped of all clothing. She knows not a single name of man or of place. Cannot read my writing, even the best written words, fabricates inspired phrases which wouldn't make sense in any language. The clearest words are disfigured. What she does best are the blanks. The page is scattered with them and that's what I correct the most easily.'

She finally produced 86 tightly typed pages, which Clemenceau calculated would make a 'brochure' of 150 pages. The published version consisted in fact of 126. It was an instant success and went through several editions. Antoine Bourdelle produced the illustrations. Clemenceau was most worried – 'They say he is a *cubist*.' No, he discovered the next day, he wasn't a cubist, 'his art is inspired by the *Boche*': he was the sculptor responsible for 'that horror which one calls the Theatre of Avenue Montaigne, pure *Greek* from Munich'. Every time Clemenceau walked down the avenue he turned his back on the building. But, a miracle, the day his publisher introduced him to the artist he was totally seduced: 'Bourdelle is a rare being, of remarkable intelligence.' Bourdelle was engaged on the spot. Charles Pons, who had been responsible for the musical version of *Le Voile du bonheur*, was then called in to put the 'brochure' to music. This was somewhat less successful: after a private audition Clemenceau wrote to Marguerite Baldensperger that he was annoyed that he would have also to sit right through the public première, all ten minutes of it. Cinematography was apparently too little advanced for a negotiation on the film rights.

But the typing, the revisions, the negotiations and the publicity never took away from him the nightmare scenario he had just outlined. 'We have under our eyes the most beautiful syndicate of bankruptcies,' he wrote to Marguerite Baldensperger in 1926. 'This country has become the property of bureaucrats.' With his health failing in September 1929, he wrote, 'I will die very unhappy at leaving our France in the hands of the Briands, the Poincarés, the Tardieus.' Or as he put it more succinctly to his personal secretary that same final year, 'Before ten years are up we will have war, Martet.'

XI

YET CLEMENCEAU'S old age was poetic. The correspondence with Marguerite Baldensperger continued unabated, filled with 'reports' on his moral state, his medical state, his sentiments: *'Je suis tout en miel à vos pieds.'* Clemenceau gave a lot of advice. When Pétain agreed to write a volume on Turenne for *Nobles vies, grandes oeuvres*, Clemenceau said don't listen: 'I would count more on a life of Pétain by Turenne than on the life of Turenne by Pétain'; Pétain, he confirmed two years later, with no book in sight, 'is a man who escapes easily.' There was sometimes anger, particularly on the day Clemenceau discovered that *ma pauvre grande chère* had arranged with an American millionaire the purchase of his flat on rue Franklin so that it could be turned into a museum at his death. But the affair was over after three days of female tears; 'I lift my veto, I yield.' He could, for his real home was now on that other French frontier, the Vendée.

Clemenceau would talk of the Vendée as an old warrior might speak of his eternal resting ground. 'The Vendée is calling me,' he told Marguerite Baldensperger one spring day in Paris. 'Life is wearing me out. I don't regard the event as tragic and right down I feel coming the final assistance of a great rest.' The end was only another beginning in which Clemenceau sought out the roots of his childhood and youth. 'Martet, I love the Vendée. Why? Because that is where I passed my youth; I know all those fields, I know all those farms, I know all those villages. I travelled by horse down all those sunken lanes.' But he noticed the changes. The lanes were being flattened and straightened, and the villages were emptying. He described with some despair in letters to Marguerite Baldensperger the way the land was being abandoned to fallow because there were too few people left to cultivate it; 'all the young have left for the town.'

So he turned his back on the land and looked out to the sea, the 'end of the world', the 'great green flood, fringed in white foam, which the warm current sends us from the Caribbean'. Clemenceau rented an isolated house on the beach of Saint-Vincent-sur-Jard.

Sand and more sand, dune after dune. There was enough life there. Over the centuries, the peasants had learned to grow every crop of the plain, save wheat, in those sands. You could find potato plots, onions, even vineyards cuddled between dunes; closer to the shore were spindle-trees and grand maritime pine whose clusters of green needle provided uncertain protection from the changing moods of a savage sky. Clemenceau grew flowers. The horticulturalists at Les Sables d'Olonne advised him against it; but he persisted and soon he was gazing at irises, roses, hydrangeas, peonies, hollyhocks, chrysanthemums, lilies, anemones – 'a tempest of flowers: it is indescribable: roses by the billion'. Clematis, wisteria and virginia creeper covered his seaside porch.

'The garden is splendid; there are flowers everywhere,' Clemenceau's valet, Albert Boulin, confided to Martet one day. 'Unfortunately it is an old shack, you know; water seeps into the bedrooms; everything is going rotten.' Even the lease referred to the place as a 'shack'. But it was all Clemenceau wanted. 'With books, flowers and the sea, I am in a *bon coin*.'

Clemenceau would travel to the Vendée by car. He said the only thing he had ever had in common with Adolphe Thiers was his hatred for trains. On the way he usually stopped off to see his friend Cristal, who owned a small château outside Orléans. Cristal, who was in his nineties, had a superb collection of wines and liqueurs, samples of which would find their way to Clemenceau's table at 'Belébat'. Clemenceau would frequently play host in the Vendée to friends, a few foreign dignitaries, and 'bits of the family' – his daughter Madeleine, his brother Albert. Guests would find him immaculately dressed: a light grey suit with a carnation in the buttonhole, the high white collar, the hat, the gloves and white shoes. The

cane, if its principal purpose was to help him walk, also provided a useful
pointer when he talked about his flowers, the distant boats and, there, just
skimming the horizon, the faint blue outline of the île de Ré.

Clemenceau had not returned to the Vendée to entertain; he was there to
contemplate, to 'affront the mystery', to examine the 'beginnings of the last
awakenings' – to write. The work Clemenceau had mentioned with such
enthusiasm during his first encounter with Marguerite Baldensperger was
Au soir de la pensée, begun shortly after his return from India and completed
and published in early 1927. Its two volumes were hardly designed for
the professional philosopher, the academic or the literary critic. Martet's
comment that he had written it for himself rather than for others is not
entirely unjust. Very few have read the book from first page to last. It
is not always clear. The first section of the chapter on 'The World and
Man' is entitled '?'. It is more an Impressionist's painting and should be
regarded as such. It is a book of the night. It is a book to keep at one's
bedside and thumb through in moments – like it was written – of intense
insomnia. He asks the big questions: 'What is it then to have lived? What
is it then to live and to die? What is it, first, to be born?' One can guess
his answers; he had repeated them throughout his lifetime. When Martet
first read Clemenceau's 1865 medical thesis in June 1928, he came back
to Clemenceau and exclaimed, 'With a distance of fifty years, it is a first
shot at *Au soir de la pensée*.' Clemenceau could hardly defend the theory of
spontaneous generation in the 1920's, but he would have liked to. Though
he cites Einstein, Planck and Rutherford a central theme of the book is one
of a great chain of being, that of his eighteenth-century masters, in which
physical sensation plays the primordial role: 'I say sensibility because it
is biologically the first stage of the reactions of the organism in contact
with the outside.' Charles Robin would have approved and Benjamin
Clemenceau would have been delighted. Evolution is discussed in his
chapter on 'Knowing' and described as 'successions of states of sensibility'.
'Dream' and 'methodical thought' are related; art and science are one.
Comte's themes of egoism and altruism are rehearsed once more. The
pages echo ideas one could find in Condorcet, Helvetius and d'Holbach.
    But it is not a book of ideology. It is a book of impressions and readings.
The sea is perpetually present, a 'rhythm of cradlesong'. There is noise
heard and silence repeated, the 'universal tumult of egoisms' countered
by an 'eternal selflessness': 'I have lived noise and here I listen to the
stifled steps of silence.' It is a book of mirrors: '"Master," cries the disciple,
"What is that God shining in majestic splendour that I discover beyond
the clouds? Doesn't he seem to you to be calling me?" And the Buddha,
smiling, replies, "It is yourself, my son."' It is also a book of margins, of
frontiers, of travel: 'In this state of mind, freed from the world and from

myself, let my last motion of presumption be to bring here the independent word of a passer-by, in the evening of thought.'

Comparing the text of *Au soir de la pensée* with the letters he wrote to Marguerite Baldensperger, one can appreciate that astonishing sense of tranquillity which characterised most of Clemenceau's last years. 'I see myself rolling again in confidence towards a future that I accept, as near as it may be, in all serenity.' He was reading a life of Nietzsche. 'I will not die mad, for I am as calm as he was over-excited.' Clemenceau asked Marguerite Baldensperger to stop sending him newspaper cuttings, 'I will never read them.' The beauty of Saint-Vincent-sur-Jard, he explained, was that it was a country where nothing happened: 'The sea and I are always looking at one another as if we were on the point of doing something, which we do not do. It is probably the last word of human wisdom.' He sat at the edge of the world where nothing sounded save the rushing of waves, the haunting scream of the seagull. If it was not paradise, the first place on earth, it was at least a sacred acre where the imagination could venture deeper, deeper, deeper into the silent tunnel that nature had laid for every man. 'Here there is nothing but mute flowers and a silent sea.'

Clemenceau's fascination with flowers was explained in an article he had written on the Vendée in the 1890's, shortly after he had lost his seat in parliament. 'Attached to their good planet, faithful to the clod of earth where the conflict of things has fixed the haphazard seed, they make out of a cradle of chance their eternal *patrie*.' Man has no power relationship with plants; they cannot answer back, their movements tell us other things. 'While the travelling troops of earth, of air and of water work hard, with great cries, at crushing the weak or at escaping the strong, moss and elm, without noisy demonstrations, follow their own law, their own destiny.'

Essential for the life of flowers was the mix of earth and water. Clemenceau said that rain was the only salutary deity. He hated the heat of the summer's sun, when 'butterflies die of apoplexy.' It was much better when it rained. 'I have just made a nice little round under the rain, pulling out the thistles which demanded the guillotine. For me, like for a flower, there is nothing more agreeable than being irrigated.'

Above all, water gave the earth movement. 'Long live the Ocean,' he wrote again to Marguerite Baldensperger, 'which sings, laughs or gets angry while the earth tries foolishly to stiffen itself.' Thanks to that unending ballet there was movement everywhere; 'I lower my eyes then lift them again: the spectacle has changed.' Like Michelet sixty-five years earlier, Clemenceau had discovered in the sea History's secret of an eternal life overcoming death.

Shortly after *Au soir de la pensée* was published, Clemenceau appears to have suffered a depression, the disease of writers and all the more serious for a man of eighty-five. 'I have tried to take up my work again and I just cannot get down to it. I have a lot of trouble breaking my vein of laziness,' he wrote on 16 May 1927. On 29 May he said he still had not found the courage to work; 'My health is not bad. But my moral equilibrium is still not what I would have wanted. One has to submit to the inevitable.' 30 May: 'I see nobody. I am indolent, heavy, lazy.' 3 June: 'I have only the time to pass from my armchair to my chaise-longue and I woke up in much pain.' 4 June: 'I write worse and worse. I am not master of the movement of my hands.' For two weeks he felt a little better, but he had great difficulty starting on his new project, his short book on Claude Monet. On 19 June he visited Adrienne, his invalid sister, now very ill. The visit brought a relapse. 'Here wind, cold, heat, everything together . . . My intellectual work is insufficient. Yesterday I was tired without reason and was ready to renounce reading and writing.' 22 June: 'I have a child's slight cold, it's almost a distraction.' 23 June: 'My cold has got worse. I coughed all night. Florand [his doctor] ordered some remedies and this evening covered me with cupping glasses. He'll be back tomorrow morning.' 28 June: 'Yesterday a very bad day and a mediocre night. This morning better, but tired. I have not finished coughing. New application of cupping glasses.' 2 July: 'A bad day yesterday, today decidedly better . . . The weather is awful . . . I feel a little tired. I am going to try to sleep. *A vous.*' His writing became worse, his phrases repetitive. Marguerite Baldensperger arrived in Paris on 11 July and stayed with Clemenceau until the 15th.

He survived. It was his doctor who died; he had a heart attack while attending to another patient.

Adrienne died in November of the same year. Then a greater shock, his younger brother Albert suddenly died in December following minor surgery. Gustave Geffroy had died unexpectedly in April 1926. Monet had died eight months later. In November 1928 came the turn of his elder sister, Emma.

It was during Clemenceau's crisis of early summer 1927 that Fernand Baldensperger started putting together the articles Clemenceau supposedly wrote from America in the 1860's. Clemenceau had his secretary, Madame Perrnoud, collect them and type them up: Clemenceau was certainly too ill at that time to check their contents himself.

In the second half of 1927 he embarked on a study of Allied war debts which never, as a separate work, saw the light of day; the text appears to have been incorporated into his posthumous *Grandeurs et misères d'une victoire*. The work on Monet, begun in all earnestness in the spring of 1928, was what really pulled him out of his black dog, and it happened quite suddenly. 'There occurred, last night, an event, Martet, – a major event!' 'Ah? What then?' 'I woke up with the desire to work. That hasn't happened to me in months, since *Au soir de la pensée.*' Clemenceau explained to Martet what he was going to do: 'Just have a look at the existence of Monet. I will tell a few stories to show how proud and courageous a man he was.'

With the Monet project finished that autumn Clemenceau entered another period of quietness, such quietness that those closest to him did not know what he was working on. He hinted to Martet that he was going to write a book on 'Decadence'; there was talk that he would travel to Greece, the islands and Asia Minor to conduct a little research on the subject. Marguerite Baldensperger asked him why he was being so mysterious. 'I have the best reasons in the world,' he replied. 'It is because I have several times changed my subject.'

Then, on 20 March 1929, Marshal Foch died. A month later the *Mémorial de Foch* appeared, damning Clemenceau. 'I am going to reply,' he told Martet. 'Now I can't take it any more. You can't ask a man to bury himself. It's awful.' Martet commented that it was a pity he had waited until Foch was dead. Clemenceau replied, 'He very well waited himself to get buried before letting loose the flood. You don't do that. I am going to give a lesson to this dead man.' Well, he had remained silent for almost nine years; but a man has to follow his nature . . . 'I am going to reply to all these fellows: Briand, Malvy, Caillaux, Poincaré, Renaudel . . . The whole band.'

It was a hard start – '*Je suis dans le marasme*' – but by mid-May the work was fully underway. 'Martet! Martet! Give me six more months of life!' He got six months and a week, with a new book of 370 pages completed.

So you want to see the grave of Georges Benjamin Clemenceau? Take a trip by car down the long straight road, past the stone cross and the *queru*, past the rough walls of rural homes which housed Protestants and Catholics, past those rocks where rebel bands waited, past the village, the *borderie* and the *métairie*, past the astonished women in their white headgear, the poor farmer leading his horse, past the fields of red buckwheat, into the heart of the *bocages*. Martet is there in the back seat chatting with the old man. Brabant is at the wheel. As the Rolls turns into the driveway of Le Colombier it begins to drizzle; the wipers thump on the windscreen.

Yes, just through that gate beyond the chicken yard. A copse of acacia. Remember? This is where Benjamin Clemenceau planted his liberty tree in 1848: this too is where Benjamin is buried. A low metal grille fence marks his grave.

Sicard's high white stele is already in place, a reproduction of a Greek Athena pointing her spear downward at the ground. Sicard had wanted to place a manuscript beneath the weapon, a goddess guarding the sacred accords of the Treaty. 'Suppress the manuscript,' Clemenceau had ordered. 'The lance of Minerva will indicate that I rest *there*.'

There? All around is a faint murmur in the wood as trees extend their boughs to take in another breath of the Ocean's winds, releasing a flight of chanting starling to the sky; a sure sign of more rain. The place? It has been dug. The younger man lifts his hat.

No, no, Martet, not now.

Look a little closer.

'Have you seen? There is the conclusion of all you will ever write on me: a hole and lots of noise for nothing,' chuckles the Tiger.

FRENCH POLITICAL GROUPS AND PARTIES, 1871–1920

FORMAL parliamentary parties did not exist in France until 1901, when the Radical Party was organised at a Paris congress. Prior to that there only existed parliamentary, and extra-parliamentary, 'groups'. An individual could belong to more than one 'group' and these 'groups' frequently changed their names.

The following table is limited to names mentioned in the text and should only be regarded as a rough guide to be used in conjunction with the index.

FRENCH POLITICAL GROUPS AND PARTIES, 1871–1920

Left	*Centre*	*Right*
1871–1881		
Extreme Left	Moderate Republicans	Orleanists Legitimists
Radicals	Conservative Republicans	Bonapartists
	Opportunists	

.............Republican Union...

1881–1901		
Extreme Left*	Opportunists	Extreme Right*
Radicals	Moderates	Bonapartists Royalists
Radical and Socialist		
Republicans		.... Unions des Droites..............
Radical Socialists		
	.... Groupes Républicains	
Socialists		
Blanquists, Possibilists		
Allemanists (Socialist		
Revolutionaries)		
Guesdists (Workers' Party)		
1901–1920		
'Socialists'	Radical Party (1901)	
	Republican Moderates	
	Democratic Left	
	Radical Socialist Left	Conservatives, 'monarchists'
Section Française de	Independent	
l'Internationale Ouvrière	Socialists	
(SFIO) (1905)		

* Obsolete, as a formal political group, after 1893.

SELECT BIBLIOGRAPHY AND SOURCES

Complete source notes and bibliography would fill over a hundred pages of print. I have limited the following lists to the most essential titles and to books that have given me pleasure to read. I have excluded all contemporary periodicals, newspapers and archival materials. Most of these can be found in the Bibliothèque Nationale (for letters and unpublished diaries, the Département des Manuscrits), the Goncourt Archives in Nancy (for many letters of Clemenceau, his family and his friends), the Bibliothèque de Documentation Internationale Contemporaine at Nanterre (especially good on the First World War), the Archives du Sénat at the Palais de Luxembourg (for the hearings and minutes of the Senate Army Committee) and the Bibliothèque Historique de la Ville de Paris.

I would particularly like to thank the Editions Gallimard for permitting me to quote from Georges Clemenceau *Lettres à une amie* (1923–1929), ed. Pierre Brive (© Editions Gallimard 1970) and the Editions Bernard Grasset for permission to quote from Mathieu Dreyfus, *L'Affaire telle que je l'ai vécue* (© Editions Bernard Grasset 1978) and Abel Ferry, *Les Carnets secrets* (1914–1918) (© Editions Bernard Grasset 1957).

BOOKS BY GEORGES CLEMENCEAU

American Reconstruction, 1865–1870, ed. Fernand Baldensperger, trans. Margaret MacVeagh. New York: Lincoln MacVeagh, The Dial Press, 1928.
Au fil des jours. Paris: Fasquelle, 1900.
Au pied de Sinaï. Paris: H. Floury, 1898.
Au soir de la pensée (2 vols.). Paris: Plon, 1927.
Aux embuscades de la vie. Paris: Fasquelle, 1919.
Claude Monet: Les Nymphéas. Paris: Plon, 1928.
Contre la justice [Dreyfus Affair, III]. Paris: Stock, 1900.
De la génération des éléments anatomiques. Paris: Ballière, 1867.
Démosthène, 384–322 av. J.-C. Paris: Plon, 1926.
Des juges [Dreyfus Affair, IV]. Paris: Stock, 1901.
Discours de guerre. Paris: Presses Universitaires de France, 1968.
Grandeurs et misères d'une victoire. Paris: Plon, 1973.
Injustice militaire [Dreyfus Affair, VI]. Paris: Stock, 1902.
Justice militaire [Dreyfus Affair, V]. Paris: Stock 1901.

La France devant l'Allemagne. Paris: Payot, 1918.

La Honte [Dreyfus Affair, VII]. Paris: Stock, 1903.

La Mêlée sociale. Paris: Fasquelle, 1919.

Le Grand Pan. Paris: Fasquelle, 1919.

Les plus forts. Paris: Fasquelle, 1921.

Lettres à une amie. Ed. Pierre Brive, Paris: Gallimard, 1970.

L'Iniquité [Dreyfus Affair, I]. Paris: Stock, 1899.

Rapport presenté à la Commission d'enquête parlementaire sur la situation des ouvriers de l'agriculture et de l'industrie en France (Grève d'Anzin): annexe au procès-verbal de la séance du 11 mars 1884 (2e annexe). Paris: Chambre des Deputés, A. Quantin, 1885. [In collaboration]

Vers la Réparation [Dreyfus Affair, II]. Paris: Stock, 1899.

OTHER BOOKS OF IMPORTANCE, INTEREST AND PLEASURE

Adam, Madame Juliette [Juliette Lamber]. *Mes souvenirs.* Vol. VI: Nos amitiés politiques avant l'abandon de la revanche; and Vol. VII: *Après l'abandon de la Revanche.* Paris: Alphonse Lemerre, 1908–10.

Ajalbert, Jean. *Clemenceau.* Paris: Gallimard, 1931.

Audoin-Rouzeau, Stéphane. *A travers leurs journaux: 14–18. Les combattants des tranchées.* Paris: A. Colin, 1986.

Becker, Jean-Jacques. *Les Français dans la Grande Guerre.* Paris: R. Laffont, 1980.

Bellanger, Claude, Godechot, Jacques, Guiral, Pierre, and Terrou, Fernand (eds.). *Histoire de la presse française.* Vol. II: *De 1815 à 1871*; and Vol. III: *De 1871 à 1940.* Paris: Presses Universitaires de France, 1969–72.

Bredin, Jean-Denis. *L'Affaire.* Paris: Julliard, 1983.

Callow, Alexander B. *The Tweed Ring.* New York: Oxford University Press, 1966.

Clemenceau-Jacquemaire, Madeleine. *Le Pot de basilic.* Paris: Jules Tallandier, 1928.

Dansette, Adrien. *L'Affaire Wilson et la chute du Président Grévy.* Paris: Perrin, 1936.

———— *Le Boulangisme, 1886–1890.* Paris: Perrin, 1938.

Daudet, Léon. *Devant la douleur: souvenirs des milieux littéraires, politiques et médiaux de 1880 à 1905.* Paris: Nouvelle Librairie National, 1915.

———— *La Vie orageuse de Clemenceau.* Paris: Albin Michel, 1938.

Dreyfus, Alfred. *Cinq années de ma vie.* Paris: François Maspero, 1982.

Dreyfus, Mathieu. *L'Affaire telle que je l'ai vécue.* Paris: Grasset, 1978.

Ducasse, Andre, Meyer, Jacques, and Perreux, Gabriel. *Vie et mort des Français, 1914–1918.* Paris: Hachette, 1962.

Duroselle, Jean-Baptiste. *Clemenceau.* Paris: Fayard, 1988.

Eksteins, Modris. *Rites of Spring: The Great War and the Birth of the Modern Age.* London: Bantam, 1989.

Ellis, Jack D. *The Early Life of Georges Clemenceau, 1841–1893.* Lawrence, Kansas: Regents Press of Kansas, 1980.

Fussell, Paul. *The Great War and Modern Memory*. New York: Oxford University Press, 1975.

Gatineau, Georges. *Des pattes du Tigre aux griffes du destin*. Paris: Presse du Mail, 1961.

Geffroy, Gustave. *Georges Clemenceau: sa vie, son œuvre*, ed. Louis Lumet. Paris: Larousse, 1932.

———— *Notes d'un journaliste: vie, littérature, théâtre*. Paris: G. Charpentier, 1887.

Goncourt, Edmond and Jules de. *Journal*. 3 vols. Paris: Robert Laffont, 1989.

Herz, Micheline. *Jewish Problems in French Literature around 1900*. Cornell University: Unpublished Ph. D. thesis, 1955 [text in French].

Horne, Alistair. *The Fall of Paris: The Siege and the Commune 1870–71*. Harmondsworth: Penguin, 1981.

———— *The Price of Glory: Verdun 1916*. Harmondsworth: Penguin, 1962.

Howard, Michael. *The Franco-Prussian War: The German Invasion of France, 1870–1871*. London: Rupert Hart-Davis, 1961.

Hyndeman, H. M. *Clemenceau: The Man and His Time*. London: Grant Richards, 1919.

Irvine, William D. *The Boulanger Affair Reconsidered: Royalism, Boulangism, and the Origins of the Radical Right in France*. New York: Oxford University Press, 1989.

Keegan, John. *The Face of Battle: A Study of Agincourt, Waterloo and the Somme*. New York: Vintage, 1977.

Lavergne, Bernard. *Les deux présidences de Jules Grévy*, ed. Jean Elleinstein. Paris: Fischbacher, 1966.

Lissagaray, Prosper-Olivier. *Histoire de la Commune de 1871*. Paris: Maspero, 1983.

Marrus, Michael R. *Les Juifs de France à l'époque de l'affaire Dreyfus*, trans. Micheline Legras. Paris: Calmann-Lévy, 1972.

Martet, Jean. *M. Clemenceau peint par lui-même*. Paris: Albin Michel, 1929.

———— *Le Silence de M. Clemenceau*. Paris: Albin Michel, 1929.

———— *Le Tigre*. Paris: Albin Michel, 1930.

Mayer, Arno J. *Politics and Diplomacy of Peacemaking: Containment and Counterrevolution at Versailles, 1918–1919*. New York: Alfred A. Knopf, 1967.

Mermeix [pseudonym for Gabriel Terrail]. *Les Coulisses de Boulangisme*. Paris: L. Cerf, 1890.

Meyer, Jacques. *La Vie quotidienne des soldats pendant la Grande Guerre*. Paris: Hachette, 1966.

Monnerville, Gaston. *Clemenceau*. Paris: Fayard, 1968.

Mordacq, General Jean-Henri. *Clemenceau au soir de la vie, 1920–1929*. 2 vols. Paris: Plon, 1933.

———— *Le Ministère Clemenceau: Journal d'un témoin*. 4 vols. Paris: Plon, 1930.

Newhall, David. *Clemenceau: A Life at War*. Lewiston, NY: Mellen, 1991.

Nicolson, Harold. *Peacemaking 1919*. London: Constable, 1933.

Pedroncini, Guy. *Les Mutineries de 1917*. Paris: Presses Universitaires de France, 1967.

Reinach, Joseph. *Histoire de l'Affaire Dreyfus*. 7 vols. Paris: Fasquelle, 1894–1908.

Simon, Jules. *Souvenirs de Quatre Septembre*. 2 vols. Paris: Michel Lévy, 1874.

Stearns, Peter. *Revolutionary Syndicalism and French Labor*. New Brunswick, N. J.: Rutgers University Press, 1971.

Sternhell, Zeev. *La Droite révolutionnaire: les origines françaises du fascisme, 1885–1914*. Paris: Le Seuil, 1978.

Tombs, Robert. *The War against Paris*. Cambridge: Cambridge University Press, 1981.

Watson, David Robin. *Georges Clemenceau: A Political Life*. London: Eyre Methuen, 1974.

Watt, Richard M. *Dare Call it Treason*. New York: Simon and Schuster, 1963.

——— *The Kings Depart: The Tragedy of Germany: Versailles and the German Revolution*. New York: Simon and Schuster, 1968.

Weber, Eugen. *Peasants into Frenchmen*. Stanford, Calif.: Stanford University Press, 1976.

Weygand, General Maxime. *Foch*. Paris: Flammarion, 1947.

Whitehurst, Felix M. *My Private Diary During the Siege of Paris*. 2 vols. London: Tinsley Brothers, 1875.

Williams, Whyte. *The Tiger of France: Conversations with Clemenceau*. New York: Duell, Sloan and Pearce, 1949.

Wilson, Trevor. *The Myriad Faces of War: Britain and the Great War, 1914–1919*. Oxford: Basil Blackwell, 1986.

Wormser, Georges. *Clemenceau vu de près*. Paris: Hachette, 1979.

——— *Georges Mandel: l'homme politique*. Paris: Plon, 1967.

——— *La République de Clemenceau*. Paris: Presses Universitaires de France, 1961.

Zeldin, Theodore. *France, 1848–1945*. 2 vols. Oxford: Clarendon Press, 1973–1977.

Zévaès, Alexandre. *Clemenceau*. Paris: Julliard, 1949.

Zuckerkandl-Szeps, Berthe. *Clemenceau tel que j'ai connu*. Algiers: Editions de la revue 'Fontaine', 1944.

INDEX